Medieval

VERSITY C

KA 0419630 9

THE MIDDLE AGES SERIES

Ruth Mazo Karras, Series Editor
Edward Peters, Founding Editor

A complete list of books in the series is available from the publisher.

Medieval Italy

Texts in Translation

Edited by

KATHERINE L. JANSEN,

JOANNA DRELL,

and

FRANCES ANDREWS

PENN

University of Pennsylvania Press

Philadelphia

UNIVERSITY OF WINCHESTER
LIBRARY

Copyright © 2009 University of Pennsylvania Press

All rights reserved. Except for brief quotations used for purposes of review or scholarly citation, none of this book may be reproduced in any form by any means without written permission from the publisher.

Published by
University of Pennsylvania Press
Philadelphia, Pennsylvania 19104-4112

Printed in the United States of America on acid-free paper

10 9 8 7 6 5 4 3 2 1

Library of Congress Cataloging-in-Publication Data

Medieval Italy : texts in translation / edited by Katherine L. Jansen,
Joanna Drell, and Frances Andrews.
   p.   cm.— (The Middle Ages series)
ISBN: 978-0-8122-4164-8 (acid-free paper)
Includes bibliographical references and index.
   1. Italy—History—476-1268—Sources.   2. Italy—History—
1268-1492—Sources.   I. Jansen, Katherine Ludwig, 1957–.
II. Drell, Joanna H., 1965–.   III. Andrews, Frances.
DG501.M535   2009
94'.01—dc22   2008051233

UNIVERSITY OF WINCHESTER

04196309 | 945.04
JAN

Contents

3: The Commercial Revolution

4: Violence, Warfare, and Peace

Contents According to
Chronology and Geography

(N) = North (Northern and Central Italy)
(S) = South (the *Regno*)

In the cases in which documents have been clustered thematically they are entered by their first chronological date. If they span centuries, they are noted in each respective century.

Twelfth Century

Fourteenth Century (*Trecento*)

Fifteenth Century (*Quattrocento*)

Introduction

Medieval Italy: Texts in Translation gathers together for the first time in one volume the primary sources in translation necessary for teaching the history of the Central and Later Middle Ages in Italy. Over the past fifty years or so, medieval Italy has been a vibrant area of scholarly research as new documents have been discovered and modern methodologies, questions, and theory have been brought to bear on well-known texts. Although the period is famous for forests of urban towers, the spirituality of Saints Francis and Clare, the fortified castles of Frederick II, and the vernacular poetry of Dante, the study of the Italian Middle Ages has until very recently been largely underrepresented in the classroom. This volume, drawing on current scholarship combined with a few "classic" texts, aims to provide a teaching tool that will both introduce students to, and deepen their understanding of, this important aspect of the medieval world, for too long eclipsed by the long shadow cast by Anglo-French topics and the "normative" Middle Ages those interests produce. In many ways, the book highlights Italy's continuities with the medieval Latin West, but it also points out the ways in which it was exceptional, particularly in regard to the cities that drove Mediterranean trade for centuries, the glittering Norman court at Palermo, the multicultural emporium of the South, the new communal forms of government, the impact of the papacy's temporal claims in central Italy, and the richly textured religious life fashioned by the laity throughout the peninsula and its islands.

In the last half-century Anglo-American scholarship, building on a distinguished tradition of Italian historiography and, in many cases, in close collaboration with Italian scholars, has produced innovative studies on a wide variety of subjects, including commerce and trade, communal politics, institutions of the *Regno*, family structure and lineage, legal culture, urbanism, religious experience and practice, and the history of everyday life, to name but a few. This dynamic field of English-language scholarship has appeared largely as monographic studies and articles, research tools, and scholarly editions of documents, rather than as teaching aids and texts in translation. Happily, all this has begun to change. In addition to Daniel Waley's *The Italian City-Republics*, J. K. Hyde's *Society and Politics in Medieval Italy*, John Larner's *Italy in the Age of Dante and Petrarch*, and Giovanni Tabacco's *The*

Struggle for Power in Medieval Italy, our long-standing "text-books," we now have the voluminous final work of Philip Jones, *The Italian City-State: From Commune to Signoria*, and two fine collections of articles for classroom use: *The Society of Norman Italy*, ed. G. A. Loud and Alex Metcalfe, and *Italy in the Central Middle Ages, 1000–1300*, ed. David Abulafia. *Medieval Italy: Texts in Translation* is envisioned to work in tandem with any and all of these texts. It is also meant to complement Trevor Dean's superb *The Towns of Italy in the Later Middle Ages*, an invaluable resource for teachers focusing on the later medieval urban environment of the central and northern peninsula. Our volume in no way aims to replace *The Towns of Italy*, but it should be noted that our collection of texts has a very different set of objectives, as it aims to provide wider chronological and geographical coverage than previously available.

The documents in this volume span the Central and Later Middle Ages, the centuries from ca. 1000 to 1400, roughly the period from the end of the invasions to the earliest years of the Medici ascent in Florence, a critical, formative period for the peninsula and its islands. We have, for pedagogical reasons, included a handful of early medieval documents—such as the one on *incastellamento*—which indicate some of the issues fundamental to an understanding of the period after 1000. But the majority of texts encompass the era when the production and preservation of documents exploded at an unprecedented pace, particularly in literate and trade-oriented medieval Italy. One of the guiding principles of this volume is that it should reflect the state of English-language scholarship so that it can be used fruitfully in conjunction with the flourishing scholarly literature. As such, this volume is very much a snapshot of the current state of research. In an effort to provide sufficient class-room based coverage and to fulfill our patient editor's request to have this collection serve as "one-stop shopping" for instructors, we have however supplemented the texts translated and published here for the first time with some classics such as the Peace of Constance of 1183 and Giovanni Villani on faction. We have also included a handful of early fifteenth-century texts to emphasize the continuities between the medieval and early modern periods while simultaneously stressing complexity, variety and diversity. The texts serve to bear witness to such continuities while calling into question the value of imposing an arbitrary date bringing down the curtain on the Middle Ages somewhere around 1348.

Medieval Italy: Texts in Translation also seeks to push geographical and disciplinary boundaries by utilizing texts that represent the distinct political, social, economic, and religious institutions distributed throughout the penin-sula. In addition to the documents which illustrate the more well-known narrative of the rise of towns in northern and central Italy, the book is strong on texts that show the growth of Rome and the papal patrimony. Drawing on the work of art and architectural historians, it is also rich in texts that document the built environment throughout the peninsula. Given Italy's strategic position at the center of the Mediterranean's "global economy," mapped as it was onto the trading networks that reached from Britain to Byzantium, it is not surprising that its role in this world has received a great deal of scholarly attention. Many of the documents in this volume treat, directly or indirectly, medieval Italy's significant contributions to the creation of this dynamic world of trade and commerce, international markets, and cross-cultural exchange. Finally, the inclusion of a number of late thirteenth- and early fourteenth-century Tuscan texts is meant to serve those who structure their courses around Dante and his world.

But what makes this reader of sources unique is that it is the first volume to incorporate the South, by means of more than a passing glance, into a larger narrative of Italian history. Thus, drawing on Hebrew, Arabic, Greek, and Lombard sources, along with documentation from the successive kingdoms of the South, this volume not only reflects the recent surge in Anglophone scholarship on the *Regno*, but also contributes to it by collecting in one place a series of important texts, many translated here into English for the first time. By including material of southern provenance, the volume speaks with ethnically and religiously diverse voices. Moreover, a distinguishing feature is that the sources in this volume are heterogeneous in terms of genre. To complement trends in recent scholarship, it relies heavily on documents of practice or use—wills, deeds, charters, inventories, and contracts—everyday documentation, usually drawn up by a notary, the materials of social history. Law codes, court cases, and legal thought also have their place, as do medical and pedagogical texts, artifacts of material culture and "high" culture alike. Nor have narrative sources been forgotten: they are represented here by chronicles, letters, sermons, and hagiographical texts. A multiplicity of evidentiary genres thus accounts for the disparate document lengths in this collection. Clearly the *vita* of a popular medieval saint, even in excerpted form, will require more space than the most basic notarial contract. Even given our broad framework, no single volume can ever hope to cover entirely or reflect accurately each and every region of the peninsula and the islands over some four hundred years of history. Inevitably, there will be those elusive texts that instructors wish we had included. As noted earlier, our choice of texts has been guided by and reflects the work of Anglophone researchers who are currently laboring in the scholarly fields of medieval Italy.

Chapters have been arranged around twelve themes, each of which ordinarily proceeds chronologically. Texts from North and South have been integrated into almost every chapter, as one of our primary objectives has been to integrate their histories into one narrative fabric. In this way fruitful comparisons can be made. Nonetheless, for those who wish to study the history of the peninsula diachronically, or in geographical units, the second table of contents, organized according to chronology and geography, will serve as a gazetteer for the reader. In addition to the topical chapters we have chosen, we are aware that these texts present many possibilities for alternative groupings and study. The topic of "identity," for example, is one that can be studied in depth by selecting documents from across the chapters in this volume.

Beginning with the deep structure of landscape, Chapter 1 looks at the countryside that was the lifeforce of the Italian cities. Issues of land leases, labor, agriculture, and the peasant economy are here brought together. The documents in Chapter 2 treat the exercise of power by secular and ecclesiastical institutions. Here the texts illustrate the development of organs of government in the communal, royal, and ecclesiastical spheres. Chapter 3 examines economic life through documents relating to trade, commerce, and finance. The perennial problem of violence and warfare is explored in Chapter 4. Chapter 5 takes up the theme of law and order by recourse to dispute processing and court cases, legal codes, and jurisprudence. Students will thus be able to compare the legal world of Roger II with, for example, fourteenth-century Florence. Focusing on the built environment and material culture, Chapter 6 provides a range of texts documenting building projects, from public works to private palaces. Rome and the patrimony of St. Peter form the thematic core of Chapter 7, while disease and medicine, particularly as it was practiced in Salerno and Bologna, are the topics of Chapter 8. Civic religion and devotional practices of the Christian tradition, the dominant religion, are the main focus of Chapter 9, followed by texts on marriage, family, and children in Chapter 10. Chapter 11 concentrates on education and erudition both inside and outside the universities. Finally, through the lens of social memory, Chapter 12 brings together texts written by individuals and communities to memorialize and commemorate their personal lives and desires, their culture and society.

From beginning to end this volume represents a grand collaborative effort on the part of the editors, authors, and translators. Furthermore, it is a multigenerational project, as between us, the 56 contributors (and three coeditors) range from junior scholars to seasoned emeriti. The volume is also a multinational enterprise with contributors from Italy, North America, Britain, Ireland, Australia, and Israel. For the most part, our translators have written the introductions to their texts, but when this is not the case the introductory paragraphs are followed by a parenthetical citation of the author.

Given such internationalism it is inevitable that the volume contains differing styles of translation and exposition. As editors we have not tried to impose a false façade of uniformity on the texts. The needs of our students have guided all our editorial interventions. As such, we have endeavored to ensure that the translations and the accompanying introductions are as clear and comprehensible as possible to modern ears. We have also attempted to pare down to the bare bones the scholarly apparatus in each article, preferring to gather in the back of the book a chronology, a set of maps, three royal genealogies, a list of popes, a bibliography, and a glossary, although it should be emphasized that some Italian terms remain recalcitrant to good English translation. Personal and place names, as all medievalists know, always pose a challenge for the translator. Place names have been rendered into modern Italian, except for cities and regions that have familiar English equivalents, such as Florence and Apulia. For the most part, we have attempted to follow the Italian editorial custom of using the vernacular form of a Latin given name. However, we have made two primary exceptions to this rule: first, when a name has been anglicized or remains in Latin by tradition (thus we use Frederick I instead of Federico I and Hostiensis instead of Enrico da Susa). Nonetheless, there are cases—particularly in the texts from the multicultural frontiers—when Latin, Greek, and Lombard names appear side-by-side. In those cases, to avoid imposing an artificial sense of homogeneity and to avoid confusion, we have sometimes had to violate our own rules.

Our hope is that this volume of translated sources from the various language groups and communities that inhabited Italy over the course of the four hundred years it covers will provide students with the raw materials to begin interpreting and crafting Italian medieval history for themselves, by confronting head-on diverse voices from a distant but endlessly fascinating past.

A Note on Dating and Currency

In a multicultural setting such as medieval Italy, dating of documents was by no means uniform. A number of regions of Christian Italy began the new year on the feast of the Annunciation with the result that the year was not ushered in until 25 March. In addition, documents were frequently dated according to the ancient system of imperial indiction, a fifteen-year cycle. Moreover, the Jewish calendar begins from the date of Creation while the Muslim system reckons from Muhammad's flight to Medina in 622 of the common era. Respecting this multiplicity of forms, we have left the dates as recorded and our translators have generously supplied the modern date equivalent. Currency and its rate of exchange present yet another challenge, as there was no standard currency used throughout the peninsula and Sicily. Moreover, the rate of exchange varied over time and place. The reader can keep in mind, however, that in the later medieval period the money of account was the *lira*, 1 *lira* = 20 *solidi/soldi* = 240 *denarii/denari* (Latin/Italian). It is also useful to know that in the mid-fourteenth century a female worker in the cloth industry typically earned about 25 *lire* a year, while a nobleman working in an important governmental position might earn 100 to 300 *lire* a year. Other currencies and coins are listed in the glossary.

Abbreviations

The following abbreviations are used frequently in text and notes:

AASS   *Acta Sanctorum*

PL   *Patrologia Latina*

RIS   *Rerum Italicarum Scriptores* (Milan edition)

RIS²   *Rerum Italicarum Scriptores* (Bologna and Citta' di Castello edition)

MGH   *Monumenta Germaniae Historica*

The Countryside and Its Dependencies

The traditional view of a "conquest" of the contado *(the land surrounding a city, its hinterland) by the developing urban centers of medieval Italy has recently been questioned by historians who wish to underline the strong ties that bound them together: after all, those who moved to the cities, feeding the burgeoning population growth of the eleventh century and beyond, came from the rural areas. Nobles who moved to live inside the urban walls held onto their rural estates; merchants who made profits in the commercial world often invested them in land. Land remained the chief form of wealth, and indeed the close dependence of all populations, whether urban or rural, on the nature of the landscape and their vulnerability to the climate cannot be overestimated. The texts in this section document some of the key elements in this relationship. Control over natural resources such as land, the production of food staples such as wheat and vines, and the importance of good husbandry are some of the themes that the texts in this section seek to illuminate. Other topics include the sometimes fraught relationships between landlords and tenants; the legal status of those tenants; the changes in the way land was exploited and rents were paid; the emergence of sharecropping; famine and food shortages; rural land donation; and the founding of "new towns" in the countryside to defend the city or hinterland.*

1. LAND LEASING AND LEGAL STATUS IN SOUTHERN ITALY THREE TEXTS (964–86)

Translated from Latin by Valerie Ramseyer

Charters are legal documents that record a variety of transactions, including sales, donations, leases, agricultural contracts, marriage agreements, and wills. The documents were written down at the request of the participants, who preserved them and relied upon them as proof of the transaction. The charters translated below are found in the archives of the abbey of the Holy Trinity of Cava, an important Benedictine monastery founded ca. 1020 and located about 10 kilometers from Salerno. A majority of the charters record transactions involving the monastery and its community, although some of the charters, especially for the period before the abbey's foundation, made their way into the Cava archives when the abbey received donations or absorbed other foundations into its monastic network.

The first text translated below is a land lease. Land could be leased under a variety of conditions. Generally, farm land was leased out in return for a portion of the produce. Grain was typically grown, as well as vines, fruit trees, and nut trees. Often sharecropping agreements from the tenth and eleventh centuries stipulated that the tenants would improve the property, usually by clearing the land and planting vines, trees, or other crops, and in return they would receive reduced payments for a specified number of years. Tenants in most sharecropping agreements were not tied to the land in any way, nor were they generally required to perform labor services. In addition to farm land, urban property was leased out for money rents, usually for residential purposes but sometimes for building shops. Finally mills on rivers were leased out, either for a money rent or for a share of the grain milled.

The second and third texts illustrate the range of legal statuses found in the documents. The main distinction—in the tenth and eleventh centuries—was between people of servile status and free people. The exact condition of servile people is unclear, and generally they show up in documents either when their masters emancipate them or when they wish to marry a free person. The Lombard laws suggest that the status of slaves could differ dramatically, depending on the type of work performed as well as the social standing of their masters; nonetheless they were in all cases legally subordinate and had to be protected and represented by their masters. Beginning in the mid-eleventh century, a new class of people arose due to the growth of commendation contracts in which free people placed themselves under the protection and authority of a church or monastery, ceding all their property to the religious house but retaining the usufruct for themselves and their heirs. These people remained technically free, but they eventually became tied to the land and needed their landlord's permission to move or alienate property. By the mid-twelfth century large landholders in the region had taken on a variety of political roles, including the right to judge disputes that arose among the tenants, the capacity to demand labor services from them, and the ability to tax all the economic activities that took place on their property.

A Land Lease from Areola (near Nocera)

April 979

In the name of the Lord, in the thirty-sixth year of the reign of our lord the glorious prince Pandolfus and the first year of his reign over the Principality of Salerno, and in the fifth year of the reign of his son lord Pandolfus, in the month of April, in the seventh year of the indiction. I, Martin, priest and abbot of the church of San Massimo, in front of the witnesses whose signatures appear below and with my advocate, the *gastald* Truppoaldus, who is one of the owners of the church (of San Massimo), had this charter redacted. By mutual agreement Nandus son of Ursus, who is called "Maino" and Peter son of Leo, who is called "Letus," and John "Ballense" son of Cicerus gave a pledge to us and they named themselves as their own guarantors. With this pledge the three men and their heirs are obliged to hold in their power for twelve years property belonging to the church [of San Massimo], which was donated to the church by Rottelmannus son of Ildeprandus and is located in San Quirico in a place called Areola [near Nocera]. And these three men will retain this property for twelve years and they will enclose it and plant vines and trees, as is right. During those twelve years, all the wine and fruit that the land produces will belong completely to them; of the grain that they cultivate they will give one-half every year to the church, paying the *terraticum* tax [a land tax] as is the custom of the place. At the end of the twelve years, the three men and their heirs will have healthy, well-cultivated vines and trees on the property, according to the possibility of the land. After those twelve years, if they want, they and their heirs can retain the land and continue to work and cultivate it, maintaining the vines and trees in good condition. At harvest time, they will let the church know, and the church will send a messenger. They will harvest the grapes and gather the fruit, as is right, and whatever wine they produce and whatever fruit they collect they will divide into three parts at the wine press: the church will receive one part and they will take two parts. The church's part of the wine will be placed in a container that the church will leave in their house, and they must take good care of the wine that is placed in their house, protecting it from fire and other damage until we [the representatives of the church] come to get it. They will also give us one-third of the grain that they cultivate, the *terraticum* tax, after the

Translated from *Codex Diplomaticus Cavensis,* ed. Michele Morcaldi, Mauro Schiani, and Sylvano de Stefano (Naples: P. Piazza/H. Hoepli, 1873–93), vol. 2, 314.

twelve years have passed. When we send our messenger to collect the wine, they will feed him according to their means. After twelve years, if these three men or their heirs no longer wish to retain the property under these conditions, they will return it to the church, keeping nothing for themselves. Likewise if they or their heirs leave the territory of Salerno to live somewhere else, the land will be returned to the church. However, if they return within three years, the land will be given back to them under the same conditions, if they so desire. But if they do not want to take back and work the land under the same conditions, then the land will revert to the power of the church, and representatives of the church may do with it whatever they please. If these men do not fulfil the terms of this agreement, or if they contradict it in any way, they or their heirs are obliged to pay the church fifty gold Constantinian *solidi*.

I, Arechisus a notary, was witness [to this agreement] and wrote this charter. Signed by Iaquintus, Ademarius, and Grimoaldus

Manumission Contract, Salerno

January 964

In the name of the Lord, in the thirty-first year of the reign of our glorious prince Gisolf [I], in the month of January, in the seventh year of the indiction. I, Magister John son of Ursus who was from Tramontana, along with a woman named Maria, who are husband and wife, inspired by the mercy of the omnipotent God and for the well-being of our souls, emancipate our slave by the name of John, who comes from the nation of the Franks. And I, Maria, do so with the consent and permission of my husband under whose guardianship I am placed. And both of us, man and wife, for the love of Christ our savior and for the salvation of our souls, with this charter grant to you John complete freedom in such a way that for the rest of our lives you will continue to serve us, man and wife, wherever and however it pleases us. However, after we die, from that day forward, you, John, will remain free, along with all your possessions legally obtained, however and wherever you want, and no one will have any power or authority over you. From that day forward you can come and go wherever and however you please without any interference from any of our heirs or any other men. And with this charter, we oblige our heirs so that if at any time after our deaths they seek to place you, the above-mentioned John, in servitude, or if they contradict this charter

Translated from *Codex Diplomaticus Cavensis,* ed. Michele Morcaldi, Mauro Schiani, and Sylvano de Stefano (Naples: P. Piazza/H. Hoepli, 1873–93), vol. 2, 225.

in any way, such an action will be null and void, and in addition they will pay twenty gold Constantinian *solidi* to you, John, or to whoever appears in your stead with this charter in hand. And for all times, just as it states, you will remain free and you will have the right to have and to hold all your possessions. Thus we asked you, Madelmus the notary, to write this charter. Enacted at Salerno.

Signed by Truppoaldus, Radechis a notary, Romoaldus, Maius, Ursus, and Truppoaldus

A Mixed Marriage

February 986

In the name of the Lord, in the third year of the reign of our lord John [II] and his son our lord Guido both glorious princes, in the month of February, in the fourteenth year of the indiction. I, Martin, priest and abbot of the church of San Massimo, in the presence of Peter the judge, by mutual agreement between myself and a freewoman by the name of Maria, declare that Maria will unite herself [in matrimony] to a slave belonging to the church [of San Massimo] by the name of Andreas son of Jordan. And I declare it legitimate for Maria to have Andreas as her husband and for them to live together on property belonging to the church and for them to have children together. And neither I nor my successors will have the authority to make these children slaves, but at all times these children will reside and live on church property exactly as other freemen do. And of the fruits of their labor, the church will take two parts and they will retain one part to do with as they like. And if they raise animals, likewise they will keep one-third to do with as they like. And Maria gave her pledge along with her advocate Domnellus and she named herself as her own guarantor. And with this pledge, if she does not fulfill the agreement as written above, or if she seeks to contradict it in any way, she will pay to me or to the church one hundred gold Constantinian *solidi*.

I, Peter the notary, was witness (to this agreement) and wrote this charter. Signed by Peter the above-mentioned judge.

Translated from *Codex Diplomaticus Cavensis,* ed. Michele Morcaldi, Mauro Schiani, and Sylvano de Stefano (Naples: P. Piazza/H. Hoepli, 1873–93), vol. 2, 383.

2. LAND, MONEY, AND GRAIN
TWO CUSTOMARY LEASES IN THE DIOCESE OF FLORENCE (1073, 1115)

Translated from Latin by George Dameron

The two documents translated below are typical examples of libelli, *traditional lease-hold contracts, which by the twelfth century were the most common type of customary lease in Tuscany. The fixed rent was usually monetary, the lease was granted in perpetuity, and both parties received copies of the contract. It is noteworthy that the first* libellus *(1073) reproduced below was not for a monetary payment; instead, it was for two* moggi *of grain (the Florentine equivalent to about 34 bushels). Most likely, the rent was charged in grain because the properties being leased were located in the Mugello valley, a major grain growing region north of Florence. After 1200, however, Tuscan contracts show more rents paid in grain as landlords attempted to take full advantage of the burgeoning grain market. Also significant about this contract is that what was being rented was the sixth part of a church, including its tithes. The leasing of churches and their income to laymen was common before the ecclesiastical reform movement began in the last quarter of the eleventh century. The second* libellus *(1115) is of interest because the tenant paid in Lucchese currency, indicating that in the early twelfth century, the Florentine countryside was clearly within the economic orbit of Lucca, a far more prosperous city than Florence at the time. Like most other ecclesiastical communities, the cathedral chapter arranged to lease out its landed holdings for an annual return.*

1. A *Libellus* Charter, Diocese of Florence (1073)

In the name of the Lord God, Amen. In the year dating from the Incarnation of our Lord, 1073, in the month of July, tenth indiction; done under auspicious circumstances. We, Abbot Raineri and Presbyter Inghizo of the monastery of San Bartoli and Santa Maria, located at Carza, according to our agreement, publicly acknowledge that we have granted to you, Bolgarello and Giovanni, twin sons of the deceased Teuza, and to Gerardo del Rustico, your nephew, certain properties for you to possess, to hold, to develop, to enjoy, and to improve. These holdings are associated with the church of Santa Maria a Paterno,[1] along with all the lands, vineyards, tithes, and income that pertain to it. Specifically, we convey to you and your heirs in its entirety a sixth part of said church, with all the possessions pertaining to it. For this property, you and your descendants (or your representative) must every year

Translated from *Regesta Chartarum Italiae*, ed. Renato Piattoli, vol. 23, *Le carte della canonica della cattedrale di Firenze (723–1149)* (Rome: Istituto storico per il medio evo, 1938), 216–17.

1. Paterno is located in the mountainous area north of the city of Florence along the river Carza.

pay us or our successors (or our representative) at our abbey one *moggio* of grain, plus one *scafilius* of barley and one *scafilius* of spelt, during the feast of the Virgin Mary. In other words, you must pay us two *moggi*, assuming that one *starius* equals eleven *panni*.[2] If, in the course of the fulfilment of these terms, we or our successors from the aforesaid church, should presume to diminish or alienate any of the mobile or immobile properties detailed here, or add to your responsibilities in this agreement, then we must pay and give to you a fine of 20 good silver *solidi*. Similarly, we declare that if we, the aforesaid twin brothers and nephew, or our heirs, should presume to violate the terms of this agreement, or if we should alienate, deteriorate, or encroach upon any properties associated with the aforesaid church or its appurtenances, then we must pay you a fine of 20 *solidi*. Done at Pietramensola, in the district of Florence, under auspicious circumstances.

Signed by hand marks of Abbot Raineri and Presbyter Inghizo, who requested a copy of this *libellus* for themselves.
Signed by hand marks of aforesaid twin brothers and nephew, who requested a copy of this *libellus* for themselves.
Signed by hand marks of Remberto of the late Rodolfo, Raineri del Vivenzio, and Martino of the late Pietro, witnesses.
I, Pietro the notary, drafted this document according to custom.

2. A *Libellus* Charter from Cintoia (28 July 1115)

In the name of the Lord our God the Eternal, Amen. In the year of the Incarnation of our Lord, 1115, on the fifth day before the Kalends of August, eighth indiction; done under auspicious conditions. I, Giambono, archpresbyter of the holy Florentine Church and head of the cathedral canons, according to our understanding, have provided to give to you, Rolando [son] of the deceased Leolo, certain properties to possess, to hold, to develop, to enjoy, and to improve. These properties constitute entire parcels of land, vineyards, and other possessions located at Potiuolo, Vico, and on our estate at Cintoia, which presbyter Rembaldus donated and confirmed to us before this time in a charter presently kept in the aforesaid church. I confirm and grant to you, Rolando, and to your heirs, in its entirety all these aforesaid lands and vineyards, along with all their associated and surrounding proper-

Translated from *Regesta Chartarum Italiae*, ed. Renato Piattoli, vol. 23, *Le carte della canonica della cattedrale di Firenze (723–1149)* (Rome: Istituto storico per il medio evo, 1938), 392–93.
2. *Moggio, starius, pannus,* and *scafilius* are all specific measurements for quantities of grain.

ties, wherever lands and vineyards are connected to the church by place and name. The same properties that presbyter Rembaldus possessed, occupied, and granted to us, I now give to you in their entirety so that you and others through you might possess and occupy them. You and your heirs are obliged every year during the Holy Week of Christmas to pay me and my successors for these properties twelve silver *denari* in good and usable Lucchese currency. This sum represents all the rent, offerings,[3] and aids that you owe us, and you pay no more. You or your representative will make the payment to us or someone appointed by us at the estate of our church. If, in the course of the fulfilment of these terms, I, as head of the cathedral chapter, or my successors, should presume to diminish or remove any of the above mentioned properties (mobile or immobile), or, if we should presume to impose on you any additional burden above and beyond what is mentioned above; or if, through our agent, you should lose these properties; or if we should presume to break the terms of this contract, then we must pay and give to you, Rolando, or to your heirs, a fine of 100 good Lucchese *solidi*. Likewise, on my part, I, Rolando, do declare, as agreed upon above, that if I or my heirs should neglect to pay the agreed upon rent every year, or if you should not receive it, or if I or my heirs should presume to alienate, deteriorate, or encroach upon these properties, then we are obliged to pay to you a fine of 100 *solidi*. We have asked for two copies of this lease contract to be made, one for each of the two parties. Done at Cintoia, in the territory of Florence, under auspicious circumstances.

3. The word, *oblias*, can also technically mean cake offerings or offerings of unconsecrated hosts.

3. A BEQUEST OF TOWN AND COUNTRYSIDE PROPERTIES IN EBOLI (1152)

Translated from Latin by David Routt

The following charter from the abbey of the Holy Trinity at Cava (Salerno) records the donation of property in 1152 by a non-noble couple. Having been moved by both divine inspiration and the preaching of the monks at Cava, the charter reveals both personal and practical desires behind the bequest. Giovanni and Trocta opted for a pre-mortem bequest that not only benefited the abbey but ensured their own material comfort for the remainder of their lives. They retained their movable property while granting the abbey their urban and countryside properties in Eboli and its environs. The couple, moreover, guaranteed their material support by keeping the use and proceeds (usufruct) from the donated property and by obliging the monastery to make good any shortfall in their needs [see #116].

In the name of the Holy and Indivisible Trinity in the year from the incarnation of our lord and savior Jesus Christ 1152 and in the twenty-second year of the reign of our lord Roger, the most glorious king of Sicily and Italy, and in the second year of lord William, the king's dearest son, in the month of July, fifteenth indiction. Since it is worthy and fitting by the laws and customs of the best men to exalt and enrich the churches of Christ, spread far and wide throughout the world, especially those in which religious communities of God's servants are governed by a rule, serving God and praying for the well-being of the souls of Christians, most of all for those to whom God had yielded power over men and lands and over supplies of goods so that Christ, God's son, our lord, the judge of everything, may protect and defend those in this present generation, may make their power firm for a long time, and may reciprocate to them the good work when we will be in his judgment. Wherefore, before me, David the judge, and witnesses came Giovanni Cap-(ut)alvus, son of the late Maraldus, with Trocta his wife, and, inflamed for good by preaching, by divine inspiration, and by the intervention and also the exhortation of the brothers, the monks of the monastery of the Holy and Indivisible Trinity, built in the most holy place of Cava, where it is called in a proper sense Mitiliano, over which, with God's protection, lord Marinus, by god's grace, [is] venerable and also holiest abbot. For the welfare of their souls, they [Giovanni and Trocta] surrendered and offered to God and the said church of the Holy and Indivisible Trinity of Cava their entire inheritance, without their movables, namely the properties of three dwellings inside

Translated from Holy Trinity of Cava, Arca XXVIII, 45, from a transcription of the original prepared by Graham A. Loud.

the city wall of Eboli in the parish of San Lorenzo, and a piece of land with a vineyard in the appurtenances of the same land Eboli in the place properly called Inbriaco, and one [piece of] land in the same appurtenance, strictly speaking in the place Pira de Marco called Cicero, and all their boundaries with possession of everything within them and their appurtenances, the recompense of their roads, and streets.

The usufruct, nevertheless, of the whole above-written inheritance [is] reserved to them as long as they will live. And, if they are unable [to draw] moderate sustenance of such a kind from the usufruct of said property, because of their want of means they should make this known to the monastery and from the monastery they ought to expect everything to the measure that is necessary for them. Indeed, after their deaths the whole above-written inheritance may revert to the right and ownership of the above-written monastery without any diminution. I ordered you, John the notary, to record all these matters in writing and I corroborated by signing with the mark of the cross of our authority.

† I who above [am] David, judge.

4. SHARECROPPING IN THE SIENESE *CONTADO* THREE TEXTS (1232, 1257, 1293)

Translated from Latin by David Routt

Present in the mezzadria *contract, a sharecropping arrangement increasingly popular in late medieval Italy, are representations of the close relationship between city and countryside and the rhythms of rural life during the economically vibrant thirteenth century. The* mezzadria *contract was a land-lease, granted by an owner to a lessee for a fixed period, in exchange for half the land's yield. These three Sienese leases demonstrate how an urban-dweller such as a shoemaker, simultaneously maintained contact with his rural interests, shed the responsibility of personal management of his lands, provisioned his urban household, and perhaps profited from a buoyant market in foodstuffs. The* mezzadria *contract, moreover, was a flexible instrument: brothers pool their lands in a single lease; another landholder consolidates and rationalizes his leases by folding expiring contracts into a single, more extensive arrangement with a new lessee; a lessor tries to maximize the return from a lease and maintain his property's agrarian integrity through precise stipulation of how the land be fertilized and through the formulaic injunction that the lessee's tending of the holding conform to the best accepted practice. The vicissitudes of inheritance and the impact of an active market in land are also evident in the fragmented character of an urban dweller's land, even within a single rural district.*

1. 22 August 1232, Siena

Bonifacio di Niccolò concedes at half for five years to Uguccione di Renaldo a vineyard and a piece of land lying near the oven of Giovanni Grassi.

I, Bonifacio di Niccolò, by notice of contract of hiring, give, concede, and lease to you, Uguccione di Renaldo, my vineyard and land lying near the oven of Giovanni Grassi, which vineyard was Piero di Cresta's, from now for five years. And I promise you up to the end of the term not to take it away, not to trouble [you], and to make no lawsuit, on the contrary to defend [it] legally if it will be necessary, under penalty of 10 *lire*, which I promise to give you, and I will consider the contract valid.

And moreover I, Uguccione, promise you to cultivate and work the said vineyard and land well. And I promise to give you half of the produce—grain and wine—with the exception of *aquarello*,[1] and I [promise] to bring and supply [the half] to your home in Siena at my expense. I promise you annu-

Translated from *Il Contratto di Mezzadria nella Toscana Medievale*, vol. 1, *Contado di Siena, Sec. XIII-1348*, ed. Giuliano Pinto and Paolo Pirillo (Florence: Olschki, 1987), 76–77, 81, 95.

1. A diluted wine frequently made from grape pulp after pressing.

ally to furnish and to carry down onto the farm twenty-five seams[2] of
dung. . . . And I will cut no trees damaging the roots. And at the end of the
term I will restore it to you staked because I receive [it] staked. [The penalty
of 10 *lire*, the formula of warranty, and the signature of the notary follow.]

2. 23 September 1257, Siena

*Arnolfino, son of the late Gualterotto, concedes in mezzadria to Ventura di Peruzzo
and to Guido Busse da Rosia for five years to start from the past kalends of August
a farm lying near Rosia.*

I, Arnolfino, son of the late lord Gualterotto, by notice of contract of hiring,
lease and concede to you Ventura di Peruzzo and Guido Busse de Rosia, in
the public eye, all my farm with vineyards that I have at Rosia, with the
exception of a field which master Barsellus keeps and the vineyard which
Johannetus di Giovanni the shoemaker keeps. The aforesaid [master Barsellus
and Johannetus di Giovanni the shoemaker] may have the field and vineyard
to keep for one year and you afterward keep [them] for four years with the
other lands and vineyards, namely the farm from the past kalends of August
for five years and the vineyards from the past feast of Saint Michael in September for five complete years. And I promise not to take away and not to concede the said farm and vineyards for the said time, et cetera [under penalty
of 100 *soldi*].

We, Ventura di Peruzzo and Guido Busse, acknowledge in truth to have
hired from you Arnolfino, son of the late lord Gualterotto, in the public eye,
the whole farm with the vineyards that you have at Rosia, namely the farm
from the past kalends of August for five complete years and the vineyards
from the past feast of Saint Michael in September for five complete years.
And we promise you from now to the said time to maintain and work the
said farm and vineyards in the manner and custom of good laborers at the
appropriate times, to furnish all seed that will be necessary for sowing on the
said farm, and not to withdraw [it] nor have it withdrawn at any time. And
we promise you to give and convey to your home in Siena half of all the grain
and new wine and the produce that there will be on said properties. And we
promise to spread for you seven seams of dung for any *sextarius* [of land]
where we will sow wheat [under penalty of 100 *soldi*].

3. 12 November 1293, Siena

Grappante di Giovanni da Calceno receives in mezzadria *for three years from Sozzo
di Orlando, shoemaker of Siena, lands and vineyards lying in the estate of Calceno.*

---

2. A seam is a quantity that can be carried by a beast of burden.

I, Grappante di Giovanni da Calceno, acknowledge to you Sozzo di Orlando, Sienese shoemaker, the recipient and stipulator for yourself and your brother Johannellus, that I leased from you, in the public eye by your giving and leasing for yourself and for him [your brother], the underwritten lands, properties, and vineyards, from now for the next three years yet to come; namely, in particular, a parcel of land lying in the place called la Croce in the estate of Calceno, at which at one [side] is [the property] of Bernardo di Becco and at the other [side the property] of Nacco and at the head [the property] of Giovanni di Urso and the road; likewise, a parcel of land and vineyard lying in Fonte Vagli of the estate of Calceno, at which at one [side is the property] of Casello di Dietisalvo and at the foot and at the head [the property] of the church of Calceno and the road; likewise, a parcel of vineyard land lying in the vale of Calceno, at which at one [side is the property] of Johannellus' heirs and at one [side] is [the property] of Giovanni di Urso and at the head [the property] of the aforesaid Bernardo and me, Grappante; likewise, a parcel of land lying in the vale of Calceno, at which at the foot [is] the trench and at one [side the land] of Johannellus' heirs and at the head the road, which are all yours, Sozzo; item, a parcel of land of the said Johanellus your brother, lying in Fontenvalli, at which at one [side] is [the property] of said Casello and at the foot the trench and at the other [side the property] of Ducco and at the head the road; or if there any others bordering on them with underwritten contracts and agreements. And you undertake to give me every year at the said time one seam of stakes, and I promise you, the recipient, as it was said, to spread onto said lands in the first year fifty-three seams of dung and afterward in each year of the said two years forty seams of dung, and at the end of said time of three years may I be able and may it be allowed to me to take half of the staked vines which I put in the said vineyard of Vagli. And I promise you, the recipient, as it was said, to work and till well the said lands and vineyards and the said parcel of land of your brother and to hoe, tend, and prune the vineyard at good and suitable times, by the practice of the good laborer lacking malice, and not to cut trees and vines perfidiously. And I promise to you also, the recipient, as it was said, to give and surrender half of all produce which is harvested and gathered from the said properties at the aforesaid Calceno at my own expense, namely of wheat and wine and any other grain and all other fruits. [The penalty of 25 *lire*, the formulas of warranty, and the signature of the notary follow.]

Figure 1. Wine measure (late thirteenth or early fourteenth century). The abbreviation *COG VINI* inscribed on the base stands for *congius vini* or *cogno* of wine, a liquid measure used for both wine and oil. Carved out of a column, the measure bears the Caetani family coat of arms of Pope Boniface VIII. It is likely that the measure was used in the marketplace on the Capitoline Hill, Rome. Rome, Musei Capitolini. (Photo: Frances Andrews)

5. BONVESIN DELLA RIVA ON MILAN
AND ITS *CONTADO* (1288)

Translated from Italian by Frances Andrews

In spite of its prose form, the description of Milan translated here belongs to a tradition of praise poems which highlighted the virtues of the cities of Italy [see #67, 115, 117]. Its author was a grammar teacher who was also a member of the Humiliati order. His fascination with statistics is particularly evident in this passage: to exalt his city he frequently resorted to numerical lists. Although Bonvesin refers to communal documentation such as tax records, to which he may well have had access, and claims the consensus of other authorities, some of his figures are controversial. Damage to the extant manuscript leaves some figures in doubt, while for others historians are skeptical about his estimates. Thus the highest modern calculation of the population of Milan by Pierre Racine proposes that including the suburbs, there may have been as many as 175,000 inhabitants, while many other historians have favored a figure as low as 60,000.[1] Even without statistical precision, Bonvesin's list indicates the great array of people and activities in the largest northern city at this date. It also underlines the importance of the relationship between the city and its contado.

FROM CHAPTER 3: PRAISE OF MILAN ON ACCOUNT OF ITS PEOPLE

Rubric 12. What can now be said of the high number of the other inhabitants of Milan and its contado?[2] Silence. He who can, let him count them. But please excuse me if I am not silent on this: since, according to my long calculations, confirmed by the assertions of many, more than 700,000 human mouths of both sexes (counting, together with the adults, all the children), live on Ambrosian lands and receive every day, from the hand of God—and the source is marvelous—"Ambrosian" food.[3]

13. Why should there not be that number, if in the heavily populated city alone there are unquestionably 150 parishes, in some of which more than 500 families certainly reside, while others have about a thousand?

14. So how many human mouths inhabit the city alone? Let him who can, count them. If he manages to do a complete count he will reach, I am con-

Translated from Bonvesin della Riva, *De magnalibus mediolani, meraviglie di Milano*, ed. and trans. Paolo Chiesa (Milan: Libri Scheiwiller, 1998), 86–95.

1. Pierre Racine, "Milan à la fin du XIIIe siècle: 60,000 ou 200,000 habitants?" *Aevum* 58 (1984): 246–63. See also Bonvesin della Riva, *De magnalibus mediolani*, 212 n. 46.

2. This passage follows an enumeration of the clergy and ecclesiastical institutions of the city.

3. This is a play on Ambrose/Ambrosian: the food of the gods and the food of the lands of Saint Ambrose, patron saint of Milan.

vinced, a total of about 200,000, since serious and accurate inquiry has proved with certainty that in the city alone, allowing for the seasons, 1,200 *moggi* of grain or more are consumed every day; and the truth of this assertion is certified by those who collect the taxes on grain ground at the mills.

15. If you want to know how many soldiers can go to war, including both veterans and new recruits, know that all together more than 40,000 men, counting by individual section, live in this city, each singly capable of handling a lance, or a sword or another weapon against the enemy.

16. I can declare how many knights prepared for war this city is able to put in the field, since at an order from the commune, more than 10,000 men, from the city and the *contado*, could easily present themselves with war horses; and so that the truth may somehow shine out more clearly by other means, even for these things said separately, I will untangle the knot one thread at a time.

17. In the city alone there are 120 legal professionals in both laws [civil and canon], and their college is not thought to have an equal in the whole world in number or wisdom. All of these, ready to issue judgments, willingly accept money from litigants.

18. There are more than 1,500 notaries, very many of whom are excellent drafters of contracts.

19. There are undoubtedly 600 messengers of the commune, whom the people call servitors.

20. There are six principal trumpeters of the commune, honorable and worthy men, who, in honor of their great city, not only possess horses, but also live a decorous life in the manner of nobles. They play the trumpet unlike any other trumpeters of the world and in a wonderful way. The terrible sound of their trumpets, well suited to the tumults of battles, and for which we have heard no parallel in the whole world, conveys both the stature and the power of this city.

21. There are twenty-eight medical experts, commonly called *fisici* [physicians].

22. Of surgeons of the different specialties there are more than 150. Many of these are excellent doctors by nature who continue the practice of surgery

learned from ancient family tradition. They have no equal in the other cities of Lombard Italy.

23. There are eight teachers of grammar; each of them has a numerous student body under his rod and as I have clearly been able to establish, they teach grammar with great labor and diligence, more than the teachers of other cities.

24. There are fourteen teachers expert in Ambrosian chant[4], from which the incidence of clerics in this city can be observed.

25. There are more than seventy elementary teachers.

26. Although there is no university [*studium generale*] in the city, copyists number more than forty. By transcribing books by hand every day, they earn their bread and other expenses.

27. As is shown in the books of the commune, there are three hundred ovens in the city baking bread for the needs of citizens. There are also many other ovens which are exempt, supplying monks or religious of both sexes; I think there are more than one hundred.

28. There are without doubt more than one thousand shopkeepers, retailing an extraordinary range of goods of all sorts.

29. The number of butchers is more than 440; in their butcher-shops excellent meat from every sort of quadruped appropriate for our consumption is sold in abundance.

30. According to their own assurances, there are more than four hundred fishermen of trout, dentex, fat eels, tench, grayling, eels, lampreys, crabs, and every other sort of fish, large and small. These they bring to the city almost every day from the lakes of our *contado* (which number more than eighteen), from the more than sixty rivers and from the almost infinite number of mountain streams.

31. The hostel keepers providing paid accommodation for foreigners number about 150.

4. Ambrosian chant: the liturgical plainchant tradition of the church of Milan.

32. There are around eighty blacksmiths shoeing quadrupeds; from this the abundance of knights and horses can be deduced. I will not try to say how many saddle-makers there are or those making bridles, spurs, or stirrups.

33. Makers of bronze bells which are hung from the collars of horses, making a sweet sound and which, as far as we know are not made elsewhere, number more than thirty; each of these has under him numerous assistants in his craft. If I also wished to list in order all the artisans of every sort, weavers of wool, linen, cotton, silk, shoemakers, tanners, tailors, smiths of all types, and then the merchants who travel all over the world for their trade and take part in fairs in other cities, or the small traders and second-hand dealers, I believe those reading or listening to this would be stupefied with amazement. The details described above relate to the city alone and let this suffice; for through them the great number of citizens and the influx of foreigners to this city may be sufficiently understood.

34. Concerning our *contado*, no one can say just how many men of different sorts live there: how many of great nobility, how many masters in the various arts, doctors, merchants, peasants [*agricolas*], artisans of all type; he who can, let him work it out in his heart. One thing I will say, even if everything else is silenced, and that is that both in the city and outside there is an abundant quantity of men of immense nobility. Of these many are called *valvassori* from *valva* meaning gate, since, when the Roman emperors lived in the Ambrosian praetorium [Milan], this was their dignity, because they were the gatekeepers of the imperial court. Others, of greater nobility, are called *capitanei* from *capite* meaning head, for they were the heads of the *pievi*. And as further corroboration of the truth of this, let he who wishes know that counting everyone in the city and *contado*, there are more than one hundred nobles who each enjoy going out hunting birds with sparrow-hawks and falcons; as for falconers, I have not been able to find their number.

35. At the end of this chapter it is worth noting, that, as in life, so in death, our citizens are magnified with honor and placed in magnificent tombs. Clear proof of this is the sign that in the city alone, both in churches and cemeteries, there are more than 2000 stone urns, some of which are made of marble, others of flint-stone or another sort of stone, each with its own cover of the same stone, and among which there are some which certainly cost more than twenty silver marks.

So now that the great wonders of the city on account of its site, habitat and inhabitants are clear, let us move on to other things.

6. GIOVANNI VILLANI ON FOOD SHORTAGES AND FAMINE IN CENTRAL ITALY (1329–30, 1347–48)

Translated from Italian by Katherine L. Jansen

Although it has been argued that medieval Italy did not experience the "Great Famine" of 1315–22, nonetheless, it did experience a number of terrible food shortages and famines throughout the fourteenth century. In the excerpts below, Giovanni Villani (d. 1348) describes those of 1329–30 and 1346–47, both of which he himself witnessed. Villani is known primarily as a Florentine chronicler; less well known is that he also held a number of important positions in the city government. In 1328, as he tells us below, he held an important municipal office charged with confronting the famine that was devastating much of the peninsula.

Book 10, Chapter 117. How the Romans Because of Famine Removed King Robert from the Lordship of the City
1328 [1329]

In these times, on 4 February [1329], Messer Guiglielmo d'Eboli, a baron of King Robert of Naples, was [ruling] Rome as senator, with 300 knights as guards of the territory. The Romans, being in the midst of a food shortage because of the great famine that was widespread throughout Italy, were complaining that King Robert was not supplying them with grain from the Kingdom of Naples, and they rose up in protest, shouting out: "Death to the Senator!" And storming the Capitoline Hill[1] they attacked it with such fury that Messer Guiglielmo, even with all his men, could not withstand the assault so that he surrendered and left his office with great humiliation and shame. And the Romans made Messers Stefano Colonna and Poncello Orsini their senators, and in order to placate the people, had their own grain and that of other Roman land-owners brought to the piazza.

Book 10, Chapter 118. How in the Same Year and the Subsequent One, There Was a Great Food Shortage in Florence and Almost All of Italy

In the aforesaid year 1328 [1329][2] through 1330 there was a great shortage of grain and foodstuffs in Florence so that one *staio* of wheat was valued at 17

Translated from *Cronica di Giovanni Villani, a miglior lezione ridotta*, ed. Ignazio Moutier, 4 vols. (Florence: Magheri, 1823), bk. 10, 156–60; bk. 12, 177–83. A new critical edition is available as *Nuova Cronica di Giovanni Villani*, ed. Giovanni Porta, 3 vols. (Parma: Guanda, 1991). Some of the first nine books have been translated by Rose E. Selfe, *Villani's Chronicle Being Selections from the First Nine Books of the Croniche Fiorentine of Giovanni Villani* (London: Archibald Constable, 1906).

1. The Senator's palace was located on the Capitoline Hill.
2. The Florentine year began 25 March.

soldi. Then that same year at 28 *soldi,* then a few days later it rose to 30 *soldi* and then at the beginning of the next year, 1329 [1330] each day it increased, so that at Easter it was worth 42 *soldi* so that from then on in most parts throughout the *contado* one *staio* of the newly harvested grain was worth one gold florin. Grain was therefore priceless, only the rich when they needed it had the money to buy it, so that there was great hardship and difficulty for the poor folk. And it was not only in Florence but all over Italy; and it was such a cruel famine, that the Perugians, Sienese, Lucchesi and Pistoians, and many other towns in Tuscany, because they did not have enough for themselves, expelled all the poor beggars from their towns. The commune of Florence, however, with wise counsel and commendable foresight, [and] with all respect to the mercy of the Lord, did not suffer in this way, but was able to support a great many of the Tuscan poor and furnish a great quantity of money to the grain deposit, sending to Sicily for grain and transporting it by sea to the port of Talamone in Maremma [Tuscany]. From there they brought it to Florence at great risk and expense (likewise from Romagna and the *contado* of Arezzo), all the while disregarding the cost, only the [need created by] the great famine. And the market rate of a bushel of wheat (with a quarter of barley mixed in) was fixed at half a gold florin. And this caused outrage among the people at Orsanmichele [the grain market] so that it was necessary for the families of the ruling lords to arm themselves with tree stumps and axes, sharpening them threateningly, in order to protect the officers and uphold the law.

And in those two years the commune of Florence lost more than 70,000 gold florins in order to sustain the people, and all this would have come to nothing if, in the end, the officials of the commune had decided not to sell grain in the marketplace, but rather to make bread for everyone in the commune's ovens. That bread was then sold every morning in three or four deposits in each of the city's six districts. Each mixed loaf weighed 6 ounces and cost 4 *denari* each. This decision was accepted and appeased the wrath of the people and the poor folk, so that at least everyone was able to have bread to survive, and such that everyone who could not afford a *staio* of wheat also had 8 or 12 *denarii* per day.

And I the writer, who was unworthy of such an office, found myself as an official for our commune along with others in this grievous time, and by the grace of God we were the masterminds of a solution and plan, which pacified the people and calmed their fury and made them happy with no scandal or alarm to the people of the city. And because of this, I can testify truthfully that in no other place did the powerful and pious citizens do so much for the poor as did the good Florentines, who, during that terrible famine, provided for the poor with their alms and provisions. And I think and believe without doubt that because of these alms and provisions made on behalf of the poor, God safeguarded us and will safeguard us from great adversity.

We have spoken at length on this subject as an example to our citizens who will [again] confront this problem, so that when [in the future] the city faces such a dangerous famine, out of reverence for God, the people can be saved and the city does not descend into madness or rebellion.

Not two decades later, Villani describes another famine that began in 1345 and afflicted much of Italy. In the excerpt below Villani recounts its devastating effects, which left the population weakened and vulnerable to the plague that struck only one year later, in which Villani himself perished.

BOOK 12, CHAPTER 73. ON THE GREAT FAMINE IN FLORENCE AND ALL AROUND IN MANY AREAS

In the aforesaid year of 1346, but beginning in October and November of 1345, because of too much rain, the sowing season was ruined, and then in April, May, and June of 1346 it rained ceaselessly, and there were such storms that for similar reasons the sowing of various crops was again ruined. And so it happened that, in many parts of Tuscany and Italy, and in Provence, and in Burgundy, and in France, a great famine was born, and also in Genoa and in Avignon in Provence, where the pope and the Roman curia were [in residence]. And so this came to pass, according to the astrologers and naturalists, because of the conjunction of Saturn and Jupiter and Mars in the sign of Aquarius, just as was mentioned earlier. Not in a hundred years had there been such a bad harvest of grain and fodder and wine and oil and everything else in this country, as there was in this year. And a *cogno* of wine [10 barrels] at the communal harvest was worth from 6 to 8 florins, and there were hardly any doves or chickens because of disease. And a brace of capon was worth one florin, 4 *lire* but you couldn't find them anyway. And fowl for Easter was 12 per brace and pigeons were 10 *soldi,* eggs were 4 or 5 *soldi* each but you couldn't find them, and oil climbed to 8 *lire* per measure. Because of disease wether, ox, and pork increased by 2 1/2 *soldi* to 13 *soldi* per pound and there was a scarcity of fruit and vegetables, all because of too much rain. For that reason, in the past, in some years, there had been scarcity but one could find food in some neighborhoods; but in this year you could scarcely find anything . . .

And there was such great necessity that most farm families abandoned their farms and because of hunger robbed each other for anything they could

find, and many of them came begging in Florence. . . . And just as in 1329
and 1340 there was great scarcity as we have already mentioned, but then you
could find some grain and some fodder in the city and the *contado* but in this
year you could find neither, especially not in the *contado*. . . .

At the beginning, the commune had 60–80 *moggi* of grain in the piazza
selling for 40 *soldi* per *staio*; and then increasing to 50, and barley selling at
40 per *staio*; but all this could not feed the many farmers who had retreated
into the city along with other needy citizens. Therefore, the officials of the
commune built in one of the cottages of the Tedaldini [family] at the San
Piero gate, a big structure—10 ovens with platforms and closed with doors—
where day and night men and women made bread for the commune without
sifting or removing the chaff, which was very rough and painful to see and to
eat. And each weighed 6 ounces, and from every *staio* you could make 9
dozen loaves, and you could bake 85–100 *moggi* of them per day. And they
were distributed at the toll of the prior's bell in the morning at the churches
and deposits throughout the city and outside of the main gates to farmers
who were near the parish of San Giovanni and the other parish gates. And
every day there were two loaves for every mouth that cost 4 *soldi* each. And
there were so many people that needed more than two loaves per head that
the officials could not control the crowd so they ordered that two loaves per
head be given to families by means of a voucher system. And by the middle
of April 1347 there were 94,000 mouths to feed every day; and we knew this
from the Master Officer of the Piazza who collected the vouchers. By now
you can judge for yourself how famine had reduced innumerable people to
be fed [by charity] in Florence, and that number does not include citizens
or their families who had other provisions and those who did not want the
communal bread, . . . nor does it include the religious orders of mendicants,
nor the poor who lived on alms who couldn't even be counted.

UNIVERSITY OF WINCHESTER
LIBRARY

Figure 2. Florentine Grain Merchant and Clients (ca. 1330–40). Miniature from *Maestro del Biadaiolo* Codex, which contains the text of *Specchio Umano* by Domenico Lenzi. Florence, Biblioteca Medicea Laurenziana, Cod. Tempi 3, fol. 2r. (Photo: Scala/Art Resource)

7. A REBELLION IN FIRENZUOLA (1402)

Translated from Latin by Samuel K. Cohn

Historians now generalize that popular rebellion in late medieval Italy occurred in towns but not in the countryside, especially in central and northern Italy, the heartland of city-state republicanism. Chroniclers, such as Gregorio Dati, recounted Florence's epic struggle of "liberty" against Milanese "tyranny" by glossing over the peasant disturbances that spread across Florence's mountainous frontiers at the beginning of the fifteenth century. Indeed, in Dati's account, the very peasants who revolted against the republic's crushing and unequal taxes in 1401–2 became Florence's most feared defenders. Dati's account continues to color our vision of the events of the Milanese-Florentine war of territorial expansion, its external as well as internal events [see #50]. But the judicial and governmental archives (provvisioni) housed in the state archives of Florence preserve records that tell another story: that the peasants of Firenzuola[1] allied themselves with the Ubaldini clan and the Milanese and Bolognese troops to resist Florentine domination and heavy, disproportionate taxation.

Our Battista [son of lord Simone, count of Piacenza], count and *podestà* of this court [the Quarter of Santa Maria Novella], sitting at our usual bench:

Lord Galeotto of Pignole [Pignuole][2]	
Troncha di Giovanni d'Ugolino of Caprile	
Guido di Guido of Pignuole	
Baldinaccio d'Albisio of Cardaccia	
Ceccho d'Ugolino di Francesco of Caprile	
Nanni d'Antonio d'Ugolino of Carda	
Activiano di Tanutio of Carda	all from the de Ubaldini family clan
Nascinbene di Federico	
Cristofano di Francesco	
Ubaldino di Guido	
Scarpecata of the Città di Castello	
Antonio d'Actaviano of Visano	

Translated from Archivio di Stato di Firenze, Podestà, no. 3886 [1402], 9r–10v [The vertical bars inserted here after names imitate those often used in notarial contracts to indicate groups from a town or a family clan.]

1. A new town and bastion built in 1332 to defend Florence from the Ubaldini lords.

2. Most of these villages—Caburaccio, Castro, Cornacchiaia, Pignole, Rapezzo, Santerno, and Tirli—were in the Alpi Fiorentine. Carda, Caprile, Coderonco, and Visano were to the east, in the mountains of Romagna.

Giovanni di Guadino of Coderoncho [Coderonco] |

Ser Vannino di Cenni |

Lippo di Ser Gini |

Giovanni di Maestro Martino |

Silvestro, called Totto di Ser Niccolai | from Caburaccio

Ser Francesco di Ser Niccolai, a priest |

Biagio di Lorenzo |

Giovannino di Magnino |

Bonono di Bertolo |

Cante and his brother | | from Cornacchiaia

Tonno and his brother |

Stefano di Fanutio |
Antonio d'Ugolino di Tani from Carda of the Ubaldini
Guido di Vannino, a cobbler from Rapezzo
Francesco di Nuccio, called Barile from Santerno

Tango di Guido |

Dominico di Chino | from Rapezzo, living in Tirli

Nanni di Tonio |

Banbo, his son | from Pignuole

Giovanni di Soccino |
Angelino del Merla
Azzino di Babbino

Cinaccio |
Giusto | di Bertino

Stefano di Viviano, called Tanaya |

Giovanni, alius Tacchone | |

Viviano, alius Nasso | his sons | from Castro

Guidoccello di Simone |

Guiduccino di Betti and |

Tonio di Mascio, alius Gnacchio |

Traitors and rebels against the Magnificent and Glorious People and Commune of Florence, men of evil habits, associations, life, and reputation . . . the above-stated in this inquest, each of them, and many others whose names at present it is better to keep silent, in the present year [1402] during the months of July and August, have been spurred on by the spirit of the devil . . . to commit and perpetrate the rebellion and betrayal described below. That is, this Galeotto Troncha of the Ubaldini clan and Cinuccio with many of the others listed above went to the city of Bologna on many, many occasions on various days, by day and at night, to talk, negotiate, and plot with Lord Jacopo del Vernio, the Duke of Milan's lieutenant in the city of Bologna and the leader of the duke's armed forces. To overthrow and rebel against the *castrum* of Firenzuola in the *contado* of Florence, on the river Santerno, surrounded by walls and moats, and located in the jurisdiction of Firenzuola, Ser Vannino ordered along with Cinaccio and many others of the indicted, saying to this lord Jacopo, the lieutenant and captain: "We have organized a plot for the take-over of this district of Firenzuola and its Alpine region, which should proceed as follows: when the bell-tower chimes, you are to have your army of foot soldiers and cavalry ready at the [entrance of] the *castrum* of Firenzuola." Ser Vannino, Cinaccio, Nasso,[3] and many others of those listed above, in whom the vicar of Firenzuola had placed great trust, went to this walled town with many others, their friends, whom they had enlisted. Armed with defensive and offensive weapons, they simply entered the town at the planned time as though all was normal. And Ser Vannino, Cinaccio, and the others named above thought that their forces were stronger than those of the *vicarius*[4] and the soldiers of the commune of Florence, who were permanently posted there. With their swords, they planned to kill the *vicarius* and the Florentine soldiers and would then lead a revolt in this walled town against the commune of Florence for the Ubaldini clan. But this time the orders and plans of Ser Vannino, Cinaccio, and the others failed to achieve these most depraved plans, plots, and intentions. They ordered the above-mentioned army [of Jacopo del Vernio] to come near to the walls of this walled-town to rebel against the Florentine troops inside Firenzuola. Ser Vannino said to the Florentine soldiers: "And with street fighting and skirmishes, we will push you out of this town, one after another, starting with the soldiers of Florence, and we will allow you to follow us to the main gate of the town, to give up your weapons, and then to flee quickly. We will then enter with all of our troops to take over the guard of this gate; we kill the *vicarius* of this town and any soldiers of the commune of Florence who remain here. Once this *vicarius* has been murdered, we will run through this town of Firenzuola, causing it to rebel against Florence, its dominion, power, and authority. We

3. By late fourteenth-century tax records (*estimi*), these were well-to-do peasants with family farms.
4. An official deputized by the commune of Florence to exercise local jurisdiction.

will further commit and perpetrate many other crimes and murders against foreigners and friends of the Commune of Florence." With all these orders, plots, decisions, and efforts firmly agreed to among them, the Highest One, who can repair all evil for the greatest good and bring about a favorable remedy, came forth and intervened: with the mediation of divine grace and with foresight, industry, and care, this lord *vicarius* of Firenzuola discovered each and every one of their plans and decisions so that they were unable to carry out their depraved and wicked plans. . . .

Not content with what they had done, this Vannino, lord Galleotto, Troncha, and Cinaccio, together with many of the other indicted realized that this lord *vicarius* had become aware of their iniquitous plans, and so they deliberated, plotted, and ordered an alternative and more effective plan to bring off their rebellion. They went to the city of Bologna for discussions with Lord Jacopo del Vernio, lieutenant and military captain and between them conducted discussions, plans, and deliberations. Then Ser Vannino, lord Galeotto, Troncha Ubaldini, Cinaccio, and many others indicted with the good wishes of this lord Jacopo del Vernio, lieutenant and captain, led a great quantity of weapons, cavalry, and foot soldiers of the duke [of Milan] into Firenzuola, including many catapults, iron assault weapons, and many other constructions built to overthrow the town of Firenzuola. They transported these things to a place, called the hilltop of Montecoloreto, which is in the Alps above Firenzuola, near the villages of Pignuole, Brento, and Brento Orsanio. And here on the summit of this hill, the indicted along with many others, whose names for the present are best to keep quiet, made, formed, and built a bastion built of wood and stone, where they remained for many days as the enemies and rebels of the city of Florence. With the pleas and support of the Ubaldini and the lieutenant of the Duke of Milan, they inflicted maximum damage, injury, and shame to the People of the Commune of Florence.

Not content with this but wishing to add even more evil deeds to those already committed, Cinaccio, together with the above-indicted Bonomo di Bertolo and many others of the foot-soldiers and cavalry of the duke, came down from the hilltop of Montecollereto and invaded a certain place called the bastion of Castro in the Florentine Alps, near the villages of Cornacchiaia, Casanuova, and le Valli, which these rebels and enemies held for the Ubaldini. They also went to a certain place called the hilltop of the Castle Giurino in these mountains, near the villages of Casanuova and Cornacchiaia. And on the summit of this hill, they built a bastion out of wood, which they held for many days at the request of the Ubaldini and the duke of Milan's lieutenant. And from this bastion, they committed and perpetrated many acts of robbery and extortion against subjects of the commune of Florence. Further, they captured and preyed on many messengers, who were sent to the lord *vicarius* with many letters from the lord priors of the guilds, the standard-bearer of justice [see **#17, 18**], and the Magnificent lords, the Ten of War of the commune of Florence.[5] On these mountaintops and from their bastions, the indicted built and set up siege weapons to invade and take over the walled town of Firenzuola. And although they were not able to execute each and every one of their commands, they brought grave damage, injury, and maximum shame to the Magnificent People and commune of Florence. . . .

None of the indicted appeared before the court; they were sentenced to be led to the usual place of justice in the city of Florence, where each of them was to be beheaded. All their property was to be confiscated and their names entered into the Book of Rebels. The sentence was promulgated on 9 December 1402.

5. Political officers and councils of the governing body of Florence.

Spheres and Structures of Power: Ecclesiastical and Secular

Throughout the medieval west, a major theme for historians is the shifting relationship of secular and sacred power and the institutions formed to express that power: here, the Church (both secular and regular), the Crown, and rural and urban lordships. Churches and the lands that went with them embodied both sacred and secular authority, and the men and women documented here were alive to how these might be used. Thus the bishop of Florence established a monastery at San Miniato in part as a way to avoid the alienation of ecclesiastical property into lay hands. At the same time both lay men and women and the clergy recognized the spiritual authority and power vested in the saints and in living holy men and women. A key theme in the documents presented here is the central and varied role of a bishop, from play-acting so that the people of Gubbio put an end to violence, visiting churches to ensure that standards were maintained (and also, not coincidentally, underlining the secular authority of a city), to representing secular government in receiving the oaths of citizens new and old. These documents also illustrate both the changing role of the bishop as new urban authorities came to the fore, and some of the difficulties of those urban entities seeking autonomy in the face of some of the great rulers of the Middle Ages, emperors such as Frederick I Barbarossa. Assessing and tracing the changing authority of these imperial rulers is indeed a central problem for historians working throughout the peninsula. Emperors were to be found legitimizing a new bishop (as here in Gubbio in the early eleventh century), issuing privileges to the emerging citizen bodies (and on occasion repealing them, as here in Cremona), but also failing to do so. Indeed, the absence of emperors, engaged elsewhere in their vast territories, allowed space first for regional lords and later for city councils to assume royal and imperial jurisdictions. Just as the papacy fought to remove imperial control over bishops, so in 1183 the cities succeeded in wresting concessions from the reluctant emperor which fundamentally changed the ground rules of government and power in northern and central Italy for the following century, and served as a legitimizing moment for the new communes. The detailed measures instituted to shore up the authority of these nascent communal authorities are also evident here—in lawsuits, oath-taking, and elaborate guarantees for fair distribution of taxation and guard duty. Similarly sophisticated administrative techniques were also characteristic of twelfth-century Sicily, where a bilingual (Arabic-Latin) boundary description records the evocative names of landmarks, reminding us of just how close to the land the population of medieval Europe remained. Land was both a means to describe the world and a source of power through the crops (and taxes) it produced. A bilingual list of taxpayers in Arabic-Greek from late twelfth-

century Corleone compares closely in intent to an appeal to the population of Lucca to pay more taxes to defend themselves against the neighboring city of Pisa at the end of the fourteenth century. The speech of the Lucca standard-bearer also epitomizes a characteristic tactic of the city governments which had come to dominate central and northern Italy—the appeal to civic patriotism and a locally shared history. But the reality of conflict is equally evident in the rise of the popolo *in the thirteenth century, a phenomenon stemming at least in part from new forms of class consciousness.*

8. THE BISHOPRIC OF FLORENCE AND THE FOUNDATION OF SAN MINIATO AL MONTE (1013)

Translated from Latin by George Dameron

The following document is the foundation charter of the episcopal proprietary mon-astery[1] [see #9] of San Miniato al Monte, located in the southern suburb of Florence on a ridge overlooking the city. The basilica is still arguably the most beautiful church in the city today. This text describes the conscious attempt on the part of the bishop to revive the cult of San Miniato (Saint Minias), who, according to tradition, was the first Christian martyr of the city. To support the community of Benedictine monks that he established on the site, Bishop Ildebrando endowed the monastery with properties that were located in the suburbs of the city as well as further afield in the Mugello, the major valley north of the city. One of the important but unstated rea-sons for the granting of these specific properties to the community was to protect certain episcopal holdings from rivals, specifically rural lords and their patrili-neages. Such a practice was not uncommon among both secular and ecclesiastical lords at this time. The revival of the cult of San Miniato accomplished a number of purposes: it served to shore up the power of the bishopric, generate offerings and attract donations to the monastery, and defend certain landed estates from rivals by placing them under the protection of the saint.

In the name of God, Amen. In the year of the Incarnation of our Lord, 1013, when Henry [II] was Emperor Augustus of the Romans, on the fifth day before the Kalends of May, 11th Indiction. While I, Ildebrando, by no merit of my own as bishop of the holy Florentine church, was visiting our own oratories of the diocese, finding many that were neglected and striving to restore them, I came upon a church not far from the city that was dedicated in honor of San Miniato the martyr. Distinguished as a monastery in antiq-uity, yet now neglected by too much age, I found that the structure was a virtual ruin. Anxiously, I began to consider how I might be able to restore it. I was burning with the greatest desire to accomplish this task, especially since I had heard that the venerable body of the above-mentioned martyr was rest-ing there. For these reasons I was eager to go to my lord the Emperor so that by his advice and assistance I might be more encouraged and better able to accomplish what I was already wishing to do. The Emperor, inspired by the mercy of God, enthusiastically shared my joy, and he instructed me to estab-

Translated from Ferdinando Ughelli, *Italia sacra de episcopis Italiae et insularum adjacent-ium*, vol. 3 (Venice: Coleti, 1718), cols. 47–48.

1. An episcopal proprietary monastery was a monastery owned by the bishop. He had the right to elect the abbot, and he controlled the properties of the institution. See John Gilchrist, "Proprietary Churches," *New Catholic Encyclopedia*, 2nd ed. (Detroit: Thomas Gale, 2003), vol. II, 771.

Figure 3. Façade of San Miniato al Monte, Florence (twelfth century). (Photo: Vanni/ Art Resource)

lish a monastic community in the aforesaid church, just as had existed in antiquity. He promised me his assistance. Returning to our diocese, having received the license of his blessing, I notified the cathedral canons, all the clergy, and the laity of our city of my plan, and I revealed to all of them in turn the counsel which I had received from the emperor and from my fellow bishops. They were all very pleased. The actual execution of this project, which I had been planning for a while, became a source of great inspiration for all. Reflecting, therefore, on the fragile nature of our mortality and the uncertain fate of our lives, and putting aside any reasons for delay, I began to set about to decide how to accomplish this project. After this desired work had gotten underway, we heard, by popular report already widely known in the area, that those precious jewels, the martyred saints, were buried visibly yet inappropriately in the aforesaid church. We thereupon came across the body of that venerable holy martyr, Miniato, as well as the bodies of several other saints, crowned with the palm of the victory of martyrdom. Such discoveries emboldened us even more. Constructing the tomb of the martyr and celebrating that most sacred treasury of holy relics, according to the best of our resources and our love of God, we re-founded and established this sacred site so that the servants of God would be able to live there. Therefore, I, Ildebrando, unworthy prelate of the holy church of Florence, for the love of God, the remedy of my soul, in the hope of a future reward, for the souls of my predecessors and successors the bishops of the city of Florence, for the souls of my lord the emperor, his famous wife, Cunegunda, for the remedy of the souls of the emperors and kings of the Kingdom of Italy, and for the souls of all those who have given or will give to this monastery, and for all Christian people, confirm and establish the often mentioned church of San Miniato the Martyr that belongs to San Giovanni [Saint John], located within the territory of the baptismal district of Santa Reparata in the city of Florence, as a monastic community.[2] With the consent and authority of the priests, cathedral canons, clergy, and with the blessing of the laity of the city of Florence, I concede in perpetuity all possessions, which to the church or monastery of San Miniato pertains or will pertain, that are necessary for these brothers to live under the rule.[3] To the abbot of those servants of God I grant and confirm in perpetuity the following: the site and the mountain where the

2. San Giovanni was one of the patron saints of the diocese (along with Saints Reparata and Zanobi), and the baptistry was named after him. Another way of rendering the Latin phrase is "within the diocese of Saint John." The phrase clearly implies that the new monastery is "under the protection of Saint John." Because it is part of the bishop's estate, it is essentially also the "property of Saint John."

3. The rule mentioned here, or set of regulations governing a monastic community, was the sixth-century Rule of Saint Benedict.

monastery is located (which in Antiquity was known as the Monte Florentinus, or the Florentine Mountain, but now is known as the Mountain of San Miniato). This comes with all the properties adjacent and attached, around, and below said mountain. I also grant to the church and monastery of San Miniato all its other properties in other locations, along with its unfree and half-free tenants of both sexes, wherever they may be found. Also included are houses, estates, oratories, landed holdings, former demesnes, woods, lands, vineyards, and all other properties pertaining to the aforesaid church, linked to it by place, settlement, name, and boundary. Similarly, I also establish and grant among its possessions the collegiate church of Sant'Andrea, located within the city of Florence near the Forum Domini Regis and the arch, along with all its associated properties, houses, estates, landed holdings, former demesnes, unfree and half-free tenants of both genders, lands, vineyards (both inside and outside the city walls), and any other holding associated with said church and monastery linked to it by location, settlement, name, or appendage. In the same way I grant the *castello* [a fortified settlement] and estate which is called Montalto, with all its attached properties. I also grant half of the *castello* that is called Montacuto, the estate called Lonnano, with all its associated possessions belonging to San Giovanni. This includes an entire oratory named after San Miniato and the fourth part of another oratory, named after San Salvatore.

I, Ildebrando, bishop of the holy church of Florence, confirm all that is written above. I, Gerardo the archpresbyter, have consented and confirmed all that is written above.

9. PROPRIETARY RELIGIOUS HOUSES IN THE DIOCESE OF SALERNO (1047–92)

Translated from Latin by Valerie Ramseyer

Before the twelfth century, the majority of religious houses in the Principality of Salerno were built and administered by individuals, often times laypeople, acting independently of the bishop or any other ecclesiastical official. These proprietary houses, as they are often referred to in English, could be bought, sold, bequeathed, and divided in the same manner as landed property [see #8]. The owners, however, were required to find clerics to administer and officiate in their houses, as well as to provide the material resources necessary to maintain and support the clergy. These proprietary houses could be monasteries, family chapels, or churches exercising the full range of pastoral duties. In some cases the bishops granted emancipation charters confirming the house's immunity from episcopal authority, although in general no such recognition from the bishop came. Notice, too, that priests frequently married and had children. The charter translated below comes from the archive of the abbey of the Holy Trinity of Cava just outside Salerno.

The following charter contains a number of inserts of earlier charters. In cases where an original survives and gives important additional information, a summary of the original charter is included in italics and brackets.

September 1092

In the name of God Eternal and our Savior Jesus Christ, in the 1092nd year since the incarnation, in the time of our lord the glorious duke Roger [Borsa], in the month of September, in the first year of the indiction. Before me John a judge, came John a cleric, son of Raidolfus a priest and abbot and he demonstrated to me that he owned two parts of some woodlands outside the city of Salerno in a place called Balnearia on which the church of Santa Lucia is built, as well as two parts of the church of Santa Lucia along with all of its wealth, both landed and movable, and he described the boundaries and measurements of the land, on which the church was built, as follows [*description of property's borders*]. . . . Then he showed six charters pertaining to the church and its property:

The first charter was written by the notary John, in the twenty-ninth year of lord Guaimarius [IV]'s rule over the Principality [of Salerno]. [January 1047]

Raidolfus, a priest and abbot, declared that out of love for omnipotent

Translated from *Le Pergamene di San Nicola di Gallucanta (secc. IX–XII)*, ed. Paolo Cherubini (Salerno: Studi Storici Meridionali, 1990), no. 115.

God he had built on his property in Balnearia a new church dedicated to Santa Lucia and that he had given to the church the piece of land on which the church was built, with all its appurtenances and roads. And this land Raidolfus had inherited from his father, Dumnellus, and his mother. In turn Raidolfus along with his brother Sesamus John, Ursus, and Ralfus sons of Lambertus and their mother, a widow, Gaita, Gualprandus son of Guaiferius and his mother Salbia, Madelmus and Altardus sons of Potus and their mother, a widow, Dilecta and Altardus' wife Aloara, and two clerics Peter and Dilectus sons of Iaquintus together, by mutual agreement and of their own free will, for the salvation and well-being of their souls and the souls of their relatives, with this charter offered to the church [of Santa Lucia] a piece of land in Balnearia in a place called Anna Cennama as well as their portion of elevated land in a place called Sant'Arcangelo. And the church will control and possess all that they have donated and the rectors of the church will do what they want with the land, along with its appurtenances and roads, just as is described in this charter signed by Theodoricus and Concilis priests.

The church would forever remain under the authority of Raidolfus and his heirs, who would appoint priests to officiate. These priests, moreover, would bring offerings to Raidolfus and his heirs on Christmas, Easter, and the feast day of Santa Lucia.

The second charter was written by the notary Romoaldus, in the thirty-third year of the rule of lord Guamarius [IV] over the Principality [of Salerno]—[November 1050].

Lord John by grace of God archbishop of the Holy See of the Archbishopric of Salerno declared that Raidolfus a priest and abbot, son of Dumnellus, constructed the above-mentioned new church dedicated to the virgin Santa Lucia on his property in Balnearia. And Lord John by agreement and with this charter conceded to and confirmed on Raidolfus the priest the whole of the church of Santa Lucia the virgin. The church would forever remain secure and free from the [power of the] archbishop, always under the authority of Raidolfus and his heirs, and neither the archbishop nor his successors would requisition the church or act contrary [to Raidolfus's rights], just as is written in this charter signed by John the archbishop, Amatus a priest and cardinal, and Iaquintus a subdeacon.

The archbishop gave Raidolfus and his heirs the right to appoint priests, monks, and clerics to serve in the church, whomever they wanted, in accordance with canon law. However, he reserved the right to bring the priests, monks, and clerics before him to judge, whenever he deemed necessary, also in accordance with canon law. In addition, if any of the church's altars was ever contaminated, the archbishop would come with holy water to reconsecrate it. The archbishop asserted that he would never demand taxes, donations, or services from the church's clergy, although Raidolfus and his heirs would pay him an annual fee of wax on the feast day of Santa Lucia.

The third charter was written by the notary John, in the twelfth year of the reign of the above-mentioned prince Gisolf [II], in the month of July, in the sixth year of the indiction. [July 1053]. Raidolfus priest and abbot on behalf of the church [of Santa Lucia], which he built, handed over to his brother Sesamus a piece of land in Balnearia. . . . [*Description of the land's borders.*] The charter was signed by Ademarius and Peter a priest.

The lease was perpetual and Sesamus was to plant fruit trees and vines over the next twelve years. For the first eight years, he was to give to the church only the terraticum *tax on the grain output. After eight years, he also had to give to the church one-half of the wine output, which he was required to transport to the rector's house, as well as the* palmenticum *tax for use of the wine press.*

The fourth charter was written by the notary Peter, in the seventeenth year of the reign of the above-mentioned prince Gisolf [II], in the month of April, in the eleventh year of the indiction [April 1058]. Raidolfus priest and abbot handed over to Marconus a priest son of Rainaldus all of the church of Santa Lucia with all its possessions, both landed and movable, and with its cells and houses, according to the terms contained in this charter signed by the notaries John and Peter.

Presumably Raidolfus handed over the church to Marconus to officiate in.

The fifth charter was written by the notary John, in the twenty-first year of the reign of prince Gisolf [II], in the month of March, in the first year of the indiction. [March 1063]. John son of Lambertus from Balnearia of his own free will with this charter and in front of witnesses sold to the above-mentioned Sesamus son of Dumnellus, and confirmed upon him perpetual possession of, a piece of land with vines located in Balnearia, in the place referred to as "a lu Puteum." [*Description of the land's borders.*] And everything pertaining to this piece of property, including its roads, would belong to Sesamus and his heirs to do with as they want, as described in this charter signed by Romoaldus and Ademarius.

John sold the land for ten gold tari.

The sixth charter was written by the notary John, in the twenty-first year of the reign of Prince Gisolf [II], in the month of March, in the first year of the indiction [March 1063]. Sesamus son of Dumnellus demonstrated with this charter of sale that he owned a piece of land with vines in Balnearia, which formerly belonged to his cousin John son of Lambertus. [*Description of the land's borders.*] Thus Sesamus, of his own free will, for the love of Almighty God, and for the salvation and well-being of his soul and the souls of his relatives, with this charter conceded and handed over this land that formerly belonged to John, as described in the charter, to the church of Santa Lucia. And [the church of] Santa Lucia would always have power over everything that pertains to this piece of property, including its roads, just as described in the charter signed by Romoaldus and Peter.

After all the above charters were shown and read, this cleric John, out of love and fear for God, of his own free will, and for the well-being of his soul and the souls of his relatives, with this charter donated to the Monastery of the Holy Confessor and Pontifex Nicolas located in Petralena and Gallucanta and headed by the monk and priest Theophilus, his two parts of the woodlands, with the borders and measurements as described above, along with two parts of the above-mentioned church of Santa Lucia, which is built on this land, and two parts of all the church's landed wealth, as described in the charters mentioned above, and two parts of all the other landed and movable wealth belonging to the church, with all its appurtenances and roads. And everything will forever be in the power of the above-mentioned abbot (Theophilus), his successors, and the monastic community to do with as they wish. However, on Christmas, on Easter, and on the feast day of Santa Lucia, the abbot, his successors, and the monastic community will give two parts of the donations collected by the church to John and his heirs, as well as two cubits of wax, to do with as they wish. For this agreement John the cleric, in the presence of respectable men, gave a pledge to the abbot [Theophilus] on behalf of the monastery and most faithfully named Leo son of Peter and Salegarda as his guarantor. With this pledge John and his heirs are obliged to defend for the abbot, his successors, and the monastic community, in all ways and at all times, the donation, as written above, against other men. In addition, permission was given to the abbot, his successors, and the monastic community to defend their rights whenever and however they wish, with the documents and rights shown above. If the above-mentioned John the cleric or his heirs do not fulfill [the terms of this agreement] as written above, or if they dare to renege on or contradict [this agreement], then due to their pledge they will be obliged to pay to the abbot, his successors, or the monastic community one hundred gold Constantinian *solidi*. The abbot [Theophilus] gave his pledge to John and named as his guarantor Ligorius son of Andreas, who now by grace of God is a monk in the monastery [of San

Nicola]. With this pledge Theophilus, his successors, and the monastic community agreed to pay (a fine) of twenty gold Constantinian *solidi* if they do not give the donations or wax to John and his heirs as written above. I, the judge John, on behalf of the monastery, asked the notary John to write this.

Signed by the judge John and the notary Grimoaldus.

10. THE COMMUNE AND BISHOP OF FLORENCE FORBID THE ALIENATION OF ECCLESIASTICAL PROPERTY (1159)

Translated from Latin by George Dameron

In 1323, three magnate families of Florence were administering the vacant bishopric after the death of Bishop Antonio d'Orso in 1321. To establish a clear account of the temporal holdings of the bishopric, they commissioned the publication of a compendium *or register of all documents pertaining to the landed properties, estates, and temporal rights of the bishopric. That register, known as the* Bullettone, *contains abbreviated versions of original documents, organized by the notaries according to locality. The entry extracted below reveals that in the middle of the twelfth century the Florentine elite (the bishop and the civic magistrates) considered the alienation (buying, selling, transferring) of church property—without proper authorization by ecclesiastical authority—to be against the security interests of the commune. Few of the urban elite had significant holdings in the countryside, but the bishop and cathedral chapter of Florence were among them. For that reason, Florentine urban leaders assumed that the potential loss of church properties in the countryside endangered secular as well as ecclesiastical security. Of particular concern was that the great rural families, or patrilineages, who still held sway over vast areas of the countryside, might accrue more property, thereby extending their power and influence.*

There exists a certain public document that includes a number of ordinances passed by the Commune and people of Florence, which includes the following: if anyone should alienate or usurp in any way the possessions of the church of Florence, from that moment on any contract between that person and the church should be considered null and void. The bishop of Florence, by virtue of his own authority and judgment, can nullify and contravene such contracts. In these cases, no Florentine judge or official may offer any assistance. This charter was drawn up in the hand of Alberto, the notary, along with several other notaries who signed here below. Dated 1158, the fourth day before the Nones of January, indiction 7.[1]

Translated from Archivio Arcivescovile, carta 171, and Archivio di Stato, Manoscritti, carta 315, ed. Pietro Santini, "Estratti dal *Bullettone*," *Documenti dell'antica costituzione di Firenze, Appendice* (Florence: Olschki, 1952), 501.
    1. The Florentine calendar began 25 March (the feast of the Annunciation). Hence this document actually dated from 1159 (common style), not 1158 (Florentine style).

11. EPISCOPAL LORDSHIP: SCENES FROM THE LIFE OF UBALDO OF GUBBIO (ca. 1160)

Translated from Latin by Maureen Miller

From at least the tenth century, bishops were important civic leaders in Italian cities. Some actually ruled their cities as counts, while the lordship of others was based on the extensive landholdings of their sees and their spiritual leadership. The life of Sant' Ubaldo, bishop of Gubbio from 1129 to 1160, provides a colorful portrait of the bishop as civic leader. This vita *was written by Ubaldo's successor in the see, Bishop Tebaldo, probably shortly after the saint's demise in 1160.*

A short time later, Bishop Stefano of blessed memory died, leaving widowed the see of Gubbio—the city, namely, of that man of God Ubaldo. When the clergy of the city, however, could not come to agreement on the election of a new bishop, the servant of God [Ubaldo] with a few of his followers went to Rome seeking to be chosen bishop by the Roman Church and consecrated by the pope himself. Indeed, the stone that the builders had rejected became the cornerstone: God made his servant Ubaldo, rejected by his fellow citizens but elected by the witness of his merits, pastor of his people. For when the aforementioned servant of God made his request along with his clergy, the Pope acquiesced instantly. Divinely instructed, the Pope himself nominated Ubaldo and ordered the clerics from Gubbio who were there to elect him their bishop. Having been thus honorably elected and then even more honorably consecrated by that same Roman Pontiff [Honorius II], Ubaldo returned to Gubbio and happily took up the episcopal seat of rulership.

A description follows of Ubaldo's virtues: he is humble, kind, affable. He mortifies his flesh, eats very little, and spurns rich clothing. He prays constantly.

One day, while the city walls were being built and they were mixing cement for this project, one of the episcopal vineyards, located just below the wall, suffered great damage. Humbly intervening, Ubaldo ordered them to stop lest further harm be done to the vines. The overseer of the work stubbornly refused and threw Ubaldo violently into the liquid cement being prepared. When the bishop got up, totally drenched [in the wet cement], he was humbly silent and with great patience, as if nothing had happened, he returned to his residence. But the citizens could not bear the injury done to their bishop: they threatened not only to destroy the house of the overseer

Translated from *AASS*, ed. Johannes Bolland et al., new ed. (Paris and Rome: Palme, 1863–), 3 May: 627–34.

and seize all that he had, but they also wanted to expel him from the city. The bishop, however, calmed the people's outburst and reserved to himself the power to punish the man, acting as if he intended to deal with him even more severely. When the accused was brought before the bishop and asked if he would obey the order [to stop work], the man promised to do whatever Ubaldo commanded, even if the bishop wished to condemn him to death. But the bishop declared that the man in no way deserved a sentence so harsh as the one proposed. The man, however, with great devotion and fearfully calling upon God as his witness, promised to do whatever the man of God commanded. The many people gathered there were stunned and waited expectantly to see what the bishop would order. Bishop Ubaldo rose up and drawing near to him who had thrown himself on the ground, said, "Give me a kiss, son, and may Almighty God forgive this and all your sins."

Another day, a violent insurrection broke out in the city plaza, and with the citizens fighting fiercely among themselves, many died there from their wounds. When blessed Ubaldo heard, he was greatly disturbed and ran quickly to the scene of the fighting. When he was unable to quell the warfare by reasoning [with the people] he rushed straightaway into the middle of the battling combatants where, among sword thrusts and a hail of stones, he immediately fell to the ground as if mortally wounded. Thinking he was dead, the people immediately threw down their arms, tore at their hair, and both men and women alike hastened to the terrible death (as they thought) of such a father. A great cry of mourning rose up to the heavens, and each one blamed himself for his death, proclaiming himself a murderer. When the man of God perceived that the war had ceased, he got up slowly and indicated with a motion of his hand that he was not wounded. And so it was that while the bishop gave himself over to death for his people, the people lived and the bishop did not perish. . . .

In the same period [1155], eleven powerful cities combined their forces and laid siege to Gubbio. The enemy forces outnumbered those of Gubbio forty to one. For three days the man of God Ubaldo led processions around the city, interceding most devoutly with Almighty God for the safety of his people. When the day of battle arrived, the holy man wisely exhorted his people to be steadfast in hope for a heavenly victory. Armed with the bishop's blessing, they went into battle. The bishop went up to the cloister roof—that is, the highest point in the town—so that he could see his people. And just as God destroyed the Amalekites when Moses prayed for Israel (Exodus 17:11–13), so when Ubaldo prayed, the Lord put to flight all the adversaries of Gubbio. At the first clash of battle, they all turned, fled, and threw down their arms. . . .

Figure 4. San Gimignano, patron saint and protector (ca. 1391). Central panel of San Gimignano altarpiece by Taddeo di Bartolo. San Gimignano, Museo Civico. (Photo: Scala/Art Resource)

The glorious Roman emperor Frederick [Barbarossa], when he was returning from Rome to his German lands, was led by enemies of the city to Gubbio. These enemies of the victorious citizens of Gubbio endeavored with pleas and gifts to incite the emperor to the destruction of the city and ruin of its people. But Almighty God, who was defending the city at the solicitude of its father [Ubaldo], filled the heart of the gentle emperor with merciful affection. For the salvation of his people there, God gave grace to blessed Ubaldo in the sight of the most serene emperor, and even more grace to the emperor in his view of blessed Ubaldo so that he understood his holiness, received him reverently, dealt with him honorably, and so that the man of God assented readily to what he proposed. The bountiful emperor gave to Ubaldo, among other gifts, a silver bowl and on bended knee he submissively commended himself to the bishop's prayers and humbly obtained the requested grace of his blessing.

12. FEDERIGO VISCONTI'S PASTORAL VISITATION TO SARDINIA (1263)

Translated from Latin by William North

The century following the Fourth Lateran Council (1215) saw a veritable explosion of texts and initiatives designed to improve pastoral care within Christendom. Central to this reform was a renewed emphasis on the importance of regular and systematic oversight of local diocesan and archdiocesan affairs by the ecclesiastical superior, a duty implicit in the bishop's title itself (episcopus = one who oversees) but often compromised by bishops' roles as important princes, lobbyists, and politicians. The episcopal or archiepiscopal visitation was a principal instrument of such oversight, and detailed accounts of visitations survive for England and France. Among the documents from medieval Italy, however, Archbishop Federigo Visconti's record of his visitation of Sardinia in 1263 to inspect the state of religious life on the island—the dioceses of which fell within his jurisdiction—is unique. It bears detailed witness to the varied activities, ceremonies, costs, and rewards of such a visitation. It also shows clearly how larger political conflicts such as that between Guelf and Ghibelline factions on the mainland or regional struggles for authority on Sardinia itself could significantly influence the success of such a pastoral visit. In its mix of sacred and secular, pastoral care and ecclesiastical power, material and spiritual gifts, Visconti's account offers a detailed look at the warp and woof of Pisa's religious life and order.

Its author and protagonist, Archbishop Federigo Visconti, was born ca. 1200 of a noble Pisan family, studied in Bologna and Paris, saw St. Francis in person, and belonged to the household of the pastorally minded Pope Innocent IV (1243–54). Because of Pisa's pro-imperial stance, Federigo, elected archbishop in 1254, was not consecrated until 1257. Dying in 1277, he is remembered for his preaching, a pastoral activity expressed in diocesan synods, statutes, and visitations, and his building projects.

1. In the year of the Lord's Incarnation 1264 [1263], in the sixth year of our consecration, we, Federigo, archbishop of the holy church of Pisa by the grace of God and the apostles, primate of all Sardinia, and legate of the Apostolic See, went to the Curia. There we sought and received general confirmation of our privileges from Lord Pope Urban IV [1261–64] in the second year of his pontificate, and also a letter [declaring] that we could freely exercise our rights in Sardinia. And so, after conducting a visitation of the city and diocese of our Pisa with solemnity and joy, at the entreaty of the *podestà*, the *anziani*, and commune of Pisa, we prepared ourselves magnificently to cross

Translated from Federigo Visconti, "Visitatio Sardinee," in *Les sermons et la visite pastorale de Federico Visconti, archévêque de Pise (1253–77)*, ed. Nicole Bériou and Isabelle le Masne de Chermont, Sources et documents d'histoire du Moyen Âge 3 (Rome: École française de Rome, 2001), 1059–68.

over to Sardinia in order to exercise the office of the primate, of our legation, and of visitation. . . .

4. While we were awaiting horses from the bishops, judges,[1] and lords of Sardinia at Cagliari, the feast of St. Mark occurred and we performed the Litanies in person together with the bishop of Sulcis. Starting from the church of the Blessed Mary [the cathedral], we went to the church of Santa Lucia; after we had sung the responsory and said a prayer to her, we went in procession to the church of San Leonardo, where we did likewise, and then on to Santa Margarita, where her gospel reading was sung, confession administered, and an indulgence of forty days was proclaimed for us and for the suffragan [bishops]. Then we continued by way of the churches of Sant'Efisio, Santa Restituta, and Sant'Anna, which were in the village of Stampace, until we arrived at the church of San Brancasio where we rested, chanted his responsory and gospel, and administered confession. Then, we returned to the church of Santa Maria through the middle of the fortress, and there celebrated the solemnities of the Mass with glory and honor, preaching to the people about how litanies of this kind developed and how they should be celebrated each year, and we decreed that from that time on what was not being done should be done.

5. The archbishop of Torres was a Cistercian monk named Brother Prosper, a Lombard by birth from Reggio who had then been in Rome or at the Curia and had been legate to Sardinia and Corsica. Because he envied us and the Commune of Pisa, he silenced the truth and sought and received [from the papacy] letters, one addressed to us saying that we were not allowed to exercise our legateship, the other to the prelates of Sardinia telling them not to obey us, since the Lord Pope did not intend to revoke [the archbishop of Torres's] legation. But the real reason [for these letters] was that the Pisans had been excommunicated because, contrary to papal mandate, they had ridden against the people of Lucca who were siding with the Church against Lord Manfred, prince and king of Sicily. The [pope's] letter, however, did not reach us in Sardinia, although the other one did reach the other prelates: for the messengers were captured at Cagliari by the castellans and were released upon the entreaty of the judge and the archbishop of Arborea. [In response to this letter], we said that, assuming that the letter was genuine, we ought to be admitted [to their dioceses] if not as legate, then as primate and patriarch of all Sardinia. And so it was done.

---

1. Beginning in the sixth century, the island was divided into first three, then four judicatures, each headed by a judge. They were located in Torres, Arborea, Gallura, and Cagliari.

6. Although we had with us horses and the aforementioned persons, we also took with us throughout Sardinia seventeen men including Lord Tancred, chaplain of Calcinaria; the parish priest of Aquis; a canon of Callaritano; Master Cortingo; Lord Bavera who was learned in the law; and twelve local men on horseback who came along in order to take care of the horses of their lords, that is to say, the nineteen of the illustrious men; Lord Giovanni Visconti, judge of Galluria (who had been sent by Fasiolo, a prudent, discerning man acting as judge for the judge himself in Callarim); the twenty-five of Count Ugolino; and the twelve of the procuracy of Count Gerard, along with seven horses of their own which the local men were riding. The judge of Arborea and his archbishop and suffragan bishops were unable to provide us with horses because they were besieging the fortress of Gutiano with an army of one thousand knights and three thousand foot soldiers in the jurisdiction of Torres, but excused themselves by letter in a very proper and courtly manner. . . .

8. On the following Friday [18 May] we rode to Olmeto. On Saturday [19 May] we reached the bishopric of Ottana, which is a suffragan bishopric of the archbishop of Torres. The aforementioned judge [of Arborea] sent us his seneschal with a *cugina*, that is to say a cook, and he had them make great preparations for us, the judge, and his company for the following day, which was Pentecost. Early the next day, the judge came to us from his host with 200 armed knights. We rode out to meet him so that, on the way back, we would be able to confer with one another at greater length as both of us rode together. When he saw us, he dismounted along with his armed knights and advanced on foot to our hand; after kissing my hand and receiving the peace, he mounted his horse again. There, too, we celebrated a solemn Mass in the company of the aforesaid judge and four bishops, namely the bishops of Sulcis, Terralba, Santa Giusta in the province of Arborea, and of Bosa in the province of Torres, and many other counts, barons, and knights of Terra Magna and Sardinia. After the word of God was preached to the people, we all ate together. Then, after much joyous feasting, the judge and his knights returned to his host, which was located twelve miles away.

This judge requested that we remain in his land of Arborea for ten more days, since he hoped in the meantime to capture the aforementioned castle [of Guziano] and then meet us and render great honor to us in person; we remained there three days [20–23 May], for the cathedral of Ottana was being dedicated, an event for which the whole region was assembling. And because the bishopric was vacant at that time, we gathered the entire clergy together and did a visitation of it, and we also decided many marriage cases there.

9. We were, however, unable to proceed safely to Sassari because of the terrible war between the judge of Arborea and the people of Sassari, for the judge said that Torres belonged to his jurisdiction and he had already attacked them with a great force; they had also pillaged each other many times. We therefore returned to Oristano [23 May], where the judge of Arborea, in addition to the honorable expenses he had already incurred for us, had the archbishop of Arborea present us with a beautiful white palfrey which the judge used to ride to Corona, along with a most noble Sardinian woven saddle. And he had all the members of our household presented with the gift of a sum of money. We believe that on our account he spent 500 pounds. This palfrey and saddle we sent on to the Roman Curia to the venerable father, Lord Ottobono, the most worthy cardinal deacon of Sant'Adriano.

Once we had made an inquiry there of both the head and the members about the bishop and chapter of Santa Giusta (for they came before us there in the palace of the judge), we rode to Terralba [24 May]. Later, on the following day, we rode to the bishopric of Alès [25–26 May], and there, after celebrating masses, preaching the Word of God, anointing many, and making a visitation of head and members, we stayed for two days. Then we rode to Furtei [27 May]; then on to the bishopric of Suelli [28–29 May], where we spent two days celebrating mass, preaching the Word of God, and anointing many young men and women. We then rode to the bishopric of Dolia [30 May], where we likewise did all of the aforementioned things. But because we received news there that the galley had returned for us, we stayed there only one day, and on the following day we arrived at Castello di Castro [31 May].

There we prepared the galley [1–17 June]. We solemnly celebrated Mass in the church of the blessed Mary and preached a sermon to the people in which we recounted the many honors which we received from both clergy and laity throughout the island of Sardinia and thanked them for the great honor and grace which they had shown us and our household there. And so on the feast day of the blessed Rainerius[2] after three in the afternoon, which was 17 June, we boarded the galley. . . .

And when we did the accounts with our treasurer, we discovered that we had spent 800 pounds from our own treasury over and above the donations, which totaled 500 pounds.

---

2. Rainerius (1117–61) was a hermit and preacher from Pisa who achieved renown for his personal austerity, healings, and conversions. Canonized by Alexander III (1159–81), he became Pisa's patron saint in the thirteenth century.

13. ORIGINS OF THE COMMUNE OF CREMONA
THREE TEXTS (996–1097)

Translated from Latin by Edward Coleman

The transition from episcopal to communal rule in cities during the eleventh century is acknowledged as a crucial development in the history of northern Italy. However, it is poorly documented. In studying communal origins virtually the only option open to historians is to consider the imperial grants issued in favor of various cities in the "pre-communal" period, paying particular attention to changes in language over time. The use of the term cives *(citizens, or perhaps citizen body) is significant, as are references to citizens' representatives (often styled* boni homines, *"good men," probably meaning respectable or law-worthy men). These latter may be seen as the predecessors of the consuls of the commune, widely documented after 1100.*

In the case of the city of Cremona imperial diplomas give a rather fuller picture than elsewhere. Cremona was a medium-sized city, strategically located in the central Po plain, and the center of a rich agricultural hinterland (contado). The city also played a significant role in river commerce on the Po, having been an important toll point since Lombard times. The tolls were collected by the bishop of Cremona, but as far back as the middle of the ninth century certain members of the city population had claimed freedom of commerce on the river in what became a long-running and bitter dispute. Opponents of the bishop—referred to on different occasions as Cremonenses, cives, *and, most significantly,* negotiatores *(merchants)—challenged the bishop in court, where they repeatedly lost their case (851, 852, 891, 910), and also through sedition and violence (916, 924). In 996 the problem assumed the dimensions of a major crisis for the bishop when a group of Cremonese citizens somehow managed to persuade the German emperor Otto III to grant to them the toll rights on the river Po that had been at the center of the by then age-old dispute. Otto soon realized his mistake and revoked the grant shortly afterward. However, tensions came to a head in the early 1030s when the citizens, probably in alliance with other anti-episcopal forces, rose in revolt against the bishop and expelled him from the city. Three diplomas issued by the emperor Conrad III around this time (one of which is translated below) appeal for order and the return of the bishop, relating in some detail what had occurred in the city. The bishop was eventually able to return, but episcopal authority was further undermined during the period ca. 1060–90 by the struggles between pro- and anti-ecclesiastical reform parties. A document issued in 1097 shows that the bishop was no longer in control although his position was still given formal deference: three named representatives accepted a grant from the Countess Matilda of Tuscany jointly on his behalf and on behalf of the city (i.e. the commune). Episcopal rule had ultimately crumbled after decades of pressure from internal and external forces of an economic, political, and religious character.*

The example of Cremona is instructive as it demonstrates that, although communes rarely emerge into the light of the historical record before ca. 1100, the changes that led to their creation can be traced back—at least in this case—for around a century. This, in turn, serves as a reminder that the formation of communes was a process rather than an event.

1. Grant of Otto III to the Citizens of Cremona (996, May 22, Rome)

In the name of the holy and indivisible Trinity, Otto [III] by divine favor emperor of the Romans. Be it known to all faithful men of God's church and to all our own loyal men, present and future, [that], through the petition of our loyal chancellor Henry, we extend our protection to all free Cremonese citizens, rich and poor in order that they may live free and secure in their city and remain protected and defended wherever they may go; and they may have the use of waters, pastures and woods on both banks of the [river] Po from the mouth of the [river] Adda as far as Vulpariolum [identified in other texts as the port of Cremona on the Po]; and they may hold and possess whatever is recognized as belonging to the state without challenge from any man, and for the salvation of our soul we command that they may conduct their business on water and on land and stop over wherever they wish without interference from anyone. Therefore we order by our imperial authority, regarding all the above mentioned, that no duke, archbishop, bishop, marquis, count, viscount, *gastald*, *sculdahis*, deacon, or any greater or lesser person of our empire and kingdom presume to molest, disturb or dispossess the aforementioned free citizens of Cremona, rich and poor, in their acquisitions or in what they may [in the future] acquire, unless through a legal judgment. They may live securely and peacefully under our imperial protection and that of our successors, and they may act as they see fit without any challenge or interference from any man. If anyone is tempted to audaciously infringe our command be it known that he will have to pay [a fine of] 1000 pounds of pure gold, half to our court and half to the aforementioned men of Cremona. In order that this order be credited and firmly observed by all we command that it be authenticated with our seal.

On 3 August of the same year a clearly embarrassed and irritated Otto III revoked the above grant, stating that "deceitful citizens of Cremona" had obtained it by fraud (MGH DD Ott. III, n. 222, 635). Two years later he went in person to Cremona, where the revocation of the original grant was read out in public and confirmed once more (MGH DD Ott. III, n. 270, 689).

Translated from *MGH DD Ott. III*, ed. Theodor von Sickel (Hannover: Hahn, 1893), n.198, 606.

2. Diploma of Conrad II to the Citizens of Cremona (ca. 1037)

In the name of the holy and indivisible Trinity. Conrad by divine favor emperor of the Romans. . . . We have learned that the citizens of Cremona have conspired and sworn oaths against the holy church of Cremona, their spiritual mother and lord, and against Landulf, of holy memory, bishop of that see and their lord, and that they expelled him from the city with great indignity and dishonor, looted his properties, razed to the ground a tower in his double-walled fortress, encircled by seven towers, and ransomed those of his household within who had not been killed, together with some faithful canons, taking everything that they had and demolishing their best houses; and they totally destroyed the old city and constructed a larger one against our authority so that they might resist us. Since not only heavenly but also earthly laws condemn such oath taking and conspiracy, those men may be deprived not only of their exterior possessions but also of their lives. Even now, stubbornly adhering to their conspiracy, they have obstructed Ubald [the new] bishop of the holy church of Cremona; they usurp his judicial authority, and withhold the rent from mills, customary tolls from ships, and ground rents without investiture [without legal title]; they pay the minimum, they seize their lands and those of their relatives which had been awarded to the church in court cases or ceded to the church in other charters, and they violently assault the bishop himself, his officials, his monks, and his clergy, killing [some of] them. They uproot woods and allow the bishop no power outside the door of his own house in contempt of our imperial sovereignty. On account of all this we wish it to be known to all faithful men of God's church present and future that in order to suppress contumacy, to eradicate so many evil customs, and mercifully to relieve the misery of the church, all landed estates of free Cremonese citizens [who have] sworn oaths and conspired, in the city or in the suburbs up to a distance of five miles, we cede and transfer by our imperial authority, in this our diploma, into full ownership of the holy church of Cremona; and that by rights the aforementioned Ubald and his successors may do whatever they see fit with all the estates of the conspirators for the benefit of the church in perpetuity. In addition to this imperial judgment we order that, concerning the lands of the conspirators, no duke, marquis, count, viscount, *sculdahis*, greater or lesser person of our kingdom presume through any kind of scheme or opportunity to dispossess or disturb the holy church of Cremona [under] bishop Ubald or any of his

Translated from *MGH DD Konr. II*, ed. Harry Bresslau and Hans Wibel (Hannover: Hahn, 1909), n. 251, 346.

successors in this see. If in the future anyone heedlessly transgresses this diploma of ours let him know that [there will be a fine of] five hundred pounds of pure gold, half to our court and half to the church whose holder has suffered the injury. In the belief that this will be truly and respectfully observed by all men we have ordered that this diploma of ours be drawn up and authenticated by our own hand and by the impression of our seal.

Conrad II issued two further diplomas regarding the situation in Cremona around the same time. In one of these (MGH DD Konr. II, n. 253, 349) he ordered the Cremonese citizens to pay compensation to the bishop for the destruction of his properties, to hand back the lands that they had usurped and also prominent members of the bishop's household who they were still holding prisoner. He also called on them to assist the bishop in bringing murderers and thieves to justice.

3. Grant of Countess Matilda of Tuscany to Cremona (1097)

On the day of Saturday in the Kalends of January, in the castle of Piadena, in the presence of the *boni homines* [good men] whose names may be read below: the Countess Matilda [see **#66**], daughter of the late Marquis Boniface [of Canossa] invested, with a rod which she held in her hands, Gotefred of Bellusco, Moricio and Cremoxano Aldioni, men of the city of Cremona, representing the church of the Blessed Virgin of Cremona [the cathedral] and the commune of the city of Cremona, in the entire county of Insula Fulcheria as a benefice, with all that belongs to the aforementioned countess in that county in its entirety. It was agreed that the *capitanei* [the highest ranking noblemen] of this church would do service to the aforementioned Countess Matilda, until a bishop was appointed to the see of Cremona who would do the due service with his *capitanei* and other knights. And if the *capitanei* of that city refused to do service, certain [other] men of the city would do service under the terms of the benefice. The aforementioned church of the Blessed Virgin and the aforementioned commune may hold the above-mentioned county henceforward as a benefice in perpetuity, as agreed, without challenge from the aforementioned countess or from her heirs or successors.

Translated from *MGH DD Die Urkunden und Briefe der Markgräfin Mathilde von Tuszien*, ed. Elke Goez and Werner Goez (Hannover: Hahn, 1998), n. 48, 150–51.

14. MECHANISMS OF COMMUNAL GOVERNMENT FIVE TEXTS (1143–84)

Translated from Latin by Frances Andrews

1. Citizenship of the Rural Aristocracy (Siena 1157)

The agreement presented here shows the city of Siena, represented by the bishop, paying to acquire the aid of a rural lord and his retinue in time of war. The pledge of a castle is presented as a guarantee of this support, as is the acquisition of a house and vineyard in the city. Citizenship is not mentioned, but the undertaking to acquire property and reside for part of the year in the city is typical of later statutory stipulations for those becoming citizens. It is noteworthy that the oath is to the bishop, not the commune, which was not yet institutionally mature enough to command recognition as a legal entity, despite the existence of consuls. This may have been particularly critical in the 1150s, as in this decade Frederick I was energetically contesting communal autonomy. Moreover, the rural aristocracy would doubtless have been comfortable pledging allegiance to the bishop as he had credibility both at the level of the city and the diocese, and—at least in theory—at the level of the empire, as bishops were by tradition and by default, agents of imperial power on the ground (except when they were explicitly opposed, as during the investiture controversy). Ranuccio undertakes to require other parties to swear to this pact also, demonstrating how the commune could exploit preexisting familial and client relationships to its advantage, bringing to their aid not just one man, but a whole consorteria.[1]

I, Ranuccio of Staggia, Bernardino and Guazolino my sons, Ottaviano and Rustico Soarzi bind as a pledge to you, Rainerio, bishop of the church of Santa Maria of Siena and to all the Sienese people, the castle called "di Strove," on pain of a double penalty.

Ranuccio ordered that this be written down, in Siena, in front of the church of Santa Maria, in the council. Malavolta Filippo, Ugolino Bosta, Malagallia Arivero, Giuseppe Ildibrandini and [16 other names] were witnesses.

If, during our lifetimes, we shall fail to observe these pacts, the pledge [the castle "di Strove"] and the tower and castle of Monteacutolo "di montemaio" shall pass under the dominion of the Sienese.

These are the pacts: we will defend the Sienese and their goods; we will aid them in the wars which they are fighting and which they will fight, espe-

---

Translated from *Regestum Senense*, ed. Fedor Schneider, Regesta chartarum Italiae 8 (Rome: Loescher, 1911), doc. 218, 82. I have also drawn on the Italian translation in Renato Bordone, *La società urbana nell'Italia comunale (secoli xi–xiv)* (Turin: Loescher, 1984), 56–57.

1. A familial circle (but not exclusively) bound by both economic and political interests.

cially in the war against the Florentines, against all enemies, and we will fight against these enemies either with the Sienese or without their aid, with the exception of the emperor, the marquis, and Count Guido of Galgano, the bishop of Volterra, the abbot of Isola, the abbot of Martoro and Martora, and I Ranuccio also personally exclude the countess Immilla. However, if such persons shall wish to make war against the Sienese, we will not aid them voluntarily against the Sienese. We will give our castles to the Sienese so that they can live there, take them, and make war from them; we will consign the tower of Monteacutulo di Montemaio within 8 days, after the inquiry by the consuls of Siena and they will commend it to the abbot of Isola and the abbot of Martoro and Martora. Within a year from 1 May next, we shall have these pacts sworn to by Beringerio Ranucci and by Paganello Soarzi and in this period they will not cause offense to the Sienese. We will live in Siena, one in the house of the Ranucci and one in the house of the sons of the Soarzi, two months of the year in times of peace with our wives and six months of the year without our wives in times of war; and in times of war we will obey the orders of the consuls. We will have all the knights of our land, our guards, and the men of Monteacutulo swear to this as we will have agreed with them. We will have Gentile, nephew of Panzo, swear to this when he reaches 14 years of age. We will buy a house and a vineyard once we have received the money from you, within a month.

2. Conditions for Being a Citizen of Milan (1184)

The difficulties involved in clarifying the status of an individual as a full citizen and subject to no other jurisdiction are illustrated here in a dispute between the Cistercian monastery of Chiaravalle outside Milan and Negro, son of Barosio of Viglione, who was living and working between the city and a mill in the Contado [see #52]. The abbot's claim to jurisdiction and taxes is supported using the traditional means of oral witnesses concerning the villein status of Negro's father and a written document, evidence of the increasing role of texts in dispute settlement in this period. Negro's counter claim, again supported by witnesses, reveals the emerging criteria for citizenship: long residence in the city in a house of his ownership and military service.

Thursday, 13 December, in the office of the consuls in Milan. Milano, called di Villa, judge and consul of Milan, pronounced sentence with the advice of his assessors in the dispute between the abbot of the monastery of Chiaravalle acting in the name of the said monastery in the person of his advocate Naza-

Translated from *Gli atti del comune di Milano fino all'anno MCCXVI*, ed. Cesare Manaresi (Milan: Capriolo and Massimino, 1919), doc. 145, and Renato Bordone, *La società urbana nell'Italia comunale (secoli xi–xiv)* (Turin: Loescher, 1984), 56–57.

rio Visconti of the city of Milan on one side, and Negro, son of the late Barosio of Viglione, on the other.

The substance of the dispute was as follows: Nazario, on behalf of the said monastery, asked that the aforesaid Negro should pay 60 *solidi* for guard-duty and be subject to his [the abbot's] jurisdiction, affirming that his father Barosio, now dead, originated from and was a villein in the place called Consonno, which belonged to the jurisdiction of the monastery, and that the same Negro lived in a mill which is near the houses of that place; he produced numerous witnesses concerning this and presented a document, at the request of the same Negro, in which it was stated that the said Barosio had been freed only from the obligation to consign to the monastery a certain number of sheaves and bundles [of grain] and other exactions [payments in recognition of monastic lordship]. Against this the same Negro asserted that his father and he himself had been citizens of Milan and maintained that he had possessed a house in Milan for a long time and that he had often done service in the army and guard-duty as a Milanese citizen; he added that the mill in which he lives is not in the territory of the above-mentioned place [Consonno], even though in the neighborhood of the houses, and in confirmation he produced witnesses in his favor who were, however, not considered sufficient.

Having heard these reasons and others, the aforesaid Milano absolved the said Negro from having to pay the said 60 *solidi* but sentenced him, as long as he should continue to live in the said mill in Consonno, to subject himself to the jurisdiction of the monastery. Thus the dispute was ended.

In the year of the incarnation of the Lord 1184, on the aforesaid day, the third indiction. Ardengo Visconti, Onrigone Pagliaro, Giovanni di Trivulzio, Quintavalle di Mama, Malgirono Pita, Manfredo di Varedo were present. . . .

I Milano, consul and judge as above, pronounced sentence and undersigned.
I Guglielmo, judge and consul, undersigned.
I Ottone Zendadario, consul of the commune of Milan, undersigned.
I Rogerio Bonafede, judge, undersigned.
And I, Ugo known as de Castagnanega, notary of the sacred palace, wrote [this document].

3. The Mechanisms of the *Estimo* of the Commune of Pisa (1162)

All governments require resources to afford defence and administration and the emerging communes were no exception. This extract, from one of the earliest surviving communal statutes, the Breve *of the consuls of Pisa in 1162, forms part of the oath of a city official, outlining the complex mechanisms and calculations involved in the assessment of property value (the* estimo *or valuation) on the basis of which citizens would be required to pay tax, the* collecta, *known in other cities as the* fodrum *or* tallia. *While those who were eligible were to be identified by others, note that the amount of property was to be identified by the tax payers themselves guaranteed by oath. As in all other aspects of communal government, much emphasis is placed on oath swearing to guarantee observance of law.*

Before the beginning of February next I will elect, without fraud, five men for each gate [district] of the city of Pisa, or more, according to the number of inhabitants of each gate, and I will have them swear that before the beginning of the following month of March they will draw up in writing, or have drawn up, the names of both males and females who live within the gate and who will have been adjudged by the majority of those elected for the gate to be such as to be subject to taxation. This list shall then be delivered to me within a month or to one of my consular colleagues; after the presentation of the lists, from 1 March for the three following months, I will have those in Pisa at that time who are of an age to consent to an oath, swear that within a month from their oath they will present in writing to the consuls, the quantity of their movable and immovable property, fiefs, leases, and the location of these, except in the case of male and female servants, equipment, horses, arms, and food stuffs: if any person has not sworn, their property [will be valued] at twice the amount or more; the property of those absent and of those who, as stated above, cannot swear because under age, will be entrusted to the valuation of the estimators so that they will value them and present them to the consuls, as decreed.

I will then have the said officers or others swear within one month that within the two months following the oath, they will valuate the property listed, divide them into four parts, and finally present the valuations and divisions to the consuls within the same months as stated; they should undertake nonetheless to concur with the majority in making the valuation and division. I will observe without fraud all that has been decreed concerning the oaths, presentation, valuation, and divisions and all this shall remain fixed, unless by the contrary wish of the senators present in the council.

4. Guard Duties at Genoa in the Mid-Twelfth Century

The early communes depended heavily on local men to provide guard duty and military service. Here the guards were to be men from villages subject to Genoa, reflecting the imposition of urban jurisdiction on the city's surrounding area (and

(3) Translated from *Statuti inediti della citta di Pisa del XII al XIV secolo*, ed. Francesco Bonaini (Florence: Vieusseux, 1870), 4–5; I have also drawn on Renato Bordone, *La società urbana nell'Italia comunale (secoli xi–xiv)* (Turin: Loescher, 1984), 262.

exempting those dependent on the citizens themselves). The terms of duty of roughly two months are typical for such service, as for many other communal offices. Those not performing a duty themselves paid taxes in both money and kind.

[1142?]

This is the guard of the city: the men of Carbonara and the men of Mostedo up to Mulini Gemelli must provide the guard for the castle of Genoa at the wall of Santa Croce from the middle of July until the beginning of the month of September; likewise the men of Casamavale, Campo Ursone, Zinistedo, Vegone, Quico, and Terralba. All those mentioned above must perform guard duties, except serfs or those who live in the property of Genoese citizens, where the city has rights of pasture.

The men of Calignano must provide the guard at Calignano, the men of San Martino and Ercle and the men of Manzasco must provide the guard at Manzasco. . . .

The men of campo Florenzano must give two *denari* of the old money of Pavia for the guard; the men of Marassi, Terpi, Monteasiano, Lugo, and Melmi must each give half a *denarius* for the guard. The men of Mortedo Soprano, and Cerreto must give a total of nine *denari* for the guard . . . the men of Pradello and Staiano must each give a measure of oil. The men of Sesto, Priano, Borzoli, and Burlo must each give a bundle of wood, the men of Langasco, Celanesio, and San Cipriano must give six pennies of the old money of Pavia for each parish. Servants and men living on property of the Genoese who provide pasture for the animals of the lords of the land are not required to provide guard service or to pay the said tariffs.

5. Oath of the Consuls of Genoa (1143)

As the communes emerged, all newly elected officials were required to swear an oath which outlined their duties as also the restrictions on their powers. The following extract from the Breve dei consoli[2] *of Genoa identifies the central duty of protection of the church and the need to work for the material advantage of the city. It also points to the shared responsibility for major decisions such as war and taxes. A reciprocal oath was sworn by all citizens to obey the consuls.*

(4) Translated from *Codice diplomatico della Repubblica di Genova*, ed. Cesare Imperiale di Sant'Angelo (Rome: Tipografia del Senato, 1936), vol. 1, doc. 120, 142–43; I have also drawn on Renato Bordone, *La società urbana nell'Italia comunale (secoli xi–xiv)* (Turin: Loescher, 1984), 113–14.

(5) Translated from *La crisi del sacro romano impero: documenti*, ed. Sergio Mochi Onory and Gianluigi Barni (Milan: Istituto Editoriale Cisalpino, 1951), 107–8.

2. The consuls swore to fulfill the duties outlined in the *Breve*, or text, related to their office. Together with the *Brevi* of other bodies in the commune these later formed the basis of city statutes.

In the name of the Lord, amen. From the day of the purification of Saint Mary [2 February] for one year, we, the consuls elected by the "commune," will praise and work for the honor of our archbishopric and our mother church and our city. . . . We will not knowingly dishonor our city nor the profit or honor of our mother church.

We will not diminish the justice of any of our co-citizens for the commune nor the justice of the commune for any of our co-citizens, but will observe justice equally and keep it as we know it to be best, reasonably and with good faith. . . .

For other matters it shall be in our judgement as we best know to be useful to our city, in good faith. . . .

We will not cause the army of the commune to be called or start a new war, or impose a ban or impose taxes on the land, unless with the counsel of the greater part of the councillors who shall be called to council by the bell and shall be in the council.

If we learn that any man of our jurisdiction is going or sending [someone] to reduce the honor of our mother church and our archbishopric, having vengeance shall be in our judgment.

15. EMPIRE AND CITIES IN THE LATE TWELFTH CENTURY: THE PEACE OF CONSTANCE AND ITS AFTERMATH: TWO TEXTS (1183, 1216)

Translated from Latin by Frances Andrews

As the communes emerged over the course of the late eleventh and early twelfth centuries, imperial power became ever less relevant. In the 1150s the new emperor, Frederick Barbarossa (d. 1190), set out to reverse the trend, reimposing imperial sovereignty and jurisdiction in northern and central Italy. Conflict with the newly autonomous cities soon followed: a league of anti-imperial towns centered on Verona was formed, expanding in 1167 to form the Lombard League, named in the peace treaty translated here. This treaty followed seven years of tense negotiations after the decisive defeat of Barbarossa's armies at the Battle of Legnano in 1176 and a preliminary peace made in 1177 in Venice between Barbarossa and the pope, Alexander III (d. 1181), who had supported the League. In the final settlement, the emperor claimed the power to invest magistrates and oaths of allegiance and retained appellate jurisdiction and the royal fodrum [see #14.3]; however, the communes acquired the "regalian customs" and other jurisdictions formerly belonging to the crown. The peace was issued as an imperial privilege, as if it were a concession to subjects now returned to grace, but the reality was a capitulation: the conflict had done more to strengthen the communes than to renew the empire. As Philip Jones put it, "the outcome of the Peace of Constance was a society of independent cities under a merely moral or symbolic imperium."[1] The concessions made at Constance were widely referred to in later Italian legislation, including the first extant law collection for Milan, the Liber Consuetudinum Mediolani *of 1216, which records the granting of jurisdiction and also one of many decisions to ignore imperial custom, in the case given here, concerning fiefs.*

1. The Peace of Constance (1183)

In the name of the holy and undivided Trinity

Frederick, by divine grace Emperor of the Romans, Augustus, and Henry VI his son, King of the Romans, Augustus, is accustomed to show grace and favor and make dispensations to subjects, with imperial clemency and mild serenity . . . however much he must and can correct the excesses of transgressions with severity, yet more he studies to rule the Roman empire in gracious peace and tranquility and . . . bring the insolence of rebels back to due loyalty

---

Translated from *La crisi del sacro romano impero: documenti*, ed. Sergio Mochi Onory and Gianluigi Barni (Milan: Istituto Editoriale Cisalpino, 1951), 96–105.

1. Philip Jones, *The Italian City-State: From Commune to Signoria* (Oxford: Clarendon Press, 1997), 339.

and devotion. . . . Therefore let all the faithful of the empire, both in the present time and in future, know that we, with our customary generosity . . . receive the League of the Lombards and their supporters, who once offended us and our empire, into the fullness of our grace . . . and we mercifully grant them our peace, ordering that the present page be undersigned and secured with our seal. Of which this is the tenor:

1. We, Frederick, Emperor of the Romans, and our son Henry, king of the Romans, grant in perpetuity to you, the cities, places, and persons of the League, the *regalia* and other customs both inside and outside the cities— that is Verona and its *castrum* and suburbs and the other cities, places and persons of the League—, so that in these cities you will hold everything as you have been accustomed until now and shall exercise without contradiction those customs which you have exercised of old . . . that is, concerning the *fodrum*, woods, pastures, bridges, water, and mills, and, as you have had of old and have, over armies, defense of the cities [and] jurisdiction over both criminal cases and those concerning money both inside and out, and in those other things which concern the benefit of the cities.

2. We wish that the *regalia* that are not granted to you shall be recognized in the following manner: the bishop of the place and men of both the city and the diocese shall choose men of good repute, believed to be suitable for this, and such as hold no special, private hatred against either the city or our majesty. They shall swear to inquire without fraud and, having inquired, to consign to our excellence those [*regalia*] which belong to us.

3. If, however, they shall consider this inquest best avoided, we request that they shall pay to us an annual payment of 2,000 marks in silver. If nevertheless, this sum shall seem excessive, it may be reduced by an appropriate amount. . . .

7. All privileges granted by us, or our messengers during the war, which prejudice or damage the cities, places or persons of the League, shall be void.

8. In those cities in which the bishop by imperial or royal privilege holds the county [as lord], if the consuls are accustomed to receive the consulate through the bishop, let them receive it from him: otherwise, let each city receive the consulate from us. Consequently, just as in each city the consuls shall be constituted by our messenger, those who are in the city or diocese shall receive investiture for up to five years. At the end of the five years, each

city shall send a messenger to our presence to receive investiture and again in future, on finishing each five-year period, they shall receive investiture from us and in between from our messenger . . . unless we shall be in Lombardy, in which case they shall receive it from us. . . .

15. All damages, losses, and injuries which we or our followers have sustained from the League or any of its members or supporters, are hereby pardoned by us and we give them the plenitude of our grace.

16. We will not stay longer than is necessary in any city or bishopric to the damage of the city.

17. Cities shall be allowed to fortify and to erect fortifications.

18. That League they now have may continue and may be renewed as often as they wish. . . .

27. All those of the League who shall swear fealty to us, shall add to the oath of fealty that they will help us in good faith to maintain possessions and rights which we have in Lombardy outside the League, if it shall be expedient and if they shall be requested to do so by us or our messenger. . . .

29. They shall pay us the customary and royal *fodrum* at the customary times whenever we enter Lombardy. . . .

There follow another thirteen clauses, including a list of the cities involved: Vercelli, Novara, Milan, Lodi, Bergamo, Brescia, Mantua, Verona, Vicenza, Padua, Treviso, Bologna, Faenza, Modena, Reggio, Parma, and Piacenza.

2. *Liber Consuetudinum Mediolani* 1216 (*The Book of the Customs of Milan*)

CHAPTER 16. ON COMBAT

These solemnities were once in use before the peace of Emperor Frederick [Barbarossa]: however they were largely banished by the peace made with Emperor Frederick, who granted full jurisdiction to the Milanese and other Lombards; thus the consul of Milan without the royal messenger, judges, disposes, and arranges judicial combat.

Translated from *La crisi del sacro romano impero. documenti*, ed. Sergio Mochi Onory and Gianluigi Barni (Milan: Istituto Editoriale Cisalpino, 1951), 147–48.

CHAPTER 25. ON THE FORM OF THE OATH OF FEALTY

We have seen what a fief is and how it is constituted and in what things and how and by whom it can be given and to whom conceded. Now let us see how it may be lost. For a benefice may be lost by many means: by chance as when a vassal dies without an heir or paternal relative, in which case the fief perishes and the things given in fee return to the lord. A vassal may also lose a fief by his own fault if he shall remain for a year and a day without requesting investiture from his lord, and this is according to the law of lord Frederick [Barbarossa]. In our custom however, the vassal does not lose the fief even if he has not sought investiture from his lord for a long time.

16. TWELFTH-CENTURY ADMINISTRATION
OF CORLEONE
TWO TEXTS (1182, 1178–83)

Translated from Arabic by Alex Metcalfe

The Muslim conquest of Sicily from the year 827 introduced a series of political, religious, social, economic and administrative shifts in the region. Knowledge of Islamic Sicily is thus fundamental for interpreting the subsequent and better-known period of the Norman kingdom, which is often understood in terms of less important territories held on the mainland. Under the Aghlabid, Fatimid, and Kalbid dynasties, not only did the population of Sicily become predominantly Arabic-speaking and Muslim, but also its new capital of Palermo became the largest and wealthiest city in what is now Europe. Although independent Muslim rule was brought to an end by the Norman-led conquest of the island which was completed by 1090, the new rulers adopted and adapted many principles of government from the Islamic world. In spite of an increasing trend toward Latinization, Arab-Muslim influence endured under the Sicilian kings (1130–94) and strongly affected the political, cultural, and administrative nerve centers of the kingdom in the royal palaces at Palermo.

After the coronation of Roger II in 1130, a highly centralized fiscal administration of the island and Calabria emerged. The main offices of the royal dīwān derived their inspiration from models found in Fatimid Cairo, but they continued to renovate and reform a complex blend of pre-existing Sicilian practices based on records kept largely in Arabic. Crown property came to be organized around two basic operations: the division of lands into provinces and their component estates whose boundaries were defined at inquests by officials with the help of local elders, and second, the compilation of lists recording the names of taxpaying household heads. Typically, these were subdivided according to their area and fiscal status. The resulting documentation is not only a uniquely rich source for understanding the development of the administration and transmission of royal authority, but also fundamentally important for the reconstruction of Sicily's shifting settlement patterns and socioreligious history during the twelfth century.

The boundary description below is taken from a large confirmation of lands granted by King William II to the church of Santa Maria Nuova in Monreale. The bilingual (Arabic-Latin) document dates from 1182. The positions of many minor localities mentioned have yet to be identified with certainty.

1. Boundary Description of Corleone (1182)

The great boundary of Qurullūn (modern Corleone) begins from the head of the river Shantaghnī from below *kūdyat al-ḥināsh* ("the hill of the

Translated from the original, Biblioteca Centrale della Regione Siciliana, Palermo 32, Edition S. Cusa, *I diplomi greci ed arabi di Sicilia* (Palermo: Lao, 1868–82; repr. Cologne: Böhlau, 1982), 179–244.

snakes"). It extends right along the river until it ends up at [the estate of] Ḥajar Zanātī. It joins the river of Ibn Zurra, to *khandaq al-gharīq* ("the sunken ditch"), to Raḥl Baḥrī ("the seaward estate") in the district of Jātū (modern San Giuseppe Iato) and which is in the hands of the inhabitants of Corleone. It descends along the river Sabāy until it joins the flow of water descending from the west of the church. The church is in the boundary of [San Giuseppe] Iato. It descends right along the river to [the place where] the water descending from Raḥl al-Thawr ("the estate of the bull") empties and rises along the Raḥl al-Thawr river to the aforesaid estate. It passes south-ward right along the river and extends to *kudyat al-sallāba* ("the hill of the cord-maker"?), to *'uyūn 'ayyāsh* ("the bread-maker's? springs"), to *faḥs al-dardār* ("the plain of the ash tree"), to Raḥl 'Abd Allāh ("'Abd Allāh's estate"), [and then] to *bāb dardār 'Amrūn* ("the pass of 'Amrūn's ash tree"). It extends along the main road up to where it leads from [the village of] Dhriyāna and continues to the pass which overlooks *'ayn al-shaḥm* ("the spring of the fat"). It turns round the woods which are at Raḥl 'Allūn ("'Allūn's estate"), rising to *bāb al-rīḥ* ("the pass of the wind") descending to [the village? of] Mālis, to the Great River descending from B.r.zū (modern Prizzi), rising right along the river to the mill of Aldhru, to *ḥārik Bū Manṣūr* ("the hill of Bu Manṣūr"), rising along the way to *muḍīq al-ṣaqāliba* ("the ford of the slaves"), rising right along the mountain to the *'uyūn al-ijrāf* ("the springs of the cliffs"), to *'ayn al-zufayzafa* ("the spring of the jujube tree") [and then] to the al-Bārid mosque. It extends to the top of the moun-tain until it arrives at the streams of water of *khandaq b.ln.bū* ("the ditch of the dove"?). From here it is joined by the boundary of Prizzi and rises in a straight line north to *kudyat al-lubūb* ("the hill of the kernels"?) where there is *ghār baqqa* ("cave of the elm tree"), rising eastward to the top of *burj lāb.lū* ("lāb.lū tower" or "outcrop") and extends along the stream of the aforesaid field. It crosses between the large rocks and [the village? of] al-Qaṣṣari. Al-Qaṣṣari is in the boundary of Corleone and the large rocks are in the boundary of Prizzi. Rising eastward along the aforesaid stream to the Dhrīyāna road, passing right along the road to *balāṭ isṭūl.s* ("the flagstones of isṭūl.s?"), the aforesaid flagstones are in the boundary of Prizzi, it extends right along the road and crosses the river descending from [the village of] Rāyā. It passes along the road to the end of the stream descending from *'ayn al-birdhawn* ("the nag's spring"), rising right along the stream to the afore-said spring. It extends to the mill of Ḥusayn ibn al-Qar'a. The mill is in the boundary of Corleone. It crosses the plain [going] straight to *muḍīq tillīs* ("wheatsack ford") which is in the lands of Ibn 'Uqāba, rising westward right along the crest to the top of the high mountain to the east of *muḍīq Iyāḍ* ('Iyāḍ's ford"). The eastern flow of water is from the road to Prizzi and extends across the land of Bū 'Ajīna to *darjat B.riyāqa al-qadīma* ("the step? hillside? of [the village? of] Old B.riyāqa"), to the mill of Ibn Ḥulīya. It extends along the way until it crosses the ruins of Old B.riyāqa above the spring. The spring is in the boundary of Prizzi. The aforesaid ruins' eastern flow of water [belongs/goes] to Prizzi. It extends north to the hill known as *ḥaddādīn B.riyāqa* ("the B.riyāqa metalworkers"), to the ditch in which the water of *'ayn al-'ullayqa* ("the spring of the brambles") descends. It extends northward to the large rock which is planted there above *ghār Bū Jarād* ("Bū Jarād's cave" or "the cave of many locusts"). It passes in a straight line north to *ḥajar Ibn 'A'jīna* ("the stone of Ibn 'Ajīna") where there is a fig tree. It extends to the hill on which there are the large stones. It passes across the drilled rock planted there which is in the plain of Ibn al-Ḍīḍ.mī. It extends between Manzil Qāsim ("Qasim's estate") and *'ayn farshaḥ* ("the parted spring"). The spring is in the boundary of Prizzi and the estate is in the boundary of Corleone. It extends right along the road to *khandaq Bin Shabīb* ("the ditch of Ibn Shabīb") along the way leading from al-Madīna (modern Palermo) to B.riyāqa. It extends north along the way to *'ayn al-injāṣa* ("the spring of the pear orchard"). It crosses the river Salla and rises right up the hill to *marqad ma'āad* ("the sheepfold [known as?] place of return"), to *ḥajar Ibn Liyāna* ("the rock of Ibn Liyāna") and extends to *nāẓūr al-ghurāb* ("the crow's nest"). It passes to *ḥārik al-ballūṭ* ("the hill of the oak tree") and it joined by Jabal Zurāra ("Zurāra's mountain") rising to the top of the mountain. The flow of water from *ḥārik al-ballūṭ* and Jabal Zurāra is south- ward and west to Corleone. The eastern and northern [flows belong/go] to [the village of] Khāṣū. It extends along the top of the mountain, descends to Qal'at Bū Samra ("the fort of Bū Samra"). The fort is in the boundary of Corleone. Descending, [it continues] in a straight line westward until it joins the river descending from *kudyat al-ḥināsh* ("the hill of the snakes"). The boundary is closed.

2. The Christians of Corleone in the Kingdom of Sicily (1178–83)

Two royal, bilingual Arabic-Greek documents from 1178 and 1183 recorded the names of almost 2,000 (mainly Muslim) taxpayers. From the town of Corleone, 354 household heads were registered, including 47 listed separately as Christians (along with a list of 6 newlyweds from among their sons and brothers). Their names were derived from a mix of Arabic and Greek, included two pig-farmers and two people called

"Muḥammad." Below, names which suggest a profession, nickname or were perhaps used figuratively have been translated literally.[1]

Abū Sayyid son of al-Thirmāsh ("from Termini?") and his brother.
Fīlib (Greek "Philippos").
Maymūn al-Baṭrālī ("from Petralia").

Yūsuf al-Bāz ("the falcon").
Yūsuf son of al-Ḥarrāth ("the plougher") and his brother.

The son of Abū l-Ḥārith.

Maymūn son of Thūfil (Greek Theophilos).
Najfūr (Greek Nikiphoros) son of Mujūna (?).
The son of al-Bāqūshī.
Abū l-Khayr son of Māgha.
 Jaʿfar al-Raḥḥāl ("the traveler").

The son of Zaytūn.
ʿAbd Allāh son of Abū l-Khubza ("the father of the loaf," "baker"?).

The son of Wārith.
Ḥammūd son of Abū Ḥajar.

Riḍwān al-Kharrāz ("the shoemaker").
Muḥammad al-Jannān ("the gardener").

Muḥammad al-Ḥarīrī ("the silk-worker").

The son of al-Majnūna ("the mad woman").
Niʿma.

al-Raffāsh(?) ("the thresher"?).
Khalīl son of al-Shamm.
The son of al-Qassāṭī ("the pot-maker").

The relative of al-ʿAmsha ("the weak-sighted/bleary-eyed woman").

The son of al-Rātiba ("the female tax-payer").
Abū l-ʿAjīn.

Abū l-Rijāl.
The son of Qālī.
Abū l-Khayr al-Khayyāṭ ("the tailor").

1. It should be also noted that some readings and meanings are as yet tentative; projects are in progress to publish new, critical editions of all the royal and private documents of Sicily in Arabic, along with translations, indices, and commentaries.

Figure 5. Greek, "Saracen," and Latin Notaries (ca. 1194–97). Miniature from Pietro da Eboli, *Liber ad honorem Augusti,* dedicated to Emperor Henry VI, the text chronicles the passage of the Norman Kingdom of Southern Italy to the Hohenstaufen dynasty. Bern, Burgerbibliothek Cod. 120.II, fol. 101r. (Photo: Bern, Burgerbibliothek)

The son of Abū l-Ḥīla.

al-Ḥāfūrī ("the ditch or well-digger").
The brother of Raqlī (Greek "Heracles").
'Alī son of M.sla.

The son of al-Rabīb ("the stepson").
Maymūn the stepson of Raqlī.
Al-Subʿ al-Naṣrānī ("the Christian").

Branqāṭ (Greek "Pankratos").

Sulaymān al-Khanzārī ("the pig-farmer").
Quzmān (Greek "Cosmas").

Niqūla (Greek "Nikolaos") al-Qaṣīr ("the short").

Abū Ghālib al-Khanzārī ("the pig-farmer").
Thūwdur (Greek "Theodoros") al-Wakīl ("administrative agent").
Khilfa son of Bārūn (Frankish 'baron' or 'Pierron").
The son of Bāsīlī (Greek "Basileios").
The son of al-Fawwāl ("the bean-seller").
Khilfa brother of Maymūn, son of Thūfil.
Khilfa son of Najfūr, son of Mujūna.
Abū Ghālib son of Najfūr, son of Mujūna.
Yūsuf brother of Abū l-Khayr, son of Magha.
Aḥmad son of Ḥammūd, son of Abū Ḥajar.

Ja'far brother of Bāsīlī's son.

17. GIOVANNI VILLANI ON THE ASCENT OF THE *POPOLO* IN FLORENCE (1250, 1293)

Translated from Italian by Katherine L. Jansen

The twelfth and thirteenth centuries constitute the period in which the popolo *rose to power throughout central and northern Italy. The word, because of its multiple but closely related meanings, defies a good English translation. Depending on the context, it can mean simply "the people" or "citizens" of a commune; however, it can also signify an intermediate social status between the nobility and the laboring classes. Moreover, in a political context, it refers to "popular" governments established by merchants and artisans in opposition to magnate or baronial interests. In the excerpts below, Giovanni Villani (1275–1348), a Florentine chronicler, describes the ascent of the* popolo *in Florence. Their first popular government, which lasted from 1250 to 1260, succeeded in establishing the "captain of the people," a rival executive officer to the* podestà. *In 1293, the second popular government succeeded in further circumscribing the power of the nobility by decreeing the* Ordinances of Justice, *a constitution in which anti-magnate laws were enacted and members of noble families were forbidden to serve in the government.*

Book 7; Chap. 39: How in Florence the "primo popolo" emerged to protect against the violence and injuries caused by the Ghibellines

1. Il Primo Popolo, 1250

[20 October 1250] . . . There was a great commotion among the Florentines because the Ghibellines who were ruling the area were crushing the people with intolerable taxes, duties, and import fees, all with very little result. And the Guelfs were scattered throughout the countryside, holding many fortresses, and making war on the city. Above and beyond all this, the Uberti family and all the other noble Ghibellines were tyrannizing the people with extortion, violence, injury. For this reason the good men of Florence united and made their headquarters at the church of San Firenze, but because of the Uberti forces they were unable to remain there so they went to the church of the Franciscans at Santa Croce, and stayed there armed, not daring to return home for fear that if they laid down their arms they would be defeated by the Uberti and the other magnates and then condemned by the [govern-

Translated from *Cronica di Giovanni Villani, a miglior lezione ridotta*, ed. Ignazio Moutier, 4 vols. (Florence: Magheri, 1823), lib. VII, chap. 39, 58–64 and lib. VIII, chap. 1, 5–7. A new critical edition is available as *Nuova Cronica di Giovanni Villani*, ed. Giovanni Porta, 3 vols. (Parma: Guanda, 1991). Some of the first nine books have been translated by Rose E. Selfe, *Villani's Chronicle Being Selections from the First Nine Books of the Croniche Fiorentine of Giovanni Villani* (London: Archibald Constable, 1906).

ment of the] *Signoria*. They then went to the fortified houses of the Anchioni in the neighborhood of San Lorenzo where with their force they elected 36 leaders of the people and removed the *podestà* and all his officials from power in Florence. And having done this without contest they ordered and decreed the [power of the] *popolo* with certain new ordinances and statutes, and they elected messer Uberto da Lucca as captain of the people, and they created 12 *anziani*[1] of the *popolo,* two for each of the six city districts, who were to lead the *popolo* and counsel the said captain. . . . And on this day the aforesaid captain gave out twenty standards to leaders representing neighborhood armed companies, so that when it was necessary every armed man would rally to the flag of his militia, and then each company would rally to the standard of the captain of the people. . . . And the principal standard of the *popolo*—the captain's—was a white and vermilion colored flag . . . [*Villani then describes the standards of all the armed companies.*] And because the *popolo* had taken over the government and the state, for the security of the people they ordered that all the towers of Florence which had a height of 120 *braccia* should be cut down to size and returned to the height of 50 *braccia* and not more [see **#57, 111**]. And so it was done, and the stones were used to build the walls around the Oltrarno district of the city.[2]

2. Il Secondo Popolo, 1293

In the year of Christ 1293 on 1 February, the city of Florence was great, powerful and content. And her citizens were fat and rich. And because of such self-satisfaction, which naturally produces pride and new problems, the citizens became arrogant and jealous such that they committed many murders, assaults, and outrages against each other. But it was above all the nobles called grandees or magnates who committed violence against the *popolo* and the powerless, in both city and countryside, assaulting them and their possessions, and occupying their property. Having had enough, certain good men—artisans and merchants of Florence who wanted the good life—set about to remedy the situation and defend themselves against the aforesaid plague. And among the leaders was an honorable man of ancient and noble *popolano* lineage, rich and powerful, who was called Giano della Bella, of the parish of San Martino, who with the counsel of the others ordered a judgment to correct the statutes and our laws, just as ancient custom had done. They decreed a number of very severe and exacting laws and statutes to control the magnates and powerful men who committed crimes against the *popo-*

1. City elders who served as councilors to the *popolo.*
2. The towers were mainly the strongholds of the magnates whom the *popolo* had just toppled.

lani, doubling the penalty for such crimes, and decreeing that one member of a magnate family should be held accountable for the actions of all others; and that two witnesses were enough to convict a malefactor of such crimes . . . and these laws were called the *Ordinances of Justice.* And so that they should be preserved and enacted, it was decreed that in addition to the six priors who now governed the city, each of the six districts should have a *gonfaloniere* [standard bearer] of justice, but one who changed every two months just as the priors do. . . . And they decreed that not one of the priors should be of a noble lineage or magnate family.

18. THE STANDARD BEARER OF LUCCA APPEALS TO LOCAL PATRIOTISM (1397)

Translated from Latin by Christine Meek

For much of the fourteenth century Lucca was ruled by various outside powers, cul-minating in a period of domination by her nearest neighbor Pisa, 1342–1369. Having obtained a grant of independence from Emperor Charles IV at great financial cost, Lucca was then administered as an independent republic and, despite what is said in this speech, enjoyed peaceful relations with Pisa for more than twenty years. By the mid-1390s, however, Lucca was again threatened by Pisa and needed to hire forces for her defense with consequent financial sacrifices [see #39]. In this speech, which unusually for Lucchese council minutes is recorded in the vernacular, the gonfaloniere[1] *attempts to persuade his fellow citizens to agree to an* estimo, *or assess-ment of each individual's resources, as a basis for dividing the sum required among the citizens [see #14.3]. His speech combines an appeal to love of liberty, an account of Lucca's unfortunate past history and the present danger, an image of Lucca as a mother in need of assistance from her children and finally a practical assertion that the burden will be by no means unbearable if shared out equitably. It is impossible to say which of these arguments proved the most effective, but the Council approved the* gonfaloniere's *proposal for an* estimo *by 109 votes to 29.*

In the name of God amen. In the year of the Lord 1397, the fifth indiction, the eighth day of June. The Major and General Council of the People and Commune of Lucca summoned by the sound of the bell and the voice of the public crier, the trumpet first having been sounded, as is customary, on the mandate of the distinguished knight, lord Peter de' Bianchi of Bologna, the honorable *podestà* of the city of Lucca and its *contado*, force and district[2] and meeting in Lucca in the palace of the dwelling and residence of the lords *anziani*[3] and *gonfaloniere di giustizia* of the People and Commune of Lucca. Present at the Council were the said lords in sufficient number and two thirds and more of the councillors of the said council and the prominent citizens

---

Translated from Archivio di Stato di Lucca, Consiglio Generale 13, Riformagioni Pubbliche, 38, 18 June 1397.

1. *Gonfaloniere di giustizia*, or Standard Bearer of Justice, the highest political office open to Lucchese citizens, chosen by a combination of election and lot to serve for a period of two months.

2. Different sections of the surrounding rural area controlled by Lucca. The district was the area within a six-mile radius of Lucca, the *contado* was the largest part of Lucchese territory divided into vicariates, and the force was a small number of outlying villages most recently acquired.

3. The *anziani* were nine in number, three from each of the three *terzieri* or wards into which Lucca was divided; they served for a two-month period alongside the *gonfaloniere*.

named below. The said lords first decided in secret vote by balls and urn[4] that this Council should be summoned and held today and that the following matters should be proposed, voted and carried into effect. In the Council then, the due formalities having been observed, the honorable man Petro Gentili, *gonfaloniere di giustizia* of the People and Commune of Lucca, proposed that the council should consult and speak on the matter indicated below which had previously been carefully considered by the said lords *anziani* and many wise citizens.

May the grace of the Holy Spirit be with us.

Honorable citizens and wise councillors. It is manifest to every man who has a true understanding and judgment of matters that liberty is among the dearest things that God placed on earth. And liberty can be recognized by its opposite, that is by servitude, and how harsh and bitter [it is] that there are many citizens alive who can and do render reliable testimony by proof and experience. Certainly it should truly be held that every good citizen would wish for death rather than to return to the hands of cruel and perfidious Pisans or any others. And who can doubt that those who govern Pisa have ever intended or continuously intend anything other than to think and plot how they can occupy our city and reduce it to servitude and place us and our liberty under their feet, that liberty which so many of our honorable citizens sought for so long and desire so much and finally obtained with the favor and grace of heaven, that is of God with the favor and grace of the Holy Church and of the Holy Empire and at inestimable cost and price to the citizens. And it is manifest that after we obtained our liberty we lived without harming any of our neighbors, always bearing many injuries with humility and patience, always seeking peace and asking for peace. But the insatiable appetite of our wicked neighbors by various tricks and deceits and by various ways and means has never wanted peace, but rather as you know has assaulted and attacked us and our lands and our men a thousand times with fire and sword with rapine, traps, and deceits, believing to achieve by warfare the end they seek, that is to put the yoke of servitude on our necks. And there is no doubt that if we continued to show patience as we have long done he would have achieved his cruel, damnable, and poisonous intention. It is therefore necessary that we come to our own assistance valiantly and defend our liberty boldly with all our strength, and to avoid exposing our peasants and citizens to the danger of death or capture. This cannot be done without men at arms,

---

4. Each councillor voted by placing in an urn a white ball for consent or a black ball for dissent.

cavalry and infantry, and they cannot be obtained or maintained without money. And the revenues of the commune are so reduced through adverse times and the cruel conditions of the world that they are not sufficient to cover the necessary expenditure. Wherefore, honorable citizens and councillors, Lucca your wretched mother, wishing to maintain herself in liberty for you, wishing to defend herself energetically against her venomous enemies, has recourse to you her dear and legitimate children [and] recommends herself to you and begs you tearfully not to allow her to perish, not to allow her to lose the name of her liberty. But that each one of you and her other children should and would support help and succor her, your dear sweet mother, each of you with what strength he can, and that you should stoutly aid, defend, and succor her in her needs, so that she be preserved in her happy liberty and you should not allow her to fall back under perfidious tyranny. Your Lucca asks no more from you than a very small part of what you can easily afford with fair distribution among the greatest, the middling, and the least, and it seems that this should be done in the following way; that is, it seems to be good, useful, and effective to make a general *estimo*, shared out equally so that each person pays his own share and no more. [He then goes on to propose three slightly different systems for making the *estimo*.]

The Commercial Revolution

This section takes its title from Robert Lopez's Commercial Revolution, *published in 1971, which argued that the period beginning in the eleventh century and ending with the Black Death of 1348 wrought changes to the European economy comparable to those brought about by the Industrial Revolution in the nineteenth century. For Lopez, the defining characteristic of the commercial revolution was the transfer of "economic leadership" from the landed class to a new group of merchant inhabitants of the city-republics of northern and central Italy. But for Lopez, the phrase signified even more. He meant it to encompass a new society, one in which the necessities of trade and business effected far-reaching transformations in the methods of doing business, the volumes of trade transacted, and the financing of it. Because of its central position in the Mediterranean, Italian merchants of central and northern Italy were at the vanguard of these transformations. The profit produced by international trade animated cities such as Pisa, Genoa, and Venice to vie with each other for domination of maritime trade routes, but it also encouraged the development of better ship-building technology and navigational instruments. Land-locked cities, not to be left out of the new profit economy, produced luxury goods for trade on the international market. Florence and Lucca were celebrated for their fine woolen and silk textiles, while cities such as Milan were known for the production of quality weaponry. Guilds emerged to regulate the production of goods and to protect their crafts and their membership. Soon they also became important sites of political power. It should be noted, however, that the "commercial revolution" outlined here was limited primarily to central and northern Italy where city-republics flourished. Although the city of Amalfi was at the forefront of maritime trade with North Africa and the East in the tenth and eleventh centuries, by the twelfth century southern Italy was ruled as a kingdom that tended to suppress communal agitation and monopolize trade. Although the* mezzogiorno *did not undergo the same economic transformations as other regions of Italy, new research is revealing evidence of urban civic identity similar to that in the North.*

The documents presented here illustrate some of these transformations as trade produced the need for documentation, regulation, the minting of standard coins for the international market, credit instruments, and legislation. This chapter also draws heavily on the papers of the most famous merchant of the period, Francesco Datini (d. 1410), whose rich archive documents almost all facets of late medieval international trade, including banking, shipping, and diplomacy. As profit was uppermost in the minds of most merchants, this chapter also includes a section on the problem of usury, excessive or illegal interest charged on loans. Ultimately the documents in this chapter show some of the ways in which the new urban economy reshaped central and northern Italian society.

19. A GENOESE APPRENTICESHIP CONTRACT (1221)

Translated from Latin by Katherine L. Jansen

Crafts, trades and professions in the Middle Ages were most often learned through apprenticeships to master craftsmen. Fathers usually chose apprenticeships for their young sons, most of whom had not yet even reached adolescence. Depending on the trade, an apprenticeship ordinarily lasted anywhere from seven to ten years, but as this contract shows, a fifteen year period was not unknown. In medieval Italy, the apprenticeship was formalized with a legal agreement, a contract drawn up by a notary, in which the terms were set out in detail and the parties agreed to abide by them or suffer the financial penalties stipulated. The Genoese contract translated below is one in which a young boy is contracted as an apprentice to a notary to serve as his assistant while learning the requisite skills of the profession.

I, Giovanni di Cogorno, for the next fifteen years contract to you master Bartholomeo, notary, my son Enrichetto to stay with you for the purpose of assisting you, and for learning your trade and lessons, with the result that he will learn to write well and compose the texts which you will teach him to write. And I promise you that I will ensure and take care that he will stay with you up to the said end [of the contract] and that he will care for and maintain your household items in good faith, and that he will not run away or quit. And if he runs away, I will have him returned to your services within three days so that he will learn the compositions that you want him to write for you. And you will teach him [to read] those books: both the *Donato* [see #103] and the Psalter according to your choice and organization of lessons. Moreover, I promise to give you for schooling and teaching of my aforesaid son, I *lira* and II *soldi* for three years; namely, an annual sum of 10 *soldi* and 3 *denari* by the Octave of the Lord.[1] Otherwise I promise the stipulated fine of 15 *lire* and accordingly, all my possessions. . . .

And I master Bartholomeo, on my part, I promise to keep your aforesaid son with me until the aforesaid end [of the contract] and to teach him accordingly and not [use him] for anything else. [And] I shall have him taught grammar, writing and reading, in good faith and without fraud, and [I agree] not to enjoin service on him that he cannot do. Otherwise, I promise [to pay] the stipulated fine of 15 *lire* and accordingly I bind myself to pledge to you all my present and future possessions.

Translated from a transcription in Giorgio Costamagna and Dino Puncuh, "Mostra storica del notariato medievale ligure," in *Atti della società Ligure di storia patria* n.s. 4 vol. 78 fasc. 1 (1964): 194, from original in Archivio di Stato di Genoa, Sezione notai, Cartolare 56, 148r.

1. The specific feast is not named; the fee was due on the eighth day after the feast, presumably the Feast of the Nativity of the Lord.

Then the two parties requested two legal instruments be made.

Made at Genoa in the church of San Lorenzo [in the presence] of witnesses Ugo Mallonus and Guilelmo Crispinus and Ansaldo Bastonus, furrier. 16 February 1221, eighth indiction.

20. GUILD REGULATIONS FOR THE OIL VENDORS AND GROCERS OF FLORENCE (1318)

Translated from Italian by Katherine L. Jansen

*By the twelfth century guilds (*arti*) were well established in many of the cities of central and northern Italy. Guilds, governed by masters, strove to regulate the production of goods and their quality along with prices, workers' salaries, and working conditions [see #41]. They simultaneously protected trades and professions and monopolized them. Significantly, guilds also served as mutual aid societies and structures for the religious life of their members insofar as they established feast-days and regulated their celebration. The most important guilds of Florence—the* arti maggiori—*were the professionals: the judges and notaries, the* Calimala *(the international cloth entrepreneurs who specialized in finished cloth), the money-changers, the wool guild, the silk guild, the doctors and apothecaries, and the furriers. After 1282 these elite guilds were those from which most of the high-ranking officials of the city were drawn. But there were other guilds as well—the fourteen minor guilds (*arti minori*), which represented such trades as the bakers, shoemakers, butchers, blacksmiths and the like. The guild regulations translated below are extracted from a set of statutes for the oil-vendors and grocers of Florence. The oil vendors were in charge of the administration of the olive presses and the selling—both wholesale and retail—of olive oil. Located just west of the baptistry, today's Piazza dell'Olio commemorates the activities of the medieval guild. The statutes were first written in Latin in 1310 but translated into Italian in 1318 to ensure that all guild members were familiar with its regulations. (See Statute LXXXIII below.) Only the vernacular version survives.*

[PROLOGUE]

In the name of God amen.

In the name of the Father, the Son, and the Holy Spirit amen. For the honor and reverence [due to] almighty God and the Blessed Mary, always a Virgin, and the most blessed Michael Archangel and St John the Baptist, and all the angels and the saints of God. And out of reverence for the Holy Roman Church and the peaceful, good, and tranquil state of the city, the commune and the people of the entire province of Florence and the lord *podestà* and the captain executor of the Ordinances of Justice [see #17], the lord priors and the *gonfalonieri* [standard bearers] of justice and their judges, knights, and notaries. And for the good and peaceful preservation of the tradesmen and the guild of oil sellers, cheese vendors, salt sellers, fodder sellers, and grocers and sellers of dried and fresh meat, and all types of dried

Translated from *Statuti delle arti degli oliandoli e pizzicagnoli e dei beccai di Firenze (1318– 1346)*, ed. Francesca Morandini (Florence: Olschki, 1961), 7–76.

meat and fish, lard, and fodder and aged and fresh *marzolino* cheese, and those who sell rope and broom-cloth,[1] glass jars, and all types of jars, pottery, and glassware and dried figs, walnuts, hazelnuts, dried and green chestnuts, pears, apples, and every other type of fruit, oranges, melons, watermelons, *panicale*,[2] shelled walnuts and fava beans and every other type of legume and fruit and shallots, ashes, soap, small tallow candles,[3] sifters and sieves and all other merchandise and groceries pertinent to this trade and the men, people, and traders in this guild.

I. On the Oath of the Men of This Trade and Guild

[I swear in] faith, without fraud, to fully obey, observe, and execute all the just commandments, which may be asked, said, or ordered of me by the rectors and consuls of this guild, who are now and will be in the future the government of the said trade, or by anyone of them from the guild party, or the notary, or anyone placed in the guild on account of honor, health, good state, or utility to the trade. And especially [I swear] to observe the chapters, statutes, ordinances, and reforms of the councillors of this guild, those already made and those that will be made in such a way that they are not contrary to the honor and government of the lord *podestà* and the captain and executor of the *Ordinances of Justice* and their judges, knights, and notaries and their courts, the lord priors of the guilds and the *gonfalonieri* of justice, and all the other officers of the city of Florence in the present and those who will come in the future. And whoever of this said trade does something contrariwise and not in obedience, as ordered by the rectors of the guild, is condemned to pay 5 *soldi piccoli* for each offense to the treasurer of the said trade, receiver of the guild. Of that fine received, one half goes to the rectors, the other half to the guild. . . .

IX. On Helping Tradesmen of This Trade and Guild

Since the rectors of this guild (by reason and occasion of their office) are held to defend each and every one of this guild from enmity, violence, [and] oppression, it is decreed, held, and ordered that if anyone from this guild suffers any violence, injury or molestation by someone not subject to this guild, for whatever reason, office or trade, the rectors of the time will be and are charged to defend, help and maintain that no one suffer either injury or harassment before the government of Florence or any other. And this will be

---

1. A rough material made from the stalks of a broom plant.
2. A type of straw from the stalks of the millet plant (*panicum italicum*) and used as fodder.
3. "Candelotti di sevo lesbio e vescovo."

done with lawyers and at the expense of the guild. And the said rectors are bound to do this under the fine of 100 *soldi piccoli*; which fine the new rectors who will succeed them in office are bound to collect under the same penalty. . . .

XVIII. On Giving Oil to the Church of Santa Maria Ughi and to Other Places

It is also decreed and ordered that the rectors of said trade, for the time they are in office, in December every year, are bound and should give and pay the church of Santa Maria Ughi,[4] or wherever the rectors of the said guild decide to donate, one storage jar of good and pure oil for the love of God and the blessed Virgin Mary. And also the said rectors and their councillors are bound to offer to the said church twelve wax candles, which should be of good wax, all of them together fair-valued at 12 *soldi piccoli*. The offering should be made each year in the month of August for the feast-day of the Virgin Mary, under the fine of 20 *soldi piccoli* for each rector and under the fine of 10 *soldi piccoli* for the treasurer.

XVIIII. On the Observance of Easter, Feast-Days, and Sundays

It is decreed and ordered that all the men and tradesmen of this guild and trade, are bound to observe and celebrate reverently the holy days of Easter and the feasts just as they are listed in order below. [This shall be done] out of honor and reverence for almighty God and the Virgin Mary and all the saints, male and female, and so that Lord God will exalt, defend, and protect the city, the commune, and the people of Florence and all the men and tradesmen of the aforesaid guild and trade, and so that the trade and the men in it may improve themselves. First, the tradesmen of the said guild are bound and must observe all Sundays; the Nativity and Resurrection of Christ; every feast-day of the Blessed Virgin Mary; All Saints day; the feasts of all the apostles; Saint Barnabas apostle; John the Baptist; the kalends of January; the day of Epiphany; the kalends of May; the Ascension of Christ; Saint Lawrence; Saint Lucy, virgin; Good Friday; Saint Michael Archangel; Holy Cross in the month of May; and at every Easter and Nativity let three days be observed; all the evangelists; Saint Mary Magdalen; Saint Salvatore; Saint Dominic; Saint Francis; Saint Reparata, virgin and martyr; Saint Zenobio, Blessed Augustine. On these solemn days, Easter week, feasts and days of reverence, or in any of those above-named and ordered for the honor of almighty God and his saints, no one of this guild should dare or presume to set up, work or open

4. A church, since destroyed, that stood near the Piazza dell'Olio.

his shop, nor to keep his shop open, only the window. And he who does not have a window may open and keep open the entrance as an exit. And he who does contrariwise against the rectors who are in office, is obliged to pay the fine of 5 *soldi piccoli*. Excepted is if anyone shows something for sale: showing, offering, and going there are not bound [by this statute]. And the rectors are bound personally to investigate each and every one of these aforesaid things on the above-cited days. . . .

XXVI. On Forcing the Women of This Trade to Obey Everything

It is decreed, ordered, deliberated, and held that all women who do or do not have husbands, who sell or buy, or who have sold or bought, or who will buy or sell in the coming period either cheese, oil, or any goods pertaining to this guild, and who have a shop to sell these goods, are held and constrained and obliged to pay and to satisfy all sums of money due for the cheese or any other goods pertaining to the said guild. And if anyone of this trade and guild receives any sum of money or anything else from a woman or her husband let him be bound and obliged to answer, respond, and satisfy the consuls of the said guild. And this clause extends to the past and to the future. . . .

XXXIII. On Not Sending, Buying, or Selling Oil

It is decreed and held that no one of this guild may dare or presume to go, or to send [anyone] to buy, or to sell oil outside of the city gates of the city of Florence, under a fine of 20 *soldi* for every offense. And the rectors are bound [by their oath] to make an investigation of these things, [and] by their power, and to condemn the guilty parties. . . .

XXXVI. On Compelling the Men of This Guild in the City and the *Contado* to Pay Taxes

The rectors of this trade and guild are also bound and should force and have forced each and every man and person practicing this trade in the *contado* and in the district of Florence to pay their part of the expenses, which the trade and guild has incurred and will incur [and] which part the rectors and councillors of this trade are bound to satisfy. . . .

XLIX. On the Burial of the Dead in This Trade

It is decreed, held, and ordered that when any tradesman of this guild dies, let the said rectors of this trade be bound, that is, let each rector be bound to order all the tradesmen of this trade and guild in his neighborhood, under a penalty of 5 *soldi piccoli* each, that they go and must go to the burial of the dead guildsman. And that all the tradesmen of this trade and guild are bound and must go to the burial of the dead guildsman at the request of the rectors, under the said penalty. And also let each and every tradesman of the said trade and guild, on that day that anyone from the said trade and guild has died, be bound to keep their shops closed just as they do on Sunday, under the penalty of 20 *soldi piccoli* each. And that the rectors, on the day that anyone of the said trade dies, under the said fine, are bound to order or to have ordered that each and every tradesman of the said trade keeps his shop closed and locked just as they do on Sunday. And let the rectors be bound to carry out these aforementioned things, on the said day that anyone dies, under the penalty of 20 *soldi piccoli* each. . . .

LIV. ON COMPELLING THE TRADESMEN OF THE *CONTADO* TO OBEY THE LAWS OF MEASURES

It is decreed and ordered that the rectors of this trade and guild are bound to ensure as are the six lords of the *biada*[5] of the city of Florence that the proper measures to measure salt and oil and those that the tradesmen of the *contado* use are and will be made right and equal to the measures that the tradesmen of Florence use. . . .

LVII. ON NOT SETTING UP A MARKET IN FRONT OF ANY TRADESMAN'S SHOP

It is held, deliberated, and ordered that no one of this trade or apprentice of this trade should dare or presume to set up a market of any type pertaining to this trade in front of the shop of anyone of this trade or any shopkeeper of this trade and guild without the permission of the shop, under the penalty of 10 *soldi piccoli* for each offense; nor should such a buyer or seller who is from another's shop or in front of someone's else's shop dare or be able to call out or make any other sign [of sale], under the penalty of 5 *soldi piccoli*. . . .

LXIII. ON SELLING OR KEEPING ON ONE TABLE OR WINDOW MEAT MIXED FROM MALE AND FEMALE ANIMALS

Then it is established, held, and ordered that no one of this trade and guild who sells such fresh meat retail should dare or presume to have, to keep, or to have had or to have kept to sell over the counter pork meat mixed with sow meat, nor the meat of a wether mixed with ewe meat, under the penalty of 40 *soldi piccoli* deducted for each and every offense to him who sells or

---

5. Officials who administrated the commune's fodder supply.

keeps it as to him who has it kept or sold. And the rectors are bound and ought to inquire and have inquiries made by others and to punish or condemn those found guilty just as outlined above. And also so that most of the meat of the city comes from the city of Florence, let the tradesmen of this trade be able to slaughter the meat and beasts every day and to sell publicly to those who wish to buy it without prejudice or encumbrance. . . .

LXXXII. On Having a Register of All the Men of This Trade and Guild

It is also established and decreed that the rectors who are in office are bound and ought to have made a membership list of all the men and tradesmen who ply this trade in the city, *contado*, and district of Florence, inscribing in order, the villages and residences of these tradesmen of the guild, by their own oath.

LXXXIII. That All the Statutes of This Guild Should be Copied in the Vernacular

It is also established and ordered that the rectors of this trade are bound and ought to have made a copy of this constitution in the vernacular so that those who are uneducated or who do not know [Latin] grammar can read and comprehend all the chapters of this constitution in the vernacular.

21. THE VENETIAN MINT AFTER
THE BLACK DEATH: THREE TEXTS (1353)

Translated from Latin by Alan Stahl

Like many aspects of life in medieval Italy, coinage was a localized phenomenon. Each commune minted its own coins, as did many lords and even bishops and monasteries. Venice was among the leading minters of Italy and supplied trade coinage throughout the Mediterranean with its fine silver grosso, *introduced around 1200, and its gold ducat, initiated in 1285. The plague that struck Venice in 1348 carried off at least half its population, including a significant portion of the staff of its mint, whose coins served as the basis for its international trade and for the local economies of the city itself and its colonies. In the wake of the plague, many mint workers fled the city, and those who remained or returned insisted on higher pay. In 1353, the Council of Forty, one of the city's governing bodies, took a series of steps to deal with these demands; it raised the wages of most of the workers and, to pay for the added expenses, debased the coinage. The Council left unchanged the two coins used for international trade: the gold ducat and large silver* grosso. *But as shown in the first document in which the Forty debated two proposals, it chose to lower the amount of silver in the basic coin for circulation at home, the* soldino. *This coin was worth one-twentieth of a* lira *[pound]; that is, a shilling of twelve pennies in the traditional European system of 12 pennies to the shilling and 20 shillings to the pound. (A woman working in the cloth industry typically earned about 25* lire *a year; a nobleman working as the head of a state agency might earn 100 to 300* lire *a year.) After modestly debasing the coins in which Venetians were paid, three months later the Forty introduced a new coin for Venice's Aegean colonies, the* tornesello, *in which less than half as much silver would represent the same value as the new* soldino. *In this way, people living in Venice would be only slightly affected by the reduced buying power of their salaries, while people in Venice's Greek colonies— Venetian colonists and local Greek inhabitants alike—would be paid in a much worse coinage, putting them at a great monetary disadvantage compared to those paid in Venetian* soldini.

Three Proposals from the Council of Forty on Debasing the Coinage and Raising Wages

1. 8 April 1353, Council of Forty, Venice

Proposal of Michele Duodo and Donato Onoradi, advisors on mint policy. Carried.

Translated from Antonino Lombardo, ed., *Le deliberazioni del Consiglio dei XL della Repubblica di Venezia*, vol. 3, R. *Deputazione Veneta di Storia Patria*, Monumenti Storici n.s. 20 (Venice: R. Deputazione Veneta di Storia Patria,1967), 11–12, #33; 16, #43–45; 28, #93.

Figure 6a. Silver *soldino*, Venice
(1353–54). American Numismatic
Society, New York, 1984.175.1.

Figure 6b. Billon *tornesello*, Venice
(1353–54). American Numismatic
Society, New York, 1982. 125.1.

As an overall good standard must be found to bring profit to the state and
fairness to the merchants traveling and operating in the Levant, and the standard for the coinage prescribed below should be profitable both for the state
and the merchants, therefore let it be resolved that there be made a coin of
the [pure] silver alloy currently used for *mezzanini* [a Venetian coin worth
half a *grosso*] and of the customary appearance of *soldini*, of which 36 dozen
are cut from the mark [238.5 grams], and each coin is worth 12 pennies, and
that all merchants who bring silver to the mint for making this coin should
have from the state or the mint masters 392 coins for each mark of silver that
they put in the mint, and the initial of the name of the mint master shall be
engraved on this coin.

In agreement—26.

Proposal of Andrea Gabriel, advisor on mint policy.

For the benefit and profit of the state and fairness and advantage to the merchants traveling and operating in the Levant, let it be resolved that there be
made a coin of which 22 dozen are cut from the mark, each coin being worth
12 pennies, and it should be of the alloy prescribed below and of the customary appearance of *soldini*, that is that there be 5 ounces of good silver and 3
ounces of copper in each mark and that all merchants who bring silver to the
mint for making this coin should have for each mark of silver 384 of these
coins, and the initial of the name of the Mint Master shall be engraved on
this coin.

[In agreement]—9; Opposed—1; no opinion—1.

*The Council then raised the pay of the workmen who refine the silver, the adjustors
who make sure each blank is of the prescribed weight, and the strikers who stamp the
blanks with engraved dies.*

2. 30 April 1353, Council of Forty, Venice

Proposal of Michele Duodo and Donato Onoradi, advisors on mint policy.
Carried.

That the workmen should receive 48 pennies per mark and they have to purify the silver for these coins when they are made and they shall have an allowance for loss during refining of 33 pennies per hundred marks.
Carried.
That the weight adjustors should receive 22 pennies per mark.
And that the strikers shall have 32 pennies per mark.

3. 29 July 1353, Council of Forty, Venice

Proposal of the Doge, his Councillors, and the Heads of the Forty.
Carried.
For the benefit and profit of the state and our Greek colonies of Coron, Modon, Negroponte, and Crete, let it be ordered that *torneselli* be minted here, putting 8 ounces of copper to one of silver, and 320 *torneselli* be cut from the mark, and henceforth let it be resolved that as great quantities of this coin as possible be sent to these places, instructing our rectors there that they use them and make them be used in their payments there and work to have this coinage circulate, that this coin be worth 3 pennies each and be of the appearance and design chosen by the doge.
[In agreement]—29; Opposed—2; No opinion—0.

22. STATE-RUN SHIPPING IN VENICE (1398)

Translated from Latin by Eleanor A. Congdon

Among the great maritime leaders of medieval Italy—Genoa, Pisa, Amalfi, and Venice—only Venice organized any significant part of her merchant marine into a state-run shipping system. Around 1300, Venice identified several commonly sailed routes where the merchandise was of very high value but low volume, and which brought significant profit for the city and merchants. The first routes emphasized the traffic in spices through Constantinople, and to Egypt and Syria. The route to Flanders and England was developed in the mid-Trecento after the passage through the Straits of Gibraltar was opened for Christian shipping. In the Quattrocento more routes were developed, including one connecting Venice, Tunis, and Egypt. On these routes, the Senate set up the muda or fleet of galleys whose safety was assured by the large number of people on each vessel [see #43]. The Senate auctioned off the privilege to captain each galley. The director of the voyage set the tariff charged to those who shipped the merchandise, created a rigid time-frame on which the muda sailed, and promulgated regulations against private ships sailing to the target markets within a time period too close to the state fleet's schedule. The following selection is a short excerpt of the detailed instructions passed in 1398. Note that the "captain" is the fleet leader while the patroni captain the individual galleys.

Item: Because it is good to try to win the good will of the lord of Malaga [Sultan Muhammad VII of Granada], let it be ordained that the captain of the said galleys shall, if it should appear to be proper, go with the said galleys to Malaga, and, unless the ruler is absent, he should present to the sultan a selection of the merchandise on the galleys, worth a value of fifty ducats, in these goods. Should the said captain and the *patroni* not be able to remain in the port more than three days, reckoned from the time of arrival to when they must depart, in order to make the said selection, they should procure a safe conduct from the said Sultan of Granada for the galleys and ships, and the merchandise from our parts for a greater amount of time.

Translated from Archivio di Stato di Venezia, *Senato misti*, reg. 44 (copia), fol. 99r, 15 January 1398.

Figure 7. Pisan galleys and lighthouse. Romanesque bas-relief from the façade of the Duomo, Pisa. (Photo: Scala/Art Resource)

23. INTERNATIONAL NETWORKS IN THE MEDITERRANEAN (1400)

Translated from Italian by Eleanor A. Congdon

Medieval merchants depended on news from employees, compatriots, the international marketplace, and diplomats to keep them informed about the latest events that might affect their business. They had to know when to invest in a market and when to pull out based on local conditions. They also needed to know about important international events because these could affect their business. This excerpt shows that merchants thought the arrival of Timur (Tamerlane the Great) in Aleppo would affect the markets in the western Mediterranean. The speed with which this letter was written is confirmed by the unusually large and sloppy though recognizable handwriting.

Yesterday there came a brigantine [a two-masted round-bellied cargo vessel] directly from the Levant with news that Timur has entered into Syria with a great multitude of warriors. All the Venetian merchants who were in Syria have fled to Famagusta on Cyprus. And the messengers trumpet out that the whole region is engulfed in the great confusion of war. Because of that, there is concern about the prices of goods which come from the region [of northern Syria around Aleppo]. And you should seek to acquire as much cotton and spices as you can in the western Mediterranean now before the prices rise, so that you can be prepared to sell. You should invest in cotton especially in Montpellier for your and our benefit because it has fluctuated greatly in value (between 48 and 55 *lire* per unit), as well as consider investing in pepper and Meccan ginger.

Translated from Archivio di Stato di Prato, Datini Busta 927, *Carteggio Barcelona*, letter Venice to Barcelona, Commessaria di Zanobi di Taddeo Gaddi e Antonio di Ser Bartolomeo to Compagnia Francesco di Marco Datini e Simone d'Andrea, 30 August 1400.

24. TRANSPORTATION OF COMMODITIES (1401)

Translated from Italian by Eleanor A. Congdon

For merchants, one of the most important factors in business was the speed and availability of transport. Independent ship captains had control over both their cargo and their itineraries. While rules, even decrees promulgated by the pope, existed about carrying items usable for enemy weaponry, patroni *(ship captains) had the freedom to choose their cargo and the merchants with whom they associated. They did so based on speed and profitability: wood and salt were two commodities that could be used for ballast when putting together a cargo with speed.*

The ship captained by Marcho de Verzoni left here and went to Segna [on the Dalmatian coast] to load a cargo of wood, and from there carried it to Ibiza from where it will be sent all over Catalonia. The said lord Marcho arrived in Ibiza and discharged the wood and other things on his ship. . . . He had intended to load up quickly with goods waiting for transport to Venice, and to top off the cargo with salt so that he could leave promptly and not lose time.

Translated from Archivio di Stato Prato, Datini Busta 927, *Carteggio Barcelona*, letter Venice to Barcelona, Antonio Contarini di Marino di Ser Pantaleon to Compagnia Francesco di Marco Datini, 20 March 1401.

25. TWO CARGO MANIFESTS (1400, 1399)

Translated from Italian by Eleanor A. Congdon

Venice dominated international trade throughout the Middle Ages. In order to maintain this status after the fall of the last Crusader toehold in the Middle East (Acre in 1291), the government instituted a system of state-controlled galleys, the muda, *which sailed on a strict schedule with a mandate to carry the high-value but low-volume commodities classified as "spices." These goods came from one of three areas: Romania, the coast of Syria, or Egypt. Below are two cargo lists for* muda *galleys. The first, pertaining to Romania (the Venetian term for the Black and Aegean Seas) is unusual in that it tells where merchandise was loaded. The second, from Beirut, is a more typical cargo list for the major spice emporia. In these documents, spices were transported in* coli, *a measure varying with the type of commodity which here has been translated as "units." Silk textiles were measured in* fardi, *best defined as packages or bales, translated here as "package." Finally, gold and silver were measured in* groppi, *translated as "pouches."*

1. Cargo of the Two Galleys of Romania Commanded by Ser Piero Zuriani, Which Arrived in Venice 23 January 1400.

[Received] in Tana:

Rhubarb	2 units
Wax	2 units
[Raw] Silk	3 packages
Gold Ducats	1 pouch

[Received] in Vospero [modern Kertch in the Crimea]:

Silk	17 packages
Crimson silk fabric	2 units
Wormwood [used medicinally]	19 units

[Received] in Trebizond:

Pepper	1 pound
Silk	26 packages
Ginger	4 units
Manna [used medicinally]	1 unit
Crimson silk fabric	1 unit

Translated from Archivio di Stato Prato, Datini 1117: *Cariche*, 23 January 1400; 11 November 1399

Retail Spices	9 units
Sandal wood	1 unit
Trefoil	1 unit

[Received] in Constantinople:

| Wormwood | 10 units |
| Silk | 3 packages |

[Received] in Negroponte

Wax	482 units
Indigo	34 units
Silk	23 packages
Kermes[1]	17 units
Lac from Maura[2]	1 unit
Shellac	11 units

[Received] in Modon:

Silk	177 packages
Pepper	377 pounds
Ginger	45 units
Indigo	26 units
Cochineal	34 units
Retail spices	1 unit
Fusti [probably clove stalks]	10 units
Scammony [a flavoring]	1 unit
Various[3]	4 units
Ermine	1 unit
Nuts [probably walnuts]	3 units
Cloves	8 units
Tutty [a flavoring]	2 units
Silk fabric	2 units
Gold ducats	2 pouches

[Received] in Ragusa:

| Silver | 7 pouches |

1. The dried bodies of females of the insect *Coccus ilicis* that cling to certain oaks in Spain and Greece. The bodies, when ground and boiled, produce a premier type of red dye.
2. In general, lac and shellac are made from the sap of certain trees that members of the insect family *coccus* feed on. The sap crystallizes over the body of the insect and draws the pigments. Cochineal is a fine red dye made when the pigment is red.
3. This could mean miscellaneous minor spices, or it could possibly refer to vair—a fur soft enough to be used for trimming and lining garments, possibly squirrel.

[Received] in Zara:

Silver	1 pouch
Gold ducats	2 pouches

2. Cargo of Five Venetian Galleys Sailing from Beirut on 11 November 1399

Pepper	219 pounds
Ginger	2419 units
Long pepper [from India]	5 units
Cloves	677 units
Nutmeg nuts	258 units
Cinnamon	277 units
Minor spices	93 units
Clove stalks	117 units
Mace	38 units
Galingale [herb for flavoring]	15 units
Indian Ginger	4 units
Myrobalans [a type of fruit]	4 units
Sugar	69 units
Zeodary [a flavoring]	6 units
Chapelette [a type of silk]	1 unit
Chubebs [similar to pepper]	1 unit
Rock Candy	5 units
Myrrh	1 unit
Frankincense	6 units
Tutty	8 units
Spikenard	1 unit
Aloe	8 units
Sagapenum [used medicinally]	2 units
Galbanum [used medicinally]	2 units
Sarcocolla [a gum resin]	1 unit
Indigo	2 units
Scammony	5 units
Sandalwood	71 units
Orpiment[4]	5 units
Brazil-wood	23 units
Cumin	8 units
Lac	42 units

4. Arsenic trisulfide, used as a yellow pigment.

Cinnabar [a red pigment]	2 units
Buckrame[5]	127 units
Velvet	1 unit
Camphor	2 units
Silk fabric	24 units
Pearls	49 units
Figs	1 unit
Camlets[6]	11 units
Silk	18 units
Ducats	28 pouches

5. A fine material of silk or cotton.
6. A fabric made of camel or mohair.

26. A RUN ON A BANK (1400)

Translated from Italian by Eleanor A. Congdon

Banks were the vital link that allowed merchants in one city to be able to pay for goods in another. Merchants deposited their money on the understanding that the banker would endeavor to make it grow through wise investments. As with the crashes of the great Florentine banks in the mid-fourteenth century, which had made too many loans to kings who had little hope or incentive to repay, smaller banks ran into trouble when investors attempted to withdraw or shift greater amounts of specie than the bank had on hand at the moment. Such were the circumstances investors found themselves in when the plague suddenly claimed Piero Benedetto, a prominent Florentine banker living in Venice.

Ser Piero became very ill with the pestilence late Monday evening [27 September 1400] and on the 30th a rumor spread from envy that he was dead and that he had wished to petition other banks [to honor his accounts]. . . . I heard that many artisans and other Venetians, fearing for their assets, rushed to his bank to be paid. It is said that they came in such great numbers, and with their emotions running so high, that the bank staff saw they could not conduct orderly business under such conditions; [so] that night they hurried to deliver the bank's books to the "*Consoles* of the Merchants" [officials appointed by the Venetian government to regulate commerce]. It is said that they wish to pay each and every one and that they ought to be able to do so. At this point [while the bank is closed and the family conducts Piero's burial], the employees of the bank and his executors seek to contact the greater part of the bank's creditors and show clearly that they can pay everyone, and that 15,000–20,000 ducats of gold will remain to Piero's sons . . . but we have heard, and verified by speaking with some of his friends, that Piero's parents have ordered a collection of money, which is a tremendous burden to family and friends. On Monday, however, when the bank reopens with more cash on hand, it should be able to satisfy everyone who comes to the bank for money they have deposited there.

Yesterday on the 4th . . . the parents of Ser Piero finished contacting all the Florentines in this territory and . . . assured them that the bank would pass to Ser Piero's heirs and the accounts would be transferred from the old books to the new. But the parents asked that we neither delay payments due

Translated from Archivio di Stato Prato, Datini 712, *Carteggio Bologna*, letter Venice to Bologna, Bindo Piaciti to Francesco di Marco Datini e Compagnia, 2 November 1400, and 5 November 1400. Transcribed in Flavia Zaccaria, "I rapporti economici tra Venezia e Bologna alla fine Trecento (Studio su documenti dell'Archivio Datini di Prato)" (unpublished *tesi*, Florence, 1990), 59–60, 64–66.

in January or any time in the next four months, nor ask that they pay off accounts that are near to completion. . . . All of the Florentines responded graciously, and it pleases them and their honor, having been asked for the time, to grant it.

27. DEBT REMISSION (1400)

Translated from Italian by Eleanor A. Congdon

During the Trecento, a revolution occurred in the way investors conducted business. In place of the old commenda *system, where one party invested most of the money but shared equally the profits or losses with the partner who traveled with the goods, investors started using commission agents in foreign ports. They paid for orders from these agents in several ways. Coin was the simplest form of payment, but it was bulky to ship and posed a temptation for thieves. Alternatively, investors could send merchandise for direct trade or sale. They could also use one of various ways to transfer money on paper, including credit and loans. A remission involved a series of orders to transfer value in the bank ledgers from one merchant to another. A banker wrote a letter of credit based on the originating investor's assets, and then sent it by the hand of a traveling agent to a banker in another place, who would turn the credit into cash for delivery to the commission agent. The money could be used for a series of ventures, with the goal of making it grow. It would then be returned to the investor by another letter of credit. The repayment phase was referred to as a "remission." The Datini letters contain many examples of this method of transferring money. In this excerpt, the* lira *is a unit of money of account, while the* grossi *are actual coins of a much smaller denomination [see #21].*

You say, moreover, that you have received from Giovanni di Ser Nigi 20 *lire* worth of *grossi* and another 15 *lire* worth of *grossi* from Domenico d' Andrea which they remitted to your agents in Florence. And on the 28th, we shall remit these as directed.

You say, moreover, that you had a promise from Salvi di Giovanni of 20 *lire* worth of *grossi* that I shall remit to your [company] in Florence for him, and on the 30th of the past was the termination date and it was sent to the bank of Piero Benedetto, and the money is for you only now.

Translated from Archivio di Stato Prato, Datini 712, *Carteggio Bologna*, letter Venice to Bologna, Bindo Piaciti to Francesco di Marco Datini e Compagnia, 2 November 1400. Transcribed in Flavia Zaccaria, "I rapporti economici tra Venezia e Bologna alla fine Trecento (Studio su documenti dell'Archivio Datini di Prato)" (unpublished *tesi*, Florence, 1990), 59–60.

28. TRADE AND DIPLOMACY (1400)

Translated from Italian by Eleanor A. Congdon

By 1400 the great Italian trading cities, especially Venice, had formalized their dip-lomatic representation in many foreign markets into consulates, and were expand-ing their presence by opening new ones. The consul usually had a residence for himself and his household, and often rooms and warehouses reserved for use by his country's merchants. The consul negotiated import, export, and sales tariffs with the host gov-ernment and intervened on behalf of the merchants under his jurisdiction. The Venetian presence in Tunis in the 1390s was greatly affected by "Crusades" against various regions in North Africa led by the Genoese, Aragonese, Catalans, and Sicil-ians. The Tunisians imprisoned many Europeans, including a large number of Venetians, and nullified existing trade agreements. The Venetians sent a series of consuls to negotiate their release. In early 1400, the Florentine merchant, Giovanni di Bartolo, who had been based in Venice, set up shop in Tunis. The following letter describes the situation there.

I think that you ought to know from my letters that . . . I came here with the Venetian consul. He was appointed for two years. We have been here for nine months now, and I have opened a shop selling fabric and other merchandise. At the end of the two years, I do not know what will happen or how well the Venetians will do with this king, but at this moment they have finished negotiating the peace. . . . I believe that there are not more merchants here because of the piracy that prevents goods from arriving here, and because the Genoese here are in prison, and about the other imprisoned merchants there is no news.

Translated from Archivio di Stato Prato, Datini 704, *Carteggio Florence*, letter Tunis to Florence, Giovanni di Bartolo to Manno d'Albizzi, 24 February 1400.

29. PROTECTIONIST LEGISLATION (1400)

Translated from Spanish by Eleanor A. Congdon

In the thirteenth and fourteenth centuries, Italian merchants traveled throughout Europe looking for opportunities to sell textiles and items such as paper, which they manufactured, and the spices, dyes, medicines, and precious stones they acquired from Muslim lands. They also offered their services as international bankers. The Italian firms were wealthy and aggressive enough to be able to finance kings and wars. They pioneered accounting practices such as double-entry bookkeeping, credit, letters of account, and insurance that allowed them to move money easily and quickly across long distances with minimum risk and no need to move large numbers of coins. Their rise made Jewish moneylenders less important to Europe. And having found ingenious ways to make money grow, the Church had a harder time arguing against usurious practices. They had tremendous reserves of liquid capital that could be used to buy large quantities of raw materials, such as wool, before these reached the market. Naturally, the economic power upset merchants native to the markets they penetrated. Many people found it easier to blame the Italians for the state of their trade and manufacturing than to compete. Italians periodically found themselves the targets of protectionist legislation. In 1401, the Catalans forced Martin the Humane of Aragon/Catalonia to ban Italian merchants from doing business in his kingdom, but since this was against the greater interests of his kingdom, he worked to open the markets again. The legislation of 1403 lays out the rules by which Italians could resume trade. These respond to, and therefore elucidate, the causes of hostility toward Italians by the Catalans.

The lord king, just as his predecessors the kings of Aragon had done, for the good will of Florentines, Lucchese, Sienese, and other Tuscans and all Lombards, and all other Italians, had made laws and contracts applying to all his kingdom which gave advantageous tariffs, on the understanding that in order to enjoy these privileges the merchants must pay with a bolt of cloth of gold, or with precious items having the value which the king would appoint based on the value of the tariffs. And the king dictated that the cloth of gold must be paid not only by the head of a company but also by each of its employees doing business in the kingdom. The payment of the cloth of gold shall stop and the following practices shall be followed: (1) All Italian merchants and strangers from foreign lands in the kingdom shall pay a fee of three dinars per unit of value for the entrance of any merchandise into the kingdom. (2) All Italian goods arriving in the Kingdom which are intended

Translated from Pedro Lopez Elum, "El acuerdo commercial de la Corona de Aragon con los Italianos en 1403 'Dret italia,'" *Ligarzas* 7 (1975): 188–93; these pages are rubrics for the chapters of the 1403 "Dret italia."

for sale in some other part of the kingdom, shall pay the entrance fee. (3) Any goods bought by Italians anywhere in the kingdom shall pay a tax upon sale; if they are shipped from one part of the kingdom to another, they shall still pay the tax. (4) The king ordains that certain goods shall be prohibited from import and export. (5) What is more, the king prohibits all fraud, especially that where Italians seek not to pay the tax. (6) Seeing that the number of Italians in his country has multiplied, as has the amount of merchandise they bring with them, the king shall place a limit on the number of Italians allowed in his lands, and on the length of time a merchant may stay—five years—and no amount of cloth of gold shall be acceptable to change these restrictions. (7) The king, aware of the need of his citizens [to be able to compete for the raw materials of their own country, while not having money with which they can speculate on production in advance of its completion], specifies that Italians may only live and trade in certain parts of his kingdom of Aragon, his kingdom of Valencia, and his lands of Majorca, Minorca, Ibiza, and Sardinia, and do all their trading from those places. (8) Italians shall pay the import and export taxes on goods brought into the kingdom. However, goods that are in transit between markets and not for sale in the kingdom, shall only pay the export tax. (9) Italians shall bring to the king's lands only enough victuals and gold and silver to pay for their entrance tax and the export tax upon their departure. If they bring more than that, they shall pay the tax upon these items as if they were merchandise. (10) The king shall appoint the officials who will collect the taxes in the ports, and they shall collect from everyone without being molested or vexed. The king appoints a "Battle General" [a royal official] for each kingdom to oversee the tax collection in various ports, pursue fraud, and determine judgments when disputes arise about the tax.

30. USURY: SIX TEXTS (1161–1419)

Translated from Latin by Lawrin Armstrong

We define usury as an excessive or illegal rate of interest, but for medieval canon law and theology usury denoted any charge for a loan of money or commodities whose use involved their consumption, such as wine, oil, or grain. The prohibition of usury originated in the early church, but was rarely applied until the twelfth century, when the commercial revolution stimulated the growth of credit markets. A series of decrees from the Third Lateran Council (1179) to the Council of Vienne (1311) excommunicated usurers, denied them Christian burial unless they first repaid interest to their debtors (doc. 1), and forbade public authorities to license moneylenders. Although the prohibition was often ignored in practice, in the highly monetized economy of medieval Italy it potentially affected a range of transactions from simple consumption loans to commercial partnerships and interest on government bonds. One immediate effect of conciliar condemnations was that explicit references to usury in contracts became rare after the twelfth century, although a few early examples survive in notarial registers (doc. 2). "Manifest" or "notorious" usurers were often compelled on their deathbeds to make restitution of usurious profits (doc. 3). Theologians and canonists debated the applicability of the prohibition to all sectors of the economy. The canon lawyer Hostiensis (Henry of Susa; d. 1271) argued that interest on loans was licit if the lender was a merchant who did not habitually engage in moneylending (doc. 4). Others, such as the theologians Thomas Aquinas (d. 1274) and Gerard of Siena (d. ca. 1336), upheld the traditional prohibition on the grounds that usury was a violation of natural law (doc. 5). Disagreements among theorists created uncertainty among the pious about the legitimacy of many economic activities. For example, Florentine citizens were periodically compelled to lend money to the government at rates of five percent. Nevertheless debates about whether the interest paid on government bonds was usurious led the merchant Angelo Corbinelli to include a clause in his will ordering his heirs to renounce the bonds if the church declared interest on them illicit (doc. 6).

1. Decree of the Second Council of Lyons (1274) Prohibiting the Christian Burial of Usurers Who Fail to Make Restitution

Even if manifest usurers have made provision in their testaments for the restitution of specific or unspecified sums of usury that they have received, nevertheless church burial shall be denied them until complete satisfaction has been made (so far as their resources permit), either to those to whom restitution is due, if they be at hand, or to others who have the authority to accept restitution on their behalf. In the absence of both, restitution shall be made

Translated from *Corpus iuris canonici*, ed. Emil Friedberg, 2 vols. (Leipzig: Tauchnitz, 1879; repr. Graz: Akademische Druck- und Verlagsanstalt, 1955), vol. 2, cols. 1081–82 (VI 5.5.2 = II Lyons, constitution 27)

to the bishop of the place or to his vicar, or to the priest of the parish in which the testator lives in the presence of honest witnesses from the parish. . . . Alternatively, the bishop may direct a public notary to accept a suitable guarantee for the sum to be restored. If the amount of usury is known, we decree that this shall always be expressed in the guarantee; otherwise the amount shall be determined by the recipient of the guarantee. He may not, however, knowingly set this lower than the sum he believes to be due, and if he should do so, he shall be obliged to make good the difference. All members of religious orders and others who, in violation of the provisions of the present constitution, dare to admit notorious usurers to church burial we declare subject to the penalties prescribed by the Lateran Council for usurers themselves. No one may witness the testaments of notorious usurers and no one may admit them to confession or absolve them unless they make restitution or, if it is permitted, offer a suitable guarantee of restitution, so far as their resources permit. The testaments of manifest usurers drawn up in any other way are invalid and utterly void in law.

2. A Genoese Contract of 16 July 1161 That Openly Mentions Usury

I, Embrone, have taken in loan from you, Salvo of Piacenza, £ 100 Genoese, for which I shall pay you or your messenger, personally or by my messenger, £ 120 within one year; but if I wish to pay you the aforesaid £ 100 and accrued interest before the next feast of the Purification, you must accept them and for that purpose have your messenger in Genoa. If I do not so observe these conditions, I promise you, making the stipulation, the penalty of the double.

3. Testamentary Guarantee of Agostino di ser Migliorello, Usurer, Florence, 13 June 1395

Likewise, the said testator states and declares that for a period of time he practiced usury in the city of Florence and received from many people beyond the principal various sums of money as interest and usury. He further states and declares that now, having posted guarantees, he restores the aforesaid usury and repays any sums owing to absent creditors, as is detailed more fully in the guarantee redacted today in the hand of his notary. In the light of the

(2) Translated from Robert S. Lopez and Irving W. Raymond, eds. and trans., *Medieval Trade in the Mediterranean World: Illustrative Documents Translated with Introductions and Notes* (New York: Columbia University Press, 1955), 158.

(3) Translated from Archivio di Stato di Firenze, Ospedale di Santa Maria Nuova 68, fol. 45v; ed. Lawrin Armstrong, "Usury, Conscience and Public Debt: Angelo Corbinelli's Testament of 1419," in *A Renaissance of Conflicts: Visions and Revisions of Law and Society in Italy and Spain*, ed. John A. Marino and Thomas Kuehn (Toronto: Centre for Reformation and Renaissance Studies, 2004), 182, n. 35.

said restitution, the testator, in his own view, no longer possesses anything acquired by the crime of usury or by any other illicit means. Nevertheless, for the complete exoneration of his soul, just as he undertakes in the aforesaid guarantee to make restitution, he also wills, disposes, prescribes and directs in this his testament that each and every one to whom anything is owed by the said testator in the aforesaid manner or any other way shall be completely satisfied from his estate as his trustees and heirs see fit.

4. Hostiensis (Henry of Susa) on Legitimate Interest (ca. 1270)

With regard to that which is added to the principal, the seeking of legitimate damages is not prohibited, but only shameful profit or other illicit increase. Therefore I am of the view . . . that if a merchant who frequents markets and fairs and there makes big profits should, for reasons of charity, lend me, who am in great need, money that he was going to employ in trade, then I am obligated to him from that moment for his damages, provided nothing is done in fraud of usury and provided the said merchant is not in the habit of lending money at usury.

5. Gerard of Siena on Why Usury Is Prohibited (ca. 1329–36)

I say therefore that a contract of usury is wicked and bound up with vice because it causes a natural thing to transcend its nature and an artificial thing to transcend the skill that created it, which is completely contrary to nature.

By way of demonstration, it must be understood that of the things in which usury is committed some things are artificial, such as coins, which are lent according to a determinate weight or number, and others are natural, such as gold, silver, and so on, which are lent according to a determinate weight, or, like wine, oil, and grain, according to a determinate measure. Now a contract of usury causes natural things to transcend their nature and artificial things to transcend the skill that made them. That this is so is clear, for we see that nature has given natural things a fixed and determinate value, the evidence of which is that it has given them a nature such that their value can be known with certainty, as in the case of things that we are accustomed to weigh, such as gold and silver, to which God has given a nature such that their value may be measured by their weight: so long as their weight remains constant, their value also remains constant. And things that have the same nature are weighed in exactly the same way; and therefore according to their

---

(4) Translated from Hostiensis, *In Decretalium libros commentaria*, ad X 5.19.16 *Salubriter*, n. 4 (Venice: Iuntae, 1581; repr. Turin: Bottega d'Erasmo, 1965), vol. 5, fol. 58vb–59ra.
(5) Translated from Leipzig, Universitätsbibliothek, MS 894, fol. 68r–68v.

very nature their value can be known with certainty, nor can their value rise or fall provided the weight remains constant. And if their value seems to rise or fall, this is not because of some change in the value of the things themselves, but because of a change in our need of them or a change in the value of the things for which they may be exchanged. And I maintain that things which we are accustomed to measure, such as wine, grain, oil, and so on, are the same in their own way as things that are weighed. For God and nature have given such things a fixed and determinate value inasmuch as they have given them a nature such that their value may be estimated and conceived by measure: so long as their measure remains constant, their value remains constant. And because their nature is such that they are mensurable, according to their very nature their value can be known with certainty, nor can their value rise or fall except in the ways we mentioned with regard to things that are weighed.

What has just been said about mensurable and weighable things cannot be said of other natural things of whatever kind, since other natural things are not such that their value can be conceived determinately or known with certainty; indeed, it is impossible to know their value with certainty because their value is not conceived in terms of some intrinsic quality but on account of external and contingent factors, as, for example, the value of a field or a vineyard is sometimes dependent on location, sometimes on the season, sometimes on the status of the owner, or various other circumstances which may be enumerated at length. And what I say of a vineyard or a field is true of all other natural things that are not weighed or measured. And this is so because neither God nor nature has determined or assigned them a value, but rather their value is intended to fluctuate in relation to various external and contingent circumstances. With regard to the proposition, then, I maintain that a contract of usury causes natural things that are weighed or measured to transcend the nature or the value, fixed and determined by weight and measure, that they have been assigned by God or nature. For by means of this contract the usurer extracts something beyond the weight and measure of the thing lent and consequently causes such things to transcend their value with respect to their weight and measure, which is wicked and unnatural, because God and nature have assigned their value in accordance with the weight by which they are weighed and the measure by which they are measured.

It was said, moreover, that usury is not only committed in natural things that are weighed and measured, but also in artificial things that are counted, such as money. For just as the value of natural things that are weighed and measured must be conceived with regard to their weight and measure, so also is the value of artificial things that are counted, such as money, conceived with respect to number; and just as nature assigns weighable and mensurable natural things a value in accordance with their weight and measure, so also in its own way does skill assign to artificially created coins a value in accordance with their number. Therefore, if a contract of usury is wicked and unnatural because it causes natural things to transcend the value which nature assigns them according to a fixed measure and weight, it will also be wicked with regard to artificial things, such as coins, because it causes them to transcend the value that has been assigned to them by skill. And therefore it is well said that a contract of usury causes a natural thing to transcend its nature and an artificial thing the skill that made it.

6. Testament of Angelo Corbinelli, Merchant, Florence, 17 April 1419

The testator stated and declared that he never bought shares in any of the public debt[1] funds of the commune of Florence, although he is in fact described as a creditor of the commune in the public debt accounts for several sums of money and gold florins on account of compulsory loans and obligations that he himself paid, as well as those paid by his family and brothers. And because on several occasions the testator personally witnessed many masters, bachelors, and other theologians dispute whether it is licit to accept payments on the aforesaid sums, and because he both saw and heard it said that highly judicious masters and theologians hold contrary opinions on this question, he was unable to be certain in his conscience. Wishing therefore to unburden his conscience so far as possible, he willed, prescribed, and directed that if at any time a decision or declaration shall be made by the Roman church or a council or a commission of doctors appointed by the Roman church or its pastors to make a decision or declaration on whether the aforesaid payments, gifts, and compensation, which citizens universally receive from the commune on account of their fiscal obligations, are licit or not, then

Translated from Archivio di Stato di Firenze, Notarile Antecosimiano 9042, fol. 73r; ed. Lawrin Armstrong, "Usury, Conscience and Public Debt: Angelo Corbinelli's Testament of 1419," in *A Renaissance of Conflicts: Visions and Revisions of Law and Society in Italy and Spain*, ed. John A. Marino and Thomas Kuehn (Toronto: Centre for Reformation and Renaissance Studies, 2004), 230–31.

1. Citizens of Florence and other city-states were periodically obliged to make loans to the government on the basis of property assessments. After 1343, such loans were declared nonrepayable, and the cumulative debt was called the *monte comune*, or "debt mountain." Other funds, also known as *monti*, were established between 1359 and 1434. Shares in the *monte comune* usually paid 5 percent interest, but citizens could recover some of their original outlay by selling their shares at a discount on a government-regulated market. Discounted shares were popular with speculators, who, depending on the rate of discount, could earn as much as three times the standard rate.

his heirs should act in every respect in conformity with the decree, decision, determination, or conclusion of the Roman church or its council or the commission of doctors to whom the resolution of the said question has been entrusted.

Violence, Warfare, and Peace

As many of the sources in this section demonstrate, violence was a recurrent reality of medieval lives, devastating communities large and small, disrupting all aspects of economic, cultural, political, and social life. It took various forms: at one end were major military encounters such as the Battle of Tagliacozzo in 1268, which put an end to the ambitions of the Hohenstaufen in Italy. These are the battles which all students of medieval Europe are likely to remember: field battles on horse back which have made their way into standard chronologies and political narratives. Other forms of violence are less widely remembered now, but are of great interest to historians of Italy and the Italian economy, such as the sack in 881 by Arabs of the monastery of San Vincenzo al Volturno, as recorded in the twelfth century (and now a site of major of archaeological excavations).

An obvious difficulty for historians is distinguishing clearly between different forms of conflict: when is a battle not a battle? Street fighting was endemic in many urban centers and might often conform to the norms of warfare: preceded by careful planning, both involved large numbers of fighters and high levels of casualties. The rules governing behavior were also comparable. Full-scale military enterprises and small-scale skirmishes took place in a context where a fair fight and honorable behavior were important considerations, at least to the record-keepers, just as betrayal was both a reality of conflict and a means to explain and justify defeat. In both contexts, the flip side of violence, peacemaking and reconciliation, took ritualized forms and sometimes (although not always) depended on the intervention of outsiders, whether clerical or lay. Such considerations of comparability explain the selection of sources included in this section. They illustrate the mentality which created and responded to differing types of violence and the experience of that violence in various forms.

Just as the nature of violence was multiform, so were its motives: from short-term political advantage and competition for office, to invasions and revolt. Government-sanctioned violence was frequently directed outward, as both royal and urban governments sought to extend their influence in their immediate vicinity or further afield. A particular characteristic of Italian warfare was perhaps the precocious use of sea battles to promote and protect overseas trade. Equally, legalized violence was directed inward, against those designated as criminals (including heretic or infidel), or against political and commercial enemies. Indeed, in the northern cities factional violence, whether or not it was legitimized by government action, was a political and social fact, often conditioning both life in a city and relations between neighboring polities as one party harbored the exiles of another. On an ostensibly more personal scale, revenge or vendetta, often involving the killing of close neighbors, was frequently explained by chroniclers as the result of betrayal among the nobility and in particular the mistreatment of women, who otherwise appear rarely in this section, since participation in fighting was usually, but not exclusively, a male preserve. Vendetta, often invoking violation of female and family honor, was also, however, a convenient narrative technique to explain long-term political conflict, most famously as illustrated here in the case of the Guelfs and Ghibellines of Florence.

These sources both allow us to explore the experience and nature of violence and also to trace some of the changing techniques of warfare, on land and at sea. At the same time they illustrate that, while peace was the purpose and product of good government, political change often drove and was driven by conflict.

31. THE DESTRUCTION OF THE MONASTERY OF SAN VINCENZO AL VOLTURNO
(Mid-Twelfth Century)

Translated from Latin by G. A. Loud

San Vincenzo al Volturno was probably the largest and wealthiest abbey in southern Italy during the ninth century, and the abbey church and building complex had been rebuilt on a massive scale by Abbot Joshua (791–818). Not surprisingly, both it and the other great south Italian abbey of Saint Benedict at Montecassino proved tempting targets for the Muslim raiders who destabilized Italy in the years after 840. To begin with these wealthy abbeys were able to buy off the threat of attacks, but eventually the monastery of San Vincenzo was sacked by the Muslims in 881, followed by Montecassino in 883. The surviving monks of both communities took refuge in fortified towns, those of San Vincenzo at Capua and those of Montecassino first at Teano and then, after their house there was destroyed by fire ca. 910, at Capua. The monks of San Vincenzo only returned to their original monastery in 914, and those of Montecassino as late as 950. The following account comes from the early twelfth-century Chronicle of San Vincenzo al Volturno, *written by a monk called John before ca. 1115. However, it is clearly based on older sources, written much closer in time to the events in question, and provides a vivid and detailed account of the destruction of the abbey.*

When the evil race of the Agarenes[1] had wasted other parts of these lands through plunder, fire, and destruction, at length this profane crowd of unbelievers, whose hands are against all, than whom no beast is more fierce, and who were not yet satiated with human blood, turned their fury against the monastery of the holy martyr Vincenzo. It was then the custom for the monks of both the monasteries of the most blessed Vincenzo and the most blessed Benedict through the grace of charity to visit each other regularly. When therefore some brothers of the monastery of Cassino were going one day to the aforesaid monastery, as was customary, and speaking to one another about their observance, suddenly the most savage Sawdan and his minions appeared.[2] The monks heard a rumor of this, and went with the utmost haste to the *castellum* close to the monastery; although they were greatly afraid, they were able to flee in safety. When the servants of God in

---

Translated from *Chronicon Vulturnense del Monaco Giovanni*, ed. Vincenzo Federici, 3 vols. (Rome: Fonti per la Storia d'Italia, 1924–38), vol. 1, 362–65, 370.

1. A biblical name for Arabs—"the descendants of Hagar."

2. Sawdan had been the emir of Bari during the period when this port was in Muslim hands, 843–70. He was probably dead by 881, so the chronicler was in error. His name was included since he was known to be the leading figure in the attacks on southern Italy at this period.

UNIVERSITY OF WINCHESTER LIBRARY

the monastery heard this news, they hid all the treasures of the church in that very spot. They themselves were not stupefied by fear, but constant and intrepid, and encouraging each other. They left a few of the elders, venerable in age and way of life, to take shelter in the church, while the remainder, with the servants subject to them, went to meet the arrival of the foreigners. Thus they mustered at a spot near the Marble Bridge,[3] blocking the road that led to the monastery. They stood on one side [of the river] and their opponents on the other, and a fierce battle began between them. The enemy were left helpless on the opposite bank, for it was no easy matter to cross to the near side. Seizing stones and other sorts of weapon, they drove the tyrants some way back, while the dense woods and the walls assisted the courage of our men.

> No icy blood constrained their powerful muscles
> For they cut the day short by fierce fighting,
> That makes it hard for both our men and the enemy to endure.
> Swords are brandished, javelins and darts are thrown,
> And the plunder of the thief sticks fast in the sharp thorns.
> Why do I spend such a long time relating the dreadful crimes
> That the hand of the vulgar has carried out with evil intent?

However, some of the serfs of the holy monastery, exhausted by this great battle, and seeing that through the protection of Divine grace no opportunity had been given for the enemy to cross [the river], but rather that the battle line of the enemy was being fiercely struck down, deserted their lords. They secretly sloped away, abandoning their lords in the midst of the fight. They went to the king of the Saracens, begging their lives and freedom from him, and saying that they could bring him a favorable outcome and the great rewards of victory. He immediately rejoiced, seducing the minds of the serfs with golden gifts and deadly promises. These promises were accepted and an agreement was made; and without the knowledge of their lords, these evil men acted as guides to the [other] evildoers. Going by a back route, a large party of warriors suddenly rushed into the monastery from the other side, and set light to it, setting fires on every side. They also put all the elders whom they found there to the sword. Thus the blood of these holy monks was shed for Christ. The marks [of this] are clear and can be seen today, having been smeared or sprinkled on the wall of the church, on the flagstones of the floor and on the stones. Immediately after this, sheets of scarlet flame rose up on high toward the stars in heaven. When those who had rushed into

---

3. A bridge crossing the river Volturno, very near the complex of monastery buildings.

battle and labored for a whole day in a fair fight saw this, they realized that they had been betrayed, and soon they were attacked from behind by the men of this troop returning [from the church]. While the defenders wished to resist those who were in their rear, they were trapped between the two [enemy] forces, and the fortunes of battle turned against them. As the enemy pursued them violently, and they strove to fight back, they reached a stretch of ground that was for some way more level, which the inhabitants still today call "the place of headless bodies." The weapons of all were turned against them, and everybody ran, though their limbs were weary, for they could make no further resistance. They fled amid the blows of the executioners, and although many were laid low by the foreigners, a few of them remained alive. But it was better to be killed by the sword than to be led into captivity. Finally, bringing the slaughter to an end, the enemy gathered together, and guided by the serfs dug hither and thither; and they discovered all the church's treasures, which the servants of God had hidden through fear of them the day before. They divided the booty among themselves, destroyed everything around, broke many things, and cast the grain and vegetables into the river that flowed nearby. As they relaxed after their labors and rejoiced in their triumph, the most wicked Sawdan drank from the holy chalices, and ordered incense to be wafted on himself from the golden thuribles. This slaughter of the blessed monks for Christ's sake took place on Tuesday 10 October, at the second hour, when one hundred and sixty-five years had elapsed from the building of the monastery. . . .

This desolation of the monastery of the precious martyr Vincenzo continued for thirty-three years, during which it was not the habitation of man but the possession of many beasts, and the place which had formerly been raised up over many was now more humble than anywhere else. There were neither monks living there, nor was it possible for there to be an abbot, for the aforesaid time of thirty-three years, which is the same number [of years] that the Redeemer of the human race deigned to associate with men in this world, before his Passion on the most holy cross.

After this these wicked freebooters savagely wasted the province of Valeria and the Roman borders, and then crossing into Campania they came to the monastery of Cassino, which had first been destroyed by the Lombards, and then had been restored through the care and labor of the blessed fathers Paldo, Tato, and Taso, along with the venerable father Petronax. They burned it down and utterly destroyed it. They then slew with the sword all the brothers of that congregation whom they could capture, or for whom through bodily weakness flight was not easily possible, without mercy, and cruelly put them to death. They similarly set fire to the [other] monastery that was down below, slaying the venerable Abbot Bertharius on the altar of Saint Martin in the church of the Holy Savior, and rendering that place uninhabitable to men. But before the arrival of the heathen, we believe that a few of the monks had fled, and gone to the town of Teano.

32. THE GENOESE CAPTURE OF ALMERÍA (1147)

Translated from Latin by G. A. Loud

This account of the Genoese expedition to Spain during the Second Crusade was written very soon after the events in question. The author, Caffaro di Rustico (1080– ca. 1164), was one of the leading men of Genoa, who served as one of the consuls of the city six times between 1122 and 1149, and who as consul commanded a naval expedition to Minorca in 1146. He also acted as the city's ambassador on a number of occasions, notably to the First Lateran Council of 1123 and to Frederick Barbarossa's Diet of Roncaglia in 1158, where he refused the emperor's demand for hostages and tribute from the city. He was a prolific historian, the author of the Genoese annals from 1099 to 1163, and of "The Liberation of the Cities of the East," a manifesto recounting the Genoese contribution to the conquest of the Holy Land which was submitted to Pope Hadrian IV in 1155. His "Annals," formally presented to the consuls and the commune in 1152, became the basis for the official history of the city, continued by a number of other authors until 1294.

The account which follows describes the capture of Almería, on the southern coast of Spain, about 180 kilometers east of Malaga. Caffaro suggests that it became a target for the Genoese because of the piratical ravages of its inhabitants, but there were in addition commercial imperatives, which he does not mention. Almería was the principal port for Cordoba, the traditional capital of Islamic Spain, and its possession would give the Genoese a base for penetrating the markets of Al-Andalus. However, Almería was an isolated enclave within Muslim territory, too far to the south to be easily defensible, especially when Spain was invaded by the Almohads, members of a fundamentalist Berber movement from North Africa. The Muslims recaptured it in 1157. Furthermore, this expedition and the cost of defending Almería seriously strained Genoese finances, to such an extent that there was something of a social and political crisis in the city during the early 1150s.

Here begins the History of the Capture of Almería and Tortosa which were taken in the year of Our Lord 1147.

It is known to almost the whole world how formerly and for a long time Christians were captured by the Saracens of Almería, far and wide, by land and sea, and through many regions. Some were killed, and many were placed in prison and afflicted with various torments and punishments, as a result of which many for fear of suffering abandoned the law of God and called upon the diabolical name of Mahomet. As a result, however, God did not fail to exact revenge for the effusion of so much blood. For the Genoese were advised and summoned by God, through the Apostolic See, and they made an oath [to send] an army against the Saracens of Almería, and they held a

Translated from *Annali Genovesi di Caffaro e de' suoi continuatori*, ed. L. T. Belgrano (Rome: Fonti per la storia d'Italia, Rome 1890), 79–89.

parliament in which six consuls were elected from among the better sort for
the commune and four more for the pleas of the city [who acted as city
judges], through whose wisdom and leadership the city and the army would
be ruled at this time. So impressive were the character, behavior, and elo-
quence of these men, the entire motherland was guided by their sense and
leadership. Their names were Oberto Torre, Filippo di Platealonga, Balduino,
and Ansaldo Doria. These four, and two of the consuls of the pleas, Ingo and
Ansaldo Pizo, went to lead the host. Oglerio di Guidone and Guglielmo
Picamilio, along with Oberto the chancellor and Ugo, judge of the pleas,
remained to rule the city. Immediately after their election the aforesaid consuls held a parliament in which they ordered everyone who was in dispute to
swear [to observe] peace. At the instigation of the Holy Spirit all those who
were at war promptly made peace as the consuls and archbishop wished, and
kissed each other. As a result both men and women greatly rejoiced, so that
they agreed unanimously to the consuls receiving funding for the army. After
hearing the precept of God and ascertaining the will of the people, the consuls ordered all the men of the *contado* of Genoa, under oath, speedily to
provide for themselves everything that was necessary for the expedition:
abundant food to avoid want, many weapons and fine tents, beautiful and
impressive banners, and everything else that would be needed for such a project, as well as towers (*castella*), machines, and all sorts of devices for the
capture of the city. Once the warriors of the city had heard the consuls'
instructions, they furnished themselves with arms, tents and everything that
was needed, so that no army as great, fine, and well equipped had been seen
or heard of in the last thousand years. Then, after everything had been made
ready as we have described, they started their journey with sixty-three galleys
and one hundred and sixty-three other vessels. Everything had been prepared
and the journey was begun within five months.

After they had come to Porto Maone, the consul Balduino then went
ahead to Almería with fifteen galleys as an advance guard until the fleet
should arrive as a body. The Genoese arrived at Cape de Gata but not finding
the "emperor"[1] they waited there for a month in a state of great fear, since
they were outside the port. They sent Ottone di Bonovillano as an envoy to
the "emperor," who was at Baeza. The latter had given his army permission
to depart, and had with him no more than four hundred knights and a thou-

---

1. King Alfonso VII of Castile (1126–57), who claimed to be Emperor of all Spain, had
concluded an alliance with Genoa in September 1146, to the effect that they would jointly
besiege Almería in the following May, and contributing 10,000 *marobotini* toward the costs of
outfitting the Genoese fleet. (*Marabotini* or *maravedi* were alternative Spanish names for dinars,
the gold coin that was the principal unit of Islamic currency in the Middle Ages.) The attack
took place in August 1147, and Almería was captured on 17 October.

sand infantry.[2] When he heard that the Genoese fleet had arrived, he was sorry that he had given his knights license [to go home]. He told them to come [once more], but he made a delay. Meanwhile the Saracens of Almería rejoiced, and sortied from the city with fifteen galleys seeking battle. The consul Balduino, who was on guard with his galleys, then ordered his companions, namely Oberto Torre and Philippo and Ansaldo Doria, to come and make war against Almería. These companions were unhappy about [doing] this, until some troops should arrive. Meanwhile the count of Barcelona [Ramón Berenguar IV (1131–62)] came with a great ship, bringing soldiers with him, including fifty-three mounted knights. They sent a message to Balduino that he should arrive at the mosque with his galleys at daybreak and make a demonstration of wishing to do battle, so that the Saracens should leave the city for this, for the count and his knights would be at the river at dawn, on land. The fifteen galleys would be outside the Lena [River] and one galley would be stationed at the mouth of the Lena. After the Saracens came out to fight, that galley would give the signal to the knights and the fifteen [other] galleys. And so it was done.

Once the Saracens saw the men from the fifteen galleys going ashore, apparently intent on doing battle, they were afraid that there were others hiding in secret. Thus they sent two soldiers, one white and one black, to climb up onto a hillock and reconnoiter the surrounding area. They did not spot the soldiers who were in hiding, and so they made a signal with flags for the Saracens to sortie from the city and come to do battle. Forty thousand armed men promptly emerged and began to fight with the men from the fifteen galleys. The Genoese then boarded the galleys and remained there, with eight of their men being killed. Meanwhile the consul Ansaldo Doria, on the one galley that was on watch, made the signal, even though it was not at the proper time. Twenty-five galleys and the knights all set off as one, and these galleys came across others, took them along with them and acted in unison. The consuls Oberto Torre and Philippo, who were off Capo de Gata, set sail with the whole fleet. They sailed forward with twelve galleys as a vanguard, while on land the knights [marched off]. These twelve galleys made contact with the others which were at the mosque, and they moved forward to the coast. The knights then encountered the Saracens who had left the city, and fortified by divine assistance, they manfully attacked them. For fear of the galleys the Saracens wished to turn back, and they started to retreat toward the city, with the knights following them. Among the latter

---

2. The troops sent home may well have been those of the urban militias, whose term of service had expired after the capture of Baeza.

was a certain Genoese knight, called Guglielmo Pellis, who charged ahead of the others without the count's permission. First of all he killed a Saracen who was in the front rank with his lance; and then like a lion tearing with his claws at the bodies of lesser beasts he slew many others, severing the Saracens' heads all along the coast by Almería. The aforesaid consuls promptly went ashore with the men from one galley to fight the Saracens, and the men who manned the galleys near the mosque also landed. They and the knights killed more than five thousand Saracens and left them lying dead along the shore. The galleys that were out to sea also joined the battle, and they killed the Saracens fleeing to seaward. After accomplishing this, the consuls ordered both the galley crews and the soldiers to go to the Porta Lena, which they did, pitching their tents there. A council was held and they rendered thanks to God for giving [them] such a great victory.

After some discussion, the consuls decided that the galleys should be beached on the shore at Almería, and after this had been done they gave instructions for the preparation of siege engines, towers and "cats."[3] As this work was begun, the Saracens made a sortie toward the galleys, in three parties, but they were beaten, some of them were killed, and [the rest] fled back to the city. While these mangonels, towers, and "cats" were being constructed, the emperor arrived with four hundred knights and a thousand infantry. We immediately brought a "castle" and some mangonels up to appropriate and suitable places next to the city. The Saracens made an attack from a number of directions but were defeated, [but] they fought back against our towers by day and night, with mangonels, fire, and other weapons.[4] However, the Genoese remained on guard, resisted the Saracens, and invariably drove them back into the city, inflicting heavy casualties upon them. The "castles" of the Genoese captured two towers and destroyed eighteen yards of the wall. This terrified the Saracens, who had secret discussions with the emperor's envoys, namely the count of Urgel and King García.[5] They offered to give them a hundred thousand *marobotini*, and also to give hostages, if the emperor would retire from there and abandon the Genoese. When the consuls of the Genoese were informed of this, they discussed the matter and decided to attack and storm the town at dawn on the next day. When dawn arrived on the vigil of Santa Lucia they held a speedy meeting, and arranged themselves in twelve companies, each with its own banner and

---

3. Protective screens or coverings, usually made of wood and leather, and mounted on wheels, which were used to approach the walls of besieged places.

4. Mangonels were stone-throwing catapults.

5. García Ramírez IV, king of Navarre, had married an illegitimate daughter of King Alfonso in 1144.

with a thousand armed men in every company. The consuls ordered them to advance. The consuls also sent a number of messages to the emperor and to the count of Barcelona, begging them to have their men arm themselves and join in the battle so as to capture the city. Hearing this, the emperor soon arrived and found the armed companies of the Genoese [already] in the field. The consuls had instructed their warriors that when they heard the signal from the trumpets they should enter the city ready to fight, but in silence and without shouting. And so it was done. The knights followed after them, and within three hours, with the help and favor of God, and with much Saracen blood shed by the swords of the Genoese, the whole city was captured apart from the citadel. Twenty thousand Saracens were killed that day; and from one part of the city ten thousand were captured, and in the citadel twenty thousand, and then ten thousand women and children were brought to Genoa. Within four days the Saracens surrendered the citadel and themselves, and gave thirty thousand *marobotini* to ransom themselves.

The consuls retained some of the captured money, namely sixty thousand *marobotini*, for the benefit of the commune, and they paid the debt that the commune owed, namely seventeen thousand pounds. They had the rest of the money divided up among the galleys and other ships. They left Ottone de Bonovillano with a thousand men to guard the city, and after holding a council they instructed everyone [else] to leave the city with their galleys and other ships, and this was done.[6] They arrived unharmed, gloriously and triumphantly, at Barcelona; there they beached the galleys and ships and appointed a new consulate. With the agreement and permission of their fellows, two of the consuls, Oberto Torre and Ansaldo Doria, went with two galleys to Genoa, and with the money that they had brought they paid the commune's debt, and they made a new consulate at Genoa.

---

6. Three weeks after the capture of Almería, on 5 November 1147, the consuls granted the Genoese share of the city to Ottone for some thirty years, in return for a token payment for fifteen years and a half-share in its revenues for another fifteen, while he promised to provide a permanent garrison of 300 soldiers.

33. IBN AL-ATHĪR ON SICILIAN MUSLIMS UNDER CHRISTIAN RULE: *THE COMPLETE TREATMENT OF HISTORY* (mid-twelfth century)

Translated from Arabic by Joshua Birk

In the latter half of the eleventh century, Norman warriors conquered Sicily and much of southern Italy. These Latin Christians found themselves ruling over large populations of both Muslims and Greek Christians. Ibn al-Athīr, a Muslim scholar from Mosul, who lived at the tail end of the twelfth century, painted a complex picture of the relationship between the Christian lords and their Muslim subjects in his Complete Treatment of History.

4 JULY 1144–23 JUNE 1145

It is said that the lord of the island of Sicily [Roger II] dispatched raiding ships to Tripoli and that this military operation plundered and murdered. At this time there lived in Sicily a learned Muslim, a pious man. The lord of Sicily honored and venerated him. He consulted his words and gave precedence to him over any among his priests or monks, and because of this a rumor began among the people that he [Roger II] was a Muslim.

One day while he [Roger II] was sitting in his watchtower, he looked down on the sea, and at the time a small ship drew near. And it brought news to him that his forces had penetrated the lands of the Muslims, plundered, killed, and been victorious. The aforementioned Muslim was at the king's side and was dozing. The king said to him, calling him by name, "Did you hear what they said?" The Muslim responded, "No." The king replied that the troops had destroyed such-and-such a place. "Where was your Muhammad? Was he away from his land and his people?" And the Muslim answered him, "If he was away from that conquest, it is because he witnessed the fall of Edessa, which was just captured by the Muslims."[1] Some of the Franks who were there mocked him, but the king said, "Do not laugh! What he says is the truth!" Days later, news of the conquest of Edessa arrived.

29 MARCH 1153–17 MARCH 1154

In this year, the fleet of Roger, king of the Franks in Sicily, came to the city of Bone.[2] The fleet was commanded by the king's eunuch, Philip of Mahdīya.

Translated from Ibn al-Athīr, ʿIzz al-Dīn Abū al-Hasan ʿAlī ibn Muḥammad, al-Jazarī, *Kāmil fiʾ l-Tārīkh*, ed. Carolus Johannes Tornberg (Beirut: Dar Sadir, 1966), vol. 11, 100, 187.

1. In December 1144, the armies of the Muslim commander ʿImad ad-Din Zengi, Atabeg of Mosul and Aleppo, conquered the city of Edessa, the capital of the first of the crusader states.
2. A coastal city in northeastern Algeria, now Annaba.

Figure 8. Ceremonial mantle of Roger II (1133/34). The border inscription reads: "This was made in the royal factory for the good fortune, supreme honor, perfection and power, the betterment, capacity, prosperity, sublimity, glory, beauty, the increase of [his] security, fulfillment of his hopes, the goodness of [his] days and nights without end or interruption, for [his] power and guard, [his] defense and protection, good fortune, salvation, victory and excellence. In the capital of Sicily, in the 528th year [of the Hegira = 1133/4]." Translation by Jeremy Johns, 1986. The mantle was subsequently used for the coronation of Staufen rulers, Frederick II, possibly among them. Vienna, Kunsthistorisches Museum. (Photo: Erich Lessing/Art Resource)

With the assistance of Arabs, Philip besieged Bone and captured the city in the month of Rajab (22 September–21 October 1153), and took the people of Bone prisoner and seized what was within the city. However, he ignored a group of learned and pious men, so that they fled from the city to the countryside with their families and their possessions. And, after staying in Bone for ten days, Philip returned to Mahdiya accompanied by some of his captives. Then he returned to Sicily, where Roger arrested him because of his kindness toward the Muslims of Bone.

It was said that he [Philip] and all his eunuchs were secretly Muslims. People bore witness that he did not fast with the king, and that he was a Muslim. Roger assembled the bishops, the clergy, and the knights, and they sentenced Philip to be burned to death. And his annihilation by fire occurred in the month of Ramadan [20 November–19 December 1153]. This was the first injury to befall the Muslims of Sicily.

34. GIOVANNI CODAGNELLO ON FACTIONAL STRIFE IN PIACENZA (1232–35)

Translated from Latin by William North

The account of an outbreak of factional violence in Piacenza and its contado *penned by the local notary and historian Giovanni Codagnello (ca. 1199–1235) is far from the simple record of eleventh-century urban conflict that it pretends to be. Distinct from his more famous* Annals of Piacenza *that covered the period 1031–1234, Codagnello's highly circumstantial portrayal of escalating violence and spontaneous reconciliation between factions of knights (*milites*) and* popolani *(in this case non-noble foot-soldiers) seems to have been intended as a kind of moral tale composed for contemporaries in response to the severe factional violence that afflicted Piacenza from 1232 to 1235. While the narrative was most likely based on a real historical incident that Codagnello discovered in the course of his research, his account employs terms and social categories that allow it to speak directly to the social and political realities of thirteenth-century Piacenza. The text thus hovers between the eleventh and thirteenth centuries, between evidence and imagination. It thereby offers insight into how contemporaries explained factional violence and reconciliation to themselves. It also shows the interplay of past evidence and present concerns which informed the production of historical narrative in medieval Italy.*

In February of the year 1090, a great conflict arose between the *popolo* and the knights of Piacenza on the occasion of a trial by combat which at that time used to take place in the open land that was between the church of Santa Maria and the road that leads to Arcive. By some misfortune it happened that a knight was fighting most unfairly with a foot-soldier, so that the two could not be separated from each other. As they struggled in this manner, the *popolani*, seeing that the man on foot could not hold his own against the knight, threw stones and mud at the knight and—even worse—beat him with large cudgels. When they saw this, the knights who were present similarly beat and whipped the foot-soldiers.

The cry went out in all directions that there had been a breach of the peace, and all the knights of the city gathered in one part of the town, the *popolani* in another. Then there began a great battle between the two groups that lasted until the dark of night. During this battle, two knights and three members of the *popolo* died. Fighting began at dawn on the second day throughout the city; but when the knights realized that they would not be able to hold out, they abandoned the city that evening and on the following

Translated from Giovanni Codagnello, *Annales Placentini*, ed. Oswald Holder-Egger, *MGH SSRG* 23 (Hannover: Hahn, 1901), 1–3.

day took up positions throughout the castles, manors, and villas of the district of Piacenza. Later, after taking counsel, the knights decided that they would all occupy the area between Villa and Cano (except for the twenty knights whom they placed on guard duty in Roncairolo) and keep watch in those parts so that no one could enter the city either to bring or take anything away. . . . In both Rivergaro and in the lands of the Arcelli [family] they stationed twenty knights who rode up to the city every day. If they found anyone bringing anything to the city, they took away their oxen and everything they were carrying and even cut off their hands and feet. And thus things stood until the octave of Saint Michael (6 October).[1]

When the *popolani* realized that they had run out of food, they took counsel and decided to leave the city, declaring: "It is better to die in battle than to witness our own destruction and perish from starvation." Withdrawing from the city, they went first to the villa of San Giorgio and burned it. They likewise burned the villas of Carpaneto, Castrucano, Iuda, and Cario. Meanwhile, all the knights in the regions of Cornigliano, Ronco, and Viustino, along with their entire army of foot-soldiers and archers, were defending the manors and villas in those areas as best they could. But the *popolani* headed toward the region of Travazzano and burned that place. Then they besieged a fort in which there were about twenty knights along with some others in their association, and they captured Montezago and Predugia by storm.

When the knights learned that the *popolani* had moved a long way from the city, all the armed patrols, along with a whole crowd of knights, foot-soldiers and archers, rushed back to the city as quickly as possible and entered it, since the gates were open. Finding no one there except for knights and some prisoners who had remained within the city walls, they seized the city and everything in it. When the *popolani* heard this news, they were overcome by sorrow and shaken by great suffering and sadness. They returned in haste to the city walls and lodged near the church of San Lazzaro. But knights who remained outside the city attacked them with such intensity that they were unable to conduct trade.

After all this had happened, it came about by divine judgment and the will of our Lord Jesus Christ, from whom all good things come and without whom nothing can be done, that the knights, moved by mercy and piety, acknowledged their wickedness and insanity and shouted out amidst their cries and tearful sobs, "Peace, peace!" Weeping and beating their breasts

---

1. The knights' strongholds were located in the southern regions of Piacenza's *contado*, and consequently the *popolani*'s attacks concentrated in that region.

with their hands, the *popolani*, too, acknowledged their wickedness and stupidity and also exclaimed, "Peace, peace!" The knights then went outside the city walls and approached the *popolo* with tears and lamentation, and they all began to exchange the kiss of peace [see **#48**]. To be sure, perhaps there was someone at the time of such a fierce and cruel nature that he was able to hold back his tears. But who nowadays ever sees knights and foot-soldiers weeping, wailing, and beating their breasts in remorse? After entering thus into the city accompanied by voices in prayer, peace and concord were established throughout the entire city and district of Piacenza.

35. GIOVANNI VILLANI ON THE ORIGINS OF THE GUELFS AND GHIBELLINES IN FLORENCE (ca. 1300)

Translated from Italian by Katherine L. Jansen

Giovanni Villani (ca. 1280–1348) is celebrated as the author of the Nuova chronica *(New Chronicle), a history of Florence from its origins, which he intended as a narrative history comparable to the great histories written about Rome by Virgil, Sallust, and Livy. Compiled after 1300 and written in Italian, the excerpt below is Villani's account of the origins of the Guelf and Ghibelline parties in Florence. As Villani tells us, the terms themselves are probably Italianized versions of German names. Guelf seems to have derived from the Welf family, whose party adherents were nominally supporters of the pope. The Hohenstaufen castle of Waiblingen gives its name to the Ghibellines, whose supporters ordinarily sided with the empire against the papacy. It should be noted that party alignments and loyalties changed continuously as the political interests of local or regional factions shifted.*

In the year of Christ 1215, when Gherardo Orlandi was *podestà* in Florence, one Bondelmonte dei Bondelmonti, a noble citizen of Florence, promised to marry a young woman of the house of the Amidei family, honorable and notable citizens. Later, when the said Bondelmonte, who was very charming and a good horseman, was riding through the city, a lady of the house of Donati called out to him, reproaching him about the lady to whom he was betrothed, saying that she was neither beautiful nor worthy of him, and adding: "I have kept my daughter for you," whom she then showed to him. And she was indeed most beautiful. And instantly, seized by the devil, he was so taken with her, that he was betrothed and wedded to her. [Hearing the news], the Amidei kinsfolk assembled together, and nursing the shame which Bondelmonte had caused them, were filled with damnable indignation, which [soon] caused the city of Florence to be destroyed and divided. For many houses of the nobles pledged to bring shame down upon the said Bondelmonte in revenge for these wrongs. And in a council to decide how they should punish him, whether by beating or killing, Mosca de' Lamberti uttered the evil phrase: "What has been done has a head;" that is, that they should kill him. And so it was done. On Easter morning the Amidei of [the parish of] Santo Stefano assembled at their house. And the aforesaid Bondel-

Translated from *Cronica di Giovanni Villani, a miglior lezione ridotta*, ed. Ignazio Moutier, 4 vols. (Florence: Magheri, 1823), vol. I, Bk. 5, chap. XXXVIII, 256–59. A new critical edition is available as *Nuova Cronica di Giovanni Villani*, ed. Giovanni Porta, 3 vols. (Parma: Guanda, 1991). Some of the first nine books have been translated by Rose E. Selfe, *Villani's Chronicle: Being Selections from the First Nine Books of the Croniche Fiorentine of Giovanni Villani* (London: Constable, 1906).

Figure 9. Vendetta against Bondelmonte dei Bondelmonti (ca. 1341–48). Miniature from *Nuova cronica* of Giovanni Villani, attributed to the workshop of Pacino di Bonaguida. Vatican City, Biblioteca Apostolica Vaticana, MS Chigi L.VIII.296, fol. 70r. (Photo: Biblioteca Apostolica Vaticana)

monte, dressed in new white apparel and riding upon a white palfrey, having crossed the river, arrived at the foot of the Ponte Vecchio on this side, just at the foot of the pillar where the statue of Mars once stood. And Schiatta degli Uberti and Mosca Lamberti and Lambertuccio degli Amidei pulled the said Bondelmonte off his horse and attacked him. He was dragged from his horse by Schiatta degli Uberti, Mosca Lamberti, and Lambertuccio degli Amidei and further assaulted and wounded. Oderigo Fifanti sliced opened his veins and finished him off. The counts of Gangalandi were also with them.

As a result, the city rose up in arms and tumult and the death of Bondelmonte was the cause and beginning of the accursed parties of Guelfs and Ghibellines in Florence, albeit long before there were factions among the noble citizens, which existed by reason of the strife and questions between the Church and the Empire. But because of the death of Bondelmonte, all the families of the nobles and the other citizens of Florence were divided. Some took the side of the Bondelmonti, who took the side of the Guelfs, and were its leaders, and some with the Uberti, who were the leaders of the Ghibellines. Afterward much evil and disaster afflicted our city, as I will recount, and some believe that it will never end if God does not intervene. It shows that the enemy of the human race, for the sins of the Florentines, maintained power in that idol of Mars, whom the pagan Florentines once worshiped, with the result that at the foot of his statue such a murder was committed and so much evil befell the city of Florence. The accursed names of the Guelf and Ghibelline parties are said to have emerged first in Germany because two great barons of that country were at war against each other; each one had castles to defend himself. One had the name of Guelf, and the other of Ghibelline, and the war lasted so long, that all the Germans were divided, and each held to their sides. And the problem even reached the court of Rome, and all the court took part in it, and the one side was called Guelf, and the other Ghibelline. And so the names remain in Italy.

By reason of the said division these were the families of the nobles who became Guelfs in Florence and likewise the Ghibellines, counting from *sesto to sesto*.[1] In the *sesto* of Oltrarno, of the Guelfs were the Nerli, gentlemen, who dwelt at first in the Mercato Vecchio; the family of the Giacoppi, called Rossi, not however of ancient descent, but they were already on the rise; the Frescobaldi, the Bardi, the Mozzi, but just starting their ascent. The Ghibellines in the *sesto* of Oltrarno, among the nobles were the counts of Gangalandi, Obriachi, and Mannelli. In the *sesto* of San Piero Scheraggio, the Guelf nobles were the house of the Pulci, the Gherardini, the Foraboschi, the Bagnesi, the Guidalotti, the Sacchetti, the Manieri of Cuona. The Volognano, the Lucardesi, the Chiaramontesi, the Compiobbesi, the Cavalcanti were associated with them but were descended recently from merchants. The Ghibellines of the *sesto* were the family of the Uberti, which was the head of the party, the Fifanti, the Infangati, and Amidei, and [some] of the Volognano, and the Malespini, who afterward because of the outrages [committed by] the Uberti, their neighbors. They with many other families of San Piero Scheraggio became Guelfs. In the *sesto* of Borgo, the Guelfs were the family of the Bondelmonti, and they were the leaders of the party; the family of the Giandonati, the Gianfigliazzi, the family of the Scali, the Gualterotti, and the Importuni. The Ghibellines of the said *sesto* were the house of the Scolari, who were originally associated with the Bondelmonti, the house of the Guidi, of the Galli, and of the Cappiardi. In the *sesto* of San Pancrazio the Guelfs

---

1. At that time the city was divided into six administrative sections called *sesti*.

were the Bostichi, the Tornaquinci, the Vecchietti. The Ghibellines of the said *sesto* were the Lamberti, the Soldanieri, the Cipriani, the Toschi, and the Amieri, Palermini, Migliorelli, and Pigli, albeit afterward some of them became Guelfs. In the *sesto* of the Porta del Duomo, the Guelf party in those times were the Tosinghi, the Arrigucci, the Agli, the Sizii. The Ghibellines of the *sesto* were the Barucci, the Cattani of Castiglione and of Cersino, the Agolanti, and the Brunelleschi, and afterward some of them became Guelfs. In the *sesto* of the Porta San Piero the Guelf nobles were the Adimari, the Visdomini, the Donati, the Pazzi, the della Bella, the Ardinghi, and the Tedaldi who were called della Vitella. And the Cerchi had already begun to rise in status even if they were merchants. The Ghibellines of the said *sesto* were the Caponsacchi, the Lisei, the Abati, the Tedaldini, the Giuochi, the Galigari. And many other honorable families and *popolani* sided with one side or the other and they changed with the times, or changed their minds and party, all of which is too long to be recounted here. And for this reason the accursed parties emerged in Florence, even if there had been a previous secret division among the nobles, some of whom sided with the rule of the Church and others who sided with that of the Empire. Nonetheless, they were all in agreement about the common good of the commune.

36. VENDETTA IN FOURTEENTH-CENTURY SIENA (1321–46)

Translated from Latin by Trevor Dean

Revenge (vendetta) features frequently in the narrative sources of some Italian cities in the later Middle Ages. The chronicles of Tuscan cities—Florence especially— are rich sources for revenge both as a social practice and as a narrative device (explaining actions, ascribing motive). Typically, once a family group had received an attack on its honor (usually in the form of violent assault or killing), it took disproportionate revenge on individuals from the family to which the original attacker belonged. In some cities, cycles of vendetta between leading families could seriously disrupt public order. It is often assumed that vendetta was socially restricted to the elite or aristocracy, and that it was the outcome of weaknesses in the power of policing and the law courts: these extracts enable us to gauge how far these assumptions are correct. They concern mainly the exchanges of violence between two of the leading aristocratic families of Siena, the Salimbeni and Tolomei (and their various branches); but other families—such as the Piccolomini— were also drawn in.

[1321] Francesco, called "friar," the son of Messer Vanni Sinibaldi, going home to the Salimbeni palace on Tuesday evening 29 December . . . , was attacked by Balsino di Francesco Tolomei, with some accomplices, one of whom wounded him. Francesco died from his wounds. Francesco had not been on the alert, because there was peace between them for past injuries. For this deed, Balsino and the others were banished [by the commune].

[1322] Giovanni, called "Bottone," the son of Messer Salimbene, arranged to have some armed men from Florence, who came secretly, entering Siena in twos and threes just as the gates were closing. It was said that these men were sent to him by a Florentine citizen who was a friend of the Salimbeni family. The armed men stayed hidden in the Salimbeni palace. On a Tuesday evening in April, Giovanni, with some of his kinsmen and with the armed men, took up position on the piazza of the Tolomei family, securing all the exits. He then went to the rear of the Tolomei palace and placed ladders up to the windows. He and his men then entered the palace, broke down some doors, and killed Mino, Tondo, and Prina, the sons of the deceased Messer Meo Tolomei. Meanwhile, a clamor arose and the *podestà*'s family took up arms, and the government rang the alarm bell, so that most of the *popolo*

Translated from *Cronache senesi*, ed. Alessandro Lisini and Fabio Iacometti, in *RIS*[2], vol. 15, pt 6 (Bologna: Zanichelli, 1931–), 389, 391, 397, 498, 501, 505, 518, 528, 530, 549–50.

turned out, and if Giovanni had stayed any longer, he and his men would have been killed by the *popolo*. Giovanni and his men left Siena and went to Rocca. Giovanni did this deed out of revenge for Francesco di Messer Vanni Salimbeni, his kinsman. His houses were destroyed [by the commune] and he was declared a rebel.

[1322] In September the Tolomei made a great assembly of armed men, both mounted and on foot, in Siena, the reason being that they wanted to take revenge on the Salimbeni for these deaths. The Salimbeni, to defend themselves, also assembled a great number of armed men, such that the city was all in arms and the Tolomei could not achieve their aims. The *podestà* summoned some of the Tolomei leaders: they came before him and were detained in the palace. Then the *podestà* summoned the Salimbeni leaders. Messer Benuccio came first accompanied by three others on horse and foot: when they reached the Campo [the city's central piazza, see **#64**], Francesco Tolomei came up behind them on horseback with his sons and nephews, all armed. The Tolomei entered the Campo, believing that they were being followed by their own men, but the *popolo* turned on them with stones, so that the horse under Messer Francesco was killed, and they only just escaped with their lives and returned home. The *podestà* condemned Messer Francesco and his sons and nephews to pay 1,000 florins each, and the others 500 *lire*.

[1330] Monday 22 October, Messer Benuccio di Messer Benuccio and Messer Alessandro di Messer Brettacone, provost of the cathedral of Siena—both of them members of the Salimbeni family—were returning from the Valdorcia when they were assaulted on the road near San Quirico by Messer Pietro, Messer Tavennozzo and a son of Messer Francesco, all of the Tolomei family. They had in the company fourteen horsemen and twenty men on foot. When Messer Benuccio and Messer Alessandro were dead, their attackers let the servants go. As there was peace at this time between the two families, this was seen as great treachery, and great loss was felt at the death of both men, as Messer Benuccio was one of the most renowned knights in Tuscany and Messer Alessandro was a most worthy man. And there was great vengeance against the Tolomei, the greatest there had ever been in Siena. Consequently, the commune of Siena convicted some of those who had been involved in the murders: Messer Tavennozzo and Pietro were banished, and their houses were destroyed.

[1331] The Salimbeni, having received this injury, and peace having been broken, wanted to take revenge on the Tolomei, so they gathered in arms in their houses in Siena. They confronted each other at the Rossi arch and on the Tolomei piazza: there was a great battle and several died or were wounded. The Government of the Nine told its Captain of War and the *podestà* to go there with troops to separate the combatants, and this they did. Once the disturbance was settled, the Nine, learning that the Salimbeni had started it, convicted fifteen of that family to pay 6,000 *lire* within certain deadlines. They also ordered one member of the Tolomei to pay 3,000 *lire*, and forty-five others 100 florins each (15,000 *lire* in total) within a certain time, in order to avoid being declared rebels. This was in February.

One night in June, with the connivance of the priest of the parish, Agnolino Bottone and Stricca di Messer Giovanni and Meo di Cione, all members of the Salimbeni, concealed some armed men in a cellar outside Lucignano (which belonged to Messer Francesco). On the following morning, Messer Francesco Tolomei and his son and nephews left Lucignano for a walk. At that point the soldiers came out of their hiding place and attacked them, cutting Francesco to pieces, wounding his son and one of his nephews. Another boy who was with Francesco, Pietro Piccolomini, was also wounded and died shortly afterward; he had not been recognized by the Salimbeni. During the assault, Agnolino, Stricca, and Meo arrived with some horsemen, and cut the head off Francesco's corpse. They also cut many of the bodies, and then returned to the castle in Tentenano.

[1337] The Tolomei and the Salimbeni, two great houses of Sienese nobles, had long been in great enmity, and had made many killings and affrays. For this reason, the bishop of Florence came to Siena on the pope's instructions to make peace between them. This he did on 5 November, except that the faction of the Renaldi branch of the Tolomei did not consent to peace with the Salimbeni, because of the death of Messer Francesco and his son.

[1341] Siena sent infantry and cavalry to assist Florence in taking possession of the city of Lucca. . . . Their military leader was Messer Tavennozzo Tolomei: he was given the communal banner. . . . But one of the Salimbeni households took great offense at this and some of them refused to march under the leadership of Messer Tavennozzo. This was for two reasons: first, because the communal banner had been given to Tavennozzo, and not to the Salimbeni (out of grandiosity and pride, they thought that they deserved it more); and second, because there had long been great enmity between the Salimbeni and the Tolomei, with peace having been made only recently. So, for these reasons, and to show their own power and pride, the Salimbeni assembled their own army of Salimbeni knights, with many foot-soldiers and supporters, and they went at their own expense to assist Florence.

25 December: Messer Salimbene degli Scotti, a Sienese nobleman, went with some kinsmen to eat with some Tolomei. They were attacked by Vanuccio de' Saraceni . . . with twenty armed men: they wounded Messer Salimbene many times, out of personal vendetta. Within a few days, he was dead.

[1346] Bartolomeo di Socino, a wool merchant, with some accomplices, assaulted Ambrogio di Lotto, another wool merchant, with a knife. His accomplices used billhooks[1] and other weapons. They wounded Ambrogio in the face and head, and killed his son, who was with him. Bartolomeo fled toward the cathedral. Another of Ambrogio's sons, and one of his servants, ran after him, caught up with him and wounded him many times, leaving him for dead. . . . The same day, 5 December, the officers of the captain of war came and arrested Bartolomeo, and on 11 December they beheaded him.

---

1. A cutting tool with a curved blade used in Italy for pruning grapevines.

37. CHARLES OF ANJOU ON THE
BATTLE OF TAGLIACOZZO
(23 August 1268)

Introduced by Caroline Bruzelius; translated from Latin by Sean Gilsdorf

Charles I of Anjou (d. 1285), the youngest brother of King Louis IX of France, was invited by the papacy to undertake the conquest of the Kingdom of Sicily in order to remove the Hohenstaufen dynasty. At the Battle of Benevento on 26 February 1266, Charles and his troops defeated the forces of King Manfred of Sicily (d. 1266), the illegitimate son of Emperor Frederick II, and Charles thus became ruler and conqueror of the Kingdom. Two years later, however, his rule was threatened by the invasion of the last Hohenstaufen heir, Conrad II (also known as Conradin), the only child of Frederick II's eldest son, King Conrad of Sicily and Jerusalem (d. 1254), who entered the kingdom in 1268, rallying to his cause many of Charles's enemies. As described in the text below, however, the young prince and his supporters were defeated and captured in a great battle at Tagliacozzo, a site due east of Rome in the Abruzzi mountains. Conradin and several of his closest companions were captured, and the young prince was beheaded in the Piazza del Mercato in Naples later that year. The events that led to the Battle of Tagliacozzo represent one of many attempts to overthrow the rule of Charles of Anjou in the Kingdom of Sicily. There were repeated rebellions and considerable strife in the kingdom throughout his reign, culminating in the disastrous Revolt of the Vespers in 1282, which led to a protracted war, the invasion of significant parts of Calabria, Basilicata, and Apulia, and in the long run established a new and separate kingdom in Sicily under Spanish control. From 1282 onward, the island of Sicily was lost to Angevin control, and as a result the city of Naples, on the mainland, became the new capital of the Kingdom.

To the most holy father in Christ and his lord, Lord Clement [IV], by divine providence supreme pontiff of the most holy Roman and universal Church; Charles, by the grace of God King of Sicily, the Duchy of Apulia, and the Principate of Capua and Count of Anjou, Provence, and Forcalquier devoutly kisses your blessed feet with all reverence and honor.

Humbly I offer you, most merciful father, as well as the most holy Roman Church, the sweet incense of a joy long awaited by all the faithful of the world, begging that the father, "arising and eating of his son's game" [Genesis 27:31], might pay his debt of gratitude to the Most High, and that both the father and the mother might henceforth find respite from their labors. You were aware that after Conradin and his followers approached the borders of my kingdom in search of openings through which they might

Translated from Peter Herde, "Die Schlacht bei Tagliacozzo. Eine historisch-topographische Studie," *Zeitschrift für Bayerische Landesgeschichte* 25 (1962): 679–744.

secretly enter and join forces with the Saracens,[1] I constantly followed them step by step for three days and nights, kept safe and sound on my journey by the hand of God, who is my teacher and the patron of justice. Finally I observed that the enemy wished to enter through the region of Cicolano, cross through the fields of Marsica, and proceed to Sulmona. They set up their ill-fated camp on a plain between Scurcola and Monte Carce.

On Wednesday, the octave of the Assumption of the Blessed Virgin [22 August 1268] (in whose aid we most fervently trust), I led my troops from the fields of Ovindoli past Lago del Fucino[2] and the village of Avezzano, and with divine grace as my guide marched them to a hill near Albe, two short miles from the enemy, below which stretch the Palatine plains. When I saw the enemy camp, I decided to order the Christian army to set up camp on the hill, since my people and horses were exhausted from their labors. But the enemy armies, seeing my banners approaching the outer edge of their fortifications and fearing an attack, came out in full strength from their camps onto the field. When they realized that my people were ready for battle, however, they returned in great disarray whence they had come, pursued by the jeering of my men. At sunrise the next day, Thursday, the enemy suddenly emerged from his location and began to head across the river [Salto] that ran between the two armies. At these troubling signs I countered their march, which I had been carefully observing, immediately organizing my troops into battle formation on the field of the Palatine plains, and, bolstered by the divine name, marching them forth double-time.

Although I believed that the enemy troops would go on further, contrary to my wishes and those of my men, they began to set up camp on the riverbank next to the village of Pontes,[3] but without breaking ranks. Seeing that my army was setting up camp as well, they suddenly crossed the river with great force. I, however, confiding in divine protection and the aid of your prayers, called upon Christ's name to help me and charged into them quickly and manfully. After this there was bitter fighting on both sides, and the better part of the enemy was destroyed with the edge of the sword, and the few who remained, unable to withstand the power of my army, sought safety in flight. These I quickly pursued over mountain and glade, killing most of them. Indeed, the slaughter of the enemy there was so great that what happened to other persecutors of the Church on the fields of Benevento

1. Muslims joined together with Conradin's Ghibelline forces made up of Italian, Spanish, and German fighters.

2. Once the third largest lake in Italy; due to its tendency to flood the surrounding region, attempts to control it continued from the Roman period until the nineteenth century, when a vast engineering effort succeeded in draining the lake completely by 1878.

3. This village, no longer extant, stood on the eastern side of the bridge over the Salto.

can hardly be compared to it. At the time this letter is written, immediately following the victory, I cannot be certain whether Conradin and the Roman senator Henry[4] fell in battle or were able to escape. I can tell you that the senator's horse, which fled without its rider, was captured by my men.

Therefore, Mother Church should rejoice and let out a cry of praise on high to him for mercifully providing so great a triumph, one obtained by the efforts of his warriors. For now it appears that Almighty God has put an end to her troubles, and freed her from the ravenous jaws of her persecutors.

Related at the Palatine plains on 23 August of the eleventh indiction, in the fourth year of my reign.

---

4. Prince Henry of Castile, brother of King Alfonso X and erstwhile ally of Charles of Anjou; he became senator of Rome (effectively, the secular ruler of the city) in July 1267, allied himself with Conradin a few months later, and took control of the imperial party in Tuscany.

38. GIOVANNI REGINA ON ANGEVIN MILITARY SUCCESS AGAINST THE EMPIRE (1328)

Translated from Latin by Samantha Kelly

Giovanni Regina, also known as John of Naples, was a Dominican preacher closely connected to the court of Robert "the Wise," king of Naples, in the early fourteenth century. The following sermon illustrates the political support that preachers like Giovanni could provide to the ruler through preaching. Internal references indicate that it was preached in April 1328, when a royal army led by Duke Charles of Calabria, the son of King Robert, was setting off to defend the kingdom's borders from Ludwig of Bavaria, described here as "the enemy of the Church of God." The sermon urged the people of Naples to pray for the success of the Angevin army. Its first two sections offer assurances that God can and will heed the prayers of the congregation. The third section, which analyzes the divine nature of the Lord, serves also to highlight the similarities between divine lordship and the lordship of King Robert of Naples. The final section of the sermon asserts the righteousness of the Angevin army and especially of its leader, Duke Charles. Here Giovanni uses an argument much favored by late medieval dynasties: that the royal family is inherently holy and transmits sanctity through its blood. The proof, in this case, was the fact that two relatives (Charles's great-great-uncle, Louis IX of France, and his uncle Louis, bishop of Toulouse) had been canonized by the Church. Also relevant were the good deeds performed by ancestors such as Charles I, Duke Charles's great-grandfather, who had founded the Angevin dynasty in southern Italy. The sermon exemplifies efforts to marshal patriotic feeling among the populace by attributing a religious aura, and thus divine sanction, to its rulers.

Preserve your people, O Lord: Psalm [27:9]. We are all gathered here today to pray to the Lord God that he preserve the duke and his army who, as will be shown below, are the people of God. The procession and sung mass, and the preaching . . . in this congregation are for this purpose. The chosen theme, *Preserve*, etc., is quite fitting to the occasion, for in it we first invoke the highness of divine majesty (*O Lord*), second we beseech the outpouring of serene bounty (*preserve*), thirdly we expound the goodness and holiness that we have to praise (*your people*).

Regarding the first point, it must be known that when a petition is first proposed for hearing, it should possess three things which signify the name of the Lord and which inhere excellently in the Lord to whom we make our petition and by whom, later, it is to be heard. These three things are the strength of power, the splendor of knowledge or prudence, and the comeliness of mercy.

Translated from Naples, Biblioteca Nazionale, MS VIII AA 11, fols. 68v–69v.

As for the first [strength of power], it must be known that any request to someone who cannot give it, as for instance begging money from a pauper, is in vain. Moreover, according to Ambrose, "lord" is the name of Power, that is, having power over others. Beyond doubt, this power abides in God: namely, the power to give whatever is asked of him. Exodus 15 [:3], *The Lord is a warrior, "almighty" is his name.*

As for the second [splendor of knowledge or prudence], it must be known that a petition existing only in the heart . . . will never be heard. Rather, it must be known by him of whom it is to be asked. Furthermore, the name "lord" implies knowledge. According to the Philosopher [Aristotle] in *Politics*, Book 1, those vigorous in intellect are naturally lords, that is, leaders of others, even if they lack physical strength, just as, conversely, those vigorous in bodily strength and lacking in intellect are naturally slaves. In God, however, infinite knowledge adheres by virtue of which he knows perfectly not only what we ask of him, but all our needs and desires and feelings. 1 Kings 2 [:3], *The Lord is a God of knowledge, and to him thoughts are open.*

As for the third [comeliness of mercy], it must be known that he who loves his subjects and is clement or benevolent toward them deserves to be called their lord, while he who has the opposite qualities should be called a tyrant. To grant a petition, however, it is not enough to be able to do it, and to know how to do it. One must also want to do it. Thus the person to whom the petition is made shows great benevolence or clemency toward the petitioner. In God, however, is total love and mercy and benevolence toward us all, inasmuch as we are his creatures and his children, made in his image. Love naturally flows from parents toward children, or, generally speaking, from anyone toward his handiwork or achievements, as Aristotle says in *Ethics*, Book 8. The Book of Wisdom 11 [:25], *You love all things that exist, and detest none of the things you have made,* and further on [11:27], *You spare all things, for they are yours, O Lord, lover of souls.* To such a Lord, therefore, in whom is the capacity and knowledge and will to do all things that we ask of him, do we boldly make our petition. May it be granted.

But it may be argued that many prayers or petitions made to God are not granted. . . . It should be said, therefore, that a prayer is sometimes not granted, for four reasons. First, because sometimes what is asked for does not behoove the asker. . . . Second, if you ask for salvation for someone who obstructs their own salvation. . . . Third, if you do not ask with trust of obtaining [what you ask], which renders the petition unworthy to be granted. . . . Fourth, if you ask lukewarmly and without persevering. . . . But what we are now asking for pertains to the salvation and good and honor of the whole Church. And thus, if we ask faithfully and fervently, we shall receive, as it says in the Psalm [36:40], *The Lord will help them and rescue them, he will rescue them from the wicked and save them, because they have hoped in him.*

Another objection could be, if God knows all our thoughts and desires, why does he want us to beg him audibly? To this it should be answered that he wants it for two reasons. First, certainly, in order to spur interior devotion, since the mind in prayer is lifted up to God. For by exterior acts, either voices or other things such as genuflection . . . the mind is to some degree spurred toward devotion and is lifted up to God. . . . Second, since we serve God by praying to him not only with our mind but with our flesh, both of which we owe to him, just as a man holding two fiefs from the king is obliged to serve him with both. Therefore, we pray to God in this present procession on behalf of our men, not only with our minds but with our voices, saying with the Psalm [61:8], *The Lord is* our *helper* and our protector. Thus ends the first part of this sermon.

As to the second principal point, it should be known that health of the soul is to be preferred to health of the body, since the soul is a more important part of the body than the body itself. And we must pray to God for everyone—principally for their souls, as for instance [saying], "May God preserve them from sin, not permitting them to think, say, or do that which is detrimental to their well-being," and secondly for the health of their bodies, for instance, "May God spare them from violent death, epidemic or plague, hunger, and so forth." Psalm [7:11]: *God saves the upright in heart,* and again [Ps. 16:7], *You save those who hope in you.* And salvation can rightly be asked of him since saving is in his nature, belonging to him by his very name, just as advice is sought from the wise, aid from the powerful, money from the rich. . . .

As to the third principal point, it should be known that the whole army of the lord duke is the people of God generally, but the lord duke himself belongs singularly to the people of God. The first [part of the] statement is proven in two ways. First, since an army in the service of the Church of God, and consequently of God himself, is the people of God. And the aforesaid army is in the service of the Church of God, that is, against the notorious enemy of the Church of God, excommunicated and condemned as a heretic by the pope who is the vicar of God; therefore, [the duke's army is the people of God]. Second, since he who has justice on his side in war belongs to the people of God, and he who has injustice belongs to the people of the devil. But the aforesaid army has justice on its side; therefore [it is the people of God]. Psalm [99:3] *We are his people and the sheep of his pasture.* Third, moreover, the [second part of the] above statement is proven because the lord duke is of the house of France, which was and is holier than the other houses of the earth. His great-grandfather [Charles I] fought and battled with the enemies of the Church and ousted them from the Kingdom of Sicily, and from his lineage above all others, two saints were recently canonized: Saint Louis King of France, and Saint Louis the brother of our lord king [Robert]. 1 Pet. 2 [:9], *You are a chosen race, a royal priesthood*—and this applies to the latter saint, who was the firstborn of the king [Charles II] and to whom the kingdom belonged by right, and he was a priest and bishop of Toulouse—*a holy nation, God's own people*. However, just as the light of fire heats more that which is nearer, but heats also that which is distant, so through that love which is called fire—Canticles 8 [:6–7], *its flashes are the flashes of fire and flame; many waters cannot quench love*—we must pray especially and more for our men who are the people of God, as was shown above, and secondly for our enemies, that God may lead them back to grace and to obedience to the Church and to our lord king without bloodshed, and may make a non-people into a people. On this, 1 Peter 2 [:10], *Once you were not a people, but now you are God's people; once you had not received mercy, but now you have received mercy*—now by grace, and in the future by glory, may God lead us to it. Amen.

39. MATTEO VILLANI ON PEACE AND THE COMMON GOOD (fourteenth century)

Translated from Italian by William Caferro

Prompted by yet another war between Florence and Pisa (1362–64), in this excerpt, Matteo Villani, brother of Giovanni Villani and continuator of his celebrated chronicle, reflects on the nature of peace and war. Following in the Aristotelian tradition, Villani argues that peace is the outcome of good government, which by definition is opposed to tyranny. A celebrated visual analogue of this theme can be found in Ambrogio Lorenzetti's frescoes in the "Hall of the Nine" in the Palazzo Pubblico in Siena.

Naturally opposite and contrary things, once brought together, demonstrate all the more their differences. We speak of this presently, because of the failed peace between our commune and the Pisans [1363], and because of the war, initiated and pursued by them with great cleverness, to retake the [Pisan] port [see **#18**]. It is this then that is the subject of the prologue of the eleventh chapter of our treatise, taking the principle that peace faithfully observed is the sure and certain foundation and basis of earthly riches and earthly happiness. Peace is the mother of unity, of citizen concord; it engenders growth and exaltation not only in small but in still lesser things. The kings of the world govern their kingdoms benevolently in peace. The people, free and engaged in arts and business, multiply their riches, glorifying the face of their cities with riches and noble edifices. From secure marriages, grow and multiply citizens with happy aspect and full of festivity. This is true not only of people who live in liberty, but also those under the most cruel yoke of tyranny, which, by its evil nature and corrupt usage, is always the enemy and adversary, openly and secretly, of good and valorous citizens. Tyrants, on account of the fear fixed in their minds of losing their states . . . [and] not content that their perverse iniquity is visited upon their citizens, and from a desire to amplify their lordship, torment their neighbors—especially those who live in liberty—with continuous war, betrayals, and schemes. And to be able to furnish their impious resolution and execute their will, they oppress their subjects, multiplying the number of *gabelles* [indirect taxes] and collections, and imposing heavy taxes. . . .

Therefore peace is properly considered the mother of happiness and fertility, crown and nobility of the most powerful kings and lords, protection and shield of free people, and, above all, the adversary and enemy of frightful, sterile, and bloody war, through which the most lofty things are brought

Translated from Matteo Villani, *Cronica* (Rome, Multigrafica Editrice, 1980), vol. 5, 139–41.

Figure 10. Allegory of Good Government (1338–40). From left the figures represented are Peace, Fortitude, Prudence, Magnanimity, Temperance, and Justice. In the center sits the City of Siena, the embodiment of good government. At their feet are city leaders and citizens. Fresco by Ambrogio Lorenzetti in the council hall (Sala dei Nove). Siena, Palazzo Pubblico. (Photo: Scala/Art Resource)

low. How many of the most famous kings and lords in prior ages has war left staggering in extreme misery and shameful loss of life? How many famous nobles and glorious citizens has it uprooted? . . . How many provinces has it left desolated and poor, and inhabitants frightened and intimidated? Who can in a few pages comprehend the incredible and amazing things that the fury and rage of war have produced in the past centuries? War is a secret and evil seed, a receptacle for tyranny, which, like a mushroom in its soil bed, germinates and rises and tenaciously nourishes itself. Therefore well it is to abhor . . . those who through ambition or evil, or disdain or for private gain, or for vendetta or vainglory push their homeland into war. And in truth, I do not know what grace before God one who repents of such activity should find, since it is nearly impossible for such a man to gain absolution.

40. A MERCENARY SOLDIER JOHN HAWKWOOD (1369)

Translated from Italian by William Caferro

Warfare was a frequent occurrence in fourteenth-century Italy. Campaigns were often drawn-out affairs, involving substantial logistical difficulties and the management of limited resources. Tensions arose between armies and their employers over pay and strategy. The soldiers banded together in times of truce, pillaging and ravaging the countryside on their own accord. Offensives aimed as much at exerting social, political and economic pressure on enemies as at winning major victories in the field. The widespread use of mercenary soldiers, both native and foreign, further complicated the situation. One of the most notable of the foreign mercenaries was the Englishman John Hawkwood (Giovanni Acuto), who in the chronicle excerpt below is in the service of the Visconti against an alliance of Tuscan cities. In the last years of his life, however, Hawkwood fought for Florence against the Visconti and their program of territorial expansion. For his service, when he died of natural causes, Hawkwood was buried with high honors in Florence and later (1436) commemorated with a mural painted by Paolo Uccello.

In the said year of 1369, when Giovanni Malatacca, captain of the Florentine forces, was besieging San Miniato, John Hawkwood [Giovanni Acuto] left Lombardy at the instruction of messer Bernabò Visconti [his employer] and rode to Borgo a Cascina to relieve San Miniato. It was said that he had . . . *barbute* with him.[1] Because of rain and lack of supplies, Hawkwood did not go directly to San Miniato. On account of this, Giovanni Malatacca, the Florentine captain, took him as cowardly and wrote many times to Florence to say that [Hawkwood's] brigade could be beaten. Accordingly, Florentine officials urged him to defeat the brigade, and wrote letters instructing him to go forth and attack them. The captain responded, however, that it was not [yet] advisable to risk that course, because the prospects remained doubtful. Hearing this—that San Miniato could not be taken for certain and that an attack on Hawkwood was not a sure thing—wise city officials decided not to fight. But more powerful voices, those not so wise or experienced as the others, wished to fight, and wrote to the captain urging him to do so. But Malatacca did not want to launch an attack. One of the men [Schiatta del Ricco Pezzaio] who directed the Florentine war effort, leader of a group of eight citizens and two captains of the Guelf Party, went to Malatacca and

Translated from "Cronaca Fiorentina di Marchionne di Coppo Stefani," ed. Niccolò Ridolico in *RIS*[2] n.s. 30, pt. 1 (Città di Castello: S. Lapi, 1903), 271–72.
    1. A military unit consisting of two men, a knight, and a page.

told him if he did not have sufficient courage for battle he would send him the heart of an ox. Hearing this, Malatacca, shamed and not wishing to be thought cowardly (since surely he was one of the bravest men in Italy) led his army into battle. He rode out from camp to Borgo a Cascina, where he engaged Hawkwood and was defeated. Malatacca himself was taken prisoner, as were many Florentines who rode with him. Among them was Filippo di Messer Alamanno Cavicciuli, who was later ransomed. . . . City officials were greatly dismayed by the defeat.

In fear and consternation, Florence thought itself surely abandoned and greatly feared for its liberty. . . . John Hawkwood, despite having attained this great victory, did not, however, ride on to San Miniato. He did not go for several reasons: some say because of the tempestuous weather and rains, the bad roads, and the terrain of San Miniato. Hawkwood and his army went instead to Peretola, within two miles of Florence, where they hoped to foment unrest and rebellion within the city.

41. ALLIANCE IN EXILE BETWEEN THE RADICAL CIOMPI AND MAGNATES AGAINST THE FLORENTINE GUILD REPUBLIC (1379)

Translated from Latin by Samuel K. Cohn

The revolt of the Ciompi, wool workers and artisans of the popolo minuto, *is best understood as three revolts. First, on 18 June 1378 Salvestro de' Medici and others from merchant-elite families sparked a constitutional struggle that challenged the Guelf Party's political dominance.*[1] *Through the institution of* ammonite, *or denunciations, they were able to expose the Guelf Party's manipulation of government elections. This revolt was supported and may indeed have succeeded because of artisans and workers rioting in the streets of Florence, resulting in the destruction of several magnate palaces. The second revolt came a month later, (20–22 July), when workers in the wool industry, who had no guild status and therefore no representation in government or any rights as citizens, stormed the communal palace of Florence and successfully overthrew the government. First, they established an emergency government of thirty-two, comprised largely of wool workers and artisans, and then a new guild government which added three revolutionary guilds to the traditional twenty-one [see #20]. In effect, guild representation and citizenship was extended to all workers in Florence.*

At the end of August, a group of disgruntled aristocrats and wool workers, known as the "Eight of Santa Maria Novella," plotted to push the revolution further and tried to force their proposals through the government. They failed, and in reaction the government disbanded the third revolutionary guild—the Popolo di Dio, composed of the least skilled workers and apprentices of the city. Workers of the two other revolutionary guilds, however, maintained their newly won status and allied with minor and major guildsmen to form a new government. The Government of the Minor Guilds [Arti Minori] ruled Florence until the end of January 1382.

The document below from the Florentine judicial archives gives insight into the creativity of the Florentine popolo minuto, *their ideology with its emphasis on justice; their networks of communication and leadership both in Florence and with exiles in other cities; and their alliance in exile with the very forces they first rebelled against in the summer of 1378. After their defeat in early September the allies of the radical Ciompi, or Popolo di Dio, included super-magnates such as Adoardo de' Pulci who immediately after Salvestro de Medici's constitutional reforms, had plotted a counter-revolution to preserve the privileges of Florence's wealthiest and most powerful men.*[2] *The description of the conspiracies and its list of rebels and their*

---

1. By the mid-fourteenth century, the Guelf Party had become an institution of upper-class reaction to initiatives toward more egalitarian measures and broader social participation in the Florentine government.

2. See *Diario d'anonimo fiorentino dall'anno 1358 al 1389*: "Adoardo de' Pulci wanted to carry out the flag [*gonfalone*] of the [Guelf] Party to rouse the city to revolt. But it did not happen because of the good intentions of Foresse Salviati, who confronted him, and thus Florence was spared from having its citizens kill and be killed," trans. in Samuel K. Cohn, *Popular Protest in Late Medieval Europe: Italy, France, and Flanders* (Manchester: Manchester University Press, 2004).

parishes calls into question two general assumptions about the Ciompi and especially about the third revolt of late August 1378: (1) that the old Florentine elites led and manipulated the workers for the elites' own interests; and (2) that the radical phase was essentially comprised of Florence's poorest workers from San Frediano and other parishes south of the River Arno. Instead, we find more or less a city-wide representation of these workers and artisans in this document and other judicial records that prosecuted the radical rebels of the third revolt. In fact, in the document below, more of the rebels beneath the ranks of the magnates came from north of the Arno (16) than from the south (9). Finally, this is the only document concerning the Ciompi or before it to list a woman among the rebels against the Florentine commune: Lady Nicholosa de' Medici, from the parish of San Tommaso, would have hardly been from among Florence's poor and exploited.[3]

Lord Lapo, son of Lapo of Castiglionchio from the parish of San Remigio
Lord Giovanni di Pocciano di Bettolo de Coppoli of Perugia
Benedetto di Simone de Pucci from the parish of San Iacopo in Fossi
Aduaordo di Bartolommeo de Pulci from the parish of San Piero Scheraggio
Bernardo di Lippo di Cione del Cane from the parish of San Frediano
Giovanni di Bartolo di Cenne de Biliotti from the parish of San Felice in Piazza
    or Santa Felicità
Niccolò di Brunetto from the parish of Santa Trinità
Lord Alberto di Pepi d'Antonio de Albizzi from the parish of San Pier Maggiore
Mancino di Lando d'Antonio de Albizzi from the parish of San Pier Maggiore
Guereni Tribald Rosis from the parish of Santa Felicità
Pigello and Talano, sons of Lord Luigi de Adimari from the parish of Santa
    Maria Nepotecase
Tommaso son of the deceased Raneri de Cavalcanti from the parish of Santa
    Lucia Ognissanti
Bartolomeo son of the deceased Niccolò di Ridolfo from the parish of San
    Michele Berteldi
Cenni son of the deceased Nardo de Rucellai of the parish of Santa Maria
    Novella
Niccolò di Iacopo de Bordoni
Bernardo di Iacopo de Beccanugi and Luigi called "Mostone" di Bernardo from
    the parish of San Michele Bertelde
Iacopo di Bartolommeo and Lady Nicholosa de' Medici from the parish of San
    Tommaso
Niccolò di Sandro de Bardi from the parish of Santa Lucia sopr'Arno
Lord Guido di Salvi Banderie from the parish of San Pier Maggiore
Simone d'Andrea called "Morello" and Bartolommeo from the parish of San
    Paolo
Iacopo di Teste called "Testinella" from the parish of San Pier Maggiore
Matteo di Tunai called Teo from San Lorenzo

Translated from Archivio di Stato di Firenze, Atti del Capitano del Popolo, n. 1198 (1379), fol. 55r–59r.
    3. The legal formulas have not been included here. Names of the rebels have been translated from Latin into Italian but have retained the "de" before all family names to make indentification more transparent.

Matteo di Scilti from the parish of San Frediano
Andreo di Signo from the parish of San Michele Bertelde
Bingeno di Piero de Rotellari from the parish of San Pancrazio
Domenico di Bonaiuto called "Bonato Danza" now living in the parish of San
    Lorenzo in Vicchio [the *contado* of Florence],
Guido and Cecchi sons of Vanni from the parish of Santa Felicità
Cambio di Giovanni called "Carnacino" from the parish of San Niccolò
Zindo di Montino, a wool weaver from the parish of Sant'Ambrogio
Lucano, a wool comber, from the parish of San Giorgio
Cecco di Zando called "Ghinazzo" from the parish of Santa Maria in Peretola
    [the *contado* of Florence]
El Mazza, a weaver from the parish of Sant'Ambrogio
Nanni di Guccio from the parish of Sant'Ambrogio
Simone called "Compare" from the parish of San Frediano
Francesco di Suxto called "Lomperio," a wool carder from the parish of Santa
    Lucia Ognissanti
Teste the brother of Mecinelle from the parish of San Frediano
Basilio and Abraamo, sons of Matteo from the parish of San Frediano
Ormano from Padua, living in the parish of Sant'Ambrogio
El Frederica, living in the street of San Gallo [the northern part of the city]
Michele di Gofri, a wool finisher [*reveditor*] from the parish of Santa Trinità
Dino di Piero of San Donnino, a wool comber, from the parish of San Frediano
Antonio called "Cateratii," from the parish of San Lorenzo
Antonio di Becche from the parish of Sant'Ambrogio
Antonio called "Lombardo" di Schamatino, living in the street of San Gallo

All the rebels listed above in May of this year [1379] gathered together, deliberated, and plotted, first in the house of the above-mentioned Lord Lapo in the city of Padua and then in the city of Bologna, in an inn belonging to Felice the son of Amante of Florence. Here, they employed men at arms to assist [the struggle of] workers and artisans [the *popolo minuto*], then living in Florence. The action, however, came to naught. In December of 1379, the Florentine *popolo minuto* living in Bologna and who had previously assisted their fellow artisans and workers [in revolts] in Florence, elected eight from their ranks and commissioned the making of several flags. One bore the insignia of the Guelf Party. A second one was a heretical flag [*banderia falsa*]: on the upper part was painted the arms of the Guelf Party with lilies surrounding it; on the lower part were depicted two arms, one holding balances, the other, a sword broken in half with the following words written below it: "With this noble sign above I will take vengeance on anyone who attempts to wrong me." These rebels met and deliberated with these flags on 19 December 1379 in Bologna at six o'clock at night [Florentine style].

On 15 February 1380 [1379 Florentine style], they were found not guilty and were absolved of the charges.

Figure 11. Equestrian statue of Can Grande della Scala, lord of Verona (fourteenth century). Verona, Museo di Castelvecchio. (Photo: Louise Bourdua)

42. LORDSHIPS AND CITY-STATE RIVALRY IN LOMBARDY AND THE VENETO (1390–1405)

Translated from Italian by John E. Law

Rivalry between city-states was endemic in medieval Italy; this is exemplified by events in the northeast in the late fourteenth century, the major players being the signorie *(lordships) of the Visconti of Milan and the Carrara of Padua, and the Republic of Venice. The Visconti under Giangaleazzo (1385–1402) looked set to dominate the region, for example taking Padua in 1388. Under Francesco "Novello" (the Younger), the Carrara recovered their lordship in 1390, and sought to profit from Giangaleazzo's sudden death in 1402. This prompted the major military intervention of Venice from 1404, after which the Republic emerged as the dominant power in the region until the eighteenth century. These events were recorded by Clemente Miari (ca. 1360–ca. 1413), a cleric from Belluno in what is now the Veneto. His city was a pawn in the larger power game, but that very fact and the prominence of his family in regional politics, helped to make Clemente an informed observer. The following extracts are taken from an Italian version of his diary-like chronicle.*

1. Belluno Prepares to Surrender to Giangaleazzo Visconti

Visconti armies entered Padua on 21 November 1390. On 1 December, the Ghibelline faction in Belluno—to which Clemente Miari belonged—rose in rebellion, attempting to seize the political initiative from their Guelf rivals who had enjoyed the favor of the Carrara. For all the confusion, procedures were followed to give the impression that the commune had recovered its authority from the representatives of the Carrara.

Andrea di Miari and Bonaccorso his brother and Giangregorio da Bolzano and Bolzano de' Bolzano, and many others, numbering over sixty, gathered in the suburb of Campitello after one o'clock, seized the bridge to the market gate of Belluno, occupied the gate itself, [and] entered the piazza armed, shouting "Long live the people! Long live the people!" while the citizens were gathered in the Palazzo Comunale with the *podestà*. And so, in the name of the people, they took the city, changing the captains in command of Santi Ippolito e Casamatta [two fortresses in Belluno's jurisdiction], and of the city. They took the keys from the *podestà*, messer Feltrino da Savoia from Mantua and his vicar messer Antonio di Ruzzolino. And on the same day the people gathered together in the piazza under the banner of the church of Belluno, that of San Martino, and appointed as its defenders ser Giovanni da Bolzano and ser Cristoforo da Castello, citizens of Belluno. And on command the people sacked the house of Giampolastro da Padova, treasurer of the said lord of Padua.

2. Giangaleazzo's Representative Enters Belluno

The lord of Milan had received the county of Vertus in Champagne from King John of France on his marriage to the king's daughter Blanche in 1350. Great play was made of the title (Vertu) by both his friends and his enemies. Feltre, Belluno's closest neighbor sharing its cathedral status, had also accepted Visconti rule.

On the following Thursday—10 December 1390—at the first hour of darkness, the noble knight messer Count Antonio da Camisano from Crema, the representative of that most illustrious prince the count of Vertus, arrived in Belluno. The clergy, together with the Friars Minor, to the solemn sound of the church bells and singing hymns of joy, processed to meet him at the moat

Translated from Clemente Miari, *Cronaca Bellunese* (Belluno: Cavessago, 1873). The original Latin text was translated into Italian by Giovanni de Donà.

of the suburb of Campitello near Santa Maria Nuova; then with the greatest joy they returned, accompanying him to the *Palazzo Comunale*. The day before, he had made his entrance to the city of Feltre; the Saturday after—12 December—he took the lordship of Belluno, and demanded an oath of loyalty from the citizens gathered in the Palazzo.

On 13 December, Sunday and the feast of Santa Lucia, at Vespers, messer Simone da Noventa from Padua, doctor of laws, and Bonsembiante d'Onigo from Treviso, captain of the castle of Belluno for Francesco da Carrara, handed the fortress with all its munitions to the said messer Count of Camisano; he received it in the name of the above-mentioned count of Vertus and ran up the banner of the Biscione.[1] All those there and in the pay of the Carrara, swore loyalty to messer Antonio, which he accepted. The citizens of Belluno organized jousts, dances and many games.

4. Giangaleazzo's Position in the Veneto Is Challenged by Rebellion

The defense of his territorial acquisitions, and his confrontation with other Italian states, threatened to overstretch the resources of the lord of Milan, and in 1390 he faced two serious challenges to his authority in the Veneto, in Verona—which he overcame—and in Padua—which he lost.

In May 1390 the armies of our lord, the count of Vertus, lord of Milan, Feltre, and Belluno, besieged Bologna, the ally of Florence. That army remained there until 20 June, when messer Francesco da Carrara the Younger entered Padua through treachery, and occupied the city and all the fortresses of the territory except for the castle of Padua itself and Bassano. Because of this rebellion, the count moved his army from Bologna to Padua, and also dispatched the knight messer Ugolotto Biancardo da Parma with seven hundred lances (2,100 cavalry) and [an unspecified] number of foot-soldiers.

When he had reached Ostiglia, he heard that there had been a popular rebellion in Verona against the count. Hence, he abandoned his march in aid of Padua and rode by night on Verona, entered its citadel, rested his troops, and then fell on the Veronese rebels and achieved victory, driving out the citizens and subjecting the city itself to three days of sack. Having recovered Verona, he moved in force to Padua where he reinforced the citadel and castle with troops and provisions before returning to Verona.

5. Giangaleazzo's Military Victories

As suggested in the last extract, the lord of Milan's successes depended much on the employment of able condottieri, *or mercenary captains. His crushing victories over*

---

1. The principal Visconti emblem, representing a young child in the jaws of a serpent.

foreign and Italian armies caused panic among his enemies, but cheered his support-
ers in Belluno. On 25 July 1391 a French army commanded by the Count of Armag-
nac and in the pay of Florence was defeated at Alessandria; at the end of June
1402, Giangaleazzo's forces defeated a Florentine-led coalition outside Bologna and
entered the city.

ALESSANDRIA

Tuesday, 1 August 1391. To celebrate the news of the victory of our most
illustrious lord, the count of Vertus, near Alessandria, over the count of Arm-
agnac and his army on the feast-day of St. James the Apostle in July, solemn
processions were held in Belluno for three days, and the following day a
prayer was offered in all the churches; it was composed by the venerable
messer Clemente Miari, canon of Belluno and doctor in laws:

Most fearful God, unconquered fortress for those in combat and power
most feared. In these last days, hearing the prayers of that most devout and
clement prince the count of Vertus, in a most marvelous fashion you delivered his enemies into his hands. Grant to your servant—who understands the
mystery of such a gift and who always keeps his heart pure for your commands—that he will constantly merit the increase achieved from victory. And
we, your faithful and contrite servants, as we celebrate religiously the ceremonies due for such great benefits, joyfully join him in glorifying your clemency toward us. For Jesus Christ Our Lord, Amen.

BOLOGNA

On Sunday 2 July [1402], our most illustrious lord wrote to the *podestà* of
Belluno a letter about the defeat delivered at Bologna. His letter ordered
processions over three days and bonfires. That was done, and the commune
of Belluno gave eight florins to the horseman who brought the letter. Great
festivities were held in Belluno over several days.

On 8 July, our most illustrious lord the duke of Milan wrote to Belluno
saying that he had obtained the lordship of Bologna peacefully. On the Sunday, a solemn procession was held, through the city, the suburb of Campitello, and as far as Santa Maria Nuova, then returning via Santo Stefano and
then back to the city. After the contingent of clergy, there was carried in the
procession the throne, on which it was the custom to place the angel in the
celebration of the Annunciation, but with the horseman sent by the above-
mentioned most illustrious lord. He held in his hand the above-mentioned
letter which, as I have said, that same most illustrious lord had written.

6. Giangaleazzo Becomes Duke of Milan

A high point of Giangaleazzo's lordship was the purchase, on 11 May 1395, of the title of Duke of Milan from the Holy Roman Emperor Wenceslas for 100,000 florins. The ducal title added to the Visconti's prestige and to the legitimacy of his authority, but it further alarmed his Italian enemies and contributed to discrediting Wenceslas's authority in the Empire. The relatively muted comment of the chronicler may be related to the "gift" of 1,000 florins the commune of Belluno had to send to celebrate the event.

In 1395 on 7 September, that most illustrious prince, our lord, messer the count of Vertus was made duke of Milan, and crowned by representatives of the emperor. And in Milan great festivities and the most splendid tournaments were held, which almost all the princes and representatives of the communes of Italy attended.

7. The Death of the Duke of Milan

The death of Giangaleazzo Visconti came as a relief to his enemies but a shock to his supporters, among them the Ghibellines of Belluno.

On Sunday 3 September 1402, in the castle of Marignano in the jurisdiction of Milan, there died, stricken by constant fevers and swellings [bubonic plague], our most illustrious prince and lord messer Giangaleazzo, duke of Milan, count of Pavia and of Vertus, and lord of Bologna, Pisa, Siena, Perugia, etc. It could be said that the comet that appeared in March was for him.

He left behind his first-born son messer Giovanni Maria, duke of Milan and of other cities—except for those listed below—and messer Filippo Maria his second son, count of Pavia and lord of [the cities] of Verona, Vicenza, Feltre, Belluno, and Bassano; also of the cities of Vercelli, Novara, Alessandria, and Tortona, along with Valenza and Casale. And on the evening of Saturday 23 the garrison of the city of Belluno was called to defend the honor and state of the above-mentioned Filippo Maria, thanks be to God.

8. The Surrender to Venice

After Giangaleazzo's death (1402) his widow Caterina and sons Giovanni Maria and Filippo Maria—both minors—faced a number of internal and external threats. In the east their main challenger was Francesco "il Novello" Carrara, and to counter him the Visconti ceded territory to Venice. The Ghibelline and pro-Visconti party in Belluno—to which Clemente Miari belonged—was anxious to be on the winning side and to thwart their Guelf and pro-Carrara enemies. Initially the Venetians presented their intervention as being in support of their Visconti allies, but the realities of the situation soon became clear. However, as in 1388, formalities were observed and authority appeared to revert, albeit briefly, to the commune of Belluno, while the attempt was made—at least by the Ghibellines—to make the replacement of Visconti with Venetian rule appear smooth and "natural."

THE VENETIANS ARRIVE

On the following Monday (28 April 1404), the Ghibellines were determined to go out and confront the Guelfs, who were besieging the city from the suburb of Campitello. They decided to attack as follows: to place thirty archers outside the first wall, while getting the cannon and handguns ready; then they would open the gates—leaving a garrison—and attack after the guns and archers had fired. But God, wanting to prevent many evils, presented a solution. While these matters were being anxiously discussed, Venetian troops crossed over the bridge on the Piave—seventy horse and seven hundred foot and archers—coming to support our lords (the Visconti) and the Ghibellines.

THE VENETIANS ASSUME THE LORDSHIP OF BELLUNO

In the year of Our Lord 1404, on Sunday 18 May, which was the feast of Pentecost, the Venetian troops assembled in the Rudo *contrada* of Belluno; their captain and lieutenant of the Venetian Republic was the nobleman Antonio Moro, sent to take and hold the lordship of the city. The clergy, with their crosses and banners—and with the standards of the rural parishes as well—met them in procession with the people in the Piazza of Santa Croce.

And the procession was organized as follows. In front came many country people, carrying greenery, which they spread around all over the street and over the city's main piazza. After them came in procession the Friars Minor; then the crosses and banners of the rural parishes and confraternities; then the crosses and banner of the cathedral church, with the clergy and members of the chapter, singing hymns of joy; then the people of the city carrying in their hands tree branches.

Following them came some Venetians on horseback, keeping their followers in order. There then followed one hundred and fifty archers marching in threes, with six standards above their heads. And so they arrived in the piazza. There the clergy withdrew to the cemetery of the cathedral facing the piazza, and the archers circled the piazza parading their flags. Then a further six companies of shield-carriers made a similar circuit of the piazza, with the city's pipers at their head. Then on horseback came the nobleman Torresino della Porte, citizen of Treviso, the marshal of the troops, and he organized their line-up. Then some others came by on horseback, and among them someone carrying the banner of San Marco; his horse's bridle was held by Giovanni and Bartolomeo Miari, citizens of Belluno.

Then came the pipers and trumpeters, playing, and immediately after messer Antonio Moro from Venice, whose horse was guided and surrounded by eight nobles citizens of the city of Belluno, and on his entry to the piazza all the bells of the city rang out. He, too, circled the whole piazza; then he came to the Palazzo Comunale, and climbed the stairs to the hall where were gathered, together with the people, the rectors and syndics of the commune of Belluno to present him with the lordship of the city.

As soon as he had arrived the venerable canon messer Giannicolo da Bolzano gave a speech in his presence; at its end, the rectors and syndics— Clemente da Bolzano, Bonaccorso da Miero, Vittore da Bolzano, Priamo de' Spiciaroni, citizens of Belluno—presented a staff or baton to the said messer Antonio Moro, who received it on behalf of the most illustrious lordship of Venice. Then he received the keys of the city itself, then the banner of San Martino from the cathedral, and lastly the banner of the commune, as a sign that he had been presented with the lordship of the city.

Then the said messer Antonio left the palazzo to go to celebrate mass in the cathedral. The canons went to meet him at the steps of the church, and there messer Leonisio dal Doglione, dean and canon of Belluno, who was there to celebrate mass, presented him with a cross which he kissed on his knees. Then the venerable Clemente Miari, canon of Belluno and graduate in canon law, the syndic of the Chapter of Belluno, took him into the choir, to the bishop's chair, which was solemnly decorated with drapes and hangings. Then mass was solemnly celebrated, and the organs sounded, and messer Antonio presented a gold ducat. At the end of mass, the banner of the Biscione was hung over the choir representing the Visconti, and to record the unsolicited help given us by the Venetian nobleman Lodovico Giustiniano, *podestà* of Serravalle, the banner of the said *podestà* was hung alongside it.

The commune of Belluno completes the process of surrender, but the Guelf and Ghibelline representatives—suspicious of one another—travel to Venice separately.

On Saturday 7 June 1404, the commune of Belluno sent an embassy to Venice to swear fealty to that illustrious lordship, and to present there the commune's petition of surrender. And the ambassadors were—for the Ghibellines—these noble and prudent men messer Clemente da Bolzano, messer Bonaccorso Miari, messer Priamo de' Spiciaroni, and messer Vittore da Bolzano, who—well armed and provided for—set off at four o'clock by raft on the Piave, because they did not want to travel with the Guelfs, whom they did not trust. And they went all the way to Venice by water, having prepared at Ponte del Piave in the Trevigiano two armed vessels, in which they arrived in Venice. The Guelfs sent the judge messer Niccolo de' Persicini, messer Cristoforo da Castello, Giampietro da Mezzano, and Antonio de' Crepadoni, who travelled on horseback. But the Ghibellines arrived by water in Venice on Sunday 8 June at three o'clock, and presented themselves to the ducal council and were received. On the other hand, the Guelfs arrived in Venice on the following Monday.

9. Clemente Miari Petitions the Visconti for Privileges

The Visconti regime was anxious to tax its subjects, both lay and clerical, but it was open to special petitions. Clemente Miari used his apparently successful involvement in this issue to secure a privilege for his own family.

On 22 September 1396, messer Clemente Miari, graduate in law and canon of Belluno, and messer Federico, from the parish of Cesio in the diocese of Feltre, acting for the clergy of Feltre, rode to Pavia as representatives to meet our most illustrious lord the duke of Milan, asking him that tax levies should not be imposed on the clergy. Moreover, the said Clemente also secured the privilege that all the Miari, as individuals and with one companion, could carry arms throughout the duke's lands without fear of penalty.

10. Peacemaking Among Factions

Although Visconti rule drew on the partisan support of the Ghibelline families of Belluno, at times it tried to broker and secure a more general peace. The citadel referred to in the following extract was under Visconti control, and in theory, might have been seen as safe or neutral territory.

On 26 April of the same year (1397), in the citadel of Belluno, Bartolomeo Miari (from the Ghibelline faction) was playing football with many of the young men of the city. As it happened, the ball fell into the stream, and Francesco da Carrara (from the Guelf faction) went to get it. But Bartolomeo wanted to get there first, and fell in, soaking himself pretty well. Then Michele da Carrara said, "Too bad you did not drown, as your father managed to do." This was reported back to Bartolomeo, who, finding Michele in the suburb of Campitello, punched him in the neck and drew his sword to strike him, but he escaped. As a result both were detained in the Palazzo Comunale, but the next day they made peace and surety was offered of 200 ducats that they would not insult each other any more.

11. The Fall of the Carrara of Padua

The Carrara emerged as persistent and effective challengers to Venetian interests on the Italian mainland or terraferma, *and the Republic's hostility was intensified by the fact that the dynasty's rise to power earlier in the fourteenth century had been aided by Venice. The Republic saw the Carrara as clients, a position with which they became increasingly impatient. The Carrara had also sustained the Guelf faction in Belluno, and the importance of their fall for Clemente Miari can be seen in the heading and detail he gives to his account. As in the case of Belluno in 1388 and 1404, the commune of Padua was allowed to recover its authority, with the new regime appreciating the political, economic, and legal benefits to be gathered from an apparently free surrender of power.*

In the name of the Holy and Indivisible Trinity from which proceeds every right judgment.

In the year of Our Lord 1405, on 17 November, that noble and powerful man messer Giacomo di Beltramino from Vicenza, a soldier in the army of the most illustrious *Signoria* of Venice encamped before Padua, under the command of that valorous and magnificent knight messer Galeazzo [Gonzaga] of Mantua as captain general, around eight at night climbed into Padua near the gate of Santa Croce. First up the ladder was a certain Quarantotto, then a herald of the said Giovanni, then Giovanni himself, and last a companion of his.

After them, with the ladders in position, there climbed in 150 infantry, all well armed. They, climbing down the walls, came to the gate of Santa Croce and took it by force; then they ran through the whole area up to Prato della Valle. Whereupon, Galeazzo, the captain general, entered [the city] with his whole army.

Hearing this, messer Francesco da Carrara the Younger and his son messer Francesco III, rang the bells so that the people would gather in the piazza. But nobody came, because they all feared that the city would be sacked. For that reason, the aforesaid lord of Padua, seeing himself powerless, asked messer Galeazzo and the Venetian *provveditori* [representatives with the army] for a safe conduct to take him to Venice, as he wished to submit himself to the grace and mercy of that illustrious *Signoria*. On receiving it, he handed over the citadel of Padua to the captain general, who promised to return it to him if the Venetian *Signoria* refused to forgive him.

Meanwhile the citizens of Padua sent representatives to Venice and consigned their city to the *Signoria*. And messer Francesco da Carrara also wanted to go to Venice himself, but the *Signoria* would not allow him, and when he wanted to turn back to Padua he found the city handed over to Venice. Whereupon messer Galeazzo said to him: "I gave you a safe-conduct, and I brought you back to Padua as I promised. But your citizens no longer want you as their lord, so now you are my prisoner." Then, on the orders of Venice, the Carrara were taken as prisoners to the castle of Oriago fifteen miles outside Padua, where they stayed closely guarded for quite a number of days, until the *Signoria* ordered that they be brought to Venice.

So, on Monday 23 November, they were brought with a reliable escort as prisoners to Venice, and there placed with care in the monastery of San Giorgio Maggiore. On the following Tuesday they were brought before that most illustrious prince messer Michele Steno, doge of Venice, and all the council of that city, gathered in the ducal palace. Before them, the Carrara were on their knees for a long time, and then they flung themselves to the ground, asking humbly and often for grace and mercy. After some period of time, the doge began to rebuke them and remind them of all the great bene-fits they had had from Venice. Then he narrated the extremely grave errors that he, messer Francesco, had committed, and how he had broken faith, and how he had been monstrously ungrateful for all the benefits he had received. They, on the other hand, with much weeping and wailing, asked for mercy and pardon, and begged that they should not consider their mistakes, mis-deeds and pride, but should exercise mercy toward them.

Then messer the doge pronounced that, duly guarded, they should be taken back to San Giorgio. He said to them: "You will stay there until the Greater Council decides if and how to exercise mercy toward you." Weeping, they were sent back straight away.

In Belluno, solemn processions (of thanksgiving) were held for four days. And then the people organized jousts, firework displays, and bonfires. Thanks be to God.

The End of the da Carrara
All the members of the family in Venetian hands are murdered.

On Christmas eve (1405), the Most Serene Ducal Lordship of Venice changed its mind, and had Francesco da Carrara, once lord of Padua, and his sons messer Francesco III and messer Giacomo taken to a strong prison—they had previously been held in a cell without windows—and for them there was prepared in the roof of the new ducal palace, a chamber of four by six paces, with all the beams reinforced with sheets of iron.

On Monday 18 January 1406, messer Francesco da Carrara, called the Younger, once lord of Padua and then a prisoner in Venice, having been tortured by the *avogadori* [law officers] of Venice, finally died, and he was buried near the church of Santo Stefano in the said city. His body was buried with difficulty because of the crowd of young Venetian boys who wanted to stone it. But at length it was buried without any funeral celebrations.

43. MARITIME WARFARE AND PIRACY
THREE TEXTS ON GENOA AND VENICE (1380–1403)

Translated from Italian by Eleanor Congdon, Michele Pietro Ghezzo,
John R. Melville-Jones, and Andrea Rizzi

1. Gunpowder

Introduced by Eleanor A. Congdon; translated by Michele Pietro Ghezzo, John R.
Melville-Jones, and Andrea Rizzi

Gunpowder was first introduced into Europe in the late 1200s; the earliest documentation of European gunpowder weapons dates to 1326. By the middle of the century, cannon were important in sieges and battles throughout Italy, although their range, accuracy, and structural integrity were yet to be perfected. The first attempt to use gunpowder weapons onboard ships is thought to be the War of Chioggia (1379–81) fought by Venice and Genoa. The preferred type of Italian warship at this time was a war galley: a shallow-draft and low-freeboard vessel with a single mast (for propulsion on the high seas when speed was not necessary) and as many as three tiers of rowers. In battle, the objective was to bind the ships together so that the crews and accompanying warriors could fight hand-to-hand, as if on land [see #22]. Gunpowder weapons eventually made this method of warfare obsolete. The description of the War of Chioggia that follows is taken from the Morosini *Chronicle. While Morosini writes in Venetian dialect, the portion from which this selection is taken was his own translation of a Latin chronicle by Raffaino Caresini. The excerpts show that the Genoese used land-based cannon to defend their positions at Chioggia and the Venetians responded by mounting cannon on their galleys in order to attack installations and ships in the port.*

On 13 July 1380, . . . the [Genoese] galleys reached 49 in number, including a few *galedoli* [smaller lightweight galleys usually used for trade], and every day appeared about to attack our galleys, which had their prows aimed toward the gates of Chioggia. . . . The Genoese who were enclosed in Chioggia . . . from every corner were trying to damage our galleys with their cannon. . . . We had 33 galleys altogether with their crews ready at their oars for rowing and to do what was necessary. [They were] equipped with cannon and with cannon balls in great quantity.

On August 10 the [Venetian galleys of the relief force] reached Rodo and took on water . . . and 12 enemy galleys were near, that is in the harbor of Vieste [in Apulia], and being advised of our arrival . . . they fled at once. Our fleet pursued them courageously, and some of our galleys drew near,

Translated in *The Morosini Codex*, ed. Michele Pietro Ghezzo, John R. Melville-Jones, and Andrea Rizzi, vol. 2, *Marino Falier to Antonio Venier (1354–1400)* (Padova: Unipress, 2000) (vol. 3, pt. 2 of *Archivio del Litorale Adriatico*), 116–19, 130–31.

and some were killed and others wounded by cannon and crossbows from one side to the other.

2. Maritime Hostilities (Genoa and Venice, 1403)

Translated by Eleanor A. Congdon

By the end of the fourteenth century, Venice and Genoa had fought several major wars that lasted for several years and cost them dearly in resources and men. For each war fought, there were numerous small incidents that could have set off another war but were quickly solved by diplomacy. The battle of Modon was one such example. It came after the French-appointed governor of Genoa, Marshal Boucicault, had taken a large fleet to Cyprus in order to impose Genoese domination on the island. Before returning to Genoa, however, he raided the coast of Syria, where Venetian merchants bore the brunt of this aggression. The following text is a composite of the reports sent by Luca di Matteo and Paoluccio di Maestro Paolo to the Datini company office in Barcelona.

Just now a brigantine has come from Candia bearing news for the [Venetian] *Signoria*. Our armada and the galleys of the Genoese have fought a great battle near Modon. In the end, the Genoese lost three galleys and all their men; the rest of the Genoese fleet departed in a very war-like mood [on account of which] we hope they do not encounter any Venetian ships. We are fortunate that the galleys of the Romania line arrived at Modon before the battle and were not damaged, because they carry very rich cargoes of spices that will offset a little the spices lost in Syria. And we hope that a good peace can be made swiftly or it will be bad for merchants.

3. State-Sponsored Piracy

Translated by Eleanor A. Congdon

The Genoese sack of Venetian warehouses in Syria in 1403 led to a showdown between the two maritime powers at Modon, on the Peloponnesus. The Venetian fleet won the battle, blocking Genoese entry into the Adriatic. Marshal Boucicault, even before the diplomats began trying to head off a full-scale war, charged that the Venetians had started the battle. In retaliation, he authorized and encouraged all Genoese ships to attack and damage Venetian interests. The following correspondence from the Datini company reveals the ongoing hostilities from a merchant's viewpoint.

(2) Translated from Archivio di Stato di Prato, Datini 928, *Carteggio Barcelona*, letter Venice to Barcelona, Compagnia Luigi Davanzati e Luca di Matteo to Compagnia Francesco di Marco Datini e Simone d'Andrea, 27 October 1403; Archivio di Stato di Prato, Datini 928, *Carteggio Barcelona*, letter Venice to Barcelona, Paoluccio di Maestro Paolo to Compagnia Francesco di Marco Datini e d'Andrea, 27 October 1403.

(3) Translated from Archivio di Stato di Prato, Datini 928, *Carteggio Barcelona*, letter Venice to Barcelona, Antonio Contarini de Messer Marin di Ser Pantaleon to Compagnia Francesco di Marco Datini e Simone d'Andrea, 21 December 1403; Alessandro Massarri, "Lettere degli

I received your letter in which you advised me how the Genoese with two *coches* [a round ship with a big cargo hold] seized the *coche* owned by Antonio Choppo in the port of Ibiza on the fifteenth of last month. And it is well you inform me because I have on the said ship 100 bales of wool that Girolamo di Lionardo had placed on her. . . . And I hear that he placed 445 bales of wool from San Matteo and 65 bales from Majorca on the *coche* captained by Taddeo di Benedetto—may God bring it [home] safely. The said *coche* left Ibiza on 20 October, but has not been seen or heard from since. It is not known whether the ship encountered the Genoese fleet as it headed for Genoa. May God preserve it. Meanwhile, Bartolomeo Soler brought his ship back empty to Ibiza from Valencia because of the great danger posed by the Genoese, who will attack if they suspect that the vessel is Venetian or carries any Venetian goods.

I am advised about the ship of Niccolò Rosso that was taken by the Genoese ships of Niccolò da Moneglia and Girolamo Grillo. I hear that Niccolò da Moneglia attacked the ship because it was Venetian. I do not believe the ship will go to England, but that all of the goods will be unloaded here [in Bruges].

Moneglia and Grillo pounced on Rosso's ship in the port of Cadiz. They manned the vessel with members of their own crews, putting the captain and crew ashore—typical practice for corsairs of the period—and then sailed it and their own craft to Bruges. There, it was unloaded, stripped of its parts, and finally abandoned in the harbor. Rosso was able to reclaim the vessel there.

Orlandi da Bruges (1398–1410)" (thesis, Florence, 1993), 744: Datini letters Bruges to Valencia, Giovanni and Piero Benize and Co. Francesco di Marco and Luca del Sera and Co., 18 February 1404.

SECTION FIVE

Law and Order

Among the many social and intellectual changes in which Italy played a leading role, perhaps the most profound was the development of legal theory and practice—in particular, the study and reapplication of the law of the late Roman Empire, as reorganized and rationalized by the sixth-century emperor Justinian. Justinian's Corpus iuris civilis *(Body of Civil Law), a recodification of Roman law, cast a long shadow over the legal history of the peninsula. Arguably, however, the early legal history of medieval Italy was shaped more by efforts to establish order in the wake of successive Germanic invasions and the emergence of new juridical institutions. The first millennium was characterized by the use of Germanic law, often alongside Roman law and legal institutions. By the early twelfth century, contrasts between the cities of the north and the monarchical south are clearly visible in their different legislative concerns. As the texts that follow illustrate, municipal legislation in the vibrant, independent communes might range from the rights of citizenship to rules for brothels or from regulating consumption to articulating legal identity. In contrast, in the south, King Roger II's legal code harkened back to antiquity, while also recognizing the variety of legal norms practiced in the region.*

This section includes a mere sampling of the rich trove of legal texts available. The sources inspire a classic question asked in both classrooms and scholarly monographs, for which there is no easy answer: do they describe theory or practice? Nevertheless, legal sources do clearly illuminate the processes and structures in place for the practice of the law: judges and witnesses, courts and penalties, alongside the public notaries who recorded it all. The law was not static, and the texts here offer glimpses of its evolution according to society's need for social, economic, political, and moral order. While the development of legal studies in Italy is often identified with the city of Bologna, its teachers, and (later) its university, recent scholarship has focused upon the earlier period when Bologna was only one of a number of locales where "the law," both Roman and non-Roman, came to be seen as an autonomous field of intellectual (and practical) concern.

44. PROPERTY RIGHTS AND THE LEGAL SYSTEM IN SALERNO (1044)

Translated from Latin by Valerie Ramseyer

The following dispute shows many important characteristics of the eleventh-century legal system of southern Italy. First, the case was brought in front of a judge by the injured party, not by the authorities. Second, the judge did not so much impose his decision on the two parties as work together with the two men toward settlement based on evidence and the law, acceptable to both. In this case it was a matter of defining the borders between two properties, a common point of contention in late tenth–early eleventh century Italy which suggests changing ideas about private property rights. Third, both men took pledges and called guarantors. Finally, it shows the common practice of forming associations (consortia) *with other individuals for specific economic purposes.*

[February 1044]

In the name of the Lord, in the twenty-sixth year of the reign of our lord Prince Guaimarius [IV] over the Principality of Salerno, and the sixth year of his reign over Capua, Amalfi, and Sorrento, the second year of his reign over Apulia and Calabria, and the second year of the reign of his son Prince Gisolf [II], in the month of February, in the tenth year of the indiction. Count Landus son of Count Landolfus brought a case before me, Count Landus, against a cleric John, son of a priest named John, saying that John and his men trespassed on property belonging to him and his associates [*consortes*] located in Montoro and that this John and his men dug and excavated and took away produce from the land. Hearing the accusation, John responded to him, saying that he owned much property in the area of Montoro and that he was not sure which piece of land Landus was referring to. Thus I, the afore-mentioned Count Landus, after listening to these things, decided to make each man promise to do the following, and I had each man make a pledge to the other and had them name guarantors. The two men would travel to the property in question, along with a judge and notary, and Count Landus, on his own behalf and on behalf of his associates, would show to the cleric John precisely the piece of property that he accused [John of trespassing on], and then, by right and by law, they would end the dispute fairly. And Count Landus named Landus son

Translated from *Codex Diplomaticus Cavensis*, ed. Michele Morcaldi, Mauro Schiani, and Sylvano de Stefano (Naples: P. Piazzi, 1873–93), vol. 6, 1032.

of Dauferius as his guarantor, while the cleric John named Bisantius son of Truppoaldus his guarantor.

Count Landus requested that I, Dumnandus a cleric and notary, write [this charter].
Witnessed by Count Landus.

45. ROMAN LAW AND LEGAL STUDY
THREE TEXTS (ca. 1124–66)

Translated from Latin by Sean Gilsdorf

The texts included here witness the diversity of goals and attitudes that marked the rise of legal studies in medieval Italy. The first, a letter written by a Provençal monk to his abbot asking permission to study law at Pisa, reveals the reputation Italian legal studies had already gained in the early twelfth century, and the combination of intellectual and practical interests that brought students to the law (and persuaded others to aid and sponsor them).

This combination of interests is epitomized by the second document, an imperial decree issued in 1158 by the German emperor Frederick I (1123–90), which offered protection to students, in particular those studying the law. Frederick's Bolognese legal advisers sought to establish Roman law as the appropriate medium for imperial rule over the independent-minded communes of northern Italy; Frederick's decree thus was simultaneously a reward to his Bolognese advisers, an act of political patronage, and an act of imperial munificence meant both to echo the acts of the great Justinian and to be incorporated within the corpus of Roman law itself.

An example of how this law was studied and understood is provided by the final text, a short treatise or summula *written by the jurist Bulgarus of Bologna (d. ca. 1166). Bulgarus's treatment of his topic reveals the jurists' detailed knowledge of, and facility with, the Roman legal texts available to them. It also indicates, however, the willingness of the jurists to work creatively with their sources: as Hermann Kantorowicz has noted, Bulgarus' claim that "it is a greater offense to be unaware of natural law than to be ignorant of civil law" was an original one, drawing a distinction which would greatly influence later legal thinking (both civil and canonistic) on the notion of error and culpability.*

Citations to Roman law sources are abbreviated as follows: D (Digest); C (Code); Inst. (Institutes).[1]

1. Anonymous, Letter to Abbot B[ernard III] of Saint-Victor, Marseille (1124/27)

Most longed-for Father, Your Clemency should know that I previously was granted leave by the brothers of our monastery to take care of an intolerable

---

Translated from "Epistola R. monachi S. Victoris ad B. abbatem suum," in *Veterum scriptorum et monumentorum historicorum, dogmaticorum, moralium amplissima collectio*, ed. Edmond Martène and Ursin Durand (Paris: Montalant, 1724), vol. 1, 469; repr. in *PL* 151: 641–42.[2]

1. The standard edition of the texts is *Corpus Iuris Civilis*, ed. Paul Krueger, Theodor Mommsen, et al., 3 vols. (Berlin: Weidmann, 1900–1905). For English translations of the *Institutes* and *Digest*, see *Justinian's Institutes*, trans. Peter Birks and Grant McLeod (Ithaca, N.Y.: Cornell University Press, 1987), and *The Digest of Justinian*, rev. ed., 2 vols., trans. Alan Watson (Philadelphia: University of Pennsylvania Press, 1998; repr. 4 vols., 2009).

2. In *PL* 151, Migne includes without comment an excerpt from volume 7 of Antoine Rivet de la Grange et al., *Histoire littéraire de la France* (Paris: Osmont, 1724–33), which dates the

and menacing threat facing us (the nature of which I believe you now know); that I began a voyage to Rome; proceeded companionless and in utter poverty to Pavia; and set out for Rome in the company of strangers. But since the divine will did not wish me to complete the voyage that I had begun, the animal in whose cart I planned to reach Rome first became ill on the way, before dying on the spot. I thus was unable to proceed any further, but I was deeply embarrassed to return immediately with my task still incomplete. At first I hesitated about what to do, before deciding to devote myself to literary studies, and since by God's grace I had been delayed for a time in that place, I remained there for the purpose of training my mind. This, then, most beloved lord, is the reason why I, after realizing that my heart's deepest desire had come to pass, did not hurry back to you. Instead, I determined to study even more, so that I might be able to serve you better in the future, as long as I live.

Now, when I constantly see scholars in Italy, particularly ones from Provence (some of whom are monks like myself), many of them flocking to the study of the laws, and I think about our monastery continually assaulted by the lawsuits of clerics and laymen alike, and enduring the loss of its justly held possessions, I wish to have at least some knowledge of this kind. For if, by God's grace, I could become adept in such matters, I would not pursue worldly cases, but would only advance the just interests of our monastery to the best of my ability. If it should please your honor, most exalted Father, that I might dedicate myself to the study of this subject, I ask and beseech you as a supplicant to grant me your gracious permission to do so, and to send written instructions to the prior at Pisa to offer me his assistance. If I obtain what I desire from Your Mercy, I will proceed to Pisa to begin my studies, God willing. In the meantime, I will wait until the feast of Saint Michael [29 September] for Your Consolation's instructions.

Farewell.

letter to the beginning of the abbacy of Bernard (II) of Saint-Victor of Marseille (ca. 1065). Closer analysis of the text, however, indicates that the letter was written early in the abbacy of Bernard III, who took office sometime between 1124 and 1127. See Jean Dufour, Gerard Giordanengo, and André Gouron, "L'attrait des 'leges': Note sur la lettre d'un moine Victorin (vers 1124/1127)," *Studia et Documenta Historiae et Iuris* 45 (1979): 504–29, and Peter Classen, "Richterstand und Rechtswissenschaft in italienischen Kommunen des 12. Jahrhunderts," in Classen, *Studium und Gesellschaft im Mittelalter*, Schriften der Monumenta Germaniae Historica 29.(Stuttgart: Hieresmann, 1983), 39–40.

2. Frederick I Barbarossa's Imperial Decree: *Habita* (1155/58)

After carefully considering this matter together with the bishops, abbots, dukes, and all the judges and magnates of our sacred palace,[3] we bestow this pious gift upon all those who travel for the purpose of study, students and especially teachers of divine and sacred laws: namely, that they as well as their messengers may travel safely to the place where they are engaged in the study of letters and safely dwell there. Since those who do good deserve our praise and protection, we consider it appropriate that we, with particular affection, defend from every injury all whose knowledge illuminates the world and directs our subjects to obey God and us, his minister. Who among them ought not to be pitied? Made exiles through their love of knowledge, they exhaust their wealth and impoverish themselves, expose their lives to every danger, and suffer unwarranted bodily harm at the hands of the vilest men. Truly, this is a most heavy burden. Therefore, by this general and eternally enforceable law we decree that from this time forward, no one should be so bold as to inflict any injury upon students, or impose upon them any penalty stemming from a debt incurred by someone else from their province—a thing which we have heard is done on occasion, in accordance with a perverse custom. Let those rash enough to disregard this holy law know that they shall be forced to restore to the local authorities, fourfold, the goods that they have seized, and that they, marked by the infamy which this law imposes, shall be deprived of their offices [*dignitas*] forever. Nevertheless, if anyone should wish to bring a charge against these [students] on account of some matter, let him call them into the presence of their lord, their master, or the bishop of the city, to whom we have granted jurisdiction in such cases;[4] and let the choice among these [persons] be made by the student. Whoever attempts to hale them before another judge shall forfeit his case, even if it be thoroughly just, on account of his attempt. We command, moreover, that this law be added to the imperial constitutions under the title "Let no one for his father. . . ." [C. 4.13].

Translated from *Friderici I. Diplomata inde ab a. MCLVII usque ad a. MCLXVII, MGH DD F I*, 10/2, ed. Heinrich Appelt with Rainer Maria Herkenrath and Walter Koch (Hannover: Hahn, 1979), 39–40.

3. At the Imperial assembly, or Diet, held in November 1158 at the plain of Roncaglia (near Piacenza). *Habita* appears to have been based on a privilege issued by Frederick I in 1155 to the legal scholars of the Bologna *studium*; see Appelt in *Friderici I. Diplomata*, 38.

4. Frederick represents himself as the successor of Justinian, the great codifier of Roman law, who made a similar provision for those studying law at Berytus (Beirut) in his constitution *Omnem* (§10), which prefaced the *Digest*.

3. Bulgarus of Bologna (d. ca. 1166), "A Synopsis of Ignorance of the Law and the Facts"

Since "the laws ought to be understood by everyone" [C. 1.14.9] and known by everyone, it is clear that anyone who is ignorant of the law and thereby suffers some harm does not deserve any assistance. Thus, if you are unaware of the *Lex Falcidia*,[5] fail to take advantage of it, and pay out legacies[6] completely [D. 22.6.9.5; cf. Inst. 2.22, D. 35.2]—that is, you do what you should not do—or if you are unaware of the edict and fail to seek *bonorum possessio*[7] within the allotted time—that is, you neglect to do what you should do—then you cannot be helped [C. 1.18.3, D. 22.6.1.1].

You should be deprived of help even more readily if, unaware of natural law or the law of peoples, you either shamelessly summon your patron to court (i.e., do what you should not do) [C. 2.2.2] or do not show your patron the respect due to him (i.e., neglect to do what you should) [cf. D. 44.4.4.16]. Indeed, the situation of one who knows the law and one who is ignorant of it is the same.

Ignorance of the facts is a different matter [D. 22.6.2]. If you pay someone in the belief that proper arrangements had been made, or do not seek *bonorum possessio* because you did not know that a relative had died [D. 22.6.1.1], or do not show respect because you are unaware that someone is your patron, then as long as your ignorance of these things is plausible, it is appropriate for you to be excused. For while ignorance of the facts can allow one to profit, it is even more the case that it harms no one in the avoidance of loss [D. 22.6.4, 8]. Nevertheless, "a case that has been settled cannot be reopened on the basis of a factual error" [C. 1.18.7].

Sometimes it so happens that complete ignorance merits assistance. If you divide an inheritance, left to you alone, with another person and without seeking a judge (for, as it is said, "a case that has been settled cannot be reopened"), but do so in the belief that a will existed when it did not, or that a particular law applied when in fact that law had not been properly carried

Translated from "Bulgari de iuris et facti ignorantia summula," in Hermann Kantorowicz and William Warwick Buchland, *Studies in the Glossators of the Roman Law: Newly Discovered Writings of the 12th Century* (Cambridge: Cambridge University Press, 1938, repr. 1981), 244–46.

5. The *Lex Falcidia*, enacted during the reign of Augustus, prevented testators from leaving more than 3/4 of their estates in the form of legacies, thus preserving at least part of the inheritance for the heirs.

6. A legacy (*legatum*) was a distribution from an estate made to someone other than the legal heirs, specified by the testator.

7. *Bonorum possessio* ("possession of goods") referred to a form of inheritance in which a successor other than the legal heir was appointed by the praetor. Under Justinian's codification, *bonorum possessio* was assimilated into the civil law, from which it originally had been independent.

out, then you should be allowed to acquire the entire inheritance. Likewise, you are supported in cases where you pay or promise to pay, in writing, a debt which you were not obliged under law to pay, or which natural law does not require you to honor [D. 12.6.19]. In a similar fashion, you are supported when you seize something in the belief that it is yours, believing that "it is proper for an owner to take by force that which is his" [*Inst.* 4.2.1]. Since you did not seek to deceive, by the same token you are exempt from the punishment for theft.

From these examples, it can be seen that ignorance of the law disadvantages no one in the avoidance of loss [D. 22.6.8], except when something is given or promised because natural law demands it; this is the case where a legacy which the *Lex Falcidia* does not require to be made is required by the wishes of the testator (that is, naturally required), or where the statements [of an individual] make it clear that he was utterly ignorant and not just unaware of the law, and thus should be pardoned [D. 22.6.9.5]. In some other cases, it so happens that the condition of those who know the facts or the law and those ignorant of them is the same. For a false description is prejudicial to no one [cf. D. 35.1.33], just as on the contrary the seller of a defective animal is uniformly judged from the outset to be required to rescind the sale, regardless of whether he knows the law or the facts or is ignorant of them [cf. D. 21.1.2].

Thus it is clear from the previous discussion that when ignorance is claimed [as a defense], a distinction needs to be made about what you were ignorant about, that is, the facts or the law. If the facts are at issue, then there is a distinction between "plausible error" and "utter carelessness" [cf. D. 41.10.5, 22.6.6]. In cases of error about the law, there is a distinction between natural and civil law, because it is a greater offense to be unaware of natural law than to be ignorant of civil law. Likewise, there is a distinction to be made regarding whether errors in civil law have to do with criminal or business issues. It is easier to be forgiven in business dealings, as when a minor makes a loan to someone's [dependent] son [see D. 4.4.11.6, 7], but not when someone commits a crime. But it remains to be seen whether the former case requires a defense or an accusation. For if [a minor] erroneously gave money to a [dependent] son, he would not charge that the latter had accepted a loan, but rather would offer this fact in his own defense [cf. D. 22.6.9 *praef.*].[8]

8. According to the *Senatusconsultum Macedonianum* of 46 A.D., those who made loans to dependent sons (*filiifamiliae*) could not recover their money, since the latter could not legally enter into agreements without their fathers' involvement; a number of exceptions were made by later jurists, however, including cases in which minors had made such loans. Cf. D.14.6, *De senatus consulto macedoniano.*

Figure 12. Lecture on law, University of Bologna (fourteenth century). Relief from
the tomb of Matteo Gandoni (d. 1330). Bologna, Museo Civico. (Photo: Scala/Art
Resource)

Cases in which your request for aid is prejudicial also should be eliminated. You may not seek help that would contravene someone's freedom [cf.
D. 4.4.9.6], or a declared judgment, or a debt paid in accordance with natural law. Further, it should be asked whether a person might be protected by
privileges issued to him, as in the case of a soldier, who is eligible for relief
from a judgment so long as he has not yet made payment [C. 1.18.1]. Minors,
as we have seen, likewise enjoy such a privilege, and a woman who makes a
payment in ignorance of the law is assisted in those circumstances described
by earlier statutes [C. 1.18.11 and 13].

46. ODOFREDUS ANNOUNCES HIS COURSE ON ROMAN LAW AT BOLOGNA (ca. 1230)

Translated from Latin by M. Michèle Mulchahey

Because the organization of academic life at the University of Bologna was largely in the hands of the incorporated student body, the masters who sought teaching posts in the city often needed to appeal to the students themselves for contracts. Here we see the Italian jurist Odofredus (d. 1265) describing his method of teaching, his mildness toward his pupils, and the thoroughness of the coverage of Roman law he can offer, in an effort to win paying students. Odofredus was no uncredentialed newcomer to the field: he had studied under the great Accursius, who had done much to revive the study of civil law at Bologna at the turn of the thirteenth century, and had practiced as an advocate in both Italy and France before returning home to look for work as a teacher. And yet, he, too, must advertise.

If you please, I shall begin with the *Old Digest* on the eighth day after the feast of St Michael [29 September] or thereabouts and shall finish it completely, through both ordinary lectures [offered during normal morning class hours] and extraordinary lectures lectures [given at other times], by roughly the middle of August, Providence permitting. The *Code* I shall always begin within about a fortnight of the feast of St. Michael and, Providence permitting, I shall finish it, with both ordinary and extraordinary lectures, on the first of August or so. The extraordinary lectures used not to be given by the doctors. And so, with me, all scholars, including the unskilled and novices, will be able to make good progress, for they will hear the text as a whole, and neither will anything be left out, as was once done in this region, indeed it was the usual practice. I shall indeed teach the unskilled and novices, but advanced students as well: the unskilled will be able to make satisfactory progress in the stating of the case and the exposition of the letter of the law; the advanced students can become more erudite in the subtleties of questions and contradictions. I shall also read all the glosses, which was not done before my time. . . .

For it is my intention to teach you faithfully and in a kindly manner, in which instruction the following order has customarily been observed by the ancient and modern doctors, and particularly by my own master, which method I shall retain. First, I shall give you the summaries of each title before I proceed to the text; second, I shall give you as clear and explicit a statement as I can of the purport of each law contained in the title; third, I shall read the

Translated from Friedrich Karl von Savigny, *Geschichte des römischen Rechts im Mittelalter* (Heidelberg: J.C.B. Mohr, 1822), vol. 3, 501–2.

text with a view to correcting it; fourthly, I shall briefly restate the meaning of each law; fifth, I shall solve all apparent contradictions, adding any general principles of law to be extracted from the passage (which are commonly called *brocardica*) and any subtle distinctions or useful questions arising out of the law together with their solutions, as far as Divine Providence shall enable me. And if any law shall seem deserving of a review by reason of its fame or difficulty, I shall reserve it for an evening repetition.

47. THE LAWS OF KING ROGER II (ca. 1140s)

Translated from Latin by G. A. Loud

This collection of laws is the earlier of two related texts purporting to contain the legislation of King Roger (1130–54), the founder of the Kingdom of Sicily. The manuscript dates from the late twelfth century. It is believed that the text represents genuine legislation of King Roger, and possibly a law code promulgated in the 1140s. For example, we have clear evidence that a number of these laws were in operation during the mid-twelfth century, notably assize xxvii. It should be noted, however, that only some of this legislation is original. More than half the laws below were reworked versions of Roman Law precepts of Justinian, probably derived from a collection of extracts rather than directly from the Code and Digest.

I. ABOUT THE INTERPRETATION OF LAWS

We order that the laws newly promulgated by our majesty, mitigating through piety excessive harshness and thus encouraging benevolent rule, and elucidating what is obscure, should be fully observed by all. Because of the variety of different people subject to our rule, the usages, customs, and laws which have existed among them up to now are not abrogated unless what is observed in them is clearly in contradiction to our edicts here.

II. ABOUT THE PRIVILEGE OF HOLY CHURCHES

Let all those subject to our power know that it shall always be our intention to protect, defend, and augment in every way the churches of God, for which the Lord Jesus Christ shed his blood, as our predecessors were at pains to do, with their traditional generosity. As a result many and uncountable benefits have always been granted by God to their advantage. Thus we shall defend and guard inviolate all the property and possessions of the holy churches which have been entrusted to our custody, after that of God and the saints, with the temporal sword which has been granted to us by God. We commend this to [our] princes, counts, barons, and all our faithful subjects, who should know that whosoever should attempt to violate our decree shall incur the wrath of our majesty.

III. GENERAL ADMONITION

We advise princes, counts, greater and lesser barons, archbishops, bishops, abbots, and all those who have subject to them citizens, burgesses, peasants,

Translated from Biblioteca Apostolica Vaticana, MS. Vat. Lat. 8782. Much of the material of this manuscript is repeated, albeit in a different order and with some textual differences, as well as with the addition of seven extra assizes, in a Montecassino manuscript of the early thirteenth century (MS. Cassinese 468).

and men of any sort, that they should treat them decently and show themselves merciful particularly when collecting the tax owed, they should demand this in moderation, for [by doing this] they render thanks to God and great joy to us, under whose power and rule Divine providence has subjected both prelate and subject. If this should be neglected, it will be examined by our solicitude with a view to reforming for the better what has been ill done.

IV. About Royal Property

We desire that our princes, counts, all barons, archbishops, bishops, and abbots should know that whoever holds any property great or small from our *regalia* can in no way and by no ingenuity alienate, grant or sell, or diminish in whole or in part anything belonging to our *regalia* in such a way that our *regalian* rights are diminished or abolished or suffer any injury.

V. About the Sale of Holy Relics

We permit no one to sell or barter relics of martyrs or of any other saint. If anyone shall presume to do this, and the price has not yet been fixed, then nothing shall follow, if the vendor wishes to agree with the purchaser; if however money has been paid, restitution shall not be made to the purchaser, who is to hand [them] over to the fisc. It shall be the concern of our providence to punish anyone daring to infringe this, and, with the advice of the bishops, to place the relics where it shall be most suitable.

VI. Concerning Flight to a Church

We order by the present law, which shall, God willing, remain in force in perpetuity, that in all parts of our kingdom nobody in flight of whatsoever condition shall be expelled or dragged out of the most holy churches, nor shall anyone because of them exact from the venerable bishops or *yconomi* [administrators] that which is owed by them. Anyone who shall endeavor or do this shall face capital punishment or the loss of all their property. Meanwhile food shall not be denied to the fugitives. However if a serf or colonus or serf of the glebe[1] shall have fled from his lord or shall have fled with stolen property to holy places, he shall be returned to the lord with the property which he has taken, that he may be punished according to the nature of the crime which he has committed, or, if intercession has occurred, restitution shall occur piously and freely.

---

1. The three types of peasants included here were distinguished by origins and/or function.

VII. About Not Violating the Privileges of Churches

Whosoever shall dare to violate the privileges of holy church shall, once the offense is removed, pay compensation according to the harm done to the church; if he shall not be able to pay the fine to which he is condemned the matter shall be committed to the judgment of the king or the arbitration of his officials. Nevertheless he shall be subject to the providence of the king and the arbitration of his officials about the scale of the offense.

VIII. About the Privilege of Bishops

The bishops shall not be compelled to give testimony unless, however, in ecclesiastical or state cases, when authorized by necessity or royal authority.

Priests shall not be compelled to make corporal oath in [secular] matters. We order that deacons, subdeacons, and those below, placed as ministers to the holy altar, shall be strangers to servile restrictions, and we quite prohibit that priests, though not the others, be subject to personal servile dues.

IX. Concerning Illicit Conventicles

We forbid illicit conventicles to be celebrated outside a church in private houses under threat of the immediate demolition of the house if its lord has knowingly received clerics in it who celebrate new and unruly conventicles.

X. About Serfs Wishing to Become Clerics

No bishop should presume to ordain serfs without the desire and assent of the persons to whose right and power they are subject, nor [anybody] from another diocese with letters of commendation either from a bishop or from their own chapter, following the institutes of the canons.

If those with whom they are enrolled [as serfs] should be convicted of having received any reward for having given permission for their ordination, they will lose the right of adscription and the one who has given the money shall be degraded from his orders and sold with all his property on behalf of the fisc.

It so happens that on sacred occasions wickedness obstructs sacred desires and disturbs the service of God and the ministry of the church. But no evil should be allowed to hinder our laws at any time. If, for example, there shall have been priests assigned to a church in the country or in a village, and after their deaths others must be substituted, and the lords of the country place or village refuse to allow the bishop to make a substitution from among the serfs, especially when the bishop is looking for a suitable person from among these serfs it appears worthy and most just to our clemency that on the just petition of the church the lord of the serfs should be corrected by the law. But the sons of a deceased priest should be returned to the condition of serfs, without any appeal.

XI. About the Rape of Virgins

If anyone presumes to rape holy virgins veiled by God, even for the purpose of marriage, he shall suffer capital punishment, or other penalty which royal censure shall decree.

XII

No Jew or pagan shall dare either to buy or sell Christian servants, or to possess them by any title [whatsoever], or to hold them as a pledge. If he should presume to do this all his property will be confiscated to the fisc, and he shall become the servant of the Court. If he should by some wicked trick or persuasion have the servant circumcised or make him deny his faith, then he shall be punished by capital penalty.

XIII. About Those Apostatizing

We curse thoroughly those who apostatize from the Catholic faith. We pursue them with vengeance. We despoil them of all their goods. We withdraw the protection of our laws from those who break a promise or vow, we abolish their right of inheritance and cancel their every legitimate right.

XIV. About Jesters

Players and those who make jokes by bodily writhing shall not use in public either the habits of virgins dedicated to God or monastic or clerical vestments. If they should do so they shall be publicly flogged.

XV. About Wards and Orphans

Through considerations of piety many privileges are confirmed by ancient laws to wards and orphans which through passage of time have fallen into disuse. We entrust and favorably commend [these laws] to our judges since their abandonment is intolerable.

In addition we settle the equity of the laws on women, who are not less disadvantaged by the fragility of their sex. We order that they should be aided from the depths of piety both by us and by our officials, as is right and proper.

XVI. About Those Unworthily Aspiring to the Priesthood

No one should dare to seek the dignity of the priesthood by paying money, and they should receive disgrace and punishment [in recompense] for the price paid as soon as this [crime] is by their own action detected. For he who seeks this honor by such an importunate and impudent manner should be deprived of it.

XVII. ABOUT THOSE WHO COMMIT SACRILEGE

There should be no dispute about the judgment, plans, decrees, or deeds of the king, for to dispute his judgments, decrees, deeds, and plans, or whether he whom he has chosen or appointed is worthy, is comparable to sacrilege.

Many laws have punished sacrilege most severely, but the penalty must be moderated by the decision of the one who is judging, unless perhaps the temples of God have been openly and violently despoiled, or gifts and sacred vessels have been stolen at night, for in that case the crime is capital.

XVIII. ABOUT THE CRIME OF TREASON

Whosoever should start a plot, whether with one knight or with many, or on his own, or should give an undertaking or oath to a plot, that plans and prepares the murder of one of the illustrious men who are among our councilors and advisors, they have by their wish to commit evil, chosen for themselves severe legal punishment. The culprit should be struck down by the sword as guilty of treason and all their property should be confiscated by the state. Their sons should indeed receive no benefit whether by our generosity or by legal right. Let death be a blessing to them and life a punishment. If however anyone shall have denounced what has been done by the conspirators without delay, he shall promptly receive pardon and grace.

The crime of treason also encompasses those who discuss and attack the reputation of the king after his death, so that anyone who should do or be a party to this will from that day on be treated as a criminal and have no protection, but everything that they have shall be sold according to the laws of the fisc.

He who shall purge a relative of a crime deserves succession to them.

All those by whose advice hostages escape, citizens are armed, plots are fomented, tumults excited, magistrates killed, men desert from the army or flee from the enemy, allies are betrayed, military formations are cloven asunder by wicked tricks, battles lost, fortresses abandoned, help denied to allies, and other things of this type [are done] shall be considered guilty of this crime, as will he who spies on, corrupts, or publishes the king's counsels, as well as he who knowingly gives shelter and renders assistance to the enemies of the kingdom.

XIX. About New Knighthood

Consenting to divine justice, we approve what must be approved and reject the contrary. For just as good must not be exasperated, so evil should not be benefited. Therefore we order and propose this edict, that if someone should seize new knighthood contrary to the happiness, peace, and integrity of our kingdom, he will lose completely the name and profession of knight, unless perhaps he is descended from the stock of a knightly family. We order the same about those who receive the order of any profession, as for example if they obtain the authority of a judge or the office of a notary, or others similar.

XX. About Forgers

A person who alters royal letters or seals what he has written with a spurious seal should suffer capital punishment.

XXI. About Coining Money

We impose capital punishment on and confiscate the property of those coining adulterine money or knowingly receiving it; we inflict this penalty [also] on those conspiring [in this].

We deprive those who shave gold or silver coins, dye them, or in anyway diminish them of their property and their lives.

XXII

Where a case of forgery occurs, diligent inquiry shall follow promptly, with proofs, witnesses, comparison of scripts, and other indications of the truth; not only shall the accuser be examined for proofs, but the judge shall be the arbiter between both parties, that when all the evidence finally agrees he shall impose sentence. When proved, capital punishment shall follow, if a punishment of that magnitude is merited, or another penalty depending on the seriousness of the offense.

XXIII. About a Forged Document

Whoever uses a false document unwittingly shall not be punished for the crime of forgery.

Whoever furnishes a falsehood with witnesses should be punished with the penalty for forgery.

XXIV. About the Concealment of Wills

Someone who removes, conceals, destroys, or alters wills and public instruments shall be subject to the same penalty.

If anyone destroys his father's will, in order to succeed as though to one [who died] intestate, shall be deprived of the inheritance from his father.

XXV. About Public Officials

The status of the person aggravates or diminishes the punishment for fraud. Officials of the state or judges who have, during their period in office, stolen public revenues [are guilty of] the grave crime of embezzlement and shall be punished capitally, unless royal piety spares them.

XXVI. About Public Properties

Anybody who has allowed public property to be lost or diminished through his own negligence should be considered guilty and liable through his own person and property, at the discretion of royal piety.

Anybody who knowingly gives assent to what has been done shall be liable to the same legal penalty.

XXVII. About the Legitimate Celebration of Marriages[2]

Since it belongs to the care and solicitude of the kingdom to draft laws, govern the people, instruct them in morals, extirpate evil customs, it seems right and equitable to our clemency to rescind by the sternness of our edict a certain evil custom which, as though some damage or pestilence, has for a long time and up to the present crept into use by part of our people, to prevent burgeoning vices spreading to the rest. For it is contrary to custom, inconsistent with what is laid down by the holy canons, and unheard of to Christian ears to desire to contract matrimony, procreate legitimate progeny, and bind oneself indissolubly to a consort, unless seeking the favor and grace of God in these matters of marriage and "concerning Christ and the Church" as the Apostle says [Ephesians 5:32], by confirming the sacrament through the priestly ministry. Thus we decree by the present law, which (God willing) shall last in perpetuity, that it is necessary for all those wishing to contract a legitimate marriage to have the marriage solemnly celebrated after the

---

2. Emperor Frederick II would later offer the following modification of Roger II's law in his thirteenth-century law code: "TITLE XXII—A wife should not be married without license of the court: In order to preserve the honor due to our crown, we order by the present constitution that no count, baron, or knight, or anyone else who holds in chief from us baronies or fiefs registered in the records of our diwan, should dare to marry a wife without license. They should not dare to marry off their daughters, sisters, or granddaughters, or any other girls, whom they can and should arrange marriages for, or to marry off their sons with movable or immovable property, notwithstanding the contrary custom which is said to have been observed in some parts of the kingdom." *Liber Augustalis or Constitutions of Melfi Promulgated by the Emperor Frederick II for the Kingdom of Sicily in 1231*, trans. James M. Powell (Syracuse, N.Y.: Syracuse University Press, 1971), 117–18.

betrothal and each for his own measure and comfort to take the path to a church and priestly blessing.

After the examination he shall place a ring of value and they shall submit to priestly prayer, if they wish to bequeath succession [to their property] to their future heirs. Otherwise they should know that they are acting against our royal precept and would have no legitimate heirs either by will or by intestacy from those born to an illicit marriage contrary to our law; the women would have no right to the dowers proper for those legitimately married. We relax the rigor of this law to all those who have already contracted marriage at the time of its promulgation. We also relax the chain of this necessity for widows desiring to [re] marry.

XXVIII. About Adulteresses [see also #92]

Moved by the piety to which we owe our whole being, we decree by the present general law that whenever a charge of adultery or fornication is put before those who, through our foresight and enactment, control our laws, they should pay no attention to status, but should clear-sightedly note the conditions and ages, and investigate the state of mind [of the parties] to establish whether [it was] of set purpose or from advice received or because of the perils of youth that they have rushed into the act, or whether they are fallen women; [to establish] whether the womens' financial means are weak or strong, and whether they have been motivated by wilfulness or by a particularly unhappy marriage; in order that, once all these factors have been investigated, proven and clarified, either a more lenient or a more severe sentence may be passed on the crimes committed, not on the basis of the severity of the law but on that of the balance of fairness. For, if we proceed in this way, justice will tally perfectly with divine justice; nor will we be departing from that divine verdict, "with what measure ye mete, it shall be measured to you once again" [Matthew 7:1].

The harshness of the laws has been softened so that she shall not, as once, be struck down by the sword but that the property belonging to her shall be subject to confiscation, if she shall have no legitimate children from this marriage or another. For it is most unjust that those who were born at a time when the law of marriage was legally preserved should be defrauded of their inheritance. And she should certainly not be handed over to her husband whose anger would imperil her life, but rather the punishment for the violation of a marriage should be slitting of her nose, which [punishment] has been most sternly and cruelly introduced. However neither her husband nor her relations should be permitted to harm her further. If her husband is unwilling that such a penalty be inflicted on her, we will not allow a crime of this sort to go unpunished, and we order her to be publicly flogged.

Whoever allows his wife to be wanton with debauched men while he looks on or by his arrangement, cannot easily accuse her in court, since he who consents to what he could forbid opens the way to fraud.

We shall not condemn everyone who has a suspect wife as a pimp; for who rightfully disturbs the peace of another's marriage? But if we learn clearly that someone has a lascivious wife, we shall immediately from this time hold her worthy of strict punishment, and we condemn him to the penalty of infamy.

Known prostitutes shall not be thought worthy to observe these laws and shall stand absolutely immune from the judicial punishments for adultery and fornication.

XXIX. About the Same Issue

A woman who has frequently exhibited her body for sale and revealed herself publicly as a prostitute is freed from accusation of this crime [i.e., of adultery], however [while] we prohibit violence to be done to her, we forbid her to dwell among women of good reputation.

An adulterer and an adulteress cannot be charged together. Each should be charged separately and the outcome of the matter awaited; for if the adulterer is able to clear himself, the woman is free and need make no further defense. If however he shall be found guilty then let the woman in turn be accused.

The law does not make a choice of who should be first tried, but if both are present then the man shall be tried first.

Divorce must always be permitted in this accusation, and neither violence nor detention should be employed.

XXX. About Pimping

We decree by the present law that madams, namely those who solicit the chastity of another, which is the worst type of crime, should be punished as adulteresses.

We punish mothers who prostitute their virgin daughters and abandon the bonds of marriage as madams, thus their noses should be slit. For it is cruel and inhuman for them to sell the chastity of their own offspring. But if a daughter prostitutes herself and the mother only consents, the matter shall be left to the decision of the judge.

XXXI. About the Violation of Marriage

If our royal majesty's providence refuses in any way to permit one of our barons to invade the *castrum* of another within the bounds of our kingdom, or to plunder it, to make an armed attack on it or to take anything from it by fraud, to prevent him by this act depriving him of its property; then by how much more do we hold him punishable if he should presume to violate the marriage of a fellow and neighbor? It seems that the law must not tolerate this. Therefore we decree that if anyone shall be accused to us of such a deed, and it be clearly proved, they shall be deprived of all their property.

     If a husband catches his wife in the very act of adultery, then he shall be allowed to kill both the wife and the adulterer, provided that it is done without any further delay.

XXXII. About Adultery

The legal penalty for pimping binds a husband who shall seize his wife caught in the act of adultery but has allowed the adulterer to get away, unless however the latter escaped through no fault of his own.

XXXIII. About Those Failing to Make an Accusation

He who receives back his wife after the crime of adultery has been proved seems to have abandoned the accusation, and thus cannot raise any further charge.

XXXIV. About Injuries Inflicted on Private Persons

What is fully in agreement with law and reason is indeed welcome to all, and what is not agreeable to all on grounds of equity is manifestly unpleasing. For it is not to be wondered at if, when something which God has most carefully and properly placed in man is negligently and contemptuously held in no account by wrong judgment, the wise man and lover of honesty is rightly indignant. For is it any more absurd that a stricken mare be compensated when its tail is cut off, and when a most respectable man be deprived of his beard? Therefore on the suggestion and plea of the subject people of our kingdom, and realizing the defects of its laws, we pronounce this law and edict, that if any ordinary person be deliberately and intentionally deprived of his beard, then those convicted of having done this shall have the following penalty imposed, namely a fine of six golden royal *solidi*. If however this was done in a fight, without being planned beforehand, then they shall be fined three *solidi*.

XXXV. About Injuries Inflicted on Curiales

Judges should most diligently observe that they consider the dignity of *curiales* [members of the court] in any case of injury; and that they impose sentence according to the quality of the persons, both of those who were injured and of those who inflicted the injury, and where and when such a rash act was committed. They shall impose sentence according to the quality of the persons; for strictly speaking injury was done by them not to the persons themselves, but in fact should be seen as an offense to the royal dignity.

XXXVI. About Those Wishing to Become Physicians

Whoever in the future desires to become a physician should present himself to our officials and judges, for an examination according to their judgment. But, if he should rashly take this for granted, let him be consigned to prison and all his property confiscated. For this had been arranged so that subjects of our kingdom shall not be put at risk through physicians' inexperience.

XXXVII. About Kidnappers

Whoever knowingly sells a free man shall be subject to this legitimate penalty, that the person sold shall be redeemed from his property and that the criminal himself shall become a slave of our court, and the rest of his property shall be confiscated. If the man who has been sold cannot be redeemed, then he [the criminal] should be handed over as a slave to the victim's parents, and his property awarded to the court. In any case where the man who has been sold shall return, the criminal shall become a slave of the court, and his sons born after this case shall be subject to the court in perpetual slavery.

XXXVIII. About Robbers

He who, thinking his life to be in danger, shall kill an attacker or robber, ought not to fear blame for his action.

XXXIX. About Children and Madmen

If a child or madman shall kill a man without evil intent, he shall not be held accountable. For the one is excused by reason of innocence, the other by his unfortunate condition.

XL. About Theft

He who shall kill a nocturnal thief shall remain unpunished, if the latter could not be arrested while the hue and cry was raised.

XLI. About Arsonists

Whoever sets a house on fire by deceit should suffer capital punishment as an arsonist.

In criminal matters the intention shall be taken into consideration, not the result; for there is no difference between someone who kills and one who seeks to cause death.

XLII. About Those Who Throw Things

Whoever hurls himself down from on high and kills a man, and whoever incautiously and without shouting a warning hurls a branch or throws a stone or some other implement and kills a man, shall be subject to capital penalty.

XLIII. About Poison

Whoever gives, sells, or possesses evil or harmful medicines which affect the mind, or poisons, shall be subject to capital penalty.

Whoever prepares a love potion or some other harmful food, even if he harms no one, shall not go unpunished.

XLIV. If a Judge Neglects His Duty

If a judge receives money and then declares someone guilty of a crime and of death, then he shall be subject to capital punishment.

If a judge fraudulently and deceitfully hands down a sentence contrary to the laws, then he shall lose his judicial authority without hope of recovery, be branded with infamy and all his property shall be confiscated. However, if he makes a mistake in sentencing through ignorance of the law, he shall be punished for his simplicity of mind and be subject to our royal mercy and foresight.

48. A PEACE CONTRACT (1274)

Translated from Latin by Katherine L. Jansen

Although it is often thought that peace contracts were a privilege of the magnate classes, research in notarial archives shows that all classes of people, including the popolo minuto, *availed themselves of this legal remedy. Peace instruments (or agreements) were contracted by two parties wishing to put an end to mutual enmity. Drawn up by a notary and often enacted in the local parish, peace contracts allowed the disputing parties to resolve their differences without having to go to court and for minimal expense. Consequently, they were an effective means of keeping the peace and putting an end to feud and vendetta inside and outside the medieval city. The peace instrument translated below is a standard "boiler-plate" contract which, as is often the case, does not disclose why the parties were disputing in the first place. This text, from the casebook of the notary Ildebrandino d'Accatto, like most other notarial documents, was recorded in a register with hundreds of other contracts treating everything from real estate transactions to dowry settlements. Notaries, it should be observed, dealt with many matters which today would be handled by a lawyer or solicitor.*

PEACE MADE BETWEEN RINALDO DOMINICHI AND HIS SONS AND TUCCIO DE VITIANA

Made and Given.

Likewise, on the same day [11 September 1274] and enacted in the parish of Antella [about 3 miles southeast of Florence] with the witnesses Lord Bonamente of the parish of Antella and the priest-canon Aiuto and Lapo Benci and others present.

Rinaldo Dominichi and Bene, called Ceregia, and Albertescho, called Toscho, brothers and sons of the aforesaid Rinaldo (the said brothers by the consent and authorization of their father), pledging themselves to each and everything written below, are one party. And Tuccio, son of the late Guido de Vitiana is the other party. Both parties on behalf of themselves, their sons and heirs, and descendants of the male sex make and give peace, reciprocally among themselves, and a perpetual end to all malice, assaults, wounds, offenses, and blows which one party made against the other, or had made or had been made in fact on the aforesaid day in whatever way. And one party promised the other to attend to and observe in perpetuity the aforesaid peace and not to violate it or do anything for any reason or cause against it, under a fine of 50 *fiorini piccoli*. Under the pledge of his own goods, if any party,

Translated from the notarial register of Ildebrandino d'Accatto, Archivio di Stato di Firenze. *Notarile Ant.*, 11252, fol. 35r.

UNIVERSITY OF WINCHESTER
LIBRARY

violating the party of good faith, contravenes [this agreement] he is obligated
to give and to compensate both damages and expenses and to abide by the
contract. And the said parties will renounce noncustomary exceptions and
ecclesiastical privileges and all other [legal] exceptions.

Likewise, the said Tuccio promised and agreed with the aforesaid
Rinaldo and his sons thus to make and ensure that Segnorino, his brother, at
that time when he reaches legitimate age, will make peace and put an end [to
hostility] with the said Rinaldo and his sons, as outlined above. And that he
will pledge and renounce and do as the said party, as above, and under the
same penalty, etc.

49. REGULATING CONSUMPTION
AND RITUAL BEHAVIOR
FOUR TEXTS (1289–1343)

Translated from Latin by Catherine Kovesi Killerby

The late Middle Ages saw a remarkable growth in Italy's trade and manufacturing economy, in particular in the area of luxury goods. Italian governments, however, felt some ambivalence toward the new wealth and its expression in elaborate cloth-ing, gift-giving, and wedding and funeral ceremonial. While recognizing the posi-tive benefits of the luxury industry and the wealth and honor which it could bestow upon their communities, they were wary of public displays of finery and of ceremo-nial which might disrupt the social and moral status quo and dissipate sources of capital. From the thirteenth century, governments of all persuasions across the Ital-ian peninsula began to legislate against expenditure and public display, especially in women's clothing, by means of so-called sumptuary laws. The difficulties of legis-lating in this area are clearly indicated in the laws translated below with their endless subclauses. Even more problematic was enforcement, with governments using a range of methods from fines, secret denouncers, enforcement officials, and even excommunication.

1. [Bologna 1289]

Concerning the penalty for those bringing gifts to any betrothal ceremony:

It is prohibited for anyone to bring, or to send, or to have brought on their behalf, or through any other way, tricks, or means, to any betrothal cere-mony, or to any person on the occasion of their betrothal, any gift in any quantity, and anyone who contravenes this is to be penalized for each occa-sion with a fine of twenty-five bolognese *lire*. Item. We declare that neither of the betrothed, nor any other person acting for them is to receive said gifts in any way, through tricks or other means under penalty of thirty bolognese *lire* for the spouses themselves or another recipient on their behalf and the person in whose house the said gifts were received or placed. And we declare that no one is to invite more than ten men or ten women from either side: that is to say, of the groom or the bride, to any feast that is held on the occasion of a betrothal or wedding; and whoever contravenes let him be pun-ished and convicted, that is, that man who organized the party, by a fine of twenty-five bolognese *lire*. And whoever ministered the sacrament is to

Translated from L. Frati, *La vita privata di Bologna dal secolo xiii al xvii*, 2nd ed. (Bolo-gna: Zanichelli, 1928), 267–68.

denounce and accuse those contravening. And the groom cannot bring more than three companions to the feast, or, including the person of the groom himself, no more than four at the most. Item. we declare that at the time of the said feast there are not to be more than three kinds of courses, excluding fruit. And that no one is to send any other courses, or to have the feast outside the house, and whoever contravenes the aforesaid shall be condemned for each and every offense to the sum of 100 bolognese *soldi*. And anyone whosoever can denounce or accuse offenders, if the aforesaid occurs in the city or district of Bologna. And the *podestà* shall make known publicly the aforesaid throughout the city and district of Bologna, in the usual places, within fifteen days of beginning his term in office. And equally the *podestà* together with the venerable father Bishop of Bologna can decide that the venerable father should pass a sentence of excommunication against the aforesaid or any other offenders. And this sentence of excommunication is to be declared through the chapels and churches of the city and district of Bologna each year on the feasts of the birth and of the resurrection of our Lord.

2. [Brescia, mid-thirteenth century]

Item it is ordered that no woman is to go near a dead body under penalty of 100 Brescian *soldi* for each offense. And no one is to make any speech over the body. It is permitted, however, for whoever so desires to say "go and leave with the Lord," And the *podestà* must pronounce this precept in the first or second council meeting. And no pall is to be placed over any dead body.

3. [Siena, 28 June 1343]

And concerning the aforesaid [ordinance restricting the depth of décolletage], the said [sumptuary] official is obligated to go, or to send his notary, on feast days through the city to where festivities are celebrated and to other places which women frequent. And if he should come across or see any woman with a low-cut dress or which he believes to be cut lower than the measurements allowed by the present ordinance, the said official is to demand a confession from the said woman or from two or three of her companions

(2) Translated from A. Cassa, *Funerali, pompe e conviti* (Brescia: Bresciana, 1887), 35.[1]

(3) Translated from Archivio di Stato, Siena, *Statuti del Comune di Siena*, n. 28, cap. 41, transcribed in Eugenio Casanova, *La donna Senese del quattrocento nella vita privata* (Siena: Lazzeri, 1901), separately published extract from *Bullettino senese di storia patria* 8, no. 1: 65.

1. The Brescian statutes and provisions of the thirteenth century are in great disorder. All we can say with certainty is that this provision was passed sometime between 1200 and 1300.

that the said dress is indeed cut below the said measure. And, if she or her companions reply that the said dress is cut too low, she may lawfully be condemned for said offense. And, if this woman or her companions refuse to so swear they shall be considered as though they have confessed. And, if her response should be "no," so that the said official cannot make measurements of the said dress at that time, she is to be held to the law and she must remove her dress and send it to the house where the said official lives either on that day, or the following day before the third day, and said woman must swear on the Holy Gospels that the dress which she has sent to the house of the said official has in no way been altered either by herself or by any other person, either directly or indirectly.

4. [Lucca, 11 April 1337]

That no woman or female, of whatever state or condition, may dare or presume to wear on her head or on her person any pearl, in or out of her house, under penalty of losing the said pearl, and furthermore under penalty of ten *lire* for each offense; and the husband shall be held accountable for the wife, the said fine being paid from her dowry, by which it is intended that the said woman's dowry be diminished. And if she has no husband, the said fine is required to be paid by the father of the said woman or indeed by those under whose authority the woman's goods are held on behalf of the said woman. Also, she must not possess or wear on her head, inside the house or outside it, garlands or other types of head ornaments worth more than three gold florins. In the same way she shall not wear any pearl, according to the penalty stated above, to which fine she would be subject in the same manner and form. And the aforesaid does not include headcloths, braidings, little cords, or silk plaits, which may be worn as one pleases without penalty. And a permitted garland or crown must be stamped.

Also, no woman, or female, as stated above, may wear any belt, of any type or name, that exceeds the value of four gold florins, under the said penalties and means, and the said belt must be stamped. Also, no goldsmith of the city of Lucca, or its villages and district, or anyone else who lives in the city of Lucca, may dare or presume to make or manufacture any belt of gold or silver that exceeds the value of four gold florins: and goldsmiths are obligated to place in the clasp or buckle the value of the object or of the silver, under penalty of ten *lire* for each person and each offense.

Also, no woman or female may or presume to wear on her mantle, or

Translated from S. Bongi, *Bandi lucchesi del secolo decimoquarto: Tratti dal registri del R. Archivio di Stato in Lucca* (Bologna: Del Progresso, 1863), 47–54.

clothes, or furs or head coverings, in any manner or style, any ornament of gold, silver, or any other metal. With the exception that on hats that women are accustomed to wear when riding it is permitted to place clasps, but only of brass, subject to the above penalties. With the exception that they may wear without penalty their mantles and clothes and hats which have those ornaments woven of gold and silver thread, since they are in clothes already made. And if it were to happen that in place of ornaments of gold, or of silver, or of other types of metal, she wishes to have an ornament, she may place or have such an ornament, or have placed ornaments of gold or silver threads, up to the value of ten *soldi* of good money for each *braccio*, provided such ornaments are removable.

And to ensure that no fraud shall be committed by anyone, each woman, who already possesses ornamented clothing, is obligated to have it stamped by the deputed official between now and the following month.[2] Otherwise she is not permitted to wear those clothes, under the aforesaid penalty. Truly, however, she is permitted to wear any of those fabrics already stamped from the period of messer Simone Filippi, as they are, without penalty and without having to have any other stamp newly made on them.

In clothes that are in truth newly made, no ornament or decoration of gold, silver or any other metal, may be placed or worn. With the exception that it is permitted to anyone to trim or have trimmings of little ornaments made on their clothing in whatever manner they wish, and truly, if so placed they cannot attract the said penalty.

Also, no female or unmarried girl may wear any newly made dress worth more than eight *lire* of good money per *canna*, under the penalty of twenty-five *lire* for each person and each offense, the which fine must be paid according to the method described above. Also no married woman may wear any new dress worth more than fifteen *lire* of good money per *canna*, under the said penalties and manner. But it is permitted for young girls up until the time they marry, to wear clothes that have already been embroidered and cut, without penalty, as they like, and on their new clothes they may place stripes and braidings of sendal or of silk.

Also, no woman or female who has been married may wear any clothes of woolen cloth, in or out of the house, whether of one color, or mixed or indeed striped or checked or bi-colored, above the aforesaid value. On top of those clothes, or others, it is not permitted to have any novelty of any cut

---

2. Governments recognized that their laws would often mean that citizens would have to have new clothes made and so incur extra expenditure. To try to avoid this, in several cities they instituted the practice of registering clothes and ornaments that had been made before the law came into force and stamping them with a special seal.

design or embroidery, or of sendal or of braiding or of other things, and this applies to clothes that are yet to be made, and not to those clothes already made, under the same penalties and methods. Clothes made truly of simple silk, devoid of any novelty of cut or embroidery may be made, owned, or worn without penalty. And cloaks of one color or bicolored may be worn on which are placed stripes or braidings of silk or of sendal.

Also, no female or woman, of whatever condition, may dare or presume to make, or have made, or wear any new mantle, or any clothes of velvet under the said penalty and method. And these rules do not include mantles or clothes already made, which must be stamped, if not stamped already, as already stated.

Also, no woman or female above the age of nine may dare or presume to wear any clothes that have forked trains; and this does not include those forked trains that have straight seams, according to the same penalties and methods. And these points refer to those clothes that are newly being made, and not to those already made.

Also no female of whatever condition, may dare or presume to drag or pull a train along the ground on any clothes that she has on her back to a length greater than one *braccio* and a half. And the above rules pertain to those clothes that are newly being made, and not to those already made and stamped, as is stated above, under the said penalties and methods.

Also no tailor or tailoress or other person can or dare cut, sew, or work on, or have cut or sewn any clothes of the types and manner forbidden above, for themselves, or any other person, in the city or without, to any or for any citizens of Lucca, or for others, against the aforesaid manner, under the penalty of twenty-five *lire* for each item of clothing and each person contravening.

Also, no female, of whatever condition, may dare or presume to have and to wear on her back or over herself anything other than gray squirrel fur (*vaio*) under the same penalties and methods.

Also, no woman or girl over the age of seven may dare or presume to have made for her any hose by any hosier nor by any of their apprentices under penalty of one hundred *soldi*, which must be taken from the said woman or girl for each infringement. And that no hosier or his apprentice may dare or presume to make hose for any woman or girl against the stated form, under the penalty of twenty-five *lire* for each person and each offense, and the master shall be held responsible for his apprentice.

Also, at any nuptial mass that is held in any manner, no one is permitted to give, offer, or dispense any money to any person except the bride, who may alone receive a small offering, and not more, under the said penalty.

Also, no groom may give, for himself or for any other person, any wide belt, or belt hung with pendants, or any other type of belt or bag that exceeds the value of two florins, or any money, or any other thing, prior to his wife being formally led to his house; nor shall he give such things to any other person for her under the penalty of losing said gift, as well as a fine of twenty-five *lire* for each person and each contravention. And the above points do not refer to gifts which are usually given either before or as gifts for weddings. Neither do the above points refer to those things that the husband sends, or has sent on his behalf, to the wife on the vigil of her formal transfer to his house, at which the bride comes dressed and adorned to the husband: so long as they do not exceed the form and manner of the present ordinance.

Also that the gifts that are sent from the wife's side to her husband's house on the occasion of her formal transfer to his house are to be carried in coffers or chests so that no one can see them, under the penalty of ten *lire* for each person who contravenes; and that they may not give more than two coffers and one little coffer, to a combined value, between coffers and little coffer, of three florins at the most, under the said penalty. And when the bride shall come to the house of the husband, the said gift may not be exhibited in an obvious manner among the women, on the said day. And the said wife, or other person on her behalf, may not herself give, or others give on her behalf, anything to her father-in-law, or her husband's brothers and sisters, or any other person of the said husband's household or family, under the penalty of twenty-five *lire*, as well as the loss of those items.

Also, no female, or girl, or indeed any wife, whoever she may be, either from the city of Lucca or from elsewhere, if she live at Lucca, may go by horse in the city or surrounding villages and district, if not with two male companions, under the penalty of five *lire* to each one who contravenes the order; the said fine will be obliged to be paid by those who belong to the house from which the female leaves to go out. And similarly, the penalty applies to those who accompany her.

And those who denounce the woman shall have half of the penalty, and their names shall be kept secret. And the aforesaid matters do not extend to girls or females who are being formally married, who, at such times may be accompanied by whomever they want without incurring any penalty. Also, no woman or female, of whatever condition, may dare or presume to wear on her finger more than two rings, under the penalty of ten *lire* for each time; but it is permitted for one of the rings to contain a pearl.

Also no female of whatever condition, except for lay sisters, members of a third order, nuns, and religious women, may go about the city and district, with a mantle on her head, unless it is raining, in which case she may wear on her head the hem of her mantle, under penalty of 10 *lire* for each person who should contravene, and for each contravention. Except for women who are left widows, on the day their husband is buried, or indeed the day of their husband's wake, they may wear a mantle on their heads without a penalty of any kind.

Also, no maid or servant may dare or presume to wear on her head any plaits or headwear, unless it is made from her own hair, nor plaits of silk or of raw silk; nor other head cloths of silk, of whatever value, or of linen if it exceeds the value of twenty *soldi*, nor binding of any head cloth over her forehead, under the aforesaid penalty. And no maid or servant may wear low-cut clothes other than those which are appropriate for them. And these cannot have or dare to make, or have made for them any new clothing, any over-gown (*guarnaccia*) or shift (*gonnella*) or other type of clothing of which the price exceeds four *lire* of Lucchese *denari* per *canna*: the said cloth must also be of one color only, or mixed, and not any other style, under the aforesaid penalties.

And these same may not have or wear any trains, or cloak (*giubba*) nor long ribbons, or belt, in which or on which there is gold or silver; nor any ribbon or cord of silk, nor bag of silk, nor slippers (*pianelle*) or high-heeled clogs (*soccoli*) decorated in gold or silver or indeed pinchbeck, nor buttons of silver, imitation silver, or enamel on their over-gown under penalty of ten *lire* for each person and each offense, according to the methods where such contraventions are mentioned in the chapters written above. And if the said penalty cannot be paid within ten days, she shall be whipped through the city. These same restrictions, in all details, are applicable to all, including single women who live on their own in any house, who are not married, and who keep or have whores, against whom one can provide proof. And by full proof is meant that it is known through public notoriety or by four men of good status and reputation. And this chapter does not apply to widows or girls who live honestly.

50. REGULATION OF BROTHELS IN FLORENCE
TWO TEXTS (thirteenth century, 1346)

Translated from Latin by Lynn Marie Laufenberg

The following law, concerning the establishment and operation of brothels in Florence, dates from the late thirteenth century and formed part of the city's oldest surviving municipal legislation. Although prostitution was widely discouraged by ecclesiastical authorities, even the great theologian Augustine of Hippo (354–430) had advocated tolerating the practice in order to provide an outlet for the sexual impulses of unmarried males who, he argued, would otherwise turn their attention to the honorable wives and daughters of fellow citizens. The Florentine law relegated prostitutes, along with lepers and public baths, to the peripheral areas of the city. This law remained on the books, in subsequent revisions, throughout the fourteenth century. The legislation seems to have proved ineffective, however, as the second document illustrates. In 1402, the Florentine government changed its policy and licensed the first of several official, municipally sponsored brothels within the city limits. This practice was widespread throughout late medieval Europe.

1. The Thirteenth-Century Law

Concerning not maintaining brothels and prostitutes, and concerning brothel-operators and pimps, and not selling women, and the penalties for these things.

It is established and ordained that no person, of whatsoever condition or status, shall dare or presume to hold or to cause to be held or to permit in his or her own house or in another's house in the city, suburbs, or surrounding territory of Florence, a public brothel or prostitutes or any public prostitute who openly would offer her body in the service of lust for money or gain; neither near the ancient walls of the city within a thousand *braccia*, nor in the suburbs or territory within two hundred *braccia*, nor near any religious houses or any church within forty *braccia* etc. And if it should happen that any brothel, or any such public prostitute, stays or lingers within the city, suburb, or territory of Florence, let any such house in which she has stayed (with no exceptions admitted) be destroyed, and the building and furnishings revert to the commune [the government of the Florentine republic] and let such a prostitute be whipped, and the pimp who retains her be punished

Translated from Giuseppe Papaleoni, "Nuovi frammenti dell'antico Costituto Fiorentino," in *Miscellanea fiorentina di erudizione e storia*, ed. Iodoco Del Badia (Florence: S. Landi, May 1886), vol. I, 73–74. The original is located in the Archivio di Stato di Firenze, Conventi Soppressi (Convent of Santa Croce). Though undated, the manuscript was written by the notary Noro di Gozzo da Pelago, whose earliest documents date from 1279.

[with a fine of] two hundred *lire fiorini piccoli* for each prostitute. If indeed it [a brothel] is found outside of the city, suburb, or surrounding territory, but in a prohibited location as mentioned above [that is, near a convent, monastery, or church], let the pimp be punished in the aforesaid manner, and the master of such a house be fined one hundred *lire*, and the prostitutes whipped in the same manner throughout the countryside. And let the *cappellani* and rectors of the community in which, contrary to the aforesaid ordinances, a brothel is located or prostitutes are lingering, be obliged to denounce the situation to the lord *podestà* or his judges within eight days, under a penalty of twenty-five *lire*. And let four nearby neighbors, that is, two from on either side of the brothel, be required to denounce [any such occurrences] to such *cappellani*, who, if they have neglected the aforementioned, shall be fined one hundred *solidi* for each one of the neighbors [who fails to make such a report]. And any neighbor whosoever may accuse and denounce concerning the aforesaid matters; and let him have one half of the fine, and let the presumption of credibility rest with him.

I, Norus Gozzi de Pelago, judge by imperial authority and notary, have set forth all the aforesaid from the constitution of the commune of Florence, and for that purpose I have written.

2. Judicial Condemnation of a Brothel-Keeper in Late Medieval Florence (1346)

The following sentence is typical of the condemnations issued for those who violated Florentine regulations concerning brothels and prostitution. Such sentences surface in the criminal records of the republic's legal tribunals throughout the late medieval period.

Condemnation by the criminal court of the *podestà* in February 1346 of Bice, daughter of Corso Rigarotti and resident of the urban parish of San Lorenzo. The court found that

Bice . . . publicly ran a certain house located in the city of Florence, and retained in it Francisca, the woman [*femina*] of Salvestro nicknamed "Bestial," and Tessa, the concubine of Stefano di ser Giovenchio, both public prostitutes in the said parish of San Lorenzo. And Francisca and Tessa and others like them were located and stayed in the said house and openly offered their bodies in the service of lust for monetary gain to anyone wanting to know them carnally. And the aforementioned was committed by the said women as described above [in the accusation] during the *podestà*'s term in

Translated from Archivio di Stato di Firenze, *Atti del Podestà*, vol. 136, fol. 36r.

office in the present year. And concerning the foregoing, it was and is common knowledge that the house is located next to the street of San Gallo at a distance of less than five *braccia*.

An addendum states that the court determined the charges were true through examination of witness testimony. Bice was sentenced to a 500-lire fine. Unable to pay it, she was placed in the communal prison of the Stinche. On 2 May 1347 the government cancelled Bice's sentence as part of an oblation of prisoners made on 17 April 1347. Twice a year, on Easter and on the feast day of the city's patron Saint John the Baptist, the Florentine government released a certain number of prisoners from the municipal prison as an act of mercy.

51. THE LONG ARM OF THE FLORENTINE LAW
TWO TEXTS (1343, 1345)

Translated from Latin by Lynn Marie Laufenberg

The following two criminal sentences were issued by the podestà, *the supreme judicial magistrate in Florence. Both concern offenses that occurred outside the city limits, in the surrounding territory* (contado) *that was politically and legally subject to Florentine dominion. Local officials in the towns and villages of the* contado *were required to refer all serious crimes committed in the outskirts back to the courts in Florence for trial and sentencing. It should be noted that Florentine laws forbade women to enter most civic buildings, such as the* Palazzo Signoria. *They were only admitted to the judicial palace of the* podestà *if they were to be tortured. Otherwise, they conducted any legal business, such as lodging accusations, testifying, or delivering confessions, with the notary at the front doors of the palace.*

1. Sentence Issued by the *podestà* (1343)

[We condemn] . . . Lapa, widow of Pietro; Diana, widow of Bartolo di Lapo; Bertina, daughter of the deceased Conte di Lippo; Pisa, wife of Piero di Venco; Lapa, widow of Conte di Lippo; and Gianne di Lapo, son of the deceased Lippo, all residents of Signa . . .

When Argus Brandini of the parish of San Lorenzo of Florence, messenger of the commune of Florence, and Beato Tornensis and Agnolo di Nato, assistants of the lord executor of the Ordinances of Justice, were sent by Berto di Tinero of the parish of San Pietro Maggiore and by the mandate of the judge of civil cases for the quarter of Santa Croce in order to seize Niccolò, son of the deceased Piero and inhabitant of . . . Signa, on account of a debt to the said Berto di Tecino for seven gold florins, they captured the said Niccolò. And the messenger and the officers seized the said Niccolò for the debt and were taking him to the fortress of Florence to detain him there when all of the aforementioned [individuals], simultaneously and with other companions, assaulted and struck and sprang upon Agnolo and Beato with wooden clubs and an iron pitchfork and an iron spade. And some of them . . . [cried] . . . "Filthy thieves!" And the aforementioned Lapa and Diana and Bertina and Pisa and Lapa and Gianne by force and violence . . . extracted the said Niccolò, [who had been] captured for debt, from the hands of the said messenger and caused him to flee.

The rector of Signa denounced the group to the criminal judge in the court of the podestà *in Florence. None of the group answered the summons and they each were*

Translated from Archivio di Stato di Firenze, *Atti del Podestà*, vol. 23, fols. 365v–366r.

fined between 50 and 150 lire, *in absentia. (Fifty* lire *represented, very roughly, the equivalent of three to four months wages for a skilled worker in the mid-1340s.)*

2. Sentence Issued by the *podestà* (1345)

[We condemn] . . . Lippa, wife of the deceased ser Bonsignore of Montesper-toli and daughter of lord Nero de Giandonati of Florence. . . .

That the said lady Lippa, contrary to the form of the laws, statutes, and ordi-nances of the city of Florence, knowingly received, kept, and harbored in the house of her residence . . . ser Dantonio di ser Bonsignore de Montespertoli, banned and condemned by the commune of Florence personally for crimes: that is, for the homicide of Francesco, son of the deceased Tendo . . . of Montespertoli, committed by him during the term in office of the *podestà*, the magnificent and powerful man lord Giovanni Marchionis. And he was also banned and condemned in person for crimes committed by him against Stefano Tosini of Villa San Lorenzo in the district of San Miniato. Item . . . that Lippa knowingly and contrary to the form of the laws, statutes, and ordinances of the city of Florence, received, kept, and harbored in the said house of her residence . . . Nerio di ser Bonsignore de Montespertoli, banned and condemned to a fine of 400 *lire* by the commune of Florence for wrong-doing during the term of the noble man Necciolo de Gabrielibus of Gubbio, former captain and defender of the *contado* of Florence, for having received and kept the said ser Dantonio. The aforesaid matter is established by us and by our tribunal to be true . . . on account of the confession of the said Lippa . . . freely made before [the notary] by the said Lippa in front of the doors of the *podestà*'s palace.

Lippa was convicted and sentenced to pay a 60-lire fine. Since she was unable to do so, she was detained in the municipal prison.

Translated from Archivio di Stato di Firenze, *Atti del Podestà*, vol. 127, fols. 366v–367r.

52. BARTOLUS OF SASSOFERRATO ON THE MAKING OF CITIZENS (fourteenth century)

Translated from Latin by Julius Kirshner and Osvaldo Cavallar

Bartolus (1314–57), among the most authoritative Italian jurists of the Middle Ages, produced architectonic commentaries on Justinian's Corpus iuris civilis, *several legal tracts, and hundreds of legal opinions. Although the specific events leading to the composition of his opinion on citizenship remain a mystery, it is likely that the requesting party was a judicial official seeking clarification of whether or not a new citizen is a true citizen. The official requesting a legal opinion was bound by law to adhere to it in his ruling. In addition to acquiring citizenship by statute, one could become a temporary citizen because of rank and status—for example, the rank of university professors and the status of students entitled them to various privileges of citizenship during their tenures or period of studies [see #14.2]. Following Roman law, the citizenship of a legitimately born person in medieval Italy was grounded in one's place of origin* (origo), *where one's father was a citizen, not where one was accidentally born. Likewise, an adopted person acquired the citizenship of the adoptive father—a rarity, however, in the Middle Ages. Children born out of wedlock automatically became citizens of the mother's* origo. *No matter how one acquired citizenship, Bartolus determined, civil law dictates that all citizens should be treated as true citizens.*

The case is this: someone is made a citizen of a city by a statute or an enactment. The question is whether this person is truly or improperly called a citizen? Regarding this question, it should be known that being a citizen is not the result of an act of nature but of civil law. This is evident, first, from the name itself, since the term "citizen" derives from "city." Second, because a city does not arise from natural law and one does not become a citizen by simply being born there. It is the decree of civil law, therefore, that makes someone a citizen because of place of origin, rank, or adoption.[1] And it should not be said that some are citizens by nature, others by civil law. On the contrary, it should be said that all are citizens by civil law: some on account of natural origin, others on account of another reason. Consequently, if a city enacts a statute to the effect that whoever has a house in the city is a citizen, that person is truly a citizen.[2] And whoever is admitted by the city to perform

Translated from Julius Kirshner, "*Civitas sibi faciat civem*: Bartolus of Sassoferrato's Doctrine on the Making of a Citizen," *Speculum* 48 (1973): 694–713, at 713.

1. C.10.40(39). 7, *Cives quidem origo*. Bartolus supported his arguments by reference to the *Codex* and *Digesta* (see # 45).
2. D. 50.16.139, *Aedificia*; D. 50.16.190, *Provinciales*; D. 1.5.17, *In urbe Roma*.

public services is truly and properly a citizen. Since in the case at hand the person was admitted to perform public services, this person is truly and properly a citizen.[3] Therefore, this person should be treated as a citizen of the city which makes him a citizen. And so I, Bartolus of Sassoferrato, counsel.

3. D. 50.1.1, *Municipem aut.*

53. A TRIAL FOR WITCHCRAFT AT TODI (1428)

Translated from Latin by Augustine Thompson, O.P.

This trial, carried out against Matteuccia Francisci of Ripabianca, is among the oldest examples, if not the oldest of a trial for diabolical sorcery (commonly called "witchcraft") in Italy. As the canonical rule that inquisitors were not to hear cases concerning sorcery unless they hint at heresy (Boniface VIII, Liber Sextus, 5.2.8) was usually observed in Italy, this case was heard before the secular court of the Captain of the People of the City of Todi, Lorenzo de' Surdi of Rome. In comparison to southern Germany, where trials for diabolic sorcery were already common in this period, trials like this were relatively rare in Italy. There is reason to believe that the occasion of this local crackdown on sorcery was related to the anti-sorcery preaching of San Bernardino of Siena in the preceding year. Although Matteuccia did not confess to making a pact with the devil, she admits, perhaps under the threat of torture, to the other elements usually considered essential to the early modern idea of the "witch": shape-shifting, night-flight, attendance at the sabbath, and spell-casting.

The Process Against Matteuccia Francisci of the Village of Ripabianca, Charged with Witchcraft

Todi, 20 March 1428.[1]

I. In the Name of God. Amen. This is the corporal condemnation and sentence of corporal condemnation, issued, given, put in writing, pronounced, and promulgated as a sentence, by the magnificent and powerful gentleman, Lorenzo de' Surdi of this City, honorable Captain and Protector of the Peace of the city of Todi and its outer territory and district, on behalf of the Holy Roman Church and Our Most Holy Father and Lord in Christ by Divine Providence, the Lord Pope Martin V, under the direction of that eminent gentleman and expert in law, Lord Tommaso de Castiglione of Arezzo, Judge for Witchcraft of the aforementioned Lord Captain, with the consent, pleasure, and consultation of that gracious Doctor of Laws, Lord Pietro de' Ricchardini of this City, Associate of the said Lord Captain.

This has been written, corrected, translated, and published by me, Novello Scudieri of Bessano, Public Notary and now, among other offices, Notary and Secretary for Witchcraft by the deputation of the same Lord Captain, in the Year of Our Lord 1428, during the Sixth Indiction, in the reign of Our

Translated from Candida Peruzzi, "Un processo di stregoneria a Todi nel '400," *Studi Storici* 21 (1955): 7–17; the passages of Umbrian dialect are here indicated by italics. Original Todi, Archivio Communale MS (18), 20 bis, fol. 21v–23v.

1. 1429 in modern usage; the Umbrian year started on 25 March.

Holy Father and Lord in Christ by Divine Providence, the Lord Pope Martin V, on the day and month indicated below.

II. We the aforesaid Captain Lorenzo, sitting in Tribunal at our accustomed Court for the Judgment of Witchcraft at the site and location from which like corporal condemnations and sentences of corporal condemnation are accustomed to be given, pass and, by these instruments, pronounce, in the manner given, the sentence of the corporal condemnation as indicated below on Matteuccia Francisci for the faults, transgressions, and crimes of witchcraft, done, committed, and perpetrated by her, to wit:

III. We are formally proceeding, by the means and by way of investigation, against Matteuccia Francisci of the village of Ripabianca in the territory of Todi, a citizen, and considered and reputed as a citizen in conformity with the statutes of the commune of Todi, a woman of evil life and reputation, a known sorceress, charmer, spell-caster and witch, on the charge, concerning the charge, and in respect to the charge, which has not once but many times been brought to the ears and attention of the aforementioned Lord Captain and his Court, that, as a fact of common knowledge, as is evident from earlier corroborating reports coming not from hostile or suspect sources but rather from truthful individuals and persons worthy of belief, the said Matteuccia, having not God but the Enemy of the Human Race before her eyes, in 1426, 1427, 1428, and earlier from the age when she had discretion, many times and in countless places, enchanted those suffering in the body, the head, or other members, either personally or by means of tokens (such as belts, hair, and like items) that had been brought to her on behalf of many different people of various places, because of the above-indicated and other illnesses, so that she might measure the said belts with pleats and say her incantations.

IV. And that, not satisfied with the above but so as to add evil upon evil, incited by the Diabolical Spirit, in 1426 and the period immediately following: she enchanted more than twenty . . . [persons from various?] . . . places possessed by spirits or having specters, who had come personally before her, while to those absent . . . [she sent?] . . . belts or other tokens, by reciting the following words: *Every little-striker, every little-springer, every little-specter; there, let him remove it, let the earth take it, and let it harm no Christian.* She said these words three times to the one afflicted, or she measured a belt three times with pleats, which, when measured, if it was large, she folded along the three pleats. And when the above-indicated words had been said, she spat three times on the ground while holding a lighted candle in her hands.

V. And that, not satisfied with the above, incited by the Diabolical Spirit and piling evil upon evil, in the year 1426 and immediately following up to the present day, she enchanted a very great number who were suffering pains in their members, by reciting these words: *In the name of the Father, and of the Son, and of the Holy Spirit, and of Our Lady Mary with all the saints, and of Saint Peter who sets every evil aright, and of the blessed saint who was physician of the Christ who, physician and not unwise, did not abolish curing by means of the Holy Scripture, the moon, the sun, and our Lord God; may you flee accursed and not nourish yourself on blessed flesh; go off to the bottom of the sea because this soul can suffer no longer; and do not persist, do not cause defilement, do not vaunt yourself, do not cause pain, do not bring on me weakness any longer.* These above-indicated words she said three times.

VI. And that, not satisfied with the above but so as to add evil upon evil, in the above-indicated 1426 and after: she enchanted many suffering body pains, by reciting these words: *Worm, wormy creature that takes heart and soul, that takes the lungs, that takes the liver, that takes me in the nose, that takes me in the head, that takes me in the feet, that takes every good; Saint Susanna, to the outside send it out; Saint Julitta, to the outside cast it out; Saint Bruna, return to the arse, to the outside cast it out, from one to another, until none remains. Amen.* Saying these words thrice she threw three grains of salt in the fire.

VII. And that, not satisfied with the above but so as to add evil upon evil, incited by the Diabolical Spirit: she told a great number of those possessed by specters or spirits who had came to her for remedies, to get a pagan bone, that is one from the tomb of an unbaptized, and bring it to a crossroads and then, placing it there and saying the "Our Father" nine times with nine "Hail Marys," she said these words: *Pagan bone, remove it from this one, and you take it.* Having done this and leaving, she let nine days pass before she returned to that road; and if she returned within nine days, the specter would return to her. And she did this for a man from San Martino in the territory of Perugia, who was nearly a simpleton, because he had become possessed from sleeping on a certain tomb. This happened in 1426 or there about.

VIII. And that, not satisfied with the above but so as to add evil upon evil, before the arrival of Fra Bernardino [of Siena] she introduced many different people from different places to charms and spells.

IX. And that, not satisfied with the above but so as to add evil upon evil, incited by the Diabolical Spirit, she gave instruction to a very great number of men infatuated with women who came to her. And showing them a remedy, she gave them a certain bundled herb, enchanted by her incantations, which they were to give to their beloved to eat, and they were to take the wash water from their own hands and face and give it to them to drink, so that they might have their will with them and direct their love toward themselves. She has done this many times at the changing of the four seasons, from then until the present day.

X. And that, not satisfied with the above but so as to add evil upon evil, before the arrival of Fra Bernardino at the city of Todi and in 1426 and 1427, on a great number of occasions, for different people from different places, she made charms from hair wound with pieces of parchment, placing them under hearths and beds, so that women might be loved by men and vice versa, reciting these words: *I do not see you; but that one be seen, that one which is the hidden heart of the body; stay enclosed, as stayed Christ in the tomb; stay fixed, as stayed Christ crucified; return to my homeland, as Christ returned to his mother.* These words were to allow men to get their way with women and vice versa.

XI. And that, not satisfied with the above and not having God before her eyes, incited by the Diabolical Spirit, in 1426, when a certain man had drowned in the Tiber, she arranged with a certain day laborer of the Branchi [family], who was called Cortona from the city of Cortona, that this Cortona would go to the said man drowned in the Tiber and get some flesh with fat from the said drowned man and bring it to her, so that she might make a fluid from the same cooked flesh. Cortona did this and he brought it to her and they made some fluid or oil from the said flesh, which oil was used for people's aches and injuries.

XII. And that, not satisfied with the above but so as to add evil upon evil, in 1426, when the woman of a certain priest in Castelpodio of the city of Orvieto came to the said Matteuccia, saying that her said priest did not love her and would not have sex with her and that just that day he had been beating her, and asking the same Matteuccia to provide her with some remedy to make him love her again, the the same Matteuccia told her to make a certain image of wax and bring it to her; and the said woman, having done as told, brought the said image to the said Matteuccia. Having taken the image from her, the said Matteuccia and the said woman set it beside the fire, and the same image was slowly consumed. The same Matteuccia told the said woman to recite the following words: *As this wax melts, so may my love's heart melt until he does my will.* When this had been done and some time had passed, the said woman returned to the said Matteuccia and said that she had obtained whatever . . . she wanted from her said priest, and that he had fallen back in love with her.

XIII. And that, not satisfied with the above but so as to add evil upon evil, in 1420, when a certain husband and wife from the village of Collemedio in the territory of Todi arrived in the village of Ripabianca, and the said wife came to the said Matteuccia to talk about her husband, saying that he treated her badly, and asking the same Matteuccia to give her some remedy that would force her husband to make restitution for the numerous and great indignities he visited on her daily, the same Matteuccia gave the aforesaid woman an egg and the herb that is called Horse-Tail [*equisetum arvense*], and she told her to cook them together and give them to her said husband to eat, so that he would become deranged for several days. And the said woman did this and the said man was deranged to the point of insanity for three days.

XIV. And that, not satisfied with the above but so as to add evil upon evil, incited by the Diabolical Spirit, in 1427, when a certain woman by the name of Catarina from the territory of Orvieto came to the said Matteuccia, saying that she had a husband who loved her little and beat her daily and asking the same Matteuccia to give her a remedy, Matteuccia told her to make a certain image of wax and bring it to her, that is, the said image to the aforesaid Matteuccia. When she had the image, the said Matteuccia wound it with the belt of a virgin girl and told the same Catarina to put the said image under the bed of her said husband, reciting these words: *Stay by yourself, as Christ stayed by himself; stay fixed, as stayed Christ crucified; return to me, as Christ returned by himself; return to my will, as Christ returned to his homeland*. She said that these words were to be recited three times and the said image was to be placed at the head of the bed of her said husband, and he would be subject completely to her love and will.

XV. And that, not satisfied with the above but so as to add evil upon evil, in 1422 during the month of March, when there came to the same Matteuccia a certain young boy who loved as his beloved a certain young girl whom he had long wanted to have as his wife, but was unable to have her because the relatives of his beloved refused to consent since they wanted to make her the wife of another, and he requested from the same Matteuccia a remedy so that such and such would happen to prevent the aforesaid bridegroom and bride from getting along well together and having sexual relations with each other, this Matteuccia, having the Diabolical Spirit before her eyes, told the aforementioned young boy to take a certain lighted blessed candle and bring it with him to a certain crossroads and, while the groom and bride were at their wedding, to extinguish that same candle and pray using these words as well as other even worse diabolical ones: *As this candle bends in this heat, so may bridegroom and bride never be united in their love*. When this was done, she said he should place the said bent candle in a safe place, and that, as long as it stayed bent, the husband and wife would remain unable to have sexual relations. She has worked this charm for many people and in different places, and she has had it done by others.

XVI. And, on the charge, concerning the charge, and in respect to the charge that, not satisfied with the above but so as to add evil upon evil, in 1427 in the month of May, when a certain woman from the village of Pacciano in the territory of Perugia, who was infatuated with a certain man, came to the same Matteuccia and asked her to make a remedy what would make him love her so much that she could obtain whatever she wanted, the aforementioned Matteuccia told her to gather some reeds, burn them, and put their ashes in the drink and food of the one she loved, so that she might obtain whatever she wanted from him.

XVII. And that, not satisfied with the above but so as to add evil upon evil, in 1427 in the month of December, when a certain Giovanna from the village of San Martino in the territory of Perugia came to the said Matteuccia to discuss her husband, who she said was keeping a concubine, spoke to the said Matteuccia about why her said husband did not love the same Giovanna but treated her badly, and requested advice about regaining the love of her said husband, the said Matteuccia told her to get a certain reed, flavor it with sugar, and give it to her said husband to eat, and then to wash her own feet and give wine mixed with that water to him to drink.

XVIII. And that, not satisfied with the above but so as to add evil upon evil, she told a certain woman from Mercatello, who had asked a remedy from her on account of her husband because he loved her very little and was always out talking to other women, to take and burn some of her own hair and, when it was reduced to ashes, put it into her husband's food and drink, so that by so doing she might make him love her. She did this in 1427 in the month of October.

XIX. And, on the charge, concerning the charge, and in respect to the charge that, not satisfied with the above but so as to add evil upon evil, the same Matteuccia gave instructions to a great and uncountable number of women who had been beaten by their husbands and asked remedies from her to make them love them and do their will; to wit, that they take the herb which is called Horse-Tail and, having ground it up, give it to their husbands to drink or eat, reciting these words: *I give you to drink, in the name of the specter and of the enchanted spirits, and may you be unable to sleep or rest until you do what I would command you.* She did this in many different places, in particular in the territory of Perugia, in 1427 during the months of June, July, August, September, and October.

XX. And, on the charge, concerning the charge, and in respect to the charge that, not satisfied with the above but so as to add evil upon evil, in 1427 during the month of December, when certain men from the village of Panicale in the territory of Perugia came to the same Matteuccia bringing a feather wrapped in a certain piece of parchment, which they had found in a certain pillow, and saying that these appeared to be charms, because they had a certain cousin in the said village of Panicale, whom they believed to be enchanted since he was going about deranged, and they had found the said wrapped up feather in the pillow on which he slept, the said Matteuccia taking the said feather into her hands and reciting an incantation, destroyed the said charms and told them to take it back to the said village of Panicale and burn it there.

XXI. And, on the charge, concerning the charge, and in respect to the charge that, not satisfied with the above but so as to add evil upon evil, in 1427 during the month of November, when a certain woman, the wife of a certain man who was called Poverello of the Castello of Deruta came to the said Matteuccia saying that she had a certain sick son[-in-law] who could not be freed from his sickness, and that she believed he had been charmed by a certain other woman with whose husband her daughter had slept several times, the said Matteuccia told her to search under the·edge of the hearth in her daughter's house to find the charms there and burn them. A few days after this had been done, the aforesaid woman came to the same Matteuccia, along with the husband of her said daughter, and said they had found three black animals that looked like mice, which were wrapped in flax mixed with linen and hemp, and that they had burned them, just as the said Matteuccia had said.

XXII. And, on the charge, concerning the charge, and in respect to the charge that, not satisfied with the above, but so as to add evil upon evil and incited by the Diabolical Spirit, in 1427 during the month of December, when a certain maid-servant came to the same Matteuccia and said to the aforementioned Matteuccia that she was in love with a certain man, and that, if this were possible, she wanted to stir up animosity to make the said man leave his wife and love her, the aforementioned Matteuccia, to grant her what she wanted, told the said woman to wash her own hands and feet, with these inverted backward and kneeling with her feet folded backward, and, when she had so washed, to take that water and throw it where the husband and wife passed, with the idea, intention, and expectation that this would stir up animosity between the said husband and wife. That woman did this and reported to the same Matteuccia that the said water had stirred up such animosity between the husband and wife that within the boundaries established by her they could never be found together and that they hated each other mutually.

XXIII. And, on the charge, concerning the charge, and in respect to the charge that, not satisfied with the above but so as to add evil upon evil, in

1427 during the month of September, the aforementioned Matteuccia took water in which thirty herbs had been steeped, and she intimated to a certain sick man, who was afflicted in his whole body in such a way that he could not walk and who had been brought to her, that to cure himself he should throw it into the street in the said village of Ripabianca so that anyone who passed over the said water would catch the same illness and be afflicted by the same illness, and she intimated to him that the illness would leave that sick man through this potion.

XXIV. And, on the charge, concerning the charge, and in respect to the charge that, not satisfied with the above, at a great number of times, on different occasions, she performed incantations in respect to different persons from different places for the above-indicated purposes. And at various times she made charms and spells in respect to a great number of men and women from different places, intending maliciously to harm them and having before her eyes the Enemy of the Human Race.

XXV. And, on the charge, concerning the charge, and in respect to the charge that, not satisfied with the above but so as to add evil upon evil, incited by the Diabolical Spirit and not having God before her eyes, in 1427 during the month of May, when a certain woman by the name of Catarina from the village of Pieve came to the said Matteuccia so that she would give her a remedy to prevent her from becoming pregnant, because she was not married and had been sleeping many times with a certain priest of the said village and was planning to have sex daily but was afraid that, if this made her pregnant, she would be embarrassed and the fact would come to the attention of her family, the aforementioned Matteuccia told her to take the hoof of a mule and burn it, reduce it to ashes, and drink the said ashes with wine, reciting these words: *I take you in the name of the sin and of the Great Demon, that it might never stick.*

XXVI. And, on the charge, concerning the charge, and in respect to the charge that, not satisfied with the above but so as to add evil upon evil, incited by the Diabolical Spirit, on a great number of occasions, she went as a witch to abuse infants and suck the blood of nursing children at many different times and places. And she also went several times with other witches to the Night-Doings at Benevento and to other Night-Doings, by anointing themselves with a certain ointment made from the fat of a vulture, blood of an owl, blood of nursing children, and other ingredients, and by reciting: *Ointment, ointment, bring me to the Night-Doings at Benevento, over water, over wind, over all bad weather.* And then, after they had assembled, they invoked Lucifer, by reciting these words: *Oh Lucibel, demon of hell, after you were released you changed your name and have the name of Great Lucifer, come to me or send me one of your servants.* And a certain demon would immediately appear before her in the form of a goat, and she herself would turn into a mouse. And, riding on the goat, she would go to the said Night-Doings, always over graves, like a shriek of lightning. And there she would find a great number of other witches, enchanted people, hellish demons, and the Great Lucifer who presided over them. And he would order her and others to go around abusing infants and doing other evils. And then, Matteuccia, after this command was given to her, would go to the many different places that she visited under the instigation and instruction of the same devils, and there abused year-old boys and girls, sucking blood through their mouth and nose, and taking the said blood to make the above-indicated ointment.

XXVII. And, on the charge, concerning the charge, and in respect to the charge that, not satisfied with the above but so as to add evil upon evil and having the Enemy of the Human Race before her eyes, in 1422 during the month of September, the said Matteuccia, bewitched as above, went to the village of Montefalco to the house of a certain woman who was called Andreuzzia, who lived on the outskirts of the said village. And there she sucked and abused that woman's only son, who was not a year old. From this abuse and sucking the said one-year-old became sick and, being wasted, did not thrive.

XXVIII. And, on the charge, concerning the charge, and in respect to the charge that, not satisfied with the above but so as to add evil upon evil, in 1427 during the month of May, the same Matteuccia, bewitched into the form of a mouse as above, along with a witch companion of hers, went to the village of Canale in the territory of Todi, to the house of a certain woman by the name of Andrellina, who had an only son not yet six months old. And they sucked and abused that child as they were accustomed to do.

XXIX. And, on the charge, concerning the charge, and in respect to the charge that, not satisfied with the above but so as to add evil upon evil, in the aforesaid year [1427] during the month of August, she went to a certain manor which was near the village of Andria in the territory of Perugia, to the house of a certain Angelino of the said manor, and, bewitched, sucked a certain son of his, who was eight months old or thereabout.

XXX. And, on the charge, concerning the charge, and in respect to the charge that, not satisfied with the above but so as to add evil upon evil, in the previous year [1428] during the month of August, bewitched, she sucked and abused a certain daughter, aged about seven months, of a certain Andreuzzo and Catarina of the village of Rottacastello in the territory of Orvieto.

XXXI. And, on the charge, concerning the charge, and in respect to the charge that, not satisfied with the above, in 1427 during the month of May on a Thursday, she went bewitched to the manor of Rotella in the territory of Orvieto and there entered the house of a certain Mecharello of the said place. In it, she found a certain daughter of the said Mecharello sleeping in a certain cradle near the bed of the said Mecharello and she abused and sucked that same daughter of his, as she is accustomed to do.

XXXII. And that the said Matteuccia, beyond what has just been said, did sail to the said Night-Doings at Benevento, while asleep, during six months of the year, that is, during the months of April, May, August, September, March, and December, on three days of the week, that is, on Thursday, Saturday, and Sunday.

XXXIII. And that each and every aforesaid item, all reported individually, was committed and perpetrated intentionally by the above-indicated Matteuccia at the above-indicated places and times, in the said village of Ripabianca in the territory of Todi, against the will of those she injured and to their grave damage, in contempt and mockery of God and all the saints, and contrary to Divine Law, good morals, and the letter of statutory law and order in the commune of Todi. And that it has been proved to us and to our Court that, in whole and in part, everything aforesaid contained in this deposition, is true and occurred at the places and times contained in that same deposition, on account of the truthful and lawful confession made spontaneously and lawfully before us and our court by the said accused Matteuccia during her trial. And so she has spontaneously confessed and said that she has neither defense nor time to prepare one, in as much as she spurned the opportunity. The set time granted and assigned to the accused Matteuccia for preparing her whole defense concerning the aforesaid has now elapsed, and neither she nor any other is acting to respond to what is being presented fully and openly to our court or to the other matters contained in our depositions, and so on that account:

XXXIV. We, the aforesaid Captain Lorenzo, sitting as above in tribunal, following and intending to follow in the aforesaid, and concerning the aforesaid, every formality of the aforesaid legal statutes and ordinances of the commune of Todi and of the commission granted to us in this case, by these instruments, following every proper procedure, process, law, and formality that we can and must by law follow, condemn and sentence the aforesaid Matteuccia, present in person before us, in order that she be made an example and be unable to glory in her evil and wickedness or to tempt others attracted to like things, to be placed, with a miter fixed on her head and her hands tied behind her back, on a donkey, and to be led or be caused to be led to the customary public place of justice where like sentences are accustomed to be executed, or to any other place inside or outside the said city that might suit and satisfy that noble gentleman, Ser Giovanni of Lord Antonio de San Nazario of Pavia, our Knight Associate, and there let her be burned by fire in such a manner that she die immediately and her soul be separated from her body (fol. 23v).

XXXV. And let him not proceed to carry out the sentence, unless there is an order for the appropriate execution as follows:

We, the aforesaid Captain Lorenzo, sitting in Tribunal as above, charge, empower, and order Ser Giovanni of Lord Antonio of Pavia, our Knight Associate, here present, listening, and understanding, that he go with our personnel and place the said Matteuccia or cause her to be placed, with a miter fixed on her head and her hands tied behind her back, upon a donkey, and lead her or cause her to be led in person to the customary public place of justice where like sentences are accustomed to be executed, or to any other place inside or outside of the said city that might suit or satisfy the said Ser Giovanni, Knight, and there have her burned by fire in such a manner that she die immediately and her soul be separated from her body, onto the execution of our sentence. And let him present evidence of her execution to us by a public instrument, and let him say and do everything else he is bound to say and do according to the formalities of the statutes and ordinances of the said city of Todi.

XXXVI. The corporal condemnation and the sentence of corporal condemnation, issued, given, put in writing, pronounced, and promulgated as a sentence through the above said Lord Captain, sitting in Tribunal, at his accustomed Court of Witchcraft where like corporal condemnations and sentences of corporal condemnation are accustomed to be given and put forth, which is situated and located in the Great Hall in the Lower Palace of the New Residence of the said Lord Captain, which palace is located in the City of Todi in the quarter of Santa Prassede and the Parish of San Lorenzo, next to the Piazza of the Commune, opposite the Palace of the Lord Priors, during the meeting of the Public and General Council of the said city, summoned by the sounding of the bell and the voice of the herald, and convoked, gathered, and assembled in the said palace in the accustomed way, has been written, corrected, translated and published by me, Novello Scudieri of Bessano, Public Notary, and now, among other offices, Notary and Secretary for Witchcraft, deputed by the same Lord Captain, in the Year of Our Lord 1428, during the sixth indiction, in the reign of Our Holy Father and Lord in Christ by Divine Providence, the Lord Pope Martin V, on the twentieth day of the month of March, in the presence of Ser Polidoro of Todi, the Notary of the Chamber, with whom I audited the said transcript and prepared a duplicate copy, Ser Latino, Ser Corradino, Ser Guaspare, Ser Giovanni, Ser Andrea of Lorenzo, Costanzo of Mannuzio, and Matteuccio the Trumpeter of Todi, assembled, called, and enrolled as witnesses. And I, Novello Scudieri of Bessano, Public Notary by Imperial Authority, and now Notary and Secretary for Witchcraft of the aforementioned Lord Captain, and through the same Lord Captain specially deputed for the exercise of, among others, the said office, was present for each and every part of the aforesaid and, being requested to write them, here have read, corrected, and published them at the command of the said Lord Captain, and have hereto affixed my accustomed seal.

(L.S.)

My Seal, Novello, the aforesaid Notary.

XXXVII. In the same year, during the same indiction, on the twentieth day of March, the aforesaid Ser Giovanni, Knight Associate of the aforesaid Lord Captain, immediately after receiving the commission related above from the said Lord Captain, departed and, returning, reported to the said Lord Captain that he had gone with his officials and personnel and the said convicted Matteuccia, with a miter fixed on her head and her hands tied behind her back, and had placed her and caused her to be placed upon a donkey, and led her and caused her to be led in person to the customary public place of justice, where like sentences are accustomed to be executed, and there executed and caused to be executed on the person of the said convicted Matteuccia the said corporal execution, just as it was fully and completely contained in the commission that he had received in the orders from the said Lord Captain. And he asked me, Novello, the below-indicated Notary, to draw up a public instrument concerning each and every aspect of the aforesaid, to the effect that the corporal execution had been carried out by the said knight, in the presence of Alvisio of Rainaldi of the Nidoli Quarter [of the city] and the Parish of San Felice, Geliello of Marcuzzio of the Valle Quarter and the Parish of San Salvatore, Pietro of Simone of the Valle Quarter and the Parish San Quirico, Pietro of Giovanni of the Camuccia Quarter and the Parish of Santa Maria, who had been assembled, called, and enrolled as witnesses for this purpose.

XXXVIII. And I, Novello Scudieri of Bessano, Public Notary by Imperial Authority, and now Notary and Secretary for Witchcraft of the aforementioned Lord Captain, and specially deputed, through the same Lord Captain, for the exercise of, among others, the said office, was present at each and every part of the aforesaid, and being requested to write them,

I have here read, corrected, and published them at the command of the said Ser Giovanni, the aforesaid Knight, as is above evident from my accustomed seal which I have affixed.

(L.S.)

My Seal, Novello the above-said Notary.

54. A QUESTION OF IDENTITY
IN VENETIAN CRETE (1438)

Translated from Latin by Sally McKee

By the second quarter of the fifteenth century, when the following court case took place, Crete had been a Venetian colony for two hundred years. The population of the island consisted mainly of Greek-speaking adherents of the Eastern Church and descendants of western Europeans, members of the Western (Roman) Church, called Greeks and Latins respectively, in addition to Venetian colonial functionaries who came and went in two-year rotations of service. In order politically to neutralize the Greek nobility on the island, the Venetian Senate excluded Greek Cretans from all political offices and privileges and prohibited marriages between Greek and Venetian noble families. Within a generation after the conquest in 1211 and Venetian settlement, however, the Senate granted permission for a few such marriages to take place. A series of wars led by Greek noble families led to a treaty with Venice, in which the Senate granted many Greek noble families the right to marry into Venetian patrician families.

Sexual relations and marriage between Greeks and Latins on all social levels led to considerable confusion in identifying who was eligible for the status and privileges accorded exclusively to Latins. The court case below centers on Georgius Modino, who underwent a proba—*or examination—to be eligible for administrative and military offices and to gain a seat on the Great Council, the consultative body composed of the male representatives of the island's Latin landowning families. Although Greek Cretan families were barred from membership in the Great Council, several families of Greek descent nevertheless appear in the few membership lists that survive from the fourteenth century. Their membership can be explained by their adherence to the Roman Church, one important distinction in determining who was Latin and who was not. The case is of interest because it demonstrates the difficulties in claiming or ascribing ethnic identity.*

The court notary recorded the two sides of the case in Latin, even though the participants used both the Venetian dialect and probably Greek. The Venetian and Greek names, too, are rendered into Latin. Since the case translated here appears in the court register in Latin, the question arises: should "Georgius Modino" be rendered into the Venetian Zorzi or the Greek Georgos? Was Modino sincere in his claim to be of Latin descent? Or was he a Greek Cretan attempting to profit from an ambiguous, decidedly colonial problem? The lack of unanimity among the prosecutors in pressing this suit or among the court itself signals that there may have been more to the case than meets the eye in the record. The annulment of the sentence six years later creates room for even more doubt about the justice of the verdict. Therefore, to avoid imposing on the reader an answer to the interesting questions raised by the document, Modino's name and those of his relatives are left in the original Latin.

Translated from Archivio di Stato di Venezia, Archivio del Duca di Candia, *Memoriali*, Busta 31, fasc. 40, fol. 54r–55v, no day given, March 1438.

March ___, 1438

In the presence of the magnificent lord Mafeo Donado, honorable duke and captain of Crete, and his council, the nobleman ser Marco Abramo, prosecutor of the commune, has come on his own to intervene in the following matter, since the other prosecutors, the noblemen ser Torino Querini and ser Filippo Corner, do not share his opinion regarding it. With Georgius Modino herein discussed present, he caused to have read aloud the case put forth by the prosecutors regarding the above-mentioned Georgius, who has made a formal claim before the prosecutors to be recognized as one who may partake of the offices and privileges of Crete. When all the documents produced by the said Georgius were read, the prosecutor argued that Georgius is not eligible to partake of the offices, and, thus, he has not proved what he wished to prove. Consequently, [Modino] is liable for the appropriate penalty and he asked the court to rule accordingly. For, in order to be one of those who may partake of the offices and privileges of Crete, it is necessary to be Latin. From the most ancient observance, of which there is no memory to the contrary, even though they may hold fiefs, Greeks have not been given and up to today may not be given any office or benefice belonging to the nobles and feudatories of Crete. This is clear in the court's records, in which no Greek, even if a feudatory, appears who ever held the office of either garrison commander, prosecutor of the commune, magistrate, or lawyer, all of which [offices] from the beginning and to this day are conferred on Latins. Moreover, it must be conceded without prejudice that, although he calls himself a Latin, Georgius is descended from Greeks, who are excluded from such offices. As a result, he must in no way be admitted [to those offices]. That his forebears were Greek is made clear in a certain testament made by Iacobus Modino, who the said Georgius says is his great-grandfather. In the testament, drawn up by the late notary Niccolò Brisano in 1346 on the 11th day of December, fifteenth indiction, no legacy is made to any Latin person or to any Latin ecclesiastic or monastery. Instead, all his legacies, arranged according to the Greek rite, are made to Greek priests and churches. The testament reads as follows: "I leave to the papas Basilio, who officiates in the church of Odigitria in the suburb of Candia, twelve *grossi* for inscribing my name in his *codex*, etc." In explanation, the prosecutor said that Greek priests are accustomed to writing down the names of all those who leave them pious bequests and to commemorate them in the celebration of the mass. They call the written record [of those names] *condachi*, which the notary has translated as *codex*. Thus, it is abundantly clear that Iacobus, the great-grandfather of Georgius, was Greek and therefore ineligible to partake of the aforementioned offices. For, if he had been Latin, he would have left at least one mass to be celebrated in the Latin rite. Although it is true that some but not all witnesses said that his father Nicolaus and his grandfather Iacobus were Latins, it was done falsely and fraudulently in order maliciously to usurp those honors that are only bestowed on Latin feudatories. That this is the case is evident for another reason. It would be impossible to verify if they had been Latins because none of the many ancestors in his family tree appear to have held any office or participated in any council. A search through the records of the councils and officials reveals none of their names. Clearly they were ineligible, especially because during the tenure of lord Zufredo Mursin, former duke of Crete, a motion was passed in the Candiote Senate to the effect that all members of the council of Crete had to undergo a *proba* each year. In none of those *probe* carried out each year until the time of the rebellion [1363] does anyone from the family Modino appear to have qualified for membership on the council. If they had been members of the council, they would have in no way allowed the loss of such a great privilege and honor. Moreover, to join the council it was necessary to buy a fief, because that privilege was given to those buying fiefs before the prohibition of lord Filippo Belegno. The prohibition warned that if henceforth someone who was not a member of the Great Council or related to those who might be members bought a fief, he would not be nor would be considered a member of the Great Council on account of the fief he purchased. The fief that the said Georgius possesses did not pass to his ancestors by way of sale but by way of legacy, for in a certain ruling passed by the lord Guido da Canal, former duke of Crete, on 26 November 1304, mention is made that Elena, mother of Marcus and Iacobus Modino, sons of the late Iohannes, left to them the said fief. As was mentioned above, Iacobus is said to be the great-grandfather of the said Georgius. Therefore, since that fief came down to them through a legacy and not through a sale, they did not gain access to the abovementioned council, a seat in which was granted only to those who purchased their fiefs, as the prohibition cautioned. Additionally, the prosecutor said that the said fief was never recorded in the court's census of fiefs in the names of any of Georgius' ancestors because they were Greek. If they had been Latins, it would be hard to understand why not one of his ancestors was registered in the census. The prosecutor also added that admitting Georgius to the council would cause great harm to the other nobles of Crete, many of whom are greatly impoverished, for they have no way to make a living except from such offices. Many of the Greek feudatories pass themselves off as Latins in order to acquire such a privilege and honor. They take the bread and wherewithal of those who are legally worthy of them. This is thoroughly absurd. And that . . . Nicolaus Modino . . . of the said Georgius . . . would not have said he was Latin is clear, since he had himself buried in a Greek church. Indeed he shows an animosity in his will drawn up by ser Constantios Mauricha, notary, on the __th day of _____ in which he left no legacy expressly to Latin churches. He did, however, say that his wife must have his soul commemorated. She, being Greek, would not have done something that was not according to the rite of the Greeks, if she herself and her people were not truly Greek. But they pretend to be Latin out of a desire maliciously to usurp what does not belong to them by law.

In response, the above-written Georgius Modino, or in his stead, the noble man ser Vittore Valaresso, herald, answered that what Georgius endeavored to prove he succeeded in proving through witnesses and documents. There is no doubt that he is the son of Nicolaus and that Nicolaus had been the son of Iacobus and thus through witnesses and documents it is clear that Iacobus had been the son of Georgius and Georgius of Iacobus and Iacobus of Iohannes. It is also evident that the same Iacobus and his brother Marcus or Iohannes their father, had the fief in 1304. Since they possessed the fief before the prohibition of the lord Filippo Belegno, former duke of Crete, issued in 1426, they would have entered the council and participated in the offices. Likewise, the said Georgius, who legitimately traces his origins from the same Iacobus, before possessing the fief, must also have had the right to participate in those offices. It does not matter that his ancestors were never in the council, nor in any office, because at that time it was not appreciated as much as it is now. Men were content to hold their fiefs and not seek seats on the councils or offices. This is no way prejudicial to them if by right they were among those who if they wished to participate could have done so. But to the charge that they are Greeks, he showed clearly through witnesses that he, his father, and grandfather were Latins and lived according to the Latin rite. That his ancestors from his grandfather back were Latin is indisputable because if they had not been Latins they would not have had fiefs. And, acknowledging this, it is then evident that they were Latins, that is to say, Modino from Modena. Nor do the legacies made by Iacobus in his will to Greeks matter, for no will made by a Latin man can be found in which there is not a legacy made to Greeks. He said also that it does not prejudice his case if the said fief was not registered in their names. Once the fief was registered in the census, they fulfilled and continue to fulfill the oath of fidelity every year and during the *mude*, they also attend the muster of the garrison, which is to say that three times a year in the presence of the Lord Captain they swear fidelity which is as good as being registered. What's more, it is not right to say that the fief came to them through legacy and not through purchase, because in no place were the names of those who were buying fiefs and seeking office written down. And the prohibition of lord Filippo Belegno states that those buying fiefs henceforth may not gain entrance into the councils. These terms do not apply to those in the past, only in the future. In conclusion, he said that he ought to be absolved of all the charges imputed to him by the prosecutor and acknowledged as eligible for membership in the council and offices, like the other nobles of Crete.

In response to the argument that the council and offices used not to be appreciated, the prosecutor replied that the opposite was the case. For when the councils of Venice determined that the members of the council in Crete should undergo a *proba*, in each one were found more than ___, a number which is greater than the city of Candia, showing clearly that it was not despised. Furthermore, it is even clearer through the prohibition of Lord Filippo Belegno former duke of Crete and his council that the regime inferred exactly the same thing, because among the Latins holding fiefs at that time were artisans and tradesmen who, having acquired fiefs, entered the council, which the regime considered unseemly. Thus, clearly the council was much valued and everyone ran to it on account of of the honor attached. It was not despised, as the other party claims. It was also claimed that they were Latins because if they were not, they would not possess the fief. The prosecutor of the commune replied that the point was of no consequence, since there are many who are Greek and not Latin who have fiefs in the island of Crete. But although they have fiefs, because they are Greek, they did not enter the council or enter into offices or profit from them. It is alleged that they participate in the muster of the garrison, but there are the most ancient Greek nobles who have fiefs and form part of the muster of the garrison right up to today. Nevertheless, because they are Greek, their ancestors did not enter the councils nor were they admitted into offices nor are they presently admitted. It was also said that there is not a testament of a Latin man in which something is not bequeathed to Greeks and the churches of Greeks. The prosecutor conceded the point, but such bequests by a Latin to Greeks are not for celebrating masses, since they might be excommunicated by ecclesiastic censure, but they do it for the sake of an obligatory commemoration by such Greeks and for the sake of devotion to the works of churches in the villages. The argument fails in any event because they make bequests to monasteries, churches, and convents of the Latins. Those Modini do not. All their bequests are made to Greeks and for the celebration of the Divine Offices and nothing whatever to Latins, which if they had been Latins, they would not have done.

For these reasons, the lord duke and the excellent lord Mafeo Bolani councillor (the excellent lord Vittore Duodo, the other councillor, not being of the same opinion), having seen, heard, and diligently studied the arguments of the prosecutor and the response from the other party and the above-mentioned documents and witnesses, with the entire trial established in the court of the prosecutors, and the above-stated laws and allegations and duplications, the case is closed and the decision rendered that Georgius is not among those who may participate in the offices as do the nobles of Crete. As a consequence, he becomes subject to the penalty contained in the order of lord Marco Falier former duke of Crete and his council.

1448   12 May, 11th indiction. By the mandate of the lord Antonio Diedo, honorable duke of Crete, and his council, the above-written sentence was canceled by virtue of the ducal letter received on the matter, drawn up in the ducal palace on 9 November 1446. In it is found its repeal and annulment, carried out by the pleasure of the noblemen ser Tadeo Giustinian and ser Antonio de Priuli, the new auditors. The letter is recorded in the chancery.

Section Six

The Built Environment

By the central Middle Ages what were once considered public works projects devolved into the hands of local rulers and private citizens, even those concerning the basic right to water, illustrated here in a charter referring to the construction of a private bath in southern Italy. Building projects more often than not, however, focused on defensive construction, often taking the form of fortified castles and towns. Encastellation (incastellamento) soon transformed the settlement patterns of the countryside, as the Veronese documents included in this section demonstrate. Cities too were concerned with protection and surrounded themselves with circuits of walls, which often had to be expanded as their populations outgrew them, as seems to have been the case in Pavia's three rings of walls described by Opicino de Canistris. Towers, which defined the skyline of so many medieval cities, San Gimignano being the celebrated surviving example, also served defensive purposes. Indeed the tower-house came to symbolize a given family's wealth, military might, political power, and social standing. As such, tower-building often escalated into a frenzied competition which had to be controlled by legislation, as shown by the Pisan document in this section [see #17, 111].

Significantly, competition served as the impulse for a variety of building projects in late medieval Italy. In urban contexts, bishops often squared off against civic governments in contests to build the most impressive enclaves in the city: the duomo, baptistry, and bishop's palace representing ecclesiastical power on the one side and the palazzi of the podestà and capitano del popolo symbolizing the newly found secular autonomy of the commune on the other. Any or all of these buildings could become the focal point of social life and civic pride, as the documents pertaining to Parma's magnificent baptistry demonstrate. External competition also fueled building projects. Just as medieval cities vied with each other for political and economic dominance, they also competed to be the most beautiful. A city's honor and self-identity were at stake, and the Sienese knew this better than anyone else, as documents pertaining to the building of the Piazza del Campo reveal. Pride in the built environment of medieval Italy resonates still in the Italian language in the word campanilismo, which translates as "local pride." The root of the word, however, reveals its architectural etymology. Campanile means bell tower, a characteristic feature of medieval Italian skylines.

Finally, the built environment of medieval Italy benefited from expressions of religious piety on every scale. One text, in this case an inscription, records the gift of a window by a community of Jews to the synagogue of Bari, while another inscribed dedication stone commemorates the private funding of a hospital in return for indulgences. The great wealth of kings and emperors of course allowed them to express their piety and dispense patronage on an even more monumental scale. Accordingly, documentation and descriptions of building projects from the Norman and Angevin kingdoms of Sicily are also included in this section.

55. *INCASTELLAMENTO*
TWO TEXTS FROM VERONA (906, 923)

Translated from Latin by Maureen Miller

*The nearly annual incursions of Hungarian (Magyar) invaders into the Po Valley in the early tenth century stimulated the building of fortifications. This process of castle building (*incastellamento*) transformed settlement patterns and power relations in the countryside. It happened in many different ways. Since building fortifications was a royal right and since kings had a duty to protect their people, sometimes* incastellamento *occurred with or through a royal privilege (doc. 1). At other times it seems to have occurred on the initiative of property owners and residents (doc. 2). However it happened, castle building involved significant resources and created valuable resources that could yield great power.*

1. Diploma of King Berengario, Verona (24 August 906)

In the name of the eternal Lord God. King Berengario. Let the devoted astuteness of all the faithful of the holy church of God and our own, present and future, know that Ardingo, most reverend bishop [of Brescia] and our beloved archchancellor, humbly begged the clemency of our serenity to make a concession on account of the incursion of the pagans: that we grant by our authority to Audeberto, deacon of the holy Veronese church, license in perpetuity to build a castle at the place called Nogara, between the estates of Two Oaks and Tilliano, on the banks of the river Tartaro, and to transact business near the castle and within it, and to build a market. Acceding to these worthy requests, we permit the deacon Audeberto to build a castle in the aforementioned place with parapets, crenellated battlements, moats, and every kind of fortification, and we decree it be affirmed by this document. And thus, confident in our royal authority, let him [Audeberto] surround the castle with parapets, fortify it with battlements, and strengthen it with every fortification, and let him construct a market there with our license. We concede as the deacon's own property the tolls, mooring dues, taxes, and all tributes and jurisdictional fines, and all else up to this time belonging to the crown, which we grant in full by proprietary right. Moreover, let no count, viscount, state officer [*sculdahis*], estate manager [*gastald*], dean, or any person, great or small, of any dignity or order, presume to hold court in that castle, or to exact or claim anything in it for the king, or to requisition lodging by force, or compel anything to be paid from that market to the public

Translated from *Codice diplomatico veronese*, ed Vittorio Fainelli, 2 vols. (Venice: Deputazione di storia patria per le Venezie, 1940–63), vol. 2, 94–95 (no. 76), 248–50 (no. 187).

treasury. Rather, let the deacon Audeberto possess all these things by proprietary right, free of the uncertainty or threat of any power. And if anyone should be imprudently tempted to rise up audaciously against this concession so as to impede its implementation, may he be compelled to pay thirty pounds of the best gold, half to the treasury of our palace and half to the aforesaid deacon Audeberto or to whomever he shall have conceded all these things. So that this might be more truly believed and more faithfully observed, we order this to be sealed with our ring, confirming it with our own hand.

Sign of the Lord Berengario, most serene king.

The chancellor Ambrogio, instead of the bishop and archchancellor Ardingo, reviewed and signed [this decree].

Done on 9 kalends September [24 August] in the year of our Lord's incarnation 906, the 19th year of Lord Berengario, most pious king, in the ninth indiction. Enacted at Verona, in the name of Christ, happily, AMEN.

2. Charter of Agreement, Verona (923)

In the name of Christ. Eriprando archdeacon of the holy Veronese church to Alteverto and his brother Andrea, the priest Pietro Giselberto, Gotefredo called Boniperto, the cleric Teudiperto, Romano son of the deceased Verecundo, Amelberto, Gauso, Traso, Setru, Teudeberto, Ildeberto, Grauso, Berengario, Auspertocio, Leudiberto, Teudiberto, Satadino, Christoforo, Teudemario, Gariberto, Ildeberto, Albucio, Lupo, Giso, Teudiberto, Gisemperto, Zeno, Odelperto, Beto, Ursemario, Ledomartino, Betuloatula, Boniverto Fer. son of the deceased Lampo, Andrea, Boniverto, Vidale, Grauso, Ermulo, Martino, Gisemberto, Teucio, Andrea, Pietro, Adolfo, Martino, Audiberto, Getuso, Bundisberto, Ficio, Audiberto, Lunedeo, Giovanni, Guncio, Dominico, Cipriano, Egino, Usberto, Gisemperto, Buniperto, Ursu, Pietro, Garimberto of the aforesaid, Alteverto and his brother Andrea living in the city of Verona and all the rest, free men, living in the castle of Cerea: Let it be known to all that because of the persecution of the Hungarians, I, Archdeacon Eriprando demanded that you fortify this castle at Cerea, building an enclosure around the tower. Having obeyed and followed my order, enclosing where before there was no wall, it is evident how much work was carried out and, not neglecting to give thanks, we now take care to make, with the consent of our priests, this charter of firm agreement. Therefore, I, Eriprando, concede to all of you, and to your sons and heirs, what you have from our own construction within this castle now built, in order that you might apply yourselves as before—just as was already completed and divided among you and you now occupy—to build whatever shall be useful to you for holding, residing, and making accesses and entrances, without any interference from myself or my successors. This agreement holds that you shall continue to complete the wall at that castle and when you have enclosed the unfinished area with rock, you may live within it and send your movables in and out without the interference of any power. And when necessity arises, you should administer, guard, and hold the castle with care, always improving it as you are able and opportunity provides, for the safety of this holy Veronese church, whose property it is. You and your heirs shall also pay us and our successors every year on the feast of Saint Zeno, which is in the month of December, four *solidi* in good silver pennies of the type now in circulation in the city of Verona; and this rent shall be handed over and paid to our administrator at the castle by you or your messengers. And if someone from among you shall want for some necessity to sell his building, we grant license to him to sell that land and to do whatever is necessary with you or with other persons. But you shall not have license beyond this to abolish what was agreed between both parties and you affirmed concerning this land, and you must receive within the castle the lord's messenger whenever he comes and serve him as you are able, but nothing otherwise shall be imposed. Between them, the following penalty was agreed upon: if the Archdeacon Eriprando or any other of his successors or if the aforementioned men and any of their heirs try to overturn this pact or do not fulfil all that is written above, that part will pay to the faithful party a fine of one hundred silver *solidi* and, the fine having been paid, the present agreement will remain in force in perpetuity as it is written above with the appended stipulation.

Enacted in the city of Verona, happily, in the name of Christ.

I, Eriprando the archdeacon signed this agreement which I made.

+ made by the hand of Adelberto who is called Addo, and Leudiberto the miller who is called Leudo.

Rimperto son of the deceased Aciverto, who lives by Roman law, [stood as] witness.

+ made by the hand of brother Erigo, Mannutio son of the deceased Gundiberto, and Placuitio called Planzo—all called as witnesses.

I, the notary Roperto, wrote this document and completed it as it was related.

56. A BATH IN SOUTHWEST ITALY (1047)

Translated from Latin by Jill Caskey

This eleventh-century charter concerns water rights and bathing in the coastal town of Minori, in the Amalfi region, the most important maritime city of the period. Until very recently, many scholars believed that bathing was rare in the Middle Ages; some hypothesized that it was revived in the West during the Crusades, when Europeans encountered the religious, cultural, and architectural practices of Muslims and Jews in the Middle East. But this representative charter, reinforced by the evidence of manuscript images, extant buildings, and archaeological finds, calls into question such views, as it indicates that bathing and its accompanying technology and architecture flourished in the region of Amalfi long before the Crusades. This document also helps reconstruct the rhythms of daily life in a medieval town, where distinctions between private and public space were blurred and subject to negotiation, as were rights to natural resources such as fresh water, air, and light. Note that the agreement struck in this charter hinges on Christian beliefs and what can be called an economy of salvation. Money does not change hands; rather, objects used in the church liturgy to honor a local saint and intercessor help seal the deal. This translation has been made from a sixteenth-century copy of the charter, which incorrectly lists the date as 1048. Even with occasional errors of transcription or interpretation, early copies like this one are still useful to historians, particularly in cases where medieval archives or portions thereof have been destroyed. Such copies, of course, must be scrutinized carefully.

Our Orso [bishop of Minori] conducted water to the episcopal palace and also made a public bath in his gardens, as we read in a parchment of 5 November, first indiction, sixth year of the Duke Mansone after the reacquisition,[1] that we [the sixteenth-century copyist] judge to have occurred in 1048 [1047] in which Anna, patrician of our Amalfi, daughter of Mauro of Gregorio of Mauro of the Count Gregorio,[2] concedes to him the right to have water pass by her farmhouse that she possesses in our Regina Minori, with the condition

Translated from Ulrich Schwarz, *Regesta amalfitana: Die älteren Urkunden Amalfis in ihrer Überlieferung*, Quellen und Forschungen aus italienischen Archiven und Bibliotheken 58 (Tübingen: Niemeyer 1978), doc. 16, 92–93, from the sixteenth-century copy of the original, G. B. D'Afflitto, "Frammenti di Minori," 1, fol. 3, and other early modern chronicles [1047], 5 November, Amalfi.

1. That is, after Mansone II's return to power following the conquest of the region by the Lombards of Salerno. Along with other coastal towns such as Gaeta and Naples, the region of Amalfi was an autonomous political entity ruled by a duke. It gained independence from the Duchy of Naples in 839 and fell to the Normans in 1073.

2. Note that Anna is identified via four generations of ancestors. Not only did genealogy help identify her as specifically as possible in this era before surnames, but it also established her elite status, as the list ends with a count, her great-great-grandfather. In this region, long lineage constituted prestige to an unusual degree; signatories of Amalfitan documents regularly listed up to nine generations of ancestors.

that the bishop and his successors shall owe in perpetuity to this same Anna and her heirs, owners of this farmhouse, on each solemn day of our saint [Saint Trofimena] ten double wax candles, each a palm and a half wide. Similarly it is the case that the bishop or his successors shall have made a public bath for washing on the said possession of his church, using this said water there. When she or her heirs shall find themselves going to said bath to wash, so this bishop shall not be able to take any payment but shall rightly allow them to bathe for free, and furthermore allow them to take continuously however much water can be received in [flow through] a hole the size of a finger on a human hand, for use at their farmhouse.

57. BISHOP DAIBERT'S ORDER ON THE HEIGHT OF TOWERS IN PISA (1090)

Translated from Latin by Patricia Skinner

The rising prosperity and political engagement of the inhabitants of northern Italian cities in the late eleventh century gave rise to an explosion of building activity as an expression of family wealth and pride. One particular type of building, the tower-house, is emblematic of the period, and functioned both as a symbol and as a practical military fortification. Some reached extreme heights (examples survive in Bologna and San Gimignano, for example) and were used for high-level skirmishes, posing a major danger to those fighting and those in the streets below. It was in this context (and perhaps inspired partly by the Church's emphasis in the same period on the peace and truce of God), that we find a number of documents setting limits to tower heights and trying to end the violence associated with them [see #17, 111]. The most famous, from Pisa, is translated below. Its importance is attested to by the fact it survives in later Pisan legislative codes. Its author, Daibert, had become bishop of Pisa ca. 1088, having changed sides in the papal-imperial wars of the late eleventh century. It was not uncommon for bishops to take the lead in the political life of Italian cities in the early eleventh century, but his role at this late date is somewhat anomalous, and it seems that he derived his authority ultimately from the ecclesiastical sanctions he was able to impose. It is likely that the "energetic and wise men" who accompany him in the document formed the core of later secular rule in the city.

The document has no dating clause or signatures, and may thus be a draft version. But its effects are felt much later, as the Breve Consulum *(one of the earliest surviving communal statutes) of Pisa in 1162 states that the consuls had to swear to respect the* securitates *of bishops Gerard and Daibert, and the text had to be read out twice a year.*

In the name of our lord and savior Jesus Christ, I Daibertus, by divine favor the unworthy bishop of the Pisans, having with me as companions the energetic and wise men Pietro, the viscount, Rolando, and Stefano, Guinezone, Marinianus and Alberto, considering as we have the ancient disease of pride which has daily caused innumerable homicides, lies, and marriages contracted incestuously, as well as the destruction of houses and who knows how many other sinful deeds, we have agreed with the consent of the abovementioned men and all of the inhabitants of the city of Pisa, its suburbs, and Quinzica, that there should be an oath taken that you should make an agreement that

Translated from G. Rossetti, "Il lodo del vescovo Daiberto sull'altezza delle torri," in *Pisa e la Toscana occidentale nel medioevo: A Cinzio Violante nei suoi 70 anni* (Pisa: GISEM, 1991), vol. 2, 25–31.

no other house should be built higher than the tower of Stephen son of Balduinus and Lambert.

Those who live in Quinzica should not build or restore their towers any higher than the highest one of Guinzonis son of Gontolinus, nor should they contradict this order in any other way, either in land which they hold as an allod or in any other way; except in lands that they can show to be theirs and not held by any other person, and except in the top of the bridge either side. And no one should contradict this order in the ecclesiastical land nor build any higher than has been stated. In the land which is next to the Arno road. . . . And if there should be a disagreement over the height of a tower as opposed to another, then a line should be made at the top of the higher one and no further building in wood or stone take place any higher on the first one. And if anyone attempts to build any higher, then you must manfully prohibit him. And no one must take or destroy the house of anyone else, unless it is with the agreement of the commune or the greater part of the wise and good men, nor should any other man be permitted to do so. If anyone, persuaded by the devil, should contravene this regulation on height or destruction . . . then he should desist from this pride within a month or be answerable to the commune and the buildings be destroyed.

No one should build a parapet or a wooden tower or anything of wood that can be used in war either in his house or around his house, unless it is for the use of the commune of the city. Those who have them should destroy them, and you should prohibit anyone from disobeying this. If anyone has posts or other wooden poles built on top of the house in order to mount these war machines, these should be disassembled within 8 days if their owners are in Pisa. And if they are not, then they should do so within 8 days of their return. So that injury is not caused to others, no one should build wooden or stone ladders or balustrades up the [side of the] house, nor should they be permitted to lean against the house.

No one under 15 years of age will be required to take this oath. All others must take this oath within 15 days if they are in Pisa, or else within 15 days of their return.

If anyone accepts an oath from another that he should not build his house above 36 cubits more or less, without license to do so, then he should be released from that oath. If he does not wish to do so on account of perjuring himself, we order that you should help him whose house is built too high to come and speak to the commune; and he whose house contradicts should be absolved from this security against him.[1] Those who have towers higher

---

1. The meaning of this passage is obscure—the gist seems to be that people who already had houses too tall were not to be penalized or forced to take the oath for fear of perjury.

Figure 13. Garisenda and Asinelli towers, Bologna (early twelfth century). The Garisenda tower, never completed (L), is 48.16 meters and the tower of the Asinelli is (R) 97.20 meters tall. (Photo: Frances Andrews)

than the aforementioned height should make their towers match the height of the other towers according to the measurement we have set out within one month if they are in Pisa, and within a month of their return if they are not. If they refuse to do so, no one should stand surety for them.

We make an exception for the tower of Ugo the viscount and the tower of the son of Albizo and order than no one should go up farther than the height we have already set out nor injure anyone who has stood surety for them. If it happens that any of these towers injure others, except those which we have just exempted, then we wish and order that they come before the commune, that the people be absolved against him and him who has stood surety, and that the people should help in this.

Regarding the bell-tower of San Michele, we order that the abbot and the monks of that abbey should have a cupola and altar built there as there was previously, and that they should invite the bishop to consecrate it in good faith by Christmas. If they do not do so, we order that you should make the bell-tower level with the measure which we have set out above. No one else should take the bell-tower, nor go up in it, nor injure anyone from it, nor enter any other church except for the use of the city. We order also that no one of the inhabitants of Pisa or its suburbs or Quinzica should take for sale any of the tribute. We also wish you to know that whoever, inflated with the pride of the devil, should disobey this peace and concord and refuse to take the oath, then they should be excommunicated and damned and separated from the church, nor will they have any communion either in church or while at sea.

58. IBN JUBAYR'S ACCOUNT OF MESSINA AND PALERMO (1184–85)

Translated from Arabic by Alex Metcalfe,
with additional texts by Joshua Birk

The Andalusi Muslim secretary to the Almohad governor of Granada, Ibn Jubayr, wrote an eyewitness account of Sicily in Arabic on his return from pilgrimage to Mecca in 1184–85. Although the organization of the material in his travelogue, or Riḥla, *is sometimes haphazard, his memoirs and testimony from personal interviews remain a significant source for the towns and palaces of Sicily, the royal administration, and the condition of the kingdom's Muslims. (AM)*

Recollection of the city of Messina on the island of Sicily (may God almighty return it!): this city is inundated with infidel merchants and a destination for ships from all quarters with many parties there for its low prices. No Muslim has settled there; it is grim with godlessness and crammed with slaves of crosses choking its inhabitants and almost squeezing the life out of them. It is full of smells and squalor, a cold place in which the stranger will find no friendly atmosphere. Messina's markets do a brisk and lively trade with an extensive range of goods to support a life of plenty. Your day and night pass by in safety even if your face, presence and tongue are unfamiliar.

Messina rests up against the hills, the lower parts of which reach down to the ditches of the town with the sea extending before it to its southern face. Its port is the most remarkable of maritime countries because large ships approach it from so close to the land that they are almost touching it. From ship to shore a length of wood is secured over which porters pass raising cargo onto it, there being no need for launches to load or unload gear except when going to ships docked far from port. They can be seen by the land lined up like a row of horses in their stalls or stables. This is due to the extraordinary depth of the sea there which forms a three-mile strait between Messina and the mainland. On the opposite side from Messina there is a town known as Rayya [Reggio] which is a large province. This city of Messina is at the top of the island of Sicily which has a lot of cities, towns, and estates too numerous to mention. The length of this island of Sicily is seven days travel and its

Translated from *Riḥlat Ibn Jubayr* (Beirut: Dār al-Ṣādir, 1964), 296–307 (Metcalfe); *Riḥlat Ibn Jubayr* (Cairo, Yuṭlabu min Maktabat Miṣr, 1992), 422–25 (Birk) A complete English translation can be found in Ronald J. C. Broadhurst *The Travels of Ibn Jubayr*, 2nd ed. (London: Cape, 1952; repr. New Delhi: Goodword Books, 2001), 335–63. For further English translations and detailed context for the description, see Jeremy Johns, *The Arabic Administration of Norman Sicily: The Royal Dīwān* (Cambridge: Cambridge University Press, 2002), 212–15, 241–42, 295–96, and passim.

width five. It has the volcano [Mount Etna], which is shrouded in cloud due to its enormous height and is always snow-capped winter and summer.

The island exceeds description other than to say it is the daughter of al-Andalus in the extent of its estates and its great fertility and comfort. It is bursting with all sorts of produce and full of every type of fruit, but is populated by the worshippers of crosses who roam its hills and are safeguarded in their shelter. Muslims are among them as well, on their holdings and estates and are treated well in their employment and work, but they impose a tax on them which they render twice a year. They have come between them and the wealth of the land they used to have. May great and almighty God improve their condition and by his kindness make everything turn out well for their property! All its hills have orchards rich with apple trees, chestnuts, hazels, pears, and other types of fruit trees. There are no Muslims in this Messina except a few who are insignificant as their work has dried up, and so the Muslim stranger would feel alienated there.

The finest city in Sicily and the seat of its king the Muslims know as al-Madīna ["the city"] and the Christians as Balarma [Palermo]. Muslim settlers are resident there and they have mosques and their own markets in many outlying quarters. The rest of the Muslims live on the island's estates and in all its villages and other towns such as Kasrqūsa [Syracuse] and the like. However, it is the Great City [Palermo] which is home to its king, William [II], and the largest and most frequented city with Messina second. If God wills it, we will make our stay in Palermo, and from there we hold out hopes for our departure to whichever town in the Maghrib great and almighty God decrees, if he has so willed.

The character of this their king is surprising for his decent conduct, his employment of Muslims, and the use made of completely castrated slaves, all of whom, or most of whom, conceal their faith and adhere to the *sharī'a* law of Islam. He puts a lot of trust in the Muslims, relying on them in his affairs and important matters of business to the extent that even the supervisor of his kitchen is a Muslim. He also has a unit of black Muslim slaves whose commander is picked from among them. His ministers and chamberlains are eunuchs, of whom he has a large number. They are the people of his state and described as his elite. Through them radiates the splendor of his kingdom because they abound with magnificent clothes and swift horses, and each has his own retinue of slaves and attendants.

This king has imposing palaces with pretty gardens, especially in his kingdom's capital Palermo, mentioned above. At Messina he has a palace as white as a dove that dominates the shoreline. He has taken on many eunuchs and servant girls and among the Christian kings there is none more affluent, more comfortable, or more opulent than he is. He resembles Muslim kings in his immersion in the luxury of his dominion, the organization of its laws, the drawing up of its procedures, the arrangement of the standing of his men, the emphasis on the crown's pageantry, and the display of its finery. His dominion is indeed splendid. He has doctors and astrologers for whom he has great concern and tremendous enthusiasm, to the extent that whenever anyone mentions to him that a doctor or astrologer is passing through his land he orders his detention and lavishes upon him such a well-provided lifestyle that he forgets about his homeland. May God by his grace deliver Muslims from temptation! The king himself is about 30 years old. May God protect Muslims from his menace and its spread! One of the fascinating things of his nature that is said about him is that he reads and writes in Arabic. According to what one of his personal slaves told us, his motto is "Praise God, it is right to praise him," and the motto of his father is "Praise God, thanks be for his blessings." As for the slave-girls and concubines in his palace, they are all Muslim. The most surprising thing his [William II's] aforementioned eunuch told us—that is Yaḥya bin Fityān al-Ṭarraz—was that among the Christian women in his palace, the Franks have become Muslim, the aforesaid servant girls having converted them, all of which they have kept from the king. These women's doing of good deeds is truly remarkable. We heard that there had been a trembling earthquake on this island which terrified this polytheist [William]. He looked about his palace and heard only the mention of God and his messenger from the women and eunuchs. Perhaps alarm befell them by his appearance, so settling them down he told them, "Let each one of you call upon his own god and whomever you believe in!" . . .

The king has, in the aforesaid town of Messina, a dockyard that contains a countless number of ships from his fleet. He has one like that at Palermo too. We stopped off in one of the merchants' hostels and stayed there nine days. Then when it was night-time of the 12th of the aforesaid holy month and the 18th of December, we boarded a small vessel and headed for Palermo mentioned above.

[Birk translation]

Recollections of Palermo, which is the capital of Sicily (may God return it to the Muslims): Palermo is the capital of the island, the union of the benefits of both opulence and grace. It possesses all the beauty, both internal and external, that you could desire and all the necessities of life, both ripe and verdant. The city is ancient and elegant, wondrous and gracious and seductive to gaze upon. It presents its courtyards with gardens, broad roads, and thoroughfares, it pleases the eyes with the beauty of its outstanding appearance. It is a marvelous place, built in the style of Cordoba, all of it constructed from a stone known as Kaddān. A river divides the city and four springs flow into it perennially from its remote areas.

Its king adorned the city, his worldly possession, and took it as the capital of the Franks, may God destroy it. His castles are arranged around the neck of the city like necklaces strung around the throats of voluptuous girls. The king moves around the gardens and courts, between amusing diversions and games. How many palaces and constructions does he have in the city, may he not long inhabit it? How many watchtowers and lookout points? How many monasteries does he have, whose monks he makes comfortable with extensive estates, whose churches are adorned with crosses shaped of gold and silver? May God make right the destiny of this island in the near future, may he revert it to a domicile of the faith and may He transfer it from defeat to security, through his power. For he can do whatever he desires.

[Metcalfe translation]

The Muslims [of Palermo] have a remaining trace of their faith; they fill most of their mosques; they pray on hearing the prayer call and they have their own suburbs in which their quarters are separate from the Christians; the markets are full of them and they are the traders there. They have no Friday prayers because the sermon has been banned for them. At festivals they pray with their sermon addressed to the 'Abbāsid [Caliph]. They have a judge there to whom they present their legal cases and a congregational mosque in which they gather for prayer under its lights during the holy month. As for ordinary mosques, there are very many, in fact, innumerable. Most of them are meeting places for teachers of the Qur'āan. In general, they are separate from their Muslim brethren who are under the infidels' protection [*dhimma*] [as tax-paying non-Christians]. They have no security for them, for their money, their wives or their sons. May God recompense them by the design of the beauty of his goodwill!

One thing can be compared to another in some way and generally this city resembles Cordoba in that it has an old town known as "al-Qaṣr al-Qadīm," which is in the center of the new town as it is in Cordoba (may God protect it!). In the old town are buildings like imposing palaces that have balconies towering into the air that enchants the eye with their beauty.

[Birk translation]

And of the most wondrous things that we witnessed among the works of the infidels was the church [Santa Maria dell'Ammiraglio, later known as

Figure 14. San Giovanni degli Eremiti, Palermo (1130s). Church built by Roger II.
(Photo: Scala/Art Resource)

La Martorana], known as the church of the Antiochian [George of Antioch].
We beheld it on the Day of the Nativity, which, for them, is a great feast day,
on which men and women gathered to celebrate. Among all of the buildings
we saw this wondrous one defies description, for it is, without a doubt, the
most wondrous of man-made works in this world. All of its interior walls are
decorated with gold and sheets of colored marble, the likes of which we had
not seen. They were all inlaid with gold mosaic, encircled by trees of green
mosaic tiles. Arranged in the highest parts of it were well-placed curtains of
glass, whose radiant glow wrests away sight and causes temptation in the
soul. May we take refuge with God from it. We learned that its founder, for
whom the church is named, spent tremendous sums of gold on the church
and was the vizier to the grandfather of the polytheist king [Roger II]. This
church has a campanile which was built upon buttresses of colored marble.
It loomed, a cupola on top of other cupolas, all with separate columns.
Therefore it was known as the columned campanile. It is among the most

Figure 15. Coronation of Roger II of Sicily (mid-twelfth century). Mosaic in the church of the "Martorana," Palermo. (Photo: Scala/Art Resource)

wondrous of buildings which you will see. May God, in His kindness and nobility, ennoble the church with the call to prayer in the near future.

[Metcalfe translation]

The Christian women's dress in this city [Palermo] is the dress of Muslims; they are eloquent speakers of Arabic and cover themselves with veils. They go out at this aforementioned festival [Christmas] clothed in golden silk, covered in shining wraps and colorful veils, and with light gilded sandals. They appear at their churches bearing all the finery of Muslim women in their attire, henna and perfume. It reminded us, by way of a literary quip, of the poet's saying, "He who enters church one day, will find therein most tempting prey!" [literally, "antelope and gazelle"]

59. THE BAPTISTRY OF PARMA
FOURTEEN TEXTS (1196–1321)

Translated from Latin by Areli Marina

Of the dozens of free-standing baptismal buildings that dot northern Italy, one of the most distinctive is the rosy octagonal baptistry that dominates Parma's cathedral square. The construction of buildings of this type—which are seldom found outside Italy—blossomed in the eleventh, twelfth, and thirteenth centuries. This period coincided with the rise of the communes, when newly independent cities asserted their autonomy and importance by constructing a series of monumental civil and religious buildings intended to enhance their patrons' prestige.

The baptistry of Parma was begun in 1196, although construction continued in several campaigns until 1307. As is true of most free-standing Italian baptistries, Parma's central plan and octagonal form ultimately derive from the Anastasis Rotunda at the Holy Sepulcher in Jerusalem, the Lateran baptistry in Rome, and ancient Roman funerary architecture. The building's designers also drew on medieval Italian sources, particularly the baptistries of Florence and Cremona. What distinguishes the baptistry of Parma from its Italian peers are its unusual height, its elaborate cladding in the pink limestone known as rosso di Verona, and the unexpected juxtaposition of two distinct architectural styles in its façades. On the ground story of the three portal façades, the baptistry's builders adopted the Northern European architectural language of the late Romanesque and early Gothic periods complete with splayed embrasures, nested archivolts, and figurative sculptural ornamentation. On the building's five blind façades and its upper stories, the builders instead chose austere and monumental classicizing motifs, such as massive engaged columns, blind arches, and trabeated colonnades. The baptistry's exterior revetment in rosso di Verona, a material used in Parma by the ancient Romans, also emphasizes the building's Roman connections. Comparable contrasts are apparent inside the baptistry. The original concept for the baptistry's interior consisted of a classicizing program based on antique columns, multiple arched niches, and trabeated galleries. Later building campaigns superimposed a daring Gothic armature of thin colonnettes, pointed arches, and a steep ribbed cloister vault onto the existing, classicizing interior.

This seeming contradiction of architectural styles within a single building documents the tension present not only in the built environment, but also in north Italian society as a whole. In both contexts, individuals had to negotiate between the pressures of the ancient Roman tradition native to Italy, the emerging north Italian communal culture, and newer Northern European currents (including prestigious Gothic architectural forms, the practice of courtliness, and imperial values as interpreted by the German emperors). Rather than simply manifesting this conflict, the baptistry encodes it in its architecture. Like a written document it, too, is both a "text" ripe for historical investigation and a tool in our exploration of the past.

Of course, written texts are not silent on the subject of the baptistry. One pat-

Figure 16. Baptistry of Parma (1196–1307). (Photo: Areli Marina)

tern that emerges from them is the dual civic and religious function of the building. Sometimes, as in the case of text II-8, document and building together allow us to perceive one way in which a single Parmesan citizen nimbly engaged in practices with distinct northern European and Italian origins.

I. Construction History

1. Inscription on the lintel of the baptistry's northern portal, facing the piazza

In the year 1196 the aforesaid sculptor Benedictus began this work.

2. Construction of the baptistry begins

Lord Bercilius and Jordanus of San Michele of Parma were the consuls of Parma in the year 1196. And in that year the baptistry of the greater church of Parma of Blessed Mary was begun.

3. A Parmesan nobleman participates in the baptistry's foundation ceremony

Likewise I [Salimbene de Adam] heard from my father [Guido de Adam] that when the foundations were being laid for the baptistry of Parma he placed stones in the footings to record the fact that my relatives possessed houses where the baptistry was built, and after the destruction of their houses they went to Bologna and were made citizens there and called de Cocca.

4. Baptistry construction progresses, though hindered by Ezzelino da Romano's refusal to allow Parma to use any more Veronese stone for its façade

Likewise in the preceding years [before 1259] the citizens of Parma had performed many good works in their city. For they had completed the baptistry in its upper part as far as raising the roof, and it would already have been completed if Ezzelino de Romano, who was master of Verona, had not hindered them. For that baptistry was made exclusively of stone from Verona.

---

(1) Translated from Giuliano Bonazzi, ed., *Chronicon Parmense: ab anno MXXXVIII usque ad annum MCCCXXXVIII, RIS*² 9.9 (1902), 7.

(2) Translated from Salimbene de Adam, *Cronica*, ed. Giuseppe Scalia, *Corpus Christianorum, Continuatio Mediaevalis* 125–125A, 2 vols. (Turnhout: Brepols, 1998–99), vol. 1, 55. This text is also available in English translation, *The Chronicle of Salimbene de Adam*, trans. and ed. Joseph L. Baird, Giuseppe Baglivi, and John Robert Kane (Binghamton, N.Y.: Medieval and Renaissance Texts and Studies, 1986), 12.

(3) Translated from Salimbene de Adam, *Cronica*, vol. 2, 786.

(4) Translated from Bonazzi, ed., *Chronicon Parmense*, 101.

5. THE BAPTISTRY RECEIVES FURTHER EXTERIOR ORNAMENTS

Likewise at that time [1307] two small turrets were first built and erected above the baptistry of the cathedral with columns and gilded crockets[1] facing the palace of the bishop of Parma.

6. NEW CAPITALS ARE ADDED TO THE BAPTISTRY EXTERIOR

At the same time [1321] two capitals were built on the baptistry of Parma on the side facing the houses of the canons by the brothers of the workshop of the aforesaid church, and above one of them was made the figure of a lion.

II. Social History and Function

1. THE FIRST BAPTISMS TAKE PLACE IN THE NEW BAPTISTRY

And in that year [1216] on Saturday the ninth of April the first baptisms took place in the newly rebuilt baptistry of Parma. This Saturday was in fact the Saturday of Holy Week.

2. A COMMUNAL STATUTE FORBIDS "SHAMEFUL DEEDS" NEAR THE BAPTISTRY

The regulation Brother Gherardo established [in 1233] is that no one should do anything shameful near the wall of the greater church in the street beneath the spurs on the inner parts of the bulwarks of the church itself, which is below the wall of the church itself, nor near the wall of the baptistry, that is, in the street which is between the baptistry itself and the wall of the canons' house. And whoever breaks this law is to pay the penalty of three Parmesan *solidi* or he is to be placed in the chains in the square of the commune.

3. NOBLEMAN GUIDO DE ADAM'S TOMB IS INSTALLED IN FRONT OF THE BAPTISTRY

In addition my father had his own new tomb in the old square in front of the door of the baptistry, where no one had been buried up to that time, because the first [family] tomb was completely full.

---

(5) Translated from Bonazzi, ed., *Chronicon Parmense*, 164.
(6) Translated from Bonazzi, ed., *Chronicon Parmense*, 8.
(1) Translated from Amadio Ronchini, ed., *Statuta Communis Parmae ab anno MCCC-XVI ad MCCCXXV*, Monumenta historica ad provincias parmensem et placentinam pertinentia, I (Parma: Fiaccadori, 1855–56), 320.
(2) Translated from Salimbene de Adam, *Cronica*, vol. I, 79.
(3) Translated from Salimbene de Adam, *Cronica*, vol. I, 54.
1. A bud-like or foliate ornament taking the place of the Corinthian acanthus.

4. LORD BERNARDO OF OLIVERO DE ADAM'S BODY IS DISPLAYED IN STATE IN THE BAPTISTRY

In the battle of San Cesario [in 1229] Lord Bernardo of Olivero de Adam died. He was an eloquent judge and a proven soldier. His body was carried and placed in the baptistry of Parma, which was near his house. And he lay there on the bier until his friends and relatives had assembled. Afterward his body was placed in his tomb, which is in front of the door of the church of Sant'Agatha, which is the chapel of the greater church of the city of Parma, and is attached to its south facing part.

5. THE BAPTISTRY HOUSES THE SPOILS OF WAR AGAINST KING HENRY AND CREMONA

Likewise in the same year [1248] on the 13th of February a great crowd of soldiers and infantry men gathered at Colorno on account of their fear and the proximity of King Enzo.[2] Other persons, who were at home, called on the name of Jesus Christ and, admonished by the weapons of true penitence, they went out and started a fire. And the aforesaid emperor [Frederick II] was driven out with the men of Cremona and others who were following him, and robbed of all his possessions. More than three thousand of the men from Cremona and others who were there with the aforesaid emperor were captured; the number of dead was innumerable. And a wagon bearing the imperial standard belonging to the men of Cremona was taken there by the men of Parma and led and maneuvered into the baptistry by the men of Parma. Many goods of incalculable value, effects, riches, and decorations of both gold and silver and innumerable war-horses were held there, and also the golden crown of Holofernes[3] with precious jewels taken by a certain citizen of Parma called Curtopasus, and it came into the commune of Parma.

6. A STREET IS OPENED UP TO BETTER DISPLAY THE BAPTISTRY

The regulation by which the authorities are obliged to have made and broadened a street running from the south of the baptistry for eighteen feet, and by which the houses which are there are to be destroyed in order to allow

(4) Translated from Bonazzi, ed., *Chronicon Parmense*, 18.
(5) Translated from Ronchini, ed., *Statuta Communis Parmae*, 445.
2. Frederick II named his illegitimate son Enzo king of Sardinia; he is also known as Enzio.
3. The *Chronicon Parmense* is the only primary source known to me to use the epithet "crown of Holofernes" to characterize what other medieval sources describe as the imperial crown. The secondary sources are equally silent. Two explanations for the name are possible: (1) the crown lost at Victoria allegedly contained figurative sculpture—perhaps of Judith and Holofernes; or (2) the chronicler intends the reference metaphorically: Holofernes as Frederick and Parma as Judith.

the baptistry building to be seen and be entered through the gate which is there, and to permit free passage around the baptistry. The aforesaid works are to be carried out at the expense of those who stand to benefit from them, clergy as well as laity [1262].

7. INFORMAL STRATEGIES TO PROTECT THE BAPTISTRY FROM DAMAGE

Concerning the ancestry of lord Guidolino da Ençola, who lived near the greater church.

The grandfather of Lord James was called Lord Guidolino da Ençola; he was a man of middle height, rich, very well known, and deeply religious, and I [Salimbene de Adam] have seen him a thousand times. He separated himself from the rest of the da Ençola family, who lived in Borgo Santa Cristina, and went to live near the cathedral, which is the church of the glorious Virgin. There he heard mass every day—the whole daily office and the night office at opportune times. When he was not busy with his religious duties he would sit with his neighbors under the communal portico near the bishop's palace and talk about God or willingly listen to others speaking of God. He would not allow any boys to throw stones against the baptistry or the greater church to destroy the carvings or paintings. Whenever he saw them he would get angry, quickly run up and beat them with a strap, as if he had been charged with keeping guard in the same place, although he did this only for heaven and the divine love of God.

8. A MAN IS DUBBED A KNIGHT AT THE BAPTISTRY PORTAL

It is well known that this Lord Giacomo da Ençola took as his wife a certain widow from Padua who was called mistress Marchisina, whom Lord Matteo de Corigia obtained for him when he held power in Padua. From this lady lord James received as a dowry a great sum of money, which he lent at interest, from which he bought land, vineyards, and great possessions on the Pupilla estate, and he became "rich and exceedingly famous." In Parma moreover he bought my house, which was next to the baptistry, and acquired it as though it were a gift, that is, for a low price, because of the respect in which my father quite deservedly held him. Afterward Lord Giacomo was made a knight at the baptistry portal facing the square and went to Modena, to be the *podestà*. He was elected by the citizens of Modena and, before he could complete the full term of his office there he completed the term of his life.

(7) Translated from Salimbene de Adam, *Cronica*, vol. 2, 915.
(8) Translated from Salimbene de Adam, *Cronica*, vol. 2, 914.

60. CHARLES OF ANJOU ON THE FOUNDATION OF A CISTERCIAN MONASTERY NEAR SCURCOLA
(Abruzzo, 1274)

Introduced by Caroline Bruzelius;
translated from Latin by Sean Gilsdorf

Charles I of Anjou's (d. 1285) campaigns in Italy were funded by a number of sources, none of them adequate to the vast expense of the enterprise. Among the sources on which the king had counted to defray his expenses was the income from the crusading tithes declared by the papacy to support his venture. Certain orders, however, had a tradition of exemption from all crusading tithes, and among these were the Cistercians, who by the middle of the thirteenth century were perhaps the most widely spread and wealthy of monastic orders. Charles refused to accept the Cistercians' traditional immunity from taxation, and after years of litigation a settlement was reached in the fall of 1273. The king's foundation of the two new abbeys in the kingdom seems to have been a quid pro quo between royal authority and the powerful monastic order, which seems to have imposed this condition on the settlement of the dispute over tithes.

(Charles I, etc.) Written to the venerable abbot of the monastery of Casanova[1] or his representative.

Out of reverence for the Supreme Father, from whom we received the governance of this kingdom and through whom we live and reign, we plan to build a new monastery in the place where our battle against Conradin [see #61] took place, namely near the *castrum* of Pontes. Therefore we have sent to you the bearers of this letter—Brother James, our cleric and confidant Master Peter of Chaules, and our faithful men Peter of Carrelli and Simon of Angart—so that they might select a place or rather site where a fine new monastery might easily be built. We carefully beseech Your Devotion to travel with them to the place near Pontes where our battle with Conradin took place, and determine together with these your monks where a fine and spacious monastery might be easily built, carefully considering the suitability of the place, how the monastery might be made more pleasant, and where might be a good and convenient place to build it. You should think about the site and how large an estate the monastery will need; you also should carefully consider how much money it will take to build it, the most convenient place for farms to support the monastery's work, and how many

Translated from Heinrich Wilhem Schulz and Alexander Ferdinand von Quast, *Denkmaeler der Kunst des Mittelalters in Unteritalien* (Dresden: W.K.H. Schulz, 1860), vol. 4, 41–42.
    1. The Cistercian abbey of Santa Maria di Casanova was founded in 1191 on the Piana del Boltigno in Abruzzo, approximately 15 km southwest of Pescara.

ploughs and other equipment these will need. When you have completed your examination and come up with a plan for the construction of the monastery and the establishment of its farms, as well as an estimate of how much money will be needed to build the monastery and establish its farms with their appurtenances, carefully and faithfully make them known to us in writing. We also ask that Your Devotion cheerfully and honorably accept into the monastery of Casanova Brothers Peter and John of your order, whom we have sent to you. Allow them to remain with you as long as they wish, out of reverence for Our Majesty. Furthermore, we want you to know that in reply to your supplications, we have ordered our faithful representative in Apulia to allow your monastery to take 600 *salme* of grain, 300 *salme* of barley, and 100 *salme* of beans by ship from the port of Manfredonia to the monastery's pier, and to be unloaded there for the use and sustenance of your fellow brothers living in the monastery. We wish the aforesaid brothers to remain with you until the others, Brothers James, Peter of Chaules, Simon of Angart, and Peter of Carrelli return to us and describe what took place regarding the business described earlier, so that we might then make our will and pleasure known.

Given at Bari on the first of January.

61. FOUNDATION OF A FRENCH MONASTERY IN ABRUZZO: SANTA MARIA DELLA VITTORIA (1277)

Introduced by Caroline Bruzelius;
translated from Latin by Sean Gilsdorf

Although work on Charles I of Anjou's (d. 1285) two victory foundations, the Cistercian abbeys of Santa Maria della Vittoria (Blessed Mary of the Victory) and Santa Maria di Realvalle (Blessed Mary of Realvalle) began in early 1274, the official foundation documents date only to 1277 and emphasize the importance of these two foundations as centers of piety and places of burial for the immigrant French community in the Kingdom of Sicily. Ironically, the emphasis on "Frenchness" at Vittoria (and its sister monastery, Realvalle) may have in the long run been an important factor in the difficult history of these foundations. There seems always to have been a shortage of monks and lay brothers with the requisite French or Provençal origins, and little evidence of patronage by members of the local aristocracy. Indeed, the abbey of Vittoria, which commemorated the defeat of the young Hohenstaufen prince Conradin in 1268, was threatened by Emperor Henry VII's (d. 1313) army in the early fourteenth century, and the donations of land and fishing rights were bitterly contested even by the local French nobility, some of whom were relatives of the king.

The generosity of princes, renowned among men, which repays followers for their service with suitable rewards, enjoys even greater distinction when everyone strives to honor these gifts as ones freely given by the Giver of all, humbly and thankfully declaring that they have accepted them not because they require anything from us, but in order to pay a debt of praise, as it were, to the Lord of all. It is well known that we, who recognize God's great generosity toward us in the favors that we have received, and who were raised to the pinnacle of the kingdom by his grace and blessed at the beginning of our office as well as later with continuing prosperity, have enjoyed brilliant victories over our enemies, ones granted by him who is able to do such things. Not wanting to come emptyhanded before him who has bestowed such great favor upon us, but rather wishing to offer a pure and devout gift, we have ordered a monastery to be founded and newly built near Scurcola in Abruzzo, in honor of God and especially the Blessed Virgin, whose patronage we believe has helped us many times, as well as for the salvation of our soul, the souls of those who came before us and will follow us, and also of those who died in God's service carrying out the business of the Kingdom of Sicily.

Translated from Pietro Egidi, "Carlo I Angio e l'abbazia di Santa Maria della Vittoria presso Scurcola," *Archivio storico per le province napolitane* 39 (1914): 160–64.

We have decreed that this monastery henceforth be called "Blessed Mary of the Victory," and have endowed it not only with our own property, so that the rents, harvests, and incomes which it produces will provide a comfortable living for those who serve there, but with generous supplies of everything—candles as well as everything pertaining to divine worship—required for their work. Of our own good and free will we give, grant, and make over the possessions listed below to the aforementioned monastery, now underway and, with God's help, soon to be finished by us:

The *castrum* [village] of Scurcola in Abruzzo, with all rights and appurtenances to be determined by us if some question about them should happen to arise. Thus we will make an exchange with those lords who own some portion of the aforesaid village, if they are willing to trade with us; otherwise we will provide the monastery with something elsewhere of equal value in exchange for the portions in question. The *castrum* called Pontes in Abruzzo, with all rights and appurtenances likewise to be determined by us if some question should happen to arise, and under the same conditions, namely that if anyone demonstrates that he has rights of some kind over the aforesaid *castrum*, we will make an exchange with him if he wishes to do so; otherwise we will provide the monastery with something elsewhere of equal value in exchange. In the territory of Ascoli in the Capitanata,[1] twenty ploughlands of arable land, and the same number of ploughlands in the territory of Salsiburgi. In Scurcola and Pontes in Marsia, five plowlands of arable land, each plow being pulled by four oxen. Ten *milliaria* each year from the tithe of oil at Bitonto, equivalent to 400 *staria* of Bari. From the Palermo tuna fishery, 150 barrels of bluefin and the same amount of other tuna, which are to be shipped by sea at our court's expense to Gaeta. Also 500 pounds of almonds each year, to be collected at Sulmona by the bailiffs of the region. Furthermore, 500 *tumini* of salt, to be collected each year from the salt belonging to the court in the region of Pescara, and ten *cantaria* of iron, to be collected each year at the trading center in the region of Pescara. Also, the right to fish in the parts of the Lago del Fucino held by our court, and to catch as many as two boats can gather, for the use and sustenance of the personnel of the aforesaid monastery. We also grant that all the animals owned by the monastery shall be able to graze and take water throughout the entire Kingdom of Sicily, namely, throughout our demesnes, without any further need to obtain rights of pasturage or any other permission, with the exception of our enclosed lands, where we have decided not to grant such rights.

The following conditions regarding us and our heirs apply to the afore-

---

1. Ascoli Satriano, approximately 25 km south of Foggia.

said monastery and to the goods which we have granted it, to wit: the abbots and the monks of the monastery, as well as all those staying there for some other purpose, shall not come from any nation other than the kingdoms of France and Provence and the county of Forcalquier, without special leave from us or from our heirs in the Kingdom of Sicily. Moreover, even if someone from a nation other than those listed above should happen to be admitted to the aforesaid monastery with our or our heirs' permission, the person so admitted shall in no way be allowed to become abbot of the monastery without further approval from us or our heirs in the Kingdom of Sicily. If, contrary to this condition, something of the kind happens to be done by the abbots or congregation of the monastery, whether it be accepting monks or making abbots in a way other than that described above, and at our request or that of our heirs in the Kingdom the abbots and congregation are warned by a bishop chosen by us or by our heirs in the Kingdom, and after three warnings (each of which shall be two months in length, so that the third such warning will end after six months) they make no attempt to remove the monk or abbot in question, then all the goods and possessions which we have given or plan to give to the monastery, as well as the rights pertaining thereto, shall revert fully and freely to us and our heirs, and all offerings, grants, and transfers of such goods which we have made or planned to make to the aforesaid monastery shall have no validity whatsoever. Instead, by the same token we and our heirs in the Kingdom shall be permitted to take those possessions and goods as our own, without first waiting for a judgment or legal proceeding, and the abbots and monks will not be permitted to hold on to these goods, just as if they had never belonged to the aforesaid monastery, since the requisite conditions will be lacking.

Indeed, we believe it right and proper that men of the aforesaid nations should serve in this monastery, just as the athletes came forth from these nations who with their sweat and effort, and with much spilling of blood, freed the Kingdom of Sicily from the hands of its persecutors, to the glory of God and Blessed Mother Church. This will bear ample fruit for the monastery as well, when the multitudes from these nations who live in the Kingdom and are flocking to it choose all the more willingly to be buried there, as well as bestow greater favors upon it while they are alive and after they are dead. In turn, if the abbots and monks are brought in from these nations, they will be more ready and willing to labor by their prayers for us, our heirs, and others from those nations who dwell in the Kingdom or are flocking to it— more ready to do so, that is, than if they were from some other nation. Dissension and scandal will not arise, [as it would] between monks from many nations, and for this reason the virtues of charity and peace—which greatly support and strengthen the monks as they seek to serve the Lord in greater tranquility, and which (as experience has shown) even more frequently are thrown into confusion by a diversity of nations and passions—will be fostered and cultivated all the more, and the monastery will go on to profit even more in spiritual and temporal ways. For if it should happen that the differences between many nations bred disagreements within the monastery, and that these disagreements (as often happens) led to one of the abbots or monks being killed (God forbid!) through the misdeeds or machinations of the disputing parties, then the infamy of such a deed would become known beyond the mountains [in France] filling the souls of everyone with such horror and hatred that no one from the aforesaid nations[2] could ever be persuaded that they would want to enter the monastery. Instead, all would look upon it with utter terror, as a place of confusion and death. As a result, the monastery would decline temporally and spiritually due to a decrease in its divine office and offerings, leaving the praiseworthy and beneficial aims of its founder utterly unfulfilled.

Therefore, it is clear how dangerous it would be to mix together a variety of nations within the monastery, as well as how fruitful it would be for only those nations mentioned earlier to serve it. Since there are so many monasteries already established in the Kingdom of Sicily, both of this and of other orders, made up of persons from other nations, it seems only fitting that this monastery, originally established only by the aforesaid nations, should remain that way, and serve as a kind of lasting memorial to what we have founded and endowed—we who, supported by the power of those nations, took this kingdom from the hands of the enemies of the Church, to the greater glory of God. And since we as well as our Kingdom must take the greatest care to beware of the plots of our treacherous enemies, this beneficial provision removes an opportunity for evildoing from those who either support our enemies or who otherwise hate us and our heirs, and it will avoid many other expenses and result in great savings. This would not be the case if we simply had granted unfettered freedom regarding the election and admission of the monastery's abbots and monks.

Furthermore, since we are moved both by special affection and by reasoned reflection to make a special decree regarding the rule and care of this monastery, we wish and decree that this monastery of Blessed Mary of the Victory should be a dependent of the monastery of the Oratory, founded and built on our hereditary lands in the county of Anjou.[3] Let it be, as it were,

2. Namely, France, Provence, and the county of Forcalquier.
3. Notre-Dame-de-Loroux, also known as the Oratory, an early dependency of Cîteaux (no longer extant), founded in 1121 in the Loire valley midway between Angers and Saumur. Nothing remains of this site.

her special daughter, and like the monastery of the Oratory let it be the recipient of our special love, generously nurtured like one of our offspring, and treated most favorably among the other monasteries of this order. In witness to this deed, we have ordered the present privilege to be produced and given force by the seal of our hand. Given at Lagopesole[4] by Master William of Farumvilla, provost etc. of our kingdoms etc., in the year of the Lord 1277, the third day of August in the fifth indiction, the first year of our reign over Jerusalem, and the thirteenth year of our reign over Sicily.

4. In Puglia, approximately 25 km north of Potenza.

62. A CONTRACT FOR STONE WORK ON THE MONASTERY OF SANTA MARIA DI REALVALLE
(near Naples, 1279)

Introduced by Caroline Bruzelius;
translated from Latin by Sean Gilsdorf

This document, one of many that concern the construction of the two Cistercian abbeys, indicates that the labor force was divided between manual labor (not mentioned here), local sculptors (Michael of Naples and Berutus of Vico) who were to execute the pillars, and more highly skilled masons, some of whom were French, for the carving of ashlar blocks (finely cut and squared masonry blocks), corner stones, capitals, and the ribs at the vault departures, described in French as charges. This document enables us to obtain some sense of the cost of construction in the Kingdom of Sicily and provides insight into the organization of labor, in part along national lines. The monastery was located adjacent to Scafati, approximately 30 km southeast of Naples. Unfortunately, only the outer wall of the south aisle survives in place at Realvalle, and has never been excavated. The weathered capitals still in place attest, however, to the high quality of the imported craftsmanship in this part of the building.

Charles I, etc. Written to his faithful men, Peter Castaldus de Castromaris and Stephen of Donfront, overseers of expenses for work on the monastery of Santa Maria di Realvalle, etc.

We wish you to know that at Scafati on Friday, the last day of this month of June in the seventh indiction, [30 June 1279] the masters listed below contracted with our court to do the work listed below as piecework for the monastery, for an amount of money specified below. John of Zalono, William of Blesi, John of Maloctis, and Robert of Reus, at their own expense, will produce or have produced as piecework, from stone chosen by you for the purpose, 1000 ashlar blocks and cornerstones of good quality and necessary for the construction of the church. Of these, two parts will be ashlar blocks and the other third cornerstones. In return, [they will be paid] five ounces of gold, at a rate of fifteen *tari* for each hundred. If they are able to produce more than these 1000, then let them do so as needed at the same rate of compensation, in accordance with our will and pleasure.

Likewise, they will produce or have produced as piecework capitals for the columns in the middle of the church, at a rate of fifteen *tari* for each capital needed.

Translated from Heinrich Wilhem Schulz and Alexander Ferdinand von Quast, *Denkmaeler der Kunst des Mittelalters in Unteritalien* (Dresden: W.K.H. Schulz, 1860), vol. 4, 85–86.

Likewise, other capitals for the columns attached to the walls of the church, at a rate of ten *tari* for each capital needed.

Likewise, other double capitals, at a rate of twenty *tari* for each column needed.

Likewise, other stones [called *charges* in French][1] which will go atop the capitals of the aforementioned columns in the middle of the church up to where the elements of each column are separated,[2] at a rate of one ounce [of gold] for every cutting of these stones.

Likewise, other stones [called *charges d'arzeres*] which will go atop the capitals of the aforementioned columns joined to the walls, at a rate of fifteen *tari* for each cutting of these stones.

Likewise, capitals for the four larger columns in the middle of the church, at a rate of 40 *tari* for each column; also, other stones [likewise called *charges*], which will go atop the capitals of these four large columns, at a rate of two ounces of gold and twenty *tari* for each cutting of these stones, up to where the elements of these columns are separated; all of these likewise [made] from stone selected for them by you.

You should assign all of the stones suitable for these various projects to the masters in front of the workshop where it is carved. We also have promised them that we will repair, as needed, all of their iron tools that they will need to complete this work, until the aforementioned piecework is complete. If, however, any person or persons should wish to do the aforementioned piecework, either all or in part, for less money, we have reserved the right to assign it either wholly or in part to those who might wish by doing so to improve the situation of our court.

Likewise, Master Michael of Naples and Master Berutus of Vico of the Principality of Salerno similarly contracted with the court to make or have made as piecework, at their own expense, ten stone pillars of good quality, adequately supported by bases and plinths [sub-bases], up to the height at which capitals of the same type and shape ought to be placed. For performing this work, they will be paid, in daily installments, 25 ounces of gold, at a rate of two ounces of gold and fifteen *tari* for each pillar. Nevertheless, we have arranged that all of the stones needed for these pillars, their bases, and their plinths should be cut and handed over to the masters at the quarry. The aforesaid masters should have them brought, at their own expense, to the work site, and cut and finish the stones there appropriately, and put into

---

1. The *charges* are the first few blocks of stone at the departure of the vaults.
2. The separation of the elements of the column here refers to the vault departures at the top of the column shafts (reference to the stones used for the departures of the central vaults of the church).

place the stones they have cut and finished for us; the only exception to this is the capitals of the pillars themselves, which they do not have to make.

We also have told these masters that we would have you provide for them, at their request, enough masters and carts to cut and haul these stones—masters and carts, that is, which are not already assigned to other parts of this project. These latter masters should be found satisfactory by the aforesaid masters, who will pay their wages and also will rent out the carts at the same rate offered by our court to other masters and for other carts on the same project.

Therefore, we order your faithfulness to assign, at the workshop, the specified ashlar blocks and cornerstones needed for the construction [of the church] to the aforementioned John of Zalono, William of Blesi, John of Maloctis, and Robert of Reus, as long as the work goes on, and to repair as necessary the iron tools used in their work, making these repairs with the money provided to you by our court. You also should assign, at the quarry, the stones required to make the specified pillars, bases, and plinths, as well as the stonemasons, to Master Michael and Master Berutus, and provide them with the carts and masters they need to haul, cut, and shape these stones in accordance with the aforementioned agreement—ones who are not already assigned to other parts of this project, with the same wages provided to these master stonemasons as are given to other masters, and the same fees provided for these carts as for other carts on the same project, as our court has ordained.

You also should ensure that all the aforesaid master stonemasons—those who are to make the aforementioned ashlar blocks and cornerstones, as well as those by whom the pillars are to be made—perform the work they have agreed to do or have done in a careful, diligent, and proper way, without any defect whatsoever, in accordance with the aforementioned agreements, just as is described in detail above, and that you pay out the money agreed upon with them for their piecework, at the agreed-upon rates for those blocks which will be made and handed over by them, as soon the pieces are made and handed over by them to you once they have been cut, worked, and finished. This money will be provided by our court, and be paid by you without any interference whatsoever, and you are to draw up proper receipts for any payments that you make.

Thus you should take particular heed, and diligently and constantly insist, as we have said, that they perform their work carefully, diligently, and properly, without any defect whatsoever. Moreover, if any persons come forward who wish to do this work, either wholly or in part, for less money, and thereby improve the situation of our court, you should allow them to do so, and then report in writing to us and the financial officers of our court, in an orderly and detailed fashion, the names and surnames of those to whom you may already have granted the same work, as well as how much they already have done and how much they have been paid. In addition, we wish and command that if the aforementioned masters, who have agreed to produce the aforementioned 1000 ashlar blocks and cornerstones, wish once they are finished to produce others as needed, under the same terms and conditions, you should allow them to do so in the aforementioned way, by the authority provided by this document, without waiting for further instructions, giving them the required stones in front of the aforementioned workshop, paying them the aforementioned price for the ashlar blocks and cornerstones that they make, and having their iron tools repaired in the aforesaid way.

Given at Scafati on the last day of June.

63. JEWISH AND GREEK PATRONAGE IN APULIA
TWO TEXTS (1313/14, 1372/73)

Translated from Hebrew and Greek by Linda Safran

There were Jews in mainland southern Italy from at least the first century C.E., and synagogue inscriptions attest to their continued presence until the sixteenth century. Sometimes these texts record donations by individuals, such as the pavement and benches provided in 1184/85 to the synagogue at Gravina (Basilicata) by a father in memory of his son. More often they record the actions of a group, like the one responsible for construction of one of the four medieval synagogues in Trani (Apulia) in 1246/47. A short text from Bari attests to communal involvement in a more modest synagogue refurbishment. This synagogue, like others in the region, was located in the heart of the medieval city (via San Sabino leads to the Cathedral of Bari). Moses may be the artisan or, more likely, the community elder who commissioned the work. He or his forefathers came to Bari from either Trier (Germany) or Troyes (France); the correct translation from the Hebrew is uncertain. The date is given in the form of a gematria, in which letters have numerical value, as is also the case in Greek (that they are to be read as numbers rather than letters is clear from the small "V" carved above each character). Their sum provides both a word—in this case, Hadasah—and a number, 74, short for the Hebrew year 5074, which corresponds to 1313/14 C.E. The gematria word choice is not likely to be casual: Hadasah is another name for the biblical heroine Esther, who may have been invoked as a hopeful model by a community that had suffered forced conversions under the previous two Angevin kings, a situation that changed after 1309 under King Robert "the Wise."

1. A Synagogue Dedication in Bari (1313/14)

השענ הז זולח : הסדה תנש s
שייורפטד השמ דיב : סע תברנ

This window was made in the year "Hadasah," a gift of the people by the hand of Moses of Trywys.

2. A Hospital Dedication from Andrano (1372/73)

George Longo announces his patronage of a new village hospital in 1372/73, and the significance of the donation is underscored by the roster of distinguished guests at the dedication ceremony. Although the date is given according to the Byzantine reckoning, with years since the creation of the world (calculated since the sixth century as having occurred in 5509 B.C.E.) combined with the repeating fifteen-year indiction

Translated from Cesare Colafemmina, "Le testimonianze epigrafiche e archeologiche come fonte storica," *Materia Giudaica* 9 (2004): 37–52; inscription on architrave (a horizontal beam) of former synagogue on via San Sabino.

Figure 17. Dedication stone (1372/73). Greek inscription from Andrano now in the Museo Provinciale "Sigismondo Castromediano," Lecce. (Photo courtesy Antonio Cassiano, Direttore, Museo Provinciale "Sigismondo Castromediano")

UNIVERSITY OF WINCHESTER
LIBRARY

*cycle in use since Roman times, the text reveals the erosion of both Greek language and Orthodox practice in the region. Three hundred years after the Norman conquest ended Byzantine rule in Italy, a southern Italian word (*spitali*) derived from Latin (*hospitale*) is used to clarify a Greek neologism (*xenonas*), and peculiarities of spelling and grammar reveal the way the Greek language was being spoken in fourteenth-century Andrano. Three of the four bishops who witnessed the dedication occupied Roman Catholic sees; only Gallipoli remained in the possession of an Orthodox bishop. George Longo received an indulgence from his local bishop, Donadeus of Castro, for his charitable foundation; and when he calls down a curse on anyone who alienates hospital property, he invokes not the patriarch of Constantinople, but rather the Roman pope, along with the 318 Church Fathers (the theophoric Fathers cited below) who allegedly attended the first ecumenical council at Nicaea in 325. Greek culture in Italy was threatened by linguistic and religious acculturation, but the Orthodox rite would not be eradicated until the seventeenth century, and in some parts of southern Apulia (though not in Andrano) Greek is still spoken today.*

The present hostel, that is, "hospital," was built by the efforts and at the expense of George Longo and his wife, Gemma. If anyone should some day try to remove the property of the hospital he will receive the curses of the 318 theophoric Fathers and of the ecumenical Pope of Rome. This was done in the year 6881 [1373] during the eleventh indiction. // George Longo of the village of Andrano made this hospital by the will of God and invited Donadeus, bishop of Castro, John, bishop of Ugento, and John, bishop of Alessano, and Cyriakus, bishop of Gallipoli. And thus he [Donadeus] accords him [George] forty days of indulgence.

Translated from Lecce, Museo Provinciale Sigismondo Castromediano, inv. 54; limestone, 46.5 tall × 46 cm wide x 21 cm deep; Greek text on front and left side. Translation adapted from A. Jacob, "Une fondation d'hôpital à Andrano en Terre d'Otrante (inscription byzantine du Musée provincial de Lecce)," *MEFRM, Moyen Âge—Temps Modernes* 93, 2 (1981): 683 C.E 93.

64. ORDERING THE PIAZZA DEL CAMPO OF SIENA (1309)

Translated from Italian by Fabrizio Nevola

The Piazza del Campo is one of the most remarkable urban spaces created in Tre-cento Italy. Far from being an organically evolving form, its bowl-like shape, defined by the enclosing clear-cut edge of building façades, is the result of careful planning enforced through legislative measures. The piazza was the city's main civic arena; the slope focuses on the city hall (Palazzo Pubblico), which formed the scenographic backdrop to occasional ceremonial events as well as the everyday commercial life of the city, for the Campo was the main market-place [see #36]. Begun in 1298, the façade design of the city hall was established as the model that all buildings facing the piazza should imitate in statute rulings of 1309. Thus, for example, the Palazzo Sansedoni enforced this ruling with its three-light or triforium windows and the boldly contrasting use of brick and white travertine stone detailing. Unity of the façades served to underline the position of the city hall as civic centerpiece, while careful control of access-points to the piazza ensured a sense of marvel and surprise, as the vast open space of the piazza is accessed from dark alleys cut beneath the residential buildings that contour the square. Paving of the piazza was first begun in 1262, before the city hall was built, and completed in the early fourteenth century, when a succession of legislative measures improved the ambience of the area by pro-hibiting certain trades from the market on grounds of aesthetics and hygiene. The documents that follow are all selected from the city statutes of Siena, drawn up in the vernacular in 1309, although in one case earlier legislation was carried over into this volume of statutes.

(III.37) THAT IN EVERY HOUSE THAT IS BUILT AROUND THE CAMPO (FIELD) OF THE MARKET, THE WINDOWS SHOULD BE DESIGNED WITH COLUMNS

We also rule and order that if any house or palace should be built on the Campo market square, that if these houses or palaces should face onto the Campo, then these façades should be built with windows divided by colo-nettes, and have no overhanging structures. And the city magistrate (*podestà*) must ensure that this ruling is enforced. And whosoever should ignore these rulings and build a house or palace without applying said demands will be condemned by the lord magistrate of Siena to a fine of 25 *lire*. And if the magistrate should omit to apply the fine, he shall likewise have 25 *lire* detracted from his salary.

Translated from *Il Costituto del comune di Siena volgarizzato nel MCCCIX–MCCCX*, ed. Mahmoud S. Elsheikh (Città di Castello: Fondazione Monte dei Paschi di Siena, 2002), 2, 18–27, 124–25.

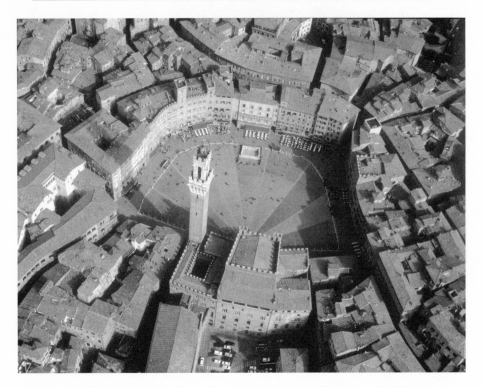

Figure 18. Piazza del Campo, Siena (fourteenth century). The Palazzo Pubblico and its bell tower are in the foreground. (Photo: Alinari/Art Resource)

(III.38) THAT NO PERMANENT BRACKETS SHOULD BE BUILT ON THE FRONT OF BUILDINGS FACING THE CAMPO

We also rule and order that no one is to have or install any permanent brackets or curtain-poles (*pertiche*), or work-benches or curtains onto the front of buildings facing onto the Campo market square, that extend beyond the awnings. And anyone who should use such brackets and curtains must ensure that these are removed every evening and in the days around Easter. And anyone who contravenes this ruling will be punished on each occasion with a fine of 5 *soldi*, half of which will be paid to the city government, and the other half to the person that denounces him.

(III.40) PERTAINING TO KEEPING THE CAMPO MARKET SQUARE CLEAR

And I order that the Campo market square should be cleared and kept clear, particularly of building materials such as stone, brick, wood, and that such materials will not be stored on the square, other than by those building on sites facing the square. In this case, they will be allowed to store materials for one month before, and one after the construction campaign is underway, provided that they continue building regularly. This ruling is suspended for eight days prior to the feast of the Assumption [15 August], and eight days following this feast, during which time the square is to be entirely cleared. And no dirt from the bellies of beasts, or any other sort, shall be allowed to be thrown on the piazza.

(III.42) That the paving around the Campo should be kept clear.

And I shall ensure that all the paving around the edge of the Campo be kept clear, and I will not permit that it be occupied by chairs, or workbenches or any other movable goods, or any other item, beyond the distance of two *braccia* from the window openings on the buildings facing the Campo. And anyone who contravenes this ruling will be punished on each occasion with a fine of 20 *soldi*.

(III.43) That neither hay nor straw shall be stored on the paving around the Campo

We also rule and order that no one is allowed to nor shall store or keep grass, hay, or straw on the paving that is laid around the Campo. And it is permitted to anyone who should find grass, hay, or straw thus stored, to remove or take this without risk of punishment.

(III.46) Regarding the filling of pot-holes on the Campo

We also rule and order that any temporary stall-holder is to fill in any hole or ditch that they make when they set up their work-benches and canopies, before they go away. And anyone who contravenes this ruling will be punished on each occasion with a fine of 5 *soldi*.

(III.51) That no barber is to practice his trade on the Campo of the market except on the feast of Santa Maria of August (the Assumption)

And I forbid that from the Kalends of January onward any barber should reside and practice his trade on the Campo of the market, from the church of San Paolo, except for on Saturday if he does not work in his shop, and the vigil and feast of Santa Maria of August (the Assumption). [Other bans applied to professions exercised on the Campo included tanners, hay, meat, leather and perhaps more surprisingly even saffron sellers.]

(III.261) THAT NO OVERHANGING JETTIES OR BALCONIES SHOULD BE ERECTED ON BUILDINGS FACING THE CAMPO

Also, with this ruling it is established that by a clause of the Statute of the Commune of Siena, that whosoever builds a house facing onto the Campo of the market, should construct windows with colonettes and not overhanging balconies or jetties (*ballatoi*), and it is also ruled by this clause that those houses that are already built around the Campo should not be modified by the addition of balconies. It is also ruled that no one, from this day forth, should build or renew or make any form of balcony or overhanging structure of any sort on buildings around the Campo, and also on any tower house or palace projecting from its walls. And whosoever should ignore these rulings will be condemned to a fine of 25 *lire*. And furthermore they will also be obliged to tear down and remove any such balcony or overhang. And this clause was ordered in the Year of Our Lord 1297 on 10 May.

65. ON THE CITY WALLS AND BUILT ENVIRONMENT OF PAVIA (1330)

Translated from Latin by Victoria Morse and William North

Opicino de Canistris (1296–ca. 1354) wrote his description of the city of Pavia in 1330 when the city was under interdict. The political circumstances are somewhat unclear, but Pavia seems first to have aligned itself with the imperial Ghibelline faction under the leadership of Azzo Visconti of Milan and then to have sheltered several of its citizens who had seized a cargo of papal tax revenue. The text can be read as an attempt to mitigate the effect of these anti-papal actions and to convince Pope John XXII of the essential religiosity of the city and its inhabitants by means of a description that highlights the city's Christian history, the religious customs and practices of its inhabitants (specifically those, like almsgiving, that could be legitimately practiced during an interdict), and the fundamental religious "infrastructure" provided by the city's churches and saints' relics. In addition, the genre of city descriptions called attention to the built environment, the surrounding countryside, and details of the city's political and social life. Two historical moments are particularly important for understanding Opicino's description of the city. Pavia was founded by the Romans, and the old city center preserved the regular Roman grid of streets (still visible today) and a functioning Roman sewer system. Around the middle of the seventh century Pavia became the capital of the northern Italian kingdom of the Lombards, and Opicino records a number of traditions about building projects that the rulers undertook in the city. Both these elements, most particularly the Lombard influence, are important in the passages about the city walls translated here. These texts show how the three sets of walls structured Opicino's experience and representation of urban space and the contribution they made to an image of the city as powerful and well defended. In the passage in which Opicino discusses the cemetery of Santa Maria in Pertica, bisected by the wall, we see him working with striking attention to archaeological evidence and interest in the physical manifestations of the Lombard past of his city. (VM)

HISTORY OF THE WALLS

This is the city which, by divine power, the Lombards preserved and selected as the capital and treasury of their kingdom, after they had destroyed and depopulated the other towns of Italy. When they had finally received the faith of Christ and established the Lombard law there, they remained at Pavia as long as their kingdom lasted, extending the walls, and they adorned the city

Translated from Opicino de Canistris [Anonymus Ticinensis], *Liber de laudibus civitatis ticinensis*, ed. Rodolfo Maiocchi and Ferruccio Quintavalle, *RIS²* n.s. 11:1 (Città di Castello: S. Lapi, 1903). Also published by Faustino Gianani, *Opicino de Canistris, l'Anonimo Ticinese* (Pavia: Tipografia Fusi, 1927; 2nd. ed. 1976). All translations are from Opicino de Canistris, *Book in Praise of Pavia*, trans. William North and Victoria Morse (New York: Italica Press, forthcoming).

with countless churches and the relics of the saints. I have discovered, however, that the second and third walls were constructed long after the end of the Lombards' kingdom.

USE OF THE THREE RINGS OF WALLS TO STRUCTURE LISTS OF THE CHURCHES AND SAINTS' RELICS CONTAINED IN THE CITY

The city is known to shine with more than one hundred and thirty churches within its three circuits of walls. Within the first circuit of inner walls which extends for a space of eighty *iugera* or more (each of which is a square of equal size and is cleansed by deep, underground sewers). . . .

DESCRIPTION OF THE WALLS

Now then, the entire city is girded with a circle of three walls, the innermost of which is wonderfully large. One exits the city, following the layout of the interior wall, through nine extremely strong, high gates; each of these has very strong doors with the rest of the wall looming overhead, double towers in certain ones, double doors in many, and a drawbridge in front of some. The first inner wall, which is quadrangular, is adorned with the same number of incredibly strong gates, except for the postern gates. The second wall, also quadrangular, is adorned with the same number of very suitable gates, although there are no doors in the first or second walls. The third wall, which is almost round, is surrounded in all directions except the south with deep and wide ditches that are always full of rushing water, and the city is adorned with fitting suburbs.

BRIDGES AND ENTRANCES TO THE CITY

Now then, the Ticino is the fourth largest river in that region after the Po, and over it, as we have said, there is a bridge which is almost half a *stadium* long, almost half covered, with walls and windows here and there, and a gate with doors on the side of the suburbs, on top of which there is the church of San Saturnino. This bridge also has pilings made of rocks and stones, and in one part has stone arches built on rocks in the water. At certain times the city also has another bridge made entirely of wood and located downstream; it has a great gate with doors at the entrance of the city. This bridge is called the Ponte Nuovo, while the other is called the Ponte Vecchio.

INSCRIPTIONS ON THE CITY WALLS

What else? The reputation of their [the Pavian] militia is widely known throughout Italy and certain large shields, which are square at the top and bottom, are called "Pavians" almost everywhere. As a consequence, these verses have been written on some of the gates of the city:

> Whoever now enters, let him say on bended knee:
> Say now, you who pass, you who touch
> The threshold of this gate:
>   Hail, O Second Rome, Imperial Head of the World.
> Thou hast conquered Thebes in war,
>   Thou hast vanquished Athens in reason.
>   Thee the nations dread,
>   To thee the powerful bow their necks.

CEMETERIES IN THE OLD CITY INTERSECTED BY THE CITY WALL

All the cemeteries are surrounded by walls; and within the third wall of the city there are, among others, three very ancient cemeteries renowned throughout the world that were, in antiquity, much larger than they are now. They are the cemetery of Saints Gervasio and Protasio, which extends even outside the aforementioned wall and its ditches; the cemetery of San Giovanni in Borgo; and the cemetery of Santa Maria in Pertica. In the middle of the cemetery of Santa Maria in Pertica is the chapel of Sant'Adriano where the Lombard kings and many other nobles are buried. This cemetery is said to have been one of the four principal cemeteries of the world, and therefore nobles from far off regions chose to be buried there and had single poles planted upon their graves with some sign by which anyone might know who was buried there. This is why even today that church is commonly called Santa Maria in Pertica [pole or staff]. Moreover, this cemetery is known to have been much larger in antiquity, because when earth was dug up far from the place where it now is, the bones of the dead were discovered as well as great jars full of earth in which cremated bodies were preserved.

Rome, the Papacy, and Papal Politics

Since the advent of Christianity, the history of Rome has been bound up with the history of the papacy. First-century witnesses attest Peter's presence in the capital and his leadership of the Christian community in Rome. By the third century, Peter was honored as the first bishop of Rome, cementing the primacy of the Roman see. Among the many concerns of the Roman pontiff was the social welfare of his city. Exemplifying the charitable impulses of his own period, Innocent III (d. 1216), established the hospital of Santo Spirito in Sassia on the left bank of the river Tiber. But as leader of the Church, the pope also had to provide for the spiritual health of pilgrims visiting the city, especially during the first Jubilee or Holy Year, proclaimed in 1300, when unprecedented numbers of religious visitors descended upon Rome.

Beginning in the eighth century, the papacy began to complement its spiritual authority with temporal power by annexing territories throughout Italy to its not inconsiderable land-holdings in the south. During the pontificate of Gregory VII (d. 1085), Matilda, countess of Canossa (d. 1115), gave protection and financial patronage to the embattled pope and, after her death, a much disputed bequest of territory in central Italy. By the late twelfth century, the patrimony of Saint Peter cut a swath through the central portion of the peninsula, becoming the basis for the papal state. The papacy also claimed lordship over the Kingdom of Sicily, which was at the heart of the decades-long contest of wills between Emperor Frederick II (d. 1250) and a succession of popes. Being a great landlord meant everything from dispatching warrior legates and mercenaries to quash rebellions to arbitrating banal disputes between tenants in the papal territories.

Rome itself was never an easy or accommodating city to rule. Roman families vied with each other to put their sons on the papal throne, creating an atmosphere of tension and violence from which not even the pope was immune. His person was not infrequently a target of violence both in life and in death and throughout the centuries Rome continued to present challenges to the papacy. The twelfth century saw a self-conscious city swept up in the heady communal movement that was spreading throughout the northern and central parts of the peninsula. In Rome, the reformer Arnald of Brescia (d. 1155) was coopted by this movement, leading a revolt against papal rule of the city and agitating for republican liberties. The rebellion proved ill-fated and was put down with the help of Frederick I Barbarossa (d. 1190), whose efforts were repaid with an imperial coronation. But republican sympathies did not lie moribund for long. In the mid-fourteenth century, led by Cola di Rienzo (d. 1354), a Roman notary of humble birth, Rome again experienced a short-lived republican moment.

66. MATILDA OF CANOSSA, PAPAL PATRON
TWO TEXTS (eleventh century)

Translated from Latin by William North

In 1082, the reform papacy under Gregory VII (d. 1085) faced crisis: Emperor Henry IV had descended into Italy with his armies to gain control of Rome and to establish his own pope, Guibert of Ravenna, and the papacy did not have the resources needed to repel him. In desperation, allies like Matilda of Canossa (d. 1115) and Bishop Anselm of Lucca (d. 1086) took the controversial step of turning to ecclesiastical and monastic treasuries for the needed funds. The following documents present one such donation, its context and consequences. The first text, drawn from a fourteenth-century prose summary of Donizo of Canossa's Life of Countess Matilda *known as the* Short History of Polirone, *offers a brief account of the immediate context of the donation. Besieged by Henry IV, Pope Gregory VII decided to turn for military aid to the Normans of southern Italy and their leader, Duke Robert Guiscard (d. 1085), with whom the Roman Church had been allied since their reconciliation in 1059.*

The second, near contemporary account records the monastery's own response to this crisis, prompted by its close relationship with its patroness, Countess Matilda of Canossa and her advisor, Bishop Anselm of Lucca, who was acting as Pope Gregory VII's representative, or vicar, in northern Italy. At the same time, its author shows equal interest in recording the amicable and profitable relations with reform-minded bishops and popes. Along with the favor of Saint Peter, these relationships also had tangible benefits for the monastery: episcopal and papal confirmation and protection of rights and privileges as well as the addition of churches to the monastery's jurisdiction (and hence the addition of their revenues to its income). It thereby offers intriguing evidence for the role of such gifts and loans in establishing enduring and reciprocal bonds of friendship between institutions and attests to the vital importance of this network of princes and prelates in safeguarding and expanding a monastery's lands and rights.

1. Life of Countess Matilda

After providing the countess with salutary advice and divine commands, [Gregory VII] said farewell and set off for Rome [in 1077]. The people of Rome went out to meet him with great exultation and welcomed him as their shepherd. Gregory then absolved all those who opposed the emperor of infidelity and perjury [in 1080]. When the emperor learned of this, he entered Italy with a great army and went here and there, crushing castles and towns; only Countess Matilda resisted him. Burning with rage, the emperor fought many battles against her, terrorized [her lands], and threatened sieges.

Translated from *Historia Comitissae Mathildis, De Gestis videlicet progenitorem ipsius et eiusdem comitissae Mathildis*, ed. Luigi Simeoni, in *RIS²* (Bologna: Zanichelli, 1930), 120–21.

But because the countess's fortresses were beyond counting, she always defended herself vigorously from the emperor's oppression.

When the emperor realized this, he hastened to the City [Rome]. When the City would not bow to his will, he besieged and devastated it and destroyed many of its walls [1082–83]. Having gained the city, Henry decreed that . . . the antipope Guibert would be called Clement [III]. Gravely offended by these developments, Pope Gregory summoned Robert Guiscard, lord of Apulia, to his aid. . . .

Meanwhile, Countess Matilda, burning with a pious heart against both the emperor and Guibert the antipope and abhorring their actions, fought many battles against them and to the best of her ability supported whoever opposed them. She was, in fact, the faithful protector of bishops, clerics, monks, and all Catholics. Indeed, all those who had been condemned, despoiled, and exiled by that emperor of idlers in this troubled time came running to her, and she supplied them with kind aid and sound counsel. Among these men was the venerable Anselm of Lucca. . . . To Anselm, Gregory VII entrusted [Countess Matilda] with a father's affection so that he might instruct her with his salutary admonitions and kind examples. [A version of the document given below follows.]

2. Matilda's Donation from the Church of Canossa

In the year of the Lord 1082, Countess Matilda and Bishop Anselm, who in those days was also vicar of Pope Gregory VII in Lombardy, asked for the church of Canossa's treasure from Abbot Gerard, who was ruling the church at that time. It was to be sent to the pope for the defense of the Roman Church, which was then suffering great persecution from the heresiarch Guibert. And so, because the aforementioned abbot and congregation of brothers had a faithful affection and love for the blessed Peter and the Roman Church, they offered their treasure to its vicar [in response] to the petition of the countess. [The treasure] was twenty-four crowns, one of them gold with a small gold crucifix on it, two altar tables of silver, the silver cover of the altar tomb of Saint Apollonius, and a large silver thurible. All this was melted down at Canossa into seven hundred pounds of silver and nine of gold.

In the end, the treasure was sent to Rome with the assent and by the will of the pope, who had received from the countess [Matilda] a donation charter regarding all of her lands. Then, when the countess asked for the

Translated from *On Treasure from the Church of Canossa That Was Sent to Rome and on the Compensation Made to the Church of Canossa*, ed. Luigi Simeoni, in *RIS* [2] 2 (Bologna: Zanichelli, 1930), 108–9.

restoration of a small amount of the treasure that had been removed, the vicar Anselm, who was then ruling this bishopric [Reggio] as well at the pope's command, placed two chapels, one in Filina and one in Casula, under [the authority] of the church of Canossa. Later, Bishop Heribert [ca. 1086–91] because he loved the Roman Church catholically, praised Bishop Anselm's action and in praising it, also confirmed it and consecrated the church of Canossa. And whatever the church rightly had in its dowry, he acknowledged; furthermore, when the Countess requested it, he placed another two chapels, one in the village of Placiola and the other in Fano, under [the authority] of this same church. Through the wish and with the support of this bishop, the church of Canossa also acquired at this time a chapel located in Gorgo from the church's patrons. In 1090, in the time of bishop [Heribert], we cleansed that church of Gorgo of thorns and snakes inside and out. Later, when Bishop Heribert wished to travel to Sicily for the profit and honor of the Queen Church, because he loved the church of Canossa with pure friendship, he received from her on loan a precious purple chasuble the color of blood with gold needlework along with an appropriate linen habit. Together [the chasuble] and the habit, he said, were worth thirty pounds. In return, he again truly confirmed everything which the church of Canossa held by right with pontifical words and promised with true faith that if he returned from Sicily alive, he would place some of the best chapels in his diocese under the authority of Canossa; if he did not happen to come back or if he lost the chasuble and habit, he would decide from which of the goods of the Queen Church the church of Canossa would have its restoration for the habit that was lent to him.

Later, after the agreement between Pope Paschal and the emperor and the death of the Countess Matilda, the church of Canossa sent the pope a tax for five years. At the same time, it sought confirmation of [its rights over] all of its churches as well as of the liberty that the Roman Church had written for it in the time of Otto I. For in this way, no bishop would ever be able to rule over it in any way, and the [new] pope might strengthen and protect it with his own apostolic privilege, just as Gregory VII had received it from the countess into the property of Saint Peter and [the monastery] had paid [the church of Rome] twenty *solidi* every year. This the most holy pope did, placing under perpetual anathema and separating from the body and blood of Christ anyone who knowingly seized by force what belongs to Saint Apollonius and who shall be found to have violated this privilege. The witnesses of this action were Lord Peter, Vincent, Peter, John, John, and Donatus, clerics of this monastery.

67. THE MARVELS OF ROME (1143)

Translated from Latin by Mary Stroll

In the twelfth century Rome was but a vestige of the ancient city, with ruins of the great monuments scattered among its inhabited and uninhabited parts. What characterized the period was a general revival of interest in the ancient world, an aspect of what scholars refer to as the "renaissance of the twelfth century." Rome manifested this "renaissance" with a great flowering of artistic activity and a renewed interest in Roman antiquity. The model of the Roman Republic provided the inspiration for the city's attempt to establish itself as a free commune, as many northern Italian cities were doing. A potent symbol of the free commune was the revival of the Roman Senate and its Senate House, now positioned on the Capitoline Hill and oriented toward the inhabited part of the city. In this context, in 1143 a canon of Saint Peter's wrote a guidebook for Roman antiquities entitled The Mirabilia *or* The Marvels of Rome, *describing foundation of the city and her chief monuments, famous places and images, which served also to glorify the city's celebrated history. This rhetorical genre, in praise of the city, became particularly popular in the thirteenth century [see #5, 115, 117].*

The first selection translated below treats the medieval legend that recounted the vision of Octavian or Augustus, in which the Tibertine Sibyl predicted the birth of Christ to the emperor. About the time of the writing of The Mirabilia *an altar commemorating this vision was constructed in the convent of Saint Mary on the Capitoline Hill. To commemorate the event, the church subsequently took the name of Santa Maria in Aracoeli (Saint Mary of the Altar of Heaven). The second selection refers to a monumental bronze statue in the piazza of the basilica and palace of Saint John Lateran, where the pope resided. Although we now know the statue to represent Marcus Aurelius, many in the medieval period believed it to be a likeness of the Emperor Constantine. In contrast, however, the* Mirabilia *author identifies the statue as a virtuous figure from the Roman Republic, which may express both a critique of the pope's claim to secular power and support of the communal movement and its attempt to revive the Roman Senate.*

I. In the time of the emperor, Octavian, the senators, seeing him of such great beauty that no one was able to look into his eyes, and of so much good fortune and peace that he made the whole world subject to himself, said to him: "We wish to adore you because the divinity is in you. If this were not so, all good fortune would not come to you." But resisting [their entreaty], he requested a delay. He called the Sibyl of Tibur to himself, and told her

Translated from *Codice topografico della città di Roma*, ed. Roberto Valentini and Giuseppe Zucchetti, vol. 3, Fonti per la storia d'Italia 90 (Rome: Senato, 1946), 3–65; 11. at 28–29; 15. at 32–33. See also *The Marvels of Rome—Mirabilia Urbis Romae*, trans. Francis Morgan Nichols, 2nd ed. (New York: Italica Press, 1986).

what the senators had said. She requested a space of three days during which she kept a strict fast. After the third day she responded to the emperor: "Lord emperor, this will certainly come to pass:

"As a sign of judgment, the earth will drip with sweat;
From heaven will come the king for all ages;
It is manifest that he will be present in the flesh
In order that he may judge the world,"
And she said other things that followed.

And on that very spot the earth opened up, and a brightness, great beyond measure, shone over him. And he saw in the heavens a certain extraordinarily beautiful virgin standing over the altar, holding a boy in her arms. Exceedingly astonished, Octavian heard a voice saying: "This is the altar of the son of God." Immediately falling to the ground, Octavian adored him.

II. At the Lateran there is a certain bronze horse that is called Constantine's, but it is not so; whoever wishes to know the truth, let him read it here. In the time of the consuls and the senators, a certain very powerful king from the East came to Italy, and besieged Rome from the area of the Lateran, inflicting the Roman people with much slaughter and war. At that time a certain armor-bearer, fine of form and virtue, bold and prudent, rose up and said to the consuls and senators: "If there were someone who would deliver you from this tribulation, what would he be deserving of from the senate?" Responding, [the consuls and senators] said to him: "Whatever he shall ask, he will soon obtain." And he said to them: "Give me 30 thousand *sesterces* [an ancient Roman coin] and after the war is over, you will make me the finest horse as a memorial of the victory." They promised to do just what he requested. And he said: "Arise in the middle of the night and arm yourselves, and stand watch within the walls, and do whatever I tell you."

The armor-bearer mounted his horse without a saddle and picked up a sickle. For several nights he saw that the king came to the foot of a certain tree to relieve himself, and that on the king's arrival, a little owl, who sat in the tree, always sang. The armor-bearer, to be sure, departed from the city, and gathered green stalks that he carried bound in a bundle in the manner of a royal guard. As soon as he heard the singing of the little owl, he approached more closely, and saw that the king had come to the tree. He went straight toward him, who had already relieved himself. The guards, who were with the king, thought that he was one of their own. They began to shout that he should get away from the king, but he did not give up on account of them. Feigning that he was moving away, he reached the king, and spurning all of

Figure 19. Bronze Equestrian Statue of Marcus Aurelius (161–180). In medieval Rome this statue stood outside the Lateran Palace. It survived destruction during the Middle Ages because it was popularly believed to have been the Emperor Constantine, hailed as the first Christian emperor. Rome, Musei Capitolini (Photo: Frances Andrews)

the guards, by his bravery he snatched the king, and bore him away. As soon as he came to the walls of the city, he began to shout: "Go forth from the gates and massacre the whole army of the king because, as you can see, I hold the king captive."

And they rushed out, killing some, and putting others to flight. Hence, the Romans acquired innumerable pounds of gold and silver. Thus, they returned in glory to the city, and what they had promised to the aforesaid armor-bearer, they paid. They handed over 30 thousand *sesterces*, and as a memorial, a gilded bronze horse without a saddle, and with the armor-bearer sitting astride, the right hand with which he had captured the king extended. As a memorial, on the head of the horse was the little owl at whose song he had achieved his victory. Also, as a memorial they placed the king himself, who was of puny stature, with his hands tied behind his back just as he had been captured, under the hoof of the horse.

68. ARNALD OF BRESCIA AT ROME (ca. 1162–66)

Translated from Latin by Thomas Carson

In 1145, Arnald, a regular canon of the Brescian church, arrived in Rome as a pilgrim. By then he had already developed a reputation as a reformer who preached against the wealth and privileges of the clergy. In Rome he encountered an incipient communal movement which aimed to establish an autonomous republican city, free from papal and imperial intervention. In 1143, in reaction to the pope's temporal claims to the suburban town of Tivoli, a Roman republic was established, the senate reconstituted, and the executive office of patricius *created. Arnald's radical preaching against the papacy's temporal power and his call for ecclesiastical poverty at first coincided with the interests of the Roman communal leaders with the result that the pope became an exile from his own city. But this "coalition" lasted only a decade as the political leaders of the commune soon distanced themselves from Arnald's most radical teachings. He was then all but abandoned at Eastertide in 1155 when Pope Hadrian IV (d. 1159) imposed an interdict on the city, threatening Rome's lucrative pilgrimage trade. Ultimately, the pope left it to Frederick I Barbarossa (1155–90), not yet crowned emperor, in collaboration with the city magistrates, to capture Arnald, execute him, and have his ashes tossed into the Tiber so that his mortal remains could inspire no marytr's cult. In mid-June the pope presided over Frederick's imperial coronation in Rome. The text excerpted below is from a Latin epic poem, written between 1162 and 1166, by an anonymous poet known to modern scholars as the "Bergamo Master." (KLJ)*

Then Arnald was residing in those regions,
Whom Brescia bore and honored overmuch.
His life was very hard and too austere;
He ate, but did not speak, with moderation.
A scholar with great confidence and knowledge,
He knew more than it was wise for him to know.
I judge that it will help your understanding
To speak about his end and what he believed:
He carped at common people and the priests,
Since he alone, he thought, lived morally,
And others were in error if they strayed
From what he taught. For nothing was above
Attack, not even actions of the pope.
He mixed the truth with falsity to please
The crowd. He damned the laymen who withheld
Their tithes as well as usury and war.
As Scripture teaches, he condemned luxury,
Dishonesty, and all the fleshly sins

Translated from *Carmen de gestis Frederici I imperatoris in Lombardia* as *Barbarossa in Italy* (New York: Italica Press, 1994), 22–32.

That blocked the path to life. No vice was flattered.
But still he acted like a foolish doctor
Who amputates both hurt and healthy limbs,
And there were very few his wrath omitted.
He censured fallen priests and Simonists
Who thought to hold their office for a price.
He said the people ought not to confess
And never take the sacraments from them.
To him the monks who disobeyed their rule
Were not entitled to the name of monk.
Infatuated by the things that perish,
The popes, he said, have spurned a higher good.
They spend their time in selling court decisions
In disregard of all their other duties.
For this he judged they'd earn eternal death,
Since sinful men were bound, he claimed, by just
One rule: To love God and their neighbor not
What evils flourish at the Roman See,
For popes, he said, had put a price on justice
And money had usurped the place of law.
From the head the evil flowed into the body
Of the Church, and every member yearned for rich
Rewards. So everything must have its price,
And what does not is held in great contempt.
This was the teaching of that famous Arnald
That pleased the masses by its novelty.
All Europe had been taken by this doctrine
Which first gathered bitter fruit in Italy.
O Brescia, you reflect your child's teaching,
Which had disturbed the peace of great Milan
And broke the easy faith of Rome's plebeians.
Wherever it was sown, it caused sedition,
Deceiving people in the guise of truth.
Although the pope desired to convert him,
His kind advice was never strong enough
To cause him to relinquish his beliefs.
In bitter language Arnald never stopped
Insulting the pope, nor would he quit his errors.
Frequent warnings often went astray,
And he rejoiced to see his fame increase.
Because his lying doctrines fooled the people,
The tearful pope desired to heal this sickness.
He found him worthy of anathema,
And hurled this doctor teaching schism from the Church,
So does the surgeon cut the rotting member
In order to protect the body's health.
But that did not restrain this master's tongue

From spreading his accustomed lies. He flayed
The church more harshly. Teaching as he taught,
He contradicted what the pope had sought.
Therefore he was reported and then jailed
By the Roman prefect acting for the king.
Then Frederick ordered him to judge this case,
And the learned doctor's doctrines were condemned.
So he discovered that he would suffer death
And fate had put a noose around his neck.
They asked him to reject his wicked theories
And be wise enough to make a full confession.
With confidence and courage that was astounding
He said his teachings seemed correct to him,
And he would not recant in face of death
Since nothing in them was absurd or harmful.
He sought a brief delay; he said he needed
Time to pray and tell his sins to Christ.
He bent his knees and raised his hands to heaven,
While sighs emerged from deep within his chest.
He spoke to God, but did not use his voice
To ask him to have mercy on his soul.
Then in a little while he stood prepared
To die, and the lictors looking on were moved
To tears by his display of piety.
Yet he was hanged, suspended by a rope.
It's said the king lamented, but too late.
What good was all your knowledge, learned Arnald?
What good your fasting and your discipline?
What good a life that is too strict and always
Spurns the easy path and carnal things?
O wretched man, what led you to attack
The church and brought you to this sorry rope?
Since that for which you suffered is condemned,
It will not quickly be restored to favor.
Your doctrines like yourself are turned to ashes,
And no relic may remain to honor you.

69. INNOCENT III TO THE HOSPITAL OF SANTO SPIRITO IN SASSIA (9 January 1208)

Translated from Latin by Brenda Bolton

Innocent III, aware that the sick and the poor in centers of urban population required care and charity, chose for his Roman foundation of Santo Spirito the model of the hospital of Saint-Esprit in Montpellier. Innocent first united the church of Santa Maria in Saxia with an abandoned hostel of English pilgrims in order to provide both endowment and site for his new hospital. In 1204, he joined Santo Spirito institutionally to Saint-Esprit, making Guy of Montpellier, as master of both foundations, responsible to the pope alone and entrusting him with the administration of these hospitals on either side of the Alps. Innocent then instituted a liturgical station on the first Sunday after Epiphany (12 January 1208) at which the sudarium or holy image of Christ's face, popularly known as the Veronica, was processed from Saint Peter's by the canons of the basilica to the hospital by the Tiber. In this stational ceremony, pilgrims and Romans alike celebrated the liturgical marriage of piety with the six corporal acts of mercy, or works of charity. Integral to this was the sermon preached by Innocent, his gift of a year's indulgence to those who attended, and his generous handouts of money to the poor and needy.

To his beloved Sons the Rector and Brothers of the Hospital of Santo Spirito in Saxia granting indulgences and privileges to them.

To commemorate the salutary wedding which at the conversion of a sinner is duly celebrated between the spirit of Man and the grace of the Creator, from which good will and actions are generated like sons and daughters, on the first Sunday after the Octave of the Epiphany, when that Gospel is read in which Jesus turned the water into wine, being invited with his disciples to the wedding where his Mother was at Cana in Galilee, turned the water into wine, we institute a solemn station at your Hospital, in which you, as a result of our institution, are given up to divine obedience. At the wedding [at Cana] there are said to have been six water pots . . . and in this Hospital, as at Cana of Galilee, a place where there is zeal for moving from vices to virtues, are to be found six water pots, that is, the six established works of mercy, feeding the hungry, supplying the thirsty with drink, gathering in the stranger, clothing the naked, visiting the infirm and attending the prisoner. . . . And those six water pots are filled up to the brim when those six works of mercy are performed to perfection; and from water is made wine when from the merit of alms the power of charity is kindled. And because we read that Jesus was

Translated from *PL* 215, col. 1270.

invited to this wedding in Cana of Galilee, where his mother was, therefore, we duly institute that an effigy of Jesus Christ be solemnly carried from the Basilica of the Blessed Peter by canons of the same to the said Hospital, where the memory of His Glorious Mother is recalled, inside a reliquary specially crafted for this with gold and silver and precious stones; a desirable object to be shown to congregations of the faithful who have met with devotion to celebrate this wedding. And so that we, who by the Lord's revelation have opened to others the venerable sacrament by its inspiration may also provide an example to be imitated by others, we grant, establish and command that for a thousand poor people coming from outside [Rome] and for three hundred people living [in Rome], seventeen pounds of normal money be given to you annually forever by the Almoner of the Supreme Pontiff, so that individuals receive three *denari*: one for bread, one for wine and the other for meat. And to the above-mentioned canons who will carry the effigy of the Savior in procession, let twelve *soldi* be given to each and a wax candle of one pound from the offerings at the *confessio* of Saint Peter. And because man does not live by bread alone but by every word that proceeds from the mouth of God, the Roman pontiff ought to be present at this Station with his cardinals and celebrate there the solemnities of masses, and deliver an exhortatory sermon concerning this celebration. So lest the faithful people return hungry from this wedding, besides material and doctrinal food, let him impart to them spiritual food also by granting an indulgence of one year's remission from the penances enjoined on them. We advise, therefore, and beseech our successors through Christ Jesus who will come to judge the living and the dead that they see to the unfailing observation of this institution which (with himself as witness) has proceeded from the fount of piety, prohibiting under the adjuration of divine judgment that it should be allowed to anyone to infringe this page of our grant, constitution, and command or by rash daring, to oppose it.

Given at Rome at Saint Peter's on 3 January in the tenth year of our pontificate.

70. A DISPUTE WITH POPE INNOCENT III OVER CUSTOMARY RIGHTS IN ALATRI (1212)

Translated from Latin by Brenda Bolton

The thirteenth century witnessed innumerable disputes between the popes and small local communities over lands previously given as pious donations to assist new and struggling religious houses. In the case of Saint Bartholomew at Trisulti, a former Benedictine abbey in the diocese of Alatri, refounded in 1204 as the first Charterhouse in the Patrimony, it was Innocent III who granted to the Carthusian brothers the forest of Eici to provide them with a barrier against intrusion from the outside world. By satisfying their quest for a remote wilderness in which to pursue the silence and tranquility they so desired, Innocent inadvertently risked depriving the inhabitants of the nearby castra *or fortified villages of Collepardo and Vico, who were increasingly dependent on what they could hunt or gather in the forests, of those customary rights of wood cutting and pasturing animals enjoyed by the communities for two hundred years. A notary's deed of 1220 reveals a previous attempt at compromise regarding the forest of Monte Furnulo, negotiated by papal representatives in September 1212, following violent attacks on each other by the Collepardesi and Vicani. The compromise allowed the inhabitants of Collepardo to use the Vicani's forest of Monte Furnulo. This particular dispute was to rumble on until the 1280s, and was replicated by peasants throughout the Italian peninsula whenever and wherever ecclesiastical or lay landlords attempted to consolidate their lands into compact estates.*

In the name of the Lord, Amen. Lord Lando de Montelongo was sworn and when questioned said that the Lord Pope Innocent had freely given the forest of Eici to the monastery of Saint Bartholomew, which that monastery stated belonged to it by right, and so the monastery peacefully retains possession of that forest by the year, in spite of the grumbling of the inhabitants of Collepardo on the grounds that they had lost all the asset of pastures and timber. The Lord Pope ordered Lord Lando de Montelongo and Lord Vita to go there and make it their concern to provide for the aforesaid inhabitants of Collepardo in the matter of pasture and timber. In the presence of the Collepardesi, they found out through good men and public instruments that as Monte Furnulo was common land so the people of Vico could claim for themselves no special control over it. Lando and Vita reported back to the Lord Pope and he caused his letter to be written on this matter and gave an

Translated from D. Atanasio Taglienti, *Il monastero di Trisulti, e il castello di Collepardo: storia e documenti* (Rome, 1985), vol. 10, 449–53; from a notary's deed, 20 March 1220 in the Archive of St. Bartholomew at Trisulti, containing the deposition of witnesses regarding Monte Furnulo which Innocent III had given in fealty to the inhabitants of Collepardo.

oral mandate that they should yield to the people of Collepardo by his authority the use of the pastures and timber on Monte Furnulo and should totally prohibit them from the forest of Eici. They faithfully followed the orders of the Lord Pope, allowing the Collepardesi to use the aforesaid Mount Furnulo, and placing the community of the people of Vico under a penalty of a hundred *lire* and one hundred *soldi* per person that they should not molest them in this in any way. The Collepardesi received that solution with alacrity, considering it agreed and valid, and with the provisions themselves fixed and having assigned useful service to them, they generously offered the gift of a thousand planks of timber.

Lord John Abioso was sworn and when questioned said that he had gone to the *castrum* of Vico with certain inhabitants of Collepardo who carried the papal letter to the community of the said *castrum*. When asked if he knew what was contained in the letter he replied that he did not know and said that they were badly received by the community of the aforesaid *castrum* of Vico. . . . A certain James was sworn and when questioned said that he had been present when Lord Lando de Montelongo and Lord Vita yielded pastures to the men of Collepardo on behalf of the Lord Pope, and timber on Monte Furnulo in recompense for the forest of Eici. James said that he had seen several legal instruments, but did not know what was contained in them, and this took place in the square of San Salvatore in the *castrum* of Collepardo. When asked who were present, he replied that nearly all the men of Collepardo and also some from Vico were there. Asked about the day, he said that it was a Sunday, as he firmly believed, but he did not remember for certain about the time, although he said that it was in winter, and that on the following day he himself and many others sent animals in order to claim their rights on the aforesaid Monte Furnulo.

. . . The Lord Pope himself, on his own authority, gave to the brothers [of Trisulti] the forest itself, giving strict instructions to the people of Collepardo that they should keep out of the wood. So the people of Collepardo, since they had completely lost the use of the wood for several years, had sent messengers to the Lord Innocent with fear asking humbly for the use of timber and pasture on Monte Furnulo for recompense and provisions. At length he granted this, writing a letter about it to them and another to the people of Vico that they should not interfere with them in this matter. The people of Collepardo, considering that this was not sufficient for them, because the people of Vico are stronger, again sent to the Lord Pope Innocent begging that through some agency they should have themselves put in possession of the mountain.

At their supplication, the Lord Pope sent Lando de Montelongo and

Vita, knights of Ferentino, who coming to Collepardo summoned the consuls of Vico there, so that in their presence they might execute the mandate of the Lord Pope, and, although the people of Vico were unwilling to listen and retired in indignation, Lord Lando declared to the people of Collepardo: "By the authority of the Lord Pope, we invest you with Furnulo, so that you may use it as your own." The people of Vico heard this before they withdrew. Then all the people of Collepardo with one accord went to the place. And Lord Rainaldo de Acuto brought with him a mattock and digging up some soil took it away with him and, with all the others, carried off timber and grass, and afterward on several occasions they sent for timber and for pasture. And the people of Vico, although much aggrieved, put up with it under protest, but requested from the Lord Pope that a prohibition be made lest taking advantage on the way to Furnulo they should destroy their enclosures and lay waste their crops. . . . Francisco Nicolas de Vico was sworn and said . . . that on a certain day, when he was taking his oxen to pasture to Monte Furnulo, he suddenly saw the inhabitants of Collepardo coming there at the same time, destroying enclosures and cutting down trees to make a way for themselves, and saying that the Lord Pope had given them Furnulo for timber and pasture and grass, and he was afraid that they would attack him.

. . . Lord Ronaldo, Lord Alberto and Lord John de Palumbaria, chaplains of the Lord Pope, and Rinaldo, subdeacon of the Lord Pope and canon of Anagni, were present to read the text and check its authenticity in the year of the Lord 1220, in the fourth year of the pontificate of Pope Honorius III, in the eighth indiction, on the twentieth day of the month of March.

And I, John, notary of the Roman Church, have written these attestations and published them.

71. PIERO DELLA VIGNA'S INVECTIVE AGAINST THE POPE (mid-thirteenth century)

Translated from Latin by Emily O'Brien

Piero della Vigna (ca. 1190–1249), raised in Capua and a master of Latin prose, served in Frederick II's imperial court (ca. 1220–49) first as notary, then justice, and later as chief spokesman and chancellor. In almost one hundred surviving letters, Piero relates much about diplomatic relations between Frederick's court, other royal houses, and the papal curia. During Piero's tenure in Frederick's court, relations between imperial and ecclesiastical authority were tense, especially with Pope Gregory IX. The text below offers a classic example of Piero's invective against the papacy. Written in Frederick's voice, and ostensibly addressed to the princes of the church— the prelates—Piero's letter epitomizes the depths to which the papal-imperial relationship had degenerated. Waging a rhetorical war, he calls the pope an antichrist, a pharisee, a great dragon. In contrast, Piero emphasizes Frederick's orthodox and devout Christianity. His use of biblical citations to support his arguments illustrates a common rhetorical device at the time. For reasons still not wholly understood— though court intrigue, jealousy, and Piero's own ambitions may have been involved—this trusted member of Frederick's entourage was cast into prison in 1249 where he was blinded. Soon afterward he committed suicide. Dante memorably cast Piero among the other suicides in his Inferno *(canto xiii), as the one who held the keys to Frederick's heart—presumably able to lock and unlock it at will.*

To all the prelates [of the church], so that they might restrain the pope from his unlawful impulses.

When the world was first created, the prudent and unutterable foresight of God . . . placed two celestial bodies in the firmament of the heavens: a greater one, and a lesser one. The greater was to preside over day, the lesser to preside over night. And these two lights are offered [by God] in the Zodiac to accomplish their respective duties, so that even if they often regard each other indirectly, one nevertheless does not offend the other. Rather, the one which is superior shares his light with the inferior one. Similarly, that same eternal foresight desired two governments in the earthly realm—that is, the priesthood and the empire—one as protection, the other as a defense. This was so that mankind, who for so long was lax in both matters, would be restrained by two cords, and thus when all sins had been reined in, peace would come

Translated from *Petri de Vineis judicis aulici et cancellarii Friderici II. imp. Epistolarum quibus res gestae ejusdem imperatori aliaque multa ad historiam ac jurisprudentiam spectantia continentur libri VI. Novam hanc editionem adjectis variis lectionibus*, ed. Joh. Rodolphus Iselius (Basel: Joh. Christ, 1740), I, chap. 31, 197–202.

to the earth. But sitting on the throne of perverse dogma, a Pharisee anointed before his accomplices with the oil of iniquity, the Roman pontiff of our age [Gregory IX], persists in trying to rid himself of this simulacrum, descended of the celestial order. Perhaps he believes that he is in harmony with those celestial bodies above, which are ruled by nature, not by their will. He intends to lead the radiance of our Majesty into eclipse, when, having transformed truth into fiction, he sends papal letters full of lies to different parts of the world; and out of habit, not out of reason, he impugns the purity of our faith. For he, pope only in name, has written that we are a beast rising out of the sea, full of blasphemous names and surrounded by [various] species of panthers.[1] But we assert that he himself is that beast, about which we read: "another red horse came out of the sea, and he who sat upon him took peace away from the earth, so that the living would kill each another." (Revelation 6:4) For from the beginning of his reign, that father, the anxious manager not of mercy but of discord, of desolation and not compassion, has roused the entire world to outrage. And let us interpret his words in the proper way: he himself is the great dragon who led astray the entire world; he is the Antichrist, whose forerunners he said we were; and he is another Balaam, hired for a price to curse us, the prince among the princes of darkness who misuse the Prophets. He is the angel springing from the abyss, holding censers filled with bitterness, to harm sea and land. For the false vicar of Christ is devoted to his tall tales that we did not pay due respect to the Christian religion and that we had said the world was deceived by three seducers. . . . But we openly acknowledge the only Son of God, coeternal and one with the Father, and with the Holy Spirit, our Lord Jesus Christ, begotten from the beginning and before the world began. With the passing of time he was sent to earth to help the human race, not by virtue of an ordained power, but by virtue of a power that ordains. He was born of a glorious virgin mother, and later suffered and died in the flesh. But his other nature, which he assumed in his mother's womb, by virtue of its divinity, rose up from the dead after three days. We are told that the body of Muhammed, however, hangs suspended in air, besieged by demons, and his soul has been delivered up to the torments of hell. His works were dark and against the law on high.[2] We know,

1. A quotation used by the pope taken from Revelation 13:1.
2. Antipathy toward Islam was an unfortunate reality during the Middle Ages. It was believed that Muslims were pagans and heretics, and that Mohammed was an Antichrist. This perspective carried over into anti-Muslim rhetoric and imagery such as that expressed by Piero. Increased awareness of and daily contact with Muslims, in no small part due to the Crusades and the creation of the Regno, further complicated relations. In so far as Muslims were condemned for their religious faith, they were also admired for their administrative practices [#16, 33] as well as their scientific, philosophical and medical knowledge [#75].

however from the Book that teaches the truth that Moses was a friend and servant of God, that he had a conversation with God himself on Mount Sinai, and that for him God set fire to a bramble bush. Through Moses, God effected signs and wonders in Egypt and for the Jewish people, and the law that was handed down showed that Moses himself was later called to glory with the chosen ones. In those matters and in others, our accuser, maliciously fomenting outrage of Mother Church against her son [Frederick II] has written these false and poisonous tracts against us for all the world to see. But if the righteousness of Apostolic judgment had not been obstructed from the inside, and if he had not preferred passion to reason, which rules over him, he would not have written such things, nor [would he have done so] at the suggestion of those who maintain that light is darkness, who say that evil is good, who believe that honey is bile . . . that true is false, when it is not. . . . The mind boggles at all these matters, and great confusion disturbs the tranquility of our mind, because you [prelates], who are the foundation and columns of the Church, the judges of righteousness, the senators of Peter's city, the hinges[3] of the world, have not altered the course of this thundering judge, as the higher planets do, when to slow the speed of a great body, they oppose themselves to it by moving in the opposite direction. In truth, Imperial success is always assailed by papal jealousy. Thus Simonides, when asked why no one envied him, replied: "Because I have done nothing successfully." And this is because good fortune has followed us in all things, thanks to God's blessing, especially when we pursued those Lombard rebels of ours to their death, whom he himself [the pope] had ordered saved.[4] This is the reason why the apostolic pontiff himself sighs, and now resolves without your counsel to thwart our success. Or perhaps the lord pope himself relishes the power to bind and loose and to use it to vex [his enemies]. But where virtue abandons power, abuse steps in. . . . Surely, if he were the true pontiff, he would be considered blameless, undefiled, set apart from sinners, one who offers sacrifices peaceably, not of his victim's quarrels but of peacemaking sacrifices. And he would offer a sweet-smelling burnt sacrifice, not a sacrifice of suffering, nor would he transform the dignity of the pontiff into wickedness. If he were the true pontiff, he would not drag the Word of God into disagreements. Nor for this reason will we be accused of being the enemy of our mother Church, holy in her origin, to which we pay respect with reverence and embrace with honor, adorned with the divine sacraments. Never-

3. Here a play on the Latin word *cardines*, as cardinals were considered the "hinges" of the church.
4. A reference to the renewed Lombard League, who unsuccessfully joined forces with the German princes and Frederick's own son, Henry VII, against the emperor in 1234–35.

theless, we deeply disapprove of eminent people, who have descended into corruption and who retreat from moderation. And because the injuries to our Majesty are not fleeting and are inflicted continuously, and because we cannot soothe our mind about these matters, nor must we in any case, we are forced into vendetta. But you [prelates], who are men appointed to give sensible counsel, possessing excellence of mind and reason, may you recall this withered adversary of ours back from his course, whose beginning was detestable, and give heed to the consequences of those matters whose causes I have outlined above. Otherwise, the whole world will suffer, just as [when] Augustus marched against his persecutor, attendant princes, and promoters; and just as he inflicted revenge for Caesar with the sword.

Figure 20. Frederick II styled as a Roman Emperor (attributed). Barletta, Museo del Castello Svevo. (Photo: Ruggiero Dicorato/Fotorudy)

72. THE JUBILEE YEAR OF 1300
THREE TEXTS

1. The Jubilee Bull (22 February 1300)

Translated from Latin by Katherine L. Jansen

Rome had been a pilgrimage destination since the early Christian period as pious pilgrims flocked to the city to venerate the heroic martyrs of the early church at their tombs. But at Christmas 1299, something very different occurred as pilgrims from all over Europe began to appear in Rome to worship at the Basilica of Saint Peter. They had heard that in return for their pious pilgrimage to Rome they would receive an indulgence, a papal pardon for their sins. However, as Jacopo Stefaneschi, cardinal-deacon of the church of San Giorgio in Velabro and right-hand man to Pope Boniface VIII reports, neither the pope nor the curia knew anything of this special dispensation. Nonetheless, the crowds in Rome continued to grow, so much so that they could hardly be ignored. On 17 January 1300, as Boniface was approaching Saint Peter's in order to celebrate the feast of the Veronica [see #69] at which he would exhibit the basilica's famous relic, the sudarium, *believed to have been the cloth with which Veronica wiped Jesus' face on the way to Golgotha, he stopped to interview some pilgrims gathered at the church. They told him how they had heard that if they came to Rome they would be rewarded with an indulgence of 100 days for every day spent in the eternal city. Not wishing to extinguish such spontaneous piety, one month later, on the feast of the chair of Saint Peter, Boniface issued the bull or papal decree entitled* Antiquorum habet fida relatio, *which put the pope's seal of approval on the pilgrimage to Rome. Significantly, the pope and his advisors had adopted as their model the ancient Jewish tradition of the Jubilee year, in which every fifty years a spiritual cleansing, centered on the notion of forgiveness, was undertaken. Thus began the celebration of the Roman Jubilee which Boniface had fixed at every hundred years, but is now celebrated by the church every twenty-five years.*

Boniface, Bishop, Servant of the Servants of God. For the certainty of the present and the memory of the future.

The trustworthy tradition of our elders affirms that great remissions and indulgences for sins are granted to those who come to the venerable basilica of the Prince of the Apostles in the city [of Rome]. According to the dignity of our office, we should willingly desire and procure salvation for each and every person; therefore, considering authentic each and all of these remissions, indulgences, and acts of grace, by our apostolic authority, we we confirm, approve and also update them with this document.

Translated from D. Quattrocchi, ed., *L'anno santo del 1300: Storie e bolle pontificie da un codice del sec. XIV del Card. Stefaneschi* (Rome: V. Salviucci, 1900), 28–29. I have been guided by the translation of Herbert Thurston, S.J., *The Holy Year of Jubilee: An Account of the History and Ceremonial of the Roman Jubilee* (London: Sands, 1900), 13–14.

So that the blessed apostles Peter and Paul may be all the more honored
as their basilicas in this city are more devoutly frequented by the faithful, and
that the faithful themselves may better experience themselves refreshed by
the abundance of spiritual gifts [attained] from this visit, We, having trusted
in the mercy of omnipotent God, the merits and authority of his apostles, the
counsel of our brethren, and in the plenitude of apostolic authority, grant to
all those penitents who visit the basilicas with reverence and who have confessed, in the present year 1300, beginning on the feast of the nativity of our
Lord Jesus Christ, recently celebrated, and to all future true penitents who
will confess their sins [and shall visit these basilicas] in subsequent centuries,
not only a full and thorough pardon, but rather the fullest pardon of all their
sins. We decree that whoever wishes to obtain these indulgences granted by
us must, if they are inhabitants of Rome, visit these same basilicas for thirty
days, either successively or at intervals, at least once a day; if they are foreigners or strangers, they must likewise visit the basilicas for fifteen days. However, one may earn more, and will the more efficiently obtain the indulgence,
if one visits the basilicas more frequently and more devoutly. Let no audacious person, therefore, dare to infringe or contravene our rescript of confirmation, approval, renewal, grant, and decree. And if any one presumes to
do so, let him know that he will incur the displeasure of almighty God and
the blessed Peter and Paul his apostles.

Dated at Rome at Saint Peter's, February 22, 1300, in the sixth year of our
pontificate.

2. Two Poems on the Jubilee by Cardinal Jacopo Stefaneschi

Translated from Latin by John Petruccione

These verses constitute one section of a dossier, entitled On the Hundredth or Jubilee
Year, *assembled and largely written by Cardinal Jacopo Stefaneschi (d. Avignon
1343). The first section, composed by the Cardinal in an extraordinarily ingenious
and contorted prose, narrates the sequence of events leading up to the granting of
the indulgence, describes the influx of pilgrims into the city and their reception by
the Romans, and discusses theological issues such as the precise scope of the indulgence
(the remission of temporal penalties on earth and in the afterlife) and the right of
the pope to grant it. The third and last section contains the text of the bull translated
above and related documents all issued by Boniface VIII. Standing between his
historical and theological disquisition on the one hand and the quotation of the
pope's official proclamations on the other, the following verses deploy the charm of
poetry to convey to the imagination and emotion of the reader the transcendent
significance of the moment. The prose sections describe and document the opportunity
represented by the indulgence, the poetry incites the reader to grasp any future indul-*

gence that may be offered. Written in the dactylic hexameter of classical pagan and medieval Christian epic, what Stefaneschi terms "heroic verse," these lines demonstrate his mastery of the meter and diction of classical poetry. Note that he feels no incongruity in launching his poetic celebration of the Jubilee with a reference to Phoebus Apollo, the Roman god of the sun.

JACOPO, CARDINAL DEACON OF SAN GIORGIO IN THE MARKETPLACE: A POEM IN HEROIC VERSE ON THE CENTENARY OR THE JUBILEE

Now dawns an age of gold as Phoebus returns this hundredth year!
Heaven shines bright with a dazzling light, for, piteous on High,
the Son of the Father eternal, in flesh from the Virgin
clothed, with blood his own, pays in full the price of sin.
Great the gift to sinners, who haste to Rome, to the portal of Peter
(His the power to unlock and to close with his key the doors of Heaven)
And pay their call to the sacred church of Paul, our guide.
Victorious, though bloodied, these two made holy the City
on one same day. Here's Rome, here prizes won from a violent
judge. Herewith heap their churches high with gifts to the saints.
Taking her cue from these, the See of Rome, supported by the might
of their intercession, jubilant at the dawn of this hundredth year,
washes away all sin. Nay more! She washes away all sin
and pardons crimes, she the source of boundless
grace—if those who, reckless, covered with grime the image divine
repent at heart, uncover their crimes,
then enter the portals of Peter and Paul, the saints our fathers:
Thirty times the citizen of Rome, the man from abroad
fifteen, while the fiery chariot churns its circling course.
Who could lie in his lair? What fool, what
laggard would not set out, not count as cool the summer's heat,
warmth winter's ice, parching dry the drizzling damp?
Yea, long's the rest, brief the task, golden always
times when pilgrims'[1] feet are covered in mud, but bright their hearts.
Let not hunger of fasting, thirst though choking,
height of mountains, depth of valleys, dripping sweat,
growing children, a lofty home, wealth you've left behind,
a wailing wife, pride in your glorious family tree,
rivers, the journey, expense, the sea, a haughty host,
weakness of age or sex, sleepless nights, or searing wind
shatter your spirit; to these does the Kingdom of Heaven lie open.
Yet none of these could cure our disease. The gracious, the lofty
Apostles' See, based on Christ's crimson blood,

Translated from the critical edition of Paul Gerhard Schmidt in Iacopo Stefaneschi, *De centesimo seu iubileo anno: La storia del primo giubileo*, ed. Claudio Leonardi (Florence: Galluzzo, 2001). Throughout, I have drawn on the notes and Italian translation provided by Antonio Placanica.
    1. Stefaneschi's word is *Romipetae*, those on their way to Rome.

'tis she who dispenses riches received from the wounds of Christ
and these our holy fathers, and thus she remits your sins.

BY THE SAME AUTHOR: ANOTHER BRIEF POEM IN HEROIC VERSE ON THE SAME TOPIC

Hear ye! Sins are wiped clear now Phoebus returns this hundredth year.
Hear ye! Contrite mouths the hidden infection of scaly sin
must bare, while through its circle the year still
spins. For fifteen days the man from abroad, Rome's citizen
for thirty must enter the shrines of our fathers,
Peter, guardian of Heaven, and Paul, kind master of gentiles.
Wide open stand the shrines where lies their ash entombed.

73. COLA DI RIENZO AND FOURTEENTH-CENTURY ROME TWELVE TEXTS (fourteenth century)

Translated from Italian and Latin by Amanda Collins

By the 1340s, two generations after the papal entourage decamped to southern France, Rome was little more than a swampy backwater with local warlords quarreling over meager resources. Such was Rome's sorry state in 1347 when Cola di Rienzo[1] (d. 1354), a humble tavern-keeper's son, seized control of the city. Gifted with a powerful sense of oratory and a taste for spectacular imperial pageantry, he promoted a dynamic, grandiose vision of a unified Italy under Rome's leadership. Cola's rule was short (7 months in 1347; 2 months in 1354), and marked by the challenges of guaranteeing local markets and securing the food supply to a city of consumers. This was complicated by the continuous factional strife created by the noble Roman families who had grown accustomed to power and revenue on a papal scale. Cola's relationship with the great barons of Rome slid dangerously from uneasy alliance, to tyranny and treachery, into open warfare. Increasing opposition from papal Avignon merely hastened Cola's fall. The tension and interplay between the various theaters of conflict—inside the city, across the distretto,[2] *among the civic stakeholders of the Italian peninsula, each demanding Cola's attention—is illustrated by the shifting perspectives of the contemporary witnesses extracted below.*

1. On Cola di Rienzo's Election

[May 1347] The citizens of the city of Rome were in a great state of internal discord, because people from other provinces were refusing to visit Rome, due to the fact they might get robbed on the road. Thus, by the whim of divine Providence, the tribune, Nicolas of Rome, was elected . . . and he expelled those who had been ruling before in their arrogance.

[June 1347] Nicolas the tribune . . . sent letters to the communes and the *signori* of Italy, telling them to send two representatives for each *signoria* and commune, because he planned to hold a general assembly, for the benefit and for the pacification of all of mankind: first, however, he was planning to be knighted.

Translated from Giulio Bertoni and Emilio Paolo Vicini, eds., *Chronicon Estense*, in *RIS²*, 2nd ed. 15, pt. 3 (Città di Castello: S. Lapi, 1907), 148–49.
   1. In the texts below he is also called Nicolas of Rome. Cola is a nickname for Nicola, Nicolas.
   2. The fifty-mile radius from the city which Rome controlled.

2. On Cola's Use of Ceremony

[August 1347] On the last day of July, the said Lord Tribune, at the hour of Vespers, ascended in triumphal style to the Lateran basilica and bathed, or was baptized, in the sacred stone font of Constantine, with full honors; as though he were an emperor, and indeed something greater than an emperor.

The said Lord Tribune had the most enormous feast prepared, for his knighting, in the aforementioned Lateran basilica—bigger than any emperor ever arranged.

3. On the Feast

There were over eighty cauldrons for this feast, to say nothing of the fifty or more, of the ladies-in-waiting to [Cola's] wife, ready to cook each course. There was also the metal horse of the lord Constantine the Emperor [see # 67], mantled in fine fur, and fixed so that wine and water poured continuously from the nostrils; no-one could work out how this had been engineered. There was an artificial castle constructed of pasta, out from which were borne platters piled with living creatures, though no-one knew how they had got in there; eventually this "lunch castle" was cut up and carried to the table for the feast.

4. On a United Italy

The magnificent knight, the lord Nicolas, tribune, rector and governor of the magnificent city, wishing to enlarge the state of the said city, had four standards consecrated, in the midst of a crowd of the people on the Piazza di San Giovanni in Laterano. One had the insignia traditionally borne by the Emperor Constantine, a white eagle on a red field with the tripartite globe below its talons. . . . Once he had placed this in the hands of the representative of the commune of Perugia, he [Cola] awarded him a ring of betrothal . . . saying, "Long live the memory of Constantine and of Perugia." On the second standard was depicted Rome in triumph, with two women: one an image of Italy, the other of the Christian Faith. He pronounced, "Long live Florence," and tried to award it to the Florentines, but no-one came forward on their behalf. The third he awarded to the commune of Siena, and the

(2) Translated from Cochetus de Chotitis (papal spy) in Konrad Burdach and Paul Piur, eds., *Briefwechsel des Cola di Rienzo*, vol. 4, *Anhang: Urkundliche quellen zur Geschichte Rienzos* (Berlin: Weidmann, 1912), letter 8, ll. 90–98.

(3) Translated from Tommaso Casini, ed., *Giovanni di Bazano: Chronicon Mutinense*, in *RIS²*, 2nd ed., 15, pt. 4 (Bologna: Zanichelli, 1919), 136.

(4) Translated from Giulio Bertoni and Emilio Paolo Vicini, eds., *Chronicon Estense*, in *RIS²*, 2nd ed. 15, pt. 3 (Città di Castello: S. Lapi, 1907), 152.

fourth to Todi. Later, the knights of the commune of Florence came to the tribune, excusing themselves for not accepting the standard, because the priors had not given them permission . . . . Then the tribune had erected a blue plaque with gold letters . . . inscribed: Nicolas the Severe and Merciful, Liberator of the City, Striver for Italy, Lover of the World and August Tribune.

5

And when the grand ceremonials and festivities of his Knighthood were over, [Cola] assembled the people, and gave a great sermon, explaining how he wanted to restore all Italy to its ancient-style obedience to Rome.

6

[August] The Senate and People of Rome possess that same authority and jurisdiction over the whole world which they enjoyed previously, in ancient times. Once again they can interpret, compile, alter, append, limit and even declare regulations and laws; they can do everything they could in the past, even revoke laws.

7. Rebellion in Rome

[September] The Colonna, Orsini, Savelli, and other nobles of the city of Rome were displeased . . . and hired an assassin to kill the tribune. When this came to the attention of the tribune, he had the killer captured and flogged . . . So the tribune sent for the nobles and interrogated them regarding this, and they confessed that it was true. Then the tribune condemned them to death, and made them put on black, and passed public death sentences on them in the presence of the people. He sent them to the place of justice, and as they went along the street they cried out, and begged for mercy.

8

The tribune had decided to decapitate all of them, in front of the assembly, to liberate the Roman people. . . . When the barons realized the plan and

---

(5) Translated from Giovanni Villani, *Nuova Cronica*, ed. Giuseppe Porta (Parma: Guanda, 1990), vol. 3, 495.

(6) Translated from "Cola di Rienzo to the Cities of Italy," in *Briefwechsel*, vol. 2, *Kritische Darstellung der Quellung zur Geschichte Rienzos* (Berlin: Weidmann, 1912), letter 41, ll. 29–34.

(7) Translated from *Chronicon Estense*, in *RIS²*, pt. 3, 154.

(8) Translated from *Anonimo Romano: Cronica*, ed. Giuseppe Porta (Milan: Adelphi, 1981), 140–41.

heard the bell ringing, they froze with fear, were unable to speak, and could not think what to do. The majority of them groveled, did penance, and took communion. His lordship Rainaldo of the Orsini and another man could not take communion because they had eaten fresh figs earlier that morning. Lord Stefano Colonna refused to confess or to take communion. He claimed he was not prepared and had not set his affairs in order.

Meanwhile one particular group of citizens, weighing up the decision Cola had made, held him back with honeyed, flattering language. Finally they persuaded him to their position, and he reversed his judgment. . . . He climbed the rostrum and delivered a beautiful speech based on the Lord's Prayer: forgive us our trespasses. Then he pardoned the barons, claiming that they wanted to serve, and be at peace with, the people. . . . He appointed some as . . . guardians of the grain supply; one he made duke of Tuscany, another duke of Campania.

These events went down badly among men of experience. People said, "This man has lit the fire with a flame he won't be able to put out." I myself would cite the proverb, "Shit—or get off the pot."

9. Cola Attacks the Barons

[November] The rebel barons tried, with five hundred cavalry and eight hundred foot soldiers, to enter the city at the San Lorenzo Gate. . . . Discovering this in advance, the tribune got the people together at night . . . ; to a man, they shouted out, crying out that they wished to march out against their enemies with weapons in their hands. Then the tribune, with about a thousand soldiers, and the entire populace . . . thus armed, at the hour of dawn on November 20, approached the said gate. The enemy, unable to stand up to the impact, was thrown into dismay, and the barons listed below were killed . . . plus seventy of their allies.

10. Cola in Exile

[August 1350] Despite vendetta among the Romans, whose murderous partisan battles involved something like eighteen hundred men, did I not get them to end the bloodletting and the climate of mutual insult and antagonism? . . . Had I not begun to achieve all this by unifying the city of Rome and the whole of Italy in a single, harmonious, peaceful, holy, and

---

(9) Translated from *Chronicon Estense*, in *RIS²*, pt. 3, 155–56.

(10) Translated from "Cola to the Archbishop of Prague," in *Briefwechsel*, vol. 2, letter 57, ll. 258–65.

indivisible alliance, by collecting and consigning consecrated standards and banners to different cities, and, to symbolize the sacred league and perfect union, by bestowing, with due solemnity, on the ambassadors of all the Italian cities, gold rings consecrated on the day of the Assumption of the Blessed Virgin Mary? . . . Yet my Lord Pope, influenced by briefings from evil men and a narrow-minded lack of generosity, viewed this union with such suspicion that the cardinals openly debated whether the union of Rome and of Italy was actually of benefit to the Church of Rome! Just listen to the partisans' tune, the song of Satan himself, a theme to horrify God and His angels.

11. Petrarch on Cola

[August 1352] Having declared himself liberty's champion, he should never have allowed the enemies of liberty to depart under arms when he could have crushed them forever; fortune has never offered such an opportunity to any ruler before. . . . He used to style himself "severe and merciful" . . . if he had decided to demonstrate mercy only to Rome's traitors in sparing their lives, he should at least have removed them of the means of causing more trouble; in particular, he should have forced them out of their grim rural castles . . . . I remember writing him a long thought-out letter about this. If he had taken any notice of its contents the Roman Republic would not be enslaved, and he would not be a prisoner today.

12. The End of Cola

[October 1354] Now I want to describe the death of the tribune. The tribune had levied a tax on wine and other commodities, which he called a "subsidy." . . . Cola de Rienzo was in bed that morning. He had washed his face. Suddenly from the northeast there came a voice crying, "Long live the people! Long live the people!" At this voice the people came through the streets from this side and that. The cry grew louder; more people gathered. At the market crossroads armed men gathered; they came from Sant'Angelo and from Ripa; they came from Colonna and from Trevi. When they had assembled the cry was changed, and they said, "Death to the traitor Cola di Rienzo!" Death!" . . . Death to the traitor who made the tax! Death! Their rage was terrible. . . . [*Cola's residence is attacked; he manages to escape dressed in disguise but his gold bracelets soon give him away.*] He could no longer

(11) Translated from Petrarch, *Familiari* XIII.6, ed. A. S. Bernardo, in Francesco Petrarca, *Letters on Familiar Matters: Rerum familiarum libri IX–XVI* (Baltimore: Johns Hopkins University Press, 1982), 250–51.

(12) Adapted from *The Life of Cola di Rienzo*, ed. and trans. John Wright (Toronto: Pontifical Institute of Mediaeval Studies, 1975), 146–52.

escape. There was no remedy but standing to mercy, to the will of others. He was taken by the arms and led without resistance through all the stairways as far as the place of the Lion, where others had heard their sentences, where he had passed sentence on others. There he was led; a silence fell . . . In silence he moved his face; he looked this way and that. Then Cecco dello Viecchio took a dagger in his hand and stabbed him in the belly.

He was the first. Immediately afterward, Lorenzo de Treio, the notary, struck his head with a sword. Then one man after another stabbed him; one struck, another swore to. He made no sound; he died at once; he felt no pain. A man came with a rope and tied his feet together. They threw him on the ground dragging him and peeling off his skin; they pierced him until he looked like a sieve. Everyone joked about it; they seemed to be at a festival. In this way he was dragged as far as San Marcello. There he was hung from a balcony by the feet; he had no head . . . His fat guts dangled from his belly . . . He hung there two days and one night. The boys threw rocks at him. On the third day, at the command of Jururta and Sciaretta della Colonna, he was dragged to the Campo dell'Austa [*where what remained of the corpse was burned*].

74. THE PACIFICATION OF THE PATRIMONY OF SAINT PETER (1355–59)

Translated from Italian by John Wright

Envisioning the return of the papacy from Avignon to Rome, Pope Innocent VI (1352–62) was preoccupied with restoring the lands of the papal state to the holy see. In the pope's absence many of its territories had fallen into the hands of local lords. Aiming to subdue these usurpers, the pope appointed the Spanish cardinal Gil Albornoz (d. 1367), in this text called Don Gilio Conchese, as his legate or representative. In the following excerpt from an anonymous fourteenth-century chronicle of Rome, in addition to Albornoz's defeat of the Malatesta of Rimini in 1355, and the submission of the city of Cesena, murderous intrigues, techniques of warfare, and a dubious papal policy of crusading against fellow Christians within Italy are described. (KLJ)

DON GILIO CONCHESE (GIL ALBORNOZ), HAVING RECOVERED NARNI AND AMELIA, MOVES AGAINST THE MALATESTI IN THE MARCH, WHERE GALEOTTO MALATESTA SURRENDERS TO HIM

Once he had finished organizing the Patrimony, the legate stayed in Orvieto for a while; he reconciled Orvieto and its district, which were very corrupt. Then he took Narni, then Amelia, and from there went on to do greater deeds: to restore order in the March, and to lower the pride of the Malatesta. Messer Malatesta was a powerful tyrant and one of the most skilful warriors of Romagna. He was lord over many cities and castles; he ruled most of the March of Ancona, whether through love or force. His brother, Messer Galeotto, guarded the frontiers and ruled the noble city of Ancona.

When Messer Galeotto heard that the legate was approaching the lands of the March, he gathered a great multitude, more than three thousand knights; he marched from Ancona to Recanati to meet the legate, along with Gentile da Magliano of Fermo and many other corporals of the March. There he waited, and announced to the legate that he might just as well not have come: he could neither equal the Malatesti nor defeat them. In reply the legate sent a note which contained only the following words: "From good warriors good peacemakers, from good peacemakers good warriors." Messer Galeotto answered, "Tell the legate not to endanger so many people; I will meet him on the field in single combat." The legate answered, "Go, tell him: here I am, ready on the field; there I will meet him myself, face to face. Let

Adapted from *The Life of Cola di Rienzo*, ed. and trans. John Wright (Toronto: Pontifical Institute of Mediaeval Studies, 1975), 111–20.

him stay where he is." Messer Galeotto answered, "Go tell my lord the legate that I will not meet him face to face; even if I should win, it would be the end of me, for he is an aged man, a prelate, fit only for the paternal care of souls."

Meanwhile the legate assembled his army on the field. Messer Galeotto Malatesta had retreated into a strong town called Paterno, between Macerata and Ancona, when behold: suddenly the noble imperial army came up behind him: Germans and Tuscans, Counts of Germany experienced in war, many crested helmets, bagpipes and kettledrums sounding. They had never rested once they began their march. When Messer Galeotto heard that these allies had joined the legate, he lost his resolution and his strength. He was helpless; he admitted defeat; he surrendered, begging the legate for mercy. The legate held him captive along with his whole army.

MALATESTA, IN ORDER TO RECOVER HIS BROTHER, PEACEFULLY RESTORES TO THE LEGATE THE CHURCH PROPERTY HE HAD SEIZED. THE CRUEL AND TYRANNICAL ACTIONS OF FRANCESCO ORDELAFFI OF FORLÌ ARE RECOUNTED

Messer Malatesta, in order to recover his brother, submitted to the legate, freely surrendering to him the city of Ancona and all the towns which he held in the March and in Romagna. Thus the Church acquired the noble city of Ancona, a seaport rich in trade and revenues. There the legate built two beautiful fortresses which stand to this day. Then he made one of his nephews Marquis and sent him to Macerata as governor of the March. He provided for the Malatesti indulgently and wisely, to enable them to live honorably and nobly from their rents. He granted them four good and famous cities, Rimini, Fano, Pesaro, and Fossombrone, four notable and powerful towns. Then he made them captains of the Church against rebels.

After this the legate went on to greater deeds and under-takings. There was a perfidious patarine[1] dog in Romagna, a rebel against the holy Church. He had been excommunicated for thirty years, his country interdicted, no Mass sung. He held many towns which belonged to the Church: the cities of Forlì, Cesena, Forlimpopolo, Castrocaro, Bertinoro, Imola, and Giaggiolo. He was tyrant over all these, along with many other castles and communes which belonged to the local inhabitants. This Francesco delli Ordelaffi was a desperate man; he had an insane hatred against prelates, never forgetting that

1. Originally the term Paterine or Paterene referred to an adherent of the eleventh-century movement that called for religious reform of the Milanese church. Over time, however, the meaning of the term changed, and as used here is a slur meaning a heretic or schismastic. See #80 for its original usage.

earlier he had been mistreated by the former legate, Messer Bettrannio dallo Poijetto, cardinal of Ostia, as was said above. He refused to submit to priests any longer. He was a perfidious obstinate tyrant.

This Francesco, when he heard the bell ring for his excommunication, immediately had the other bells rung and excommunicated the pope and the cardinals, and, what was worse, he had stuffed paper effigies of the pope and the cardinals burned in the piazza. Conversing with his well-born friends he said, "So: we are excommunicated; our bread, though, and our meat, and the wine we drink won't taste any the worse or be any the less wholesome for that." He treated the priests and the monks in the following way. The bishop who pronounced the excommunication was insulted and driven from the city. Then the captain forced the clergy to say mass. Most of them did, despite the interdict. Fourteen clerics, seven religious and seven secular, refused to say mass and received holy martyrdom: seven of them were hanged by the gullet and seven of them were flayed. But Francesco was closely bound to the people of Forlì, and dearly loved; he behaved as if he were pious and charitable: he gave dowries to orphans, found husbands for girls, and helped those of the poor people who were his friends.

THE LEGATE, AFTER HAVING TAKEN UP ARMS AGAINST ORDELAFFI, IS RECALLED BY THE POPE, WHO SENDS THE ABBOT OF BURGUNDY AS NEW LEGATE

Now I turn to the war. Don Gilio Conchese of Spain established his head-quarters and residence in Ancona, and to strengthen his forces proclaimed a crusade. I myself heard it announced: remission of penalty and guilt to who-ever took the cross or gave aid. Now the legate moved against the dog captain of Forlì, Francesco delli Ordelaffi. Before setting up his camp he prepared everything necessary for the army.

The legate sent bishops, knights, and other worthy people to persuade the captain not to persevere in his error. He heard the exhortations in silence; that night he made a foray from Forlì and plundered the lands of the Church; he took loot and prisoners. He made no other response. The legate, recognizing the hardened heart of Ordelaffi, set up camp against the city of Cesena. The Malatesti were corporals and leaders of the army. There were twelve thousand crusaders and thirty thousand mercenaries; out of these two separate armies were formed. The army made great devastation and damage: at the sound of trumpets three thousand plunderers with banners ravaged the enemy land and then withdrew: a memorable deed. Meanwhile the Holy Father sent express letters ordering Don Gilio to return to Provence. The reason for this was that the Count of Savoy, with his great company of three thousand soldiers, was plundering the whole of Provence: he was seizing towns, robbing, and kidnapping people. Before Don Gilio left another legate arrived, a wealthy French landowner, strong and powerful.

The captain had a son named Messer Janni and another named Messer Lodovico. Messer Lodovico approached his father and humbly beseeched him, saying, "Father, in God's name I beg you not to contend with the Church, and not to stand against God. Let us obey these commands; let us be obedient. I am certain that the legate is considerate; he will treat us as well as he has treated the Malatesti. He will allow us enough to live well and honorably." To these humble words the proud father replied, "You are a bastard, or else you were switched at baptism to spite me." The son, after hearing his father's violent answer, turned to leave. Then his father threw a long naked knife at his back, and wounded him in the kidneys; before midnight his son Lodovico died from this wound.

While the new legate, the abbot, prepared himself for war, Messer Gilio was not idle. He attacked Cesena, and set up three bastions at intervals of ten miles each. The legates returned to Rimini.

[1357] Cesena is taken by the legate through the work of four citizens

Madonna Cia, the wife of the captain of Forlì, was in Cesena, inside the castle, with her nephews and a large group of mercenaries. To this Madonna Cia the captain wrote a letter which said, "Cia, be cautious and take good care of the city of Cesena." Madonna Cia replied, "My lord, be content to take good care of Forlì, and I shall take good care of Cesena." The captain wrote another letter, the gist of which was, "Cia, we command you to cut off the heads of four plebeians of Cesena, Janni Zaganella, Jacovo delli Vastardi, Palazzino, and Bertonuccio, all Guelfs, whose loyalty we suspect."

When the lady received this letter, she did not follow her husband's orders at once. She investigated these four citizens with the greatest care and diligence, and found that they were good and loyal men. She took counsel with two of her husband's most loyal friends, Scaraglino, a nobleman, and Giorgio delli Tumberti. She showed them the letter, and they said, "Madam, we find no reason that these men should lose their lives. We know of no plots they are forming. If these men lose their lives, the people are liable to become indignant. We suggest, therefore, that you postpone this judgment. Meanwhile we shall watch their behavior closely. At the least sign of trouble we shall take immediate action: we shall arrest them and execute them after an open trial." The lady followed the advice of her husband's two noble friends, and put aside her investigation into sedition.

All this was done in secret, and in secret it was revealed to the four plebeians. Then they formed a conspiracy and planned a revolution in the city. Janni Zaganella made the arrangements among his friends. He rode on his pony throughout the town, stirring up one man after another. One morning, when the plot was still recent, Jacovo delli Vastardi and his neighbors ran to the gate which is called Troygate and seized it. Bertonuccio and Palazzino aroused the people and barricaded the city; then they sent two hostlers to the Hungarian soldiers who were occupying the bastions at Savignano nearby. They came quickly.

When Madonna Cia heard the commotion, she knew that the people had arisen; she immediately ordered her mercenaries, cavalry and infantry, to take up their arms and overrun the city. But this was impossible: the town was barricaded, the people armed, the city gate taken, the towers fortified, and furthermore the knights had come to the aid of the people. There in the setting of the sun were eight hundred Hungarian archers who had been occupying the bastions at Savignano; they came flying, a lively people, drawn up in battle order. They did not enter Cesena, but circled the city, now approaching, now withdrawing, to encourage the citizens. Seeing this Madonna Cia withdrew her mercenaries, retreated to the citadel, and there held out. This citadel is part of the city; it is surrounded by a strong wall, and contains the communal piazza, the palace, the tower, and great private houses; it is set rather high above the city, which is low-lying. Madonna Cia, angry at her loss, turned her wrath on the two counselors, her husband's friends, Giorgio delli Tumberti and Scaraglino; she had them beheaded. Her husband disapproved of this deed.

CAPTURE OF THE CITADEL OF CESENA AND IMPRISONMENT OF MADONNA CIA, WIFE OF ORDELAFFI

When dawn broke on the next day, behold: the Malatesti arrived with a great army to help the citizens. Troygate was surrendered to them, and they entered Cesena. Now Madonna Cia was besieged in the citadel. Then the Fiumone castle was surrendered. The Malatesti fought hard at the citadel: they made forays, they threw fire inside, they raised catapults and threw rocks and stones. It was useless: the defenders had plenty of water, and there was a strong tower above the citadel gate.

The legate ordered undermining, a hard, expensive, and time-consuming job. A tunnel was dug under the cistern of the citadel, the cistern was broken, and the water was lost. Then they brought the tunnel under the main tower of the piazza. They set fire to the struts, and the tower collapsed with a great crash. Now the tunnel was extended to the tower above the gate, which protected the citadel's entrance. Madonna Cia, angry at this, did not know what to do. She selected those of the citizens within the citadel whom she most mistrusted and put them in the tower above the gate, saying, "If the tower falls, it falls on you." The tower stood on its struts; it trembled.

Meanwhile the legate, Don Gilio, was passing through the district with a great company of soldiers; he came to Cesena to see how the tunneling and the siege works were progressing. Then about five hundred women came pouring out of Cesena, tearing their hair, beating their breasts, weeping, and lamenting. They made a great noise. They fell on their knees before the legate and pled for mercy. The legate, not knowing the reason for this bitter weeping, asked why they were doing it. The women answered, "legate, our husbands, brothers, and kinsmen are imprisoned in the tower above the gate. The tunnel is completed; if the tower falls, the men will perish. Therefore we beg in God's name that you delay setting fire to the struts."

The legate realized that Madonna Cia doubted herself, that her resolution was broken. He held negotiations with her and recovered the people of Cesena who had been put in the tower. Then they set fire to the tower; in a little while it fell, along with part of the citadel wall. So the wall was breached, and they could enter; nevertheless they entered calmly, not furiously.

The legate took Madonna Cia prisoner, along with her son and two nephews. Madonna Cia refused to be released, fearful of her husband's quick temper. Rather she begged insistently that the Church protect her. The masters of the tunneling, the catapults, and the other devices cost three thousand florins a day. The soldiers cost twelve thousand florins a day. The legate entered Cesena and took the town for the Church. This was how the city of Cesena in Romagna was recovered.

[1358] The legate repeatedly declares a crusade against Ordelaffi, and finally strips him of Faenza and Bertinoro

Now the legate prepared to attack the city of Forlì. First he collected a strong and copious army. Meanwhile news spread of the imprisonment of Madonna Cia, who had been sent to Ancona under guard. One of her daughters, a noblewoman, married to a great man of the March, appeared before her father in tears, with her arms folded; falling on her knees she said to him, "Father, my lord, please do not allow my mother, so great a lady, to remain a prisoner in the hands of others. I beg you, do the will of the holy Church."

The captain's only response to these words was this: he seized this daughter of his by the hair and with a knife he parted her head from her body.

After the capture of Cesena the legate sent to the captain, saying, "Captain, return what is not yours. I am returning your wife, your son, and your nephews to you." To these words the captain replied, "Tell the legate that I used to believe he was a wise man; now I consider him a stupid ox. Tell him that if I had captured him, the way he has captured my people, I would have hanged him by the gullet three days ago." His soul hardened against such a perverse patarine heretic, Don Gilio, the old legate, departed for Provence. When the company of the Count of Savoy heard that Don Gilio was approaching the borders, it melted away like a bit of snow in the hot sun.

The new legate, the abbot of Burgundy, remained in Romagna. This abbot besieged Forlì with an army of private soldiers. For many years he declared the crusade; the cross was preached through all Italy. He lopped the grain and and cut down the vineyards, trees, and olive orchards; he struck at every point, at every hour. Because of this fervent war the captain and his sworn allies, the Manfredi, lost Faenza; he also lost Bertinoro. Then he retreated to the citadel of Forlì.

During the siege of Forlì many crusaders, who had come to gain indulgence by fighting these schismatics, were captured. The captured crusaders would be brought before Francesco, who would say to them, "You carry the cross; the cross is made of cloth; cloth wears out. I want you to carry crosses which will not wear out." Then a red-hot iron of the form of a cross would be prepared; with it he would brand the soles of their feet, and so, after robbing them, he would let them go. Many other crusaders were captured; to these he would say, "You have come to save your souls; if I let you go perhaps you will return to your earlier sins. It would be better for you to die while in a state of contrition. God will receive you into His city." Saying this, he would have them flayed, hanged, beheaded, impaled, and torn to pieces, to die of various martyrdoms.

The war lasted for many years. To maintain it the crusade was proclaimed many times. Just recently, in the year of our Lord 1358, in January, it was proclaimed in the city of Tivoli.

Disease and Medical Practice

*During the Middle Ages, western medicine developed in no small part through con-
tact with the texts of Muslim scholars such as Avicenna (Ibn Sina, d. 1037) and
Averröes (Ibn Rushd, d. 1198). To this end, two uniquely Italian contributions were
the integration of Arab medical knowledge, and the subsequent dissemination of
that knowledge throughout Italy and beyond. In particular, by the twelfth century,
the city of Salerno was a flourishing and highly regarded center of medical learning,
in terms of both theory and practice. The Salernitan texts included here address a
number of fundamental issues such as the translation of Arabic texts, obstetrical
procedures, pharmacology and herbal medicine, and anatomical study through dissection (in this case, a pig). By the fourteenth century, a system for the formal licensing of doctors of both sexes was developed in the Kingdom of Naples. The influence
of south Italian practice is evident in the early fifteenth-century texts from the University of Bologna. The selections included here range from descriptions of advance-
ments in dissection and surgery, to the curriculum for doctors-in-training. The
latter includes a culturally syncretic syllabus of Arab, Latin, and Greek authors—as
well as the study of decidedly non-Christian astrological texts.*

 *Between the heyday of Salerno's medical school and the development of a medi-
cal curriculum at the University of Bologna occurred one of the worst epidemiological catastrophes in history: the "Black Death," or simply "the Plague." This highly
contagious disease swept up the Italian peninsula from Sicily in 1347–48, quickly
spreading throughout Europe with unparalleled and memorable fury, and eventually killed between one-third and two-thirds of the population. It would take many
years and repeated outbreaks for Europeans to come to grips with the endemic and
pandemic character of the pestilence, explanations for which varied from God's
wrath to the (mis-) alignment of the planets. However, in his account of plague in
Germany and Brabant (1357–58), Matteo Villani hints at an incipient understanding about the transmission of and immunity against the disease, even the possibility
that the plague was not simply one disease.*

75. MEDICINE IN SOUTHERN ITALY, TWELFTH–FOURTEENTH CENTURIES: SIX TEXTS

Translated from Latin by Monica H. Green

Medieval Italy's earliest claim to prominence in the history of medicine comes from the southern half of the peninsula. There, from the mid-eleventh to the early thirteenth century, an unprecedented explosion in medical activity took place. Southern Italy would remain an important locus of medical practice well beyond the end of the medieval period, but its largest "international" impact was due to the wealth of theoretical and practical writings it bequeathed to the rest of Europe during this early period. These would remain foundational texts in medical training and practice for the rest of the Middle Ages.

Southern Italian medicine was characterized by the adoption of practices, theories, and texts coming out of the Arabic world, which added a new patina of science to earlier empirical traditions. Constantine the African [d. before 1098/1099], a translator from Arabic to Latin (Text I) can primarily claim credit for making the wealth of Arabic medicine available to Christian Europe in the late eleventh century. However, two other trends were already in play at the time of his arrival. On the one hand, Arabic medical learning and techniques were being independently adopted by Latin- and Greek-speaking Christians on Sicily and in Calabria, probably through oral transmission. On the other hand, already beginning in the middle of the eleventh century there were attempts to improve the comprehensibility of medical texts that had circulated in Latin since late antiquity and to enlarge that corpus with new translations from the Greek. Constantine's translations thus served to consolidate efforts to systematize medical knowledge that would be centered, from the early twelfth century on, at the Lombard city of Salerno, just south of Naples on the Amalfitan coast.

The so-called "school" of Salerno was in this period not a legal or physical entity so much as a circle of masters (and at least one mistress) and students; together they developed new forms of teaching and thinking about health and disease. Salernitan physicians were already renowned in the eleventh century for their empirical skills, and this reputation in no respect diminished in the twelfth century. What did change was that now Salernitan practitioners wrote down summaries of their practices. The obstetrical instructions presented here (II) are an example of this empiricism. Although female practitioners clearly treated men, just as male practitioners prescribed for some gynecological and obstetrical conditions, there seems to have been a distinct sexual division of labor when it came to actually touching the female genitalia. It is likely that the present excerpt comes from the work of the famous Trota of Salerno, or perhaps from some other female practitioners who compiled her work.

Empirical concerns also led to the creation of practical works of medicine by male authors on topics such as diagnosing by urines, controlling diet, or developing proper bedside manners. Many of these works became authoritative throughout the rest of medieval Europe. Some, like the pharmaceutical textbook Circa instans *(III), moved beyond straightforward descriptions of clinical practices—"do this, mix that"—and synthesized the new theoretical learning into handbooks that were both clinically useful and instructive of basic principles of the new rationalized medicine. Other texts focused strictly on theoretical instruction; that is, teaching the "hidden principles" of medicine: the four elements, the four humors, and other aspects of the body not directly accessible to sensory perception. One of the areas of instruction was basic anatomy, which was taught by means of dissections of pigs (IV).*

*The final selection (V) shows one of the longer-term social consequences of the advanced medical teaching in southern Italy. Whereas in the eleventh century a practitioner gained a reputation by the simple clinical efficacy of his or her treatments (to say that he or she "cured many people" was the ultimate praise), by the early thirteenth century the medical learning of Salerno had won out by convincing many people that theoretical knowledge was in and of itself a valuable commodity. Practitioners moved from calling themselves simply "healers" (*medici*) to "healers and persons learned in science" (*medici et phisici*), the latter term referring to knowledge of the natural world. Perhaps influenced by Muslim practices, within a decade after King Roger II relocated the Norman capital to Palermo he instituted a regulation that "whoever in the future desires to become a physician should present himself to our officials and judges for an examination according to their judgment" [see #47]. Roger's grandson, Emperor Frederick II, would go further, stipulating in 1231 that any physician must be "approved in a convened public examination by the Masters of Salerno." Thus, although many practitioners who obtained licenses (including the two licensees included below) in fact never attended a university, the institution of licensing confirmed that physicians and surgeons with theoretical training were best able to assess the competence of all other practitioners.*

Learned traditions of medical practice in southern Italy would continue through the end of the Middle Ages, but the south would produce few major medical innovations in later years that could match the hugely influential work that came out of Montecassino and Salerno in the eleventh and twelfth centuries.

I. Biography of Constantine the African by Peter the Deacon (mid-twelfth century)

Constantine the African, a Benedictine monk (d. before 1098/99), was the first of several translators over the course of the eleventh through thirteenth centuries who would make available in Latin the wealth of medical learning, including some texts of the second-century writer Galen, that the Arabic-speaking world had cultivated in the intervening centuries. Originally from North Africa, well-traveled and obviously knowledgeable about medical substances (he may have been a spice merchant), Constantine arrived in Salerno sometime before 1077 and soon established himself as a monk at Montecassino. Constantine translated only a tiny fraction of the Arabic medical corpus into Latin (some two dozen works in all), yet the theoretical sophistication of these texts infused new life into the Salernitans' nascent attempts to estab-

lish a truly philosophical medicine, one that grounded therapy on a rational understanding of the "hidden" workings of the body.

The following account of Constantine's life is found in a collection of biographies of Cassinese figures, Peter the Deacon's mid-twelfth-century On Famous Men. *Although quite fanciful in many respects, it does give a sense of how radically transformative this new body of learning must have seemed to his contemporaries. Most of Constantine's known works are included in Peter the Deacon's bibliography; among those missing is one of Constantine's earliest works, a treatise on stomach ailments dedicated to one of his patrons, Archbishop Alfanus of Salerno.*

Constantine the African was a monk of this same monastery [Montecassino]. He was fully learned in all philosophical studies, a master of East and West, a new and shining Hippocrates. He left Carthage [Tunis], whence he originated, and sought out Babylonia,[1] in which [place] he became fully learned in the grammar, dialectic, rhetoric, geometry, arithmetic, mathematics, astronomy, necromancy, music, and medicine of the Chaldeans, Arabs, Persians, and Saracens. Departing from there, he went to India and gave himself over to perfecting himself at their schools. And then, when he was fully trained in the arts, he sought out Ethiopia, and there he studied the disciplines of the Ethiopians. And when he was sufficiently full of their learning as well, he set out for Egypt, and there he was fully instructed in all the arts of the Egyptians. Having completed all these studies in the space of 39 years, he returned to Africa. But when the Africans saw that he was so fully learned in all the studies of the races, they hatched a plan to kill him. Hearing of this, Constantine secretly left by boat and came to Salerno, where he remained for some time impoverished. Then he was recognized by the brother of the king of the Babylonians who had come there, and he was held in great honor by [the Norman] count Robert [Guiscard]. Leaving there, Constantine sought out the monastery of Montecassino, where he was most willingly accepted by the abbot Desiderius, and he was made a monk.

Now established at this monastery, he translated a number of books from the diverse languages of the races, among which especially are the following:

(1)   the *Pantegni* (which is divided into twelve books), in which is explained that which the physician ought to know;

Translated from Peter the Deacon, *De viris illustribus* 23, ed. Herbert Bloch, in Bloch, *Monte Cassino in the Middle Ages*, 3 vols. (Cambridge, Mass.: Harvard University Press, 1986), vol. 1, 127–29.
    1. *Babilonia* is normally interpreted in medieval usage as referring to Cairo. Note that later it is said that Constantine traveled to Egypt, as if that were an entirely different place.

(2)   the *Practica* [of the *Pantegni*], in which is explained how the physician should maintain health and treat infirmity (which is [also] divided into twelve books);

(3)   the *Book of Degrees* [that is, of simple medicines];

(4)   *Diet of Foods*;

(5)   the *Book of Fevers*, which he translated from the Arabic language;

(6)   the *Book of Urines*;

(7)   *On Interior Organs*;

(8)   *On [Sexual] Intercourse*;

(9)   the *Viaticum*, which is divided into seven parts: the first on diseases arising in the head; then on disease of the face; on the instruments [of respiration]; on infirmities of the stomach and intestines; on infirmities of the liver, kidneys, bladder, spleen, and bile; on those which arise in the generative members; on all those which arise on the exterior of the skin;

(10) a commentary on the [Hippocratic] *Aphorisms*;

(11) the book, the *Tegni* ["The Art (of Medicine)"];

(12) the *Megategni*;

(13) the *Microtegni*;

(14) an *Antidotarium* [a compendium of compound medicines];

(15) a *Debate Between Plato and Hippocrates on Various Opinions*;

(16) *On Simple Medicines*;

(17) *On Women's Matters*, that is, on the organs and bodies of women;

(18) *On Pulses*;

(19) *Prognostics*;

(20) *On Experiments* [or, perhaps more correctly, "tried-and-true remedies"];

(21) *Glosses on Herbs and Spices*;

(22) *Surgery*;

(23) *Book of Medicines for the Eyes*.

This man spent forty years pursuing the studies of diverse races. He died in Montecassino recently, an old man full of days. He lived during the time of the above-mentioned emperors [the late eleventh century].

II. Trota (?), Obstetrical Excerpts from the Salernitan Compendium, *On the Treatment of Diseases* (ca. 1180–1200)

Some women developed considerable expertise in women's medicine. One of these was the most famous Salernitan female practitioner Trota (or Trocta). She wrote her own collection of practical remedies (her Practica, *which covers almost every aspect of medicine save surgery), and her work forms the basis of the* Treatments of Women, *a collection of gynecological, obstetrical, and cosmetic remedies that would ultimately form the core of the so-called Trotula ensemble. The following passages on obstetrics come from the compendium* On the Treatment of Diseases. *They are not explicitly attributed to Trota here, but they bear a strong resemblance to the obstetrical practices described in her authentic work. These passages are distinctive in presenting the only "hands-on" obstetrical procedures in the whole corpus of Salernitan literature.*

On inducing and hastening birth. To induce birth, have marsh mallow[2] boiled in water, and let the woman be suffumigated with its vapor. And let the marsh mallow plant be put on her pubis. Likewise, provoke sneezing with any sort of powder, the mouth and nose being constricted with the hand. Likewise, if the woman is unable to give birth, cut the little skin of the lower parts [the perineum] with a fingernail and thus she will give birth. Afterward, to repair the [ripped] flesh, cook marsh mallow well and place it on the rupture of the little piece of flesh. Having done this, sew it with a needle and a red thread. Then for three days put on it some rue and mugwort mixed with an egg. On the fourth day, take some [Armenian] bole, dragon's blood,[3] and comfrey, and powder them and apply them to the rupture. But first let her bathe herself and let her beware of cold and exercise. I say [to do] this when this rupture occurs from the vagina to the anus. But when it is made with the fingernail, there is no need of such medicine. . . .

On the purgation of the woman after birth. For a woman who is not freely purged after birth: press out the juice of the leaves of a leek or borage and mix it with oil, and let her drink it. And immediately she will be purged.

Likewise for pain of the woman caused by the child or in giving birth to a dead fetus. For pain caused by the child or from giving birth to a dead fetus, take balsam and offer it to the patient with warm water; she will be freed and the dead fetus will be expelled. Likewise, take pennyroyal oil or musk oil, [and give it] in the same manner with warm water. Likewise, if after birth the woman suffers pain, take the tips of elder and the leaves of great plantain, and let her press out the juice. And let her make little wafers from this, and from eggs, and let her eat them. And let her drink wine and she will be cured.

. . . If, on the other hand, the woman is [not] able to give birth immediately and the child is still alive, let her take marsh mallow and cook it in water,

Translated from *De egritudinum curatione,* in *Collectio Salernitana ossia documenti inediti, e trattati di medicina appartenenti alla scuola medica salernitana,* ed. Salvatore de Renzi, 5 vols. (Naples: Filiatre-Sebezio, 1852–59; repr. Bologna: Forni, 1967), vol. 2, 346–47.
    2. Marsh mallow (in Latin, *malva*) is a plant (*Althaea officinalis* L.), not the sweet confection we are more familiar with.
    3. Armenian bole is a kind of earth used medicinally since Antiquity. Dragon's blood is a red gum or resin from a variety of species.

and from this water let her wash herself and let her be fomented; then let her make for herself a fumigation of spikenard in [hot] water, or [placed] upon hot coals.

[If] after the child is born the afterbirth cannot be expelled, give her immediately to drink the juice of leek with oil. If this does not work, make her lie with her face turned away, and anoint the belly with oil, always drawing the belly toward the vagina. Then wash both her feet and, standing and holding her feet up high, place your foot between her groin and the ground. And thus holding her, put two or three of your fingers on the umbilical cord and, twisting it, draw it away from the vagina, and thus [the afterbirth] will come out. After the woman is completely emptied out, let her be bathed and let her belly be kept tied with a washed cloth stretching from the pelvic area up to the chest, taking care to avoid cold because if the uterus senses it, it will swell up and many infirmities will result. Let her eat good and pleasant-smelling foods. Likewise for pain after birth, boil strong wine and henbane and bran, and place it upon the pelvic area and behind.

III. Mattheus Platearius (attributed), *Circa instans* (mid-twelfth century)

The Circa instans *ascribed to Mattheus Platearius was the chief authority on* materia medica *(pharmaceutical ingredients) in later medieval Europe. The title refers simply to the opening words of the text, "Concerning the present [topic of simple medicines]." "Simples" were substances that had not yet been compounded with other materials (we would today call them the "active ingredients" of a medicine). The* Circa instans *describes and lists the medicinal uses of various plant, animal, and mineral substances. Arranged in alphabetical order, the* Circa instans *identified the "properties" of the substance in terms of degrees of hotness or coldness, wetness or dryness. The notion of "degrees" of medicines had been formulated in the second century by the great Greek physician Galen of Pergamum (129–ca. 217 C.E.), but it was through Constantine the African's translations that the theory was brought to Latin Europe. These substances, according to Galen, were not "cold" or "hot" or "wet" or "dry" to the touch, but induced a warming or chilling or moistening or drying effect on the body when used medicinally. On the basic principle that "opposites are cured by opposites," a "hot" condition (like fever) would be treated by a cooling substance, like mandrake. A "cold" condition, like paralysis or anything characterized by a predominance of phlegm, would be treated with something "hot," such as agaric.*

The effect of the Circa instans *throughout Europe is hard to exaggerate. Extant in Latin in several hundred copies, it was also translated into all the major European languages. Laws often stipulated that apothecaries must have a copy in their shop. It served as the basis of an elaborated herbal, the* Treatise on Herbs, *the first herbal to be illustrated from life since late antiquity.*

Figure 21. Pharmaceutical Ingredients (late fifteenth century). Miniature from a French translation of the *Circa Instans* or *Book of Simple Medicines* ascribed to Mattheus Platearius (twelfth-century Salernitan physician). St. Petersburg, National Library of Russia. (Photo: Erich Lessing/Art Resource)

The following three excerpts show several characteristic aspects of Salernitan medicine. The first passage, on aloe wood, offers some insight into the world of "counterfeit drugs" in twelfth-century southern Italy. The second excerpt, on mandrake, shows how Platearius incorporated older lore about medicinal substances into his work. The final excerpt, a description of sugar and its properties, shows one of the ways in which European Christians had taken up a relatively "new" substance into their pharmacopeia. Never mentioned in earlier medieval Latin medicine, sugar came into use after the Norman conquerors of Sicily took over the island's Arab sugar mills as part of their booty at the end of the eleventh century. A new kind of medicine that could be prepared from sugar was syrups, a word that itself comes from the Arabic.

(a) **Aloe wood.** Aloe wood is hot and dry in the second degree. It is found in the great river of upper Babylon with which the river of Paradise is conjoined.[4] . . .

There are three kinds of aloe wood, as Constantine says. One is found on an island called Cume, and it is more praiseworthy than the rest. The second is found on an island called Camearum, and it is less praiseworthy. The third is found on an island called Rame, and it is the worst. The first, which is the best, we recognize by its ponderous weight. The better quality is aromatic, has a somewhat bitter taste, [and] is blackish or reddish in color; upon grinding by the teeth it is not entirely resistant, and while one is chewing it immediately an aromatic odor seems to touch the brain and in a certain way fill it.

The second type is less weighty, nor so bitter or odoriferous, and even in these respects only moderately. The third kind is slightly whitish, hardly bitter to the point that it has almost no taste or smell at all, unless it is made by artifice, in which case it is called *feruleum*.

It is falsified thus: in the mountains of Amalfi a wood, similar to aloe wood in its weight, nodular, and mildly aromatic, is found, which is called wild aloe wood by certain people. This is rubbed vigorously with lead or tin so that it imitates the color of gold by the added superfluity. So that it might be made bitter and a little bit reddish, afterward it is placed in wine with a decoction of powder of the best aloe wood, with a little bit of musk added, so that it might be made especially aromatic. When made thus, it is hardly ever distinguished from the best quality. But it is, in fact, able to be distinguished because it is extremely hard, it resists completely any chewing by the teeth, and what is inside tastes bitter when chewed.

Translated from *Das Arzneidrogenbuch "Circa instans" in einer Fassung des XIII. Jahrhunderts aus der Universitätsbibliothek Erlangen: Text und Kommentar als Beitrag zur Pflanzen- und Drogenkunde des Mittelalters*, ed. Hans Wölfel (Berlin: A. Preilipper, 1939), 1, 4, 75–76, 118.
4. Here, however, he seems to mean Babilonia in the biblical sense.

Aloe wood strengthens the stomach, enables digestion, and is good against debility of the stomach, heart, and brain, against cardiac affliction and fainting, against retention of the menses, and against all afflictions and debilities of the heart arising from coldness. Wine with a decoction of aloe wood strengthens the digestion and warms up a cold stomach, and if it should be abhorrent [to the patient], let a small amount of aloe wood be placed whole into wine at night. In the morning, let the wine be administered at the same time as a decoction of aloe wood, cloves, and mastic; this enables digestion, and strengthens the stomach and head. . . .

Against fainting and debility of the brain, let there be given a syrup made from rose water in which the powder of aloe wood, bones of deer heart, cloves, and roses have been cooked. With sugar added, let the above-mentioned powders be given with syrup made from rose water and sugar. A suffumigation of aloe wood, received by the woman below through a funnel, provokes the menses and treats uterine suffocation very well when the woman is wrapped all around with sheets so that the fume does not reach the nostrils.[5] Likewise, *trifera magna*[6] with wine decocted with aloe wood provokes the menses. When its fume is received through the nostrils, it warms a chilled brain and strengthens the debility. And so that I might conclude briefly its praises, it strengthens all members of the debilitated body when powdered. Mix aloe wood, cloves, and deer heart bone with oil and anoint the head of a rooster, and in that day and night it will not sing.

(b) **Mandrake.** Mandrake is cold and dry, but its degree is not specified by the authorities. There are two kinds: male and female. The female has rough leaves. Certain people say that [the female kind] is better suited to medicinal use, but we use [both kinds] indiscriminately. Certain people say that the female kind is formed in both the manner and shape of a woman, while the masculine is in the manner of a man. But this is false, for plants never approach human shape. Certain ones are, however, worked over into such shapes, or so we hear from rustics. The bark of the root is [the part] principally appropriate to medicinal use, second, the "apple" [of the plant], third the leaves. The bark of the roots, once gathered, can be preserved for four years, retaining its efficacy. The bark has the power to constrict, cool, and to a certain extent mortify, because it has a hypnotic power, that is, somniferous.

---

5. Uterine suffocation was thought to be caused by either retained menstrual blood or the woman's own seed that corrupts inside the body. For further details on the condition and treatment, see Monica H. Green, ed. and trans., *The Trotula: A Medieval Compendium of Women's Medicine* (Philadelphia: University of Pennsylvania Press, 2001), 22–30.

6. A compound medicine made of, among other things, opium. Its chief virtues are gynecological. See Green, ed., *The Trotula*, 133–34.

For provoking sleep in [cases of] acute fevers, let powder of the bark be mixed with the milk of a woman and egg white, and let it be applied to the forehead and temples.

For pain of the head caused by heat, crushed leaves [of mandrake] should be placed upon the temples. Let them also be anointed with mandrake oil, which is made thus: having ground the "apples" of the mandrake in common oil, let them be macerated for a long time. Afterward, make a little decoction and let it be strained. This mandrake oil is said to be good for provoking sleep and for pain of the head from hot humors, if the forehead and temple are anointed with it. Also, it represses the feverish heat if the pulse points are anointed.

For hot apostemes [tumors or swellings], first let there be made an anointing with this same oil, which represses the matter [collecting in the tumor]. The fruit and leaves should be plastered [onto the patient], or at least a powder with the juice of any sort of cold herb.

For flux of the belly and an onset of bile, let the belly and entire spine be anointed with the above-mentioned oil, and let a small amount be injected by means of an enema.

(c) **Sugar.** Sugar is hot and moist in the second degree, more or less. It has the power to cool and humidify, to nourish and to relax. In syrups, if there are two pounds of sugar, let there be one of water; if there is more than that of water, it will not harm unless due to continual cooking. Sugar is made in this manner from honey cane in lands beyond the seas, in Sicily, and in Spain: around the time of the feast of the blessed John the Baptist [24 June] the native peoples take honey cane, which is very similar to other kinds of cane, except that its inside is solid and sweet (as opposed to marsh cane, which is hollow and tasteless); they cut it into tiny little pieces through the middle, and they grind it. After having ground it, they put it in a copper kettle and make it boil on a slow fire until it becomes thick and foamy, from which foam [some] sugar is made. Fake sugar is lighter than [real sugar] and inside it is full of holes, by which one is able to discern it from the other. Whence I recommend that in a large sale of sugar, the cone of sugar be broken and tasted.[7] For if inside it is very porous and in taste does not seem to be very sweet, if it dissolves in the mouth and does not crack upon chewing, you should know that it is false and full of foam. They make good sugar from the above-mentioned thick liquid [remaining after cooking], which once it has

7. Platearius regularly offers comments on how to differentiate real from fake or poor quality simples.

cooled slightly, is placed in a round vase in the sun. And as much from the heat as from the long cooking, it turns into hard and white sugar. This can be kept for five years in a place that is not too cold and not too hot. Its use is necessary in many things, namely, in confections of medicines for those suffering from acute fevers, and in syrups. . . . And note that a lot of sugar is good for thirsty travelers if it is offered when they do not have liquid in a hot region. And it is good for consumptives and asthmatics when put in their food and drink, for it rectifies their emaciation and lubricates their dryness.

IV. Copho (attributed), *Anatomy of the Pig* (twelfth century)

This work is the earliest of three twelfth-century Salernitan anatomical texts that purported to give instructions for anatomizing a pig. As is explained in the text here, the argument for doing so was the resemblance of the pig's internal (primarily visceral) anatomy to that of humans. Although human dissection had been per- formed in ancient Alexandria during the Hellenistic period, the practice seems to have died out and was not reestablished in Europe until the late thirteenth century. The two sections that are translated reflect, first, the justification for the work and the instructions for opening the neck of the pig. The following section on the uterus goes into much more physiological (and theoretical) detail, and is clearly talking more about imagined processes in the human body than what is being observed in the anatomized pig.

Because the entire composition of the interior members of the human body was unknown, it pleased the ancients, and especially Galen, to make manifest the positions of the interior organs of brute animals by means of anatomy. And because among brute animals certain ones, like the monkey, are similar to us in their external structures, while others, such as the pig, are similar in their internal structures, in regard to the position of the internal organs none were found so similar [to humans] as pigs. And so we have determined that dissection will be made upon them.

Anatomy is the right division, which is made thus: you ought to place the pig down [with its belly up], [and] you should cut it open through the middle of its throat. And then the tongue appears in front of you, which on both the right and the left sides is tied down with nerves which are called "motive nerves," and from underneath there arise to the tongue nerves which are called "reverse nerves," because when they arrive from the brain to the lung, they turn back to the tongue, by which the tongue moves in making sounds. Next to them are certain glandulous pieces of flesh which are

Translated from Karl Sudhoff in "Die erste Tieranatomie von Salerno und ein neuer saler- nitanischer Anatomietext," *Archiv für Geschichte der Mathematik, der Naturwissenschaften, und der Technik* 10 (1927): 136–54.

called *pharynges*, and their swelling is called the same thing. But next to that there are large glands, in which the humor is collected which causes hoarseness. On the roots of the tongue there are two passages, the tracheal tube, by which air passes to the lung, and the esophagus, by which food is dispatched to the stomach. And the tracheal tube lies above the esophagus, upon which is a certain cartilage which is called the epiglottis, which sometimes closes so that food and drink cannot descend through it, and [sometimes] opens, so that air enters and exits.

The text then continues with the organs of the thorax and the abdomen.

Now the anatomy of the uterus ought to be seen. It is known that Nature arranged this organ in women so that whatever superfluity of the whole body is generated in them might be sent out through this organ at the accustomed time, just like bilge-water, and hence women naturally have menstruation. This organ is, moreover, the field of our nature, which is cultivated so that it might bear fruit. [For] just as sometimes into good soil there is thrown seed which clings to life [and] which through the action of Nature—with the heat working together and the spirit mediating inside—splits open in the manner of a grain and sends out little branches, so certain roots or mouths infix the [human] seed into the uterus and administer nutriment to it and to the fetus being formed. And thus transformed by these actions into a foodstore, as you have often heard said by me (if you remember), the future fetus is generated and grows.

The uterus is situated above the intestine, and above its neck is the bladder and under it is the rectum and below it is the vagina. Now you ought to divide the uterus through the middle of its mouth and you will find two testicles, through which the female seed is transmitted to the uterus, so that from it and the male seed a fetus might be formed. The uterus has seven cells,[8] and if [the animal] is pregnant, you will find in it a fetus, above which you will see a certain tunic, just like a kind of shirt, which is called the secundine, which breaks when the fetus kicks its way to the exit. [The secundine] is tied to the uterus and the fetus, and the nourishment runs through it by means of veins that penetrate it, passing from the uterus to the fetus. And these little passageways, by which the fetus is tied, are called cotyledons.[9] There is also a certain large vessel called the umbilicus, which is broken off

8. The seven-cell theory is first found here in Copho's work and in an anonymous work entitled *On the Seed* (*De spermate*), which may have been another of Constantine's translations. Males were believed to form in the three cells on the right, females in the three (colder) ones on the left, and hermaphrodites in the middle.

9. See Green, ed., *The Trotula*, 90, III.

from the uterus and, when the fetus comes out, it comes out with the fetus. And then midwives tie it next to the belly at the length of four fingers, from the ligature of which bloody inflammations [sometimes] arise.

V. Medical Licenses from the Kingdom of Naples

Southern Italy was the first area of medieval Europe to establish formal licensing of medical practitioners. University training per se was not a requirement. (If it had been, neither of the following two practitioners would have ever received approval.) Rather, the authority of rational medicine as it was taught and practiced at Salerno gave the "masters" there (and later at Naples as well) the authority to assess the qualifications of all other medical practitioners in the kingdom. In these two excerpts, King Robert of Naples (d. 1343) [see # 109] and his granddaughter Queen Giovanna I (d. 1382) issue formal approval for Bernard of Casale Santa Maria and Maria Incarnata of Naples, respectively, to practice their trade in specified locations of the kingdom. Bernard's license shows how an unlettered (ydiota) practitioner could gain the right to practice certain limited procedures, while Maria Incarnata's demonstrates the continuing sexual division of labor that reserved "hands-on" aspects of women's medicine to female practitioners out of concern with morality. Although not explicitly called ydiota, as were some other women who received licenses, there is nothing in Maria's license to suggest that she has any book learning. Rather, like most surgeons in this period (male and female), her learning has come through practice.

1. FOR BERNARD OF CASALE SANTA MARIA (1330)

Robert [King of Sicily], etc. To all those throughout the provinces of Terra di Lavoro and the county of Molise and Capitanata who will be reading this letter, his faithful servants, greetings, etc. Physicians were established by divine ordinance for curing sick bodies; so that they might be proficient in the office of practical procedures, they are selected by the provident science of medicine by approved physicians who assist Us. Clearly, master Bernard of Casale Santa Maria, an unlettered surgeon, Our faithful and lawful servant, born from a faithful family [as acknowledged] by public written testimony of the municipality of Bagnoli[10] (whose praiseworthy testimony Our Court receives), and whom We had diligently examined by our surgeons, is found to be experienced in [treating] bones. Hence, having first received from him the customary oath of fidelity sworn on the holy Gospels of God, that accord-

---

Translated from: Raffaele Calvanico, *Fonti per la storia della medicina e della chirurgia per il regno di Napoli nel periodo angioino (a. 1273–1410)* (Naples: Arte Tipografica, 1962), 222–23, 261.

10. The Latin phrase is *per testimoniale publicum scriptum universitatis castri Balneoli.* Bagnoli is an area rich in thermal baths, lying on the coast of the Bay of Naples between Naples itself and the more famous baths of Pozzuoli.

ing to the traditions of this same art he will practice faithfully, We are led to concede to him by the tenor of the present letter a license to treat and to practice on bones broken in the arms and legs, throughout the whole of the above-said provinces. We order, by Our faith, that this same Bernard shall be free to treat and to practice on the aforementioned broken bones of the arms and legs throughout each of the lands and places of these provinces to the honor and fidelity of Us and Our heirs and to the utility of Our faithful servants of these same provinces, no impediment or obstacle withstanding. Given at Naples by John Grillo of Salerno, etc., the year of Our Lord 1330, the ninth day of May, of the thirteenth indiction, the twenty-first year of our reign.

2. ON SURGERY. FOR MARIA INCARNATA (1343)

Giovanna, etc. To all those throughout the province of Terra di Lavoro and the County of Molise who will be reading these letters both now and in the future, her faithful servants, greetings, etc. With respect to the public weal as it relates to the upstanding women of Our [kingdom], We have been attentive and We are mindful in how much modesty recommends honesty of morals. Clearly, Maria Incarnata of Naples, Our faithful servant, present in Our Court has proved that [she] is competent in the principal exercise of surgery, in the treatment of wounds and apostemes [tumors]. She conducts herself with circumspect judgment in such cases, because of which she has supplicated Our Highness most attentively that We might deign to concede to her a license to practice on diseases or conditions of this kind. Because, therefore, by trustworthy testimony presented to Our Court, it is clearly found that the above-said Maria is faithful and comes from a worthy family and, having been examined by our surgeons, she is found to be competent in treating the above-said illnesses. Although it should be alien to female propriety to be interested in the affairs of men lest they rush into things abusive of matronly shame and for this reason they risk the sin of forbidden transgression, [nevertheless] because the office of medicine is expediently conceded to women by an unspoken rule of law, it being noted that females, by their honesty of character, are more suited than men to treat sick women, especially in their own diseases, We, having first received from this same Maria the customary oath of fidelity sworn on the Gospels and [the promise] that she will faithfully treat [patients] according to the traditions of this art, impart to her a license to treat and to practice on the mentioned afflictions throughout the whole of the abovesaid principality, by the counsel and consent of the glorious lady, Lady Sancia, by the grace of God Queen of Jerusalem and Sicily, reverend lady mother, administrator and our principal governor, and by the public authority of our other administrators. Therefore by Our faith from the counsel and assent of the above-mentioned, We command that it be ordered that in so far as this same Maria treats and practices on the above-said diseases through the whole of the above-said principality, to the honor of Us and Our heirs and the utility of Our faithful servants of these same provinces, you should permit her freely [to do so], posing no impediment or obstruction to her. Given at Naples by Adenulf Cumano of Naples, professor of civil law, Vice Protonotarius of the Kingdom of Sicily, in the year of Our Lord 1343, the seventh day of May of the eleventh indiction, the first year of our reign.

76. MATTEO VILLANI ON PLAGUE AND MALARIA (1357–58)

Translated from Italian by Samuel K. Cohn

For some time, historians have associated Matteo Villani (d. 1363) with the plague and have used his chronicle to analyze its moral consequences. Their use of his chronicle, however, has been limited to a consideration of the first strike of plague, when, similar to the Sienese chronicler Agnolo di Tura del Grasso and Giovanni Boccaccio, he divided the world into two camps—the few who learned from God's wrath and thus became more pious, and the many who did not, who now more than ever lived for pleasure and sin. Few, if any, have examined Matteo's descriptions and comments about the other plagues he reported either from his vast foreign correspondence or from first-hand experience—those of 1357–58, 1360, 1361–63—the last of which felled him. The passage below is significant for four reasons: first, it shows an elementary awareness of the human potential to acquire immunity to the medieval plague (unlike modern bubonic plague, Yersinia pestis, for which humans have no immunity nor can they acquire it). Second, contemporaries of the medieval world did not see all diseases alike and call them plague, as modern historians of medicine often claim; rather, doctors and chroniclers made distinctions, and these distinctions were based on elementary epidemiological observations such as how fast the disease killed or how contagiously it spread. Third, these contemporaries were not tied to seeing the world of diseases through the prism of classical knowledge; instead, the Black Death and its recurring strikes caused them to question doctrine. Fourth, theories of miasma (that diseases originated and spread because of the corruption of air) did not prevent contemporaries such as Villani from observing that diseases also could spread from person to person; in his terms one "spotted" another.

Although the arm of God still stretched out over the world of sinners, they had not corrected or mended their ways, despite his terrible judgment over the entire known world. To whip them into adopting a more wholesome life, in the autumn of this year [1357] he once again inflicted the pestilence of the swellings in the groin on them; its scourge blew in with the westward winds. It struck Brussels with particular severity; more than 1,500 citizens died in October and November, not counting women and children, who also died in great numbers. With a similar severity it infested Antwerp, Louvain, and others cities of Brabant. But it did not touch Flanders, because on the previous strike this area had been severely stricken, and therefore Brabant now felt it much more. And for the same reason, it now struck Germany around Basel

Translated from Matteo Villani, *Cronica con la continuazione di Filippo Villani*, ed. Giuseppe Porta (Parma: Guanda, 1995), vol. II, book 8, chapter CVIII.

and other cities and towns in Bohemia and Prague, where the first plague had not been serious.

At this time, diseases of tertiary, *quartene*,[1] and other fevers with long-drawn-out illnesses afflicted our territory, in the Valdelsa, Valdarno di sotto,[2] and Chianti, somewhat like in the previous year, from which few died. This baffled the people of the Valdelsa and Chianti, since they had good and pure air; nonetheless, for two years they infected one another with similar diseases, and no one could identify any single cause for this occurrence.

1. Today, this term refers to *Plasdomium malaria*, which causes periods of fever for seventy-two hours at two-day intervals.
2. Valdesa was the region along the Elsa river south of Florence on the western border of the Chianti. Its center was Barberino Valdelsa. Valdarno di sotto was along the Arno river west of Florence.

77. THE CURRICULUM IN ARTS AND MEDICINE AT BOLOGNA (early fifteenth century)

Translated from Latin by M. Michèle Mulchahey

Famed for legal studies, the studium *at Bologna also taught the arts and medicine, as the syllabus below clearly indicates. The notable absence in the curriculum of many Italian universities was theology: Queen of Sciences and the dominant faculty at the University of Paris, theology was taught in Bologna only through the schools of the friars and other religious until the mid-fifteenth century. This affected the shape of the arts curriculum, which at Bologna was seen as training preparatory more for medicine than for theology, and thus more emphasis was placed on Aristotelian natural philosophy less on metaphysics and psychology. It also explains the inclusion of lectures on astrology, which was considered relevant to medical prognostication but banned by the ecclesiastical authorities.*

LECTURES IN PHILOSOPHY

Ordinary	Extraordinary
First Year	
Aristotle, *Physics*, entire	Aristotle, *On Generation and Corruption*, Bk II
Aristotle, *On Generation and Corruption*, Bk I	Aristotle, *On Sleep and Waking*
	(Ps.-)Aristotle, *Physiognomy*
Second Year	
Aristotle, *On Heaven and Earth*	Averroës, *On the Substance of the Universe*
Aristotle, *Meteorology*	Aristotle, *On Memory and Reminiscence*
Aristotle, *On Sense and Sensation*	Aristotle, *On Inspiration and Respiration*
Third Year	
Aristotle, *On the Soul* (except the errors of its first book)	Aristotle, *Metaphysics* (part of Bk IV)
	(Ps.-)Aristotle, *On the Brevity of Life*
Aristotle, *Metaphysics* (Proemium only of Bk I, and Bks II, V–XII)	Aristotle, *The Cause and Movement of Animals*

LECTURES IN MEDICINE

Ordinary	Extraordinary
First Year	
Avicenna, *Canon*, Bk I (except the Anatomy and Chapters on the seasons and the second fen, and only these chapters of the third fen: The Necessity of Death, Diseases of Infants, What to Eat and Drink, As to Water and Wine, Sleep and Waking)	Avicenna, *Canon*, Bk IV, fen 2, and Bk II
	Galen, *On Inner Spaces* (except Bk II)
	Regimen of Health
	Galen, *Critical Days*, Bk II
	Aphorisms of Hippocrates (except Particula VII)

Compiled and translated from Carlo Malagola, *Statuti delle università e dei collegi dello studio bolognese* (Bologna: Zanichelli, 1888), rubric 68, 274–75.

Galen, *On Differences of Fevers*
Galen, *Of a Bad State of Health*
Galen, *Of Simple Medicines* (except Bk VI)
Galen, *Critical Days*, Bk I

Second Year

Galen, *Tegni*
Hippocrates, *Prognostics* (without commentary)
Hippocrates, *On Acute Diseases* (without commentary and omitting Bk IV)
Avicenna, *On the Powers of the Heart*, in part
Galen, *On Accident and Disease*
Galen, *On the Crisis*
Galen, *Critical Days*, Bk III
Galen, *To Glauco: On Fevers*, Tract I
Galen, *De tabe*
Galen, *On the Utility of Breathing*

Avicenna, *Canon* (portions noted as in First Year)
Galen, *On Differences of Fevers*
Galen, *Of a Bad State of Health*
Avicenna, *Canon*, Bk IV, fen 2
Galen, *On Simple Medicine* (except Bk VI)
Galen, *Critical Days*, Bk I

Third Year

Aphorisms of Hippocrates (except Particula VII)
Hippocrates, *Therapeutic*, Bks VII–XIII
Averroës, *Colliget*, in part
Galen, *On Natural Virtues*, in part

Galen, *Tegni*
Hippocrates, *Prognostics* (without commentary)
Hippocrates, *On Acute Diseases* (without commentary and omitting Bk IV)
Galen, *On the Powers of the Heart*, in part
Galen, *On the Crisis*
Galen, *Critical Days*, Bk III
Galen, *To Glauco: On Fevers*, Tract I
Galen, *On States of Health*

Fourth Year

Avicenna, *Canon* (as in First Year)
Avicenna, *Canon*, Bk IV, fen I and Bk II
Galen, *On Inner Spaces*
Regimen of Health
Hippocrates, *On Nature*

Aphorisms of Hippocrates (except Particula VII)
Hippocrates, *Therapeutic*, Bks VII–XIII
Averroës, *Colliget*, in part
Galen, *On Natural Virtues*, in part

LECTURES IN ASTROLOGY

First Year

Al-Khwarismi, *Algorismus*, on fractions and integers
Euclid, *Geometry*, Bk I, with Commentary of Campanus
Alfonsine Tables, with Canons
Theory of Planets

Second Year

John of Sacrobosco, *On the Sphere*
Euclid, *Geometry*, Bk II
John de Lineriis, *Canons and Tables*
Messahala, *On the Astrolabe*

Third Year

Alcabitius, *Introduction to Astrology*
Ptolemy, *Centiloquium*, with Commentary of Haly
Euclid, *Geometry*, Bk III
Treatise on the Quadrant

Fourth Year

Ptolemy, *Quadripartitus*, entire
William of England, *On Urine Unseen*
Ptolemy, *Almagest*, Dictio III

78. DISSECTION AT BOLOGNA (early fifteenth century)

Translated from Latin by M. Michèle Mulchahey

Dissection is often thought of as having been an unauthorized, if not shady, study in the Middle Ages, requiring questionable strategies on the part of students of anatomy for gaining access to corpses [see #75.4]. This statute from the University of Bologna shows the extent to which human dissection—of both male and female bodies—had been regularized as part of the curriculum of the Italian medical faculties by the fifteenth century.

Since the performing of dissection pertains to and enhances the work and progress of scholars, and quarrels and rumors have often arisen over the search for and locating of bodies of which dissection might be made, the syndics have decreed and ordered that any doctor or scholar or any other person shall not dare or presume to obtain a dead body for himself for the purpose of dissection, unless he has first obtained permission from the current rector of the university. Furthermore, when the said license is requested, the rector is bound and required when giving permission to doctors and scholars to give due attention to precedence and to observe the rules. Also, not more than 20 persons may attend the dissection of the body of a male, and not more than 30 the dissection of a female. And no one may attend a dissection unless he has been a student of medicine for two full years and is in his third year of study, even if he attended classes extraordinarily. Also, he who has attended the dissection of a man once cannot attend another that same year; he who has attended twice may not attend again in Bologna, except the dissection of a woman, which he may observe once and once only, whether or not he has seen a man being dissected.

Moreover, the said 20 or 30 who may attend and observe a dissection are to be chosen and selected in the following manner: namely, for the anatomizing of a man, five from the nation of the Lombards, four from the nation of the Tuscans, four from the nation of the Romans, three from the nation of the Ultramontanes, and three Bolognesi. And for the dissection of a woman there shall be chosen eight from the nation of the Lombards, seven from the nation of the Tuscans, seven from the nation of the Romans, five from the nation of the Ultramontanes, and three Bolognesi—excepting always that the rector may attend any dissection with one companion, even if that exceeds the aforesaid limit and notwithstanding the rule that he who

Translated from Carlo Malagola, *Statuti delle università e dei collegi dello studio bolognese* (Bologna: Zanichelli, 1888), rubric 96, 289–90.

has seen a dissection once in a given year may not attend again that year. Furthermore, he who has received a license to attend from the rector shall also have the choice of inviting whom he will, so long as the terms of this statute are observed.

Also, let no one dare to request permission to perform a dissection from a rector at the time of his election in the church of San Francesco under pain of five pounds Bolognese. Immediately after accepting office, however, the rector should publish throughout the schools the names of those to whom he has granted a license to dissect, so that it may be known to all, with a fine of 10 pounds Bolognese to be imposed on the rector for failing to observe this procedure and for not enforcing it. A fine of 100 *soldi* Bolognese will also be imposed on each scholar who offends against any of the aforesaid statutes.

Also, any doctor who has been asked by the scholars to perform a dissection in the manner and form described above must do so, even if he has already performed one that year, and his stipend shall be 100 *soldi* Bolognese. The said expenses and any others that may be incurred incidentally shall be divided equally among the scholars who are to attend, so that not more than 16 pounds Bolognese be spent for the dissection of a man and not more than 20 for that of a woman, under penalty to each doctor of 100 *soldi* Bolognese, the one exception being that the one who has undertaken the arrangements and made the expenditures, together with one associate he shall name, shall be wholly freed from the said expenses. And before the dissection begins, the rector shall summon before him the scholar to whom he gave permission for the dissection, and shall require him to take an oath that he will make the expenditures in good faith and without fraud, and that he will submit them to the scholars witnessing the dissection, under penalty to the rector then holding office of 10 pounds Bolognese.

79. SURGERY AT BOLOGNA (1405)

Translated from Latin by M. Michèle Mulchahey

The medieval distinction between the physicus *or* physician, *the university-trained master skilled in Aristotelian natural philosophy and theoretical medicine, and the* medicus, *the actual medical practitioner, had a long history. That this distinction was beginning to be eroded in Italy by the fifteenth century is hinted at in this statute from the University of Bologna. Masters of surgery now appear alongside masters of medicine in university legislation, and, as the previous document showed, dissection was clearly being carried out in the medical faculty. At the same time, however, surgery was still being taught predominantly through classic textbooks and scholastic pedagogy, including schoolroom debates over surgical terminology and methodology.*

Further, the syndics decreed that the doctors lecturing on surgery ought to lecture in the following way, namely, that every year, when the university opens, they shall begin in the first course of lectures to read the *Surgery* of Bruno and, after finishing it, to read the *Surgery* of Galen. For the second course, they shall lecture on the *Surgery* of Avicenna and after that the seventh book of *Almansor*. Moreover, each doctor giving ordinary lectures in surgery should lecture in the afternoon at the nineteenth hour.

Further, they decreed that the divisions of the texts into sections should be determined by one of the doctors lecturing in surgery, so that the same number of sections is assigned as are assigned in the other sciences. And each doctor giving lectures shall observe the section divisions and complete and cover them as assigned, under penalty of 20 *soldi* Bolognese for each offense. Also, each doctor lecturing in surgery is required to dispute two questions in surgery, or more, each year, just as the doctors lecturing in medicine are bound to do; and also each is required to put them in final form, in clear writing and on good paper, and to submit them to the general beadles as a permanent record to be guarded and kept by the beadles. Each doctor is to hold these disputations in the afternoon, unless a feast day falls during the week and on the day on which he intended to dispute, in which case he may dispute in the morning, provided no lecturer in medicine is disputing then. Moreover, he is required to dispute only over surgery and surgical terms, under the penalty stipulated in the statutes. Further, no one shall presume to take part in any academic function while the doctors of surgery are disputing, and the rector and the doctors of medicine are required to attend their dispu-

Translated from Carlo Malagola, *Statuti delle università e dei collegi dello studio bolognese* (Bologna: Zanichelli, 1888), rubric 35, 247–48.

tations as others are, and to be there from start to finish, and to take part in the debate just as they do at other disputations, under penalty of 20 *soldi* for each offender. Likewise, each doctor lecturing in surgery shall be required to meet all the same obligations as doctors in the other sciences. Moreover, they shall receive 20 *soldi* Bolognese for their labor and salary from every person attending their lectures on the subject, with a fine of five pounds Bolognese being exacted from each of the said doctors each time he offends in any of the aforesaid matters.

Varieties of Religious Experience: The Christian Tradition

The length and complexity of the texts included in this section reflect the central importance of the Latin Christian tradition to religious life in medieval Italy, whose small Jewish, Greek, and Muslim communities are documented elsewhere in this volume [see #16, 33, 47, 54, 58, 63, 110, 113, 114]. The voices of churchmen dominated discussions of religious life in this period, despite increased access to reading and writing, particularly in the burgeoning population centers of northern and central Italy. Their literary skills were put to work describing religious experience on both sides of the line distinguishing "faithful and faithless," as the first writer in this chapter, Andrea da Strumi, put it. Clerics were keen to criticize lay assumption of authority in matters of religion, but the increasingly creative engagement of lay people in religious life is clearly evident here in activities such as membership of the confraternity to which a layman, Albertanus of Brescia, preached in 1250. Albertanus was one of a rare but growing breed, challenging the clerical monopoly on teaching of the faith, just as in rather different ways both the Milanese "Pataria" and the Humiliati had done in earlier centuries. The urgent need for evidence of divine approval, if not direction, when claiming religious authority is perhaps particularly clear in accounts of the holy lives of lay women and men. These were presented as models for the behavior of the laity in general: facing adversity, even death, with patience, caring for the poor and sick, and above all rejecting the values of the world, especially the wealth of the merchant and noble classes from which they came. In an effort both to ascertain and to assert the truth more convincingly, churchmen subjected these lives to legal trial in the form of canonization inquests and also continuously insisted on the veracity of their own accounts, citing numerous witnesses and the effectiveness of miracles and intercession. That this effort was not superfluous is underlined by the skepticism about devotional practices expressed by writers such as Franco Sacchetti, some of whose witty criticism of saints' cults and the veneration of their images is included here. This provides an alternative view of the "modern saint," Umiliana de' Cerchi, whose more conventional Vita *(life), written by a Franciscan, is also presented below. Sacchetti was particularly acute, but his expression of personal doubt about practices cannot have been unusual; indeed, clerical writers and preachers continually complained of the misguided behavior of the ordinary faithful. Not infrequently, in addition to their pastoral sermons, preachers were called upon to bless affairs of "the state," as the sermon of the Neapolitan preacher, Giovanni Regina, so well demonstrates [see #38].*

As well as documenting the frequency and range of causes of controversy or the dangers of life as a senior churchman caught in the political tension between empire and papacy, the documents here also reveal the life of the church at its most ordinary, illustrating for example, the dogged determination of a parish priest whose career, like that of many of his contemporaries, was endlessly disrupted by political change. At the same time, they demonstrate the continuing imaginative enthusiasm of men and women for religion and devotional practices: turning murdered bishops into saints, turning to saints as civic patrons, or for cures, going on pilgrimage to saints' shrines, joining confraternities to praise them or engaging in alms-giving in the name of Christian charity.

80. THE *PATARIA*: ANDREA DA STRUMI'S PASSION OF ARIALDO (late eleventh century)

Translated from Latin by William North

The Pataria—*a term of derision used by its opponents and probably meaning "rag-picker"—was the longest (1057–75) and most violent of the popular responses to the call for ecclesiastical reform in the eleventh century. At its heart, the* Pataria *attacked two practices that were, it is generally agreed, widespread in the archdiocese of Milan. First, it sought to end the accepted or even openly acknowledged practice of clerical marriage/concubinage, a practice that wove clerics deep into the dense fabric of desires and concerns of lay society and thereby compromised their ability to be spiritual leaders and providers of saving sacraments. Second, the* Pataria *sought to end simony, the practice of receiving a spiritual office or role in exchange for a payment of some kind, whether money or service, a custom that many considered not only sinful but heretical. Although they received little support from most of the established clergy or the archbishop, two clerics from the lower Milanese nobility, Arialdo (d. 1066) and Landulf (d. 1062), did receive sustained encouragement from the Roman curia and pope and, thus encouraged, pursued an aggressive campaign of preaching, liturgies, institutional reorganization, and popular action against clerics who refused to correct their ways. For a considerable period of time they were highly successful in mobilizing popular support, especially within the city of Milan itself. When Landulf died, Erlembald, a knight and lay brother, took his place as Arialdo's companion and aide, and they both continued to work for reform, though seemingly with more aggressive tactics. When Arialdo was brutally murdered in 1066, Erlembald continued the struggle until he too was eventually killed in 1075 in one of the many street battles that characterized the period. Throughout the conflict, the politics of the* Pataria *intersected with numerous related, but distinct, tensions and developments that were restructuring eleventh-century Italy: the ecclesiastical primacy of Roman authority versus local traditions and self-determination; the struggle between pope and emperor over the emperor's rights within the church and influence in Italy; strife among the social classes in Milan that had, a decade earlier, erupted in civil unrest; the emerging roles of papal legates and the cardinalate as potent political players; and changing notions of the proper relationship between authoritative texts and living institutions.*

Andrea da Strumi's Passion of Arialdo *intended to preserve for posterity the memory of a new saint and a martyr in the cause of ecclesiastical reform and an admired spiritual leader and friend. Indeed, Andrea's work is particularly notable in the many quasi-verbatim speeches of Arialdo and others he purports to include. Yet, inasmuch as he begins writing his hagiography soon after the death of Erlembald in 1075, when the* Pataria's *strength had been broken, his narrative may also have been intended to commemorate, even as it criticized, the movement itself as a vital part of Milan's religious history. The text offers insight not only into two divergent responses to the* Pataria's *demand for clerical reform but also into the social, cultural, and institutional dynamics of a popular religious movement and the place of historical and hagiographical texts in preserving social memory in medieval Italy.*

[Prologue] Venerable father Rudolf, you ordered me to write down the passion of the blessed martyr Arialdo. . . . Whoever shall read this life should know that in it I have said absolutely nothing that I have not learned from the accounts of reliable men, namely Melchior, his faithful brother, or Bonvesino, his most faithful servant who served him loyally from the cradle. . . . Furthermore, since many of Arialdo's words and deeds [recorded] in this book may be useful for edification, I pray that you shall give it to the twelve monasteries over which the heavenly judge has placed you so that, when they hear what others in our time have said and suffered in defense of truth, they, too, shall be kindled to say such things and, if necessary, suffer such things for this same truth.

2. Now then, in a village name Cucciago situated between Milan and Como . . . the people say that there lived a man called Bezo and his wife Beza, both noble by birth but even more noble by virtue of their good character. Indeed, the many deeds of these holy people lead us to pause awhile in praising them, since we all know that the praise of a tall building is always easier, if there is clear certainty about the firmness of its foundation. Now then, Bezo and Beza considered the driving force behind wicked men, namely unbridled greed, to be so odious that, among their other good deeds, although they possessed great wealth in servants and horses, [they did not allow] a single one of their servants to dare to place a bale of hay, stolen or taken by force from another's field, before their horses. Furthermore, they so hated pride, which is the driving force behind the devil, that although they might easily have threatened their neighbors in every way and could not have been restrained by any of them if they did not wish it, they behaved as though they were among the least of them and submitted willingly to all their just agreements. Yet because it is a small thing for someone not to do wicked deeds, unless he devotes his energy to good works, they focused so much on the needs of the poor and the sick that there was not one of their neighbors lying on his bed, weighed down by illness, who was not visited by Beza of worthy memory and nourished from her wealth, if they needed it. Furthermore, in the benefits that she constantly gave to the rest of the orphans and the needy, her life was so pleasing to God and men that the poor themselves

Translated from Andrea da Strumi, *Arialdo: Passione del Santo Martire Milanese*, ed. and trans. Marco Navoni (Milan: Jaca Books 1994), 52–104, 128–30 (Latin text on even pages).

talked to each other about her, saying: *If she dies, it is clearly unfitting for us to live.*

3. . . . When Beza bore her son, they called him Arialdo, made him a cleric, and diligently sent him to the schools until there were no more masters in the province who could teach him anything new. And when, as is the custom with schoolboys, he returned home from time to time and his sisters presented themselves to his gaze, adorned more elegantly than usual, Arialdo—as I know from his mother who often told the story—drove them from his sight saying: *This is Satan's trap!*

4. Arialdo devoted himself unceasingly to his studies at schools in various places until he had attained both an excellent knowledge of the liberal arts and divine letters and adulthood. At that time, however, the ecclesiastical order was corrupted by so many errors that hardly anyone could be found who was truly in his proper place. Some served the pleasures of the hunt, wandering about with hounds and hawks, others were tavern-keepers and wicked overseers, while still others were impious usurers. Almost all led shameful lives either with wives who had been acknowledged publicly or with concubines. All were seeking not the good of Christ but rather their own good. [Philippians 2:21] For—and this neither can nor should be said or heard without lamentation—all were so deeply implicated in the heresy of simony that from the least to the greatest there was no order or clerical rank that could be had unless it was bought just as a pig is bought. And what is worse, there was no one at that time who took a stand against such perversity. Indeed, even though they were in fact hungry wolves, they were considered to be true shepherds.

It was, of course, to uncover and correct this perversity that God undoubtedly sent Arialdo to Milan, where this kind of iniquity was the more pervasive, as Milan was more populous than other cities. For Arialdo was, as we have said, well trained in divine laws. Once he entered the city, he began to speak in this way to the people who gathered to hear his words:

> My beloved friends, I want to begin speaking with what I know you already know so that little by little I may introduce you to what you do not know but most certainly ought to know. Now then, I believe that you know that until the coming of Christ the human race was blind, not in the eyes of the body but in those of the heart. It was blind because it believed that what was false was true, when it said to stone, wood, and metal: "You are my God." But the highest eternal light, through which

all things were made and in which all things find their being, had so
much compassion for the blindness and wretchedness of the human race
that, far from sending an angel to remove this blindness from the people's hearts, he himself came down from heaven, took on flesh, and willingly mounted the cross of death in order to expel this blindness
completely from people's heart. In the days of his flesh, he chose as many
men as he foresaw before the dawn of time would suffice to illuminate
the world. Once every shadow of falsity was expelled from their hearts,
he illuminated them with his eternal light, sent them throughout the
world, and ordered them to carry everywhere the light which they had
received, and then he returned to the Father whence he had come. Now
then, this highest, eternal, and living light left on earth two sources by
which those who were to be illuminated would be illuminated and ever
remain beacons of light until the end of time. . . . Do you want to know
what these sources are? The Word of God and the lives of the doctors
[of the Church]. . . . Therefore the Lord has placed one light before
them, and another before you. To those to whom he has given the
knowledge of Scripture and whom he has chosen to be his ministers, he
has laid down that they always live as brilliant lights according to the
light of his Word, and he has decreed that their life be the scripture for
you who cannot read. But through the treachery of the enemy of the
human race as well as through the consequences of our own negligence
and sin, the doctors have lost their light by turning back [to their old
life] and so you have lost your light. But although the enemy took the
truth of their sanctity away from them, he permitted them to retain the
outward semblance of it in order to deceive you with greater certainty.
I say this with a sorrowful groan not to shame but to caution you. . . .
For just as those deceived long ago believed rocks and wood to be gods,
so you suppose your priests to be true priests, even though it is readily
admitted that they are false. How do we know this? Do you want to
know how? We are in the shadows, and to see this more clearly, let us
walk into the light. Into what light? Into the Word of God. Behold,
Christ cries out: Learn from me because I am meek and humble of heart.
[Matthew 11: 29] And again, He says about himself: The son of man has
nowhere to lay his head. [Matthew 8:20; Luke 9:58] and: Blessed are the
poor in spirit for theirs is the kingdom of heaven. [Matthew 5:3] In contrast, as you can see, those of your priests who can make themselves
richer in earthly possessions, more exalted by building towers and
houses, prouder in honors, and more beautiful in their soft and elegant
clothing . . . these are the ones thought to be more blessed! Behold,

they, as you know, openly take wives like laymen, pursue fornication like wicked laymen, and are all the more energetic in pursuing these things as they are less weighed down by earthly labor, since they live off the gift of God. Christ, in contrast, seeks and desires such great purity in his ministers that he condemns the crime of fornication not only in deed but also in the heart when he says: he who sees a woman and desires her has already committed adultery in his heart. [Matthew 5:28] My dear friends, return to your hearts, return and learn how to accept the true and reject the false. I have tried to lead your priests back to their own light but I have been unable. But so that I may lead you to yours, I have come to you now and I shall either succeed or I am prepared to surrender my life to the sword for your salvation.

When the man of God expressed these and many similar thoughts, almost all the common people were so kindled by his words that those whom they had formerly venerated as ministers of Christ, they condemned and declared enemies of God and deceivers of souls.

5. While this was occurring, it also happened that a certain cleric named Landulf arose in the midst of the crowd, a man from the best people in the city in both rank and birth as well as a very powerful and eloquent speaker, and he asked for silence. When it was granted, he burst out in a joyful voice and said:

Before you all I thank omnipotent God that he allowed me to hear just now things that have long burned in my heart. For although I knew and lamented these things, I remained silent because there was no one with whom I might speak about them. But now, my dearest lord Arialdo, because the gift of God has given you to me, know that I have been given by him to you and that from now on, whatever you shall say or do about this matter, I, too, shall do and say. And I am fully prepared to lay down my life for the salvation of my brothers just as you have declared yourself willing to lay down yours.

When the people who were already believers heard this, they rejoiced and grew strong in the praise of God. The opposition grew weak and failed. Arialdo, the servant of God, his eyes and hands raised to heaven, gave great and due thanks to the giver of all good things.

6. Then, after him, there arose a layman named Nazarius, a minter by profession, whose life was greatly praised by all, even though he was married. He

asked for silence, and when silence fell, he offered the following response in the presence of all:

> Lord Arialdo, that what you say is true and useful not only the wise but any fool can see. For who is so foolish that he cannot see clearly that the life of those men should be superior and different from mine whom I summon to my home to bless it, whom I feed according to my ability, to whom I offer a gift after kissing their hands, and from whom I receive all the sacraments for which I expect eternal life? But as we all observe, their way of life is clearly not cleaner but filthier. But you should know that this wickedness is so deeply rooted, and of such long standing, that it is almost imposible to tear it out and then only with great effort. But now, because the Giver of all good things has given me so many goods that can satisfy both of us. I beg you by the omnipotent Lord that you deign to enter my house and from then on enjoy all my wealth just as I do, so that I and this entire people may be freed from this error by your constant exhortation and be strengthened in every truth. Take care lest you pay too much attention to the noble blood from which you arose and to the great wealth with which you shine, lest perchance, in despising the oath with which I entreated you, you seem to seek not the things of God but your own. . . .

Then, because Arialdo and Landulf exhorted the people with faithful and constant teaching, . . . there was no one left who was not compelled to give up such great wickedness . . .

7. At the same time, the faithful decided to send Landulf to Rome for the synod, since their rivals were heading there to accuse them falsely. But he was not allowed to go beyond Piacenza, since he was thoroughly beaten up there by an impious man and so returned to Milan. But Arialdo, the servant of God, although he undertook the same journey, avoided the treachery of all the enemies who lay in wait all around to kill him and, with God's protection, arrived in Rome unharmed. He presented himself before the highest pontiff, and after he told him about the movement that had just begun and the pope conferred great honors upon him, the pope ordered him to receive the divine mysteries only from certain priests and, with an irresistible order, commanded him to continue the work that was now underway and to persist in it with vigor until either he eliminated completely these wicked deeds that were rife within the ecclesiastical family, or he offered to shed his own blood for Christ by his enemies. Obedient in all things, he returned to Milan and pursued

the aforementioned cause in a fitting and constant way together with the companion that God had given him, and from then on their teaching had both authority and truth.

8. When the impious clerics of the city saw this, they met secretly and decided to kill Landulf, since he was of better birth, thinking that in this way they would frighten Arialdo into silence. To commit so foul a deed, they selected a certain bold cleric and promised that if he would snuff out Landulf, they would make him free from cares with a very great reward. Once he had acquired a large executioner's sword—a sword I later saw many times—and poisoned it for a swifter kill, he secretly began to follow Landulf over the course of Maundy Thursday, Good Friday, and even on the Holy Day of Easter. (I know that I am telling the truth even if I do not know whether I have got the order exactly right.) But because on these days he was never able to find Landulf without crowds of people around him, it was only on the Monday after Easter that he finally carried out his impious yet long desired wish. At dawn on that day, he found Landulf praying alone in front of a certain altar. The impious ingredients that he brought with him— namely, the sword and the poison—he combined on the spot. Then, sneaking up on Landulf from behind, he struck him hard in the neck and then immediately fled. Yet, it was the will of God that, although he was swift to flee, he was nevertheless captured at the basilica's exit by a certain crippled man. Then, a loud hue and cry went out, and the people quickly assembled to find out the reason for all the racket. When they learned the reason, they surrounded the wicked cleric and discovered that he had a flask full of poison. Then, lamenting the one who had been struck, they took both victim and assailant to Landulf's house, all the while awaiting death suddenly to befall him. But at that moment, omnipotent God showed evidence of a great miracle, namely that he made the poison have no more effect on the servant of God than if it were water. For the cleric claimed that he had tested it on many sheep and all of them died as soon as they ate it. O wondrous power of the Lord! that after the poison touched this man, it was unable to harm anyone. After rendering due thanks to God, Landulf released unharmed his clerical assailant, warning him never again to attempt such a great act of presumption. Meanwhile when the cleric considered the fact that his carefully planned efforts had been clearly rendered impotent by God and that his servants had rendered unto him good for evil, he was struck by heartfelt remorse, sought forgiveness, turned in the real authors of this great crime, promised that he would never try anything like it again, and finally departed. . . .

10. At this time the servants of Christ, perceiving that the entire population was very ready to heed whatever they said, began to speak openly about simony, a subject about which they had hitherto remained silent. And although Landulf was the more eloquent of the two, Arialdo was the stronger in both learning and sanctity and it was he who preached to the people the following sermon about and against simony:

> We should give thanks to omnipotent God, dearest friends, who has given you to wish what He wishes. We wish you to know that the great effort that we have made until now against the insolence of married and adulterous priests, we have done more out of necessity than by our own wish. For it matters little to us whether heretics have wives or not.

When he saw that the crowds were looking at him and wondering why he said this, he added:

> Dearest friends, you have heard it said when the Acts of the Apostles was read that Simon the magician came to the apostle Peter and asked him for the grace of the Holy Spirit in exchange for payment. The evangelist Luke who described what the blessed Peter said to him in response immediately added: "Your money shall be with you in hell, because you thought that the gift of God could be had for money" [Acts 8:20]. . . . Behold, the wicked crime that the prince of the apostles handed over to eternal perdition as an idea alone holds such power throughout almost the entire world that no one arrives at episcopal, abbatial, or any other ecclesiastical office except by means of it. Who shall not be struck dumb in sorrowful amazement at what I am about to say: Behold, Christ the true Lord, the good pastor, gave to his flock a good and salutary command but this has been cast into such profound oblivion that there appears to be no one now who dares to recall it. Do you want to hear what it is? "What you receive freely, give freely." [Matthew 10: 8] In contrast, that impious idea, which wickedly arose once in the heart of the impious Simon and was then condemned by the great apostle together with its author, has now been spread everywhere with such solemnity that almost no one approaches the office of the altar, unless he first does in deed what he has likewise contemplated iniquitously in his heart and until he subjects himself all the more deeply to the same curse, since it is known to be worse to do evil than to contemplate it. Would that this curse only strike those who presumed to buy or sell the gift of God with a bold and impious heart! But in this case, so noxious

is the crime that not only those who do it and those who consent to it but even those who do not resist it and fight against those who do it are bound by the same punishment, so that they shall share in the curse that Peter imposed on Simon. And lest you think I am lying, hear what the blessed Ambrose, our patron, thinks about it.[1] He says in fact: "Let those who think that they can buy the rank of priest with money know that they have received leprosy. . . . Thus you may see throughout the Church those whom not merits but money have advanced to the rank of the episcopacy.[2] . . . There are three orders in the holy Church: the first, those who preach, the second, those who are continent, and the third those who are married. The first should fight with tireless exhortation against simony, while you who are married and live by the work of your hands should each day persist in works of almsgiving in order that omnipotent God may repel and destroy this heresy from the holy Church. Now whoever belongs to these three orders and has not fought ardently against the heresy of simony with these works of justice, you shall have . . . the same punishment that Simon the magician now has. For if those to whom the duty and knowledge to preach has been committed, remain silent for some reason, not only the continent, whose preaching should be all the freer and truer as it is clear that they are freed from all secular matters and are deeply learned through constant meditation upon sacred law, but you, too, who are private persons and ignorant of scripture, should beware of this iniquity in whatever shared converse you can. . . .

While the blessed Arialdo was saying this and much like it, the salvation-bearing sword was undoubtedly sent to that place that divides the faithful from the faithless and about which the Lord said: "I have not come to bring peace but the sword" [Matthew 10:34]. Now then, Guido, who was said to be the archbishop, the majority of clerics and knights, and many iniquitous men from the lower ranks of the *popolo* went away in secret and said to each other:

> If this doctrine bears fruit, life will not be worth living for ourselves and our children. For what else is our life if not the benefices that we buy and sell constantly? It is better for us therefore to die resisting this new teaching than to allow it to come to fruition.

1. Ambrose (d. 397), bishop and patron saint of Milan.
2. Andrea here has Arialdo quoting a sermon by Pseudo-Ambrose edited under the title *On the Office of Priest*.

The blessed Arialdo answered them as follows:

> . . . I entreat you through him to separate yourselves completely from the company of false priests, for there should be no company, communion, or society between light and darkness, faithful and unfaithful, Christ and Belial. . . . [Despise] the company of all heretics, faithfully seek out good and faithful pastors from him and know without a doubt that you shall receive them.

At these words, many men and women were so kindled [with pious zeal] that they not only despised all acts of the simoniacs but also absolutely would not pray with them in the same oratory. In these days, if you were to walk through the city, you would hear scarcely anything but debate on this matter. Some excused the simoniacal heresy, others condemned it constantly, and no wonder since one house was faithful, another completely unfaithful, in a third the mother and one son were believers, while the father and another son were unbelieving. And the entire city was permeated and filled with confusion and contention. . . .

14. There were two clerics who had long before received the mark of clerical status in the church of Santa Maria Secreta. But neither of them could receive its benefice until, as was customary in this place [Milan], the priest of this church died. It just so happened that he died at this time. But although the cleric who had been first assigned to the church ought to have received it, if only he offered the payment that had been established by evil custom, he nevertheless hesitated to do so because he believed the words of the man of God [Arialdo]. The other cleric, who was second in line for the benefice, was not so scrupulous and, ashamed before neither God nor man, was not afraid to acquire the church with money. When this news reached Arialdo, the man of God, he summoned the cleric and said this to him: "Foul usurper, why have you not feared to commit this crime after you heard me teaching that one who buys or sells what is sacred is a heretic?" The cleric grew silent and did not know what to say to excuse his behavior. But since he was now utterly despised by his neighbors, he finally said: "Now that I heard a clear explanation, I see that I have done wrong but I don't know what to do now, because the abbot of San Vittore to whom I gave almost everything I had for this benefice, does not fear God enough so that he will return to me the money he received, and if I don't have this money, I shall not have the wherewithal for even a modest existence."

The man of God said to him: "How much did you give him?"

"Twelve pounds of silver."

The man of God replied: "And if they are returned to you, will you willingly give up what you wrongly purchased?"

"Most willingly," the fellow answered.

Then that good disciple, imitating his pious master, carried out in deed what he said in word: from his own patrimony he took the whole twelve pounds of silver and gave them all to the priest and thus made it so that the other man freely held this church which belonged to him by right.

15. At this time, Arialdo's companion Landulf died but left behind his brother Erlembald, a prudent and faithful person, albeit a layman. Having recently returned from Jerusalem, Erlembald wanted to leave the world and give himself over to the monastic life. But since he perceived his faith and constancy, Arialdo started to promise Erlembald that he would gain greater status in the eyes of God if he delayed entering a monastery and joined with him in defending the catholic faith and resisting heretics and the enemies of Christ. Erlembald wished to determine whether he dared to trust in what Arialdo was promising him and so, in the company of a number of the faithful, he set off for Rome, not traveling by the royal road but going by way of those worshiping God in the desert and asking all of them about this matter. After all those aflame with the true and pure faith had given him a judgment that agreed with the blessed Arialdo's, he finally reached Rome. There, Pope Alexander [II] and the cardinals ordered him to return [to Milan] with an inescapable command and to resist Christ's enemies bravely with Arialdo in defense of justice even to the point of shedding his own blood. And they gave him a banner on behalf of the blessed Peter so that when the madness of the heretics raged beyond measure, he might tame them holding it in his hand. With what constancy he fulfilled this command over the course of eighteen years, my tongue is unable to describe fully and my pen unfit to express. For before the eyes of the world, Erlembald was like a duke arrayed in fine clothes and surrounded by knights and arms, but in secret before God he was like a hermit in the wilderness, dressed in woolens. I saw him wash the feet of the poor, something that I do not recall ever having seen before. For as he went about the city surrounded by a great retinue of loyal followers who willingly obeyed him, he would gaze with horror upon the poor and the sick. Secretly he used then to tell one of his servants to remain behind and bring the poor man to his house. Once the visitors had departed, water was brought and, girded in linen, he rinsed and cleansed the poor man's feet with great veneration. Then, laying his body down upon the ground, he placed his head beneath the poor man's feet and in this way he made it so that the

poor beggar got to trample a bit upon him, who was rich. Then he ate with him in honor and abundance. Over time, I saw him perform this holy act with twelve poor men. Indeed, so aflame with the zeal for God was he that the man of God Arialdo often used to talk about him when he was not there and say with a sigh: "Alas! Save for Erlembald and Nazarius, I find scarcely a cleric who does not try to persuade me in some way under a false sense of discretion to remain silent so that the simoniacs and adulterers can freely commit works of the devil." I am aware of many other good things about Erlembald from our close acquaintance but because he was recently crowned with martyrdom in defense of justice, I shall leave them for another book and another author, because I want to finish the life of Arialdo swiftly. . . .

21. On the following night the wicked faction again met with Guido, saying:

> These misfortunes should not discourage us in any way. For the mob is quickly altered and is easily inclined in different directions. We are, indeed, certain that we are absolutely unable to snuff out Arialdo in the city. Therefore our wit and wisdom must find some other plan that he shall not be able to escape. Also, prudent men of ours should be placed in different places throughout the city who shall have large amounts of money that we give them and which they shall secretly distribute among the people by night. But during the days, setting all business aside, let us meet constantly. And let us continue to do this until, our numbers greatly multiplied, we are able to drive him forcibly from the city. And when this happens, with traps set everywhere, he shall be captured and once captured killed. If we don't do all this, we will never have peace. What more is there to say?

For fifteen days, therefore, there were two continuous and ardent assemblies of people: one of the faithful at the church of Rozo, the other at the bishop's court. But the wicked faction grew greatly because of the money given to the people during the night. And as it grew through iniquity, the faithful gradually grew tired and began not to attend. . . . But although the impious clamored with insane rage against him, they did not dare to do in any way what they were threatening, because whenever they attempted to rise up against the servant of Christ, their heads suffered for it. Therefore they issued an iniquitous public order that, as long as Arialdo remained in the city, any cleric who celebrated the mystery [the mass] publicly or sounded the bells or any layman who allowed this to be done in his church, would not only be deprived of his property but also of his life. . . .

22. From the place of his capture, Arialdo sang the psalms. At Staziona, he was separated from the soldiers . . . and was handed over to five fierce servants who spoke to him while they were leading him to his death, saying: "Arialdo, why don't you deny what you have said until now and proclaim that our lord is the true bishop? For if you were to do this, you could perhaps be able to go on living." But he replied: "God forbid that the crown which I have acquired during my life by speaking the truth, I lose at the end of my life by lying. For I do not know whether you are leading me to my death, but if you are, know that I shall greatly harm your lord not only in the future life but also in the present." And then they said: "Do you see that big mountain over there? If it was made of gold and you were to give me the whole thing, there is no way that you would live." When he heard this, he arose and began to sing aloud a hymn to the holy apostles Peter and Paul. When he was finished, they arrived at the remote spot where they were heading. Taking him from the ship, they placed him sitting and bound atop a rock. Going a short distance away, they began to discuss the situation, saying: "What are we going to do? If we kill a great man like him, our souls shall never again find relief, but if we don't kill him, we shall die all the same." While they were hesitating over these questions, they spied a ship coming swiftly toward them bearing two people. They said to each other: "Let's wait for them. Perhaps they are bringers of good news." But the niece of the wicked Guido, who was from that time on called Jezabel and Herodias, after she ordered the five servants to kill the servant of God, had summoned two clerics whom she knew longed especially for Arialdo's death and spoke to them thus: "Take up your swords and persecute your enemy swiftly, lest perchance he seduce the others and live." It was these two who were arriving by boat. Once they had reached the others and disembarked, they said: "Where is Arialdo?" [The servants] answered: "He is dead." The clerics said: "We were ordered to see him, dead or alive." And looking around, they saw him sitting bound upon a rock. They rushed at him avidly, like famished lion cubs upon prey. With swords bared, one seized one ear, the other the other ear, saying: "Tell us, you gallows rogue, if our lord is the true archbishop. Arialdo answered: He is not and never was, because the calling of an archbishop is neither in him now nor was it ever." Then those merciless clerics cut off both his ears. But Arialdo, his eyes raised to heaven, said: "I thank you, Christ, that today you have deigned to number me among your martyrs." He was then asked again whether Guido was the true archbishop. Maintaining his usual constancy of spirit, he said: "He is not." They immediately cut off his nose and upper lip. Then they gouged out both eyes. Then they cut off his right hand, saying: "This is the hand that wrote the letters sent to Rome." Thereupon they cut off his

genitals, saying: "Until now you have been a preacher of chastity, now you shall be chaste." Then they tore out his tongue out of his throat, saying: "Now be silent [tongue] that troubled and dispersed the families of clerics." In this way that holy soul was released from the flesh . . . .

26. For ten years the blessed levite and martyr Arialdo lived, fighting the good fight for Christ; he offered ten of his body's members at the hands of the wicked, eight when he was killed, two lest he be recognized. He lay ten months at the bottom of the lake safe and sound; the lake [then] brought him forth ten miles closer to us than it received him. For ten summer days Christ preserved him in the church of Saint Ambrose for all to see and, in the tenth year after this, He joined him to Erlembald, his faithful companion, in the kingdom of heaven, as I believe, after his life was cut short at the hands of wicked men. In this tenth year, these texts were written in praise of Christ and his servant Arialdo. The blessed levite and martyr of Christ Arialdo suffered on 27 June in the year of the Lord's incarnation 1066, when Pope Alexander II presided over the apostolic see and our lord Jesus Christ reigned with the Father, Son, and Holy Spirit for ever and ever. Amen.

81. TESTIMONY ON THE MIRACLES OF BISHOP GIOVANNI CACCIAFRONTE OF VICENZA (1226)

Translated from Latin by Patricia Skinner

Born Giovanni Sordi in Cremona, he entered the Benedictine Order and became abbot of San Lorenzo in Cremona in 1155. When the papacy entered into its struggle with Emperor Frederick I Barbarossa, Giovanni sided with the Holy See and was banished. He retired and became a hermit near Mantua. In 1174 he was elevated to the office of bishop of Mantua after its bishop was deposed. In 1177, the former incumbent repented and wished to be reinstated; Giovanni resigned in his favor and transferred to the see of Vicenza. On 16 March 1184 he was murdered. He had fought to recover church property near Vicenza at Brendola, which had been confiscated and it is thought that his murderer was hired by the Sonaglio family of Brendola; dying in the service of the church he is regarded as a martyr. His body was translated in 1441 into the cathedral chapel of the Incoronata or Gonfalone in Vicenza cathedral: his tomb depicts his murder. Giovanni's life is in many ways typical of the difficulties faced by bishops in Italy in the eleventh and twelfth centuries, as they found themselves caught up in the turbulent relationship between the papacy and successive German emperors. The resumption—or perhaps continuation—of hostilities during Frederick I's reign meant that many northern Italian prelates found themselves having to choose between the two sides. In a broader context, Europe saw a spate of episcopal murders in the twelfth century. The document which follows is a canonization inquest. By the thirteenth century, the process of being recognized as a saint, which up until the early twelfth century had largely depended on the discretion of the local bishop, had become a formal procedure overseen by the papacy, with papal representatives being sent to inquire about the merits of the candidate. Pope Alexander III (d. 1181) is credited with having enforced this requirement, although historians disagree as to whether his opinion was a novel piece of ecclesiastical legislation. Witnesses were called and asked to make statements about what they knew of the prospective saint's qualities during his/her lifetime and after death. As we shall see, the testimony of clerics was favored over lay people, and that of men over women. Nevertheless, the document is informative not only about the criteria used to judge sanctity in this period, but also, in passing, about the lives of the men and women called to testify.

JANUARY 1224, VICENZA

Here are the attestations and inquisitions made by master Jordan, by the grace of God bishop of Padua, and brother Joachim the prior of Santa Maria

Translated from Franco Scarmoncin, ed., *I documenti dell'Archivio Capitolare di Vicenza (1083–1259)*, no. 34 (Rome: Viella, 1999), 82–89; earlier edition in Alessandro Schiavo, *Della vita e dei tempi del B. Giovanni Cacciafronte Cremonese, vescovo di Mantova e poi di Vicenza: Memoria* (Vicenza: Paroni, 1866), 244–50.

in Vangio at Padua, and brother Albert the prior of Santo Spirito in Verona, delegated by the lord pope as judges and inquisitors about the life, honesty, and miracles of Giovanni Cacciafronte, of good memory, former bishop of Vicenza. 1224, 12th indiction, in the month of January.

The priest Aldigerius de Quinto of the diocese of Vicenza, having sworn, said: "I know that it was a good 40 years ago, or thereabouts, that lord Giovanni of good memory, once the bishop of Vicenza, ordained me as a cleric, and I saw and knew him well and I was employed with him, and the common knowledge during his lifetime was that he was a man of good reputation and opinions and he led an honest life and he celebrated the catholic and divine offices regularly, and he loved good catholic men and hated the bad and heretics, and I know that he had brought to this region some theologian from Lombardy, whose name I do not know, who had to lecture in theology in this land, and this was the time of his death." When asked how long he saw and knew him he replied, "About two years, and the common knowledge was that he constantly saved and maintained the goods and rights of the episcopate and that he died because of this maintenance and conservation of the goods and rights of the episcopate."

The priest Sigonfredus de Lançade of the district of Vicenza swore and said, "I know that it is 40 years or so ago that lord Giovanni of good memory, once the bishop of Vicenza, died, and it was said and the common knowledge was that he died for the sake of maintaining and saving the rights of the bishopric and church of Vicenza, and I know certainly that for two years before he was killed I knew him because I was employed in his curia with a brother of his; and at that time when I knew him he was held and believed to be a good, catholic man of the greatest charity and he regularly celebrated the divine offices and diligently loved the church and hated those who hate the church."

Henry, priest of Credatio in the district and diocese of Vicenza, said under oath that he saw and knew lord Giovanni, former bishop of Vicenza and that he was his butler for four years and stayed with him until he was killed, and he said that he was killed for maintaining the liberty of the church and the rights of the bishopric, and because he maintained the poor people of the villa Maladi who were being destroyed by the rich and nobles and magnates, who were occupying their lands and those of the bishopric. . . . Also he said that [Giovanni] was a man of extremely good reputation and opinions and charitable, because on the same day that he was killed he was going with him to the schools of theology which he had set up, and he was waylaid by a certain poor man, in front of the gate of the bishopric opposite the church, who asked him for a coat for the sake of God; and he said,

"Henry, go and buy him a coat." And [Henry] replied, "I shall go"; and he said again "I *shall* go" because he did not wish to leave him for fear of his enemies, who were threatening to kill him. And the lord bishop said, "Unless you go and buy him a coat I won't go anywhere." And after I saw his determination I grew angry with the poor man and the lord bishop stood there watching after me while he could still see me, and at that hour while I was away he was killed, and now I return with the coat, but I am not with him any more in the storeroom[1] and I give the coat to the poor man and standing there I heard a noise and I went out in a hurry and when I reached him he was already dead, and wishing to take his body the killers followed me and would not let me take it. Also he said that [Giovanni] regularly celebrated the divine offices and was a good preacher and kindly, and in time of famine he had collected all of the bishopric's grain at the bishop's palace and divided it among the poor and infirm; and he rebuilt the city street of porta San Felice, through which no-one could pass without great effort and labor; and he said that he [Henry] was always with him in the evening and put him to bed and took off his shoes, but he never took off his hose nor the linen shirt which he wore next to his skin tied with a rope belt; and he was an honest man and lived an honest life . . . ; and he greatly extended and improved the bishopric while he lived; and always every Holy Thursday he made me, the butler, buy clothes and give and divide them among many poor people, and he had a number of poor people assembled, sometimes 12 and sometimes 20 more or less just as they could be found, and he washed their feet.

The priest Americus of San Pietro of the city of Vicenza and its district said on oath, "I know that for a good six years I saw and knew master Giovanni, former bishop of Vicenza, and I know that he ordained me a cleric, and I know firmly that he was a man of the greatest charity and of good faith and he lived an honest life, and regularly and with the greatest devotion celebrated the divine office, and he remained wherever it was being celebrated, and he loved the church and all catholics very much, and he hated Patarenes and heretics and all those believing in them." Asked how he knew this he replied, "Through common knowledge and because I worked with him, and I believe firmly and know that he was killed for maintaining and saving the legal rights of the bishopric, and this was the common knowledge."

Berta Nicolai de Planeciis of the district of Lacu under oath said that her husband Nicholas had lain in bed on account of illness for 12 years, so that he could neither raise himself in any way by a belt or rope hung low where

---

1. *Canipa*, the term used here, could also mean treasury/wine cellar/tavern.

he could take hold of it, nor any other way. . . . And when he heard how God by the merit of the blessed Giovanni, former bishop of Vicenza, was showing miracles, he very much wanted and continued wanting to come to his tomb, and he made a vow to come to the tomb, and next he decided to come to that which he had chosen, and thus he was put on a beast, because he could not come on foot, and was led to the saint, and his children came with him and they spent the night there at the tomb with him for two nights, and thus it happened by God's mercy that he, remaining in prayer at the tomb, by the merit of the blessed Giovanni, was liberated and stood freely for two years less a week with me and I with him, thanks to the glorious liberation of the lord God himself and the blessed Giovanni, former bishop of Vicenza, testifying to this until by the will of God he was taken from this world to the other. And the same Berta said that after Nicholas was liberated he would go to the fields with her and their children and work, a thing he had not been able to do for 12 years; and she saw that he was liberated at the tomb from Good Friday [onward], and there were three years to come as she believes, thus that on the next Wednesday after Easter Sunday he came to the village of Planeciis rightly . . . freed, and she said that she firmly believed that he had been freed by the merits of the blessed Giovanni, and of this there was common knowledge as there had been many witnesses present.

The priest Avancius of the same village and district on oath said and confirmed that everything that Berta had said there present about the infirmity of the said Nicholas was true, how he saw him thus infirm after he had been priest in that territory for close on two years, and afterward he came to the tomb of blessed Giovanni the bishop, and he returned to the village, and how he saw him well and going and coming and doing business just like everyone else, on account of which he was very happy and believed firmly that he had been freed by the merits of blessed Giovanni, and the common knowledge and three witnesses prove this miracle.

Lanfranco Panis Milius, citizen of Vicenza district, said on his oath that when God through the merit of the blessed Giovanni began to perform miracles he had been the guardian of his tomb and saw how the said Nicholas was led there on a beast to the great church of Santa Maria in Vicenza, and carried in arms to the tomb of the blessed Giovanni, former bishop of Vicenza because he could not lift himself from his middle downward, and he had two crutches and standing there in prayer he stayed for two nights, but on the second of those nights around dawn he called me to put him equally far from the other people because he was weak and he said to me, "Master Lanfranco, accept this crutch from me because through the mercy of God and the merits of the blessed Giovanni I am standing erect, so that I can go, and just now I went and tried through the whole church to see if I could move well and I [can] and I believe, if God wills, that I shall soon give you the other crutch." And thus I saw afterward that he went home on foot with one crutch, and after a few days he returned to the aforementioned San Giovanni, and came right to me, and gave me the other crutch, and so I firmly believe that God freed him through the merits of the blessed Giovanni, former bishop of Vicenza.

Corbello de Barbarano of the district of Vicenza swore and said that he was greatly constrained and beset by deafness, and it was more or less three years that he had suffered this infirmity from Lent to Easter, and after Easter I know that I made a vow to come to the tomb of San Giovanni because I heard that God was making miracles through him, and so I came to the tomb and stood there from the evening throughout the night to the next day praying, and at dawn many standing there and seeing me called me and laughed at me, because they knew me to be deaf, and I answered them, at which they greatly glorified God the Father in great wonderment, and this through the grace of God just as I know and feel I am freed, and I hear just as you can hear and just like any man.

Armengarda, called Teuda, wife of this same Corbello confirmed on oath that everything he had said to those present about his infirmity, and how much time she had seen him, heard him and knew him, and about the liberation, just as she was present when he was freed, was all true.

Master Burgensis, the doctor of the city of Vicenza, swore and said, "I know that once a great infirmity afflicted a small son of mine in the eyes, so that he could not see in any way." And one day his wife was extremely sad about this son, and he said to his wife that she should not get upset about this because it was necessary and she should bear this which was God's will, and he said that his wife one day, which he cannot remember exactly, made a vow to God and to the blessed Giovanni, former bishop of Vicenza, that if her son was liberated she would give two [ex voto] silver eyes and carry them to the tomb of San Giovanni, and this vow evidently having been made in continence, the boy was freed from the abovementioned infirmity by the merit of San Giovanni. . . .

Maria of Albertino of the district of Padua said under oath that when her husband Alberto son of the late Bonacorso, now a minor friar, was healthy and happy as he said, he went to the church of Santa Maria. When he was at the tomb of the blessed Giovanni he said to a crowd of women standing there, "O good foolish women, what are you doing? You might just as well pray to that [piece of] wood," and then he went to the market hall and bought fish and came home and prepared the fish himself. And when it was dinnertime on the Wednesday, because he was fasting he did not have lunch . . . ; however, he told me to have lunch and I went to eat and he went to the house of a tailor friend of his and threw himself down on the bed there; and I, seeking him, went and found him ill and saw that a great fever of plague was invading him, and then I persuaded him to be brought home and thus he lay, and did not eat or drink until the Friday, and that night, recovered a little and having been purged he said, "Maria, certainly I see now how the lord blessed Giovanni freed me and I shall vow to him a candle of my same height." And she responded, "Certainly, good husband, and I already vowed one and will go and look for one." And so I went and made a candle and wanted to take it to the saint, and he said, "No, because I want to take it," and I said, "Who will take you there?" And he replied, "Trivisio and Albrigeto my friends—go and get them." And I went for them, and around evening they took him to the saint and straightway he began to sweat and was totally covered in water, and sustaining a great fever he stayed there all night in prayer until the morning, and then by the mercy of God he was freed and went on his own feet to San Salvatore to hear the mass of the friars minor, and came home well and happy; and I was very happy and I know firmly and believe that he was freed through the merits of the Blessed Giovanni, and from reverence for him he was made one of the order of the Friars Minor and has been living and praying with them for over two years.

Trivisio and Albrigeto, the friends of the abovementioned Albertino of the aforementioned district, said under oath that they were with the aforementioned Albertino when he laughed at the women praying at the tomb of the blessed Giovanni and that he that night fell ill and was close to death, and that they visited him while ill just as a friend does for another, and that they brought him ill and weak to the church, and afterward saw him cured and everything that Maria said there, in their presence, was true and they confirmed it. And they said and believe firmly that out of the reverence for the blessed Giovanni, former bishop of Vicenza who cured him from his illness he mended his ways and joined the order of the Friars Minor and follows them in way of life and prayers.

I, Alexander, Secretary of the Sacred Palace and afterward of Lord Frederick, King of the Romans, wrote down all these sayings and testimonies as I heard them from all these principal persons and witnesses in good faith and without fraud and alongside Turpin, notary of Padua, and by the order of the lord bishop of Padua and his fellow judges and put them all in public form.

+ I, Turpin, son of the late Gnatius, notary of the Sacred Palace set down the sayings of the above witnesses and principals alongside the aforementioned Alexander, notary, and these writings, by the order of the above inquisitors of the lord pope I corroborated with my sign.

82. THE LIFE OF RAYMOND "THE PALMER" OF PIACENZA (1212)

Translated from Latin by Kenneth Baxter Wolf

Raymond "the Palmer" of Piacenza (1140–1200) is a good example of what André Vauchez has termed a "saint of charity and manual labor."[1] Lay saints like Raymond were to be found in many northern and central Italian cities between the years 1180 and 1280, gaining their reputations by tending to the needs of the poor and sick while at the same time embracing lives of poverty for themselves. Why they emerged at this particular time and in this particular region is not entirely clear, though in general terms it is safe to say that the rapid urbanization experienced in this time and place resulted in new kinds of social and economic problems that in turn spawned creative spiritual responses. Raymond's particular path to sanctity, however, began not with acts of charity but with a series of pilgrimages. His adopted epithet "Palmer" is the English form of the Latin palmarius (alternatively, palmerius), referring to someone who had completed the pilgrimage to the Holy Land, returning with a palm frond in hand as a symbol of his achievement. Raymond ultimately gave up the life of a pilgrim and returned home to found a hospice-hospital in 1178 and tend to the needs of the poor and pilgrims in Piacenza. Raymond's career inspired an unusually detailed vita *authored in 1212 by a man named Rufino at the encouragement of Raymond's son.[2] Raymond's existence is corroborated by the chronicler Giovanni de Mussis, whose* Chronicon Placentinum *records the death of the saint—"a man of great charity and hospitality"—in 1202.*

The Author's Preface and the Dedication of the Work

. . . I will draw only upon those things to which I or you were witnesses, or those things witnessed by others who have sworn to their veracity with a hand on the sacred gospels. Let us, therefore, in the name of God, set in order what we have been describing, dividing it into appropriate chapters.

Translated from *AASS* (1686–1736), Jul. 6, ed. Peter van der Bosch, 645–57.

1. André Vauchez, *Sainthood in the Later Middle Ages*, trans. Jean Birrell (Cambridge: Cambridge University Press, 1997). This introduction is largely borrowed from Kenneth B. Wolf, *The Poverty of Riches: Saint Francis of Assisi Reconsidered* (Oxford: Oxford University Press, 2003), 72.

2. *AASS* Jul 6:645–57. The original Latin version of Rufino's life, housed in archives of the convent of Saint Raymond in Piacenza, was misplaced sometime after it was loaned (1525) to the nearby Dominican house for the purposes of producing a vernacular version. A futile search for the original in 1728 ultimately led the Bollandist Peter Bosch to translate the Italian version back into Latin for inclusion in the *Acta Sanctorum*.

CHAPTER 1: THE HOMELAND, PARENTS, AND CONDITION OF SAINT
RAYMOND; THE DEATH OF HIS FATHER; HIS PILGRIMAGE WITH HIS
WIDOWED MOTHER TO THE HOLY LAND, AND HIS RETURN

5. As regards his homeland, blessed Raymond was a Piacenzan, being born
in the city of Piacenza itself. He had parents who were neither illustrious in
origin nor completely lowborn. They were private citizens who were neither
rich nor poor in domestic terms. The blessed father [that is, Raymond] was
of medium height and slender of body. Though thin and reduced, he was
agile and expedient when it came to getting things done. He had an adroit
mind, equipped with an innate prudence and a wonderfully temperate can-
dor, which might even be seen as a dove-like simplicity. He shrank from
distrust as well as from joking, and knew neither shrewdness nor simulation
when dealing with people. He was a man of good and sincere faith with
reference to whom you might aptly cite the scripture that reads: "Behold an
Israelite in whom there is no guile" [John 1: 47].

6. Raymond's mother educated and reared her child at home. But when he
had reached approximately twelve years of age, he was sent off by his father
to a workshop, not to dedicate himself to letters or learning, but to apply
himself to his father's servile and ignoble craft and to learn those things necessary to engage in commerce. This was a kind of skill that could not be
mastered through argumentation; those who wished to become shoemakers
were led not by science but by conjecture. It is however true that any craft
would have been displeasing to that remarkable young man. Nevertheless,
though born for a higher purpose than this, Raymond had to keep his suffering to himself. Being under the power of his father, the boy had to tolerate
this craft for some time. But so doing he submitted to the mandate of God,
who demanded, by divine law, that honor and obedience be given to one's
parents.

7. Blessed Raymond had already reached the years of puberty or adolescence—which begin in the fourteenth year—when his father passed from this
brief life to his celestial homeland. The holy young man [Raymond], considering himself to have been liberated, decided to say farewell to the dark workshop, not so that he could pursue a life of leisure or prostitute himself to
vices as ordinary adolescents are wont to do, but to adhere more closely to
his Savior through a life consecrated with all his heart to divine obedience.
So as to burn more deeply with love for the blessed Jesus Christ, he decided
to take a pilgrimage to the Holy Sepulcher and to visit the sacred places that
are in Jerusalem as well as those to be found nearby. But he did not wish to

set out before he had consulted his widowed mother and she had given him her approval. Coming to see her one day, he entered a room with her alone and addressed her in this manner: "My dearest and most beloved mother, I give infinite thanks to my Creator, who has inspired me with the idea that I should leave such distasteful matters and profane skills to profane men; that I should leave this land, say farewell to all my friends and relatives, and, embracing the cross of our sweet Savior Jesus, visit the Lord's Sepulcher as a pilgrim. The only thing that troubles me, my dear mother, is your care, for you are alone and widowed and have no other solace or refuge aside from me, your only son. Though I love you, consider what it says in the scripture: 'He who loves his father or mother more than me, is not worthy of my grace' [Matthew 10:37]. Therefore, mother, I beg you. Do not be the reason why I give up the grace of my Savior, but instead send me off with your permission and your blessing."

8. Hearing this, his most pious mother, drenched by her own copious tears, embraced her son and burst forth with these words: "O my dear and only light! O sole support of your wretched, widowed mother! Do not suffer for my sake. You could not have said anything more pleasing to me, especially at this time, finding myself released from the bonds of marriage, having no children—aside from you, who are already reared and no longer a boy—and being advanced in age. I had already decided to dedicate what remains of my life to the divine offices and to visiting holy places and have asked that such grace be granted to me from the Creator [Luke 2:36–7]. Be of good cheer, my son! We shall go together to the Holy Sepulcher. Only death will keep me from it!"

9. . . . Then, with an eye to fulfilling their vows, they arranged everything that was necessary for the pilgrimage and, after saying goodbye to their friends and relatives, they approached the most venerable bishop [Hugo (1155–66)] of the city of Piacenza and said: "Most revered father and shepherd, we have decided to leave and travel abroad to the Holy Sepulcher. With our hands held out together in the shape of a cross, we ask for that which pilgrims of this kind are wont to ask." When the bishop recognized the reasonableness of the request made by this mother and her son, he placed a red cross on their chests. "Behold," he said, "the sign that will keep you safe from all danger. May the most clement Savior guide you there and bring you back unharmed. May you be mindful of your homeland when you are praying there."

10. Having gathered everything together, they left, though not without many tears on the part of their relatives, neighbors, and friends. After facing many dangers and expending great effort, on land as well as sea, they finally reached the destination for which they longed. As they explored the most holy city of Jerusalem, both of them overflowing with a most tender sense of piety, they contemplated in their souls the obstinate cruelty of the Jews, who were so blinded at that time that they surrendered the very author of life to his death. . . .[3]

11. After these two suppliants had visited the holy sites of Jerusalem and kissed them a thousand times and more, they made their way to the town of Bethlehem to venerate the palace—that is to say, the stable—of the Son of the most chaste Virgin . . . . From there they went to the most holy and precious tomb of the glorious Virgin, located in the Valley of Jehosaphat; then to Bethany to the house of the beloved Magdalen, whom they regarded as most fortunate in so far as she sat at the feet of the sweet Master and listened to his divine and wise words. After many days had passed and they had gone around to all the holy places, they began to think of returning to their homeland, so after they visited the sacred places again, sprinkling them with their tears one last time, they made their way back to the coast so that they could return by ship to Italy and once again see their homeland. . . .

On the way back home, first Raymond and then his mother grew seriously ill. He recovered, but she died in Italy before reaching Piacenza.

17. Once his dear mother had been buried, good Raymond, seeing that he had been left all alone, directed his soul toward the Lord God and said, weeping: "O how wretched I am now that both my father and mother have left me. But I trust that you, Lord, will adopt me." . . . So good Raymond set out on his journey home, dressed in the garb of a pilgrim—such as those who return from the Holy Sepulcher customarily wear—and displaying certain signs: a red cross on his pure chest and a palm branch in his hand—the latter of which leading him to assume the surname "Palmer." There are those who think that his family was already called "Palmer," but there is no clear evidence to report on this matter. When he finally arrived at Piacenza, before

3. Anti-Judaism was a fact of the Christian Middle Ages. It was believed that the Jews were symbolically blind since they had refused to see the "light" of the Christian Gospel. Hence visual representations of the allegorical figure of the Synagogue often depicted a female figure blindfolded. Church doctrine of the period also taught that the Jews were responsible for the death of Jesus Christ, a teaching finally repudiated in 1965 at the Second Vatican Council with the Declaration, "Nostra aetate" ("In Our Era"). [Eds.]

heading to his own home, he made his way to the cathedral. There he presented himself, with the symbols of his pilgrimage, to the most venerable bishop. . . .

18. A few days after his return to his homeland, Raymond's relatives began to suggest the following to him: "Brother Raymond, if you continue to live alone as a single man, you will have to work very hard, for you have no one to take care of your affairs. Let us assist you in taking a wife.[4] Remember that married people are also capable of serving God; In fact marriage was instituted by God" [Genesis 2:24]. Good Raymond allowed himself to be persuaded. Indeed Divine Goodness permitted it, so that his servant would experience the miseries that he [and his wife], joined in matrimony, would have to suffer, with her needing to be governed and the household needing to be administered, and the children needing to be fed and reared. So Raymond married and, knowing that his patrimony would not be enough to support a family, returned to the workshop, to that trade—that is, shoemaking—that he had learned at the command of his father. He turned to it completely and, without deceit or avarice, made enough to feed himself, his wife, and his children, with enough left over to be generous in his almsgiving to the poor.

19. But the craft of shoemaking was not pleasing to Raymond, since it diverted his soul from its spiritual purpose. So during those few hours that he was able to carve out by applying himself with greater intensity to his work, he exerted himself with regard to matters of the soul. He did this especially in anticipation of holy days, so that he could converse with religious men, outstanding in their probity and their teaching, for Raymond was inspired by the desire to familiarize himself with divine law and sacred letters. Indeed he made such progress in that area that even though he was unlettered—which is not to say that he lacked the gift of divine wisdom—he appeared to be the most learned of those connected to God and to the Catholic religion. In order to turn profane men—especially those who practiced his particular craft—away from lascivious stories and useless amusements, he would, on holy days, chose for himself a certain workshop, where he would preach, in an informal way and with the great ardor of his charity, to his fellows, the true teachings of God's holy law. Thus he shared with them the reasons for living according to divine precepts, for following virtue, and for fleeing vice.

4. The Latin suggests that the relatives were offering to represent him, perhaps providing surety on his behalf, in the negotiations to secure a marriage contract.

20. It was not long before the fame of good Raymond had grown to the point that, on holy days, as soon as they had ascertained in which house or workshop he could be found, many would rush there to hear his ardent words. Some asked him to hold the assembly in a public place, even in the piazza itself. But this humble servant of God refused to do so, asserting repeatedly that that was the duty of priests and learned men; that errors could creep into his words, since he was not a man educated in letters.[5] Knowing himself well, Raymond would not acquiesce to counsel of this kind. Nevertheless, so homey and humble were the exhortations that he delivered in the presence of his colleagues in the workshop, that whenever they pondered a certain religious matter, they would rush to none other than good Raymond, their father and spiritual leader.

21. This servant in the works of God organized his life according to the example of holy Tobias:[6] modest in eating, assiduous in almsgiving, and indefatigable with regard to fasting, prayer, and the divine offices. He rehearsed the confession of his sins often and with a truly contrite heart so that he might enjoy the sacred mass, which was followed by a flood of his tears. For the entire time that he lived in his body on earth, he was busy directing his whole mind toward heaven. He dressed modestly as was his custom. He corrected and taught his wife like a daughter, loved her like a sister, and venerated her like a mother. From her he received a number of children. It was his habit to offer them to the Lord God, author of all good things, as each was being immersed in the sacred font. He would say: "These ones bear your image, Lord. You bestowed them on me; now I present them to you, since they were created by you. Their life and death is in your hands." . . .

22. Knowing that his servant would not be able to apply himself with all his heart to the efforts of a spiritual life given the bonds of marriage and the concerns associated with rearing children, the good Creator took pity on him and sought to give him some freedom from all this. So within the space of a single year, He gathered up all Raymond's young children from this life. Given the instinctive love that a father has for his children, it grieved Ray-

---

5. Here Rufino is careful to underscore Raymond's deference to church authority, realizing that his readers might wonder why a layman was preaching when this was a privilege reserved for the clergy. Saint Francis of Assisi (d. 1226), another layman who felt inspired to preach, was permitted by Pope Innocent III to preach only penance.

6. The reference is to the first chapter of the apocryphal Old Testament book of Tobit (also known as Tobias), which describes the fidelity of Tobit (Tobias the elder) to the Law, despite living in captivity under Assyrian rule.

mond to lose his. But he concluded that it had happened in accordance with the divine will and so he acquiesced completely. . . .

23. The death of his children extinguished in blessed Raymond all desire associated with this life. Seeking to dedicate himself completely to God, he encouraged his wife to agree to maintain sexual continence from that point on. For the time was at hand in which it was appropriate for them both to transfer all their love to God, not to work to create new offspring. But she, being little drawn to celestial things, impudently responded: "When I become a nun, I will heed your warnings. But for now it is as a wife—and not as a widow or a nun—that I am governed by you." Being prudent, and noting his wife's imperfection and peril, the servant of God did not want to push her in a troublesome fashion. So they lived together in peace and without sin.[7]

24. It happened by divine providence that his wife bore yet another child and Raymond saw himself returning to the servitude [of the world]. One day, when his wife was out, he picked up his child, just as he lay there, all wrapped up in his cradle, and made for Piacenza and the church of Saint Brigid, where he often attended the divine office in the presence of the sacred image of the cross. Lifting the small boy up as high as he was able, he prayed: "My Lord and Savior, you who open your arms to all those who flee to you, I beg you, just as you took my five sons up to you at a tender age, receiving them as co-heirs to eternal happiness, deign to accept my new little son, who was unexpectedly given to me by you. I beg you to do this, my Savior, so that he will not be separated from his brothers. But if you have decreed for him a longer life, then let me offer and dedicate him right now, chaste and pure, to this servant of holy religion [Saint Brigid], to whom I wish him one day to be assigned." His prayers completed, Raymond secretly returned the child to its cradle, saying nothing about this to his wife.

25. After offering his young son to the most sweet Savior, the desire was fixed even deeper in Raymond's breast to strive, in so far as he was able, for perpetual continence. But he did not wish to cross his wife, knowing that she was unlikely to give her consent. In the end the Lord God, in his wisdom, opened up another path for Raymond to achieve his goal. He permitted Raymond's wife to be afflicted with an incurable disease, so that she would by

7. Which is not to say that they abstained from sex, as the following passages make clear. The point Rufino is making is simply that whatever sexual relations they had from that point on were licit in the eyes of the church insofar as they occurred within the bonds of marriage.

no means be able to engage in any more conjugal activity. As a result, the servant of God was able to fulfill his vow without upsetting his wife and without sinning. . . . [Following the death of his wife,] Blessed Raymond, released from the bonds of marriage, then confirmed his intention to live in perpetual chastity and continence.

CHAPTER 3: HAVING LEFT EVERYTHING BEHIND, HE SETS OUT ON PILGRIMAGES, UNTIL, COMMANDED BY CHRIST TO RETURN, HE DEDICATES HIMSELF COMPLETELY TO WORKS OF MERCY IN HIS OWN HOMELAND ACCORDING TO THE INSTRUCTIONS HE RECEIVED FROM HIM

26. Seeing himself unburdened from his father, his mother, his wife, and his children—with the exception of his youngest child—the servant of God relentlessly turned his soul inward and totally shook off his concern and desire for fleeting things. Since it was clear to him that rearing his little son would be a hindrance for him, he was divinely inspired to approach his parents-in-law. Carrying the small child in his arms, he deposited him in their presence, saying: "To you, my honorable and dear father-in-law, and to you, my mother-in-law, I offer and commend this little child, born of your daughter and me. I beseech you to take care that he be reared correctly and be educated, imbued with good letters, so that he will turn out to be religious and upright and useful, for I have offered him to the blessed Jesus Christ. I am placing all my resources at your disposal. Spend them for the good of my son who is now yours. For my part I am bound and determined to renounce the world and to head off for those holy places where the bodies of the saints are honored, especially to Rome and to the church of Saint James in Galicia [Santiago de Compostela], to Saint Anthony's, and to the other most celebrated places.[8] I will never return here nor will you ever see me again. I will not let myself be detained any longer. I will apply whatever remains of my life to undertaking pilgrimages continuously. I have asked my Savior to grant me only one thing: that my journey finally come to an end where his most holy body—born from the most pure Virgin—was buried. . . .

28. Setting out from Piacenza, Raymond did not stop before he had reached the church of Saint James in Galicia. All the while he supported himself through begging, always with great patience and a humble soul. After paying his respects to the body of the most holy Apostle, he made his way back

8. According to legend, the body of Saint James the Apostle was miraculously conveyed to the northwestern corner of Spain, where it became the endpoint of the famous Camino de Santiago ("the path of Saint James") pilgrimage route. The most important cult of Saint Antony the hermit (d. 356) in the Latin west was situated in Vienne.

toward Italy, by way of the relics of the most holy Magdalen and from there to that bitter place of penance not far from Marseilles.[9] Then he hastened through Provence, to the bodies of the "Three Marys" and those of Saints Martha and Lazarus.[10] He then made his way to Saint Anthony and Saint Bernard.[11] Once he had entered Italy again, he venerated whatever pious sites he could find there, especially the relics of Saint Augustine in the region of Pavia. He then went on to Rome, where he was able to spend several days visiting the sacred remains of the Prince of the Apostles and of the most holy martyrs and virgins. He then decided to visit Jerusalem a second time, planning to stay in that holy place for the rest of his life. But, lo and behold, while he was waiting for an opportunity to cross the sea, he received an admonition from our Savior, which we will now recount.

29. When blessed Raymond was in Rome, sleeping under a certain portico at Saint Peter's basilica in the manner of a poor pilgrim, blessed Jesus Christ appeared to him dressed as if he were on a pilgrimage, just as he had formerly appeared to the two disciples on the way to Emmaus [Luke 24:13–35], and spoke to him as follows: "My servant Raymond, your requests have been pleasing to me, so up until now I have respected your pious wishes to go on pilgrimage, and for that reason I liberated you from your servitude to your wife and children. But now you have seen all of the most pleasing holy places and nothing of your vow remains except to return to my holy Sepulcher. This plan is not acceptable to me. Instead I want you to occupy yourself with works of mercy, for such things are more pleasing to me and more helpful to you. You should not think that the kind of pilgrimages and pious exercises [in which you have been engaging thus far] will be held in particular regard by me at the time of judgment, when I will say: "Come, blessed of my Father. Take possession of the kingdom of heaven. I was hungry and you gave me something to eat; I was thirsty and you gave me something to drink; I was naked and you clothed me; I was sick and you visited me; I was in jail and you ransomed me" [Matthew 25:34–36]. And so I do not want you, my son, to travel about the world any more. I want you to return to your homeland of Piacenza, where there are so many poor people and so many who are sick

9. From the mid-eleventh century, the abbey church of Vézeley claimed to have Mary Magdalen's body. In the thirteenth century, a shrine in Aix-en-Provence staked rival claims for her relics, while legends also maintained that after the death of Christ she had lived out a life of penance in the caverns of La Saint-Baume about 25 miles from Marseilles.

10. The so-called "three Marys" are the three women of that name who are mentioned in the Gospels as having been the first to discover that Jesus' tomb was empty. A later legend had these three sailing to southern France, where they spread the faith. The focal point of the cult was Saintes Maries de la Mer in the Camargue on the south-central coast of France.

11. In Clairvaux, where Bernard was abbot until his death in 1153.

and oppressed by various calamities, all of whom beg for my mercy; for there is no one there to help them. You will go and I will be there with you and I will give you grace so that you will be able to lead the rich to almsgiving, rival parties to peace, and those who have strayed—especially wayward women—to a proper way of life."

31. "You will return to Piacenza and there you will commence using these symbols of your pious purpose: You will dress in a garment the color of the sky that extends down to the middle of your legs, with loose sleeves and no hood. You will always carry my cross over your shoulder, executing every act of piety in its name and under its power. You will establish through your own effort a pious place for the indigent and for pilgrims. Inscribed with your name, it will remain in perpetual memory of its founder. Rise and do what I say. Do not despair. Leave Rome, where you are wasting your time and energy, and make your way to your own country." . . . When he finally came to Piacenza . . . [Raymond] went to the bishop [Teobaldo, 1167–92] whose blessing he sought. "Most venerable father," he said, "though I had decided in my heart never to return to my homeland again, my Savior urged me to do just that and, with your permission, to dedicate myself completely—in the name of the holy cross—to seeking alms for the indigent, to gathering together poor pilgrims, and to reconciling enemies. I can do none of these things without your good will. Therefore I beseech you, most venerable father, by the command and words of my Savior, to reach out your helping hands for the sake of this most holy exercise, for which I admit I am completely unworthy." . . .

34. When Raymond realized that in order to fulfill this task properly he would need a holy and sizeable space, he selected a dwelling next to the Canonry of the Twelve Apostles—granted to him by these same canons—that was big enough for collecting alms and well suited for offering hospitality to the poor of both sexes, whether pilgrims or sick people. Having obtained this, blessed Raymond began to search the entire city for indigent people whose shame or infirmity prevented them from begging. Once he had secured information about people of this type, he openly sought alms for them throughout the entire city, carrying his cross on his shoulder. . . .

35. A huge crowd of beggars rushed toward him, pleading for some portion of the alms that he had collected. The blessed servant of God said to them: "Why not go and ask for alms as you are wont to do? You are neither too sick nor unaccustomed to the shame of it." They called back to him: "We do

beg, but we get nothing for our efforts." When he heard this, the blessed Raymond's sense of charity was ignited and he roused himself against the hard-heartedness of the wealthy. Taking up the holy cross on his shoulder, he ordered the pitiful ones to follow him and, made his way from one cross-roads to the next, shouting: "Help, help, O cruel and heard-hearted Christians, for I am dying of hunger while you live in abundance." The citizens, especially the women, were struck by his voice. Some hurried to their windows, others rushed from their previously locked doors into the street, saying: "Come, Raymond, come and eat. Do not torture yourself so." But he, stepping forward, responded: "I do not have just this one mouth—which, by the way, I willingly allow to be vexed with hunger; in truth I have many mouths, as many as you see before you dying of hunger. Therefore I entreat you, through this most holy cross, to have mercy on the poor of Jesus Christ." Saying this, he lifted the blessed cross into the air. Having witnessed such charity on the part of the servant of God, everyone was moved to pity and kindly gave aid to the miserable flock of beggars. Raymond's reputation grew in such a short time, that all who were afflicted, infirm, or poor, both those who suffered in public as well as those who were hidden from view, regarded him as a surrogate father and protector. Moreover many pious men left their homes and came to him so that they might bring their collective effort to bear on such a holy task by gathering alms and ministering to the sick and especially to the pilgrims who were welcomed there as guests.

36. Blessed Raymond observed that beyond the acts of mercy that needed to be performed, he also needed to provide shelter for men and for women. So as to avoid giving the group any occasion for sin or disgrace, he decided to separate the men's and the women's quarters. He did this by assigning the women to a particular domicile adjacent to the Canonry of the Twelve Apostles, which was somewhat better furnished and yet more closed off. To this shelter Raymond admitted not only female pilgrims but also impoverished [female] citizens of Piacenza who were destitute of all property. Raymond did not hesitate to accept even those women who had come from dens of iniquity, hoping that he might make them repent for their sins and desire to lead a life of chastity. He guided them by mature and blameless example, having committed them to the custody of matrons of great purity.

37. After a reasonable amount of time [spent in the hospice], Raymond would ask each of these women what type of life she wanted to lead from then on. Some responded that they thought themselves more suited to marriage, whereby they could pursue with greater security their plans to lead

honest lives. Raymond himself provided for the wishes of these, collecting dowries for them from upright men. Others replied that they wished to continue to cultivate the chaste life that they had been living. Raymond took care to have them admitted to decent, cloistered monasteries, knowing full well how hard it would be to preserve their virtue unimpaired in the outside world, especially when only a short time ago they were used to such baseness. There were also those who wanted to deviate from his chaste counsel and return to their prior shame. Whenever this great servant of God became aware of this, he would chastise such women with the most humane words, using his great spirit to exhort them to shame. "Consider, daughters," he would say, "how unhappy your condition is. If you return to such filthy activities, you will by all means prostitute your honor, you will lose your souls, you will be bound to the infamy of men, and you will die in misery. I beseech you, my daughters, on behalf of this holy cross, on behalf of the most pure Virgin, and on behalf of Jesus Christ himself, who deigned to die for you: take pity on your own souls and be not unmindful of such a great favor." Some of these women ultimately yielded to his ardent persuasion, but others remained obdurate. These he quietly expelled from his hospice lest they succeed in infecting the more upright women with the disease of their shameful example.

CHAPTER 4: HIS CHARITY TOWARD WIDOWS AND ORPHANS, TOWARD PEOPLE IN CONFLICT, TOWARD CAPTIVES, AND TOWARD SICK AND DESTITUTE CHILDREN. HIS HOLY DEATH

38. His sincere sanctity produced such respect for blessed Raymond, that poor people, widows, orphans, and others rushed to him—the common parent and protector of all the wretched—whenever they were wrongly vexed by others and were unable to obtain justice at the hands of judges and magnates. They called out: "Servant of God, help us. We lack the money we need to go to contend with our adversaries in judgment." Informed of such an injury, Raymond became inflamed and, like another Elijah,[12] welcomed the sorrowful ones, saying: "Remember, sons, that those who undergo adversity out of love of their Creator are blessed. So have heart and be hopeful. You will not be without my assistance." . . .

39. . . . Raymond made his way to the tribunal and there, taking the cross in his hands, he spoke out about injustice in the presence of the judges: "Love and administer justice to the needy, O you judges who judge here on earth.

12. The quintessential prophet of Israel, described in 1 Kings 17–19, 21:17–29.

Remember that you too will be placed in judgment, judged by him who died for you on the cross. Remember that after this life you will not be doing the judging; instead you will be the ones being judged." Raymond added the holiness of his life to the power and weightiness of his words, so that the magnates and the prefect of the city did not interrupt him. And when he managed to get himself heard, these same men accomplished many things. Indeed, if the city faced a particular difficulty or danger, these same ones would treat blessed Raymond as if he were a prophet, often deferring to his judgment with regard to what ought be done.

40. Raymond held peace—without which, he knew, nothing else could be preserved—in such high regard that when he sensed contention or hatred between people, he would not rest until he had recalled them to concord. He was wont to use the following supplication: "Are you ignorant, my children, that the Son of God himself descended from heaven to earth and that he was placed on a most cruel cross, so that he might reconcile men to God? Why then do you want to be enemies to one another? Those who have enemies never have peace." . . . Not a few, influenced by his pious warnings, referred the causes of their dissension to good Raymond so that he could put an end to them. Bestowing upon them the gift of his prudent counsel, he quickly restored them to grace.

41. Raymond could by no mean tolerate the factions and divisions that he saw tearing apart the citizens [of Piacenza]. . . . Good Raymond then made his way to public places, and when he noticed factions rising up and making an uproar and cursing one another, he called out, all the while crying and burdened down by his cross: "Woe to you, seditious Piacenza! God has already prepared a scourge with which to beat you. You will be plundered and set on fire. You will lose your fortunes and your lives. Because your body is torn apart, you do not revere God." This prophecy of the Servant of God turned out to be true, as the people of Piacenza learned first-hand after Raymond's death.[13]

42. In blessed Raymond's time, Piacenza was torn not only by internal hatred, but by external wars. Cities were armed for mutual destruction, with armies from each side being compelled to fight. The people of Cremona in particular did just that against the people of Piacenza. When Raymond first

---

13. Piacenza did experience a papal interdict after a violation of clerical immunity, but the contemporary chronicles are silent about any fire or plundering suffered by the people of Piacenza between Raymond's death and 1212, when Rufino was writing.

learned that such armies were being assembled, he left Piacenza, armed only with his most holy cross. Going out to meet both battle lines, he cried out in a tearful voice: "My brothers, look to Him [that is, Christ on the cross], who did not hesitate to die to keep you from dying.[14] Why do you rush toward death, invading or attacking your neighbors for the sake of transitory wealth? Why do you hasten to inflict injury for things that are not eternal? Come, now! Remember that you are Christians; imitate your Savior! Forgive, forgive, and make peace! Commit the whole matter to me, whom you should consider to be the fairest of arbiters." And so, rushing first to one army and then to the next, Raymond strove to achieve concord. His efforts were not displeasing to the leaders of Piacenza, but those of Cremona drove off the servant of God with threats and no few lashes.

43. Raymond bore this all patiently, but still modestly assigned some blame [to the people of Cremona] when he said: "I seek only peace and you repay me with insults. My Savior will judge between your cause and mine." These words enraged the people of Cremona even more, so that they dragged Raymond to Cremona and put him in jail so that they would no longer be bothered by him. There Raymond directed his cries up toward heaven—cries which everyone present could hear—saying: "My Savior, I commend your paupers back to you. I fear they will die of hunger while I am detained here as a captive. I am prepared to undergo not only the discomforts of prison, but even death. May you direct the hostile souls of both of these peoples toward peace. Forgive the people of Cremona, Lord, who threw me into this place. For they do not know what is in store for them." Scarcely had the citizens of Cremona heard this when, having been made aware of the exceptional sanctity of blessed Raymond, they made arrangements to free him and restore him to his own people. Fearing the avenging presence of God, they begged forgiveness for the injuries he had sustained. Indeed, the terror of divine judgment remained with those who had confined him to prison, to the point that when the life of Blessed Raymond had ended, they visited his tomb as suppliants to obtain forgiveness from him. They feared him even more after he was dead than they had feared him when he was still alive, well aware of how powerful and terrible God can be through his saints.

44. Many times it happened that blessed Raymond would see a large crowd of mounted men preparing to compete in Trojan games, or some other kind

14. Raymond was directing the attention of the armies to his cross and having them ponder Jesus' death on it.

of gladiatorial contest in which brawling, injury, and murder were common-place. Being so alien to these ludicrous contests, his entire being would become agitated and he would rebuke them, saying: "Our Savior does not want you to exercise your fury by engaging in the games of brutal, savage beasts. He wants you to establish ones that are decent, peaceful, and civil; ones that serve to relax the soul. He does not want anyone risking his life out of a desire for empty glory but for the safe-keeping of the fatherland and for the authority of divine law. If the love of your Savior has touched you, be concerned about saving your souls as well as your bodies and leave these pernicious contests behind." So he spoke. But because the crowd was full of youths, who are typically excited by the fervor of blood and the thirst for glory, his admonishment was in vain. He used to make his way to the most venerable bishop and to the city magistrate, not leaving until they followed him to the site of such a contest with the intention of disrupting and breaking up the games through their intervention. Raymond did not care that his actions were displeasing to those unstable and inconsiderate youths, for in the process he had subverted such occasions of sin.

45. Blessed Raymond was assiduous in visiting prisoners, bringing with him those things that were suitable for healing the bodies of these wretched ones, so that he could prepare them to accept his cure for their souls. After they had recovered their strength, he offered them the following words: "My sons, the end of this life is not the same for everyone: one may die in bed, another in war, another at sea, another in solitude; this one might die a spontaneous death, that one might meet a violent death. Do not give up your hope and your souls based on the type of death that you are facing, lest you be fright-ened by those things that can kill the body but which, after that, cannot do anything else to you" [Matthew 10:28]. Instead fear that which, after you are dead, has the power to send people to hell, just as my Savior, who was sacri-ficed for your sake on this most cruel cross, said [Matthew 10:28]. Make the decision, my sons, to change your lives and your ways from this point on. Place your faith in the mercy of the Savior. To the extent that I am able, I will not allow you to be abandoned."

46. The power of his prayer, which flowed forth from Raymond's most ardent charity, was such that he found no one, no matter how much his soul had been given over to shameful things, whom he could not convert to piety and patience. Inspired by God, Raymond understood when their penance was serious and their intention to do good was solid. He knew that they would someday, through their holy works and the illustrious examples that

they provided, prove useful to the people of God. He begged for the release of such as these in the presence of the judges and officials. "Lord judge," he used to say: "I have fathered a spiritual son who has much to offer Christian society. I beg you, through this holy cross—which gave true life to us, decorated by the death of the Son of the most pure Virgin—I beg you to give him to me. You will not be sorry. He will most certainly be a comfort to the entire city." The judges, moved by the well-known sanctity of the man and by the voice of God speaking through him, assented without hesitation to what he asked of them. Many who were released remained steadfast in their virtue, attentively weighing the dangers of secular life, and, at the urging of blessed Raymond, embracing the religious life at the Canonry of the Twelve Apostles, where they most faithfully served God.

47. If I were to try to describe one by one all of blessed Raymond's virtues, all his labors, and each of his pious works, an entire year would not be sufficient for the task. So I think it will suffice to have briefly culled a few from them, for the glory of God and his saint and as an example to those living now as well as to those who will come in the future. I will not mention how many times he came upon children here and there who had been abandoned and secretly cast aside; children whom he carried—often two at a time, one in each arm, lest they perish in their misery, all the while crying out of pity—back to his hospice to nurture with his care. Nor will I say how many sick people, especially foreigners and pilgrims, destitute and on the street without any resources, he carried on his own back. These things I pass over, so that I might move on to describe the laudable and blessed end of his life.

48. When that time arrived, the time that Divine Mercy had preordained both for bringing to an end and for generously rewarding the toil and anguish of his servant, Raymond was seized by a serious fever. Since it only got worse with each passing day, this blessed one sensed that the time of his passing was near. So he asked that he be given the sacrament, which he received from the hands of the good priests in that place. Fortified in this way, he handed over all the cares and concerns of his hospice to his associates, who had, for twenty-two straight years, provided faithful labor to him in his pious efforts on behalf of the poor of Jesus Christ.[15] He spoke to those whom he summoned to his room in the following manner: "My brothers and comrades in these pious labors, keep my most holy cross before my eyes and listen

15. Raymond's date of death on 26 July 1200, at age sixty, makes him approximately 38 years old at the time of the foundation of the hospital in 1178.

to me. I give thanks first to you, my Savior, and to you, most holy cross, for I see that my pilgrimage and the course of my laborious life are now leading me to their long desired end. Next, I thank you, O faithful companions, who did and accomplished so much with me, feeding and strengthening the poor, to whom I gave birth in the spirit of charity. Now I beseech you through this most holy cross in which I have placed all my hope: do not grow cold or be intimidated by the labors undertaken thus far. I bequeath to you this place along with my needy ones, and at the same time I am entrusting you with this most holy cross. Place your faith in it; it will not be found wanting in the midst of any holy undertaking. The time is at hand for me to return to my Savior, from whom I—trusting not in my own merit but in his infinite kindness—expect eternal mercy."

50. Blessed Raymond was already on the verge of death when the image of his son, who was present with him at the time, came into his mind. "Come here, son," he said. "Reach out your hand to me and give me the kiss that you owe your parent. Then promise to do what I ask." His son approached and, with tears pouring from his eyes, kissed his father. Then blessed Raymond said: "If you wish me to die content, then renounce the world and embrace the religious life on behalf of which I long ago removed you from your crib and presented you at the Church of Saint Brigid in the presence of the image of my Savior.[16] I have often admonished you about this, but up to now you have not fulfilled my wish. Do not put this off any longer, my son. Consider how the contours of this world are passing away and how death awaits nearby. Do not place your trust in the world's comfort and wealth. Think about real riches and how those who follow voluntary poverty will abound in them while greedy rich men will become beggars. May my Lord bless you, son. Now close my eyes." Having said this, turning his serene face to the holy cross, he said: "In your arms and by your name and your power, I pass from this world to my Savior and Creator." And thus Raymond's most holy soul departed, led by holy angels. . . .

51. . . . Such was the happy death of blessed Raymond "the Palmer" of Piacenza in the year 1200, the 26th of July, in the sixtieth year of his life . . . .

52. Scarcely had that most holy soul departed when the news spread throughout the entire city: blessed Raymond had passed on from this life. The most important men in the city, the nobles, and the venerable matrons,

---

16. Raymond's son Gerard converted shortly thereafter, becoming a canon at the church of the Twelve Apostles and the caretaker of his father's tomb.

all hastened to his residence, not to mourn but to venerate the dead man and to commend themselves to the Servant of God, who was already, in their opinion, blessed and powerful in the presence of the Savior as a result of his great merit. What a marvelous thing it was, beyond all imagination, to see the princes of the city, counts, and nobles all prostrated before the body of this little poor man. In their feelings of incredible piety, they struggled with one another, some to touch or kiss his hand, others his foot, and still others to obtain a piece cut from his garment. This rush to the body lasted for three days, after which it was decreed by the city leaders that the body be deposited in a precious sarcophagus to be put in the Canonry of the Twelve Apostles, in a place of honor, where it could be humbly approached and venerated by the faithful. They did not doubt that our Creator would illuminate the merits of our servant [Raymond] with great prodigies, which did, in fact, come to pass.

55. After the holy body had been placed, as we just now described, in the canonry, a huge crowd of Christians, both inhabitants of the city and outsiders, rushed to it, seeking help for their illnesses and other evils. Nor was there any lack of obvious miracles, through which the Lord made manifest the sanctity of His servant. The abundance of things, of money, of images that were offered there day after day was astounding, to the point where the leaders of the city, seeing this, considered selecting honest and pious men, especially from among the dear companions of blessed Raymond, whom they could charge with the responsibility of using these offerings to support the paupers in Raymond's hospice. And this was in fact done. Indeed, the quantity and quality of the offerings turned out to be so great that they alone sufficed for this purpose.[17] Indeed it brought back to mind what blessed Raymond had told them not long ago: that it would be easier for him to feed the poor as a dead man than it had been for him to do so when he was alive.

56. A few days later, when the city magistrates observed that this great flow of gifts was continuing unabated, they decreed that a "Hospice of Saint Raymond" (which still bears this name today) be established. So that they might do it in such a way that would be welcomed by the poor, they designated Raymond as its patron and protector so that it would remain as an eternal memorial to this Servant of God. Also hastening to his tomb were no few people from Cremona, who, as we said above, had afflicted the Servant of

17. In other words, there was no more need to go out looking for alms the way Raymond used to do.

God with lies, lashings, and prison when he had come to them to lead them to a peaceful settlement. These ones came prepared with much self-deprecation and, with fists pummeling their chests, begged for his forgiveness. They were terrified lest the blessed one invoke vengeance from the hand of God, saying: "Lord, avenge the injuries and oppressions suffered by your servant."

57. So many and so great were the signs and prodigies that the divine power displayed through the merits of its servant Raymond—the sick being healed, those possessed by demons being liberated, and those in peril on the sea, on rivers, in wars, in prisons, on journeys, as well as those suffering from any of the various other calamities to which this life is exposed, being succored— that it would be impossible to recount all of them even with a level of industry far beyond my own. I reckon that it will be sufficient if I draw attention to a few of the many, both to prove Raymond's sanctity and to encourage and delight the piety of the faithful, giving these same ones something to use for preaching and convincing their descendants about the sanctity of this servant of God. I want everyone who might read this account to know that I have recorded no miracle here without it being verified by the sworn testimony of mature men worthy of confidence.

58. In the upper reaches of Italy, in an area referred to as Piedmont, there was a certain German named Ogerius who, on the feast of the Lord's nativity, ate cabbage cooked with ox meat. Unfortunately it happened that a piece of bone lay hidden mixed up in the stew. The man was eating the food so voraciously that he swallowed the bone along with the cabbage. The bone went down into his stomach and stuck there, tormenting the poor man for many days, the doctors being ignorant of the cause of the malady. While he was suffering from this pain, it happened that a certain fellow citizen of his had come to Piacenza to visit the tomb of the blessed Raymond, so that he might see the marvelous prodigies. When he returned to Piedmont, he recounted all that he had seen and heard to Ogerius, who immediately conceived of a vow: he promised that if somehow he might be made well again, he would go to Piacenza himself and visit the tomb of this blessed man, bearing pious gifts in hand. Scarcely had he made the promise than he vomited up the bone into his hand. He carried the bone with him and after he had venerated the holy sepulcher as promised he asked that it be hung up so that it might bear witness to this worthy miracle.

The author goes on to recount eight additional miracles.

65. . . . These few prodigies have been related here only for the sake of confirming the merit and virtue of blessed Raymond. I am not young enough to

review, nor is my memory great enough to grasp, or my hand and pen sufficient to record all the other miracles that are so well-known all throughout
Lombardy. Those miracles that exceed my powers to recount, I leave to ora-
tors—among whom I am the least—more learned than I.

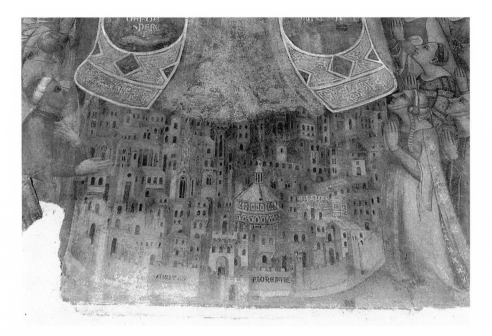

Figure 22. Lay devotees of the Madonna della Misericordia flank the first known image of the city of Florence (1342). Maestro del Bigallo, Florence, Loggia del Bigallo. (Photo: Frances Andrews)

83. LIFE OF UMILIANA DE' CERCHI (1246)

Translated from Latin by Anne M. Schuchman

The Franciscan friar Vito da Cortona completed the earliest vita *of Umiliana in 1246. According to this* vita, *she was born in 1219 to the prominent Florentine banker Oliviero Cerchi and his first wife. Umiliana was married when she was sixteen in what was probably a political union. About a month after her marriage she began to shun the trappings of her well-to-do society, and instead dedicated her time and resources to the poor and sick, while forming ties with other religious laywomen. Widowed five years later, Umiliana returned to the Cerchi household, leaving her children with her husband's relatives. She refused a second marriage, and was eventually defrauded of her dowry by her father. Umiliana took up residence in the tower of the family's palazzo, leaving only to attend mass or visit the poor and sick. Although she desired to enter a local Franciscan convent, she did not become a nun, but instead created a sort of cloister for herself out of her room. In doing so, according to her hagiographer, Umiliana established a model for all pious laypeople of how to live in the world while remaining detached from its temptations. Her religious devotion turned from outward works of charity to visions, prophecy, and miracles. Umiliana died 19 May 1246, five years after her self-imposed enclosure, after a protracted illness, surrounded by devout laywomen (male family members and clergy were conspicuously absent). She was buried in the Franciscan church of Santa Croce in Florence, where less than three months later her remains were moved to a more prominent position, indicating that her fame had already begun to spread. The popularity of her cult waxed and waned over the next several centuries, culminating in her beatification in 1694.*

Saints' lives, like that of Umiliana, can be a valuable resource for historians as well as literary scholars, although their use is not without its difficulties. Since vitae *were explicitly written to demonstrate a person's holiness, they often reveal more about the author's perception of sanctity than about the saint. Yet in these individual characterizations a broader understanding of the relationship between the human and divine can be uncovered. In addition,* vitae *can provide historical information about people who might otherwise have escaped record. Umiliana's* vita, *for instance, offers intriguing details regarding the varieties of religious practises followed by laywomen, practices that are highlighted in the following selections. The* vita *begins with a list of thirty-four witnesses, most of whom were women whose marital, religious, and social status varied widely. While the author was a male cleric, most of his information came from firsthand interviews with laywomen, a feature he himself emphasized to underscore his text's authenticity. Thus this* vita *offered women an indirect opportunity to describe their own lives while contributing to a portrait of Umiliana as a saint.*

CHAPTER I

Umiliana's works of charity during her marriage were met with disapproval, and thus she went to great lengths to avoid detection.

A lady by the name of Umiliana, daughter of Olivierio Cerchi, a Florentine, was married by her parents when she was sixteen. And as if filled with God, one month after she joined her husband she began to spurn the ostentation and ornamentation of that age, such that she did not make herself up. The care for her clothes, which was a sign of respect for her husband, was not a joy for her, but a heavy cross . . . her sister-in-law, who feared God, encouraged her in this . . .

Since she was not able to prepare food [for the poor] because of various

---

Translated from the earliest fourteenth-century Latin *vita*, Florence, Biblioteca Medicea-Laurenziana, Cod. 27 Dext. 11, and the seventeenth-century edition in *AASS*, 6 May (Antwerp, 1685), 385–400.[1]

1. In general I have given preference to the older manuscript except for the chapter divisions, which are a later addition. An Italian translation of this *vita*, primarily based on a manuscript found in the Biblioteca Nazionale of Florence, *Nuovi Acquisti* 1099 (formerly *Ricasoli* 128), was published by Giuseppe DeLuca in *Prosatori Minori del Trecento: Scrittori di Religione*, vol. 1 (Milan and Naples: Riccardo Ricciardi, 1954; repr. Turin: Einaudi, 1977), 723–68.

duties at home and the crowd of the family and the conversation of the men and women, she silently prepared [it] at night . . . And at sunrise, not looking for the pomp and honor and vanity of the world, but almost as a servant of God, she joined her sister-in-law, who was her participant and her secret ally in this . . . they went around in the city to the place of the poor, sick and well, distributing this food . . .

CHAPTER 2

Following her husband's death, Umiliana returned to her father's house where she refused remarriage. The loss of her dowry limited her outward charity and thus her spiritual life turned inward.

The whole first year after her return to her father's house, she heard the divine office every day without fail, and she busied herself in works of piety. . . . In the second year however she withdrew from such lengthy visits, and she raised herself incredibly higher. And since it was not enough for her to occupy herself with those who were so poor, she pronounced this vow: "Lord, you knew that to the extent that I could I have given to you with great generosity. Now, deprived of my means, I entrust to you my whole body and soul." From then on, burning, inflamed by divine love, she longed for the solitary life . . . and to give herself with love to God as she promised . . .

She wanted to enter the convent of Santa Maria of Monticello[2] . . . but God, who had decreed another path for her, did not permit it. God in fact was unwilling that the lighted lamp should remain hidden any longer under the bushel; therefore he placed her upon a candelabra so that the height of her life might be an example. . . . She was in fact the vessel chosen by the Lord and the precious stone upon which he should found the construction of the heavenly Jerusalem . . . Divine wisdom, wanting to construct her house . . . sent her servants, that is, the founders of the different orders . . . and together with them she also sent this marvelous foundress of a new life and of a holy spirituality. Others, with the guidance of the Holy Spirit . . . distinguished their orders with different customs and with the habit of honesty. She kept the habit of honesty of the Third Order, directed toward the same kingdom according to the form of the other religious orders. . . . What did she lack in the monastic life, she who lived in continuous silence and in full observance? What less did she have than the holy hermits, she who found her solitude in the heart of a great city, and changed the nuptial bed into a prison?

2. The Franciscan convent of Florence.

UNIVERSITY OF WINCHESTER
LIBRARY

What minor hardships did she bear in respect to the holy sisters of San Damiano, she who lived so soberly as far as food and drink. . . . In what way could she better follow the way of the friars minor, she who observed so perfectly the gospel of Christ? In fact dividing all that she had with others, she gave everything to the poor, and with faith she placed her body and her soul in God. Others served the Lord after abandoning worldly life and paternal household, fleeing into solitude. This one, taking solitude in her father's house, nobly fighting, conquered the world and vice in the middle of the world [itself]. . . . If she did not leave her father's house and dress herself in widow's clothes, she did not stay for herself . . . but God did not permit it. He wanted, in fact, with her example to draw the lazy ones out of the world . . . so that no one from the greatest to the least would have any excuse that he could not serve God as much as possible in his own home and secular habit. . . . She was instructed with healthful advice by God and the friars minor, and above all Friar Michael, who was her instructor in the way of devotion. . . .

Following a series of miraculous visions, Umiliana incurred the wrath of Satan who sought to stop her devotion. He presented the images of dead bodies before her to distract her from prayer, but Umiliana ignored them. The devil then reverted to his true form, that of a giant serpent. Umiliana ordered him to depart in the name of Jesus, which he did, but later another serpent arrived.

After several days, Satan sent her a huge serpent who terrified her, not incorporeal, as the other had been, nor pretended or imagined, but real, truly terrible, and horrendous. He was always nearby at her prayers and when she rested he kept his tail at her feet, and his head at her face . . . so that she was not able to pray or sleep in peace. In fact, when she went to sleep, she always rolled her clothes around her feet and tied a belt around them, so that the serpent could not enter from her feet, and touch her naked body in any way. . . . Patiently enduring this for many days . . . she said . . . to the serpent who remained near her: "I command you, serpent, in the name of Jesus my delight, to coil yourself up immediately here by my hands." At that the serpent, lowering his head, immediately rolled his tail and body to his head, as he had been ordered. The blessed Umiliana . . . lifted him up, praising and blessing God saying: "Blessed be that love that made you so very strong." And carrying him to a window of the tower, she commanded him saying, "Go on your way and stay no more with me, because you are useless and fruitless." This said, the serpent quickly left.

CHAPTER 3

Umiliana cured many of both physical and spiritual problems. She was of the utmost humility and patience, and appeared to be in continuous devotion.

Indeed she used to say to others: "I want you to transcend three grades: that is that you first mourn your sin and time lost [in sin]; second that you deplore ingratitude, because you did not acknowledge the grace of God and lament the passion of Lord Jesus; third that you meditate on Divinity and rejoice, just as God has shown you." She encouraged some to peace, others to patience; she proposed the lives of saints to others . . . she urged others to [be] faithful to the life of solitude, saying, "Consider your home the solitude of the woods, and the wild beasts as your family, and among them you will be just as in the woods, maintaining silence and pursuing constant prayer." Humble Umiliana, the example of humility, counseled that anyone who wanted to surmount the highest things should make a foundation in humility. . . . Truly she spoke as the imitator of the mirror of all humility, that is the glorious Virgin, because she was compelled with all her mind to imitate her along the paths of humility. . . . And it is worth marveling that after she began to know God no word was ever uttered from her mouth except of great humility. And although she burned inside this way because of divine love, she did not dare to offer sermons on God, except sometimes, beseeched, she humbly uttered two or three words about the divine fire. . . .

And on the road, going to receive the sacrament of the body of Christ, she besought her companions not to say anything to her, saying: God is everywhere and he can be received everywhere . . . if only He finds a place prepared for Him. Thus if you want to make me happy do not distract me [by] speaking; since often on the road, being among the creatures, or listening to preaching and the holy office, I have found my Lord with the same fullness as in my cell in the midst of prayers and orations. . . .

CHAPTER 4

Umiliana's sufferings were closely related to her ecstatic experiences. She received many gifts from God, including the spirit of prophecy and the ability to cure illnesses.

One day she happened to lift her eyes [because of] the fury of a runaway horse on the road . . . and [she] suddenly saw the seated horseman. Then, due to the pain in her heart, she rushed forth with disturbed words saying: "Oh if only I were blind, Lord, so that I should no longer see such things." Another day, walking on the road, she heard someone [say], "Why did you not take a nice man, with whom you could happily enjoy and rejoice in the delights of this world. . . ." She responded: "If only I were blind and deaf, so that I would not hear such things again." . . . Since the sense of hearing does not have a natural obstacle, one often happens to hear things that are displeasing . . . therefore she tightly stuffed cotton in her ears so as not to hear the noises and vanities of the world.

. . . She also desired to be enclosed in her tower, saying: "I wish my father would thus enclose me in this tower for Christ's name, so that neither doorway nor window should remain." She said that about her father and not others . . . because at times her father had threatened to wall up the door of the tower, because she did not live according to his will about remarriage. And he [wanted] . . . her to live in a new house near Sant'Ambrogio . . . and her cousin Galgano wanted to live in that tower, in Blessed Umiliana's cell, with his wife. . . . But that blessed one did not want to leave it, because of the grace that the Holy Spirit had [given] her. For this mistreatment both were gravely struck by God, Galgano to bodily death; perhaps not the soul, since by the prayer of the Holy Umiliana he was deemed worthy to receive the sacrament of penance. Her father truly would have been seriously harmed, had the saint not protected him with her prayers to God.

She desired to be in harsh mountains and in deserts and solitude, in inaccessible places where she might have only herbs for sustenance, and might freely meditate on God as she desired, and might burst out in praise and pious effusions for the love of the highest love, Jesus Christ. She called herself imprisoned, because she could not release what she had inside. And she often called the cell a hell because of the . . . devil's bitter trials . . . although out of the love of Christ she freely remained in it.

CHAPTER 5

Umiliana's visions and raptures increased during her final illness. Finally she embraced a happy death.

Umiliana longed to see Jesus as a child, a vision that was granted her. While she was visiting a very sick boy, Umiliana offered to take on his illness. As she lay suffering in her bed, a small boy appeared in Umiliana's room, although the door to her cell was locked from the inside. When she saw him she felt a great joy, believing that he was truly a messenger of the highest King; and . . . she said: "Oh sweetest love, oh dearest boy! Do you only know how to play?" And the boy, with a tranquil look, responded to her: "What else do you want me to do?" And the blessed Umiliana humbly said: "I want you to tell me something good about God." And the boy said: "Do you think it is right to speak of oneself?" And with these words Baby Jesus disappeared, leaving her completely cured of the illness. Blessed the eyes that saw what you saw, happy Umiliana! To other saints and elect of God some angel was sent, so that they might be comforted in the Lord. To you Jesus is sent, blessed fruit of the Virgin's womb, only son of the highest Father, whom you desired to see with your whole heart . . .

Blessed Umiliana humbly asked God to die on a Saturday, out of reverence for Our Lady, and that no one from her father's house be present at her death, which she obtained . . . [She] asked those who watched over her . . . to buy a tunic to carefully cover her naked feet, so they might not be touched in any way by mortals. The lover of honesty could not bear a hint of dishonesty even [while] dead. She truly foresaw the devotion and faith . . . that people were going to feel about her, tearing the fabric of her funeral clothes out of devotion. . . . Oh mirror of holiness, formed of all humility, example of chastity, path of honesty, sower of devotion, rule of obedience, solace of poverty, defender of patience!

. . . Nearing the hour of her death the devil was present, visibly appearing to her, terrifyingly awaiting the parting of soul from body. When she saw him stand before her she began to cry out loudly and berate him saying: "What are you doing here, cruel beast and evil adversary? What are you waiting for? Depart from me, enemy. Go away, since you will have nothing from me. But here is my Lady at hand, who will now present her sweetest Son to me with glory." And she threatened him not only with words but with her hands, fending him off and saying: "I say go away quickly, miserable one, since my Lady is with me, who will instantly destroy and tear you and your underhanded machinations apart."

. . . And her companion quickly ran to the portrait of Our Lady, where there was a lock of hair of the worthiest Mother [of God], and brought blessed candles that she lit, keeping them in the shape of a cross. And she placed the portrait, the image of the Lady, and the crucifix upon her breast. The candles illuminated her, and the incense perfumed, and she sprinkled holy water upon her head. When these were done she spoke to the devil . . . saying: "Go away from me, iniquitous one, and henceforth do not dare bother me in any way." And that said the devil, beaten and confused, departed. And she rested in complete tranquility. And opening her eyes and seeing that portrait placed upon her breast, she placed [it] with honor in the silk cloth of her mantle and positioned it better upon her breast. Resting all Saturday night, and the coldness of the extremities in her whole body worsening, [on] Saturday without a cry . . . she gave her soul to heaven, at the hour she was used to taking the body of the Lord, that is, at dawn . . . the nineteenth day of May . . . We believe she was immediately separated from the flesh without purgation, [and] went to God, as the present writings manifest.

Appended to the vita *is a series of post-mortem apparitions and miracles compiled by the friars Vito da Cortona and Hippolytus of Florence. Not surprisingly, these accounts, which go up to 1253, reveal that the beneficiaries of Umiliana's graces as well as the chief proponents of her cult were Franciscans and laywomen.*

84. FRANCO SACCHETTI ON "MODERN SAINTS" (ca. 1365)

Translated from Italian by Catherine Lawless

This letter was written by the Florentine poet and writer Franco Sacchetti (ca. 1335–1400) to a friend in Perugia. The letter concerns various trends in popular devotion which disturbed or amused Sacchetti. Chief of these was the proliferation of individuals venerated as saints. The later Middle Ages saw an increase not only in the number of saints officially canonized, but also in the types of individual deemed worthy of veneration. Instead of saints being only those closely tied to religious orders, and often of royal birth, many lay saints of humble birth were being canonized. This development was stimulated by the mendicant orders, and by an increased level of lay participation in religious life. Clerical celibacy and virginity were no longer requirements for either male or female saints; many of these individuals— characterized by André Vauchez as "new saints"—were in fact married or widowed. Sacchetti's letter is also interesting for what it tells us both about his views on what constituted sanctity and the role of images in late medieval devotion. The letter opens with a discussion of images of Pope Urban V (d. 1370), who, like many Sacchetti mentions, was never formally canonized as a saint.

Dearest friend.The aforementioned letter began around the time of the year 1365, when, as is believed, Pope Urban V and Charles, king of Bohemia, emperor, secretly discussed some things together in Avignon, so that they could direct the world.

Urban V, the first pope whom I ever saw painted, was in a panel painting in our own San Giovanni of Florence, which can still be seen today, that had, lighted in front of it, a torch [of wax] worth two *lire* and the crucified Christ, which was not far from it, had a miserable little candle worth a *denaro*. So I said to certain people who were in that place: "I see too well how, as we turn earthly matters around all day, so we wish to turn divine matters." And if someone who knew nothing of divine matters were asked which of the paintings represented the king of eternal life he would surely believe that it was Pope Urban, given the painting and its illumination. But the crucified Christ with the little candle worked a great miracle: one of the town's important men who had placed that panel painting [of Urban V] in the church soon afterward lost his money and status [and] fell into such poverty, that he ended his life in a vile hospital finding neither relative nor friend to help him. Indeed it can be said, that by not having recommended himself to the great-

Translated from Franco Sacchetti, *Opere*, ed. Aldo Borlenghi (Milan: Rizzoli, 1957), 1113–18.

est advocate, he lost [his] possessions and himself. . . . In conclusion, I do
not hold and do not deny that he [Urban V] could not be or that he is not a
saint; rather, I say that the men and women running to paint that which the
Holy Church has not made public and certain, even the religious who consent to it through avarice, do so in order to attract attention to themselves.

*Here Sacchetti makes clear that he appreciates the differences between officially rec-
ognized saints and those merely considered saints. This distinction was shown in
contemporary painting: saints were crowned with a disk-like halo while* beati
(blessed) were represented with golden rays issuing from their heads.

But let us leave Pope Urban, and come to a point which you make to
me, which is what Ghino marquis of Cittadella says, that these new saints
make him lose faith in the old ones. And is what this gentleman says not true?
And who can be certain that there are not quite a few who doubt that the
other saints began in this way and that in the fullness of time the rays of the
head can be converted to a halo, and the *beato* to a saint? How should we
believe in our priests who put the bodies of such *beati* high up, and make
lights and images of wax, while Our Lord and the Virgin Mary are painted
below, close to the ground and the dirt, without any light? And still worse,
that in many places the chimeras of worldly sinners are painted high above
Our Lady, with false verses, showing them to have been great valiant men to
the world.

*In the following passage Sacchetti discusses some of these "new saints" and contrasts
them with "old saints" such as Augustine and Benedict. Gerard of Villamagna was
a Franciscan tertiary who died in 1245, and whose cult was also claimed by the
Knights of Jerusalem. He was first buried in the Jerusalemite church of San Jacopo
in Campo Corbolini and was then transferred to Villamagna. The disputes over
which order he belonged to reflect the fluid situation of thirteenth-century devotional
movements; many of the "new saints" were in fact claimed by the major orders only
after their deaths. Gerard was not a saint in Sacchetti's time, being canonized only
in 1833. Umiliana de' Cerchi (1219–46) was a member of a prominent Florentine
family who refused to remarry upon widowhood [see #83]. Like Gerardo, she was
not a Franciscan tertiary, as she died long before the Franciscan Third Order was
officially founded, but her* vita *was written by a Franciscan, Vito of Cortona, and
her cult rapidly became associated with the Franciscan order. The blessed Giovanna
could be Vanna of Orvieto, a Dominican tertiary who died in 1306, or another
blessed Giovanna associated with the Dominicans of Santa Maria Novella, who died
in 1333. The two cults are often confused. Villana dei Botti died in 1361. She was
never officially a Dominican tertiary, but her cult was supervised by the Dominicans
of Santa Maria Novella, with whom she was associated.*

They allow everything in order to draw [attention] to themselves. The Franciscans in the city of Florence have the body of . . . Saint Gerard of Villamagna and that of Saint Umiliana de' Cerchi, who from *beati* have become *santi*, and much wax is offered to them all, where Our Lord and the Apostles have none, and likewise neither does Saint Francis. And the Dominicans have Blessed Giovanna painted with a jar of oil, claiming that, when she gave oil to God, it always appeared to increase in the jar (perhaps in July when it expanded with the heat); they have Blessed Villana, who was my neighbor, and was a young Florentine girl; although she always went about dressed just like the others, and they already have a feast day for her, whereas Saint Dominic stands on his own. The Hermits [of Saint Augustine] have Saint Barduccio, and others; and the Carmelites and the other orders are similarly full of them, and Saint Augustine and Saint Benedict are not visited, for the people all run to new things.

Sacchetti here questions the role of images, and in particular the Volto Santo of Lucca. This was a cross on which Christ's features were said to have been miraculously imprinted after the Crucifixion. It was taken in procession through Lucca every 14 September—the feast of the Holy Cross. He also discusses the popular belief that an uncorrupted body is a mark of sanctity and somewhat cynically suggests that the earth of Cortona may be responsible for the vast number of saints in the area.

And do they not make a big fuss over these things in other cities? As a matter of fact! And I will not hold back from saying this [just] because the Volto Santo has been in the city of Lucca for a long time; [but] was there never anyone who questioned this belief? Who knows if it is the image of Our Lord? With all due respect, Christ's was the most beautiful and best proportioned body that ever was, and did not have frighteningly crossed eyes. It is not [so] surprising that I can state this with confidence, because I have heard the Franciscans, Masters Nicola and Ruggero, both great Sicilian theologians, speak openly against those who trust in images for intercession. . . . Blessed Ugolino and Blessed Margaret of Cortona are exhibited in great reliquaries shown on their [feast] days [and it can be seen that] the bodies are uncorrupted, and for this they are sanctified; on the other hand the clergy say that an excommunicated body remains uncorrupted forever.[1] Be that as it may, I believe that Cortona is very old land, and there have been quite a

1. The Beato Ugolino referred to is probably Ugolino of Cortona, an Augustinian friar, who died in 1370. It could also, however, refer to Ugolino of Gualdo, another Augustinian friar who died in 1260. Margaret of Cortona was a lay woman who lived a life of penitence after witnessing the death of her noble lover. She died in 1297 and her cult was appropriated by the Franciscan order.

few martyrs there: Saint Renzo of Imola, Saint Peter Fabiani of Faenza, Saint James of Forlì, and Saint Marcellinus, and Beata Nicolina of Pesaro, it is quite likely that these were martyred by the Romagnols.[2] And there are so many others that their catalogue is already half as long as that of the early saints and I could not [possibly] count them.

Pescione is a character who also appears in Sacchetti's Trecentonovelle, *a collection of short stories. Suora Scotta was clearly one of a number of women who lived anchoritic lives near or beside churches and religious foundations.*

. . . And I remember that at my place near Florence, there was a pleasant man, a rhyme-maker called Pescione, who was blind. One day a piece of news came that within the monastery, a Sister Scotta had died and was performing great miracles [and] everyone was traveling there. This Pescione asked me for a guide to go and touch the body, so that he might receive the grace of sight. I had him brought there, and as it turned out, he returned with his nose almost broken or half-cut in such a way that, in addition to being blind, he [now] went about scarred forever. I asked another peasant who lived near me, who was returning from [viewing] this Sister, if she had performed miracles. Yes, he replied. A bag of five florins had been snatched from him and he had returned lighter than he had gone. Rather large pieces of wax are brought to this Sister for such miracles, especially by women.

In this passage Sacchetti discusses the various miraculous images of the Madonna in Florence: images that spoke, bled, or performed miracles. Santa Maria de Cigoli and Santa Maria de la Selva are both in the Florentine contado, *or hinterland, while Santa Maria Primerana is in Fiesole. But the best-known miraculous images are those in Santa Maria Impruneta, Orsanmichele, and Santissima Annunziata. The Santa Maria Impruneta image, painted sometime in the thirteenth century, began to work miracles around 1340; its miraculous powers, however, were usually only active when the image was taken in procession throughout the city of Florence. Orsanmichele was originally a grain market, built on the site of an old oratory dedicated to Saint Michael, hence the name. It became the focus of devotion around 1291, when an image of the Madonna painted on a pillar began to work miracles. The image of the Annunciation in Santissima Annunziata also began to work miracles in the fourteenth century. There were also several small chapels on the Ponte Rubaconte, often attached to cells inhabited by anchoritic women. Santa Maria*

2. James of Forlì may be James the Venetian, a Dominican friar who died in 1314. Saint Marcellinus of Forlí, another Dominican friar, died in 1397. Nicolina of Pesaro is almost certainly Michelina of Pesaro, a Franciscan tertiary who died in 1356. Renzo (probably short for Lorenzo) of Imola is not known. Saint Peter Damian's relics were in Faenza, but Peter Fabiani remains unidentified.

delle Grazie was built there in 1371 to house a miraculous fresco of the Virgin and Child.

I could write too much if I wanted to talk about [just] how many places this error is found. And the pope does not attend to it: he has greater things to do. And the new middle classes abandon old things, and go to the new ones. How many changes have been in my city even in the figure of Our Lady! There was a time when everyone ran to Santa Maria de Cigoli; then they went to Santa Maria de la Selva, then the fame of Santa Maria in Pruneta [Impruneta] grew; then [they went to] Fiesole and Santa Maria Primerana; and then to Our Lady of Orsanmichele; then all were abandoned, and everyone gathered with great ceremony at the Annunziata de' Servi, at which, by one means or another so many images have been affixed that, if the walls had not been reinforced a short while ago, they would be in danger of collapsing along with the roof. Now everyone is drawn to a little chapel, which is called Santa Maria de le Grazie on the Rubaconte bridge, made to resemble the sepulcher of Christ. All the people go to it [and] because the place is so small, nearly every day the wax offerings have to be taken away to make way for more.

85. THE HUMILIATI: FIVE TEXTS
(1184–thirteenth century)

Translated from Latin by Frances Andrews

The first account of the Humiliati, written by an anonymous chronicler in Laon in northern France, provides an outsider's view of this group of north Italian religious enthusiasts. He refers to two activities which were to become trademarks of heresy and prompted their excommunication: rejection of oath-taking and preaching without authority. They were anathematized as heretics in the papal decree Ad abolendam *of 1184 alongside other groups listed by name. However, as demonstrated by the succinct gloss on a papal decretal by the Bolognese canon lawyer Tancred, working in the early thirteenth century, condemnation did not last. In 1201 the Humiliati returned to the Catholic fold and established an order of regular and tertiary religious, including both clergy and lay men and women. Such wholesale transition from condemned heretics to approved professional religious was extremely unusual. Their preaching against heresy, however, proved highly effective, as observed fifteen years later by a traveler through the region, Jacques de Vitry, a canon of Liège and later cardinal. By the middle of the century their communities had multiplied vastly and extended across northern and central Italy, from Tuscany to the Veneto and Piedmont. The numbers provided here by Bonvesin della Riva, exaggerate somewhat, but nonetheless draw attention to the continuing importance of Milan and its region in the history of the order. These brief references to the Humiliati are typical of the fragmentary sources that must be pieced together in order to trace the history of the new religious movements.*

1. The Laon Chronicle Description (early thirteenth century)

In the year of grace 1178 [1179] . . . At that time there were certain citizens of Lombard towns who lived at home with their families, chose a distinctive form of religious life, refrained from lies, oaths, and law suits, were satisfied with plain clothing, and argued for the catholic faith. They approached the pope and besought him to confirm their form of life [*propositum*]. To whom the pope granted that everything [they did] should be done with humility and honesty, but he expressly forbade them to hold private meetings or to presume to preach in public. But spurning the apostolic command, they became disobedient, for which they suffered excommunication. They called themselves Humiliati because they did not use colored cloth for clothing, but restricted themselves to plain dress.

Translated from Anonymous of Laon, *Chronicon universale*, ed. Georg Waitz, *MGH SS*, xxvi (Hannover: Hahn, 1882), 449–50.

2. The Condemnation (1184)

We [Pope Lucius III] decree that Cathars and Patarenes and those who men-
daciously assume the false name of Humiliati or Poor of Lyons, Passagines,
Josephines and Arnaldists, shall be subject to perpetual anathema.

3. A Gloss on the Condemnation (early thirteenth century)

Today the Humiliati have been received into the Church because they sinned
in nothing, except that they condemned oath-takers. Tancred.

4. Jacques de Vitry's Description (early 1220s)

For now the formidable heretics who are called Patarenes [see **#74, 80**] are
overcome and, thus powerfully and openly exposing their deceits, they [the
Humiliati] wisely convince the impious and incredulous using divine scripture and publicly confound them, so that now they [the Patarenes] do not
dare to appear before them, and many of them, recognizing their errors,
having returned to the faith of Christ, have joined themselves to these brothers. Thus those who were masters of error have become disciples of truth.

5. Bonvesin della Riva's Description (c. 1288)

In the city and *contado*, there are also as many as 220 houses of the second
order of the Humiliati of both sexes, in which the number of persons leading
the religious life and working with their own hands is high. Amongst these
the Brera is the principal one. The canonries of this same order, as has been
said, are seven. . . .

There are also houses of religious women of poverty, among them the
most noble religious women of Sant'Apollinare of the order of the blessed
Francis, who stand out for their honesty, sanctity, nobility, and number.
What should I say of the various orders of brothers, that is of the militia of
Saint Mary, the brethren of the third order of the Humiliati and the order of
penance, living with their own households who comprise, counting them all,
both within [the city] and outside, more than seven hundred? And I shall say
nothing of the high number of women among them. What can be said of all

(2) Translated from "Ad abolendam," in *Texte zur Inquisition*, ed. Kurt-Viktor Selge,
Texte zur Kirchen- und Theologiegeschichte 4 (Gutersloh: Mohn, 1967), 26.
(3) Translated from Gloss on I Comp 5.6.11 (X. 5. 7. 9) s.v. "Humiliati." Admont, Stifts-
bibliothek MS 22 fol. 72va.
(4) Translated from *The Historia Occidentalis of Jacques de Vitry, a Critical Edition*, ed.
J. F. Hinnebusch, Spicilegium Friburgense 17 (Freiburg: University Press, 1972), chap. 28, 146.
(5) Translated from Paolo Chiesa, *De magnalibus mediolani: meraviglie di Milano* (Milan:
Scheiwiller, 1998), chap. 3, 82–85.

the others living in religious habits, of whom some have given themselves and their property to regular houses or serve them in the habit of *conversi*, while others serve individual churches; others lead the life of hermits or recluses served by their own *conversi*; others in other ways, living separately from secular men? Of their great number I shall recall nothing special.

86. ALBERTANUS OF BRESCIA
A SERMON TO A CONFRATERNITY (1250)

Introduced by James M. Powell;
translated from Latin by Gregory W. Ahlquist

*Albertanus of Brescia (ca. 1200–1251) first appears in the historical record in a docu-
ment renewing the Lombard League in 1226. In 1238, he served as captain defending
the town of Gavardo against the advancing forces of Emperor Frederick II. He was
captured and imprisoned in Cremona, an event that marked the beginning of his
writing career. He was a man of considerable learning, widely read in Augustine's*
City of God, *Seneca's letters, and other contemporary and classical sources. The
extent of his legal education, though he cited legal sources in his works, remains
controversial. He served as a* causidicus *or legal counselor in Brescia. His first treatise, entitled* On Love and Delight in God and Neighbor *(De amore et dilectione
dei et proximi) marked him as an original thinker, concerned about the nature of
society. In 1243, he journeyed to Genoa in company with his fellow Brescian, Eman-
uele di Maggi, the new* podestà *of that city. While there he delivered a sermon to a
confraternity of notaries and* causidici, *which served in part as inspiration for his
second treatise,* The Art of Speech and Silence *(De doctrina loquendi et tacendi),
written in 1245, a book of advice for those involved in the law and public affairs that
remained popular into the sixteenth century. His most famous work,* The Book of
Consolation and Advice *(Liber consolationis et consilii) served as the basis for
Chaucer's Tale of Melibee. His major importance is as a social theorist. He developed
an early theory of consent based on his experience in communal affairs, his involvement in a confraternity of fellow* causidici, *and his knowledge of law. In 1250, he
delivered a series of sermons in the Franciscan church of San Giorgio in Brescia,
which constituted a very early commentary on a confraternity rule, perhaps the
earliest we have. Although preaching was forbidden to the laity, moral exhortation
was not. The following sermon or exhortation articulates the goals and aspirations
of confraternal life.*

SERMON DELIVERED ON ILLUMINATION ON BOTH SPIRITUAL AND BODILY
REFRESHMENT AND WHAT IS NECESSARY FOR REFRESHMENT

Pray to God, brothers, that by the ministry of his holiness, through me, his
useless and unworthy servant, he may administer something of use to you
today.

My brothers, gathered here as is usual, we will consider the rule of our

Adapted from Gregory W. Ahlquist, "The Four Sermons of Albertanus of Brescia: An
Edition" (M.A. thesis, History, Syracuse University, 1997). Biblical citations from *Sermones
Quattuor: Albertanus Brixiensis* (critical edition), ed. Marta Ferrari (Lonato [Brescia]: Fondazi-
one Ugo da Como, 1950.

congregation, investigating some useful things concerning it. Indeed, the rule of our congregation has a three-fold basis. The first is illumination; for we are accustomed to gather here to meet as the oil is purchased by which the sacred place is illuminated. The second basis is spiritual refreshment, which we are accustomed to receive from the friars here with devotion. The third is bodily refreshment, which we should take here with charity. We will examine all of these individually.

Concerning illumination we need to know that those who want to shine their light for others, should have light within themselves. For, without light, man is said to be almost blind and "if the blind should lead the blind, both will fall in the pit" [Matthew 15:14] as the Truth itself testifies in the Gospel. So that we may therefore have the true light and can bring it to others, it must be known that, just as in our usual corporeal light we need four things, namely: fire and oil and a pure vessel in which the oil is poured and can be burned, and the burning itself, likewise the four previously said things should be present in the spiritual light.

For we should have fire; this is to carry God in our hearts, to hold the memory and to be warmed by his loves. And Saint Paul states well the nature of god as fire in the Epistle to the Hebrews, when he says: "Indeed our god is a consuming fire" [Hebrews 12:29] for he consumes all of our sins. For he is the fire, who inflamed and illuminated the apostles on the day of the Pentecost. For he is the fire, who appeared to Moses in the bush. He is the pillar of fire who led the Israelite people through the desert. Moreover, he is the fire holding burning coals, which melt our hearts, hard to make good, about which the prophet says, "sharp arrows of the powerful, with burning coals" [Psalm 120:4] These are the coals we should heap upon the heads of our enemies as Saint Paul says in the Epistle to the Romans: "If your enemy is hungry, feed him: if he is thirsty, give drink to him, indeed in doing this, you will heap coals of fire upon his head." [Romans 12:20].

But we should have oil, this is the light of good works and works of charity. This is the oil about which it is said in the Gospel about the ten virgins, of whom five were prudent, but five foolish. The wise ones prepared their lamps with oil and entered into marriages with a spouse. The foolish ones had not taken the oil with them and thus they were excluded from the marriages and it was said to them: "Amen I say to you, I do not know you" [Matthew 25:12].

This oil should be pure and mixed with nothing rotten, in order that a strong and pure light can be drawn out of it. For, when we do works of charity, we should not do this mixed with vainglory. For this reason, it is said in the Gospel: "When you give alms, do not announce it with a trumpet, but in secret, that your left hand does not know what your right is doing: and your father, who sees in secret, will pay you back" [Matthew 6:2–4]. For God is not unmindful to works of charity, but on the day of judgment he will say: "I hungered, and you gave me to eat: I thirsted, and you gave me to drink: I was naked, and you clothed me: I was a stranger and you sheltered me: I was sick and in jail, and you visited me" [Matthew 25:35–36]. "Come and occupy the kingdom." [Matthew 25:34] etc.

Indeed, you should not do works of this kind with reluctance or for impression, but happily. For, as Augustine says: "Whoever gives to a poor person not to refresh the belly of the needy one, but to remove the weariness of the one asking, loses both the deed and the reward." And clearly works of charity are rightly compared to oil, because, just as oil placed on any liquid rises to the top, whether it is placed on top, or placed underneath, so charity and its works surpass all other virtues. Wherefore Saint Paul says, in the First Epistle to the Corinthians: "Now however, these three remain, faith, hope and charity: but the greatest of these is charity" [1 Corinthians 13:13] . . .

[Another] matter ought to intervene: this is any pure body, which is burned; that is our bodies should be pure in order that the previously mentioned oil is well poured into these bodies and they can be set on fire. For we should purify them and remove all corruption of sins from us through the works of penitence, of which there are seven namely: solicitude, defense, indignation, fear, desire, emulation, punishment. Of these Saint Paul made mention of all in the second Epistle to the Corinthians, around the middle, where he says: "For what according to God is sadness, penitence" [2 Corinthians 7:10], etc. For we should have solicitude to correct what we have done wrongly. We should make or keep a defense, because we should defend ourselves from the preceding faults.

We should indeed always have fear lest perhaps we fall and we revert to our earlier state, because "Blessed is the man who is always fearful" [Proverbs 28:14]. "For the beginning of wisdom is the fear of the Lord" [Psalms 111:10] as the Prophet said and also as a certain philosopher has said: "He who fears God, all things fear him; but he who does not fear God, fears everything. And another has said: "The fear of the Lord should be your business, and profit will come to you without labor."[1]

We should indeed always have the desire to be advanced to something better.

We should indeed have emulation, namely of the saints, because we should always imitate them.

---

1. For these two citations Ferrari cites Petrus Alfonsi, *Disciplina clericalis*, ed. Alfons Hilka and Werner Söderhjelm (Heidelberg: C. Winter, 1911), 2.

We should indeed endure punishment; this is to afflict our body with vigils and fasts and other good works. And if through the previously mentioned works of penance, our bodies shall have been cleansed, the oil could well have been poured into them, and they could well be burned for the love of God. A fourth matter is also necessary for true illumination, as I have said, namely the burning itself. For Luke said in the Gospel: "I came to send fire on the land, and what do I wish except that it be set on fire?" [Luke 12:49]. The fire of the love of Christ should burn in our hearts through the arousal of these very bodies in respect to works of charity; you do this in a way that however much it is always aroused, so much greater it is set on fire and is built into a larger flame as Isaiah the prophet testifies, when he says: "When you pour out your spirit to the hungry, and satisfy the afflicted spirit, your light is raised in darkness and your darknesses will be as the noonday. And the Lord God will always give you rest, he will save your spirit in splendor, and he will free your bones, and he will be like a watered garden and a living fountain, whose waters will not cease" [Isaiah 58: 10–11]. And again in the same way he said: "Break up your bread for the hungry, and if you see someone naked, clothe him and lead the needy and the vagrant into your own home: and despise not your flesh. And then your light will break forth like the morning and your health will quickly spring forth" [Isaiah 58:7–8]. For Tobit also said: "Give alms from your substance and do not turn your face from the poor: for thus will it happen that the face of God will not be turned from you" [Tobit 4:7] whose face is true light, as Saint John says; "He was the true light, that enlightens every man coming into this world" [John 1:9]. And again Tobias said the same thing: "When you can, be merciful. If you have much, give liberally: if little, be zealous to impart from that little. For your reward will be a good treasure on the day of necessity; for alms free one from every sin and death, and do not allow the soul to go in darkness" [Tobit 4:8–10]. And so, with an aroused and kindled light in us, it can be said with the Prophet: "Light for us is shown to the just, and happiness for the right in the heart." [Psalms 97:11] Indeed to serve God is true happiness. Whereupon Solomon said: "The light of the eyes brings happiness to the spirit: and good news heals bones" [Proverbs 15:30]. And also it can be said with Saint Paul: "You were sometimes in the darkness, now however you are light in the Lord. Walk as children of light: moreover the fruit of light is in all goodness and justice and truth" [Ephesians 5:8–9]. . . .

Now we advance to the second basis for the rule of our congregation, namely: to treat spiritual refreshment, as we are accustomed to receive here from the brothers with devotion. About this we ought to know that, just as we should have bread and water and wine and other foods in bodily refreshment, so also we should have the previously mentioned things in spiritual refreshment.

We should have the bread, namely of life and understanding, about which one reads in the Book of Wisdom. The bread of life is the bread of tears and compunction about sin. About this bread the Prophet says: "You fed us with the bread of tears: and for drink you gave us tears in measure" [Psalms 79:6]. Through this bread we arrive at the bread of life, that is, to Christ, who said: "I am the living bread, who has descended from heaven" [John 6:51]. . . . We should have the water of wisdom, as I have said, and of heavenly teaching which is the water Christ promised the Samaritan, saying: "I will give you water, spring up into eternal life" [John 4:14].

We should truly have the wine of compunction for our sins. About this wine the Prophet says: "You give us the wine of compunction to drink" [Psalms 60:3]. Through this wine we arrive at a pure wine, that, at a heavenly mystery, which is mixed in the New and Old Testament. Of this pure wine, the chalice in the hand of the Lord is full, as the Prophet says: "He humbles this man, he raises this man: because in the hand of the Lord is a full cup of pure wine mixed" [Psalm 75:7–8].

But we should have other foods for full refreshment, that is every word of God and about God. For, as he said: "Man does not live on bread alone, but by every word, which proceeds from the mouth of God" [Matthew 4:4]. For our foods should do and fulfill his words and his will, who sent us, as he says about himself; for he said: "My food is that I may do his will, who sent me" [John 4:34].

Now we approach the third part of the rule of our congregation; this is about bodily refreshment, as we are accustomed to receive here with charity. Concerning which, we should preserve moderation, before refreshment and during refreshment and after refreshment.

Before refreshment we should preserve seven things, which are to be understood in these verses: "Let there be fear during banquets, a blessing, a reading, time, a brief sermon, a happy face, a part given to the needy."

We should certainly have fear, when a banquet is placed before us, lest we eat too much or in some way offend the Lord, according to that, "Blessed is the man, who is always afraid" [Proverbs 28:14]. If Adam had feared, he would not have been ejected from Paradise.

A blessing should intervene, according to that, "He blessed and broke" [Mark 6:41; Matthew 14:19].

Then reading and time should intervene, because we should, if we are religious, order a reading before our presence and wait for the sacred third hour, before we go into the banquet: as we read about these two matters in the *Decretum 44 c.12*.

The sermon should truly be brief, in the same manner that: "within many words, sin is not absent" [Proverbs 10:19], and indeed according to Cato, who said: "Say little in a banquet."[2]

We should indeed have a happy face according to Saint Paul who says: "God loves a happy giver" [2 Corinthians 9:7], and again: "And he shows mercy in happiness" [Romans 12:8]. And also, according to the saying of Jesus Syrac [Jesus, son of Sirach or Ben Sira, author of Ecclesiasticus], who said: "In every gift make your face happy" [Ecclesiasticus 35:8].

Part also is given to the needy, according to the word of the Lord when He says: "Give alms, and everything will be given to you" [Luke 11:41], and also according to the word of a certain wise man, who said: "Whoever you are at the table, first think about the poor man; for when you feed him, friend, you feed God; God hides in the guise of the poor" [cf. Luke 14:13].

Four things, however, should be avoided in refreshment, but are very much present. Indeed four things ought to be avoided, and they are contained in this verse: "Pleasures, slander, drunkenness, grumbling should be avoided." Pleasures should be avoided. For we should not desire pleasures or pleasurable foods, though we can use them, if they are consumed without desire, as it is read in Decretum 41 c.2 "Delicie."

Slander should be avoided, because we should not complain about the foods, neither about the makers of them, nor anyone else, according to the saying of Saint Paul: "Slander no one" [James 4:11].

Excess above all should be avoided, according to the word of Saint Paul saying: "Not in excess and drunkenness" [Romans 13:13].

Complaining should be avoided, according to the saying of Saint Paul, in the First Epistle to the Corinthians: "In order that you will not have complained, just as some of them have complained, and were destroyed by the destroyer" [1 Corinthians 10:1], and according to Solomon saying: "Beware of complaining, protest nothing, since an obscure response will not go into a vacuum" [Wisdom 1:11].

Indeed, there ought to be many things in refreshment: we should keep moderation in quality and in the quantity and variety of food.

In quantity, because we should not eat too much. For Seneca said in "On the formula for the honest life": "Neither consume to excess nor drink to drunkenness. May refreshment be easy: not for pleasure, but you assent to

2. Ferrari cites *Catonis Disticha*, ed. Marcus Boas and H. J. Boschuyser (Amsterdam: North Holland, 1952).

food. Hunger excites your palate, not tastes."[3] "Therefore hold this healthy and moderate rule of life so that you only give in to the body in so far as it is sufficient for good health" [Seneca, *Epistulae*, 1, 8, 5] as he also said in his letters.

We should truly keep moderation in quality, because we should not care about the quality of the foods, but, if they seemed harsh to us or not well cooked, we should expect hunger, according to Seneca, who said in his *Epistles*: "Hunger renders bad bread as good and soft and therefore it must not be eaten before it is necessary" [*Epistulae* 9, 4, 22].

We should truly keep moderation in a multitude and variety of foods. Jesus Syrac said: "Do not be greedy at every feast, and do not eat everything in sight."[Ecclesiasticus 37:29] For in much food there is infirmity; and he also spoke thus about drink: "Moderate drink is healthy for the body and soul. For drinking much wine makes irrationality and anger and much ruin." [Ecclesiasticus 31:25–27] And Seneca said in the *Epistles*, "Various foods are contrary to good health and alien from our bodies" [*Epistulae*, 18, 108, 18]. . . .

After refreshment, therefore, we should keep moderation, which is contained in this verse: "after we eat the food, we give thanks to Christ," [Acts 27:35] as in the *Decretum 44*, "Non liceat."

Preserving the aforesaid things with devotion, the Lord willing, we will be refreshed at the table of Christ, in the kingdom of God, to which he leads us, who lives and reigns without end through all ages. Amen.

3. Ferrari cites Martini Episcopi Bracarensis, *Opera Omnia*, ed. C. W. Barlow, Papers and Monographs of the American Academy in Rome 12 (New Haven, Conn.: Yale University Press 1950), 242.

87. THE CONFRATERNITY OF THE MISERICORDIA MAGGIORE IN BERGAMO THREE TEXTS (1282–1362)

Translated from Latin by Roisin Cossar

Confraternities, or associations of devout people (often lay people), who gathered together for prayer or worship, had existed on the Italian peninsula since the early Middle Ages. But it was not until the twelfth century that these pious associations began to experience their great period of growth, spurred on by a laity determined to play an active role in their own religious lives. Although confraternities continued to fulfill their original function as brotherhoods of religious devotion, now, in the later medieval period, they also served their local communities as distributors of charity. In these three extracts from the archive of the confraternity of the Misericordia Maggiore in Bergamo, founded in the thirteenth century by local clerics and lay people, the organization's charitable efforts are highlighted. The first document, a list of paupers who received alms in 1282, reveals the identities of the confraternity's clients in the thirteenth century. The second document, an extract from one of the confraternity's fourteenth-century expense books, suggests that the confraternity's officials sometimes responded to individual needs in its charitable distributions. The final text is a petition to the confraternity from three "shamefaced" paupers, members of the aristocratic Bonghi family, asking for support in 1385. The Misericordia's response suggests growing tensions between the confraternity and some of the poor in Bergamo.

I. A List of Paupers (1282)

In the name of God, amen. These are the poor and needy of the neighborhoods and city and burgs of Bergamo provided by the men named below; that is, two men per neighborhood, who were elected by the minister and cellarer of this company to give alms to the poor in their own neighborhoods. These paupers are to receive Bergamasque cloth bought with money given by lord Bonaventure de Pappis from a legacy left by lord Grazio, his late brother.

i. These are the poor receiving alms from Gualdrico Bagocho and Brother Pietro Choqui of the neighborhoods of Sant'Antonio.
First, Dona Anexia, the widow of Andrea da Bondo (given 7 *braccia* [of cloth])
and Donasenda di Ambrosio Andriani ([cloth] given)
and Lanfrancho, who lives in the house of the Asperini ([[cloth] given)

Translated from Bergamo, Biblioteca Civica (BCBg), MIA archivio 718, 45r–v.

Figure 23. Venetian Confraternity of St. John the Evangelist at the feet of the nursing Madonna (fourteenth century). Panel painting by Giovanni da Bologna. Venice, Accademia. (Photo: Cameraphoto Arte, Venice/Art Resource)

and a certain girl who lives in the house of Bonomo Peterzani ([cloth] given)
and Totescha Rampi, the sister of Fene ([cloth] given)
and Richelda who lives in the house of Carissimo the miller ([cloth] given)
and Guglielma, the widow of Martino Macie ([cloth] given)
and Gerardo di Pietro Ducis ([cloth] given)
and Carina, who lives in the house of Alberico Predemollo ([cloth] given)
and Caracossa Giordane ([cloth] given)

2. These are the poor receiving alms from Musso di Musso and Giovanni da Gorle of the neighborhood of Sant'Alessandro de la Croce.
First, Ser Martino who lives in the house of Acurso de la Fornace ([cloth] given)
and the *incarzelata* [recluse] who lives in the house of Santa Caterina ([cloth] given)
and Zanino, the son of Martino Colderari ([cloth] given)
and the wife of Martino, the son of Celicio of Sorlascho ([cloth] given)
and Bella, the daughter of Drusiollo, who lives in the house of the Fadini ([cloth] given)
and Ser Giovanni dei Avis, from Clusone ([cloth] given)
and Floramons, who lives near the bridge of Priviolo ([cloth] given 7 *braccia*)
and Zanino, the son of Drusiollo della Ranica ([cloth] given)
and two children of Bonetta da Nembro ([cloth] given)
and Ser Alberico da Sorisolle ([cloth] given)

3. These are the poor receiving alms from Alberto Savini and Enrico Agegario in the neighborhood of San Michele del Pozzo Bianco.
First, Poma Guillelmi da Valcamonica ([cloth] given)
and Orsillia, the widow of Venture Gisalberici ([cloth] given)
and Salva, the widow of Vezaniche ([cloth] given)
and Martino da Ruspino ([cloth] given)
and Poma da Vicomercato ([cloth] given)
and Teutaldo da Zogno ([cloth] given)
and the boy who lives in the house of the Lombardi ([cloth] given)
and the son of Arduyno da Foro ([cloth] given)
and one of the children of Betto dei Asinis ([cloth] given 7 *braccia*)
and the wife of Enrico the servant ([cloth] given)

. . . all of the cloth, which totaled four pieces, was distributed by all of the good men and persons on Friday the fourth departing day of November [27 November] and the following Saturday, 1282. And the recipients received five *quartae* [2/3 of a meter] of cloth each at least, except for those who received more, namely one per neighborhood who received 7 *braccia* as was noted above.

II. Charitable Expenses of the Confraternity (1361 and 1362)

5 ¹/₂ *soldi* for Barono da Zogno, which Barono spent in burying Antonio da Verdello, whose head was cut off in the month of January.

2 *lire* for Alessandro da Crema for his female servant to marry for the love of God on 14 July.

4 *soldi* for Bisesco Batalia da Curno to buy medicine for a pauper whose head was broken in the town of Curno.

6 *lire* and 8 *soldi* for Bono da Urniano to help redeem prisoners who were captured by the men of lord Cane de la Scala of Verona. The prisoners were brought to the town of Gredeniano in the district of Brescia.

10 *soldi* for a certain woman called Paxina who wishes to go to Rome on the abovementioned day [4 March 1361].

2 *lire* for Cresole, of the Astino valley, since his house was destroyed, to his misfortune.

4 bushels of wheat for Bruna da Urio who nursed the son of Betono da Urio, since he is an infant and an orphan, and also because Betono made the [confraternal] company his heir after the death of his son.

4 *lire* and 16 *soldi* for Master Donato d'Alme, who treated and cured the son of the late Betono da Urio, of the burg of Sant'Andrea, who was *crevatus*.[1] Betono desired that if his son died this confraternity would succeed him as Betono's heir, and this son has nothing of his own, since Maffeus da Urio is his guardian and is in the prison of the commune of Bergamo because he abused his guardianship.

A loan of 1 *lira* and 12 *soldi* to Zinino, the servant of Marchetto da Mappello [an official of the Misericordia] on the word of Marchetto and at his request.

2 *soldi* for Giovanni dei Mersis, who carried a cross before those who were decapitated on the kalends of August [1 August].

III. A Petition from the Bonghi Family

THE BONGHIS' REQUEST

In Christ's name, to you, the minister, cellarer, councillors, and other officials of the company of the Misericordia Maggiore of Bergamo, from Antonio,

---

(II) Translated from BCBg, MIA archivio 1383 bis, various folios.
(III) Translated from Archivio di Stato di Bergamo, Notarile, G. Fanconi, busta 117b, 12–27.
　　1. *Crevatus* may refer to a hernia.

Tomasso, and Giacomo, brothers of the Bonghi family. The petitioners state that since lord Pietro Bonghi, whose estate is held by the [confraternal] company, wanted his estate to provide for the poor, especially members of the Bonghi family, and since the said petitioners are members of that family, and they are poor, having fifteen small children whom they must feed and not enough income [40 *lire* annually] on which to live with dignity, they ask that the company provide them and their children with aid appropriate to their status and station in life, including, among other things, the ownership of two pieces of land in the territories called La Martinella and La Cornella.

THE CONFRATERNITY'S RESPONSE

The confraternity does not have enough money even to support poor men with an annual income of only 5 *lire*, but instead it seeks to assist the aged and infirm confined to bed, poor beggar women in labor, poor shamefaced girls who wish to marry, and other pious and needy causes to which it is committed. Thus, the confraternity cannot manage to support those who have 40 *lire* of income annually. Moreover, the said company has already rented the brothers [Bonghi] the properties in La Martinella and La Cornella at a reduced rent, asking 20 *lire* less than the usual fair price of 47 *lire* annually for these properties . . . furthermore, the [confraternal] company states that lord Pietro Bonghi would not have provided this assistance for the brothers if he were alive.

88. CIVIC VENERATION OF THE SAINTS AT SIENA
SIX TEXTS (1326–39)

Translated from Latin by Diana Webb

All Italian cities made public provision for the veneration of the saints. Every city observed the major festivals of the Christian year and honored the great saints, but each also had its supreme patron (not always the patron of the cathedral) and its "own" saints, ancient bishops and local martyrs often among them, who were regarded as emblems of civic identity. This civic "pantheon" was not static; as the documents translated here show, new saints, especially if they had some connection with the city, might be added to it [see #84]. There were many holidays, some observed just by the law courts and others by all the citizens, when there was a cessation of "all servile labor," but the festival of the supreme local patron saint naturally received special attention. On this occasion the citizens, and also representatives of subject cities and rural communities, were legally required to process with prescribed offerings to the church where the cult was centered, as did the civic magistrates and officials.

Siena's supreme patron was the Virgin and the major civic festival of the year was the Feast of the Assumption (15 August). In the late 1320s the Sienese government was also honoring several other saints, including an ancient martyr, Ansano, who began to receive official offerings in 1326, and also certain new saints, especially Ambrogio Sansedoni and Pier Pettinaio, who were venerated by the local Dominicans and Franciscans respectively. In late 1328, as one of a package of economy measures, it was proposed that the supreme magistrates of the commune (the "Nine") should no longer attend or send an offering to any religious festival. In response, the orders of friars argued strongly that the city benefited from doing honor to the largest possible number of heavenly patrons. It will be noted that such issues were dealt with precisely like any other legislative matter: proposals were laid before the General Council and voted on in the same way. For a time, the friars prevailed; but later in the 1330s, in a new edition of the city statutes, it was laid down that the supreme magistrates would attend only the Feast of the Assumption in honor of the Virgin. The important effect was to emphasize the unique importance of the Virgin and of her major festival rather than to achieve a significant budgetary saving.

1. 26 October 1326: A Petition Is Presented to the "Nine" of Siena

It is submitted in the presence of you, the Nine Lords Governors and Defenders of the commune and people of the city of Siena, and requested with the utmost urgency and devotion by many of your fellow citizens, that (remembering how our Lord, through the prayers and merits of blessed Ansano, patron of the said city, miraculously converted our forefathers, who

Translated from Archivio di Stato di Siena, Consiglio Generale 103, fols. 94v–97.

at the time were followers of the perfidy of the devil, to the faith and afterward delivered her from various perils), out of reverence for so great a saint, and as your predecessors have ordained in respect of several other saints, you should ordain that every year in perpetuity his holy solemnity [Ansano] should be devoutly celebrated in your city of Siena and that all citizens should cease from all servile labor. The *podestà* or vicar, the captain, the Lords Nine and each and every official of the commune should be obliged to venerate the blessed Ansano with fitting [candle] lights on his feast-day. The offerings which are then brought by the aforesaid officials should go to the officials of the Opera[1] of the glorious Virgin to be converted into ornaments for the saint's most blessed relics and otherwise as shall seem befitting to them and their councilors.

In response, the Nine put a proposal to the General Council which reproduced the petition almost word for word, with the following addition:

The lights, offerings, and expenses shall be in money of the commune of Siena and must not exceed the quantity or sum of £25 of Sienese pennies. And in order to meet the aforesaid expenses, the chamberlain and four overseers of the commune of Siena shall be bound every year in perpetuity to lay out the sum stated on the aforesaid lights. And whoever is the head of the Opera of Saint Mary shall, on taking up his office, swear on the holy gospels, physically touching the book, to expend that offering whole and entire and without any diminution and to convert it solely to the honor and adornment of the body of blessed Ansano, with the counsel and consent of the officials, the lords Nine, and four councillors of the aforesaid head of the Opera, every year, and not otherwise or in any other way. And every year he shall be bound to render account when he presents the accounts of the Opera of works of St. Mary.

2. 12 November 1328: The Consiglio Generale Resolves

that the Lords Nine may not go in person to any festival or send or offer any tapers, candles, offering of money, etc.

3. 16 February 1329: The Dominicans of Siena Submit a Petition

The prior and brethren of the convent of the Order of Preachers of Siena and also many men of the city of Siena reverently and humbly request that, as

Translated from Consiglio Generale 106, fols. 88–92.
Translated from Consiglio Generale 107, fols. 33r–v; printed in *AASS* Mar., vol. 3, 243.
1. This was the Office of Works, a body of laymen responsible for looking after the fabric and finance of the church.

your reverences well know, a certain ordinance has been made whereby it is provided that the office of the Lords Nine and the other officials of the said commune cannot go to any festival except according to the form of the statutes: which was and is, in truth, contrary to the mind and intention both of yourselves and of those who made that ordinance and of all Sienese, because, in fact, there is nothing in the statutes of the commune of Siena to say that the officials should go to any festival. Therefore, if they were to follow the new ordinance, the said officials could not go to the festivity of the blessed Virgin Mary in the month of August, nor to the feast of Sant'Ambrogio of Siena, as has been the custom for the last forty years and more. It is therefore clear that those who made the aforesaid new ordinance were contravening their own will and that of all Sienese, as they have openly said to us on several occasions, adding that they would never had made it if they had known or dreamed that it would in any way detract from the aforesaid festivals; for it was their belief, as they affirmed, that several statutes stated that the office of the Lords Nine and the other oft-mentioned officials should go to festivals and especially to the two above-mentioned; whereas in truth there is no statute which says anything on this subject, as was stated above. Furthermore, there is no city in Tuscany which does not have its own saint whom it venerates with some solemnity. And, as it is to be firmly hoped and believed that the veneration of the saints which has hitherto been performed in the city of Siena by the said commune and officials has conferred many benefits on the said commune, they beg and beseech as humbly as they may, for both the good and the honor of the aforesaid city, that you should present this petition to the General Council and propose in it that the said officials should and must go, as has hitherto been the custom, to the feast of Sant'Ambrogio, your most noble fellow citizen; whom you have known, whom you have heard, whom your hands have touched, through whom the words of eternal life were most abundantly manifested and expounded to this city.

4. On the Same Day the Franciscans Also Present a Petition

Another petition was presented to the said office of the Lords Nine, to the following effect: In the presence of you, the prudent Lords Nine, governors and defenders of the commune, people and city of Siena, it is set forth and related on behalf of the brethren and convent of the Friars Minor of Siena: that it is now a long time from the time the blessed Pier [Pettinaio] departed from the earth to heaven, that the office of the lords Nine and the other

Translated from Consiglio Generale 107 fol. 34; printed in *Miscellanea Francescana* 5 (1890): 52.

officials of the commune, in consideration of the merits of San Pier Pettinaio, and of his sanctity and the miracles, which the Heavenly Father publicly manifests on his behalf and wishing to do special honor to the Heavenly Father in his person, have been accustomed on the feast of that saint to go to the church of the aforementioned brethren and hear the divine office and there devoutly remain for the holy office. Wherefore, as blessed Pier was a native of this city, and because of his birth and natural love has a special care for the city and its citizens, and by his sanctity and merits, as we must believe, has obtained favors from God, and because the city will be the better safeguarded the more distinguished advocates it has with the supreme defender, that is God himself, and because it is to the honor of the city and its citizens that so great a saint came forth from among them, it is requested that in honor of the divine majesty and of San Pier aforesaid, this good and honorable custom should by some means become law and the due honor hitherto done to this saint should be increased and so that this increase may infallibly take place that it should please you to establish, by your own decree and also, if necessary, by decree of the Council of the Bell[2] of this commune, that the Lords Nine for the time being, with the lord *podestà* and the other officials of the city aforesaid shall be bound every year on the day of the feast of the aforementioned San Pier to go in the morning to hear the office at the church of blessed Francis and San Pier aforesaid, in the place of the said brothers, honorably as shall seem appropriate for such great magistrates. And that saint will be, as he is, forever a foremost advocate for the city with the Highest.

5. 20 February 1329: A Similar Petition Is Presented by the Augustinian Hermits

As it is well known to all Sienese that the blessed Agostino Novello of the said holy order, whose body is in the church of the said place in Siena, on account both of his sanctity and of the great love and affection which he had for the commune of Siena and every individual and person of that commune, is rightly to be honored by that commune, especially as it is to be believed, indeed held as a certainty, that he is constantly a great advocate in the heavenly court for the commune and city of Siena and its peaceful condition; as it is said that a certain ordinance was recently made in the commune of Siena, contrary to the intention and mind of the good men of the city, whereby the officials are prohibited from going to any feast except to those mentioned in

Translated from *Consiglio Generale* 107, fols. 39v–40; printed in André Vauchez, "La commune di Sienne, les Ordres Mendiants et le culte des saints, histoire et enseignements d'une crise (novembre 1328–avril 1329)," *Mélanges de l'école française de Rome* 899 (1977): 765–66.

2. The chief deliberative and legislative body of the commune.

the statutes, and the statutes make no mention of any feast, you are devoutly and humbly asked that, out of reverence for God and in consideration of the merits of the blessed Agostino aforementioned, the meaning of whose name is "increase," you should present or send this petition or put it before the General Council of the Bell, and have it proposed there that you and the other officials of the said commune, both present and future, may legitimately, notwithstanding any previous ordinance, visit that church for that feast and on any day of the feast of the blessed Agostino Novello, with that company and honors which shall seem most appropriate, so that almighty God, through the merits and prayers of the blessed Agostino aforesaid, may guard the commune of Siena against all adversities and preserve its peaceful state and increase and augment it from good to better.

6. 1337/9. Revised Statutes of Siena

Distinction 4, r. 31. That feasts should be honored by the commune.

The Lord Nine may not leave the palace in which they are for the time being resident unless in accordance with the preceding chapter. And if they or any one of them for any reason [other] than those stipulated in the said chapter should wish to leave the palace, it shall not be permitted unless on the advice and with express consent, by a two-thirds majority of a formal vote of the Lords Nine themselves and the officials of the commune, with this express prohibition, that neither they nor any one of them may go to any festival save the festival of the Blessed and Glorious Virgin in the month of August, on pain of [a fine of] £50 to be levied by the *podestà* from each person who so contravenes. Other festivities to which the Lords Nine have been accustomed to go shall be honored by the commune of Siena in this manner, to wit, that the rectors and all the foreign officials and all the magistrates of Siena, *except* the Lords Nine, shall go in the accustomed manner with the others, each year, to the feast of the blessed Ansano and to the feast of the blessed Ambrogio, accompanied by the members of the Council of the Bell and by other Sienese citizens who wish to accompany them. To other festivals which the Lords Nine used to attend there shall go only the chamberlain of the Biccherna[3] with a religious companion and the four overseers, each bearing his candle. And nevertheless, to all of these festivals, both of saints Ansano and Ambrogio and any others, six wax tapers of ten pounds weight each may be carried, in holders painted with the arms of the commune, at the expense

Translated from Archivio di Stato di Siena, Statuti 26, fol. 205r.
3. Chief financial office.

of the commune, to be left in the church in which the festival takes place, to give light to the Body of Our Lord Jesus Christ; and those in charge of this church must devote the said tapers to this purpose and if they do not do so that church shall be deprived of the tapers in perpetuity.

89. OPICINO DE CANISTRIS
CONFESSIONS OF A PARISH PRIEST (1336)

Translated from Latin by Victoria Morse

Opicino de Canistris (1296–ca. 1354) was a parish priest, manuscript illuminator, and religious writer from Pavia, a small city in Lombardy. Opicino wrote the auto-biographical notes translated here in Avignon, most likely in 1336, after he had fled Pavia for political reasons and had taken up the position of writing-clerk in the papal Penitentiary, the office that absolved penitents of those sins that only the pope could forgive. The work takes the form of notes entered into a circular calendar, surrounded by the symbols of the four evangelists, centered on a drawing of the Virgin Mary, and overlaid on a sketch map of northern Italy.[1] It is one drawing (fol. 11r) in a series of fifty-two, done in ink on parchment. The overall purpose of the manuscript has been debated, but it seems fundamentally to aim at making visible the structures of the Christian spiritual universe against the backdrop of the physical world, expressed by various forms of maps, calendars, and other schematic drawings. At a personal level, Opicino's autobiographical writings present him as a former sinner who was reformed by divine intervention; the illness recorded in the text translated here marks the beginning of this conversion experience.

The account of Opicino's life is sometimes cryptic, because he wrote not a con-nected narrative but rather a series of "entries" inserted into a temporal framework which often obscures connections and developments. In addition, he tended (like many contemporaries) to couch ideas in biblical phrases or the language of prophecy. Nevertheless, several dominant themes emerge. Crucial background to his life is the ongoing struggle between the Guelf and Ghibelline factions in northern Italy and especially the attempts of Ghibelline Milan, under the leadership of the Visconti family, to annex Pavia, which had been an independent city state until this period. Above all, however, Opicino was interested in tracing his development as a priest, and in doing so he offers a unique portrait of the education and concerns of a member of the parish clergy, a group notoriously difficult for modern historians to know except at the driest institutional level. In notes that should probably be under-stood more as a confession than as autobiography in the modern sense, Opicino recounted the stages of his education in the urban schools of Pavia and the nearby towns of Lomello, Bassignana, and (farther afield) Biella. He was especially con-cerned to explain the course of his education and eventual ordination to the priest-hood and how these were affected by his family's economic and political problems. This text underscores the importance, by the early fourteenth century, of schools run by individual masters where clerics and lay students alike would receive a basic education, although other evidence suggests that apprenticeship was also a common route to the priesthood. Singing was a crucial area of study, along with basic literacy

---

1. For this reason the formatting of the translation that follows has numerous breaks. These are maintained to enable the reader to perceive the original circular structure. The head-ings here are by Opicino.

[see #19, 102, 103] and, ideally, some knowledge of canon law [see #45, 46] and theology. Opicino's life shows the difficulty of keeping up such studies in the face of economic troubles. A boy normally could only be made a cleric if he had some guaranteed means of support; for Opicino this was originally his family patrimony. As the family's financial situation worsened, his education was frequently interrupted, and he worked at a number of different jobs to support himself and his family. Ultimately the canons of the cathedral had to support the final stages of his education, and he carefully noted his income as the rector of Santa Maria Cappella, which seems to have been quite low by contemporary standards. The political turmoil enveloping Pavia as Opicino grew up was an equal hindrance: he had to interrupt his studies as his family alternately fled and returned to Pavia, it made it impossible for him to receive holy orders in the diocese, and it generated a set of more nebulous concerns about the proper exercise of the priestly function in a city under interdict and politically at odds with the papacy.

Finally driven into permanent exile in 1328, Opicino joined a host of other poor clerics seeking papal support in Avignon. His spiritual writings, which he produced even during some of the most troubled years of his life, provided him with a means of winning the pope's favor and appointment to a position that supported him decently during the later years of his life.

1296   24 March   Conception in iniquity from a legitimate marriage.[2]
              December 24   Birth in sin at Lomello.

1297   1 January   Circumcision from my sins for the adoption of the son of God.[3]

              1 July   Circumcision from excesses according to the contents of nature.[4]

[1298–99: no entries]

1300   ca. 10 April   At the time when I cracked my forehead on a rock, I remember that I was nursed and weaned in Biella and opened my eyes to vanities and miseries. I remember that on returning home, I met people from France coming [to Rome] for the general indulgence[5] [see **#86**].

Translated from Opicino de Canistris, Autobiographical Notes, from his untitled manuscript Biblioteca Apostolica Vaticana, MS Pal. Lat. 1993, fol. 11r. Edited by Richard Salomon, *Opicinus de Canistris: Weltbild und Bekenntnisse eines avignonesischen Klerikers des 14. Jahrhunderts*, with additional material by A. Heimann and R. Krautheimer, Studies of the Warburg Institute 1a, 1b (London: Warburg Institute, 1936), 205–20. Corrections to the text made by the translator have been noted below. I have maintained Salomon's dating and layout of the entries, even though it not always clear that individual entries should be tied to the months Salomon indicates.

2. Cf. Psalm 50:7: "In iniquities I was conceived, and in sin my mother conceived me."
3. Baptism.
4. This passage is puzzling, but alludes to the circumcision of John the Baptist, which, according to Luke 1:59, was celebrated eight days after his birth on June 24.
5. This was the year of the Jubilee declared by Boniface VIII.

[1301: no entry]

1302 (January) In this year Christ the Lord was shown to me crucified by my grandmother, in order that I might believe that he was the true lord, and from then on I have never believed otherwise.

BOYHOOD

1303 (January) I was told the time of my age, on what day and at what hour I was born. Since I was forced to attend the schools, I was able to learn nothing.

1304 (January) Sent back to Biella and forced to return to the schools, I barely learned to read or sound out words.
    (End of April) I played childishly with my younger sister, although I ought to have been rebuked. In that place [Biella] I was confirmed with her by the bishop of Vercelli.

1305 (January) When I returned home [to Pavia], my intellect was wondrously opened—which would have been unbelievable to many people, if there had not been witnesses. Yet I still was learning against my will.
    (End of April) I was not able to resist childish vices, and I liked the leisure of feast days better than studying my letters.
    11 November The adversity of my house began in Biella.

1306 (January) I began to understand how the years of the Lord should be computed.
    2 September I was made a cleric by our bishop solely on the basis of my patrimony.

1307 (January) I was admonished in a dream to study harder.
    mid-February I changed masters many times. At that time I heard hardly anyone swearing by the body or blood of Christ, as thousands do now each day in vain. Already at that time, they were beginning to consider Christ's gospels worthless, so that they inclined me little by little to utter so great a sacrilege.[6]
    (October) We were transferred to the town of Bassignana.
    11 November I was sent to a school of grammar at Lomello.

1308 I changed to the school of this same master in Bassignana. There, because I learned miraculously without effort and was compelled to teach others, I devoted more attention to drawing images.

---

  6. In a note at the margin, Opicino clarifies that he (and others) began to swear by the Gospels.

1309   Mid-February   At this time I began for the first time to go to con-
            fession with shame.
            (May)   In the town of Bassignana, I heard for the first time the
            modern diabolical names of the factions, which were named differ-
            ently at that time.[7]

1310   22 August   Near the town of Bassignana I was placed for a time in
            charge of the tolls from the bridge over the Po river.
            (October)   I was sent back to the school of this same master in
            Pavia, our hometown.

ADOLESCENCE

1311   (May)   I was sent to the school for writing, of which art I have
            retained a modest amount.
            1 June   A great conflict arose in the city when the Emperor Henry
            [VII] was near Brescia.[8] As my age increased, so did my wickedness;
            I was already bound by many vices.
            (October)   I was sent back to the town of Bassignana, when the
            emperor returned to Pavia.[9]
            Beg. of November   I returned to Pavia, having been sick for three
            months with a quartan fever.

1312   (January)   I was sent to the school of another master in grammar
            and logic.

1313   May   I was sent to school for singing, not voluntarily but against
            my will, and therefore I took little care over this art.

1314   Mid-February   At this time, since merciful judgment upon my
            house grew strong, I was forced to leave the schools entirely.
            May   I heard a little of the art of medicine [see #77]. Many times
            I was sent during the night to guard the city walls [see #14.4],
            Beg. July   I began to teach the son of a certain count from Ger-
            many who was captive there [in Pavia] with his father.
            15 August   At this time I was forced to stay with the wife of the
            then lord of this city who was a captive in Milan to teach their
            daughters letters, and I made very little progress with them. Will-
            ingly,

1315   (January)   Out of my zeal for the wretched faction which is called

    7. This may refer to the gradual adoption of the terms Guelf and Ghibelline in place of
more local names for the factions.
    8. Siege of Brescia, 19 May–5 September.
    9. 6–15 October 1311.

"the church faction," I involved myself knowingly in many illicit activities but stopped short of bloodshed and sacrilegious blows. Although some of them were excommunicate and all were under interdict, I associated with them except in crime.

(May)   I began to learn the art of playing musical instruments for the purpose of instructing these daughters. I learned a modest amount, I profited them very little.

8 October   When the city was captured by the opposing faction, after I accompanied that lady on that night in secret to [the monastery of Santa Maria de] Josapath, I never saw her or her children again. I remained with another lord.

1316   18 January   I journeyed to the city of Genoa with my entire house, some members sooner, some later. I stayed for a modest time with someone to instruct their children.

End of April   For several months I lived with a certain master in the grammatical arts for a share of the profit.

June   I was still struggling with the flesh; many times I was conquered with my own consent.

8 July   Outside the adversity of my house was increasing.

3 September   A definition of the last judgment was revealed to me in my dreams. From that time on the mercy of the Lord began to restrain me from vices. I began to learn how to illuminate books for my own sustenance and that of my family. Amid the labors of this job I snatched moments to study the theological books that I received for illumination.

1317   (January)   Little by little I gathered the spirit of the divine words to my memory. Already at this time in that peaceful Genoa, I had cast our diabolical factions into oblivion.

5 May   My brother, a very simple fellow not yet at puberty, was killed by accident. I was patient, I moved on easily.

3 September   Everything went wrong in my father's hands, both in his person and in his affairs.

26 October   When my father died, I perhaps would have bound myself to the religious life with my brothers, if an alien country had not restrained me with affection for my widowed mother.

1318   (January)   From that day on I began to open my inner eyes to the reason of the faith.

11 April   I returned from Genoa to Pavia with my mother, brother, and my sisters, from adversity to adversity. I found my homeland

bound by sentences of excommunication and interdict, just as it still is.[10] During this twofold adversity in both my homeland and my affairs, I lived by the labor of my hands and was comforted internally in spirit. Little by little I began to say the hours of the Blessed Virgin Mary.

October   I was promoted while still a simple cleric to a chaplaincy in the cathedral church. There I was received as a pauper and, supported by the lords [the canons], I learned the office of this church. In vain I went to Milan to receive orders.

1319   January   I would not have been able to live on the income that I was to receive without the support of the lords. I began to hear decretals [study canon law] in Pavia

2/3 March   I received the four minor orders in Bologna from its bishop.

End of March   I received the subdiaconate and the diaconate from the bishop of Bobbio between Milan and Lodi.

(May)   When I heard the decretals, I understood almost nothing except the divine things.

27 May   I first sang the Gospel.[11]

15 August   I sang the Gospel a second time.

2 December   I began the *Book in Verse on the Parables of Christ*. End of December/

1320   (January)   I went in vain to Milan to be ordained priest.

27 February   I was transferred to the diocese of Piacenza for the occasion, and I received the priesthood in Parma through its bishop.

30 March   I sang my first mass in the church of Pavia. I began to baptize.

(July)   I published my *Treatise on the Ten Commandments*, amid the labors of my hands by which I was living. . . . [12]

YOUTH

1321   (October)   Sometimes I learned decretals, sometimes theology more by listening than by reading. My conscience began to be plagued by many inextricable scruples which would continue for many years. Nonetheless, I continued in my divine studies.

10. The details of Pavia's interdict remain somewhat unclear; the city's final absolution did not take place until 1341.

11. To sing the Gospel was one of the duties of a deacon.

12. I have omitted a short section on the technicalities of the interdict.

1322	(January) I was busy with many treatises on divine matters.

8 October   While passing through Pavia, Fra Agostino [Gazotto] of the order of Preachers, the most pious man, having been transferred from the bishopric of Zagreb to that of Lucera, saw and admonished me with the greatest kindness and praised works of my writing.

1323   5 February   I received the care of another's parish for a time with a license but without income.

21 October   I was elected to the chaplaincy of San Rafaelo in the church of San Giovanni in Borgo, which I renounced after a short time. I was elected to the parish of Santa Maria Capella and, once confirmed by order of the bishop, I entered into my office. At first, I began to preach there immediately. In this church I found many contradictions, on account of which I wounded my conscience sometimes out of ignorance, sometimes violently, sometimes out of fear. Truly it would take too long to speak of these things. Meanwhile I thought about divine matters and wrote many books and treatises. From the income of this church I never received more than ten or eight florins, since I had no church except that one. I completed the *Book on the Lord's Passion According to the Four Evangelists* and thought much about that material.

[1325–27: no entries]

1328   11 July   I left Pavia, went to Tortona, then Valenza and Alexandria; I stayed for a time in Valenza.[13]

3 August   On this day I was judged to be dead on account of illness. I recovered. Supported like a pauper, I preached in Valenza and learned the sacraments, some of which I did not know because of the sentence of our interdict.

1329   (January)   In Valenza, I compiled a small work on the poverty of Christ. I published a small book in meter on the virtues of Christ.

mid-February   I corrected the small work on the poverty of Christ; I finished the *Lamentations of the Virgin Mary.*

April   I first came to Avignon in tremendous poverty. For a month I worked on the illumination of a book of a certain protonotary of the pope. After that I begged with the poor clerics. (June) After a general absolution by the penitentiaries, Pope John XXII received

---

13. These were nearby towns in the hands of the papal forces fighting against the Ghibelline powers of northern Italy.

and saw the aforementioned book, although he did not know I was present.

(3 June)   He provided for me.[14] I returned to Valenza with the *Book on the Preeminence of Spiritual Rule* which I had already started in Avignon.[15]

8 September   I completed that second book of [spiritual] rule.

September End   I returned again to the curia.

10 October   I appeared before the lord pope, who looked upon me kindly.

24 October   On this day I transcribed the corrected copy of this book, which I had promised to give to the lord pope. He again provided for me in the future. Amid the strains of poverty, after the aforementioned absolutions [earlier in 1329] my conscience became much more subtle.[16]

PERFECT AGE

1330   (January)   Since affliction was piled upon affliction, I abstained entirely from divine offices, since I received nothing from the Penitentiaries nor from the Major Penitentiary.

5 March   Finally, after some difficulties, I was absolved by the chamberlain of the Lord Pope. In the meantime I completed a *Treatise on the Lord's Prayer*.

(May)   Several times I had supplications carried to the Lord Pope and several times he ordered that I appear before him, but nothing was done about it. I was present three times at masses and sermons of the Lord Pope in the cathedral at different times.

24 August   I made a brief [written] confession of my sins.

13 September   In a dream, I saw a terrifying vision of the sacrament of the eucharist. I wrote the *Book Describing Pavia*. In the midst of my distress, the Lord Pope received the *Book on the Preeminence of Spiritual Rule* which I sent to him.

14. The pope granted him the future expectation of a benefice in Pavia, but no immediate income.

15. This work is extant and has been partially published in *Unbekannte kirchenpolitische Streitschriften aus der Zeit Ludwigs des Bayern (1327–1354)*, ed. Richard Scholz, vol. 2 (Rome: Loescher, 1914), 89–104.

16. Opicino never explains what sin he had committed that necessitated absolution by the Penitentiary. Comments in one of his other works suggest that he may have committed simony by complying with local custom and making a payment upon taking up his benefice in Pavia.

4 December   The Lord Pope provided me with my present office [as a writing-clerk in the Penitentiary]. It came into my heart

1331   (January)   to make images of the ecclesiastical hierarchy. When I was received in the writing office [of the Penitentiary] an accusation was raised against me. The same thing happened, in Pavia, to my younger sister concerning her reception in a noble monastery to which the Lord Pope had provided her. For my case there were about fourteen witnesses. For several years this case was maintained against me with scarcely a break except perhaps for a three-year period. Anything that I acquire beyond decent food and clothing I spend on this kind of business. Aside from my position I have no other patrimony. I have only a poor parish: when I was resident there I repeatedly suffered Egyptian servitude; in absentia I receive nothing, but it provides for a certain vicar in my stead. My sister, fearing to enter the monastery from which she was blocked, was received into another with no charge.

1332   12 November   I completed the *Book of the Seven Prayers of the Virgin Mary*.

1333   1 February   I finished the *Book of the Promotions of the Virgin Mary*.

1334   17 January   In obedience to the Lord Pope, I worked at his palace for a month with my colleagues.

31 March   On this day came the illness. After I had received the necessary sacraments, I lay as if dead for a third of the month. Coming back to life, I found myself paralyzed in my limbs. I believe that I improved because of the testimony of obedience to the keys [of Saint Peter].

3 June   On this day, after vespers, I saw with my servant a certain vase in the clouds.[17] I was still mute and weak on my right [side] from the illness and I miraculously lost a large part of my literal memory.

15 August   On this night, I saw in my sleep the Virgin Mary sitting sadly on the ground with her son in her lap. After this tribulation, she restored to me through her merits as to Job from the loss of spiritual wealth which I had prodigally dissipated from adolescence not more letters but double the spirit.

4 December   On this day Pope John XXII passed away.

17. This vision refers to that in Acts 10:11.

THE YEAR OF EXPECTATION[18]

1335   8 January   Consecration of the Lord Pope Benedict XII.

1 February   From this time on I gradually turned aside from our office because of the weakness of our right hand which was, in spiritual work, stronger than before. From this time on, I made all these images with this right hand without any human aid.

25 April   My mother passed from this world.

20 May   My true weaning: when I learned of my mother's death.

18 December   The Lord Pope

THE YEAR OF RETRIBUTION

1336   (January)   Benedict XII justly and fittingly suspended us from our vain expectation.[19]

1 March   The first complaint against me has been once again revived and truly burdens me with expenses.

(May)   Although my literal knowledge has been lost, spiritual knowledge was restored to me twice over. My right hand is weak in temporal affairs, but strong in spiritual ones.

1 June   On this day the work of this vessel has been completed.

One of the marginal notes continues Opicino's assessment of his spiritual development and its relationship to his early education.

After I had been made a cleric without the title of a church and with only a secular patrimony, I lived in secular fashion among secular concerns. Had the grace of God not withdrawn me from them, I would have remained in these miseries. I became accustomed to lies. I never took pleasure in the divine offices. Gradually I began to go to listen to preaching and I willingly heard about the divine scriptures from the secular masters in the schools. I felt distaste for grammar and greater boredom for logic. I took pleasure in learning the art of composing letters with masters and especially in verses and rhythms without masters. Likewise, I took pleasure in hearing fables, in reciting them, in reading in books in the Italian and French vernacular, and in translating into these idioms from Latin letters.

18. The initial "headings" refer to the standard ages of human life, but the last two appear to be inventions of Opicino's, referring to the events of his life.

19. Benedict canceled the expected benefices granted by his predecessor.

SECTION TEN

Marriage, Family, and Children

The history of Italy, in both legend and fact, is often told through the stories of families: from the Caesars of ancient Rome, to the Medici of Renaissance Florence, to the Sicilian mafia of Godfather fame. The family is a fundamental social unit the study of which not only has an intrinsic value, but is also central to the understanding of larger economic, political, cultural, and religious developments.

The texts in this section reveal the concerns and complexities of families in medieval Italy, and the sources that historians are currently using to unravel webs of kinship. Scholars of the medieval Italian family demonstrate how kinship relations could be the nexus for marriage alliances, the multigenerational transmission of power, and the manipulation of claims of loyalty, property, and marriage. Of major interest is the emphasis on the patrilineage and the consequent effective disinheritance of women. Issues treated here include inheritance practices, marriage and dowry customs, concerns about consanguinity, fertility, affective ties, and childrearing. The texts also raise questions about the legal position of women, the jurisdiction in defining a family unit (church or government), and family strategies employed in response to demographic and economic change. Furthermore, the texts demonstrate a shared concern over the preservation of family honor. Anything that might potentially tarnish family reputation, such as adultery or illegitimacy, earns sharp rebuke or penalty for its clouding of the blood line.

90. FAMILY AND MARRIAGE IN LOMBARD SALERNO THREE TEXTS (1008–78)

Translated from Latin by Valerie Ramseyer

The following charters show us a number of laws and customs relating to marriage and the legal status of women in southern Italy. First of all, they demonstrate that Lombard women were always under the protection of men, generally close relatives such as fathers, husbands, or brothers. When Lombard women appeared in legal documents, they did so in the presence of and with the permission of their mundual-dus, *a male who acted as their legal guardian. Second, the charters describe the tradition of the morning gift (*morgengabe*), a Lombard custom in which husbands gave their wives one-fourth of all their possessions, present and future, on the morning after the nuptials. The husband was also required to treat his wife justly and take good care of her, or pay a hefty fine to her male relatives. Notice, too, that two different legal traditions existed in the Principality of Salerno: some people lived under Roman law, and others under Lombard law, although overlap between the two traditions was common. Under Roman law women did not need guardians, nor did they receive the* morgengabe.

1. Betrothal Contract

September 1008

In the name of the Lord, in the twentieth year of the reign of our lord the glorious prince Guaimarius [III], in the month of September, in the seventh year of the indiction. I, Falcus son of Maraldus, before the witnesses whose signatures appear at the end of the document, declare that I received a pledge from Balsamus, with the permission of his father Rinardus, that he [Balsamus] would take my sister, Gemma, as his lawful wife and that on the day after the nuptials, he would give to her in writing the *morgengabe*, which is one-fourth of all his possessions, as required by the law and custom of the Lombard people who [always] give [the *morgengabe*] to their wives on the day after the nuptials. If, on that day, he does not give a written agreement [of the *morgengabe*] to my sister, or if he does not want to take her as his lawful wife, he must pay me one hundred gold Constantinian *solidi* and then, by compulsion, he will nonetheless take [Gemma] as his lawful wife and give her the *morgengabe*. He also pledged never to mistreat her, and to keep and take care of her according to his means. If he is ever suspected of mistreating her, and is accused [of doing so] by us, and if he then refuses to take an oath

Translated from the original, Archives of the Abbey of the Holy Trinity of Cava, Arca V, 107; Edition: *Codex Diplomaticus Cavensis*, ed. Michele Morcaldi, Mauro Schiani, and Silvano de Stefano (Naples: P. Piazza/H. Hoepli, 1873–93), vol. 4, 609.

[denying the charges] with his relatives, as required by law, in a place where we have prepared the gospels, he will be obliged to pay to us or whoever appears with this charter in hand fifty gold Constantinian *solidi*, and he will then be compelled to keep her and take good care of her according to his means just as he promised. . . . In addition, with this pledge, Balsamus promised that if my sister is ever seized by anyone whosoever, and is taken outside the city or its walls, he will be required to pay two-thirds of whatever ransom we must pay to get her back, and we will pay the other one-third. And with the greatest of vigilance he will search for her throughout Italy in order to pay [the ransom] and bring her home. If he does not want to pay [her ransom], he is obliged to give me and my heirs thirty gold Constantinian *solidi* and then by compulsion to pay her ransom and bring her back. But if he is unable to find her or is unable to pay the ransom requested, in such a case he must swear before us as required by law that he wanted to pay the ransom to get her back but was unable to do so, and then he will be absolved of any wrongdoing and he will return to us the money that we had given him [for the ransom]. If Balsamus does not fulfill the terms (of this agreement), or if he goes against it in any way, with his pledge he is obliged to pay to me and my heirs, or whomever appears with this charter in hand, twenty gold Constantinian *solidi* and afterward he must fulfill the terms. Balsamus pledged to uphold everything written above, and he named Maraldus son of Maraldus as his guarantor.

I, the notary Roderissus, was present and wrote this charter
Witnessed by Iaquintus a priest and Mirandus

2. *Morgengabe* and *Mundium*

May 1026

In the name of the Lord, in the thirty-eighth year of the reign of our lord Guaimarius [III], and in the eighth year of the reign of his son lord Guaimarius [IV], both glorious princes, in the month of May, in the ninth year of the indiction. I, a woman by the name of Alferada, daughter of Roccus and wife of Sesamus son of John, declare that my husband, with a written charter, sold to a woman by the name of Tanda daughter of John "Atrianense" and wife of Leone son of Sergio "Mangnanarum" two pieces of land with vines in Giovi, which he got from my father Roccus; and the [two pieces of land] have the following borders and measurements [description of prop-

Translated from *Codex Diplomaticus Cavensis*, ed. Michele Morcaldi, Mauro Schiani, and Silvano de Stefano (Naples: P. Piazza/H. Hoepli, 1873–93), vol. 5, 782.

erty's borders]. . . . And my husband sold to Tanda both these pieces of land, as described above, along with their roads and springs, and he did so in such a way that she can do with the land as she pleases. Of this property, one-fourth pertains to me as my *morgengabe*, as seen in the *morgengabe* agreement that my husband had written down. I thus hereby agree to confer upon Tanda all of my one-fourth. So I, Alferada, of my own free will, before the witnesses whose signatures are found at the end of the document, and with the consent and free will of my husband under whose protection [*mundium*] I am placed, agree to give to you [Tanda] all of the one-fourth that pertains to me of this property. And no part of the property as described above, neither the appurtenances, nor the roads, nor the springs will remain to me, but instead will belong to you and your heirs forever, firmly and securely, to have, possess, and utilize and to do with as you like. To cement this gift, I received from you [Tanda], with your husband present, in accordance with Lombard law, a countergift [*launegilt*] in the form of a tunic; and with this payment, and according to the law and custom of you Romans, and as prescribed among us by the *launegilt* [this agreement was executed], just as agreed upon by us. I, Alferada, along with my husband, by common consent gave a pledge to you, and we named ourselves as our own guarantors. And with this pledge we promise to pay a fine of ten gold Constantinian *solidi* [if we do not uphold the agreement.] And we asked the notary Rodelgrimus to write this [charter] for you. Enacted at Salerno. Witnessed by the notary John and the notary Alderissus.

3. Domestic Abuse

July 1078

In the name of God Eternal and our Savior Jesus Christ. In the 1079th year since the incarnation, in the time of our lord the most glorious duke Robert [Guiscard], in the month of July, in the second year of the indiction. Before me, Sico, a count and judge, were present John a notary son of Pandone, and John son of Ursus "Atrianese" who is called "Infresatore." And in the hand of John the notary was a document written by John the notary as follows:

In the 1078th year since the incarnation of the Lord, in the time of our lord Robert [Guiscard], in the month of August, in the first year of the indiction.

Translated from *Codex Diplomaticus Cavensis*, ed. Simeone Leone and Giovanni Vitolo (Cava dei Tirreni: Badia di Cava, 1984–90), vol. 10, 102, 118.

Before me [Sico count and judge] John son of Ursus "Atrianese" gave a
pledge to Sergio, son of Maurus "Atrianese," naming John "Atrianese" son
of Constantine, son of Count Marinus, most faithfully as his guarantor. And
with this pledge he agreed to take Anna daughter of the above-mentioned
Maurus as his lawful wife and to give to her, in writing, one-fourth of everything he owned and would in the future own, both landed and movable
wealth, and Anna would be free to do what she wanted with it according to
the law. He promised to provide Anna with a quiet and peaceful life with him
and to take good care of her, just as other men like him take good care of
their wives. He promised never to mistreat her, and if he mistreated her and
was compelled by Sergio or his heirs or whoever appeared with this charter
in hand to come to a place where the Gospels were prepared, and if then he
refused to swear on the bible that he did not mistreat her, in accordance with
the law, each and every time it occurred, he would be required to pay to
Sergio or his heir or whoever appeared with this charter in hand twenty gold
Constantinian *solidi*. . . .

After this document was shown, John the notary and John son of Ursus said
that John the notary a few days ago had accused John son of Ursus of having
mistreated his wife Anna and that John son of Ursus had not dared to swear
[to the contrary] as required by the above-mentioned document. Thus John
son of Ursus owed John the notary twenty gold Constantinian *solidi*; however, he did not have the money to pay him as agreed. So instead John son
of Ursus handed over with this charter to John the notary, whose wife Mucza
is Anna's sister, his portion of the land that Constantina daughter of John
"Atrianese" wife of Iaquintus son of Peter had sold to John and his brothers
Sergio and Constantine . . . , as well as all of the land that he owned outside
the city [of Salerno] in the locations of Troccle, which is also called Gattu-
mortu, and Transboneis . . . (John son of Ursus then showed a number of
charters relating to the property.) And this land will always be in the power
of John son of Pandone and his heirs and they can do with it what they want.
This [John] son of Ursus gave his pledge to this [John] son of Pandone, and
most faithfully named John son of Constantine son of Count Marinus as his
guarantor, and by this pledge [John] the son of Ursus obliged himself and
his heirs to always defend the land for [John] the son of Pandone and his
heirs against others. He [John son of Ursus] also gave permission to [John]
son of Pandone and his heirs that whenever they wanted they would have the
power to protect their land, however they wished, with the rights and charters shown above. If John son of Ursus and his heirs do not fulfill their pledge
or if they presume to renege on it or contradict it in any way, then John and

his heirs will be required to pay to John son of Pandone and his heirs one hundred gold Constantinian *solidi* and afterward to fulfill [the agreement] as written above.

And I, Sico the judge, asked you, John the notary, to write this [charter]
Signed by Sico the judge.

91. GEOFFREY MALATERRA ON THE MARRIAGE OF MATILDA AND RAYMOND OF TOULOUSE TWO TEXTS (ca. 1080)

Translated from Latin by G. A. Loud

Geoffrey Malaterra's The Deeds of Count Roger of Sicily *was completed between 1098 and the count's death in 1101. It is our principal contemporary source for the Norman conquest of Calabria in the 1050s and of the island of Sicily in the years between 1061 and 1091. The author was a monk of the abbey of Sant'Agatha in Catania, founded by Count Roger (d. 1101) in or about 1091. It is not surprising, therefore, that his account took a very favorable view of the count, and especially praised him for his* strenuitas—*a Latin word which implies bravery, and also determination and persistence—it is here translated as "valor." The account below is a romanticized and literary one, with much stress on "love," but it reveals something of how a diplomatic marriage was negotiated in the Middle Ages. From the point of view of Count Roger, a marriage between his daughter and an important French territorial ruler marked a significant step along the road to achieving respectability for a man who had begun his career as a warlord with little more than a sword and a strong right arm to his name. In fact, Matilda died childless, and subsequently, in 1094, Raymond IV married a daughter of King Alfonso VI of Castile. However, Roger was subsequently able to marry other daughters to the sons of the German emperor and the king of Hungary, showing that he had become a figure of major importance in late eleventh-century Christendom.*

1. Prose and Poetry on the Marriage of Matilda of Sicily and Raymond of Provence

Meanwhile, news of the reputation for valor of Count Roger of the Sicilians came to the celebrated Count Raymond of Provence [later count of Toulouse]. Hearing of this, he [Raymond] sent envoys of a rank suitable for such an important matter to this great prince, asking that he might be joined in marriage to Matilda, the count's daughter by his first wife, a young but very beautiful girl. The count acceded to this request, and the agreement was subsequently confirmed by oaths from both parties. Once the nuptial day was decided, the count rewarded the envoys who had come with many gifts, as was the custom. They then made a speedy return to their lord and informed him that his request had been granted. He was extremely pleased by this, for the tidings of her beauty which he had heard from them left him burning

Translated from Gaufredus Malaterra, *De rebus gestis Rogerii Calabriae et Siciliae comitis,* ed. Ernesto Pontieri, *RIS²,* V(i) (Bologna: Zanichelli, 1927–28), book III, chaps. 22–23, 70–71.

with love and desire for her—and when he was informed of the date for their marriage he was at pains to bring forward the day of his departure for Sicily.

On his arrival the count [Roger] received him with proper ceremony. The agreements were renewed and the girl's dowry was recorded in a chirograph document.[1] The betrothal was celebrated in the presence of bishops from both parties, with prayers by the bishops and holy and catholic rites. The bond between the young man and woman developed little by little, and then (as is customary) grew immeasurably after their first night together.

The marriage was celebrated with elaborate and costly ceremonies, and afterwards the bride's father kept his son-in-law with him for quite some time. But eventually he showed his affection with generous gifts, as the occasion demanded, both to him and to those who accompanied him, one for each of them according to what he knew of their rank, and with the ships now ready and the sea calm, he took leave of him and his daughter. With sails very carefully set and a following wind, they quickly returned whence they had come, taking the bride with them.

Geoffrey then, as he often did, moved into verse. One suspects that he did this more to show his mastery of different literary styles than for any other purpose—he used a variety of different meters for the various poems in his work.

> The daughter forsook her father, and was not ashamed to leave her mother;
> She delights in her union with a foreign count.
> She leaves the land where she was raised and somewhere else gains her,
> Many mothers suffer this fate when their daughters grow up,
> Nor is the one who has been
> Brought up gone into the possession of a friendly relative.
> She is now under the authority of a foreigner rather than her father.
> Neither do I condemn this overmuch, although I portray such things;
> Nor do I avoid it by omission, since she does this joined to a husband
> [Whom] she loves and by entering into a fair and charming agreement.
> For those whom the law has joined, no sentence can put asunder:
> That issue should grow, because by not doing this the race would perish.
> A virgin is given forth and joined to her first man,
> By such an event two may become as one flesh.
> Divine law orders this, not anything strange.
> Scripture shows us those things which the future brings:
> She who is joined as a wife in a stronger love
> Thinks less of her father—she even thinks less of her mother,
> Hence the lineage is preserved by this law of marriage.

1. A chirograph was a sheet of parchment on which two copies of the same document were written, one for each of the two parties to the agreement. The parchment was then cut, irregularly, to separate the two copies. The irregularity was so that, in case fraud was suspected, the two copies could then be fitted together to check their authenticity.

2. Geoffrey Malaterra on the Grief of Count Roger of Sicily on the Death of His Son Jordan, and Then the Joy That Followed the Birth of Another Son, Simon

Despite two marriages, Count Roger lacked a legitimate male heir, and thus it was assumed that his illegitimate son Jordan, who had been his chief lieutenant in the later stages of the conquest of Sicily, would be his heir—though Malaterra is clear that he had not been formally designated as such. However, Jordan died in September 1092. Finally, in 1093/4 the problem of the succession was solved when Roger had a son by his third wife, Adelaide of Savona, whose birth prompted Geoffrey once again to turn to verse in celebration. (This son Simon succeeded his father when the latter died in 1101, but himself died at the age of eleven or twelve in 1105, and the eventual ruler of the county was Roger's second son by Adelaide, Roger II, born probably in 1096 and from 1130 the first king of Sicily.)

The count's son Jordan was popular with everyone because of his valor, and many people conjectured that he was the count's heir, since Geoffrey had been afflicted by leprosy, and the count had no other male child. But he was struck down by a fever at Syracuse, a city under his jurisdiction. When his father was told about this, he hastened to get there before he died, but the disease grew worse, and Jordan's last moment arrived faster than did his father.

The count entered the city, and as he saw his son's funeral rites he was seized with unbearable sadness. All those who were with him shared his grief and broke into tearful lamentation. Many were moved to tears much more by the father's grief than by Jordan's death. The whole city resounded to tearful wailing, to such an extent that it caused tears even among the Saracens, the enemies of our race, not indeed out of real love, but rather because of kindly emotions stirred when they saw the sadness afflicting our people. . . .

> Deprived of his son by mortal illness, the bereaved father,
> Lest he lament, lacking the joy of parenthood,
> Is blessed with an offspring. As if blooming by heavenly provision
> The mother's joyful womb is made fruitful, swells, and becomes heavy:
> The child grows as the birth approaches.
> Father and Mother both pray to God that it will be a boy.
> While his seed is growing, he makes all sorts of vows.
> Let the fetus now be safe within the mother's belly!
> After nine months of expectancy, the womb hastens to give fruit.
> A child is plucked forth: nobody is sad, all are joyful.
> The nurses are happy at the breaking of the waters.

Translated from Gaufredus Malaterra, *De rebus gestis Rogerii Calabriae et Siciliae comitis*, ed. Ernesto Pontieri, *RIS²*, V(i) (Bologna: Zanichelli 1927–28), book IV, chaps. 18–19, 97–98.

The announcement that a boy is born brings forth new joy!
The mother hears it and rejoices, there is no need for sorrow;
They hasten and announce the joyful news to the happy father!
Who claps his hands, rejoicing that his prayers are answered.
He grants requests, and rewards the messenger with rich presents,
He orders more such gifts, and is pleased to be generous to the poor.
Let the pain of death, once heavy and strong, from the loss of a son
Be softened and forgotten by hope with this joyful birth.
At the font, as his brow is anointed with chrism, he is named Simon,
The count has an heir: a future duke is furnished for Sicily,
The Calabrians choose for themselves to be subject to his sword.
And since it is given to him to be a father, he fulfills his every vow.

92. FREDERICK II'S LEGISLATION ON ADULTERY AND PROSTITUTION (1231)

Translated from Latin by James M. Powell

Like King Roger II and the Emperor Justinian before him, Frederick II in 1231 promulgated a law code (the Liber Augustalis*) in which the subjects of adultery and prostitution were addressed. However, as the following examples suggest, Frederick II was not concerned about female morality or family legitimacy. In the case of his adultery legislation—borrowed from his predecessor King William of Sicily— Frederick aimed to distinguish between secular and ecclesiastical jurisdiction in the judgment of such cases. With respect to madams, Frederick elaborated Roger II's laws [see #47] by imposing harsher punishments on madams who particularly exploited women living without benefit of a guardian. Finally, in his legislation about a mother who prostitutes her daughter, again elaborating Roger II's prior law, Frederick proposed a more sympathetic understanding of the reasons why a woman might allow herself to be exploited in such a way. (JD)*

TITLE LXXXIII (60)

How adulteries should be corrected

[King William]

The complaints of some of the prelates of our kingdom have informed our majesty that their churches are being deprived and suffering a loss in their rights over adulteries, which the justiciars, chamberlains, and bailiffs of our kingdom do not permit to be judged in the church court as they should and about the persons of clerics whom they judge and jail like laymen. If this is true, it appears serious and displeases us. For it is not suitable, and we do not desire, that those matters that should be judged and corrected in the church should be punished or judged and corrected by others. Therefore, we order and firmly command that from now on justiciars, chamberlains, and bailiffs should not become involved in the judgments of those tried for adulteries. But if anyone from the parish of some church has been accused or has been caught in the act of adultery, he should stand for the judgment of the church in which these adulteries should be judged, and he should be judged and corrected by the court of that church, unless the adultery was committed with insult and violence. But if this happens, he should be judged by the church whose judging belongs to the church. Whatever belongs in a secular court, that is, insult and violence, should be judged in our court. In addition,

Translated and adapted from *Liber Augustalis* or *Constitutions of Melfi Promulgated by the Emperor Frederick II for the Kingdom of Sicily in 1231*, Book 3, trans. James M. Powell (Syracuse, N.Y.: Syracuse University Press, 1971), 147–48.

we order that all our officials should provide aid for the correction of adulteries to all prelates who have need.

LXXXIV (61)

About madams

[The Emperor Frederick]

We order that madams, who solicit the shame of wives, daughters, sisters, and finally all virgins and honest women that some good man has inside the walls of his house, should be punished by the slitting of their noses as are adulteresses according to the statutes of our grandfather of divine memory, King Roger. But we order that those who attract the minds of women, who, since they have lived freely and were under no one's protection, have given themselves to the wills and pleasures of men at any time (though it is, not really believable that they would desire to give themselves for the first time), should be beaten after they have been convicted by legitimate proof of committing such acts, and they should be marked on the forehead in recognition of the crime they have attempted. Such madams should know for sure that if they attempt to repeat what they have done again, they will certainly and without doubt be subjected to the slitting of their noses.

TITLE LXXXV (62)

About the penalty for a mother who prostitutes her daughter publicly

[The same Augustus]

We order that mothers who publicly prostitute daughters should be subject to the penalty of having their noses slit, which was established by the divine King Roger. But we believe that it is not only unjust but cruel for other mothers, who give their consent, and for their daughters, who may not be able to marry a husband because of their poverty but who also cannot even sustain life, to be subject to this penalty when they expose themselves to the pleasures of some man who gives them sustenance for life and other favors.

93. THE *CUSTOMS OF SALERNO* ON DOWRIES (1251)

Translated from Latin by Joanna Drell

The Customs of Salerno is the earliest extant customary tract from southern Italy, dating from 1251. Other tracts exist from Naples, Amalfi, Gaeta, and Benevento. Most customary tracts treat comparable issues, including marriage, dowries, and inheritance. Differences seem to stem from diverse local traditions, making the tracts valuable indicators of civic consciousness and regional identity. The Salerno Customs reflect but do not necessarily repeat Lombard practice, despite the fact that this period witnessed the revival of Roman law. In the Principality of Salerno charters dating back several centuries attest to the influence of the Customs, with explicit reference to acts completed "according to the customs of Salerno." The excerpts that follow are distinctive in that they distinguish between dowries and marriage gifts, or reverse dowries, among people from different social classes. For example, wealthy women are provided with sheets made from more costly fabrics than are other women. Furthermore, the text expresses a fixed relationship between the dowry and the marriage gift or reverse dowry. Out of concern not to exceed the prescribed limits of the marriage gift, the text begins by mentioning the exchange rates of different coinage at the time. It goes on to suggest ways the wealthy can circumvent the legal limits by excluding certain valuables from the calculation. Finally, the text reveals that dowries and marriage gifts could include combinations of movables (goods and cash), and immovables (land) that were not strictly prescribed.

These are the customs of the city of Salerno. Just as laws have been made, are made, and will be made inviolable forever, likewise, customs are inviolable . . .

I. THE GRANTING OF THE DOWRY

The granting of dowry in the city of Salerno in ancient times was given in the princely currency [*solidi*] which [dowry] at that time equaled one pound of silver, and every *solidus* was worth four *tari*, and each one corresponded in weight and measure to twenty *grana* [grains], counted at the rate of twelve golden grains of current Sicilian money.[1]

II. IN WHAT MANNER THE AFOREMENTIONED DOWRIES WERE GRANTED

As dowry, the *solidi* were worth twelve and one-half times every ounce of the principality's money. Next was the presentation of the marriage gift. One hundred *solidi* of marriage gift were worth one hundred *solidi* of wrought gold, valued at two ounces of gold of the usual money in the aforesaid princi-

Translated from Romualdo Trifone, *I frammenti delle consuetudini di Salerno* (Rome: Athenaeum, 1919), 18–19, 115–16.

1. Presumably each *tari*—though it is unclear in the text.

pality. And, thus, for any one hundred *solidi* it was forbidden to give more than the prescribed number of two ounces of gold of the native money. And the rate of any ounce of wrought gold was worth twenty *solidi*. These *solidi* were worth and are worth one ounce and eighteen *tareni* of our money of Sicily.

Indeed, fifty *solidi* were to be paid from the *solidi* of the marriage gift, for which were offered any movable goods, reins/girdle/belt [*corrigia*], woven silk cloths, a bed, or vessels—excluding wrought gold. Among the nobles of Salerno, a marriage gift of a bed without silken borders is worth nothing, [but] knives and empty cauldrons made in gold are not excluded. Luxury utensils, painted vessels, vessels for pleasurable use, and the like are not counted among such things by the patrician Salernitan people. The common people, however, may fairly receive linens, silken shirts, curtains, or a bed with and without silken borders, copper vessels, [and] chests, which all pertain to the marriage gift.

94. DISPUTED MARRIAGE IN BOLOGNA
(ca. late thirteenth century)

Translated from Latin by Lynn Marie Laufenberg

The following passage comes from a collection of Quaestiones, or "Questions," that formed one of the types of texts used by university masters for the teaching of Roman (civil) or canon law. Though they are framed as hypothetical questions, they often reflect the kinds of actual dilemmas that judges confronted in the courts. Alberto de Gandino (d. ca. 1305) was a practicing judge in central Italy who authored the earliest surviving treatise on criminal law. This text is taken from his work on the statute law of the Italian city states. In larger cities, the bishop would preside over the ecclesiastical courts there. Throughout Italy, secular and church courts usually existed and operated side by side [see #45, 46, 95].

Question 39: It is established that the existence of a marriage cannot be proved by a smaller number of witnesses than seven. Is it valid even if it is done to the contrary? The inquiry rests with the *podestà* etc.

. . . It is established in Bologna [in the statutes of 1250] that a valid marriage cannot be proved by a smaller number than seven witnesses, and if anyone has done otherwise, let him be punished with a fine of 50 *lire*. A certain man demanded a certain woman as his wife in the presence of the bishop and proved the marriage by two witnesses. The woman herself accused this man before the *podestà*, and asked that he be punished, because he had acted contrary to the statute. The *podestà*'s judge, having heard this, detained him; the bishop's vicar sent word to the *podestà* that he should not interfere in this matter, because marriage cases are spiritual cases and pertain to the ecclesiastical judge, as in the *Liber Extra* on consanguinity and affinity [I.4.14.1];[1] and the statute is contrary to the freedom of the church, and hence is not valid. . . . Moreover, the law of God could not be removed by a [civil] statute, because an equal thing does not have authority over another equal and so much more so a lesser thing does not have authority over a greater one, as in the *Digest* concerning judicial authority, l. "for the magistrate" [Dig. 4.8.4]. But the Bolognese jurists have ruled in this question, since the question is between the commune of Bologna and the bishop, that the statute aptly has force, because statutes should be able to discern the law of God and of the Gospels, as is said: "in the mouths of two or three [people]

Translated from Alberto de Gandino, *Quaestiones statutorum*, ed. Henrico Solmio, Bibliotheca juridica medii aevi 3 (Bologna: Monti, 1901), 174.

1. This text refers to the degrees of relation, whether by blood (consanguinity) or by marriage (affinity), within which the Church prohibited two people from marrying or they would be considered to have committed incest [see #95].

abides every word," according to the *Liber Extra* on witnesses . . . [2.20.28].
Human law, however, distinguishes between a contract and a will, because
regarding the validity of contracts two witnesses suffice, as in the *Digest*, concerning witnesses . . . [Dig. 22.5.12]; regarding wills, five witnesses [suffice]:
see the *Codex*, concerning wills . . . [Cod. 6.33.27]; and add that it is noted
in the *Liber Extra* concerning witnesses [2.20.28].

95. TREES OF CONSANGUINITY
AND AFFINITY (ca. 1310–30)

Introduced by Robert Gibbs

A significant feature of many canon law manuscripts and often their most ambitious or even only figurative enrichment is a pair of tree-shaped tables (arbores) of the degrees of consanguinity and affinity, which enable the viewer to trace the degrees of relationship within which marriage was prohibited by the Church. Consanguinity defines blood relationships considered to be incestuous, at least in the first two or three degrees. Affinity defines relationships by marriage within which the Judeo-Christian tradition also precluded further intermarriage [see #94]. The Church inherited from its Judaic roots barriers to overlaying a spiritual relationship with a physical one, and relatives by both baptismal and marriage sacraments were thus constrained. Canonical counting of degrees was more exclusive than its source in the Roman [civil] law of Justinian, precluding marriage between second cousins rather than permitting it between first cousins as the civil Law did. In both systems marriage between direct descendants and ancestors was absolutely precluded: between parents and children, grandparents and grandchildren, etc. But the civil law counted degrees up to the common ancestor and back down to the partner. The canonists simply counted up to the common ancestor. These relationships were complex and far from obvious; tabulation was therefore needed. Sometimes the trees are merely diagrams, but often they are held or drawn over imposing representations of a standing man for the consanguinity tree and a married couple for the affinity tree. It is easy to date individual copies of the Arbores *before the 1215 Lateran Council or after: the stem and branches of the consanguinity tree show 7 stages or 6 stages beyond Ego (self), numbered II–VII, or 4 after 1215, when the prohibited degrees were reduced. A series of glosses intended for use in the Schools were written through the course of the thirteenth century, but the work of the major Bolognese canonist Giovanni d'Andrea, written ca. 1300 came to replace all the rest. From the mid-thirteenth century therefore, the* Arbores *generally appear surrounded by text, as a visual text glossed like the rest of the manuscript. The copy reproduced here is an example from Bologna around 1320, part of a local tradition which began in the twelfth century and came to a close in the city in the late fourteenth century. It is illuminated by the "Seneca Master," who worked on the choirbooks of the Dominicans in Bologna and was one of the more productive university illuminators between 1310 and 1330. The gray-haired consanguinity figure is shown with a miniver-lined doctor's cap (Figure 24). Christ and perhaps the Virgin Mary have been inserted into the facing affinity table (Figure 25). Consanguinity is surrounded by tondi (round paintings) with assorted children and lawyers, lions devouring oxen, centaurs, and a mother with her baby partnered at the base of the tree by a very obsequious, aged scholar or lawyer with his reference book. A married couple frame the Affinity tree, and Christ and presumably his mother (neither with a halo) are framed by what are perhaps four Ages of Man.*

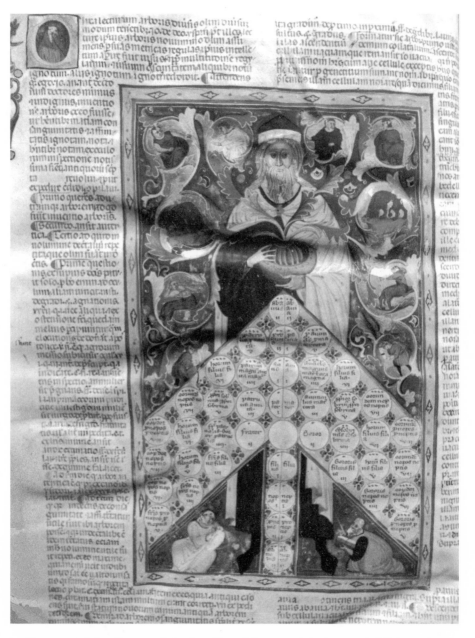

Figure 24. *Arbor Consanguinitatis* or *Tree of Consanguinity* (ca. 1320). Miniature by the Seneca Master (Bologna) in Giovanni d' Andrea, *Apparatus super Arbores*, included within the *Liber Sextus*, MS. Barth. 10, fol., 102v. (Photo courtesy Frankfurt am Main, Universitätsbibliothek Johann Christian Senckenberg)

Figure 25. *Arbor Affinitatis* or *Tree of Affinity* (ca. 1320). Miniature by the Seneca Master (Bologna) in Giovanni d' Andrea, *Apparatus super Arbores*, included within the *Liber Sextus*, MS. Barth. 10, fol., 103r. (Photo courtesy Frankfurt am Main, Universitätsbibliothek Johann Christian Senckenberg)

96. MARRIAGE, FAMILY, AND CHILDREN IN THE DATINI FAMILY NINE TEXTS (1375–1401)

Translated from Italian by Eleanor A. Congdon

In the heart of Prato's historic center stands the palazzo of Francesco di Marco Datini (d. 1410), begun in 1383. Decorated with frescoes by Andrea di Taddeo Gaddi, son of the prize pupil of Giotto, the massive building advertised to the people of his hometown that Datini had returned from his early career in Avignon as a successful and rich merchant. He proceeded, over the remaining twenty-eight years of his life and career, to create companies in important mercantile centers, such as Florence, Avignon, Genoa, and Pisa. His will stipulated that anything in his house at the time of his death had to remain there in perpetuity. The resulting treasure trove for historians contains almost 153,000 merchant letters and over 700 ledgers. These provide a window into the family life of a great merchant in addition to information about trade, finance, shipping, and the aftermath of the Black Death.

1. An Illegitimate Child (1375)

At the age of fifteen, in 1350, Francesco di Marco Datini went to Avignon to learn his trade as a merchant by acting as an agent for his guardian Piero di Giunta. His foster mother, Mona Piera di Pratese, wrote frequently using Niccolozzo as her scribe. Her usual topics were to urge Datini to return to Prato and to marry. Here, instead, she reacts to the news of the birth of his first illegitimate child, who died four months later.

Francesco! Mona Piera and I, Niccolozzo Ser Naldo di Prato, give you greetings and wish that this letter shall find you well and cheerful, and your dear brother as well. On the 18th, Mona Piera received your letter, and replies here briefly. We read that God has given you your first child. We are overjoyed and we are grateful to God that we can know of this happy event. We very much wish, however, that you had chosen to make this child legitimate because that would be a greater honor to God, and we pray that you will make the matter right for all the world to see. . . . Mona Piera sends you 10,000 good wishes for your part and all joy for your baby.

2. Datini Finds a Wife (1376)

Almost one year later, Francesco di Marco Datini sent word to his foster mother, Mona Piera di Pratese, that he had found a wife. The girl turned out to be the child

(1) Translated from Archivio di Stato di Prato, Datini Busta 1101, *Carteggio familiare e privato*, Filze Niccolozzo di Ser Naldo, letter from Prato to Avignon, Niccolozzo di Ser Naldo to Francesco di Marco, 20 September 1375.

of a Florentine noble who had been exiled for leading a rebellion against the city's government.

I believe that God ordained, when I was born, that I should have as a wife a Florentine. I waited, and I believe that I have found her. She is a girl called Margherita, whose father was Domenicho Bandini. He lost his head in Florence some time ago when he was found guilty of wishing to give Florence to another government. The mother of this girl is Mona Dianore from the ancient family of Gherardini. She remains here in Avignon with her three sons and three daughters. She has given one of her daughters in marriage to the merchant Niccholo del Ammanato, who has a company with Messer Pazino in Florence.

3. A. Fertility Remedy

In the 1380s, Margherita Datini tried every possible medicine and potion in order to conceive a child, but she proved to be barren. This particular concoction (a laxative), recorded as an item in the household expenses, is from the period when she was trying especially hard to find a way to become pregnant.

For a purgative medicine that treats constipation, made from anise, spike lavender, and a special ingredient, for Margherita at the suggestion of Maestro Belino and commended as effective in his book; carried here by Simone di Andrea; the price was 10 *solidi*.

4. Another Illegitimate Child (1390)

In 1390, Francesco di Marco Datini moved to Pistoia in order to escape a recurrence of the plague. He left his barren wife Margherita back in Prato, but took some of the family's servants with him. He soon had a liaison with one of them, Ghirighora, who became pregnant. In the following selection, Niccolò di Piero di Giunta updates Francesco on the arrangements made for Ghirighora.

The reason for this letter is to tell you that I have sent the necessary money which we have agreed will be suitable for Cristofano di Merchatto to take Ghirighora into his home, knowing what state she is in. I have made assur-

(2) Translated from Archivio di Stato di Prato, Datini Busta 1114, *Carteggio familiare e privato*, Filze Carte to Mona Piera di Pratese, letter from Avignon to Prato, Francesco di Marco Datini to Mona Piera di Pratese, 28 August 1376.

(3) Translated from Archivio di Stato di Prato, Datini Busta 214, *Spese di Casa 1390–1394*, Filze 6, "Medicines of Marcho di Tano, 1386," fol. 4r.

(4) Translated from Archivio di Stato di Prato. Datini Busta 1099 *Carteggio di carte di Niccolò di Piero di Giunta*, letter from Prato to Pistoia, Niccolò di Piero di Giunta to Francesco di Marco Datini, 28 September 1390.

ances to him that Ghirighora and the child shall be taken care of and not ill-treated in your household, and that she will have fabric for clothes and whatever else she needs as befits and portrays your honor and status should anything happen to him.

5. Another Illegitimate Child (1392)

The following three excerpts refer to the care of Ginevra, Francesco di Marco Datini's only illegitimate child to survive. After years of failing to conceive a child of her own, Margherita eventually adopted Ginevra as her own. In these passages Ginevra is not named for two reasons. The first is that she was being raised by "milk parents" (couples who cared for babies, including breast-feeding) until she was past the first few highly dangerous years of life. The second reason she remained unnamed was that at this time Francesco had yet to acknowledge his illegitimate daughter to his wife Margherita. The first excerpt is from an account book, the others from a ricordanza, *a commonplace book.*

Debit on the 15th of May 1392 to be paid for a coverlet, a petticoat and six shirts to be sent to Monte Lupo for the young girl written about before.

The personal account of Francesco di Marco: debit on the 15th of May 1392, 56 *solidi* that we paid for a coverlet, a petticoat and 6 shirts for the young girl, whom we sent to Monte Lupo; carrying cost 14 *solidi*, 8 *denari*.

Debit on the 10th of March 1395: 2 florins 14 *soldi* 4 *denari*, for 1 2/3 *braccia* of pale blue fabric for the anonymous valued one, and 2 1/2 *braccia* of scarlet fabric to send to Monte Lupo by the hand of Giovanni Sodermi.

6. Milk Parents (1395)

When Ginevra had reached the age of four, Datini decided that she should join his household. In the following letter, suffused with paternal love for the child in his care, Ginevra's milk father replies to Datini's summons.

I received your letter where you say to send your daughter Ginevra to you with the carrier of the letter, yet you do not allow her to bring anything with her from here. The love that my wife and I have for her has become as if she was our own child. For this reason, and because she is a good child and it

(5) Translated from Archivio di Stato di Prato, Datini Busta 557, *Libro Nero di Francesco di Marco e Stoldo di Lorenzo in Prato 1390–1394*, fol. 79v; Archivio di Stato di Prato, Datini Busta 613, *Quadernaccio Memoriale Ricordanza Proprio Segnata A*, fol. 176r, 184r.

(6) Translated from Archivio di Stato di Prato, Datini 1109 II, *Carteggio Prato*, Filze Piero di Strenna, letter from Montelupo to Prato, Piero di Strenna to Francesco di Marco, 8 August 1395.

makes her very frightened that you do not wish her to bring those things she finds dear, I write you that she and I will come to Florence together. May God guard you always. If there is anything I can do to be pleasing, I am at your command.

7. Wet Nursing (1397)

Although Margherita Datini could not bear children herself, she knew much about how to care for them. When the wife of a Datini employee gave birth, Margherita wrote the following letter about how the child should be cared for in the first years. Middle- and upper-class women did not usually nurse their own children; instead they put their infants in the care of a milk-mother, a bailia, *usually a woman who had recently given birth but who had lost the child. Children remained in the milk-mother's care anywhere from a few weeks to a few years, but many died during this period because of inadequate sanitation, poor hygiene, and accidents. In this letter, Margherita reminds Datini that nursing is critical to an infant's survival.*

The messenger said that the father of the child cannot be located, and that one day has already been lost, and tomorrow will be another. Therefore I wish that you should hire a good milk-mother. It is not fitting that one of your employees, whose activities help the success of our company, should lose his child because he is not present at its birth. Pay the cost for a good *bailia* instead of saving money on several less expensive ones so that the child will not be exposed to so many conditions [illnesses]. If you find a good one, the child should stay with her for twenty-eight months or more, having milk for a year and two months or more if it remains good and plentiful. If the *bailia* turns out not to be good, the child should be moved to a better one at once. I have already looked throughout Prato, but did not find a good one.

8. Extended Family (1398)

Margherita treated all the children in her household as if they were her own and a reflection of the Datini family. The Chaterina named in this passage lived in the Datini household but was not otherwise related.

I trusted you with acquiring Chaterina's petticoat and that you would have something appropriate made for her. What you sent, in my opinion, is not

(7) Translated from Archivio di Stato di Prato, Datini Busta 1089 (I), *Lettere di Monna Margherita a lui e altri (1384–1418)*, Filze Margherita to Francesco, letter from Prato to Firenze, Mona Margherita to Francesco di Marco, 5 April 1397.

(8) Translated from Archivio di Stato di Prato, Datini Busta 1089 (I), *Lettere di Monna Margherita a lui e altri (1384–1418)*, Filze Margherita in Prato to Francesco in Florence, 20 March 1398.

appropriate for several reasons. She ought to have an outfit befitting her father, and, considering that he is in a poor state of health, to us because we raise her. It is clear to me that you do not guard, as you ought, our reputation, but give more attention instead to the mule. There needs to be much more beautiful fabric on Chaterina's petticoat. The child of Monna Stroza di Carlo should not be seen to have better clothes than my Chaterina's!

9. Extended Family (1401)

The Black Death was not a one-time event: it returned many times over the course of the fourteenth and fifteenth centuries [see #76]. Families soon developed strategies by which to avoid possible exposure; here, Datini details his strategy of moving to a "clean" city. Note that the idea of family for a wealthy merchant included people from his business and his household employees, along with his wife and children.

Ricordanza that on 27 June 1400 we left Florence with all of our family to come to Bologna in order to flee the great death that was in Florence. We arrived here on 29 June all safe and healthy in this manner: Francesco di Marco of Prato on his mule, Mona Margherita on the mule being led by our [employee] Andrea that we presented to Guido di Messer Tomasso [who had found their quarters in Bologna] . . . [and six others including Datini's partner Stoldo di Lorenzo and the servant Nanni di Martino], Margherita's slave Lucia on the mule with a covering to facilitate riding, together with Andrea [her husband] . . . Ginevra and Nanna [a household servant and here Ginevra's traveling companion] together on another mule, also with a covering, and others.

Translated from Archivio di Stato di Prato, Datini 613, *Quadernaccio Memoriale Ricordanza Propria Segnata A*, fol. 60r.

97. MARRIAGE, DOWRY, AND REMARRIAGE IN THE SASSETTI HOUSEHOLD (1384–97)

Translated from Italian by Isabelle Chabot

In his diary, the Florentine merchant Paolo Sassetti recounts the marriage of his orphaned niece Lena in the spring of 1384. The groom, a widower with a young child, was about forty years old, while the bride was seventeen. The text shows precisely the different stages of negotiation and ritual accompanying a marriage alliance of the urban elite: the private agreement between the families, officialized in a public ceremony in a church; the celebration of the nuptial rite with the exchange of consent and the gift of a ring to the woman in her home; the transfer of the bride to her husband's house where the wedding party was celebrated; and the "return" of the bride to her parents' home before the new couple began their married life. This text also shows that marriage and remarriage were a collective responsibility of the men of the family. Women, being legally constrained, were not involved in the important decisions that concerned their person and their goods (here, a substantial dowry).

[1384][1]

Memory: that we married Lena, daughter of the late Bernardo our brother, with the mediation of Andrea, son of messer Francesco Salviati, and Filippo, son of the master Tebaldo, who was the [marriage] broker.

On 20 March 1383 [1384], we secured and agreed with the said Andrea di messer Francesco Salviati, and in the presence of the said Filippo di maestro Tebaldo, mediator and [marriage] broker, that the said Lena (may God bless her and all of us) should be the wife of Lodovico, son of Filippo Fabrini Tolosini, a young man between 36 and 40 years old, with a dowry worth 700 gold florins, made up of money and *trousseau*. And this was the agreement with the said Andrea di messer Francesco.

Then, on Wednesday 30 March 1384, in the name of God and peace and consolation for both them and us, we swore and promised her in the church of the Badia of Florence. The contract was written by the notary ser Michele of ser Aldobrando and the mediators for the dowry were Andrea di messer Francesco Salviati and Ghino di Bernardo d'Anselmo.

Then, on Sunday 3 April 1384, the said Lodovico, her husband, went to see her and gave her the ring [and] the contract was written by the said ser Michele.

Then, on 30 April 1384, we gave him in cash, by means of Ugo, son of

Translated from Archivio di Stato di Firenze, *Carte strozziane*, II ser. 4 (1363–1400), fols. 69v–75r, 111v–112r.

1. In Florence the year began on 25 March.

Domenico Vecchietti, 500 gold florins as part of the dowry we must give him without any receipt.

Then, on 11 May 1384, we gave him in cash, by the mean of Ugo son of Domenico Vecchietti, 130 gold florins as part of the dowry we must give him without any receipt.

Then, on 12 May 1384, we sent two new marriage chests that contained the following items and their estimated value:

2 strong boxes with coffer and two small boxes—15 gold florins, 10 *soldi*

1 two-colored silk dress, red and pink, we valued it at 20 florins

1 two-colored woolen garment, we valued it at 10 florins

1 hair ornament decorated with pearls, like a little tiara, we valued at 15 florins

1 hair ornament of little buttons, we valued at 4 florins

Sum we gave to Lena for her dowry, trousseau and cash: 700 florins, 10 *soldi*.

And on the same day, in the name of God and of good fortune, we sent her, dressed in a red silk dress, to her husband on a brown horse of messer Antonio son of messer Niccholaio Alberti, escorted by messer Forese Salviati and by messer Filippo Maghalotti. And our servant Uliva went with her to be her maid. God give her good fortune and comfort to us.

And in addition to the said items and money, we gave her, besides her dowry, for gifts given to Lena:

1 dress, not estimated, 2 gold florins, 10 *soldi*

8 shirts . . .

18 bonnets, worth 5 gold florins, 20 *soldi*

2 embroidered caps, 2 florins

1 new basin, __florins, 17 *soldi*

1 little ewer we had at home, estimated at 10 *soldi*

She stood in her husband's house for the wedding on Thursday and Friday 12–13 May and on Saturday 14 May, in the name of God and good fortune, she came back to our house accompanied by women because a new law of the commune prohibited men to participate.[2] And the women were Bartolomea, wife of Tommaso di Giovanni Pantaleoni, and Sandra our sister.

Then, on 20 May 1384, we gave a lunch on the morning of Ascension day to celebrate the return of Lena. We had to delay giving this lunch because the said Lena went with the daughter of messer Ghirighoro Tornaquinci, our niece, when she married the son of Vieri di Migliore Guadagni, who married her on Sunday, 15 May 1384.

---

2. A new sumptuary law was published in April 1384.

On 28 May 1384, we gave 3 florins to Filippo di maestro Tedaldo mediator and broker of this blessed marriage for his mediation and mercy; Tommaso di Federigho Sassetti brought the money to his home in San Pier
Maggiore on Saturday night.

Again, we gave Lena for her to give [as gifts] to her husband's home:

    1 silver belt, weight 5 ounces worth, *soldi* 28 per ounce, to give to the
        young boy born from Lodovico's first marriage, 4 gold florins, 24
        soldi

    1.5 *braccia* of dark fabric for stockings for Lena

    1.5 *braccia* of woolen fabric to give to the male servant of the house, it
        cost 1 florin, 6 *soldi*, 3 *denari*

    2 linen veils, one to give to the slave, the other to the wetnurse, it cost
        2 *soldi*

We also gave, besides the said items:

    a silver and coral string of *paternoster* [beads] with pearl buttons, worth
        3 florins

    a silver belt, worth 4 florins

    a little bag, worth 3 florins

    a book of prayers to the Virgin, worth 4 florins

    a little knife with a silver cap, worth 2 florins

and other things, ribbons, roses, mirror, little combs and other little things.

    cash we gave her for shoes, 1 florin

    cash to give to the child . . . 15 *soldi*

    cash . . for her bag, 5 *soldi*

1393

    More about our Lena's wedding when she got married. . . .

    In addition to what we have mentioned [above], we gave to the said
Lena and we spent on dinners owed to our kinfolks, that is,

    a deep red woolen dress with black bone buttons, estimated at 8 florins

    a two-colored woolen dress with silver buttons, estimated at 8 florins

    We gave a lunch for the following women and men the morning when
we betrothed her on 4 April 1384:

    ser Michele di ser Aldobrando di ser Albizzo

    Cambio di Arrigo, our brother-in-law

    Tommaso di Giovanni Pantaleoni

    Ugo di Domenico Vecchietti

    Domenicho di Franceschino, called "Lanza"

    monna Ghostanza wife of Lippo Guidalotto

    monna Sandra widow of Ghinozo de' Pazzi

monna Bartolomea wife of Tommaso Pantaleoni
monna Piera wife of Ugho Vecchietti
monna _____ wife of Benedetto d'Uberto Benvenuti
monna Bartolomea wife of Sinibaldo Sassetti

And then we gave another lunch when Lena returned home, and this was on 20 May 1384, and the following men and women were invited:

Lodovico, husband of the said Lena
Tolosino Tolosini who came on behalf of his company
ser Giovanni Bencini di Albizzo
Manente Sassetti
Ugho di Domenicho Vecchietti
Tommaso di Giovanni Pantaleoni
Filippo di Piero d'Anselmo
Filippo di Ghinozo de' Pazzi
Cambio di Arrigo Fei, our brother-in-law
monna Sandra wife of Ghinozo de' Pazzi
monna Sandra wife of Morello Bonamicchi
monna Lisabetta wife of Federico Sassetti
monna Sandra, our sister
monna Lena our niece, [daughter] of Bernardo our brother.

On 15 May 1385, Lodovico Tolosini, Lena's husband, acknowledged having received the dowry of 700 florins, for which his brother Filippo stood as the legal guarantor; they both promised that their brother Gieri would also guarantee the restitution of the dowry for the next eight months, but he probably did not do it.

And then, God was pleased to call the said Lodovico to him, whose soul our Lord God has given peace. He died in Catalonia, in the city of Valencia, on 2 July 1395. Gieri and others of the Tolosini family informed us on 10 September 1395, on Friday night at 2 o'clock. And we brought Lena back [to our family] on the same morning according to the Florentine custom. And we remained with sadness and damage. And we also found that he had not written a will and we remain without having recovered the dowry. Then, on 19 April 1396, we obtained a copy of the dowry contract, written on vellum, and we paid 3 gold florins to ser Michele di ser Aldobrando and we are keeping it with us at home.

LENA'S SECOND MARRIAGE (1397)

1397

Memory: that we remarried Lena, daughter of the late Bernardo our brother, with the mediation of Lorenzo di Carlo Strozzi our kinsman and friend, to

Iacopo di Paolo Covoni with a dowry of 700 gold florins, which he received in this way, as we will say:

It is true that we had to bring a lawsuit against Gieri di Filippo Tolosini, Lodovico's brother, may God forgive him, who was Lena's first husband, and [in so doing] Gieri and I had to spend some money. And then Gieri changed his mind and dropped the case and we were pleased. On 6 November 1396, Gieri and I gave up the lawsuit, on 7 November 1396, we arbitrated an agreement with Bartolo di Bellozzo on our side and the said Gieri on the other side, and the said Bartolo acted as Lena's procurator [legal representative]. The arbitrators of this agreement were Bartolomeo de' Medici and Perozo di Luca Bonagiunta.

It followed that, on their order, we dropped the lawsuit in the court [of the *podestà*]. Then, on 7 November 1397, the said Gieri guaranteed to pay [us] 700 florins [for the dowry]. He did so, so that there would be no legal action or reason to claim the goods or property of Ludovico.

98. FAMILY AND CHILDREN IN THE *LIBRO DI RICORDI* OF LUCA DA PANZANO (1425–46)

Translated from Italian by Anthony Molho

Luca da Panzano, born in 1393, was the scion of an old family hailing from the village of Panzano in Tuscany. The family's fortunes had fallen on hard times, yet, with much hard work, especially in his commercial activities as a silk merchant, and with considerable good fortune, Luca was able to reacquire many of the family's old estates, and to emerge as a prosperous and successful citizen, and a highly respected member of his society. The text translated below refers to his own marriage, and to the births of his numerous children, excerpted from his libro di ricordi, *a term difficult to translate, the most proximate English equivalent would be "chap book," an account of personal, family, and, on occasion, public events recorded by the author of such a book. In the original full text of his* libro di ricordi, *Luca combined both family and business data on the same page. The punctiliousness necessary in keeping a merchant's account book was transferred to nearly all other aspects of such merchant's lives, their activities documented in their books with the precision of the incomes and expenses incurred in Luca's silk shop.*

One aspect of these passages may be worth commenting. It is Luca's meticulous and systematic attempt to create a complex web of personal relations with people who were drawn into his emotional and symbolic worlds as a result of his children's birth. For every one of his children, at the time of her or his baptism, a small group of people were asked to enter Luca's social universe. These were the newborn child's godparents. These people—asked to assume the moral responsibility of baptizing one of Luca's newborn babies—covered the entire range of social positions in the city and the surrounding country. Among them one finds wet nurses, themselves wives of poor and modest peasants, and illustrious personages such as Messer Lionardo Bruni, the city's chancellor and Luca's neighbor. By becoming godparents to Luca's children, these people had created a bond with Luca and his family. And by accepting their generosity, Luca had himself become obligated to them. Thus, throughout these passages—as is the case with Luca's entire libro di ricordi—*one encounters a man who was constantly drawn into other people's lives, while constantly inviting and welcoming this engagement himself.*

I took my wife.

I recall that on 23 September 1425[1] I, Luca, took as my wife Lucrezia, daughter of the late Salvadore di Biondi del Caccia, and I must have as dowry for the said Lucrezia one thousand gold florins, and I agreed to this.

Ser Lorenzo di Paolo, Florentine notary, drafted the oath made with

Translated from Archivio di Stato di Firenze, Carte Strozziane, ser. II, no. 9

1. The new year began on 25 March; thus Luca's daughter Alessandra, who, as he records, was born 18 March 1438 and died 25 March 1439, at her death was only one week old.

her, back in June, on _____ 1425 in the church of Santa Maria sopra Porta, and the dowry referred to was for one thousand florins, with the exact sum left up to Lionardo di Ridolfo de' Bardi and Bernardo di Bartolomeo Gherardi.

I paid the tax of 1018 florins on 31 October 1425. Giuliano di Bartolo Gini and Luca da Panzano and company, silk merchants, paid to Zanobi di Lionardo Altoviti, cashier of the Contract [Tax], 26 florins, 2 *lire*, 18 *soldi piccoli*. The said Giuliano and company were registered as creditors in my book marked A, *carta* 162. It appears in the book of the Tax of contracts marked S, on *carta*[2] 236.

I posted surety for the said dowry on _____ 1426, ser Lorenzo di Paolo drew up the deed in the house of Michele di Salvadore, Tommaso and Matteo di Matteo di messer Luca da Panzano, for 1018 florins.

I shall note below the children I shall have from Lucrezia, my wife.

A boy, to whom I gave as name Antonio; he was born on 6 November 1426, I gave him to wet nurse in Sesto, [recorded] in this book, *carta* 38.

A girl, whom I named Catelana and Filippa, born on 14 October 1427; I gave her to wet nurse in Panzano, in this book on *carta* _____; she died on _____ 1429, she is buried in Panzano.

A girl whom I named Gostanza; she was born on 6 December 1428, I gave her to wet nurse to Matteo di Monna Cara at San Miniato a Monte, registered in this on *carta*_____.

A girl whom I named Marietta and Giovanna, she was born on 14 May, 1430, I gave her to wet nurse to Mona Mea di Salvadore, she lives in San Giusto a Ema.

A girl whom I named Catelana, she was born on 19 May 1431, she lived 46 days, she is buried in Santa Croce in our large tomb, on 23 June 1431.

A boy whom I named Niccolò and Giovanni, he was born on holy Saturday, on 19 April 1432, I gave him to wet nurse to Nanni di Cenni da Sesto on 23 April 1432, [recorded] in the book marked A *carta* 248.

A girl born to me on 5 June 1433, I named her Maddalena and Salvestra, I gave to wet nurse in the Val di Pesa, she entered the convent of San Girolamo in San Gimignano.

She died in the said monastery on 26 July 1449.

A boy, whom I named Francesco, born on 26 September 1434, and on that morning many families were armed, and with them popular families, and then on _____ September the Palace convened by bell a Parliament and they

---

2. I keep the term *carta* used by the author. Literally it means sheet, and refers to either the front or back page of a sheet of paper.

elected merchants to a special committee, and sent to exile several citizens; I gave him to wet nurse to Monna Mea di Valdarno at 5 *lire* a month, she is in Florence. May God give him luck, and he was born early on Sunday morning.

We shall continue with the children I shall have in this, ahead on *carta* 90.

+ MCCCCXXXV on the day 13 of August.

Children I shall have.

I find myself with six live children of Lucrezia my wife, of whom I made reference above on *carta* 28, three male and three female.

On 24 August of the said 1435, at 7 hours, in the night of San Bartolomeo, Lucrezia my wife bore me a boy; he was baptized for the love of God in San Giovanni on 26 August 1435, I gave him to wet nurse as it appears in my notebook on *carta* 38; I gave him the name of Salvadore, for he was a good man and a good merchant, may God grant him good luck; then at the baptismal font the person who baptized him gave him the name of Bartolomeo and Salvadore, and Salvadore comes first because my wife remade her father's name.

He died on 18 November 1458, I make a notation in this, *carta* 195.

They named him Salvadore and Bartolomeo.

On 12 May 1437, a Sunday, a boy was borne to me, I named him Michele and Giovanni, and Michele should go first for the name of Michele Benenati, who in everything was one of the most punctual merchants in the universe; he amassed great credit for having been a great almsgiver, and he had grand buildings made for God; he was like a father to me and to all of us, and he died back on 8 March 1436, and I, Luca, went all the way to San Gimignano to have him buried, and I honored him greatly.

On 18 March 1438 at twenty hours, the said Lucrezia, my wife, bore me a girl; on the 19th, she was baptized at San Giovanni for the love of God by monna Felice, widow of Fronlio, mace bearer, and by monna Maria da Monte Gonzi, my son Michele's wet nurse; she was named Alessandra for the name of my wife Lucrezia's mother; the above said Monna Maria, who was also our godmother gave her the breast for the little while she lived.

She died on 25 March 1439, buried in Santa Croce.

On 17 July 1440 at 6 hours at night, on Sunday, Lucrezia, my wife, bore me a girl; I had her named Mattea and Niccolaia, for my mother who died last May; she was baptized in San Giovanni on the 18th of the said month at about the third hour; she was baptized for the love of God by Messer Lionardo di Francesco Bruni and other women and by a messenger of the Signori, who is named Malandrino, who is the Signori's messenger at the

Office of the 5 del Contado;[3] and at that time I was among the 5; I gave her to wet nurse on 26 July 1440, as it appears in my notebook, *carta* 212.

On 15 January 1441 at 20 hours on a Monday, the said wife bore me a girl, while I was *podestà* in Sesto;[4] I had her named Sandra and Antonia. Sandra comes first, as the name of my said wife's mother. She was baptized for the love of God in the baptismal font of Sesto, on _____ of January. Monna Nanna del Salinbancha, iron monger, baptized her.

We shall follow with children I shall have, in this, ahead in *carta* 112.

Children I shall have. It is above, also on *carta* 109.

I find myself on this day with 5 boys and 5 girls, born of Lucrezia my wife, as it appears above on *carta* 90.

On 8 August 1443 Lucrezia my wife bore me a girl, at about the day's Ave Maria; I gave her the name Bartolomea and Simona, for the daughter of Antonio di messer Luca, who was the wife of Betto di Giuliano Gini, and she was named Bartolomea for my father's mother, who had been Messer Bindo di Messer Oddo Altoviti's daughter; I had her baptized for the love of God; and I gave her as the second name Simona, because she was born within two days of San Lorenzo.

On 21 October 1445 the said wife bore me a boy according to the person who delivered him; he was baptized at home and I gave him the name of Giovanni; the woman who delivered him said that he was stillborn; he was buried at San Simone in an unmarked grave; and the mother was as close to the brink of death as one could be, and before his birth she lost about one fourth of a barrel of blood. The Lord and the Virgin Mary, and Saint Anthony of Padua gave her this grace because she was a good woman. She then died in this birth.

My above mentioned wife died on 5 November 1445 in this birth on Friday night at two and a half hours; and in this on *carta* 123 I make note where she is buried and the honor done to her, and may God have pity on her soul, for she was a worthy and good wife, and she died with good reputation before God and the world.

+ MCCCCXLV on 5 November.

I recall that Lucrezia, my wife, of whom today on this day I have 11 children, died on the said day, Friday, at two and a half hours on Friday night, which grieves me as much as if I had died myself. For she was with me 20 years, one month, and 10 days, and for her I devoutly pray to God that he

---

3. The Cinque del Contado (the Five Officials on the Contado) were responsible for the administration of the rural areas governed directly by Florence.

4. Sesto is a locality a few kilometers to the west of Florence.

grant her true pardon. She died during childbirth, and gave birth to a boy who it was said had died in her body, and yet, because it was said he breathed, he was baptized at home, and named Giovanni, and buried in San Simone, he is not in the sacristy.

I had my daughter Gostanza and monna Caterina, daughter of the late Salvadore del Caccia and widow of Filippo di Ghezzo dressed with 14 *braccia* of cloth for a mantle and gave a pair of veils to each one, and a towel to each.

I had the vigil celebrated by priests and monks at home on Saturday morning, at 11 hours, and she was buried on the said day, 6 November 1445, in Santa Croce, in the tomb of our Messer Luca, in the church, on the side of the basin of the holy water.

On the 8th I had the masses celebrated in Santa Croce, with as many candles and as much incense as was possible, and in the presence of many relatives and friends. And this woman's death was a great loss, and it displeased all the people of Florence because she was a good wife and sweet wife, with good manner, and she was liked by whoever knew her. And I believe that this soul went to the feet of the servants of God, because in her death she showed great humility and patience, for she was sick 15 days after she gave birth to the boy. May God in his great charity have accepted her in the place of his angels; I take note in this, on *carta* 112, of the children I have had of her.

On 16 May 1446, I, Luca da Panzano, ordered that 30 masses of Saint Gregory begin, in succession, one each morning, for the cure and salvation of the soul of Lucrezia, my late wife, which I asked that brother Attaviano del Mangano friar of Santa Croce of Florence and my confessor, celebrate, to whom today I gave 2 torches of wax, each of which weighed one *libra*, to keep lit during the masses he must celebrate in Santa Croce, where the said Lucrezia is buried.

I gave to the said brother Attaviano, per payment of his labor, about one half a *braccio* of specially made alexandrine velvet.

Education and Erudition

During the centuries of dislocation and instability that followed the Roman Empire's collapse, the principal bastions of literate and literary culture were ecclesiastical institutions, in particular monasteries. Monasteries such as Montecassino, Bobbio, and Nonantola developed great scriptoria *which painstakingly copied out manuscripts for liturgical use and, importantly, as teaching and devotional aids. But ecclesiastical institutions were neither intended nor able to meet the increasing demand for education in the later medieval period. As such, municipal schools which focused on reading,* abacus *(practical mathematics), and grammar emerged to meet the demands of medieval Italy's urban centers that needed a literate and numerate class for governing and commercial enterprise. By 1300 municipal schools had triumphed, effectively replacing ecclesiastical schools that had once catered to a lay clientele, while apprenticeships and private tutors also continued to teach basic skills. Those who wished to join religious orders, however, trained at monastic schools which by the thirteenth century were now rivaled by the* studia *of the mendicant orders. Universities, a product of the high Middle Ages, developed early on the Italian peninsula.* Universitas *means "guild," and the majority of early Italian universities were student guilds, with strict guidelines for how parties should conduct themselves and perform their duties. Unlike the great universities of England and France that specialized in the speculative fields of theology and philosophy, the most celebrated Italian universities focused on the practical sciences of law and medicine. The development of the legal curriculum at the University of Bologna (1088) was the result of the revival of Roman law based on Justinian's* Corpus iuris civilis, *while the University of Naples, founded by Frederick II in 1224, was occasioned by the intersection of Latin, Greek, and Arabic knowledge in the multicultural south. From grammar school basics to the founding of the first law school, the texts in this chapter cover both curricular content and such practical matters as books, schools, contracting a tutor, the skills for household management, even a graduation speech. The section also includes a selection of documents that demonstrate the high level of erudition that could be attained by the lay elite.*

I. LOCAL SCHOOLS AND
ELEMENTARY EDUCATION

99. GIOVANNI VILLANI ON THE SCHOOLS OF FLORENCE (late 1330s)

Translated from Italian by M. Michèle Mulchahey

One of the most famous descriptions of the extent of elementary schooling in medieval Italy occurs in the Florentine Giovanni Villani's Nuova cronica *(XI, 94). Amid boasts about Florence's growing population, and the number of its churches and other institutions, Villani includes a brief census of the educational opportunities the city provided for both boys and girls. It should be noted that female literacy is taken for granted.*

We find that there are from eight to ten thousand boys and girls learning to read. Of boys studying *abbaco* [practical mathematics] and arithmetic, there are from 1,000 to 1,200 in six schools. And those studying Latin and logic in four large schools number from 550 to 600. . . .

Translated from Giovanni Villani, *Nuova cronica*, ed. Giuseppe Porta, vol. 2 (Parma: Guanda, 1990).

100. SCHOOLING FOR A GIRL (1399, 1402)

Translated from Latin by Eleanor A. Congdon

*Ginevra Datini, the illegitimate daughter of Francesco di Marco Datini, was edu-
cated as was appropriate for the daughter of a successful merchant. It was expected
that she would eventually have to run a household, and possibly her husband's business affairs while he was away from home, which required the skills of reading and
writing. The excerpts below are taken from Datini's* ricordanza *or commonplace
book.*

Today, 31 October 1399, I gave to my Ginevra one florin's worth of copper
for her to give to Mona Mattea, who teaches her to read at Santa Maria
Novella.

Today, 20 February 1402, Francesco di Marco gave to Ginevra, his daughter,
one new florin that she is to give to the mistress who teaches her to read, and
those other subjects, which have been asked of her, for her salary.

Translated from Archivio di Stato di Prato, Datini Busta 613, *Quadernaccio Memoriale
Ricordanza Proprio Segnata A*, fol. 23v; Archivio di Stato di Prato, Datini Busta 614, *Francesco
di Marco Datini Proprio (1401–1404)*, fol. 5v.

101. GRAMMAR SCHOOL
TWO TEXTS (1360s, 1406)

Translated from Italian by M. Michèle Mulchahey

1. Merchant Bartolomeo di Niccolò dei Valori Reminisces About His Early Education (1360s)

*Florentine merchant Bartolomeo di Niccolò dei Valori has left us a striking descrip-
tion of the schooling that set him on the path to a commercial career. Nearly sixty
when he wrote his recollections of his life, Bartolomeo di Niccolò is recalling events
that took place beginning when he was a boy of nine or ten. He describes four years
of grammar education, which meant that he was taught Latin, followed by a few
months of training in a school of abbaco, where he learned basic arithmetic and
calculation [see #99, 104].*

In October 1363, once the plague had subsided, I, Bartolomeo, set myself to
learn grammar at the school of Master Manoello. And there I remained until
the end of the month of May of 1367, and then in June of the same year I set
myself to learn *abbaco* with Master Tomaso di Davizzo dei Corbizzi, so as to
know how to keep accounts. And there I stayed until February of 1368, when
I put myself to work at the booth of Bernardo di Cino Bartolini, a banker in
the New Market.

2. The Humanist Vespasiano da Bisticci Describes the Similar Early Education of Banker Gianozzo Manetti Forty Years Later (1406)

*Although renowned as a humanist and as the librarian who helped such Renaissance
collectors as Cosimo de' Medici and the future Pope Nicholas V gather manuscripts for
their libraries, Vespasiano da Bisticci provides evidence of the continuity in Italian
elementary education from the medieval period through the early years of the fifteenth
century. While humanistic interests may have shifted the emphases in higher education,
the practical character of mercantile schooling clearly remained constant.*

His father Bernardo sent him to learn reading and writing when he was still
quite young, as was the custom in the city of Florence. And in a short time
he had learned everything necessary to one who was to become a merchant,
so he was moved on to learn *abbaco*. And in a few months he learned all there
was to know of that discipline as well. At the age of ten he went to work in
the bank.

---

(1) Translated from Florence, Biblioteca Nazionale Centrale, MS Panciatichi 134, fol. 1r.
(2) Translated from Florence, Biblioteca Nazionale Centrale, MS Panciatichi 134, fol. 1r.

102. LEARNING TO READ: *LA TAVOLA*
(ca. mid-fourteenth century)

Translated from Latin by M. Michèle Mulchahey

Boys and girls in Italy first learned to read Latin and to parse basic abbreviations by means of "la tavola," the tablet, or what in English is known as a hornbook. This was a small wooden board into which the alphabet had been incised directly, or to which had been attached a piece of parchment with the letters written out on it. A thin sheet of transparent horn was then placed over the parchment to protect it from the children's fingers as they traced and retraced the letters. The most common contents of the tavola were the alphabet itself, including examples of letters that had more than one medieval form—straight-backed and uncial d, short and tall s, regular and round r—and some basic syllabic combinations, together with one or two common prayers. Memorization was the key here; actual reading began with the Psalter.

Jesus. Mary.

+ Alphabet: a b c d 6 e f g h i j k l m
n o p q r 2 s f t u v x y z
7 9 2/ b⁹ [= et con- -rum -bus]

Ba	be	bi	bo	bu		Ca	ce	ci	co	cu
Da	de	di	do	du		Fa	fe	fi	fo	fu
Ga	ge	gi	go	gu		Ia	ie	ij	io	iu
La	le	li	lo	lu		Ma	me	mi	mo	mu
Na	ni	ne	no	nu		Pa	pe	pi	po	pu

Translated from a Primer without title (Perugia: Petrumiacobum, 1578); today in the New York Public Library.

103. LEARNING TO LATINIZE: *DONADELLO*
(ca. mid-fourteenth century)

Translated from Latin by M. Michèle Mulchahey

After children had learned their alphabet and begun to read by using the tavola and the Psalter, they moved on to elementary Latin grammar. There were several grammar textbooks available to medieval teachers in Italy, but all were based on the primer in dialogue form that had been penned by Aelius Donatus in the fifth century, and came to be known simply as "Donatus," or, in Tuscan usage, by the diminutive "Donadello." The version that circulated most widely in Italy was one that opened with the words "I am the door for the unlettered" (Ianua sum rudibus). *The opening lines are reproduced here.*

I am the door for the unlettered who desire to learn the first art.
Nor will anyone be properly trained without me.
For I teach gender and case, species and number, and
the pattern for those parts of speech that are inflected.
I bring order to the remaining parts, demonstrating what agrees best with what.
And no usage is left that I shall not teach.
Read on, then, O unlettered reader, and apply yourself to study,
For you can learn many things with a bit of study.

What part of speech is it? A noun. Why is it a noun?. Because it signifies a substance, or an individual or common quality, and exhibits case. How many qualities do nouns have? Five: species, gender, number, figure, case. What is one sort of species? Primitive. Why is it called that? Because it is derived from nothing else. What other sort of species is there? Derivative. Why is it called that? Because it derives from something else, as "poet" from *poesis.* What is the gender of the noun "poet"? Masculine. Why? Because the pronoun that precedes it when declining it is the singular article *hic.* What is another gender? Feminine. Why? Because the pronoun that precedes it when declining it is the singular article *haec.* Is there another gender? Neuter. Why is it so called? Because the pronoun that precedes it when declining it is the singular article *hoc.* . . .

Translated from *Aelii Donati Grammaticale introductorium . . . (Ianua sum rudibus)* (Milan: Franciscus Paganellus, 1597), Trivulziano H 1898/1.

104. LEARNING TO RECKON: LEONARDO FIBONACCI'S *BOOK OF ABBACO* (1202; revised 1228)

Translated from Latin by M. Michèle Mulchahey

Leonardo Fibonacci wrote an encyclopedia of mathematics specifically adapted to the needs of merchants, his Liber abbaci, *around 1202. Abbreviated vernacular versions of it began appearing in Italy towards the end of the century, and the first schools of* abbaco *at about the same time. Abbaco treatises like Fibonacci's usually began by introducing the system of Hindu-Arabic numerals, defining terms such as addition and multiplication, and then presented numerous mathematical problems. The use of an abacus was not assumed: these were problems to be solved on paper using various techniques of calculation, including algorism and algebra. Below are examples of the problems Fibonacci set; the last results in the famous "Fibonacci Sequence."*

PROBLEM 1 (*The lion that was in a pit*). A pit was 50 hand's breadths in depth. A lion climbed up the pit 1/7 of a hand's breadth and fell back 1/9 of a hand's breadth. How long would it take the lion to get out of the pit? . . .

PROBLEM 3 (*A voyage*). A certain man doing business in Lucca doubled his money there, and then spent 12 *denari*. Thereupon, leaving Lucca, he went to Florence; there he also doubled his money, and spent 12 *denari*. Returning at length to Pisa, he again doubled his money and spent 12 *denari*. Nothing now remained to him. How much did he have in the beginning? . . .

PROBLEM 4 (*An inheritance*). A man whose end was approaching summoned his sons and said, "Divide my money as I shall prescribe." To his eldest son he said, "You are to have one bezant and a seventh of what is left." To his second son he said, "Take two bezants and a seventh of what remains." To the third son, "You are to take three bezants and a seventh of what is left." Thus he gave each son one bezant more than the previous son and a seventh of what remained, and to the last son all that was left. After following their father's instructions with care, the sons found that they had shared their inheritance equally. How many sons were there, and how large was the estate? . . .

PROBLEM 26 (*How many pairs of rabbits are produced in one year from a single pair*). A man had a pair of rabbits together in an enclosed place, and one wishes to know how many rabbits are produced from the pair in one

Translated from Florence, Biblioteca Nazionale Centrale, MS. Conv. Soppr. C.1.2616, the basis for the edition by Baldassarre Boncompagni, *Liber abbaci di Leonardo Pisano* . . . (Rome: Tipografia delle scienze mathematiche e fisiche, 1857).

year, when it is the nature of them to bear another pair in a single month, and in the second month those born to bear also.

Because the above-mentioned pair in the first month bore, you will double the number of pairs; thus in one month there will be 2 pairs. One of these, namely the first, bears in the second month, and thus there are in the second month 3 pairs; of these in one month two are pregnant, and in the third month 2 pairs of rabbits are born, and thus there are 5 pairs in the month; in this month 3 pairs are pregnant, and in the fourth month there are 8 pairs, of which 5 pairs bear another 5 pairs; these are added to the 8 pairs making 13 pairs in the fifth month; these 5 pairs that are born in this month do not mate in this month, but another 8 pairs are pregnant, and thus there are in the sixth month 21 pairs; to these are added the 13 pairs that are born in the seventh month; there will be 34 pairs in this month; to this are added the 21 pairs that are born in the eighth month; there will be 55 pairs in this month; to these are added the 34 pairs that are born in the ninth month; there will be 89 pairs in this month; to these are added again the 55 pairs that are born in the tenth month; there will be 144 pairs in this month; to these are added again the 89 pairs that are born in the eleventh month; there will be 233 pairs in this month. To these are still added the 144 pairs that are born in the last month; there will be 377 pairs, and this many pairs are produced from the above-written pair in the mentioned place at the end of the one year. You can indeed see in the margin how we operated, namely that we added the first number to the second, namely the 1 to the 2, and the second to the third, and the third to the fourth, and the fourth to the fifth, and thus one after another until we added the tenth to the eleventh, namely the 144 to the 233, and we had the above-written sum of rabbits, namely 377, and thus you can in order find it for an unending number of months.

II. THE UNIVERSITY OF BOLOGNA

105. *UNIVERSITAS*: A PAPAL BULL IN FAVOR OF THE UNIVERSITY OF BOLOGNA (1220)

Translated from Latin by M. Michèle Mulchahey

The universitates *or universities of medieval Europe were essentially guilds of masters and students who had organized themselves for purposes of study. The relations between the universities and the cities in which they operated were often strained, as the towns attempted to impose local jurisdiction over the universities and the scholars sought a degree of independence. Bologna became an important center for legal studies from the mid-twelfth century onward, and the development of its university provided a pattern for a number of daughter institutions throughout Italy. Indeed, many of the universities of northern and central Italy were founded as secessions from Bologna, at times when the city's scholars moved their schools to other locations in protest. The papal bull here captures a particular moment in the early quarrels between town and gown in Bologna. Following what was a nearly total dispersion of the city's schools between 1217 and 1220, Pope Honorius III—a former archdeacon of Bologna—has stepped in to defend the university's rights. The settlement was, however, only temporary: by 1222 the scholars had departed again, this time for Padua, which would become the most prominent offshoot of the Bologna schools.*

TO THE PEOPLE OF BOLOGNA

Having understood from the report of our venerable brother the Bishop of Ostia the devotion that you all bear toward the Roman Church, we are eager to procure those things that pertain to your salvation and honor, and also recognize that you are obedient children ever ready to obey the Church's commands and are willing enough to pull yourselves back from those actions that cloud your reputation and may bring about your disadvantage and downfall. Since, beyond enjoying the infinite benefits that the study of letters has bestowed upon you, your city is famous above all others because of her *studium* [a center of learning], and her name is proclaimed throughout the whole world, and she is become another Bethlehem—that is to say, "the house of bread" that is broken for the little ones of this house, from which the leaders who guide the Lord's people go forth, since those trained in this *studium* are appointed to the care of souls—you should not only stop punishing the scholars, but should, in fact, shower honors upon on them, being aware that they have freely singled out your city as their place of study, which was humble before but now surpasses nearly all the cities of the region

Translated from Hastings Rashdall, *The Universities of Europe in the Middle Ages*, vol. 1, *Salerno, Bologna, Paris* (Oxford: Clarendon Press, 1936), Appendix D.

because of the riches they have brought to her. Indeed, we have had explained to us by members of the university itself how you—not showing them due respect, and attempting to turn their gift to you into a debt, their freedom into slavery—have legislated that if any of them is discovered making or to have made a separate contract or agreement to transfer the *studium* from Bologna to another place, and if any scholar should obligate any other scholar in any way that enables him to force him to depart from the city of Bologna in order to study elsewhere, he shall be perpetually banned, and all his goods that he possesses in Bologna or its environs will be confiscated, and half of them given to the one who has informed against him. Furthermore, the scholars are not permitted to have a university or rectors, unless this new regulation is imposed on them by oath, namely, that they will not aid in the transfer of the *studium* to another locale, nor compel any scholar to leave the aforesaid city in order to study elsewhere. And they shall never alter this regulation with or without their advice; and if anyone shall do otherwise he shall be likewise banned and his goods confiscated. Also, within two months of taking office, the *podestà* is bound to make the rectors and scholars swear to this regulation, if there are rectors currently serving, or within fifteen days of the election of new rectors and the presentation of the statutes of the university of the scholars; nor shall they permit any Bolognese or foreigner to join their university until he has first sworn that he will not offer any "extraordinary" lectures elsewhere. And so, with this, the noble man, Guglielmo da Pusterula, the *podestà*, having seized the opportunity you provided him, usurping this unlawful jurisdiction over them, attempted to infringe the scholars' freedom; and, on the pretext of insisting on the right to make them swear to observe these regulations, tried to harass them in many ways.

But since statutes of this sort are beyond doubt unfair and manifestly stand in the way of academic freedom, and an oath to observe them is not binding, inasmuch as observing them is wrong and to do so is neither right nor just, we have decided that the same Guglielmo is to be advised and exhorted, and send him apostolic letters that command to this effect, that he will henceforth not harass the aforesaid scholars contrary to the freedom they have had up until now, or infringe the said freedom in any way on the basis of these statutes, which we determine are to be quashed as unfair, so that their study may not be impeded but rather may flourish to the honor of God, the profit of the students, and the glory of the city itself. And let not anyone presume to attempt to induce us to think otherwise in this matter. Regarding which we advise and exhort your community that, having carefully considered the profits and honor accruing to you and your city from the scholars, that you embrace them with the arms of charity, and do not henceforth harass them contrary to their ancient and traditional freedom on the pretext of these statutes, which ought rather to be called unstatutory. Nor shall you allow them to be harassed henceforth by the said *podestà*, having rescinded the aforesaid oath from this time forward, permitting them to enjoy their wonted freedom, so that with minds at rest they can apply themselves to scholastic endeavors, and we can commend your devotion to the Lord. But if you should do otherwise, which we do not believe you will, we shall be forced against our will to show to you our harsher face.

Given at Viterbo, Ides of April, the fourth year of our Pontificate.

106. DUTIES OF THE RECTORS OF THE *UNIVERSITATES* AT BOLOGNA (1317–47)

Translated from Latin by M. Michèle Mulchahey

Despite the efforts of Bologna's civic leaders to prevent the scholars who had gathered in the city from organizing effectively, the students did prevail. At the beginning of the thirteenth century there were, in fact, four universitates of scholars at Bologna, as the students from the various regions formed themselves into separate societies— the Lombards, the Ultramontanes, the Tuscans, and the Romans. By the fourteenth century these four universitates had been amalgamated into two, the Ultramontanes and the Cismontanes, and it is to these two universities and their rectors that the document here refers. It should be stressed, that, unlike the universities of northern Europe, which were formed as societies of masters concerned to protect their professional prerogatives and to monitor teaching standards within an essentially ecclesiastical environment, Bologna and the other Italian universities were student organizations designed to protect the students' interest.

Putting the honor of charity into action, we have decreed that the rector of one university shall accompany the newly elected rector of the other university to his house and conduct him through his university in the usual manner accompanied by trumpets. Also the new rectors shall be required to have read all the statutes within the first month of their incumbency. They shall also be required to visit each new *podestà* and captain of the commune of Bologna within ten days of their having taken up the office of *podestà* or captain, and to commend and present the university to them. Also the rectors are required to make all scribes, illuminators, correctors of texts, and mixers of colors and palimpsestors of books, binders, dealers in paper, and those who otherwise make their living from the university and its scholars swear that they will be subject to the rectors and to the university, and that they will serve everyone faithfully. They shall also be required on the first, second, or third day after the opening of the university when there are no lectures to convoke the university, and to have the statutes read out, at least the third book. At the opening of the university they shall also have read out in classes those statutes that pertain to doctors and their classes, and which describe the method and order of lectures. Also let them take care that they do not enter in their matriculation lists as scholars those who do not study law, or who do not take the oath, unless they refuse to do so for a valid reason approved by the rectors. They are also required, whenever asked to do so by a scholar, to have

Translated from Carlo Malagola, *Statuti delle università e dei collegi dello studio Bolognese* (Bologna: Zanichelli, 1888), 13–14.

read out in classes any statute that is particularly applicable to that scholar. Nor shall the aforesaid statute be read out except by a notary of the university or, if he cannot do so, by the beadle, who shall be bound to read it at the command of either rector, even if the other forbids it. The rectors are also required by such means as shall seem appropriate to them to arrange that the bells that are rung for the convenience of the scholars are rung in a manner, at the time, and at intervals that are acceptable, and they shall take especial care that the ringing of the bells for the review [session] is done at the appropriate hour and for the right length of time. In April they shall also have an announcement made in classes through the university notary that, if anyone wishes to say anything or criticize any official of the university, he may report to the rectors and councilors of the university. Also, the rectors are required to ensure that the doctors' salaries are paid after 1 November. And if these salaries have not been paid by the 1st of January, they shall be required to hold meetings with the councilors regarding this matter at least once a week and discuss the ways and means of paying their wages. But if they have not been paid by the 1st of March, from that point on the rectors, together with the councilors, shall have the full authority of the university in this matter, and, failing any action on the part of the university, they or a quorum of them can do all that the university itself should do. But they do not have the authority to suspend the operations of the university, although the whole university can be assembled to do this at the request of those who are paid salaries. Also, the rectors are required to demand payment of the pecuniary fines incurred by doctors, scholars, or others enjoying the privileges of the university within ten days of the infraction; and every person who knows of any penalty incurred that is overlooked and not exacted is bound to report it to the rector; otherwise the rector himself shall be fined the same amount by the syndics at the close of his term of office; nor can any proposal to remit the said fines be proposed in council or to the university. Moreover, half of the fines shall go to both universities and half to both rectors, nor can the rectors remit their share. Also, the entrance fees for those who come to Bologna are common to both universities. Also, when one rector is requested by the other to arrange a meeting of his councilors with the whole university, the rector is required to do so; and the beadle is required to convoke the university whenever one rector together with a majority of the councilors of either university so orders, even if the other rector and a majority of the other councilors forbid it. He may not otherwise convoke the university, except in the cases stated in the statutes, unless the councilors have previously agreed to call the meeting. . . .

Also the rectors shall have all the documents now in the university's possession transcribed within a month of the publication of the statutes, unless the sheer quantity of material demands more time. Furthermore, any documents that are drawn up in future will also be transcribed within a month of their receipt, and in both cases the originals shall be preserved in the university chest or ark, so that they may not perish as others have perished . . .

Also, four times a year the rectors shall investigate whether the university chapel situated in Borgo San Mamolo operates as it should. If they do not, they are liable to correction, and either the bishop or his vicar will make a report in the appropriate manner. We further stipulate that within ten days of surrendering their office the outgoing rectors should hand over to the new rectors delegated to their office the items of university property that are in the university chest at the church of the Friars Preachers, and then an inventory of them shall be made by the notary of the university, which they must also hand over to their successors. Those who are negligent in this shall incur a fine of 20 pounds Bolognese to be collected by the new rectors and syndics and given to both universities, and if they fail to pay, they shall be punished with a further appropriate penalty.

107. RULES GOVERNING BOOKSELLERS AT BOLOGNA (FROM *STATUTES OF THE JURISTS*, 1317–47)

Translated from Latin by M. Michèle Mulchahey

One of the great innovations of the medieval period came in the form of a new method for the rapid reproduction of texts that was developed at the universities. It was known as the pecia *or "piece" system, because it was based on the idea of circulating individual quires, i.e. pieces, of unbound manuscripts for students to copy. Exemplars of texts that were important within the university curriculum were supplied to the booksellers, or stationers, who made a number of copies for their shops; these they left unbound and rented out piece by piece to those wishing to make their own copies for schoolroom use. The* peciarii *described here are officials of the university whose task it was to maintain a sort of quality control of the* peciae *being rented out. The system resulted in a quite remarkable diffusion of scholastic texts, whose accuracy was ensured both by the university's monitoring and by the fact that texts that were "read" in class would have been corrected by the owner as lectures went along.*

We have decreed that each year on a day selected by the syndics there shall be chosen by the rectors and councilors from the bosom of our university six good men, clear-sighted and wise, who bear the marks of clerical orders and of whom three are Ultramontane and three Cismontane, to be *peciarii* to the number of six, and they shall be chosen by the same form by which electors are chosen. . . . Once elected, they shall have full freedom and jurisdiction in the matter of *peciae*, taking cognizance of all cases involving *peciae* and corrupt texts, also pronouncing and executing sentence. As regards defects in *peciae* they may, and should, demand an oath from certain scribes and correctors that they will report any *peciae* they find that are corrupt. We desire that a stationer shall incur a fine of ten *soldi* Bolognese for each corrupt *pecia* he gives out, and for each offense; he shall also be required to reimburse the scholar double what the scholar paid for the rental of the *pecia*. Half the fine shall go to the university, half of the remaining half to the *peciarii*, the remainder to the informant.

Moreover, these same *peciarii* shall see and examine all the *peciae* and quires of all the stationers on certain feast days at some place determined by them, requiring beforehand an oath from all the stationers that they will bring to the place designated by the *peciarii* all the exemplars of *peciae* or

Translated from Carlo Malagola, *Statuti delle università e dei collegi dello studio bolognese* (Bologna: Zanichelli, 1888), 20–21.

quires that they rent out, and will conceal none. To this place all stationers are required to bring any exemplars they have without fraud and without deceit. And if the majority of the said six *peciarii* judge that there is any shortcoming in need of correction, they shall see to it that the *peciae* are corrected at the expense of the stationers to whom they belong by correctors designated by the six themselves. Any doctor or scholar may be asked to lend his own copy of a text for this purpose, if he has a good one, at the request of four of the *peciarii*, and of the rectors. And if, after the need has been judged to be critical, the scholar or doctor refuses to lend his copy even for use within his own house, he shall be penalized with a fine of five pounds Bolognese to be paid to our university. And if any copies are not assessed, the stationers shall be required to assess them. And if any stationers shall have neglected to do so, for each offense they shall incur a fine of five pounds Bolognese to be given to the use of our university; and no scholar ought to accept *peciae* or quires made from such a copy or correct a text according to it henceforth, under penalty of ten *soldi* Bolognese and a perpetual ban, and the rectors then in office shall be required to enforce the said penalty at the request of the said six *peciarii*, as noted above, by virtue of their personal oath. And the *peciarii* should pay the correctors of the *peciae*, and are required to receive the money from the stationers in the presence of the correctors and to pay it immediately to the correctors, nor shall the stationer pay the correctors directly.

Figure 26. Castel del Monte (ca. 1240–50), hunting lodge of Frederick II. (Photo: Joanna Drell)

III. ROYAL EDUCATION

108. FREDERICK II: *ON THE ART OF HUNTING WITH BIRDS* (ca. 1248)

Introduced by Joanna Drell; translated from Latin by Casey A. Wood and F. Marjorie Fyfe

Among scholars Emperor Frederick II of Hohenstaufen (1194–1250) has been a controversial figure; however, no-one has denied his passion for hunting, falconry in particular. Frederick's royal household included a large contingent of royal falconers, and he built magnificent castles in Apulia for his hunting expeditions, most famously his octagonal Castel del Monte. But for Frederick, hunting was more than sport a marker of noble status; it was the subject of intense study and scientific inquiry. For more than thirty years Frederick II gathered texts and information on the subject, completing by 1248 a treatise, On the Art of Hunting with Birds. *Although Frederick drew on Aristotle's recently translated corpus of treatises on animals, he was a critical reader of those works. In addition, he was guided by the expertise of falconers from the East—most notably the works of the Arab falconer, Moamym. Ultimately, however, Frederick based many of his conclusions on his own observations and practices.The topics that Frederick discusses in his multivolume work range from the behavior of birds in the wild, to falconry, to the training of the falconers. The selections included below offer a glimpse of Frederick's passion, as well as the theoretical and empirical basis for his text. (JD)*

INTRODUCTION

We had proposed for a long time to present our theories in a work such as this, but deferred the task for nearly thirty years because we felt our insufficient experience and need of continued preparation. However, as time passed and we heard no report that any other writer had anticipated us and donated to the world a full account of such material as we have been enabled to gather for the work, we finally decided to publish our own account of falconry. Certain branches of the art have, it is true, been explored by various other persons in the practice alone, and accounts thereof have been published, but with a lamentable want of mastery of the general topic.

We have investigated and studied with the greatest solicitude and in minute detail all that relates to this art, exercising both mind and body so that we might eventually be qualified to describe and interpret the fruits of knowledge acquired from our own experiences or gleaned from others. For example, we, at great expense, summoned from the four quarters of the earth masters in the practice of the art of falconry. We entertained these experts in our own domains, meantime seeking their opinions, weighing the importance of their knowledge, and endeavoring to retain in memory the more valuable of their words and deeds.

As the ruler of a large kingdom and an extensive empire we were very often hampered by arduous and intricate governmental duties, but despite these handicaps we did not lay aside our self-imposed task and were successful in committing to writing at the proper time the elements of the art. Inter alia, we discovered by hard-won experience that the deductions of Aristotle, whom we followed when they appealed to our reason, were not entirely to be relied upon, more particularly in his descriptions of the characters of certain birds.

There is another reason why we do not follow implicitly the Prince of Philosophers: he was ignorant of the practice of falconry—an art which to us has ever been a pleasing occupation, and with the details of which we are well acquainted. In his work, the *Liber Animalium*, we find many quotations from other authors whose statements he did not verify and who, in their

Adapted from Frederick II of Hohenstaufen, *The Art of Falconry*, trans. and ed. Casey A. Wood and F. Marjorie Fyfe (Stanford, Calif.: Stanford University Press, 1943), 3–6, 56–58, 75–76, 143–44.

turn, were not speaking from experience. Entire conviction of the truth never follows mere hearsay. . . .

We beg every nobleman who by reason of his rank should be interested in the contents of this work to order it read and explained to him by some master of the science. At the same time we crave indulgence for any ambiguity in our presentation of the subject. This art, like all other avocations, has its own peculiar vocabulary; and, inasmuch as the exact terms we require cannot be found in Latin grammars, we have substituted for them the terms that in our opinion best express our meaning.

Our main thesis, then, is *The Art of Falconry*, and this we have divided into two cardinal sections. The first contains the argument, by which we mean contemplative thought, or theory; the second illustrates practice, which portrays experimental action. In addition, a third subsection contains a part of the argument and includes certain data pertaining to both theory and practice. Our purpose is to present the facts as we find them. Up to the present time the subject of falconry has been devoid of both artistic and scientific treatment. . . .

The author of this treatise, the august Frederick II, Emperor of the Romans, King of Jerusalem and of Sicily, is a lover of wisdom with a philosophic and speculative mind.

The work called *The Art of Falconry* has manifold and far-reaching uses. The pursuit of falconry enables nobles and rulers disturbed and worried by the cares of state to find relief in the pleasures of the chase. The poor, as well as the less noble [the minor nobility], by following this avocation may earn some of the necessities of life, and both classes will find in bird life attractive manifestations of the processes of nature. The whole subject of falconry falls within the realm of natural science, for it deals with the nature of bird life. It will be apparent, however, that certain theories derived from written sources are modified by the experiences set forth in this book.

The title of our work is "The Book of the Divine Augustus, Frederick II, Emperor of the Romans, King of Jerusalem and Sicily, *De arte venandi cum avibus*, an Analytical Inquiry into the Natural Phenomena Manifest in Hawking."

BOOK I: THE STRUCTURE AND HABITS OF BIRDS. CHAPTER XXIII–I:
OF THE FUNCTIONS OF AVIAN ORGANS

. . . We shall now consider various external and internal organs that distinguish birds as members either of a species or of a genus.

Structural differences the young bird inherits chiefly from his ancestors.

If all birds were uniformly constructed, their members would exhibit in detail a corresponding uniformity of function, no matter how many species were represented; but avian organs show a great diversity in form and appearance, so much so that individuals may be distinguished one from another. These variations are at times so marked that they at once divide bird life into various categories.

The avian body, like that of any other aquatic and terrestrial animal, may be divided into cellular (homogeneous) and organic (functional) parts. The cellular parts are those that are constructed of similar elements, like bones, cartilages, nerves, the cardiac ligaments, blood vessels, flesh, and fat, and the tissues of the skin, feathers, and nails. We shall say little concerning each of these substances, merely mentioning them when we discuss the nature of the organs of which they form a part. The internal organs of birds do not vary greatly from one species to another in their component tissues. . . .

One should not conclude that the functions of the members determine their conformation, since that would be to attribute the cause a posteriori rather than a priori. Organs come first, according to their nature; then their characteristics, which are manifested through action and function, just as action depends upon the objective. As functions are determined by characteristics, and characteristics are derived from members, obviously functions depend upon organs. . . .

It must be held, then, that for each species and each individual of the species, Nature has provided and made, of convenient, suitable material, organs adapted to individual requirements. By means of these organs the individual has perfected the functions needful for himself. It follows, also, that each individual, in accordance with the particular form of his organs and the characteristics inherent in them, seeks to perform by means of each organ whatever task is most suitable to the form of that organ.

The external parts of birds that are of a sensitive nature are chiefly the head, eyes, ears, nasal cavities, mandibles, shoulder blades, joints, sides, belly, rump, hips, shinbones, feet, toes, back, thighs, external breathing apparatus, tail, oil glands, and other related parts.

The internal organs are the meninges, brain, vertebral canal, tongue, other parts of the mouth, bronchial tubes, lungs, heart, cardiac ventricles, diaphragm, esophagus, larynx and vocal cords, intestines, stomach, spleen, liver, kidneys, testes, uterus, and many other organs.

We shall now discuss this list of both internal and external avian organs (by which birds consume their food and digest it and by which they avoid dangers, live in their dwelling places, fly about in space, and change their habitats) and shall include matters that it is necessary to study for the purpose of writing about the treatment of their diseases.

Indeed, birds have particular organs for definite functions, examples of which are many. One organ may serve a single purpose or more than one; or several organs may be required to carry on but one function. That we may avoid needless prolixity in our discussion of these topics we shall mention only those organs and functions that are pertinent to our thesis, beginning with the bird's head. . . .

BOOK II: OF FALCONS USED IN HUNTING
CHAPTER XLII—HOW TO CARRY A FALCON ON THE HAND

After one has thoroughly studied all that has been taught him in previous chapters, he may more readily learn how the eyas [nestling hawk] should be trained to stand on the fist and how she may be carried about.

The first positions to be practiced are the following: The falconer's upper arm as far as the elbow should be allowed to hang loosely at the side of the body. It must not be held so close that it reflects every movement of the body, otherwise the bird is more likely to be disturbed. The lower arm is kept at a right angle to the upper arm, and the hand is extended in a straight line with the arm and not moved either forward or back. The outstretched thumb is laid on the forefinger and the latter is bent to touch the last joint of the thumb, exactly as an Abacist monk would make the sign for the number 70; then pressing the remaining three fingers against the palm of the hand, one makes the sign of the figure 3. A combination of these poses, that is, the bending of the index finger on the last joint of the thumb and the pressing of the other three fingers against the palm of the hand forms the Abacist figure 73, and from these combined positions we have the proper posture of the hand and arm for holding a falcon while she is being carried about.

The falcon should be held during transport opposite the shoulder, for when without her hood (or unseeled) she must be held out of sight of the carrier's face until she is manned, since it is in the nature of the bird greatly to dislike the human countenance.

The foregoing rules apply equally to both hands and arms of the falconer or his assistant in transporting hunting birds; and he should learn to carry the falcon on either fist, for he must bear the bird on his right hand if the wind blows from the left side and on the left hand if it comes from the right. In this way the falcon's breast is always exposed to the breeze that does not ruffle the feathers of the tail and back, nor those of the rest of her body. A disturbance of her plumage she will not stand, but will always turn herself about to avoid it.

In some countries falcons are borne only on the right hand. The exponents of this method severely criticize any other. We firmly hold that hunting birds should be carried afield on either fist exactly in conformity with the regulations just laid down, and for the reasons given. . . .

109. A GRADUATION SERMON OF ROBERT OF ANJOU, KING OF NAPLES (fourteenth century)

Translated from Latin by Samantha Kelly

Robert of Anjou (1309–43) ruled the Kingdom of Naples, the County of Provence, and much of Piedmont in the early fourteenth century, in close alliance with the papacy [see #75.5]. He was well known for his patronage of artists and scholars, and contributed to his own reputation for erudition by collecting a large library and composing learned treatises. Most unusually, he preached more than 250 sermons over the course of his reign, on religious holidays and for various state occasions. This form of oratory, which was officially restricted to clergy, communicated a sacred and erudite aura well suited to Robert's reputation as "the Wise." The following sermon illustrates the multiple ways the king burnished and publicized his own ideal image. The occasion itself—the graduation of a royal officer from the University of Naples—presented Robert not only as patron of scholars but, in the king's role as official head of the university, as a first among equals in the scholarly community. Further, the sermon's content not only celebrated the erudition of the honoree but showcased the king's own: its learned references include traditional sacred texts such as the Bible and Saint Augustine, a variety of classical and Arabic writings, and the foundational civil law text of the Middle Ages, Justinian's Corpus iuris civilis. The broader project of royal self-promotion exemplified in this sermon illustrates that the assertion of political legitimacy—in this case, through the image of a wise and therefore judicious and pious ruler—was a central priority not only in the newer and presumably more fragile republics and signorie *of northern Italy, but in the southern kingdom as well.*

A ROYAL SERMON FOR THE GRADUATION OF LORD BARTHOLOMEW, COUNT OF SALERNO AND ROYAL COUNCILLOR, IN CANON LAW

If you seek wisdom like silver and search for it like treasure, then you will understand the fear of the Lord and find the knowledge of God (Proverbs 2 [:4–5]). These words reveal five things in succession. For they propose (1) the pursuit of study in order to obtain the riches of knowledge, through the search for instruction: *If you seek wisdom;* (2) the spread of knowledge through the act of learning [and] through the cultivation of expertise: *search for it;* (3) a comparison of knowledge's value to the acquisition of wealth, through the [metaphor of] accumulation of money: *like silver* and *like treasure;* (4) the benefits gained by reverence and pious fear: *then you will understand the fear of the Lord;* (5) the resulting prize of a vision of knowledge in the fullness of its splendor, since it says, *you will find the knowledge of God.* . . .

Translated from Rome, Biblioteca Angelica, MS 151, fols. 172r–175v.

Figure 27. Robert of Naples receiving the crown of the Kingdom of Naples from his brother St. Louis of Toulouse (ca. 1317). Altarpiece by Simone Martini celebrating the sanctity of the Angevin dynasty. Naples, Museo Nazionale di Capodimonte (Photo: Alinari/Art Resource)

On the first point, it should be understood that wisdom can be defined in seven ways. First, in a common way, according to which wisdom is equivalent to philosophy in name, inasmuch as philosophy is the love of wisdom; nor do they differ except inasmuch as one seeks and the other is the thing sought, according to what Seneca writes in Epistle 91 [*sic*: 89]. This is evident, too, in the fact that the same categorization that suits philosophy—that is, into moral, natural, and rational, as Seneca says in the same letter—is fitting to wisdom. Furthermore, according to Plato, both are divided into active and speculative, as Augustine notes in *The City of God*, Book 8, Chapter 3 [sic: 4].

Second, and in a more common way, wisdom is defined as knowledge. According to this definition, wisdom and knowledge both aim for the same thing, and this agrees with the definition of Cicero in *Tusculan Disputations*: "The knowledge of things divine and human and acquaintance with the cause of each of them." Or according to Al-Ghazali, in *Metaphysics*, Book 3, Chapter 9, wisdom is the true understanding of things, with certainty about what is. Knowledge, truly, is defined by Avicenna in this universal way in the first book of *Physics*, Chapter 9: it is the comprehension of what is, as it is. . . .

Third, wisdom can be defined in the most common way, as including not only the level of knowledge (as knowledge is generally understood) but even the level of art. And [it includes art] in two senses, according to Aristotle in *Ethics*, Book 6: that is, the particular sense, according to which we call someone a wise man in a certain art, and the universal sense, by which we mean someone is wise in any art whatever. In this way wisdom applies to Homer, too, and to the architects of Rome, [who] have been called most wise in terms of manual tasks.

Fourth, wisdom can be understood in an appropriate way, that is, as the principal intellectual virtue and, as it were, the head of other virtues, according to Aristotle in *Ethics*, Book 6. . . . And according to Avicenna in *Physics*, Book 1, Chapter 1, as well as Aristotle at the start of *Metaphysics*, wisdom is about first principles and highest causes.

Whence also, fifth, wisdom can more appropriately be called metaphysical and divine, according to Aristotle at the beginning of *Metaphysics*.

Sixth, wisdom can most appropriately be called theology since it is most divine and treats of divine and highest causes—not, like philosophy, through human investigation, whereby many falsehoods are mixed with truths, but by divine means, that is, by revelation, according to which nothing false can result. Whence the passage from Ecclesiasticus 24 [:4] can properly be applied: *I dwelt in the highest heavens*, etc.

Seventh, it can be understood through its qualities, applying [the name of] wisdom, under certain conditions, to legal knowledge. Nor is it to be wondered at if legal knowledge takes this name, as an effect takes the name of its cause, and a daughter the name of her mother. Indeed, Proverbs 8 [:15] says, *Through me kings reign and rulers decree what is just.* And according to Cicero in *Tusculan Disputations*, Book 4, wisdom is the knowledge of things divine and human. But [legal knowledge], too, deals with divine things, as is clear from the title[s] at the beginning of the Codex, like "On the Trinity and Catholic faith," and it deals with the sites of worship, like "About sacrosanct churches." . . . And it deals with human things, that is, with regulating their actions. There are indeed some regulations regarding human actions. Similarly, since—as was said above—the terms "philosophy" and "wisdom" are equivalent, and philosophers investigate them [both] and reduce them to categories, as is clear in the beginning of the Codex, so it is evident that the term "wisdom" properly applies to legal knowledge. Even more does the term "philosophy" apply to canon law, which is based in theology.

With that said about the definition of wisdom, more remains to be said about the study of it. We must therefore investigate wisdom in two regards. First [we must investigate] the loving example of preaching which is a great gift of God. Indeed, wisdom or philosophy is fitting [in this context] since it is a gift of God greater than which nothing could be given, according to Augustine in *The City of God*, Book 22 chapter 22. On this point Cicero says in *Tusculan Disputations*, Book 1, that philosophy, which is the mother of the arts, cannot exist except as a gift of the gods. Similarly, the wise man Ecclesiasticus in his preface says, *All wisdom is from the lord God* [Ecclesiasticus 1:1]. . . .

Second, [we must investigate] the zealous diligence of application, or the perfect good of the mind, and search for what wisdom is since it is difficult to know it. For according to the Philosopher [Aristotle] in *Metaphysics*, Book 2, Chapter 1, the contemplation of the truth is difficult, as is the understanding of it, according to Seneca, *On Benefits*, Book 4. And nevertheless one must not desist from the investigation of it, for it is precious and good. Whence in Ecclesiastes 1 [:12–13] is written, *I Ecclesiastes was king of Israel in Jerusalem, and resolved in my mind to inquire into and investigate wisdom.* But above all one must not cease in this quest, for [truth] is revealed through those who love it. The Book of Wisdom 6 [:13], *wisdom is easily seen through those who love it and is revealed through those who search for it.* Moreover, this quest is undertaken by means of study, which should be continual and assiduous. As Seneca says in Epistle 2, "you must linger among and imitate a certain number of master thinkers if you would possess ideas that shall win a firm hold in your mind." . . .

Regarding the fifth principal point—where our theme mentions the

UNIVERSITY OF WINCHESTER
LIBRARY

resulting prize of a vision of knowledge in the fullness of its splendor, since it says, *you will discover the knowledge of God*—this knowledge of God is the blessed life, that is, the clear recognition of God. As it says in John 17 [:3], *this is life eternal, that they may know you, O Lord, who sent Jesus Christ*. Moreover, it is clear from Seneca's letter to Lucilius that the pursuit of wisdom is necessary for the blessed life, for blessed life is effected as perfect wisdom . . . The Book of Wisdom, 10 [:10] [speaks] of this: *He gave him the knowledge of the saints*. And this is the aforesaid [knowledge], about which our theme says, in conclusion, *and you will find the knowledge of God*. To this life and knowledge may we be led by Jesus Christ, who is blessed for ever and ever. Amen.

Social Memory, History, Commemoration

Recent scholarship has suggested that history and memory are not the distinct categories that we have traditionally believed them to be. That is, theorists of "social memory" argue that the memory of the past—be it individual or collective—is conditioned by the social context of the present, and that the writing of history is not exempt from these considerations. With these insights in mind, this chapter has grouped together texts which treat in various ways the subject of memory. The texts range from chronicle excerpts such as those from Bari, Oria (Genealogy of Ahimaaz), and Parthenope (Naples). It should be noted that the chroniclers do not merely document events, they shape the way their readers think about those events through their selection of sources, choice of language, interpretive explanations, and narrative structures. Although of a very different genre, the same might be said about the song of Philipoctus de Caserta, hardly an impartial view of Angevin rule of fourteenth-century Naples, and Henry of Rimini's paean to the city of Venice. In a different but related vein, the wills from Gaeta and Bologna included here, along with the bilingual Jewish tombstone inscription from Oria, the foundation document from a Byzantine monastery in Calabria, the pious donations made to two Paduan chapels, and the church inventories from Cortona each demonstrate individual acts of self-commemoration, the active shaping of memory and identity for family, community, and posterity.

110. A BILINGUAL JEWISH TOMBSTONE INSCRIPTION IN ORIA (eighth century)

Translated from Hebrew and Latin by Linda Safran

Members of the Jewish community at Oria produced the earliest Hebrew texts in western Europe. Shabbetai Donnolo (a friend of Abbot Nilus of Rossano, who founded the monastery of Grottaferrata) wrote medical, astrological, and philosophical works in the tenth century, and the Genealogy *or* Scroll of Ahimaaz *[see #114] further attests to the vigorous intellectual and religious life there. Liturgical poems (piyyutim) that are still included in Jewish prayerbooks were written in Oria by some of Ahimaaz's distinguished forebears. There is still a "rione Giudea" (Jewish quarter) in Oria, but no Jews have lived there since at least the mid sixteenth-century expulsion of the Jews under the Aragonese kings.*

This bilingual tombstone, dated on epigraphic grounds to the eighth century, is important evidence for the proximity of the Jewish and Christian communities of early medieval Oria. A menorah and two shofars (ceremonial horns) decorate three sides of the stone; on the fourth vertical side is a carefully carved Hebrew epitaph, and on the top is a Latin text. The adjacent epitaphs give slightly different information. The Latin text (1) is more concerned with establishing kinship and status, as it gives Anna's title and that of her father, while the Hebrew (2) focuses on Hannah's religious virtues and hopes for her eventual resurrection. The author of the Hebrew text, Samuel, is preserved as an acrostic in the initial letters of his rhymed verses (all the lines end in −NA). The carver of the tombstone was comfortable with Hebrew but not with Latin: he began carving from the right rather than the left; the N is consistently rendered backwards; and the <ES> at the beginning of the third line and the second LVI are meaningless repetitions of the letters immediately above. Despite these errors, both texts were meant to be read and understood by literate Christians and Jews, whose burial areas in Oria were probably contiguous.

1. IC REQUI-
ESCIT D(OMI)NA
<ES> ANNA FILI-
A R(EBBITIS) GULIU ET-
ATE LVI ANI-
NI LVI.

Here rests Lady Anna, daughter of Rabbi Julius, age 56 years.

Found in Oria in the nineteenth century; now in Biblioteca Comunale De Pace-Lombardi. Limestone, 46 cm tall; Hebrew text field 24 cm tall, Latin text 14 cm square. Translation adapted from C. Colfemmina, "Note su di una iscrizione ebraico-latina di Oria," *Vetera Christianorum* 25, 2 (1988): 641–51, and David Noy, *Jewish Inscriptions of Western Europe*, vol. 1, *Italy (Excluding the City of Rome), Spain and Gaul* (Cambridge: Cambridge University Press, 1993), no. 195.

‫| הנובנ השא | הפ תבכוש .2‬
‫| הנמא תווצמ | לכב תנכומ.‬
‫| הנינח לא || ינפ אצמתו‬
‫.הנמ | ימ תציקיל‬
‫הנח | הרתפנש וז‬
‫הנש ו נ | תב‬

Here lies a prudent woman, ready in all the precepts of the faith. May she find the benevolent face of God upon the reawakening; who can count [the progeny of Jacob]? She who died is Hannah, age [lit. "daughter"] 56 years.

Figure 28. Bilingual Hebrew-Latin tombstone (eighth century). Latin inscription now in the Biblioteca Comunale "De Pace-Lombardi," Oria. Hebrew inscription now in a private home, via San Sabino, Bari. (Photo courtesy Biblioteca Comunale "De Pace-Lombardi," Oria and the Mayor of Oria)

111. COMPOSITE CHRONICLES
FROM BARI, ca. 1000–1117

Translated from Latin by Tehmina Goskar and Patricia Skinner

The history of the city of Bari can be seen as a microcosm of southern Italian history as a whole between the ninth and twelfth centuries. Ancient in origin, it formed the focus of Lombard, Byzantine, Frankish, and Arab interests in the early Middle Ages. The eleventh century saw repeated attempts by the Byzantines to regain authority in the city, and visible factions emerge within the Barese population itself. These events in turn aided the Norman conquest of the city in 1071. The translation that follows is a selection from an amalgamation of the three surviving narrative histories from the city. The Bari Annals *focus on the early history of the city until 1042; the text attributed to Lupus Protospatharius runs from the ninth century to 1102 and makes use of the earlier annals; the* Bari Anonymous *seems to follow Lupus for the early years, but continues beyond his end date. Taken together, all three provide a strong sense not only of the interest in events at Bari, but of a wider perspective taking in much of Apulia and the Mediterranean. The annals also reveal a tower-centered tension similar to that between rival families as northern Italian cities in this period. In addition, they provide a different perspective on the Norman conquest of the South, so often reconstructed from the fuller viewpoints of the victors. That said, these are still challenging and sometimes contradictory sources: their individual interests are apparent in what they include, and what they omit. Reading them in a composite translation reveals their inconsistencies.*

The sections that follow describe the tense relations among Byzantine, Saracen, and Lombard forces in and around the city of Bari, characterized by fierce raids, sudden alliances, and temporary truces. Abbreviations: Entries by date only: Bari Annals; *LP:* Lupus Protospatharius; *AB:* Bari Anonymous.

LP987—Sergius the *protospatharius* was killed by the Baresi on 15 February and Adralistus by Nicholas the judge on 15 August. There was a solar eclipse.

AB987—XV indiction. Sergius the *protospatharius* was killed by the Baresi. And Adralistus was killed in the same year by the judge Nicholas.

LP988—I indiction. The Saracens sacked the Barese suburbs and led men and women to Sicily as slaves.

LP/AB991—[AB: IV indiction.] Count Atto[1] clashed with the Saracens in Taranto and here he died with many Baresi.

Translated from *MGH Scriptores*, vol. V (Hannover: Hahn, 1844) VV, 51–63; *RIS*, V (Milan, 1724), 145–56.
1. LP972 mentions a certain Atto, son of the marquis Trasmund, who fought the Saracens at Taranto.

LP992—A great famine in all Italy and a dearth of grain.

LP994—Matera was besieged for three months by the Saracens and conquered in the fourth.

AB994—VII indiction. Matera was besieged by the Saracens and was conquered after four months.

996—Matera was besieged for three months on end by the iniquitous race of the Saracens who finally took it by force in the fourth month, that is, December. In this city a woman ate her son.

LP1002—Caid Safi besieged Bari from 2 March until Saint Luke's day in the month of October. Then it was liberated by Pietro (II Orseolo) doge of the Venetians.[2]

AB1002—XV indiction. In this year, in May, Safi the apostate arrived and besieged Bari until the day of Saint Luke the apostle. The city was freed by the intervention of the Madonna and of Peter, doge of Venice.

LP1009—Much snow fell and the olive trees dried up and fish and birds died. In May an uprising happened. In August the Saracens took Cosenza having broken the treaty in the name of Caid Safi.

AB1009—VII indiction.

1013—On 11 April Bari was besieged by the *catepan*[3] Basil, called Sardoniti [Mesardonites] who after 61 days made peace with the Baresi and entered the castle of Bari, which is now the seat of the Greek magnates [now the site of the basilica of San Nicola, the former "court of the *catepan*"].

AB1013—XI indiction.

LP1015—In February a comet appeared. King Samuel [of Bulgaria] died and his son reigned.

AB1015—XIII indiction. King Samuel died and after him reigned his son.

LP1016—The son of Samuel was killed by his cousin, son of Aronis, who

2. Venice was developing her naval power in the Adriatic. In 1002, Doge Pietro II Orseolo led the naval expedition that drove the Saracens from Bari.

3. *Catepan*: the Byzantine Emperor Nicephorus Phocas had appointed a "*catepan* of Italy" to replace the *strategos* (the military leader of the Byzantine theme or administrative territory of the Lombards) as representative of Byzantine rule in the region in the 960s. The change does not appear to have had much effect in reinforcing Byzantine rule, as this entry demonstrates.

took the kingdom. The city of Salerno was besieged by the Saracens by sea and by land. However, they achieved nothing.

AB1016—XIV indiction. The Saracens besieged Salerno by sea and land.

Though sources on the arrival of the first Normans in southern Italy do not agree on all the details, most mention a role played by Melo (or Melus) of Bari, a local Lombard nobleman. The following passages detail some of Melo's actions, as well as the rising profile of the Normans.

LP1017—The *catepan* Mesardonites died in Bitonto. In November Leo, brother of Argiros died. In May the *catepan* Tornichios descended. The *cubicularius* [bed-chamber servant, chamberlain] Leo Pasiano engaged in battle against Melo and the Normans. Once again on 22 July the said *catepan* Tornichios engaged in battle, but Melo and the Normans won. Here Pasiano died.

AB1017—XV indiction. The *catepan* Andronicus (Tornikios) arrived, fought against Melo and Melo won.

LP1018—I indiction. The *catepan* Basil Bugiano descended, and in December the patrician Abalanti and Ligorius Topoterites engaged in battle at Trani and here Johannnizius the *protospatharius* was killed, while Romoald was taken and deported to Constantinople.

AB1018—I indiction. The *catepan* Basil Bugiano and patrician Abalanti arrived and . . . Johannizius the *protospatharius* was killed in battle at Trani and Romoald was deported to Constantinople.

LP1019—The aforesaid Bugiano [the *catepan* Basil] in October engaged in battle with the Franks and won. Melo fled with some Franks to the emperor Henry [II, r. 1014–24]. This battle took place near the city of Canne.

AB1019—II indiction Bugiano the *catepan* fought against the Franks [Normans] at Canne and won. Melo fled and took refuge with the emperor Henry.

1021 [actually 1019]—Basil Vulcanus [Bugiano] engaged in battle with the Franks and defeated them at Canne.

LP1021—Datto [brother-in-law of Melo] was captured and entered the city of Bari on 15 June riding an ass.

AB1021—IV indiction. Datto was taken and entered Bari on the rump of an ass.

LP1022—In March emperor Henry arrived in Benevento and besieged Troia in the Capitanate.

AB1022—V indiction.

1027—Ispo [Oreste] the *chitonitus*[4] came to Italy with a large army of Russians, Vandals, Turks, Bulgarians, Vlachs, Macedonians and others in order to conquer Sicily. Reggio was rebuilt by the *catepan* Vulcanus. But by his numerous sins the emperor Basil died in the second year; and everything went backward without having achieved anything.

AB1027—X indiction. In September San Nicola de Monte was built.

1041—The *protospatharius* and the *catepan* Michael Dochiano the younger came here to the Lombard Kingdom from Sicily. In November he entered Bari and sent four men to the gallows, having them hanged on the walls of Bitonto. On 17 March a battle took place between the Normans and the Greeks near the river Olivento. And here many Russians and Opsikions fell. In truth the same Dochiano and part of the army, which had saved itself from the battle, turned in flight in the direction of Montepeloso. Then, in May, all the Greeks united in a single army near Monte Maggiore, next to the river Ofanto, and at dawn of the fourth day engaged in battle. Many Anatolians, Opsikions, Russians, Thracians, Calabrians, Longobards, and Dauni died there. The priest Angelus, bishop of Troia, and Stephen, bishop of Acerenza were also killed there. In fact, as all those who were aware of the events report, there participated more than two thousand on the side of the Normans, whereas the Greeks, without counting the servants, were a good eighteen thousand. Michael, in the end, returned from here humiliated, with a few survivors left half dead by the fear of the Normans, who did every sort of violence, and he wrote to Sicily and the poor Macedonians and Paulicians and Calabrians came and united with each other at the foot of Montepeloso. Then the *catepan*, son of Bugiano, came to Apulia. Michael, on the orders of the emperor, returned to Sicily whence he came.

LP 1041—Dochiano came from Sicily and went to Ascoli; and in the month of March Arduin the Lombard called the Normans to the city of Melfi, in Apulia, and the said Dochiano engaged in battle with the Normans. The Greeks were defeated and in May, on a Wednesday, once again the Normans fought with the Greeks and Dochiano fled towards Bari.

AB1041—IX indiction. The *catepan* Michael Dochiano came from Sicily, and for the homicide which the same auxiliaries had committed he went to

4. A Byzantine honorific title.

Ascoli and there impaled a man. The same *catepan* came to Bitonto, impaled three men, and blinded four others. Arduin the Lombard entered Melfi, where there was a lieutenant of the same *catepan*, and assembled as many Franks as he could and raised a rebellion against the same *catepan*. The Greeks were defeated and so the same *catepan* sought refuge in Bari.

1042—In this year on 3 September the Greek army came out from Montepe-loso and the Normans came out from the castle of Monte Serico; between the two mountains there began a terrible clash, during which all the poor Macedonians were killed and few survived from the rest of the army. Here Bugiano was taken prisoner and led through all of Apulia ending up in the city of Benevento. In fact, as all who were present at this battle say truly, the Normans were seven hundred whereas the Greeks were ten thousand. Following this third clash, the Materans and the Baresi [and, according to William of Apulia, Monopoli and Giovinazzo too] came to an agreement with the Franks, since there was no one who could save them from their hands. Then, in February, the Normans and the Baresi elected as their prince and lord, Argiros, son of Melo. In April the *magister* Maniaces came to Taranto and reorganised all of the Greek army and made camp in the locality called Tara. Argiros wrote to the Normans in Aversa and Melfi, and all those who arrived at Mottola were around 7,000. Now, the iniquitous Maniaces, with all the enemy ranks, terrified by an immense fear, ran away during the night and shut himself away in Taranto. But the Normans, since they were standing in front of the landward gate calling for battle and since there was no-one there to oppose them, plundered all of the land of Oria and then returned to their own territory. In June, since the poor Giovinazzesi had concluded a pact with the Greeks in Trani, prince Argiros besieged miserable Giovinazzo with the Normans and Baresi. On the third day they conquered it and ransacked it of everything, while the Greeks in this city were killed. In truth the same prince after various pleas succeeded in liberating many men and women from the hands of the Normans. Then in truth, since the Tranesi would not stop damaging the Baresi, in the last week of the month of June, the prince together with the Normans and Baresi besieged Trani for thirty-six days. They tormented it with both attacks and with other calamities. In fact, they had built here a wooden tower the like of which had never been seen with human eyes even up to our own day. But the same Argiros, having received in the meantime an imperial letter which conferred on him the titles of patrician and *catepan* and *vestis*, ordered the war machines burnt. And returning to Bari with his fellow citizens, he gave praise to the holy emperor Constantine Monomachos [r. 1042–55]. But I will tell you more about that presently. I will report instead the story of the impious Maniaces. So, as I have said, he drove back the Normans from his borders, and assembling the army, in the month of June Maniaces left in the night for Matera. Here, the wicked man, in front of all the Materans, had killed all the men who had been captured in the camps and elsewhere who were more than two hundred. The iniquitous man did not fear to do the same thing in a second raid against Monopoli.

LP 1042—Esaugusto came in August and on 3 September clashed with the Normans. He was taken prisoner and from here was deported to Melfi. In the month of December the emperor Michael died and the Caesar, his nephew, was elected, who was also called Michael. In the month of February the Barese Argiros was named prince and duke of Italy. In the month of April the *magister* Maniaces came down to Taranto and in June sacked Monopoli, and set off towards the city of Matera and here inflicted a huge massacre. In September William was elected count of Matera. In this year the said Caesar Michael was deposed from the kingdom and blinded through the orders of the sisters Zoë and Theodora; Constantine Monomachos was named emperor. On 3 July Giovinazzo was taken by duke Argiros. In the month of August Argiros went to besiege Trani and held it under siege for a month.

AB 1042—X indiction. The *catepan* Esaugusto, son of Bugiano, came down, and once more clashed with the Normans and their duke Atenolf of Benevento below Montepeloso, and the Greeks were defeated and the *catepan* was taken as a prisoner to Benevento. Dochiano went to Sicily and Argiros became prince. The emperor Michael died and Caesar Michael, his nephew, ascended the throne and sent Maniaces to Apulia. After five months these miserable people blinded him and Zoë exiled him. And Constantine Monomachos ascended the throne. Argiros besieged Giovinazzo and took it through a betrayal from within. Maniaces proclaimed himself emperor in Italy and attacked the city of Monopoli, taking prisoner on the battlefields many men and having them decapitated in front of the gate. Similarly, he had 200 men killed in the city of Matera. Argiros departed for Trani and besieged it by sea and land and had built there a very high tower of wood and other siege machines to take the city. Whilst these events were going on, emperor Monomachos sent Theodoret bearing imperial orders and title of patrician to Argiros, who therefore burned all his siege engines and re-entered Bari.

By now the Normans, led by Robert Guiscard and other sons of Tancred of Hauteville, had successfully acquired scattered territories across the southern Italian pen-

insula through a combination of military strength and marriage alliances. In 1061 they launched their conquest of Sicily; Bari would be their prize in 1072.

LP1070—In the month of January, in Brindisi, a great massacre was perpetrated; in fact, since the Normans desired to take it, forty of them with another forty-three reinforcements fell in an ambush and the heads of all were taken to the emperor.

AB1070—VIII indiction. On Sunday 18 July the patrician Bisantius was killed by iniquitous men and then the houses of Melipezzo were burned and destroyed.

LP1072—10 June: Duke Robert [Guiscard the Norman] entered Palermo in Sicily.

AB1072—X indiction. Palermo was conquered by the duke on 10 January. In July emperor Diogenes was captured and killed.

LP1077—The city of Salerno was besieged and taken by Robert the Norman duke.

LP1083—This year, 517 years have passed since the Lombards entered Italy; the 28th year of the solar cycle was completed, the seventeenth year of the lunar cycle, the first nine-yearly cycle and the eleventh phase of the moon. At this time the Romans, getting rid of Pope Gregory [VII, r. 1073–85], sent an ambassador to the above-mentioned king [Henry] so that he might come to Rome; but the duke anticipating this, sent to Rome more than 30,000 gold coins to reconcile them to himself and the pope, which happened. Nevertheless the king, when he came to Rome, where the church of the prince of the apostles originated, took all of the region the other side of the Tiber. In June, leaving there his council with his son in the castle which he had built to unsettle Pope [Gregory] who had walled himself in the Lateran and on Mount Celio, with forty hostages he left Rome in the direction of Tuscany. In May the duke besieged Canne, a city in Apulia, and in July took it.

AB1083—VI indiction. The duke collected a tribute of *solidi* from the Baresi and caused them many torments and made confiscations; he attacked the city of Canne and, after the attack, took it with force on 10 July.

LP1084—Duke Robert [Guiscard], reuniting a large army of Normans, Lombards and other people, turned toward Rome to free Pope Gregory held under tough siege; this was done. In fact coming to Rome he conquered the greater part of the city and from here bravely rescued the pope and brought him to Salerno.

AB1084—VII indiction. He destroyed Canne and once more extorted many *solidi* in Bari and headed for Rome; he entered the city, seized pope Hilde-brand [Gregory VII] and took him away with him.

LP1085—The duke with a large apparatus of ships and with an innumerable army reached Brindisi, and here, having built a fleet, entered the Adriatic Sea and reached the island of Cassiopeia where the Venetian fleet and the son of the doge of Venice with very many ships confronted his force aggressively but, colliding in a naval battle, the Normans came out victorious. In this battle fell more than 5000 men, then five ships were captured, two sank with men, and those who could not flee from the sword were swallowed by the whirlpool of the sea. In May of this year Pope Gregory, while residing in Salerno, finished his last day and, while he was passing away, much hail fell and there was such a thunderstorm that everyone thought of abandoning their lives because of the violence of the whirlwind. In the month of July, while residing in the place that came to be called "veneti victi" since the Venetians were defeated, and while his army was on the island of Kefalonia so as to take a city, and he himself was closed up in this place with part of the army, preparing to besiege the royal city (Constantinople), with an enormous contingent of ships and soldiers, the the duke died of dysentery by the will of the most merciful and omnipotent God, who dissipates and objects to the thoughts and the projects of princes which are not in harmony with his own.

AB1085—VIII indiction. In October Robert [Guiscard] went to Greece. In January he had a naval battle with the Venetians and won. Pope Hildebrand died in Salerno. In July, on the day of Saint Alexius, duke Robert died in Kefalonia.

LP1086—Roger [Borsa], son of Duke Robert, was made duke.

AB1086—IX indiction.

LP1087—In the month of May the body of the most blessed Nicholas, arch-bishop of Myra [Smyrna], purloined by some Baresi from the above-men-tioned city of Mira, was brought to Bari, capital of Apulia. In this year Abbot Desiderius of Saint Benedict of Montecassino, with the support of some noble Romans, was made pope of Rome while the antipope Clement, the bishop of Ravenna, still lived.

AB1087—X indiction. On 9 May our Baresi carried back the body of the most blessed Saint Nicholas.

LP1088—In September there was through all of Apulia a great earthquake, such that it was related in some places that towers and houses had collapsed.

Now began at exactly that point the war between dukes Roger [Borsa] and Bohemond his [half-] brother [both were sons of Robert Guiscard]. In this year Syracuse, once the capital of Sicily, was taken by Count Roger I [brother of Robert Guiscard], where it is said, the siege was prolonged so excessively that both men and children were eaten.

AB1088—XI indiction. On 10 September, Friday, there was a great earthquake through all our territory, so great as to shake the foundations.

LP1089—In Melfi a synod was held of all the bishops of Apulia, Calabria, and the Abruzzo. Duke Roger also came here with all the counts of Apulia and Calabria and of other provinces. And in the course of this synod it was decided that the sacred truce of God be observed on the part of all vassals. In this year Ursus archbishop of Bari died and Pope Urban [II, r. 1088–99] came to Bari and here consecrated the church of Saint Nicholas, and the archbishop Elias, while the said pope Clement still lived; Pope Urban consecrated the cathedral of Brindisi.

AB1089—XII indiction. Archbishop Urso died and Elias was elected, and Bari welcomed Bohemond as its lord.

LP1091—A truce of God was sworn by the Normans. And 6291 years have completed since the creation of the world (Epact 19/29).[5]

LP1092—While the city of Oria was besieged by Bohemond, with the help of a few, the Oritani beat off the siege and since the same Bohemond fled, they seized all of his siege machinery and even the banners.

LP1093—In October Eugenia abbess of the monastery of Saint Benedict died in Matera and in the same month Pope Urban reached Matera with a large following and stayed in the abbey of Saint Eustasius.

LP1095—The night of a Thursday in April, all over Apulia there were seen to fall unexpectedly from the sky little flames like stars, and they filled up all the surface of the land. From this moment the people of Frankia [Francia] and of all parts of Italy started to depart toward the sepulcher of the Lord bearing on their right shoulder, together with weapons, the sign of the cross.

AB1095—III indiction. In January the Baresi gave an oath to the lord archbishop Elias, promising to listen to him, and to obey him in all that he might command for the common salvation.

---

5. *Epact 19/29*. An epact was a complicated dating system used to calculate the date of Easter by establishing the position of the year in a nineteen-year cycle. C. R. Cheney, ed., *Handbook of Dates for Students of English History* (London: Royal Historical Society, 1961), 8.

LP1096—Roger, count of Sicily, with twenty thousand Saracens and with an enormous contingent of soldiers, and with all the counts of Apulia, besieged Amalfi. Since the siege persisted, through divine inspiration Bohemond with other counts and with more than 500 knights abandoned the siege, after having put the sign of the cross on the right shoulder of his tunic. They passed over the sea to reach Constantinople to fight against the pagans with the help of Emperor Alexius, then turned toward Jerusalem, to the sacred sepulcher of our Redeemer Jesus Christ.

AB1096—IV indiction.

LP1097—Bohemond, with the count of Sant' Egidio, the count of Normandy, and other western lords and with innumerable men, left in April, moving from the city of Constantinople, passed over the sea and conquered all the territory that the Turks had taken away from the emperor, and in the clash that took place with the Turks Christ granted the victory to his Christians. It is said that the pagan forces were 140,000. The battle happened near the city of Nicaea.

AB1097—V indiction. Inspired by God many westerners—kings, counts, princes with their numerous armies, on horseback and on foot, large and small, rich and poor, old, young and children with many women, bishops and priests, abbots, monks, hermits—with great courage and with the consent of pope Urban, placed on their clothes the sign of the Holy Cross. And some marched across the land of Hungary as far as Constantinople; others departed on ships. . . .

LP1099—In October Pope Urban held a general synod in Bari and here 185 bishops convened. In June, on the festival of the apostle Peter, Jerusalem was taken by the Christians and all those who were found in the city were killed. It is said that 200,000 men were killed. Then the Christians elected Godfrey of Bouillon (1061–1100) as king, who had been duke of the Swabians. In July Pope Urban died and Pope Paschal II [r. 1099–1118] was elected.

AB1099—VII indiction. On 3 October Pope Urban came with many bishops, archbishops, and abbots and counts. They entered Bari and were welcomed with great deference; Elias, our archbishop, prepared a marvelous papal throne in the church of the Most Blessed Nicholas, confessor of Christ. And he held a synod here for a week. After eight days they went in peace. In July pope Urban died and Paschal became pope. In the same month Jerusalem was taken by the force of the Christians who, through the love of the Holy Sepulcher, had gone there, and all the pagans were put to the sword.

AB1115—VIII indiction. Pascal, son of Passaro, and Nicholas Tirra his nephew, son of Sergius called Ungrulo, sent two men by night who, having placed a wooden ladder on the house of Nicholas Garzone, went up secretly and silently onto the tower of the sons of Melo de Giovanni patrician. The guard of the tower was standing on the floor below that which they had reached and, coming down the stairs of the tower unseen, they tied up the guard and, having taken the tower they destroyed three floors of it. As a result there were many fights and scuffles among the citizens on both sides, during which several young men were killed.

AB1117—X indiction. Peter Johannizzi and Nicholas of Giovanni Usura and their faction destroyed the tower of Saint Nicholas, which was next to the tower of Nicholas of Melipezza. In the rubble Nicholas of Giovanni Usura and a large group of Baresi nobles died. In the same year the tower of Maio of Polignano was consigned to Peter Johannizzi by the guardian of the sister of Grimoald of Guaragna; Peter had the traitor thrown from the top. Indeed in entrusting it he drove the Saracen guardian from the tower from a great height to the ground; and eight days after he took the tower he had it knocked down.

112. WILL OF DOCIBILIS I OF GAETA (906)

Translated from Latin by Patricia Skinner

The city of Gaeta lies on a rocky peninsula in southern Lazio. Site of a small fortifi-cation, it grew in size and importance in the ninth century as the Tyrrhenian coast came under attack from the Arabs, and provided a refuge for the inhabitants of the nearby much older city of Formia. Gaeta, like Amalfi and their much larger neigh-bor Naples, was nominally under Byzantine rule, but all three cities were effectively independent by the latter part of the ninth century. The remainder of central-south-ern Italy was under Lombard rule, although the Lombard polity, like the Byzantine, was suffering major political upheaval and fragmentation. The tenth century would see this process continue, before the Lombards began an aggressive expansion from Capua and Salerno which was cut short only by the arrival of the Normans in the eleventh century. Docibilis I, whose will is translated below, was the first autono-mous ruler of Gaeta, although as I have shown in my study of the city, he had close relations with the rulers of Naples, and his will is still dated by Byzantine imperial rule.[1] His family would rule the city and its limited territory (previously papal patrimonial lands) for well over a century, until eclipsed by the Capuans in the 1030s. Even then, several branches of the family still appear in the Gaetan charters. Docibilis's will has been compared to the much better known (and earlier) document of doge Giustiniano Partecipazio of Venice, both revealing extensive fortunes. In fact, if Docibilis's rise was based on disposable wealth, he very rapidly turned it into landed resources, particularly an interest in monopolizing the market in mills in the territory, and his major resource, as his will reveals, was his sheer number of living heirs to expand and carry on the family's interests. In common with other testamentary sources, however, we should not assume that this document includes his entire fortune, but instead expresses the testator's wishes for how his residual wealth (once Roman inheritance laws were satisfied) was to be distributed.

In the name of our lord Jesus Christ, in the 28th year of the reign of our lords Leo and Alexander the purple-born, crowned by God magnificent and serene emperors, in the month of February in the 9th indiction at Gaeta.

A passage follows on the fragility of human life and the need to ensure the health of body and soul.

Thus I Docibilis, *ypatus*[2] of this city of Gaeta, walking on my feet, healthy of body and with whole mind, called you Stefano, priest of the holy Gaetan

---

Translated from *Codex Diplomaticus Cajetanus*, vol. 1 (Montecassino: Montis Casini, 1887), document 19.

1. Patricia Skinner. *Family Power in Southern Italy: The Duchy of Gaeta and Its Neighbours, 850–1139* (Cambridge: Cambridge University Press, 1995), 32–34.

2. A Byzantine honorific title equivalent to the Latin *consul*; it did not automatically con-vey any right to rule.

church, and am now speaking my will in front of you, asking you to write it down. And I have asked witnesses to sign so that what is in this charter deed will be written and done and tied up and executed as I order.

I wish and order first that the church of San Michele Archangelo which I newly built should have a pair of oxen, 2 more oxen, 2 slaves, cows, money, pigs, and land both inherited from my relatives and bought at San Lorenzo; and land in the estates under my control [*domus culta*] also inherited and built; and in Cessano; and a cemetery in the *domus culta*; and 4 *modia* at the just *modium* of arable land bought from Giovanni Fusco; and give to the church the silver I gave him; and the vineyard next to it with the garden on the side of San Teodoro; also 2 storehouses in Bica and the watermill at Pampilinum; and let the church take a portion of the mules as my sons would.

I have given 500 Byzantine *solidi* for my soul to redeem captives and for masses to be sung and for the monasteries and the poor.

I order and wish that all that I gave to Bona my daughter—gold, silver, silk cloths, male and female slaves, bronze, and all the other things—should remain firmly and stably [hers]; along with a house at the gate with the tower which I bought from Stefano the priest; also the land with the walls next to the tower *de Georgia* (on the other side is the house of Leo the priest); and the tower next to the foot of the Long Tower in front of the gate.

I wish that all I gave to my daughter Maria—gold, silver, silk cloths, male and female slaves, bronze—should remain firmly and stably [hers]; let her have the old and new house which I bought from Megalu the nun and the land up to the new wall, and that which I bought from the priest as a gift from the foundations to the top of the roof. Let the abovementioned Maria and her sister Bona have the oven next to the house of Ardavastus.

I wish and order that all I gave to Eufimia my daughter—gold, silver, bronze, silk cloths, movables of value, male and female slaves—should remain firmly and stably [hers]; also let her have the house which I built for her at the port.

I wish and order that all I gave to Giovanni *ypatus* my son—gold, silver, bronze, silk cloths, *specie*,[3] male and female slaves—be firm and stable; also the house with the bath and tower where he lives; also the house which was Aelisabetha's next to it which he bought. Let him also have the house which I bought where Cristoforo lives; let him have the whole garden in the high

---

3. *Specie*: translated as "spices" by Robert S. Lopez and Irving W. Raymond, *Medieval Trade in the Mediterranean World: Illustrative Documents*, Records of Western Civilization Series (New York: Columbia University Press, repr. 2001). I prefer their alternatives "coins" or "assorted wares"; clearly it is used to denote small movables of high value.

place; let the named Giovanni *ypatus* my son have the tower *a Mare* which I bought from Rampho de Dimitri and Bono Gallici.

I wish and order that all I gave to my son Leo—gold, silver, bronze, silk cloths, male and female slaves, and the house where he lives with the cistern and four entrances and all its appurtenances [should remain firmly and stably his]; and the small piece of land in front of it; let him also have the house which belonged to the brothers Teofilo and Giovanni de Urese with its court-yard and all its appurtenances; let him have sole ownership of the land on the Monte where once there was a house with a small piece of land and where there is now a garden which was Marino de Ramfo's.

I wish and order that all I have given to my son Anatolius—gold, silver, bronze, silk cloths, male and female slaves—should be firm and stable. Let him also have the house where he lives from the foundations to the roof and the half upper floor which we obtained from Mammalo; and let him have the house which I bought from Leuthera daughter of Giovanni Gorgone; let him have the wine-cellar; let him have the house of the women's quarters and the mill with the kitchen; but he does not have the right to build further on the women's quarters or the kitchen; let him have the mill with its equipment and mechanism and the wooden board.

I wish and order that all I gave to Megalu my daughter—gold, silver, bronze, silk cloths, male and female slaves—be firmly and stably [hers]; let her also have the house I built for her in the port. I wish and it pleases me that the gable-end wall of the house above the road to the west where the oven was should be communal with the house of Megalu my daughter.

And here I record that if any of my sons or daughters should lose any of what has been willed to them, let them have total justice.

I wish that the land and estates outside the city which I don't recall should be divided between all of my children each with their portion. Here I record that whatever charters of concession I made to my children should be firm and stable. I wish that all the charters about land and estates bought outside the city in my name or my wife's should be demesne land and shared by all my sons and daughters.

It pleases me that the gable-end walls of the house at the port where the oven was should be common with the house of Megalu my daughter, and my son-in-law Stefano has no right to close off the gate, but let him have from the wall of the kitchen; and let him build upward as much as he pleases.

I wish Giovanni *ypatus* my son to have the land with walls which begins at the Platea Maiore road, and let him build on this land a hospital for visitors.

It pleases me that the priest of Sant'Angelo should keep an eternal regi-men of singing a mass every day for me and another for my wife Matrona.

And let him feed 2 visitors every day; and if he does not do so may Leo my son, to whom I have left the church [see below], consider this and take from him the grain ration and ransom 2 captives for my soul; and if he does not take the grain ration may the price of this labor be given from the said church. Let Leo my son have the care of the said church and appoint the priest and everything else; may he be a Judas if he appoints a priest who has a woman, unless that man is chaste.

I wish and it pleases me that all the work I did in the church of San Silviniano, confessor of Christ—the pavement, the marble crenellations, the roof beams, and the storehouse, on which I spent more than 120 Beneventan *solidi*, and the processional cross with gold and gems weighing 15 ounces— [should remain firm]; and let this church have 20 *modia* of land in Casari; and let it be in the care of Leo to appoint the priest and the deacon with his heirs. Also the church of Sant'Angelo should be in Leo's care and that of his heirs for ever. And if what I do not believe happens and some great or small person should arise who wishes to take the church of San Silviniano from the power of my son Leo or his heirs, let him [Leo] take out the cross and all the land and all I have spent there.

I wish that Eufimia and Megalu should have the land above the church of Sant'Irene. The land is bordered by the garden of the heirs of Adeodatus to the east, the vineyard of Gemmus to the west, above it to the south is the public road down to where the house of Vitulus was.

I wish Fermipertulus to be freed. I gave him 10 Byzantine *solidi*; let him also have 2 pairs of oxen and all his household goods and half of the land in the Platea Maiore under the road up to the old wall which I got from Bonus my father-in-law, which is bordered on one side by the land of Cristofero de Andrea and on the other by the house of Basil the count which the *coloni* [tenants] bought; with its small piece of land in front of the courtyard of Basil's house.

I wish and order that Leo *vicedominus* [farm manager] be freed and have a pair of oxen and a mule and the other half of the land in the Platea Maiore with Fermipertulus.

Let Petrulus the miller be freed with his wife and household goods; let him have a pregnant cow and a veal calf.

Let Lupo the pigman be freed with his wife and have an ox.

And all that we have in Vivano, wherever it came from, should be my son Leo's; and let him have the vineyard and empty land in the close in Casale.

Let San Silviniano's have the land outside the gate, because the church has two-thirds there and I have the other third.

Let Petrulus be free with all his household goods; and let him have the land with walls at Pertusillum, and let him have a foal . . . ; let him have the vineyard and land either bought or inherited in Paniano. Let him divide the Paniano land with Paolo his semi-free servant.

Let Paolo be free with his household goods and have the land at Ripa with walls. Let him have a horse and a mule and the land at Paniano shared with Pietro.

Let Formosula be freed with her household goods. Let her have the land above the roofless house in the Platea Maiore where I said a hospital is to be built; and let her gain access to it via the steps of Giovanni Buffo or in front of the cellar of Leontacius. This land is bordered on one side by that of Leontacius, on the second side by that of Constantine son of Leo, on the third side by the land of Ardavastus. Let Formosula also have the lower ground floor of the Long Tower which I bought from Alagernus, and the land which I gave to the church of San Silviniano at Casari bordering Letitia's at the point where I showed the priest, and from the stone which we fixed to Serape where I showed the priest.

Let all the gold, silver, houses, cloths, and specie that I gave to my sons and daughters remain firmly and stably [theirs] and let no-one seek anything from another from the lands outside the city.

If anyone acts against my will, may he share the same fate as Judas traitor of our Lord, and pay 10 pounds of bright gold, and may my will be firm.

Written at my order by Stefano the priest and scribe of this city in the abovementioned month and ninth indiction.

I wish that the charters I made to my sons and daughter be firm.

And let 30 *modia* of grain coming from the mill of Pampilinum go to Sant'Angelo for visitors, for my soul and that of Matrona my wife, and let Leo my son take care of this.

[The sign of Docibilis *ypatus*, Stefano the priest, and six witnesses.]

113. FOUNDATION OF A MONASTERY IN BYZANTINE CALABRIA (1053/54)

Translated from Greek and Italian by Adele Cilento and David Routt

In the Byzantine Empire, monasteries and churches were often founded by laymen, sometimes functionaries of the local administration who, in exchange for the material support for the foundation, requested prayers for themselves and their families. Important evidence of this custom appears in a document drafted in the theme of Calabria, one of the two provinces held by Byzantium through the mid-eleventh century in southern Italy (the other was the theme of Lombardy, corresponding roughly to present-day Apulia and a portion of Basilicata). In the document, called a homologia—*a generic term indicating any type of agreement between parties—numerous important people appear as witnesses who, together with the donor himself, can be numbered among the* archontes *[the powerful] of Byzantine provincial society. Besides Cyril who holds the position of commander of troops, two witnesses appear with the title of* protospatharios, *and also a* tassiarca, *a subordinate official in the provincial governor's office. There are, moreover, four representatives of the ecclesiastical hierarchy who quite rightly regarded themselves as members of the* theme's *elite. The document clearly attests, therefore, to the connections and the coincidence of interests among the exponents of civil authority and of the members of the religious hierarchy in a provincial area of the empire.*

HOMOLOGIA, 1053–54, CALABRIA

† Mark of the hand of Cirillo, *spatharocandidatos* and *domestikos,*[1] of the troops of the Ungari.

In the name of the Father and of the Son and of the Holy Spirit. The above-written Cirillo, *spatharocandidatos* and *domestikos,* marking with his own name and by his own hand the sign of the honored and salvific cross, beyond all compulsion and necessity, with clarity to you, Leonzio, monk *kourator;* and Cosma, monk *papas;*[2] and Vitale, monk.

As has often been requested by you with prayer, I concede to you one of my lands located at Fella in the *saline* [saltpans] of the *theme* of Calabria. This plot of land borders on the hill with the stream that descends from

Translated from Messina, Archivio di Stato, Fondo Medinaceli, Sivilgia 64–1308; Edition: A. Guillou, C. Rognoni, "Une nouvelle foundation monastique dans le thème de Calabre," *Byzantinische Zeitschrift* 84/85 (1991–92): 423–29.

1. Noble title (*spatharocandidatos*) accompanied by the indication of the position of commander (*domestikos*) of a little-known military corps called Ungari, perhaps for the ethnicity of its soldiers.

2. *kourator:* term of broad meaning, here perhaps employed for matters negotiated by the monastery with other people; *papas:* probably a monastic official who negotiated the monastery's affairs with the outside world.

Fineles and likewise surrounds the vicinity. This [is] for the purpose of constructing a residence and planting a vineyard and some gardens and sowing and possibly building for yourself a mill or anything else. In exchange you will allow me to build a church in that place, at my expense, to pray unceasingly for me and my relations and my children. You will not appropriate any of it for yourself and you will not violate the canons and you will not defraud me by transferring this place given to you by me to an unknown person and, if they tempt you to do this, I will have the authority to chase you out, and after me my heirs also [will be able to do] so. Whatever this place contributes or creates will remain completely for my church. And when by ill destiny the *egumeno* [abbot] dies, you will be allowed to make another *egumeno* with my approval and my advice; and, should the same happen after me, also with my heirs. All this is established and ratified by me in the presence of the assembled eminent and reliable witnesses, who sign by their own hands. If you act well and in keeping with the canons, you will not be able to be driven out either by me or by my heirs. If something evil is done against you, and, if this happens from my part against you, may I be driven away from the faith of Christ and may you be free to take legal proceedings against me.

Written by the hand of Filippo, humble priest . . .

Costantine *protospatharios* and *epì Manglabiou*,[3] judge, signs with his own hand the *homologia* of the same Cyril.

+ [I] Panchario Kontonikitas, *protospatharios*, being witness of the *homologia* of the lord Cyril, sign with my hand.

+ Komitas, priest and *ekdikos*,[4] witness, signs.

+ Giovanni, deacon and *carthophylax*,[5] witness, signs.

+ Teodoro, *tassiarca* of the *Bizineoi*[6] . . . witness.

+ Christodoulos, humble priest and *klerikos*,[7] witness, signs.

+ Thomas, humble deacon "chart . . ." and *klerikos*, witness, signs with his own hand.[8]

3. Initially a position as guard in the imperial corps armed with a cudgel, which indicates in all probability the designation of a membership preceding the deed's ratification: that is to say, Constantine had been part of the imperial corps of the Manglaviti when he was named judge of the *theme* of Calabria, the province's highest judicial authority.

4. The *ekdikos* of the cathedral was equivalent in function to the attorney of the ecclesiastical tribunal.

5. The *carthophylax* was the head of the episcopal chancery and, therefore, the bishop's principal assistant.

6. Term that indicates the geographic origin of the armed corps commanded by the *tassiarca*.

7. *Klerikoi*, clerks of the cathedral, were officials of a bishop or archbishop who were paid with a private landed income.

8. On the reverse of the document, beyond a few scattered words: "Seal of Cyril *spatharocandidatos*, Leonzio *egumeno*, Vitale *egumeno*."

114. *THE SCROLL OR GENEALOGY OF AHIMAAZ BEN PALTIEL*: JEWISH LEARNING, MYTH, AND IDEALS IN AN UNCERTAIN SALENTINE WORLD (1054)

Translated from Hebrew by J. H. Chajes and Kenneth Stow

This short text, about 800 lines in all, was composed in the year 1054. Its author, one Ahimaaz ben Paltiel, about whom we know nothing except what his Genealogy tells us, was seeking to aggrandize his past. It survived in a single manuscript resting in the Cathedral of Toledo, and was discovered near the end of the nineteenth century. The text makes us privy to Jewish life in southern Italy, especially the tension of Jews living in a society where outside pressure comes from Christian and Islamic sources. The author is extremely skilled: this is storytelling at its best, but it is also a social and cultural record. It is not the historical record some would make of it. Ahimaaz begins by extolling the magical—and Talmudic—prowess of his scholarly progenitor, Abu Aaron. The scion of the secular head of the Jews of Babylonia (now Iraq), Abu Aaron begins his wanderings upon being exiled by his father for abusing his preternatural gifts. He arrives in Italy, at Gaeta, off the beaten track about 60 miles south of Rome, on the Appian Way. Jewish communities were scattered along this commercially important route. The bulk of Italian Jewish communities, apart from Rome (where Jews had lived since well before the time of Julius Caesar), were then in the south, in Apulia, and especially the Salentine Peninsula (the heel of the boot). Later Jews, in Ashkenaz (the German Rhineland), would say that "The Torah came forth from Bari, the word of the Lord from Otranto." The culture Abu Aaron is ascribed with having brought from the East is thus the source of later Ashkenazi Jewish culture and memory. The Hebrew text is rhymed prose. We will not attempt to imitate it, although something of the cadence is preserved.

Jewish learning, whether Talmudic or otherwise, took place in large university-like academies in "Babylonia." In the West, including southern Italy, the preferred format was the small studium, *noted for intellectual debate, rather than formal lecturing, as in the East. At the time of Abu Aaron, nonetheless, the West still depended on the East for deeper knowledge and texts. Aaron's arrival marks the start of a change toward Western intellectual and spiritual independence; this is really Ahimaaz' point in these stories.*

From there [Gaeta], Aaron went in strides to Oria. There he found tents, embedded as rivers, and as trees planted and flourishing on waters. There were schools of learning and inquiry solidly rooted as cedars. Resting on the

Translated from the Hebrew edition by Benjamin Klar (Jerusalem, 1944, repr. 1974). An earlier English translation is *The Chronicle of Ahimaaz*, trans. Marcus Salzman (New York: Columbia University Press, 1924).

waters as babbling brooks, [their scholars] contending and persuading [one another, with the tenacity of combatants] in a head-on war. Teaching the tradition publicly . . . the sons of Rabbi Amitai, my forefathers Rabbis Shefatyah and Rabbi Hananel.

Ahimaaz claims that these rabbis exercised the functions of deciding capital cases, something no Jewish tribunal had been empowered to do since antiquity. He really means their learning was extremely sophisticated.

There was one Theophilos, who committed a great trespass and was guilty of adultery with a married woman. And the leaders of the community sat and judged, and they sentenced Theophilos to end his days by strangulation [as the halachah, Jewish law, prescribes].

It is the political issues, mixed with magic, nonetheless, that we must deal with first. This story closely parallels a talmudic one [BT Meilah 17b] involving R. Shimon bar Yohai and the demonic possession of another emperor's daughter. In both stories, the exorcism has political consequences: in this case, the Jews of Oria are spared forced conversion to Christianity.

The Basileus [emperor of Byzantium] had a daughter, whom he loved as the apple of his eye. But a demon afflicted her, and he was unable to cure her. He secretly summoned Rabbi Shefatyah and pleaded with him, saying: "Help me, Shefatyah, heal my daughter's illness." "Surely I will do this," Shefatyah replied, "with the help of Almighty God. But do you [Basil]," he asked, "have a special place [of ritual cleanliness] where there is no [idolatrous] abomination?" Said the emperor, "the Bucoleon [a palace on the Sea of Marmora in Byzantium] is appropriate" and the garden is mine. He inspected it and found it suitable; the Bucoleon was favorable in his eyes, since its name means "lion's mouth." So it was to there that [Shefatyah] led the maiden. And he adjured the demon in the Name of Him Who dwells on High, and in the Name of Him Who moves heaven and earth, and in the Name of Him Who founded the Earth on Wisdom, and in the Name of Him Who forms mountains and seas, and in the Name of Him Who suspends the Earth over the void. And the demon cried, "Why are you being so beneficent to the daughter of the evil one, whose evil has been so great and who has so often done evil to the people saved [by the Lord]. The Lord has given her over to me, to subjugate her and to shatter her. Now leave me alone, for I will not leave my place." To which, [Shefatyah] replied, "To your words I pay no heed. Depart, in the name of God, so that [Basil] might know that there is a God in Israel." Straightaway, the demon departed, fleeing swiftly.

Shefatyah, however, caught it and inserted it into a lead vessel that covered it completely, which he then sealed with the name of its Creator and flung into the sea, where it sank in the mighty waters. The maiden then went quietly, relieved, and in peace, to the emperor and empress.

The overjoyed Basil tries to convert Shefatyah to Christianity, but Shefatyah refuses, asking not to be "cast in the wasteland." Ahimaaz has already called the Church of Hagia Sofia a "house of impurity." Such names and attitudes are typical of relations between medieval Christians and Jews. Christian laws had said Judaism and idolatry were identical.[1] Jews said the same of Christianity. We know there were hard times for Jews under Byzantine rule in Italy from about 875 to 930, roughly the time of Shefatyah.[2] Ahimaaz's family chronicle thus becomes one great polemic about Judaism's virtues and Christianity's failings.

To the emperor's question, what did he wish, Shefatyah replied in distress and in bitter tears: "If my lord cares for Shefatyah, leave those who busy themselves with wisdom in peace, and do not remove them from the Torah of God, to expel them to the wasteland, in mourning and oppression. And if you do not want to do my will in all of this, at least do one thing for my sake: Let there be no forced conversion in my city [of Oria]." The Emperor angrily called out from his throat: "Had I not sent my seal and sworn, he said, I would do you evil, just now and in this instant. But what can I do, for I have . . . [given my word]? And I cannot renege from what I have inscribed." And he [issued an edict sealed with] a decorative golden seal, that in Oria there would be no forced conversion and sent [Shefatyah] home with honor and in peace to his place and his chamber.

Then the evil Basil dictated oppression in all his lands; he sent minions to make forced converts—to pressure them and to compel them [to abandon the true] faith, to turn them back to his vanities [but Oria was spared].

Ahimaaz has one step more to go in extolling the virtues of his ancestors, alluding to their role in heralding a messianic time. Such allusions are most evident in the tales about Paltiel, Ahimaaz' greatest hero and ancestor. In the narrative, Paltiel is made a Jewish ruler, a vizier, something Islamic law forbids. However, Christian standards, too, said Jews were to possess no rule. Paltiel contradicts this claim. It is precisely this restoration of Jewish power that belies the truth of other religions and is a sign of the messiah's immanence. Who was he? A real Paltiel, or one like him,

1. Amnon Linder, *The Jews in Legal Sources of the Early Middle Ages* (Detroit: Wayne State University Press, 1997), no. 502, *Christianorum ad aras.*
2. See Steven Bowman, *The Jews in Byzantium (1204–1453)* (University: University of Alabama Press, 1985).

*there likely was. But Ahimaaz's Paltiel was clearly modeled after Ahimaaz's con-
temporary, the Jewish Granadan Vizier and General Samuel the Prince.*

Rabbi Hasadiah the son of Rabbi Hananel [son-in-law of Rabbi Shefa-
tyah] had a son named Paltiel, and Paltiel, in turn, fathered a son named
Hananel, as well as a daughter named Cassia, who greatly feared God. Cassia
gave birth to a son named Paltiel, one who knew how to read the stars [an
astrologer].

Now, in those days, [roughly, the mid-tenth century], the Ishmaelites
[the standard Jewish negative euphemism for Muslims, descended from
Ismail] set out with their armies. Their leader was the emir al-Muizz.[3] They
coursed through Italy and destroyed Calabria and they came to Oria on the
edge of Apulia. They assaulted the city, destroyed its [Byzantine] garrison,
and placed it under siege. . . . It fell, . . . and the remaining few were taken
captive. The Emir inquired about the family of Shefatyah. He sent for them,
and they brought them before him and God made the Emir merciful. God
extended his grace to Rabbi Paltiel, and he ingratiated Paltiel to Al-Muizz,
his prince.

Paltiel and al-Muizz go out one night and read in the stars that the
Emir's star had swallowed three others. Al-Muizz asked Paltiel, "what have
you understood?" And Paltiel replied: "speak first." The emir then said:
"The stars are three cities, Taranto, Otranto, and Bari, which will be mine."
Paltiel, in turn, said: "No, my lord, for I saw a great thing. The first star
means you will rule Sicily, the second Ifriqiyah [roughly, Libya], and the
third, Babylonia."[4] Instantly, the emir embraced Paltiel and kissed him on
the head. He removed his signet ring, gave it to Paltiel, and swore in his
favor: "Should it be as you said, should your words be confirmed, you will
reign over my household, throughout my kingdom and my realm."

*The Genealogy concludes with stories of attacks on Oria by a "king of the Arabians."
Ahimaaz's family is dispersed to Capua, near Naples, from where Ahimaaz has
returned, to Oria, to begin anew. Ahimaaz's story is like that which another Orian,
the early tenth-century physician and naturalist Shabbetai Donnolo, tells of himself.
Donnolo's work,* The Book, Enlighten Me, *or* Make Me Wise *(in matters of mysti-
cism and science) asserts the congruity between Jewish and non-Jewish speculative
knowledge. This is an element to which Ahimaaz barely alludes; nevertheless, there
seems to have been a common world of scientific and astrological knowledge that all*

3. Al-Muizz (r 953–975) was a Shiite Fatimid ruler. In 969, he conquered Egypt and
founded Cairo; in 956, his naval forces inflicted a severe defeat on the Byzantines of Southern
Italy.

4. Babylonia is the standard medieval Hebrew name for Mesopotamia, modern Iraq,
using, therefore, the region's biblical name, full of memories for Jews.

traditions shared. Donnolo could learn from non-Jews with no fear. The wisdom of the stars was, as Donnolo saw it, identical to that taught by the sage Samuel the Preacher. This was the key. Donnolo could be as radical as he liked, as long as he was convinced that the wisdom of the stars, planets, and constellations was consonant with his own tradition.

I Shabbetai bar Abraham, known by the name of Donnolo the physician, with the help of the eternal God, who gives wisdom and understanding and knowledge, sought to achieve something of worth, and I took heed to write many books. I set my heart to inquiry, and to seek by wisdom that which the seasons have brought about. I was exiled from my city Oria, the land of my birth, by an army of Ishmaelites. This was on the second day of the week, at the fourth hour of the day [after sunrise] the hour of Mars, on the ninth day of the [Hebrew] moon of Tamuz [in the summer], in the year 4685 from the creation [hence, 925], in the eleventh year of the 247th lunar cycle [a nineteen-year cycle used to calculate the new moon]. Ten wise and righteous rabbis were killed, may their memory be for a blessing. Rabbis Hasadiah, son of Hananel the Great and Righteous, our relative, a relative of my grandfather called Rabbi Yoel, and [others of Ahimaaz's family].

I Shabbetai was redeemed in Taranto, with money from my fathers [his family], when I was twelve years old. They then exiled my "fathers" to Palermo and Ifriqiyah. I, however, remained in the Kingdom of the Romans [Byzantines]. "Then I looked on all the works my hands had wrought and on the labors I labored to do" (Ecclesiastes 2:11) for there was no hard work "of those who have seen affliction" (Lamentations 3:1) that I did not turn to, and "behold, all was vanity and vexation of spirit and there was no profit under the sun" (Ecclesiastes 2:11). "Then I saw that the advantage of wisdom over ignorance was like that of light over darkness (ibid.). . . . Thus I labored greatly to be apprenticed [to a scholar] and to learn the science of medicine and the science of the stars and constellations. I copied for myself books from those of the ancient scholars of Israel. However, I could find not one wise man of the Jews in these parts who understood these ancient [scientific] books. Some of the wise men of Israel were in the habit of saying of the books describing the constellations written by Jews that they were worthless. That was because they did not understand them. The [real] books of wisdom about constellations and stars were to be found among the Gentiles. The thinking in these books differs from that in books written by Jews. Thus my heart led me to know, to peruse, to search out the science of the Greeks, and the science of the Ishmaelites, and the science of Babylonia and India. And I was not in peace until I myself could copy books of science of Greece and

Macedonia, in their own script, their language, and as they were understood. I investigated, too, the [writings of] many sages of Babylonia [Mesopotamia] and India, and searched them deeply. I found them identical in every detail that pertained to the wisdom of the stars and planets with the books written by Jews. In every case, their thinking was the same, and correct. Yet I also realized from these books that all the wisdom of the stars and constellations is based on the *Baraita of Samuel the Preacher*.[5] The books of the sages of the nations also agree with what this *Baraita* says. But Samuel made his book exceedingly opaque. And after I copied those books, I traveled around the various lands to find the wise men of the nations who know the wisdom of the stars and the constellations, to apprentice myself before them, of whom I found one or two. Afterward, I found a wise man of Babylonia, whose name was Bagdash, a great expert in the wisdom of the stars and the planets.[6] He also knew [astronomical] calculation and [how] to understand what was, what would be, and [the ways of] the stars and the constellations. All his wisdom jibed perfectly with the *Baraita of Samuel*, and with all the books of Israel, and with all the books of the Greeks and Macedonians. His wisdom was well known. And after I had experienced many times the wisdom of this man, which he derived from calculating the stars, and the "dragon"[7] and the constellations, things which had been and also things that would be, then I persuaded him with much money and many gifts to teach me the traditions about the stars and the calculations of the constellations. He taught me to recognize in the skies twelve constellations and five planets, their risings, their settings, their zenith and their nadir. He taught me, too, the rules of observing the constellations, explaining which were beneficial, which malevolent, and how, by measuring the shadow cast by the rod, as written in *Baraita of Samuel,* the star and the constellation which are lords of the hour can be known, so that any question may be asked and answered.

And after I had studied with this wise man and became experienced and understood well what was written truly, I set my intelligence to understand every book that came to hand, and I amassed all their wisdom together with that of the wise man of Babylonia [who had taught me] his learning. All of which I have written down clearly in [this] book called *Hakhmoni: Make Me Wise.*

---

5. Otherwise anonymous, in J. D. Eistenstein, ed., *Otsar Midrashim* (New York: Eisenstein, 1915), 542–47.

6. Andrew Sharf has identified Bagdash with the physician Abu Ja'far ibn al-Jazzar of Kayrawan (ca. 929–1009); see Sharf, *The Universe of Shabbetai Donnolo* (Warminster: Aris and Phillips, 1976), 130, n. 45.

7. *Teli*, a mythic rendering of the Ptolemaic *axis mundi*, the axis of the universe.

Figure 29. Doge's palace, southern facade (thirteenth century with later additions), Venice. (Photo: Scala/Art Resource)

115. HENRY OF RIMINI'S PAEAN TO VENICE (ca. 1300)

Translated from Latin by John E. Law

Henry was a Dominican friar. Not much is known about his life—in 1308 he served on a Venetian embassy, when the Republic was seeking to avoid excommunication for its attack on Ferrara, a papal fief, and a possible date for his death is 1314. His description of Venice is found in the discussion of justice in his treatise on the cardinal virtues written ca. 1300, a treatise which enjoyed a wide circulation in the fourteenth and fifteenth centuries. Its positive and at times eulogistic tone, possibly born from his diplomatic experience, makes it one of the earliest examples of the "myth of Venice"; all the basic elements of the "myth" are found here: the excellence of the Republic's "mixed" constitution; its peace and security; its cosmopolitanism; its social harmony; the consequences of its unusual situation; its piety; its industry [see #5, 67, 117].

Among all the states which are to be found today among Christian people, that of the Venetians appears to come closest to the "mixed constitution." For in it, around four hundred are admitted to the public councils from the nobility and even from the worthy people; of these, some of the more prudent are chosen to elect the prince. And they choose somebody from among the noble Venetians to elevate as their doge. But he, elected from the magnates, governs the state along with six who are called Councillors, and forty who almost have the position of *anziani* of the people. Nor do those who rule the city with the doge remain always in office, but every member of the Council at statutory times is elected to hold the offices of Councillor and *anziano*. And so each one of those elected to the Council has some part in the government, which virtually has something of each of the three principal types of constitution. For, in so far as one is set over all, it could be called a monarchy; in so far as a few of the leading citizens elect the Doge and govern the state with him, and are elected to this position at various times it could also be called an oligarchy; in so far as these leading citizens, ducal electors, councillors and members of the Forty are elected from the whole Council, the constitution has something of a popular regime, for there are in the Council not only the greater nobles, but also many of the worthy people.

These Venetians enjoy such peace and security that nobody is ever driven into exile by a hostile faction; immigrants and refugees are offered sanctuary; there is no oppression or invasion from foreign parts. Everything is secure. Murder and the shedding of blood are never, or only rarely, heard of. Subject to no man, the people enjoy the fullest liberty. Indeed, the doge they create is so bound by statute that he cannot be any more eminent than the people want him to be.

In the sea waters, which surround them on all sides, they have built buildings of great number, beauty, and luxury. They teach their young men the ways of the sea, with all its dangers and difficulties, so necessary is it for their livelihood; however, they involve those who are older in the affairs of state. Instead of horses, they have oars; for oxen they have boats. Everything is traded in cash, even drinking water. Nobody here is born a slave, nor is anyone even hired. Everyone defends on his own behalf the freedom of the fatherland, and seeks his livelihood with the sweat of his own brow. They are

Translated from J. E. Law and D. Robey, "The Venetian Myth and the *De Repubblica Veneta* of Pier Paolo Vergerio," *Rinascimento* ser. 2, 25 (1975): 52–56.

most audacious and skilled in naval warfare, striving at one and the same time for the glory of the state and for their own reputations.

Food supplies are carried there from many parts of the world, and those commodities which are not found in distant places, they transport to many areas of the west. They dress magnificently, but they are moderate in their eating habits lest trading be interrupted or affairs of state disturbed by debauchery; they have no inns. They are devoted in their care of churches and truly love God's name. They care for the poor. In Venice, there are many hospitals for the destitute and fine monasteries dedicated to the worship of the saints; both are supported by public and private endowments and alms. They leave a tenth of their liquid assets, which constitutes almost all their material possessions, to the poor and to the furtherance of Christian observance. They are good Catholics and totally free from any taint of heresy. They never commit inhuman and monstrous crimes, and are not influenced by the habits of their neighbors. No usury is permitted in the city. They do not observe the common law, but follow their own statutes, suited to their own constitution; when their statutes prove inadequate, they turn not to foreign laws but to the customs of their ancestors.

They are deeply loyal to the state, which every citizen tries to preserve in its wealth and dignity. In turn, the state tries to maintain the wide freedoms and singular immunities enjoyed, not only by the citizens, but even by the plebeians. If anyone encounters trouble abroad, he soon receives help either with the arrival of ducal letters or public ambassadors, or by the threat of reprisals, so that he is freed from his difficulties. Poor but worthy citizens depend for advancement on salaried offices; many are supported from common funds.

116. FOUR BOLOGNESE WILLS (1337)

Translated from Latin by Shona Kelly Wray

Wills are a valuable source for reconstructing the mental outlook or disposition of medieval people. The following are the testaments of a butcher, a baker, a porter, and a laborer, living in the city of Bologna in 1337. As non-elite wills they are simple, with few bequests and instructions—only the technical language of stock legal phrases has been omitted from the translation. Although these men had little property to leave for charitable purposes, they all provide instructions for the future of their family through dowry and institution of a universal heir. The standard inheritance pattern of late medieval urban Italy, as confirmed by the laws of intestacy,[1] was to divide the inheritance equally among sons. Daughters received dowries, but were not named heirs. However, it is clear from these wills that testators had more leeway than the laws suggest: daughters are named with their brothers as heirs. As they were not provided with a dowry, they were most likely expected to use their share of the inheritance for that purpose. These wills also show a certain amount of flexibility regarding bequests made to wives. Typically the husband returned the wife's dowry, but tried to compel her not to demand it back by offering a usufruct over house and all his goods as long as she remained "chaste and widowed," lived with her children, and "did not seek her dowry." These wills, however, show that not all husbands made these claims. Translated from Bologna's city notarial registers, the Libri Memoriali, *these wills are copies of originals drawn up by a notary, with seven witnesses present in the home of the testator. These names have been translated in the first example. If the testator was ill—and most were—a member of the clergy had to be present to confirm his identity and mental capacity. Within two days after the will was redacted, the notary and testator, or his proctors if he was too ill, went to the city's office of the* Memoriali *to register the will, pay a city tax, and then deposit it for future recording, which is what we read today.*

1. A Butcher's Will

1 February, 1337. Vilano di Bonaventura, a butcher of the parish of San Giuseppe, by the grace of Christ, healthy in mind and senses, but sick in body, with this nuncupative[2] testament first leaves, for his soul, 10 Bolognese pounds of which he wishes some to be spent [in recompense] for ill-gotten gains as his executor sees fit and the rest to be spent for the benefit of his soul according to the wishes of his executor. He chooses and names as executor his son, Nicola. . . . He leaves to his wife, donna Francesca, daughter of the late Giovanni, 50 pounds which he received as her dowry. As further legacy he leaves to her one chest and one mattress belonging to him. He

---

Translated from Archivio di Stato di Bologna (ASB), *Memoriali*, vol. 191, fol. 126v.

1. Laws governing succession when there is no will.
2. An oral will made by the testator before witnesses, subsequently written down.

leaves to donna Gesia, wife of his son Nicola, 100 pounds which he had received from her as her dowry. In all his other goods and in all present and future actions he institutes as his universal heirs, in equal portions, his children Nicola, Giuseppe, Giovanni, Andrea, and Margarita [4 sons and 1 daughter]. And this he asserts to be his last will and he wants it to be valid by testamentary law. . . . Redacted in Bologna in the home of the testator with friar Angello of Florence and friar Tommaso of Bologna, both of the order of Servites of Bologna, who recognize the testator to be healthy in mind. Also present as witnesses are Pietro Bertolomei of the parish of Santa Maria Maggiore, Maxello, called Castra, di Giovanni of the parish of San Giuseppe, Cambio di Meloghini de Ranfredis of the same parish, Jacopo di Benati of Castenaxio, Jacopo di Nicola of San Giuseppe, Nicola di Bertolatio dei Tolomeis of the said parish, and Fillippo di Benzevene de Castro Francho, all called as witnesses by the said testator, who since he was sick appointed friar Angello and Pietro as his proctors in order that the aforesaid be declared, written, and registered in the *Memoriali* of the commune of Bologna. From the instrument of the notary, Manfredo di Gerardi de Sexto. And so the aforesaid proctors, friars, and notary went, declared, and deposed and had the aforesaid written and notations were given on the aforesaid day of the aforesaid year.

2. A Laborer's Will

3 September 1337. Albertino di Ser Petro, laborer, of the parish of Santa Maria degli Alemanni, by grace of Christ, healthy in mind and sense but sick in body, not wishing to die intestate, devolves all his goods and things by the present nuncupative testament in this manner, namely he leaves 20 *solidi* [in recompense] for ill-gotten gains. Then he leaves for the benefit of his soul 10 *solidi* to friar Alberto, his confessor, of the order of friars of Santa Maria degli Alemanni. He leaves to his confessor 3 *solidi* for the singing of masses. He wants his confessor to arrange for his funeral and burial which he wants to be at the church of Santa Maria degli Alemanni. As legacy he leaves his nephew Luciolo 20 *solidi*. And in order to carry out these wishes he chooses as his executor Giovanni di Giovanni of the parish of Santa Maria degli Alemanni, giving and conceding to him full and free power to sell, etc. He leaves to his wife, Margarita di Giovanni, her dowry which was 23 Bolognese pounds. In all of his property, movable and landed, in laws and actions in the present and the future, he names as his heir his wife, Margarita, and asserts that this is his last will which he wishes to be valid by testamentary law. . . .

Translated from ASB, *Memoriali*, vol. 192, fol. 7r.

Redacted in the *guardia* [zone outside the walls] of the city of Bologna near the church of Santa Maria di Ponte Maggiore in the parish of Santa Maria degli Alemanni in the house of the said testator with present as witness friar Alberto from the order of Santa Maria degli Angeli, chaplain and priest of that church, who says that he recognizes the testator and he is of sound mind and able to make a will. [Also appearing are eight witnesses all from the testator's home parish along with a barber, Nicola di Giovanni, of the parish of San Biagio.] From the instrument of the notary, Bertolomeo di Jacopo di Bertolomeo. Thus the healthy testator and the notary went, declared and had the aforesaid written down on the same day.

3. A Porter's Will

In the name of our lord amen. 15 February, 1337. Berto di Alberti, porter of the parish of Santa Maria Maddalena, healthy in mind and sense but weak in body, makes his testament with these words. First he leaves to his wife, Gisella di Marco de Abellis, her dowry which was and is 36 Bolognese pounds. In all his other property, movable and landed, in rights and actions of the present and future he names his son, Antonio, who is called Tumolo. And he asserts that he wants this to be his last will which he wants to be valid by testamentary law. . . . Redacted in Bologna in the aforesaid parish in the house in which the said testator abides, with don Alberto, priest and chaplain of the church of Santa Maria Maddalena present who declared that the testator was of sound and composed mind. [Also present are four men from his home parish, a barber-surgeon and another man from the adjacent parish of Santa Maria Mascarella, and a seventh witness from the nearby parish of Santa Cecilia].

4. A Baker's Will

7 September 1337. Bertucio di Giovanni, baker of the parish of San Sigismondo, by grace of Christ, healthy in mind and senses, but weak in body, disposes all his goods and things with this nuncupative will in this manner. First, wishing to provide for the health of his soul, he leaves 5 Bolognese pounds [in recompense] for ill-gotten gains of which 20 *solidi* must be given each year, beginning from the day of the death of the testator until the money runs out, to the Ospedale dei Battuti or dei Devoti and for the poor of that hospital. Then he leaves to the priest, Pagano, the chaplain and canon of the church of San Sigismondo 10 *solidi*. He wishes that his burial be at the church

(3) Translated from ASB, *Memoriali*, vol. 192, fols. 340r–v.
(4) Translated from ASB, *Memoriali*, vol. 193, fol. 462r.

of San Sigismondo with expenses as necessary. He names as executors his wife, Isotta di Arardi Benasi, and Jacopo di Jacopo, a spice-seller, to whom he gives full and free power to sell and alienate his goods as they see fit. Then he leaves to Isotta her dowry which was 20 Bolognese pounds which he confesses to have received from her. He bequeaths also a legacy of 20 pounds and gives her authority and usufruct of all his goods as long as she remains chaste and honest and lives with his children as a widow and does not ask for her dowry and wants to live with her children. But if it happens that she does not want to live with the children, then she shall have only her dowry and the legacy of 20 pounds and no other legacy of usufruct. He names as his universal heirs Giovanni, Bertolomeo, Agnesia, and Caterina his sons and daughters, in equal portions. And he asserts that he wishes this to be his last will . . . From the instrument of the notary, Vinciguere di Bertolomeo. Redacted in the home of the testator with the priest Pagano, chaplain and canon of the church of San Sigismondo who asserts that he knows the testator and that he is of sound mind. [Also present are seven witnesses coming from six different parishes consisting of a spice-dealer, a barber-surgeon, a master carpenter, an agricultural worker, a tailor, a weaver, and a cotton worker. Because the testator was sick, he named a proctor who went with the priest and notary to the Office of the *Memoriali* to register the contract on the same day.]

117. *CHRONICLE OF PARTHENOPE*
(Naples, early fourteenth century)

Translated from Latin by Samantha Kelly

Composed by an unknown author in the early fourteenth century, the Chronicle of Parthenope *was the first civic-centered history to appear in Naples in over four centuries. It drew on numerous classical and medieval sources, as well as popular legend, to recount the history of the city from its origins to the twelfth century, and enjoyed considerable popularity. In addition to inspiring two "sequels" that carried the story through the fourteenth century, the* Chronicle *was frequently copied and cited in later histories of the fifteenth to seventeenth centuries. Like the chronicles and encomia of northern Italian cities, the* Chronicle *stressed the virtues which made the city and its people superior to others. These were standard rhetorical devices of medieval narratives of place [see #5, 67, 115]. Notable figures in the following passages are the freedom-loving ancient Greeks who founded the city, the Roman poet Virgil who made it his home (and who was celebrated in the Middle Ages as a benevolent magician), and Constantine, the first Christian emperor of Rome.*

On the city of Naples, which has acquired the greatest fame among the other cities of the world on account of the multitude of its knights and of their sumptuous and delightful riches. The following facts have been told in many volumes and chronicles, and are briefly compiled here.

CHAPTER ONE. HOW THE NOBLEMEN OF THE CITY OF EUBOEA IN THE PROVINCE OF CHALCIS CAME TO THE ISLAND OF PROCIDA, ALSO CALLED PITHECUSA, AND BUILT CUMAE

At the time when the Athenian philosopher Solon and Draco of Lacedaemonia, each a legislator in his city, drafted laws such that all Greece could be subjected to them, the peoples, noblemen, and lords of the city of Euboea in the province of Chalcis, indignant at being constrained by such laws, decided to leave their homeland and settle elsewhere. And so they did, passing many harbors and coasts with their large complement of ships; and a series of great storms brought them to Sicily, as Livy recounts in the eighth book of *Ab urbe condita* ["On the Founding of the City"].[1] Ovid, for his part, says in the *Metamorphoses* that they disembarked on the island of Pithecusa, or Aenaria: Pithecusae [situated on a barren hill] called from the name of its inhabitants.[2] And once the aforesaid people, noblemen, and lords prudently realized that

Translated from the edition of Antonio Altamura, *Cronaca di Partenope* (Naples: Società Editrice Napoletana, 1974), with additional textual notes.
1. Cf. Livy, *Ab urbe condita*, Book 8, Chapter 22.
2. Ovid, *Metamorphoses*, Book 14, line 90.

the island was not capable of supporting them, they discussed it among themselves and sought out the harbors of Cumae, which were not yet called Cumae. Disembarking, therefore, from their ships into the harbor, they found a pregnant woman sleeping, which they considered a good omen. And because of this omen [indicating] that they would greatly multiply, they named the city that they were about to build Cumae, since "Cumae" in Greek and Latin means "to sleep". . . .

CHAPTER THREE. HOW BECAUSE OF THE PLAGUE IN THE CITY [OF CUMAE] THEY CAME TO THE SITE OF THE TOMB OF PARTHENOPE, WHERE NAPLES NOW STANDS

After the city of Cumae had been built and populated by the settlers from Chalcis and Euboea, a great plague came upon its inhabitants, either through the pollution of the nearby lakes or through divine will, such that in the end the city was almost destroyed. Seeing this, many citizens, lacking any medical remedy to the plague, decided to move their homes, and so they did. And they came to the tomb or temple of Parthenope, and in the temple and in the surrounding fields they waited with their families for the pestilence to pass. And because of the temperate air there and the sweetness of the site— because, also, of the fright they had just suffered—they did not want to return to Cumae when the plague had passed. But most of those who had remained near Cumae were constrained to return ashamedly to the city.

CHAPTER FOUR. HOW IN ACCORDANCE WITH THE WORDS OF APOLLO THEY DID NOT RETURN TO CUMAE BUT REMAINED IN PARTHENOPE AND STARTED TO BUILD

The Cumaeans who had left Cumae for fear of the plague and who had returned in shame to their homes, were assailed ten years later by a second plague much fiercer than the first. And since they had escaped the first plague by moving their homes and finding a salubrious site, they [now] went to the temple of Apollo to ask what they should do. The oracle's response was that they should seek out and search for Parthenope and build their homes there, since from their seed the city would grow in number and go from good to better, and it would be greatly honored and become the most famous of cities. And this was done, but not by all, since some people, who farmed the land, could not so easily move their homes and did not wish to leave. But the majority of the noblemen and lords, taking their movable goods, searched for and sought out Parthenope, and each began to build there according to his own ability and means.

CHAPTER FIVE. HOW NAPLES TOOK ITS NAME FROM A WOMAN NAMED
PARTHENOPE

The temple of Parthenope took its name from an unmarried, virgin girl
named Parthenope, a girl of excellent and very great beauty who was the
daughter of the king of Sicily. Coming with many ships to Baia, she fell ill by
chance and died in that very spot, and there she was buried. And on account
of the tomb, a temple was built there, and later the city, which deserved to
be called Parthenope. So say Isidore and Papias, and Virgil in the fourth book
of the *Georgics* ("In those days I, Virgil, was nursed by sweet Parthenope")
and Ovid, in the third [*sic*] book of *Metamorphoses* ("Parthenope, for soft
pleasures founded").[3]

CHAPTER SIX. HOW TIBERIUS JULIUS TARSUS DECIDED, ON ACCOUNT OF
THE INFIGHTING OF THE CITIZENS, TO LEAVE AND BUILD ANOTHER CITY
ON THE HILL OF SANT'ELMO

After the city was built and given the name of Parthenope, the citizens lived
for a long time in peace and tranquility. And since no large city can remain
in peace for very long, if it does not have external enemies it will find internal
ones among its different families. Thus, due to the city's very riches and
abundance, disagreements and feuds grew up between them. And as a result
a young man named Tiberius Julius Tarsus, who shone among the citizens
on account of his nobility, wealth, and virtue, decided to separate from the
others and, along with some of his followers, to build a new city not far from
Parthenope. And this place, according to what is written, was laid across the
slopes at the foot of Mount Falerno, which is now called Sant'Elmo[4] by the
people. . . .

CHAPTER EIGHT. HOW THE CITY OF NAPLES CAME TO LOSE THE
NAME OF PARTHENOPE

After the city called "Neapolis" [new city] in Greek had been built, the Par-
thenopean city started gradually to lose its name; and it came to pass that
when people wished to refer to Parthenope they called it "Paleopolis" in
Greek, which in Latin means "old city," since "pale" in Greek is the same as
"old" in Latin. And Naples was populated by the people of Paleopolis, as
Livy affirms in Book Six [*sic*] of "From the Founding of the City."

3. Virgil, *Georgics*, Book 4, lines 563–64; Ovid, *Metamorphoses*, Book 15, lines 711–12.
4. Sant'Eramo (Saint Erasmus), more commonly called Sant'Elmo.

CHAPTER EIGHTEEN. HOW VIRGIL DISPELLED THE BAD AIR FROM
NAPLES BY MAGIC

On account of the swamps in this city, there were at that time many flies,
such that they seemed to breed disease. Virgil, because of his great affection
for the city and its citizens, used his arts of necromancy under [the influence
of] certain planets and stars to make a golden fly as large as a frog. And
through its efficacy and power all the flies in the city fled, according to what
Alexander, who saw this golden fly in a window in the Castel Capuana, attests
in his work. And Gervase, in his chronicle called *The Imperial Responses*,
proves that it was so.[5] Afterward, this fly was taken away to the castle of Cicala
and lost its power. . . .

CHAPTER TWENTY-EIGHT. HOW VIRGIL REMOVED THE SERPENTS
FROM NAPLES

At Porta Nolana (which is now called Forcella) in Naples is a stone road
artificially constructed and laid out, and on this road Virgil placed a seal [that]
mysteriously destroyed every species of serpent and of other poisonous worm.
And God in his mercy has continued to maintain this to the present day, such
that in caves and trenches that are dug underground to build houses or wells,
no snake or other worm has ever been found alive or dead, unless it was
brought in unintentionally with wood or hay. And while in Naples Virgil, at
the age of twenty-four, composed the *Georgics* to instruct the Neapolitans,
born as they are in a fertile and abundant homeland. In this book he
explained how and when to plow and cultivate and sow the the fields, and
when to plant and cut trees. As he himself says at the end of the work, "At
that time I was nurtured by sweet Parthenope, most noble in its leisure and
flourishing in studies." And this Virgil, who was of the Lombard race, was
born in a Mantuan village called Pettacula. He became renowned in the time
of Julius Caesar and under Octavian, and died in the 25th year of Octavian's
rule in the city of Brindisi, whence his body was later stolen by the Calabrians
and brought to Naples. And he was buried in the place now called Santa
Maria dell'Itria, in a tomb in the form of a small square temple with four
corners made of tiles. His epitaph of ancient letters was engraved and embel-
lished at the base of a marble [slab], and this marble was still intact in the
year 1326. The epitaph consisted of two verses, which said in an epigram,
"Mantua bore me, the Calabrians stole me, now Naples holds me." This
Virgil wrote in verse the *Bucolics*, the *Georgics*, and the *Aeneid*. . . .

---

5. These works are Alexander Neckham's *De rerum natura* of the late twelfth century and
Gervase of Tilbury's early thirteenth-century *Otia imperialia*, a widely read medieval compendium of historical, geographical, and physical information.

CHAPTER FORTY-TWO. HOW EMPEROR CONSTANTINE, ON HIS WAY TO GREECE WITH POPE SILVESTER, APPOINTED OFFICIALS AND DIGNITARIES TO THE PRINCIPAL CHURCH OF NAPLES

When some time had passed and the emperor [Constantine] wished to sail to Greece, he came to Naples with Pope Silvester and resided there for many months while his ships were outfitted for the journey. And the more often he heard mass in the mother church of Naples, the more devoted to it he became, and he endowed and enriched it with many possessions and lands and greatly beautified it, and raised it up by establishing, through Saint Zonio, its canons: that is, seven prebendary priests and seven prebendary deacons, to whom the emperor gave lands and possessions. Further, he gave to the church the *cimonarca* or the cimonarcal office, following the custom of the early Church and of the archbishoprics of Greece.[6] For in every metropolitan or archiepiscopal church of Greece there is a *cimonarca*, since they do not have other dignities such as provost, cantor, archdeacon, and other similar offices. And to say *cimonarca* in Greek is to say "prince of ceremonies and sacrifices" in Latin, which shows that the *cimonarca* performs the most important office in the church, and thus the name reflects the office. In no church of Italy, nor indeed in all the world from the rising to the setting sun, is there any church that has this office of the *cimonarca*, except the church of Naples and that of Milan. On Holy Saturday six dignitaries of six Greek churches, all built in Naples and endowed by the aforesaid emperor Constantine, are obliged to come to the cathedral of Naples and to sing or read six Greek lessons, and on Easter Sunday they are obliged to assist the *cimonarca* and to sing the Credo in the Greek vernacular and according to the Greek rite, and they must perform some acts that are called *squarcase* in the Latin vernacular.[7] The aforesaid six churches are the church of San Giorgio di Mercato, the church of San Gennaro a Diaconia, the church of Santi Giovanni e Paolo, the church of Sant'Andrea a Nido, the church of Santa Maria Rotonda and the church of Santa Maria a Cosmedin; and it is no wonder that these are the rich churches in Naples, since they were endowed by the emperor. And let it be known to everyone that other churches, similar to these and with their own charters can be found in the city of Constantinople, which the aforesaid emperor made so magnificent with numerous priests and holy offices.

6. An office of the early Greek Church equivalent to a treasurer, the *cimonarca* (or cimili-arca) was, in medieval Naples, an honor given to the archpriest or head of the cathedral chapter.
7. "Squarcase" or "squarastase": probably a religious drama or reenactment.

118. PHILIPOCTUS DE CASERTA'S SONG TEXT ON LOUIS, DUKE OF ANJOU (ca. 1382)

Translated from French by Yolanda Plumley

Nothing certain is known about the biography of the poet-composer Philipoctus de Caserta, other than what his name suggests, that he originated from the kingdom of Naples. He is known to us today as the author of five French-texted songs, a mass movement, and also two attributed treatises, one on the art of writing musical counterpoint, the other concerning music notation practice. All these works survive exclusively in Italian manuscripts, and it is clear that Philipoctus was well known in Italian circles by the early fifteenth century. However, it seems plausible that his songs were written during a period spent in Avignon, because they are written in the musical style and notation that was current there in the 1380s and '90s, and they are transmitted with other songs that originated in the orbit of the papal and French princely courts during those years. Philipoctus' songs feature the hallmarks of the late fourteenth-century French musical style that has come to be known in recent years as ars subtilior *(the "more subtle art," in relation to the classic fourteenth-century style known as* ars nova*). They are all scored for three parts (comprising a texted voice, and two untexted accompanying parts) and are characterized by a virtuosic rhythmic style that includes extensive syncopation and intricate cross-rhythms. The notation is typical of this* ars subtilior *repertory, featuring the note shapes that had been current through the fourteenth century amplified by new ones to encode the complex rhythmic proportions and small note values.*

Of the five song-texts, three support the notion of a connection with Avignon through their political content. One praises Pope Clement VII (r. 1378–94), another cites the motto of Bernabò Visconti, ruler of Milan (d. 1385), while the third, the one presented here, alludes to the French prince Louis, duke of Anjou (d. 1384). The three works may well have been written at a similar time, since their three dedicatees formed an alliance to rescue Queen Giovanna of Naples following her capture by Charles of Durazzo. The song-text refers to the capture and imprisonment of Queen Giovanna, alias "Adriane the wise," at the hands of Durazzo (represented as "Theseus") which took place in 1382. Before her submission, the Queen had appealed for succor to the French king who pledged support for a military campaign to be led by his uncle, Louis of Anjou. Alliances were soon made with Visconti, Clement VII and others. It seems likely the song dates from this time, and its author may have travelled to Avignon in the retinue of one of the many Neapolitans who went there to meet with Giovanna's allies during this period. Louis of Anjou was crowned king of Naples and Sicily in Avignon by Pope Clement and in September 1382, he set off on the ill-fated campaign, shortly after learning belatedly that the Queen had already met her death at the hands of her captor. Louis failed in his mission, and died at Bari in 1384.

The obscure language of the song's text is typical of the songs of this repertory in ballade *form. The* ballade *was especially favored in this period for lyrics of an elabo-*

rate and ambitious nature as regards their content and language; musical settings, like this one, match this with a correspondingly complex musical style. The political protagonists are represented in the text by classical figures. Particularly intriguing is the refrain line, where there is a double allusion to Louis of Anjou: it can be read as saying that Giovanna's territory cannot be saved without an army covered by lilies; but reading literally, covering "O" with "LIS" renders the name "Lois." The fleur-de-lis mentioned both here and at the beginning of the third stanza was the heraldic symbol of the French Angevin kings and princes.

Through the great sense of Adriane the wise
Theseus was protected from danger
When in his turn he had to brave the expedition
To the house of Daedalus.
Afterwards he betrayed her and wanted to exile her;
He robbed her of a jewel of great value,
That she cannot recover without an army covered in lilies.

Adriane is of such noble lineage
And so powerful that one can pronounce it.
The jewel that she obtained through her own inheritance
Theseus struggled to usurp
And in order to have it, he puts it in great peril;
If she doesn't get help, she'll lose the jewel,
That she cannot recover without an army covered in lilies.

But the lily is so high born,
Handsome to behold, pleasant in deportment,
Rich in power, and so perfectly brave,
That the lady can call upon his virtue.
She need not wish for Roland nor Hector
To save the jewel of great worth
That she cannot recover without an army covered in lilies.

Translated from song text in Bibliothèque Chantilly, Musée Condé MS 564, fol. 37v.

119. GIFT-GIVING IN PADUAN CHURCHES FOUR TEXTS (1374–1405)

Translated from Latin by Louise Bourdua

Patronage of a chapel provided lay patrons with a locus of memory and guarantees of prayers for their and their loved ones' souls in exchange for gifts. The mendicant churches were particularly popular targets for such donations. The following documents concern the gifts acquired for the furnishing of altars in the Santo, the church of the Franciscans in Padua that was also the burial site for the second Franciscan saint, Anthony of Padua, and a major pilgrimage center already in the late thirteenth century. Donors to chapels could therefore hope for prayers from pilgrims as well as locals and family members. Francesco Turchetto, whose gifts are listed below, was a key member of the Carrara "inner circle" of Padua. He headed the treasury of Francesco il Vecchio from 1365 to 1382, and played a full role in the major events of this court during the last quarter of the fourteenth century. Bonifacio Lupi, marquis of Soragna, was a wealthy and successful soldier of fortune whose family had been exiled from Parma because of their Guelf associations. As a distinguished military leader and diplomat, he participated in all noteworthy politico-military events of the second half of the fourteenth century in northern Italy. The last thirty years of his life were tied to the Carrara court, not only because of a maternal family connection but also as a trusted councilor and ambassador for Francesco il Vecchio. The date and manner of his death, around 1389–90, remain shrouded in mystery and controversy.

1. Francesco Turchetto's Donation to the Church of Saint Anthony

The first note, drawn up on 2 April 1379, records gifts presented by Francesco Turchetto to the sacristan Almerico at the church of Saint Anthony of Padua. This donation by the patron follows the initial concession of rights at the altar of Saint Francis granted on 8 December 1378. Holders of such rights were expected to provide all the equipment necessary to celebrate mass: an altar, a chalice with paten (the cup for the wine and the plate for the Eucharistic wafer), a missal, an altar frontal (the cloth which draped the front of the altar) and vestments for the celebrant. Indeed the concession of a chapel was not deemed valid unless all these furnishings had been supplied. This particular receipt of 1379 survives because it was produced as evidence during a seventeenth-century dispute surrounding the patronage rights of the Turchetto family.

[The following gifts] were assigned to friar Almerico of Padua, sacristan in the convent of Saint Antony of Padua, in the presence of brothers Bartolo-

Translated from *Archivio Sartori: Documenti di storia e arte francescana*, vol. 1, *Basilica e Convento del Santo*, ed. Giuvanni Luisetto (Padua: Basilica del Santo, 1983), 566.

Figure 30. Chapel of St. James of Compostela. Bonifacio Lupi's decorative program, 1377–79. Padua, Basilica del Santo (Photo: Louise Bourdua)

meo of San Giorgio of Padua, vicar of the provincial minister of the province of Saint Anthony, Nicola of Lendinara, guardian of the said convent of Saint Anthony, Alberto of Monselice, Antonio de Porcu, and Pietro Penacii. They were presented to the altar of Saint Francis by the wise and discrete man, ser Francesco Turchetto, referendary[1] of the magnificent lord Francesco de Carrara lord of Padua. First, a chalice of gilt silver with enamels on the foot, a knop [a small rounded central knob on the stem of the chalice] and a paten of great value weighing 63 ounces; item, a beautiful missal well strengthened and of great worth; item, a vestment of green velvet with a fringe complete with alb, stole, and belt, [which is] very beautiful and of great worth; Brother Bartolomeo of San Giorgio wrote this.

2. Bonifacio Lupi's Gift to the Church of Saint Anthony

In the following extract, Bonifacio Lupi spends hundreds of ducats purchasing furnishings for his family chapel of St James of Compostela located opposite that of Saint

1. An officer who procured and sent diplomas and decrees.

Anthony. In this transaction, one of many, for the chapel was lavishly endowed and painted by Altichiero between 1377 and 1379, he employs no fewer than three agents: Jacopo dall' Olio (Francesco da Carrara's former treasurer), Domenico della Seta and Corradino Lovo. The other participants represent Francesco da Carrara, the ruler of Padua, who controlled expenditure tightly in his city-state during times of war. It can generally be said that the wealthier the donor, the more numerous the agents. These "middlemen" acted as intermediaries and carried out a variety of tasks, from witnessing a legal act, ensuring that the correct amount of money was dispensed, or choosing a work of art or craftsman.

A. 1379

Written below are certain monies spent for the furnishing of the chapel. First for vestments of which there are six pieces, bought by Jacopo da l'Olio and paid to Guglielmo notary at the office of messer Luca Casale, factor of the lord [Francesco da Carrara] and counted by Domenico della Seta, in the name of messer Bonifacio in the chancery of the said messer Luca, in the presence of Coradino Lovo and according to the wishes of messer Antonio da Moncalero, vicar of the lord [Francesco Carrara] and of Francesco Turchetto, servant of the said lord. On the 26th day of November, 100 gold ducats. . . . Item a chalice and a paten and a corporal with its cover worked and a small towel to place on top of the said chalice . . . 28 ducats

B. CHURCH INVENTORY RECORDING THE LUPI CHALICE

One of the Lupi gifts, a silver chalice with enamels and its paten, can be clearly identified in the third document here, taken from the first inventory of the church and convent, drawn up in 1396. This was a serious business, conducted by a large group of friars and laymen including a goldsmith. The purpose was to record all valuable movable objects and books (though excluding paintings unless they held relics), their basic materials, any identifying marks such as coat of arms or subject matter, their weight (if gold and silver) and any relics they contained.

Item, a chalice of silver with gilt paten with a corporal and a purse to hold the corporal; on the chalice there are sixteen enamels on the foot and knop, of which four display the arms of the Lupi, [its] weight is 29 ounces and a quarter, [and it is] reserved for the chapel of the lord Bonifacio Lupi.

    (A) Translated from *Archivio Sartori: Documenti di Storia e Arte Francescana*, vol. 1, *Basilica e Convento del Santo*, ed. Giuvanni Luisetto (Padua: Basilica del Santo, 1983), 471.
    (B) Translated from G. Baldassin Molli, *La sacrestia del Santo e il suo tesoro nell'inventario del 1396* (Padua: Prato, 2002), 106.

C. LUPI'S GIFTS CONTINUE AT THE CHURCH OF SAN FERMO

Finally, gift-giving could extend beyond the deathbed. Some seventeen years after Bonifacio Lupi's death, his spouse, Caterina dei Francesi di Staggia, continued to provide liturgical furnishings displaying her late husband's coat of arms. The last document is an excerpt from her will dated 19 July 1405 and records a vestment ordered for their former parish church of San Fermo in Padua, a pious donation meant to aid in the salvation of the souls of both benefactors.

[19 July 1405] And on the said vestment which will be given to the said church, the arms of the illustrious lord knight Bonifacio Lupi who was her husband, accompanied by the arms of the said testatrix.

Translated from Louise Bourdua, *The Franciscans and Art Patronage in Late Medieval Italy* (Cambridge: Cambridge University Press, 2004), 205 n. 196.

120. CHURCH INVENTORIES FROM CORTONA TWO TEXTS (1429)

Translated from Latin by Daniel E. Bornstein

The following inventories come from two churches in the diocese of Cortona, at the border between Tuscany and Umbria. Both inventories were redacted in 1429, as part of a comprehensive effort to document the furnishings of all churches in the diocese and the rectories attached to them. That project was never completed; some churches never provided inventories, and those that did offered lists of varying degrees of thoroughness. The inventory of Sant'Eusebio, for instance, is obviously far less complete than that for San Giorgio. Its cursory list of household furnishings includes bedding but no bed, bowls and spoons but no table at which to eat; and we must suppose that the rector of Sant'Eusebio had both a bed and a table. Still, the differences between the furnishings of San Giorgio and Sant'Eusebio suggest something of the contrasting level of resources—material, cultural, and spiritual—available in city and countryside

The church of San Giorgio was not particularly large or wealthy. Though inside the city walls, it served a relatively sparsely populated parish high on the hill above the center of town. The parish was suppressed in 1630 and its population aggregated with the nearby parish of San Cristoforo; the church of San Giorgio itself was torn down in 1661, making it impossible to speak with any certainty about its size or appearance. We may guess that it was roughly on the scale of the church of San Cristoforo (or Sant'Eusebio, for that matter): a single nave twenty meters long and seven wide, capable of accommodating perhaps 100–150 families.

Sant'Eusebio sits in the plain not far from the base of the hill of Cortona, about five kilometers west of the city. In addition to serving the peasants whose houses clustered in the locality known as Il Sodo, it functioned as the pieve of its district. Its priest thus had several other churches, with their officiating priests, subject to him. Given its proximity to the city and its position in the organizational structure of the diocese, the poverty of its furnishings is striking.

1. Inventory of the Church of San Giorgio of Cortona

In the bell tower of the said church, two ringing bells

Item, a small ringing bell beside the altar

Item, a little bell for giving communion

In the body of the said church, two altars of two sections apiece, for saying mass

Item, in the main altar, a small coffer for the sacraments that can be locked

Translated from Archivi storici ecclesiastici di Cortona, Archivi della curia, scaffale XIV, pachetto 1: Visite pastorali, 1337–1435; fols. 1596–1600r (= 170r–171r in modern numeration).

with a key, inside of which are two small vials with relics, and two old white bands of nettle-cloth or rather of silk, and a tin vial for holy oil

Item, an enameled chalice all of gilded silver with San Giorgio on the paten

Item, a small chalice of gilded copper with a silver cup

Item, a small tabernacle of gilded copper for giving communion

Item, two crosses, one in the modern style and the other in the ancient style

Item, a small Virgin Mary of gilded wood

Item, a missal[1] bound in parchment, and a votive one in Parisian lettering in parchment

Item, a missal bound in rag copy-paper of various sorts

Item, a large breviary without the psalter, bound with boards

Item, a breviary on quarto folio, in parchment, equipped with a psalter and hymnal and all in order, bound with boards

Item, a psalter on quarto folio, in parchment, fully equipped and in order, also bound with boards

Item, a small piece of a breviary on octavo folio, in parchment

Item, a small *summa* of penitence on octavo folio, in parchment

Item, an ordinary missal, folio, in parchment

Item, a piece of an ordinary with musical notation for the night office, folio, in parchment

Item, a piece of antiphonal with musical notation in modern style for the office of the nativity of Christ, in scraped parchment, folio

Item, a piece of antiphonal with modern notation for the mass with the common of the saints and other offices, folio, in parchment

Item, a quarto folio notebook, in parchment, with the nocturns of the dead in Parisian lettering

Item, an old common of the saints with musical notation, in parchment, on quarto folio

Item, a notebook of quarto folio parchment with musical notation for the office of Corpus Christi

Item, a notebook of quarto folio, in parchment, with musical notation for the *Kyrie eleison*

---

1. The missal is a book containing the prayers and rites used by the priest in celebrating mass. The ordinary refers to the common items or texts of the Mass; the proper of the mass refers to those texts that are specific to particular masses, such as that for the dead. The breviary contains all the texts needed for the recitation of the daily Divine Office—psalms, hymns, prayers, lessons, and so on—without chant. Certain hymns, prayers, and lessons are common to all celebrations of the Divine Office; others—the proper of the seasons, or the proper of the saints—are specific to a particular liturgical season or celebration. An antiphonal is a choir book containing the psalms and scripture verses sung during the Divine Office. An epistolary contains the passages from the New Testament epistles read during the Divine Office. A psalter contains the text of the psalms.

Item, beside the altar, two chests in the form of benches with two latches, with bases and backs

Item, a large studded chest next to the altar

Item, an old large studded chest for vestments

Item, a large choral reading stand, and a small one for the epistolary

Item, two handles for crosses, large and small

Item, a pedestal for the cross on the altar

Item, a pair of stands for candles

Item, an aspergillum for holy water

Item, a gilded thurible

Item, two small chests for hosts

Item, a pair of candlesticks for the altar, each of iron

Item, a pair of heavy candlesticks for in front of the altar at night

Item, three cushions for the altar: one of blue linen embroidered in gold with roses and leaves; another of violet cloth woven with golden deer; and the other of red silk with a pattern of flies

Item, in all, three tiny pillows for missals

Item, an altar frontal of light blue linen embroidered with gold roses

Item, an altar frontal of violet silk all woven with golden deer

Item, an altar frontal of blood red wool worked with waves, with silk acacias, and with trefoils

Item, two altar frontals striped with red and yellow silk

Item, an altar frontal striped with yellow and violet silk

Item, an altar frontal of green wool, with red and yellow waves

Item, an altar frontal of wool striped blue and white, with little green and blue flowers

Item, an altar frontal of black wool with three crosses of multicolored cloth

Item, a woolen cover for the dead, black, with two white crosses

Item, a cover for the large reading stand, of striped violet cloth with a yellow fringe around the edge

Item, a runner of cloth woven with various colors with a towel as backing, bordered with a fringe of twisted silk in various colors

Item, a runner of light blue wool embroidered in gold with roses and foliage

Item, a runner of deep blue cloth with a towel as backing, worked with shields and peacocks in silk

Item, a runner lined with linen, with a hempen fringe of various colors

Item, a cover of red cloth woven with green snakes

Item, a cover of cloth woven with finches on a field of gold

Item, a cover of blue cloth finely woven with white feathers

Item, an old cover of silk woven with birds of violet silk

Item, between small and large, old and new, ten pairs of corporals

Item, a chasuble of red velvet,[2] with a blue orphrey embroidered with golden roses

Item, a chasuble of white velvet, with a red orphrey embroidered with golden doves

Item, a chasuble of green silk striped with stripes of various colors

Item, a chasuble of blue silk with an old orphrey woven with gold checks

Item, a white linen chasuble, with an orphrey of red striped with white

Item, an old chasuble of red silk

Item, a chasuble of black serge, or rather blue, with an orphrey striped with red

Item, an old quilted chasuble of yellow silk, with linen backing and a golden fringe

Item, an alb furnished with red, green and black apparels, striped with white

Item, an alb furnished with green apparels, striped with various colors

Item, an alb furnished with green apparels, striped obliquely

Item, an alb furnished with black and yellow striped apparels

Item, an alb furnished with pure green apparels

Item, an alb furnished with pure yellow apparels

Item, an alb furnished with light yellow apparels

Item, an alb furnished with green apparels with violet and blue-violet stripes

Item, a new alb with the amice, with apparels of blue silk

Item, a pluvial of white silk with a scapular of red velvet and with a gold cross

Item, an old pluvial of violet silk striped with gold

Item, four large surplices, some good and some worn, and one small one

Item, a new linen cloth for the altar woven with birds, with three bands at each end

Item, a piece of cloth striped with various colors

Item, six other cloths, some good and some so-so, also for the altar

Item, a long striped towel for giving communion

Item, sixteen towels in all, counting good and bad, torn and whole, small and large, of every quality and kind

Item, in all, twelve small towels for the altar, counting small towels for the chalice and handkerchiefs, small and good and bad, whole or torn

2. The colors of a priest's vestments changed with the liturgical season. Red, the color of blood and of fire, was used for the feast-days of martyrs and for Pentecost Sunday. White, the color of purity, was used for the seasons of Christmas and Easter. Green, the color of vegetation (and hence of life) and of hope, was used for the season of Epiphany and the period following Pentecost. Purple, the color of royalty, was used for Advent and Lent; because purple dye was very costly, a dark blue or violet was sometimes substituted for it.

Item, one towel with wide bands of red silk
Item, two more small towels with bands and other work in silk
Item, a linen cover for the crucifix cut in a cross with little black crosses
Item, a small box for hosts
Item, a pair of irons for making hosts

In the kitchen, an old studded chest
Item, an old chain for the fire
Item, two irons for the fire, one for hanging and the other a tripod
Item, three spits, two middle-sized and one small
Item, a shovel and a pair of tongs for the fire
Item, a sharp cheese grater
Item, two old pans, one middle-sized and the other small
Item, two stone mortars, one large and the other small
Item, a small box for beating lard, with two steel knives
Item, two plates, one large and the other small
Item, a medium-sized cauldron
Item, two tin bowls, with two small bowls for seasonings
Item, tableware, large and small, consisting of ten trenchers [wooden plat-
    ters] and fifteen bowls, including small bowls for seasonings
Item, a dining table with four legs, and two small tables
Item, two iron lamps and one iron ladle
In the living room, a table with two tripods, eight feet long
Item, with solid benches all around
Item, a linen chest with a small chest inside
Item, a bench with an old cover for a back
Item, two small plaited baskets for bread, and two small plates for sweets or
    for fruit
Item, between plain hand cloths and cotton napkins, five in all
Item, between towels and hand towels, another five

In the storeroom, an old tub of 25 *some* that stays in place[3]
Item, another old tub of 13 *some*
Item, an old cask of 25 *barili*[4]
Item, another old cask of fourteen *barili*
Item, an old cask of twelve *barili*
Item, an old cask of ten *barili*

---

3. *Soma* (plural: *some*) was a unit of bulk measure equal to about 2.8 bushels.
4. *Barile* (plural: *barili*) was a unit of liquid measure equal to about 12 gallons.

Item, an old cask of eight *barili*

Item, a small cask of five *barili*

Item, a rather good small cask of four *barili*

Item, a slender small cask of four *barili*

Item, a little cask of three *barili*

Item, a small old tub of seven *barili*

Item, two charred tubs that were small casks, one of four *barili* and the other of five

Item, a barrel of 25 pints

Item, a dogwood hook for casks

Item, two old bins for grain, one of 28 *staia* and the other of 30

Item, some iron tools, amounting to six pieces of hardware: an old hatchet, a new spade, a hoe, a worn-out sickle, a new axe, and a pruning hook

Item, a weeder for the garden, forked on one side

Item, a large pruning hook with handle

Item, a hammer for walling

Item, two gimlets, one large and the other small, for making peg-holes

Item, a new wood saw

Item, a pair of large tongs

Item, a medium-sized steelyard for weighing

In the bedroom, an old bed frame with a large course sack of straw and an old down mattress and a rather good red pillowcase

Item, a down pillow for a down bolster, with a new white pillowcase

Item, an old coverlet of chicken feathers, with a small bolster and red pillowcase

Item, two covers, one white and the other red, all torn

Item, a down pillow with a red silk pillowcase

Item, two pairs of old linens

Item, a hamper for linens, small and old

Item, a solid bench at the foot of the said bed frame

2. Inventory of the *Pieve* of Sant'Eusebio, in the Countryside of Cortona, on the Aforesaid Date and Year [1429]

First, a large coarse linen altar cloth, painted, old

Item, an old cloth on the altar

Item, three small striped cloths for the altar, old

Item, an old chasuble of yellow silk, equipped with alb and amice

Item, a chasuble of blue silk, old and worn, equipped with everything

Item, a small chalice with a silver cup and another of copper, and one corporal

Item, half a missal, old, in the ancient manner

Item, a piece of an old missal, without the epistles

Item, a small piece of a votive missal

Item, a little book for baptizing

Item, two little cushions for the altar, small and old

Item, a small bell for giving communion

Item, a copy of the indulgence for the *pieve*

Item, a small box in which the said indulgence is kept

Item, an aspergillum

Item, an iron lantern, broken

Item, an old cross with a linen cover

Item, a thurible for incense

Item, a small chest for the hosts

Item, an old piece of cloth painted for use as an altar cloth

Item, a cloth to drape the table for the dead, worn, striped with red and blue-violet

Item, a towel, old and worn

Item, a large new surplice

Item, a small clerical tunic, old

Item, two pieces of bed linens, old and sad

Item, a small chest, old

Item, two iron candlesticks for the altar

Item, a table knife, old, all of iron

Item, three old trenchers, four bowls, seven small bowls, a copper ladle, a pestle, an old lantern, a pot, and a mortar

Chronology

11th c.	Amalfi emerges as an important maritime city
1000–1030	First Normans arrive in southern Italy; 1030 first Norman capital established at Aversa [**#111**]
1013	Foundation of San Miniato al Monte near Florence [**#8**]
1017	Pisan-Genoese alliance captures Sardinia from Muslims
1046	Synod of Sutri
1053	Battle of Civitate (Normans, led by Robert Guiscard, defeat forces of Pope Leo IX)
1054	The *Genealogy* of Ahimaaz ben Paltiel is composed [**#114**]
1057–75	*Pataria* active in Milan [**# 80**]
1059	Treaty of Melfi. Pope Nicholas II recognizes Robert Guiscard as vassal of St. Peter in return for protection
1061–91	Norman conquest of Sicily by Robert Guiscard and Roger I
1071	Norman conquest of Bari by Robert Guiscard
1077	Benevento (last of the Lombard strongholds) annexed to papal territories
	Norman conquest of Salerno by Robert Guiscard
	Pope Gregory VII absolves Emperor Henry IV at the fortress of Canossa belonging to Matilda of Tuscany [on Matilda see **#13.3, 66**]
1080	Marriage of Matilda of Sicily and Raymond of Toulouse [**#91**]
1085	Pope Gregory VII (r. 1073–85) dies in exile in Salerno, having been rescued from the emperor by an army led by Robert Guiscard (d. 1085)
1087	The Baresi bring the relics of St. Nicholas from Smyrna
1090	Bishop Daibert of Pisa set limits on the height of towers in the city [**#57**]
1096	Siege of Amalfi
12th c.	Medical school flourishes in Salerno; study of law gives rise to University of Bologna; communes emerge in central and northern Italy [**#46, 75, 77, 78, 79**]
1115	Death of Matilda of Tuscany, who bequeaths extensive holdings throughout central and northern Italy to the papacy

1130	Coronation of Roger II approved by Pope Anacletus II, an "antipope"
1139	Innocent II confirms Roger II's royal title as king of Sicily
1140s	Roger II's law code probably promulgated [#47]
1143	A canon of St. Peter's wrote *Marvels of Rome* [#67]
1147	Capture of Almería and Tortosa by the Genoese [#32]
1154	Death of Roger II
1155	Death of Arnald of Brescia [#68]
	Imperial coronation of Frederick I Barbarossa in Rome
1155/58	Frederick I issues the decree *Habita*, protecting students of Bologna [#45]
1158	Diet of Roncaglia, Frederick I Barbarossa
1162	Frederick I Barbarossa destroys Milan
1166	Death of William I of Sicily
1167	Formation of the Lombard League, alliance of 36 northern cities
1176	Battle of Legnano (Defeat of Frederick I Barbarossa by Lombard League)
1183	Peace of Constance, Frederick I Barbarossa's settlement with Lombard League [#15]
1184	Marriage of Constance of Sicily and Henry VI
	Condemnation of heretical groups including the Humiliati in *ad abolendum* [#85]
1184–85	Ibn Jubayr's travels to Mecca via Sicily [#58]
1190	Death of Frederick I Barbarossa
1194	Birth of Frederick II
1196	Construction begun on the baptistry of Parma [#59]
1200	Death of Raymond 'the Palmer' of Piacenza [#82]
1201	Approval of the *Humiliati* [#85]
1208	Institution of the procession of the *Veronica* in Rome [#69, 72]
1209 ca.	First, oral, approval of Franciscans
1216	*Liber consuetudinum Mediolani* (Book of the Customs of Milan) [#15]
1220	Imperial coronation of Frederick II
1221	Death of Dominic of Calaruega in Bologna
1222	Foundation of University of Padua
1224	Foundation of University of Naples
1226	Death of Francis of Assisi

1231	*Constitutions of Melfi* (*Liber Augustalis*) promulgated by Frederick II [**#92**]
1245	First Council of Lyons
1246	Death of Umiliana de' Cerchi [**#83**]
1248	Frederick II completes his *On the Art of Hunting with Birds* [**#108**]
1250	Death of Frederick II
	Government of Primo Popolo at Florence (until 1260) [**#17**]
1251	*Customs of Salerno* issued [**#93**]
1253	Death of Clare of Assisi
1255	Construction begun on Palazzo del *Podestà* (now Bargello) in Florence
1260	Battle of Montaperti (Florentine Guelfs defeated by Sienese Ghibellines)
1263	Federigo Visconti's pastoral visitation of Sardinia [**#12**]
1266	Battle of Benevento (Charles I of Anjou defeats Manfred, son of Frederick II)
1268	Battle of Tagliacozzo. Execution of Conradin [**#37**]
1274	Second Council of Lyons [**#30**]
1277	Lordship (*signoria*) of Visconti family in Milan
1282	Sicilian Vespers (Rebellion against Angevin rule in Sicily)
1284	Battle of Meloria, Genoa defeats Pisa
1287	Government of "the Nine" (*Nove*) established at Siena (until 1355) [**#88**]
1282	Sacred Ordinances (anti-magnate legislation) issued in Bologna
1293	Ordinances of Justice decreed in Florence [**#17, 20**]
1297	"Serrata" in Venice (restriction of Great Council membership to noble families)
1298	Palazzo Pubblico begun in Siena [**#64**]
1300	First Roman Jubilee (Holy Year) [**#72**]
early 14th c.	Composition of the *Chronicle of Parthenope* in Naples [**#117**]
1305	Pope moves residence to Avignon
1321	Death of Dante
1336	Opicino de Canistris writes an account of his life [**#89**]
1338	Lordship (*signoria*) of Carrara in Padua (until 1405)
1343	Death of Robert of Naples [**#109**]
1347–48	Black Death arrives
1354	Death of Cola di Rienzo [**#73**]

1378	Ciompi Rebellion in Florence [**#41**]
	Pope returns to Rome from Avignon
1378–81	War of Chioggia, Venice defeats Genoa [**#43**]
1380	Death of Catherine of Siena
1400	Death of Franco Sacchetti [**#84**]
1402	Peasant rebellion in Firenzuola [**#7**]
1405	Padua falls to Venice [**#42**]
1410	Death of Francesco di Marco Datini [**#96**]
1434	Medici family dominates Florentine politics
1447	End of Visconti lordship in Milan

Map 1. Italian cities of the Middle Ages.

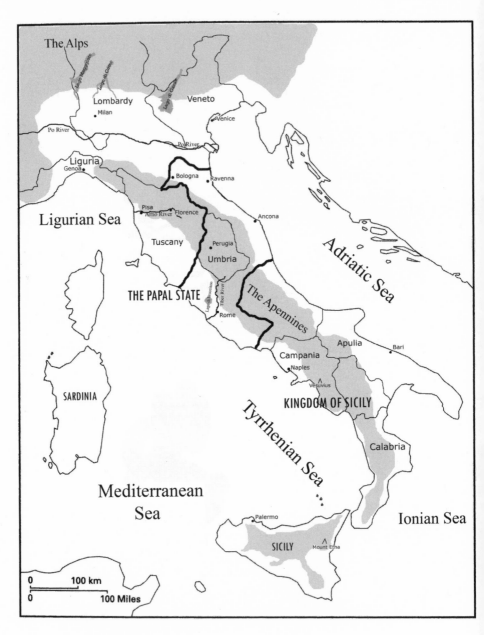

Map 2. Regional map of Italy, ca. 1300.

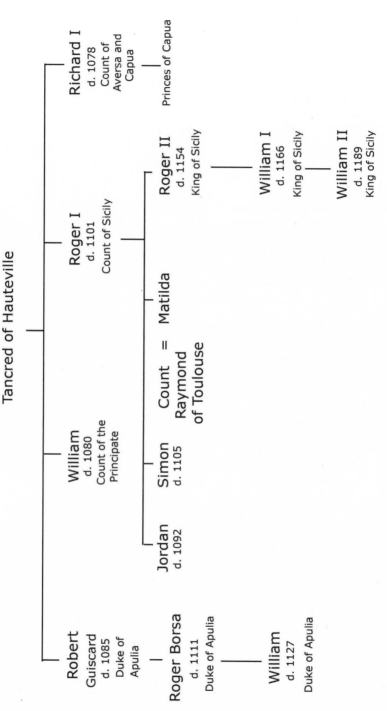

The Norman Lineage

Tancred of Hauteville

Robert
Guiscard
d. 1085
Duke of
Apulia

William
d. 1080
Count of the
Principate

Roger I
d. 1101
Count of Sicily

Richard I
d. 1078
Count of
Aversa and
Capua

Roger Borsa
d. 1111
Duke of Apulia

Jordan
d. 1092

Simon
d. 1105

Count = Matilda
Raymond
of Toulouse

Roger II
d. 1154
King of Sicily

Princes of Capua

William
d. 1127
Duke of Apulia

William I
d. 1166
King of Sicily

William II
d. 1189
King of Sicily

Genealogical Table 1. The Norman lineage in Southern Italy.

The Norman and Hohenstaufen Lineage

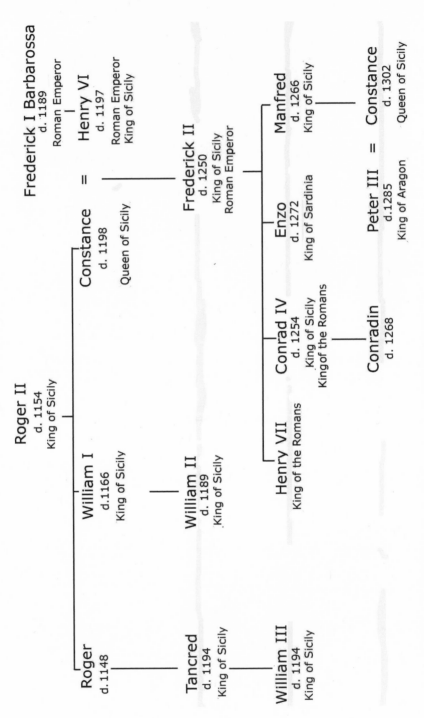

Genealogical Table 2. The Norman kings of Sicily and the Hohenstaufen lineage.

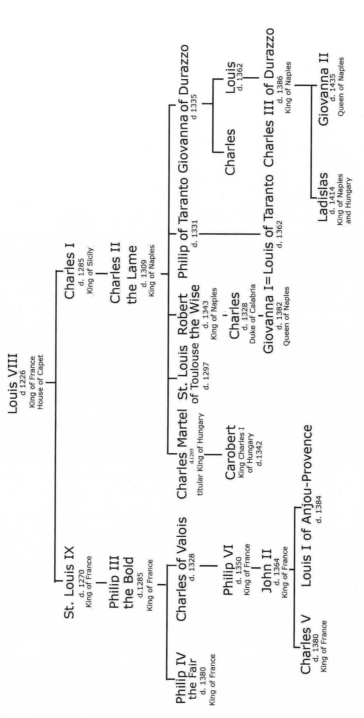

Genealogical Table 3. The Angevin rulers of Sicily and Naples and the Capetian lineage.

Medieval Popes ca. 950–1430

Names of antipopes are in italics.

Agapitus II (946–55)
John XII (955–64)
Leo VIII (963–65)
Benedict V (964–66)
John XIII (965–72)
Benedict VI (973–74)
Boniface VII (974, 984–85)
Benedict VII (974–83)
John XIV (983–84)
John XV (985–96)
Gregory V (996–99)
John XVI (997–98)
Sylvester II (999–1003)
John XVII (1003)
John XVIII (1004–9)
Sergius IV (1009–12)
Gregory VI (1012)
Benedict VIII (1012–24)
John XIX (1024–32)
Benedict IX (1032–44, 1045, 1047–48)
Sylvester III (1045)
Gregory VI (1045–46)
Clement II (1046–47)
Damasus II (1048)
Leo IX (1049–54)
Victor II (1055–57)
Stephen IX (1057–58)
Benedict X (1058–59)
Nicholas II (1058–61)
Alexander II (1061–73)
Honorius II (1061–72)
Gregory VII (1073–85)
Clement III (1080–1100)

Victor III (1086–87)
Urban II (1088–99)
Paschal II (1099–1118)
Theodoric (1100–1102)
Albert (1102)
Sylvester IV (1105–11)
Gelasius II (1118–19)
Gregory VIII (1118–21)
Calixtus II (1119–24)
Honorius II (1124–30)
Celestine II (1124)
Innocent II (1130–43)
Anacletus II (1130–38)
Victor IV (1138)
Celestine II (1143–44)
Lucius II (1144–45)
Eugenius III (1145–53)
Anastasius IV (1153–54)
Hadrian IV (1154–59)
Alexander III (1159–81)
Victor IV (1159–64)
Paschal III (1164–68)
Calixtus III (1168–78)
Innocent III (1179–80)
Lucius III (1181–85)
Urban III (1185–87)
Gregory VIII (1187)
Clement III (1187–91)
Celestine III (1191–98)
Innocent III (1198–1216)
Honorius III (1216–27)
Gregory IX (1227–41)
Celestine IV (1241)

Innocent IV (1243–54)

Alexander IV (1254–61)

Urban IV (1261–64)

Clement IV (1265–68)

Gregory X (1271–76)

Innocent V (1276)

Hadrian V (1276)

John XXI (1276–77)

Nicholas III (1277–80)

Martin IV (1281–85)

Honorius IV (1285–87)

Nicholas IV (1288–92)

Celestine V (1294)

Boniface VIII (1294–1303)

Benedict XI (1303–4)

Clement V (1305–14)

John XXII (1316–34, Avignon)

Nicholas V (1328–30, Rome)

Benedict XII (1334–42, Avignon)

Clement VI (1342–52, Avignon)

Innocent VI (1352–62, Avignon)

Urban V (1362–70, Avignon)

Gregory XI (1370–77, Avignon; 1377–78, Rome)

Urban VI (1378–89)

Clement VII (1378–94, Avignon)

Boniface IX (1389–1404)

Benedict XIII (1378–94, Avignon)

Innocent VII (1404–6)

Gregory XII (1406–15)

Alexander V (1409–10, Bologna)

John XXII (1410–1415, Bologna)

Martin V (1417–31)

Clement VIII (1423–29)

Glossary

Abbaco—The final element of early education for those headed into commercial careers in medieval Italy. This was not the theoretical arithmetic and geometry of the university, but the practical mathematics that was first elaborated in the Christian West by Leonardo Fibonacci (c. 1170–1240), a Pisan official who had studied Arab mathematics in North Africa and who played a major role in popularizing Hindu-Arabic numerals in the West.

Alb—A white liturgical vestment with long, tapered sleeves.

Allod—Land not owing any service or payment to an overlord.

Anziano/i—Derived from the word for elder, an *anziano* was generally a judicial magistrate. Each city nuanced the position a bit differently; in Lucca in the fourteenth century, for example, there were nine in number, three from each of the three *terzieri* or wards into which Lucca was divided, and they served for a two-month period alongside the Gonfaloniere.

Archivolt—One of a collection of concentric ornamental moldings around an arch.

Arimanno/i—Derived from a Lombard term for free man, the *arimanni* were a military/warrior class.

Arte/i—Guild—a collective association of merchants, artisans, or craftsmen organized to regulate the production of goods, and to protect members' economic, political, and social interests.

Arti maggiori/minori—In Florence, the *arti maggiori* or major guilds were the seven dominant guilds, which included the wool guild, the Calimala [see below], silk guild, furriers, money changers, doctors and apothecaries, and judges and notaries. The *arti minori*, or lesser guilds, were the guilds of craftsmen, including butchers, shoemakers, smiths, and stone masons.

Avvogadore/i—A high-ranking law officer, such as in Venice, charged with the duties of prosecuting attorney for the state.

Braccio/a—Linear measure used for building or cloth. Initially defined as the length of both arms extended, measured from middle finger-tip to finger-tip (*braccio* means arm). The precise measurement varied from place to place, but in late medieval Florence, one *braccio* equaled approximately a yard or ¹/₃ or ¹/₄ of a *canna*.

Breve Consulum—One of the earliest surviving communal statutes of Pisa (1162).

Calimala—The Arte di Calimala, made up of international traders, was the wealthy wool-importers' guild, which specialized in finishing imported woolen fabric.

Canna/e—Linear measure used commonly for cloth and land, often divided into *braccia* or *piedi*. 3–4 *braccia* = 1 *canna*.

Cantarium/a—"Hundredweight," used throughout the Mediterranean for bulk shipping of goods long distance. Its exact weight varied depending on the type of pound (*libbra*) in use, and varied from 100 to 250 *libbre*.

Cantaro/i—Italianization of *cantarium*.

Capitano del popolo—Executive officer of the *popolo*, usually a foreigner, designated to balance the power of the *podestà* and the magnates and to defend the rights of the *popolo* and the *arti*.

Cappellano/i—Chaplain; or in Florence, a neighborhood or parish official who was responsible for reporting any suspicious or illegal activities in his district to the central judicial magistrates.

Castellum—Castle, fort, or stronghold, but usage can extend to mean a fortified settlement or village (diminutive of *castrum*).

Castrum—Ordinarily a fortified settlement or a village, but can also be used in a more restricted sense to mean castle, fort, fortress.

Chasuble—Principal, outermost clerical vestment worn for celebrating mass.

Civis/es—Citizen.

Colo/i—Measure for spices, translated in these documents as "units."

Confessio—Originally used to designate the tomb of a martyr; later, the altar over a martyr's tomb or the high altar of the basilica erected over the martyr's burial place.

Consorteria/e—An association of individuals who joined together for specific economic, familial, or military purposes.

Consuls—The chief magistrates of the early communes, usually elected, often by, and from, a very narrow oligarchy. They were elected for periods ranging from six months to one year.

Contado—Agricultural territories and hinterland of a city, often divided into smaller subdivisions called vicariates. In Lucca, for example, the *contado* was comprised of the "district," an area within a six-mile radius nearest to Lucca, while the "force" was a small number of more recently reacquired outlying villages.

Contrada/e—A neighborhood, quarter, or administrative district of a city, often dominated by a group of allied families and their supporters.

Converso/a—A lay member of a religious community, living a life of penance.

Crockets—Bud-like or foliate ornaments taking the place of the Corinthian acanthus leaves in capitals or placed at the edges of architectural elements.

Decretals—Papal decisions or rescripts in letter form. See also *Liber extra* below.

Decretum Gratiani—Or *Concordia discordantium canonum* (Concordance of Discordant Canons), a repertoire of church law, drawn from various sources, and compiled ca. 1140, by Gratian, who is thought to have been a teacher of canon law at the University of Bologna. The *Decretum* became a textbook for students of canon law in the Middle Ages.

Doge—The doge was the head of the Venetian state, elected to that office for life from among the Venetian nobility. The title was also used in Genoa.

Donatus—The primer in dialogue form penned by Aelius Donatus in the fifth century, which was the basis for grammar textbooks available to medieval teachers in Italy; in Tuscan usage, known by the diminutive *Donadello*.

Embrasure—The flared, recessed opening of a door or window.

Estimo—A general tax assessment of the citizens' resources that then served as a basis for the division of expenditure among them. The usual method was to appoint a number of boards of assessors to make separate financial assessments of each citizen. A final figure was reached by eliminating the highest and the lowest and averaging the others.

Executor of Justice—An important judicial official in medieval Florence. The office was created in 1307 as a result of the ascendancy of the *popolo* in the 1290s. The executor, who himself had to be a *popolano*, was responsible for enforcing the Ordinances of Justice and for protecting members of the *popolo* from the violence of the magnates.

Fardo/i—Measure for silk textiles, translated here as "package."

Fideles—Loyal or faithful followers, retainers, vassals.

Fiorino/i piccolo/i—The common silver currency of Florence in which fines, wages, and most prices were calculated.

Fiorino/i (florin)—The gold florin constituted one of two monetary systems used in Florence; the other was the silver *lira*. The exchange rate between the two systems fluctuated throughout the Middle Ages. Normally, items of high value such as real estate and dowries were calculated

in florins. Wages, consumer goods, and legal fines were usually reckoned
in *lira*.

Gastald—An estate manager.

Ghibelline—A loose political label for local or regional factions who nominally supported the cause of the western emperor and his allies in Italy,
in opposition to the Guelfs (see below), but who ordinarily furthered
the interests of a local or regional faction.

Gonfaloniere di Giustizia—Standard Bearer of Justice. The highest civil magistrate in many Italian communes of the late thirteenth and fourteenth
centuries. In Lucca, for example, he was chosen by a combination of
election and lot to serve for a period of two months.

Gonfaloniere/i—Standard-bearers.

Groppo/i—Measure of gold and silver, translated here as "pouches."

Grosso/i—A big silver penny, minted by the Venetians, among others.

Guelfs—A loose political label for local or regional factions who nominally
supported the cause of the papacy and its allies in Italy, in opposition to
the Ghibellines (see above), but who ordinarily furthered the interests
of a local or regional faction.

Incastellamento—Literally "encastellation": creating new settlements (sometimes fortified) to provide local control and protection.

Indiction—A method of dating in fifteen-year cycles beginning 1 September
each year.

Indulgence—Declaration issued by a pope, bishop, or council that decreed
that one's time in purgatory would be shortened by a specific number
of days or years in return for meritorious works or specific devotions. It
was predicated on the obligations of the sacrament of penance.

Invitato/i—Refers to prominent or experienced citizens who were not members of a council at a particular time, and were "invited" to participate
and vote in the council.

Iugerum/a—Roman land measurement, the equivalent of about two-thirds
of an acre.

Liber extra—Or *Decretales Gregorii IX* (*Decretals of Gregory IX*), a collection
of papal and conciliar legislation from Gratian up to the pontificate of
Pope Gregory IX. Authorized by the same pope, it was published in 1234
and became part of the *Corpus iuris canonici* (the official collection of
ecclesiastical law).

Lira/e—Money equivalent to one pound of silver; more often a money of
account than a minted coin, the *lira* contained 20 shillings (*solidi*), each
of which in turn contained 12 pennies (*denarii*), making a sum of 240
pennies (*denarii*) to the *lira*.

Litanies—Formal prayers involving responses from the congregation; also a
    liturgical procession with singing.

Martyrology—A calendar of martyr-saints' feast days.

Materia medica—Pharmaceutical ingredients.

Messer—Title of address for knights and noblemen, similar to "Sir."

Mezzadria—A sharecropping contract whereby an owner grants land to a
    lessee for a fixed period, in exchange for half the land's yield.

Mezzogiorno—The Italian south; southern Italy.

Miliarium (*migliaio*)—Generic term for 1,000 units of any item, used for
    both weight and volume.

Modius (*moggio*)—A standard large measure of capacity used for grain. The
    term can also be used to describe the amount of land that can be sown
    with a *modius* of grain. In Florence it was equivalent to about 34 bushels.

Muda—A system of state-controlled galley convoys which sailed on a strict
    schedule with a mandate to carry the high-value but low-volume com-
    modities classified as "spices." Galleys commonly carried 200 men (a
    conservative figure) and were powered by both rowers and sails, the for-
    mer providing more mobility because of the overall design.

Mundium—Legal power of guardianship over a woman. In Lombard society
    a woman's *mundium* was normally held by her father (or brother if the
    father was dead) until she married, when her husband took it over. This
    power of guardianship also applied to male children before they came of
    age.

Mundualdus—A male of legal age who acted as the legal representative of a
    woman in Lombard legal matters, a tradition that carried over into later
    judicial systems.

Necrology—Announcement or listing of the death dates of members of a
    community, often a religious house. Comprised sometimes of a mere
    name and death date, at other times a short biography, they served to
    memorialize the dead for the community and posterity.

Negotiatores—merchants, bankers, factors

(The) Nine (*Nove*)—The Nine Governors and Defenders of the Commune
    and People of Siena were the main government committee between 1287
    and 1355, sitting for two-month terms of office.

Ordinances of Justice—A series of laws first enacted in 1293 by the Florentine
    popolo. The Ordinances excluded magnates from holding office, placed
    heavy restrictions on their activities, and subjected them to especially
    harsh penalties for lawlessness.

Palazzo Comunale—The town hall where administrative offices were housed and civic business conducted. Known also in different regions as the Palazzo Pubblico or the Palazzo della Ragione.

Papal State—The temporal property of the papacy, which expanded in a process of recovery, from Bologna to southern Lazio.

Patrimony of St. Peter—The core of the temporal property of the popes; an assemblage of lands centered on Rome, based on the ancient duchies of Rome and Spoleto. According to the donation of 817 made by Louis the Pious to Pope Paschal I, its northern frontier included Aquapendente and Radicofani, while the River Liri at Ceprano marked the southernmost boundary. It included the Sabina, a less well-defined area eastward to the Apennines.

Patrono/i—In maritime terminology, a technical word for what we now call a sea captain; "captain" meant a squadron leader.

Pievano—The priest of a *pieve*.

Pieve—From the Latin *plebs* (people), the term describes an ecclesiastical unit that could range in size from an entire diocese (in the early Middle Ages) to a parish or even a small congregation of the faithful. Often used to define a baptismal church.

Podestà—An official, appointed by the commune as executive officer heading the civic government. His powers were both judicial and military. His term lasted no longer than a year, a practice adopted to help combat conflicts of interest, judicial corruption, and factionalism.

Popolano/i—Term used to refer to members of the *popolo*, or non-nobles, which included both the middling merchant class (*popolo grasso*) and the artisan class (*popolo minuto*) within the commune. In some places, because of their historical roles in a city's military forces, members of the *popolo* are also referred to as "footsoldiers," or *pedites*, in contrast to nobles who are called *milites* or "knights." Nobles sometimes associated with the *popolani* for political reasons.

Popolo—The term used to describe the portion of the populace who were not members of the noble class. In a political context this refers not to the people but to a governing party or faction whose leaders were qualified by property ownership and guild membership. Members of the *popolo* were distinguished from the magnates, members of legally designated families descended from very old, aristocratic feudal lineages, which in the late thirteenth century became a legal designation. Struggles between the *popolo* and magnates dominated the political history of the cities of central and northern Italy.

Postills—A type of biblical commentary.

Primicerius—The head of a bishop's clergy.

Proprietary houses—Proprietary religious houses might be monasteries, family chapels, or churches exercising the full range of pastoral duties. They were privately built and could be bought, sold, bequeathed, and divided in the same manner as landed property. The founder also had the right to nominate the ecclesiastics associated with the institution (*iuspatronatus*). In some cases bishops granted emancipation charters confirming a house's immunity from episcopal authority, although in general no such recognition from the bishop was acquired.

Provveditore/i—Ordinarily, a term used for administrative officials. In late medieval Venice, however it was a a government official attached to an army to direct its commander and to protect the state's interest

Provvisioni—Judicial and governmental archives, especially records of council meetings.

Quattrocento—Fifteenth century (1400s)

Regalia—The rights, privileges, and/or symbols of royalty or high office.

Regular canons—Clergy who lived according to a rule, often that of St. Augustine, following the common life, and held property collectively.

Responsory—Derived from the Latin verb *respondere*, "to respond or answer," a responsory consists of a series of statements, often derived from Scripture, spoken or sung in answer to another verse. Responsories occur in both the mass and the divine office.

Revetment—Stone facing

Salma/e—As a cubic measure, usually for grain. It varied from place to place but the *salma* was equal to 16 *tumuli*, or approximately 8 hectoliters (23 bushels).

Sculdahis—A Lombard magistrate.

Ser—Title commonly used for notaries.

Sesterce—An ancient Roman silver coin.

Sextarius/i—Measure of volume equaling one-sixteenth of a *modius*.

Signoria/e—A governing authority or lordship, which, when in the hands of one individual, was frequently associated with the decline of the communes.

*Signore/*i—Lord.

Stadium/a—Roman distance measurement; a furlong.

Starium/a (*Staio/a*)—The standard unit of measure for oil, the *starium* held from 5 to 10 liters; the size of this and other weights and measures varied between towns and regions.

Studium/a—A center of learning and training associated with the mendicant friars.

Suffragan—Derived from the word *suffragor* meaning "to aid," this term describes the bishops subordinate to an archbishop.

Synod—An official assembly or council of clergy convened by a bishop.

Tari—The gold *tari* was the standard currency of the Sicilian kingdom from the eleventh to thirteenth centuries, with thirty *tari* to an *uncia* (ounce) of gold.

Tavola—Small wooden board or a wax tablet into which the alphabet had been incised directly, or to which had been attached a piece of parchment with the letters written out on it.

Thurible—A vessel used for burning incense during liturgical services and usually suspended on chains so that it can be swung.

Trabeated—An opening or arcade constructed with horizontal beams or lintels instead of arches

Trecento—Fourteenth Century (1300s)

Triduum—Literally "a three day period," but more specifically it refers to the three days before Easter Sunday.

Tuminus/i (*tomolo/i*)—A measure of dry capacity equivalent to approximately 50 liters (a bit more than a bushel)

Usufruct—The right to use proceeds from a piece of property; literally "the use of fruits."

Usury—Usually defined as an excessive or illegal rate of interest, but for medieval canon law and theology, usury denoted any charge for a loan of money or commodities whose use involved their consumption, such as wine, oil, or grain. Lending money at interest over time was considered unacceptable because time was a commodity which could not be purchased.

Vicarius—An official deputized by a city to exercise local jurisdiction in its subject territories.

Villein—An unfree peasant whose status was usually marked by liability to render labor service to a lord.

Zenodochium—Guest house with status of religious house under supervision of a bishop.

Many of the definitions for weights and measures derive from Ronald Edward Zupko, *Italian Weights and Measures from the Middle Ages to the Nineteenth Century* (Philadelphia: American Philosophical Society, 1981) and Florence Edler, *Glossary of Medieval Terms of Business: Italian Series* (Cambridge, Mass.: Medieval Academy of America, 1934).

Further Reading

This selected bibliography focuses on English language works on medieval Italy. It privileges monographs, surveys, and volumes of collected essays. For the student with Italian language skills, each of the items listed below generally contains bibliographical references to the vast, rich Italian bibliography not cited here. Although many of the titles listed below are useful reading for more than one subject, for reasons of space they are not repeated after the first citation.

GENERAL HISTORY AND COLLECTED ESSAYS

Beyond Florence: The Contours of Medieval and Early Modern Italy. Ed. Paula Findlen, Michelle M. Fontaine, and Duane J. Osheim. Stanford, Calif.: Stanford University Press, 2003.

Italy in the Central Middle Ages. Ed. David Abulafia. Oxford: Oxford University Press, 2004.

Medieval Italy: An Encyclopedia. Ed. Christopher Kleinhenz. New York: Routledge, 2003.

The New Cambridge Medieval History. Ed. Rosamond McKitterick. 7 vols. Vol. 5, *ca. 1198–1300.* Ed. David Abulafia. Cambridge: Cambridge University Press, 1995–2005.

The Origins of the State in Italy, 1300–1600. Ed. Julius Kirshner. Chicago: University of Chicago Press, 1996.

Portraits of Medieval and Renaissance Living: Essays in Memory of David Herlihy. Ed. Samuel K. Cohn, Jr., and Steven A. Epstein. Ann Arbor: University of Michigan Press, 1996.

The Society of Norman Italy. Ed. G. A. Loud and Alex Metcalfe. Leiden: Brill, 2002.

Towns and Townspeople in Medieval and Renaissance Europe: Essays in Memory of J. K. Hyde. Ed. Brian S. Pullan and Susan Reynolds. *Bulletin of the John Rylands University Library* 72 (1990).

BACKGROUND: EARLY MEDIEVAL ITALY

Italy in the Early Middle Ages. Ed. Cristina La Rocca. Oxford: Oxford University Press, 2002.

Kreutz, Barbara. *Before the Normans: Southern Italy in the Ninth and Tenth Centuries.* Philadelphia: University of Pennsylvania Press, 1991.

Ramseyer, Valerie. *Transformation of a Religious Landscape: Medieval Southern Italy, 950–1150*. Ithaca, N.Y.: Cornell University Press, 2006.

Squatriti, Paolo. *Water and Society in Early Medieval Italy: AD 400–1000*. Cambridge: Cambridge University Press, 1998.

Wickham, Chris. *Early Medieval Italy: Central Power and Local Authority*. Ann Arbor: University of Michigan Press, 1989.

———. *Framing the Early Middle Ages: Europe and the Mediterranean, 400–800*. Oxford: Oxford University Press, 2005.

Southern Italy

Abulafia, David. *Italy, Sicily, and the Mediterranean, 1100–1400*. London: Variorum, 1987.

———. *The Western Mediterranean Kingdoms, 1200–1500: The Struggle for Dominion*. New York: Longman, 1997.

Houben, Hubert. *Roger II of Sicily: A Ruler Between East and West*. Trans. G. A. Loud and Diane Milburn. Cambridge: Cambridge University Press, 2002.

Loud, G. A. *The Age of Robert Guiscard: Southern Italy and the Norman Conquest*. New York: Longman, 2000.

———. *Conquerors and Churchmen in Norman Italy*. Brookfield, Vt.: Ashgate/Variorum, 1999.

Matthew, Donald. *The Norman Kingdom of Sicily*. Cambridge: Cambridge University Press, 1992.

Oldfield, Paul. *City and Community in Norman Italy*. Cambridge: Cambridge University Press, 2009.

Northern and Central Italy with an Emphasis on Cities

Becker, Marvin B. *Florentine Studies: Selected Writings of Marvin B. Becker*. Ed. James Banker and Carol Lansing. Ann Arbor: University of Michigan Press, 2002.

Brucker, Gene A. *The Civic World of Early Renaissance Florence*. Princeton, N.J.: Princeton University Press, 1977.

Crouzet-Pavan, Elisabeth. *Venice Triumphant: The Horizons of a Myth*. Baltimore: Johns Hopkins University Press, 2002.

Dean, Trevor. *Land and Power in Late Medieval Ferrara: The Rule of the Este, 1350–1450*. Cambridge: Cambridge University Press, 2002.

———. *The Towns of Italy in the Later Middle Ages*. Manchester: Manchester University Press, 2000.

Epstein, Steven. *Genoa and the Genoese, 958–1528*. Chapel Hill: University of North Carolina Press, 1996.

Florentine Studies: Politics and Society in Renaissance Florence. Ed. Nicolai Rubinstein. Evanston, Ill: Northwestern University Press, 1968.

Grundman, John P. *The Popolo at Perugia, 1139–1309*. Perugia: Deputazione per la storia patria per l'Umbria, 1992.

Herlihy, David. *Cities and Society in Medieval Italy*. London: Variorum: 1980.

———. *Pisa in the Early Renaissance: A Study of Urban Growth*. New Haven, Conn.: Yale University Press, 1958.

———. *Medieval and Renaissance Pistoia: The Social History of an Italian Town, 1200–1430*. New Haven, Conn.: Yale University Press, 1967.

Hyde, J. K. *Padua in the Age of Dante*. New York: Barnes and Noble, 1966.

———. *Society and Politics in Medieval Italy: The Evolution of the Civil Life, 1000–1350*. New York: Macmillan, 1973.

Jones, Philip J. *The Italian City-State: From Commune to Signoria*. Oxford: Clarendon Press, 1997.

Lane, Frederic C. *Venice: A Maritime Republic*. Baltimore: Johns Hopkins University Press, 1973.

Larner, John. *Culture and Society in Italy, 1290–1420*. New York: Scribner: 1971.

———. *Italy in the Age of Dante and Petrarch, 1216–1380*. New York: Longman, 1980.

Meek, Christine. *Lucca, 1369–1400: Politics and Society in an Early Renaissance City-State*. Oxford: Oxford University Press, 1978.

Norman, Diana. *Siena and the Virgin: Art and Politics in a Late Medieval City State*. New Haven, Conn.: Yale University Press, 1999.

Schumann, Reinhold. *Authority and the Commune, Parma 833–1133*. Parma: Deputazione per la storia patria per le provincie parmensi, 1973.

Venice Reconsidered: The History and Civilization of an Italian City-State, 1297–1797. Ed. John Martin and Dennis Romano. Baltimore: Johns Hopkins University Press, 2000.

Waley, Daniel. *The Italian City-Republics*. New York: McGraw-Hill, 1969. 3rd ed. 1988.

———. *Mediaeval Orvieto: The Political History of an Italian City-State*. Cambridge: Cambridge University Press, 1952.

———. *Siena and the Sienese in the Thirteenth Century*. Cambridge: Cambridge University Press, 1991.

SECTION I. THE COUNTRYSIDE AND ITS DEPENDENCIES

Chittolini, Giorgio. "A Geography of the 'Contadi' in Communal Italy." Trans. Shona Wray Kelly in *Portraits of Medieval and Renaissance Living: Essays in Memory of David Herlihy*. Ed. Samuel K. Cohn, Jr., and Steven A. Epstein. Ann Arbor: University of Michigan Press, 1996.

City and Countryside in Late Medieval and Renaissance Italy: Essays Presented to Philip Jones. Ed. Trevor Dean and Chris Wickham. London: Hambledon, 1990.

Cohn, Samuel K. *Creating the Florentine State: Peasants and Rebellion, 1348–1434*. Cambridge: Cambridge University Press, 1999.

———. *Lust for Liberty: The Politics of Social Revolt in Medieval Europe, 1200–1425*. Cambridge, Mass.: Harvard University Press, 2006.

Dameron, George. *Florence and Its Church in the Age of Dante*. Philadelphia: University of Pennsylvania Press, 2005.

Herlihy, David. "Santa Maria Impruneta: A Rural Commune in the Late Middle Ages." In *Florentine Studies: Politics and Society in Renaissance Florence*, ed. Nicolai Rubinstein. Evanston, Ill: Northwestern University Press, 1968. Repr. in

UNIVERSITY OF WINCHESTER LIBRARY

Herlihy, *Cities and Society in Medieval Italy*. London: Variorum, 1980. Article III.

Jones, Philip J. "From Manor to Mezzadria. A Tuscan Case-Study in the Medieval Origins of Modern Agrarian Society." In *Florentine Studies: Politics and Society in Renaissance Florence*, ed. Nicolai Rubinstein. Evanston, Ill: Northwestern University Press, 1968. 193–241.

———. "Medieval Agrarian Society in Its Prime 2: Italy." In *The Cambridge Economic History of Europe*, ed. M. M. Postan. 2nd ed. Vol. 1, *The Agrarian Life of the Middle Ages*. Cambridge: Cambridge University Press, 1966. 340–432.

——— . "A Tuscan Monastic Lordship in the later Middle Ages: Camaldoli." *Journal of Ecclesiastical History* 5 (1954): 168–83.

Waley, Daniel. "A Commune and Its Subject Territory in the Thirteenth Century: Law and Power in the Sienese Contado." In *Diritto e potere nella storia Europea: in onore di Bruno Paradisi*. Florence: Olschki, 1982. 305–11.

Wickham, Chris. *Community and Clientele in Twelfth-Century Tuscany: The Origins of the Rural Commune in the Plain of Lucca*. Oxford: Clarendon Press, 1998.

———. *The Mountains and the City: The Tuscan Apennines in the Early Middle Ages*. Oxford: Clarendon Press, 1988.

———. "Rural Communes and the City of Lucca at the Beginning of the Thirteenth Century." In *City and Countryside in Medieval and Renaissance Italy: Essays Presented to Philip Jones*, ed. Trevor Dean and Chris Wickham. London: Hambledon, 1990. 1–12.

Section 2. Spheres and Structures of Power: Ecclesiastical and Secular

Andrews, Frances. "Regular Observance and Communal Life: Siena and the Employment of Religious" In *Pope, Church and City: Essays in Honour of Brenda M. Bolton*, ed. Frances Andrews, Christoph Egger, and Constance Rousseau. Leiden: Brill, 2004. 357–83.

Backman, Clifford R. *The Decline and Fall of Medieval Sicily: Politics, Religion and Economy in the Reign of Frederick III, 1296–1337*. Cambridge: Cambridge University Press, 1996.

Baron, Hans. *The Crisis of the Early Renaissance*. 2 vols. Princeton, N.J.: Princeton University Press, 1955. Rev. ed. 1966.

Becker, Marvin. *Medieval Italy: Constraints and Creativity*. Bloomington: Indiana University Press, 1981.

Bowsky, William. *Finance of the Commune of Siena, 1287–1355*. Oxford: Clarendon Press, 1970.

———. *Henry VII in Italy: The Conflict of Empire and City State, 1310–1313*. Lincoln: University of Nebraska Press, 1960.

———. *A Medieval Italian Commune: Siena Under the Nine, 1287–1355*. Berkeley: University of California Press, 1981.

Brentano, Robert. *A New World in a Small Place: Church and Religion in the Diocese of Rieti, 1188–1378*. Berkeley: University of California Press, 1994.

Brucker, Gene A. *The Civic World of Early Renaissance Florence*. Princeton, N.J.: Princeton University Press, 1977.

Cohn, Samuel K. *The Laboring Classes in Renaissance Florence*. New York: Academic Press, 1980.

Coleman, Edward. "Cities and Communes." In *Italy in the Central Middle Ages*, ed. David Abulafia. Oxford: Oxford University Press, 2004.

———. "The Italian Communes: Recent Work and Current Trends." *Journal of Medieval History* 24, 4 (1999): 373–97.

Cowdrey, H. E. J. *The Age of Abbot Desiderius: Montecassino, the Papacy and the Normans in the Eleventh and Early Twelfth Centuries*. Oxford: Clarendon Press, 1983.

Fisher, C. B. "The Pisan Clergy and an Awakening of Historical Interest in an Italian Commune." *Studies in Medieval and Renaissance History* 3 (1966): 141–219.

Foote, David. *Lordship, Reform, and the Development of Civil Society in Medieval Italy: The Bishopric of Orvieto, 1100–1250*. Notre Dame, Ind.: University of Notre Dame Press, 2004.

Johns, Jeremy. *Arabic Administration in Norman Sicily: The Royal Diwan*. Cambridge: Cambridge University Press, 2002.

Jones, Philip J. "Communes and Despots: The City-State in Late Medieval Italy." *Transactions of the Royal Historical Society* 5th ser. 15 (1965): 71–96.

Kohl, Benjamin G. *Padua Under the Carrara 1318–1405*. Baltimore: Johns Hopkins University Press, 1998.

Lansing, Carol. *The Florentine Magnates: Lineage and Faction in a Medieval Commune*. Princeton, N.J.: Princeton University Press, 1991.

Loud, G. A. *Conquerors and Churchmen in Norman Italy*. Brookfield, Vt.: Ashgate/Variorum, 1999.

———. "The Norman Conquest and South Italian Society: How 'Norman' Was the Norman Conquest of Southern Italy?" *Nottingham Medieval Studies* 25 (1981). Repr. in Loud, *Conquerors and Churchmen in Norman Italy*. Brookfield, Vt.: Ashgate/Variorum, 1999. 3–34.

———. *Montecassino and Benevento in the Middle Ages: Essays in South Italian Church History*. Brookfield, Vt.: Ashgate/Variorum, 2000.

Martines, Lauro. *Power and Imagination: City-States in Renaissance Italy*. Baltimore: Johns Hopkins University Press, 1988.

Meek, Christine. *The Commune of Lucca Under Pisan Rule, 1342–1369*. Cambridge, Mass.: Medieval Academy of America, 1980.

Metcalfe, Alex. *Muslims and Christians in Norman Sicily: Arabic Speakers and the End of Islam*. New York: Routledge, 2003.

Miller, Maureen. *Verona: The Formation of a Medieval Church: Ecclesiastical Change in Verona, 950–1150*. Ithaca, N.Y.: Cornell University Press, 1993.

Munz, Peter. *Frederick Barbarossa: A Study in Medieval Politics*. Ithaca, N.Y.: Cornell University Press, 1969.

Najemy, John M. *Corporatism and Consensus in Florentine Electoral Politics, 1280–1400*. Chapel Hill: University of North Carolina Press, 1982.

———. *A History of Florence*. Malden, Mass.: Blackwell, 2006.

Oldfield, Paul. "Citizenship and Community in Southern Italy c. 1100–1220." *Papers of the British School at Rome* 74 (2006): 323–38.

———. "Urban Government in Southern Italy, c. 1085–c. 1127." *English Historical Review* 122 (2007): 579–608.

Osheim, Duane. *An Italian Lordship: The Bishopric of Lucca in the Late Middle Ages.* Berkeley: University of California Press, 1977.

Rubinstein, Nicolai. *Political Thought and the Language of Politics: Art and Politics.* Ed. Giovannni Ciappelli. Studies in Italian History in the Middle Ages and Renaissance 1. Rome: Edizioni di Storia e Letteratura, 2004.

Skinner, Patricia. "When Was Southern Italy 'Feudal?'" In *Il feudalesimo nell'alto medioevo.* Settimane di Studio sull'Alto Medioevo 47. Spoleto: Centro italiano di studi dell'alto medioevo, 2000. 309–45.

Tabacco, Giovanni. *The Struggle for Power in Medieval Italy: Structures of Political Rule.* Trans. Rosalind Brown. Cambridge: Cambridge University Press, 1984.

Takayama, Hiroshi. *The Administration of the Norman Kingdom of Sicily.* Leiden: Brill, 1993.

Taylor, Julie. *Muslims in Medieval Italy: The Colony at Lucera.* Lanham, Md.: Lexington Books, 2003.

Trexler, Richard. *Power and Dependence in Renaissance Florence.* 3 vols. Vol. 3, *The Workers of Renaissance Florence.* Binghamton, N.Y.: Medieval and Renaissance Texts and Studies, 1993.

Wickham, Chris. *Land and Power: Studies in Italian and European Social History, 400–1200.* London: British School at Rome, 1994.

SECTION 3. THE COMMERCIAL REVOLUTION

Abulafia, David. *Commerce and Conquest in the Mediterranean, 1100–1400.* Brookfield, Vt.: Variorum, 1993.

———. *The Two Italies: Economic Relations Between the Norman Kingdom of Sicily and the Northern Communes.* Cambridge: Cambridge University Press, 1977.

Armstrong, Lawrin. *Usury and Public Debt in Early Renaissance Florence: Lorenzo Ridolfi on the "Monte Commune".* Toronto: University of Toronto Press, 2003.

Blomquist, Thomas W. *Merchant Families, Banking, and Money in Medieval Lucca.* Burlington, Vt.: Ashgate/Variorum, 2005.

Cipolla, Carlo. *The Monetary Policy of Fourteenth-Century Florence.* Berkeley: University of California, 1982.

Epstein, Stephan R. *An Island for Itself: Economic Development and Social Change in Late Medieval Sicily.* Cambridge: Cambridge University Press, 1992.

Epstein, Steven. *Wage Labor and Guilds in Medieval Europe.* Chapel Hill: University of North Carolina Press, 1991.

Glossary of Mediaeval Terms of Business: Italian Series: 1200–1600. Ed. Florence Edler. Cambridge, Mass.: Medieval Academy of America, 1934. Repr. New York: Kraus, 1970.

Grierson, Philip and Lucia Travaini. *Medieval European Coinage: With a Catalogue of the Coins in the Fitzwilliam Museum, Cambridge.* Vol. 14, *South Italy, Sicily, Sardinia.* Cambridge: Cambridge University Press, 1998. Vols. 12 (*Northern Italy*) and 13 (*Central Italy*) are forthcoming.

Hunt, Edwin S. *The Medieval Super-Companies: A Study of the Peruzzi Company of Florence.* Cambridge: Cambridge University Press, 1994.

Hunt, Edwin S. and James M. Murray. *A History of Business in Medieval Europe, 1200–1550*. Cambridge: Cambridge University Press, 1999.

Italian Weights and Measures from the Middle Ages to the Nineteenth Century. Ed. Ronald Edward Zupko. Philadelphia: American Philosophical Society, 1981.

Kedar, B. Z. *Merchants in Crisis: Genoese and Venetian Men of Affairs and the Fourteenth-Century Depression*. New Haven, Conn.: Yale University Press, 1976.

Lane, Frederic C. *Venetian Ships and Shipbuilders of the Renaissance*. Baltimore: Johns Hopkins University Press, 1934. Repr. 1992.

Lane, Frederic C. and Reinhold C. Mueller. *Money and Banking in Medieval and Renaissance Venice*. Baltimore: Johns Hopkins University Press, 1985.

Lopez, Robert. *The Commercial Revolution in the Middle Ages, 950–1350*. Cambridge: Cambridge University Press, 1976.

Luzzatto, Gino. *An Economic History of Italy from the Fall of the Roman Empire to the Beginning of the Sixteenth Century*. Trans. Philip Jones. New York: Barnes and Noble, 1961.

Mackenney, Richard. *Tradesmen and Traders: The World of the Guilds in Venice and Europe, c. 1250–1650*. Totowa, N.J.: Barnes and Noble, 1987.

Marshall, Richard K. *The Local Merchants of Prato: Small Entrepreneurs in the Late Medieval Economy*. Baltimore: Johns Hopkins University Press, 1999.

Mazzaoui, Maureen F. *The Italian Cotton Industry in the Later Middle Ages, 1100–1600*. Cambridge: Cambridge University Press, 1981.

Medieval Trade in the Mediterranean World. Ed. Robert S. Lopez and Irving W. Raymond. New York: Columbia University Press, 1955.

Origo, Iris. *The Merchant of Prato: Francesco di Marco Datini, 1335–1410*. New York: Knopf, 1957. Repr. London: Penguin, 1992.

Stahl, Alan M. *Zecca: The Mint of Venice in the Middle Ages*. Baltimore: Johns Hopkins University Press, 2000.

Stuard, Susan Mosher. *Gilding the Market: Luxury and Fashion in Fourteenth-Century Italy*. Philadelphia: University of Pennsylvania Press, 2006.

SECTION 4. VIOLENCE, WARFARE, AND PEACE

Caferro, William. *John Hawkwood: An English Mercenary in Fourteenth-Century Italy*. Baltimore: Johns Hopkins University Press, 2006.

———. *Mercenary Companies and the Decline of Siena*. Baltimore: Johns Hopkins University Press, 1998.

Dean, Trevor. "Marriage and Mutilation: Vendetta in Late Medieval Italy." *Past and Present* 157 (November 1997): 3–36.

Dunbabin, Jean. *Charles I of Anjou: Power, Kinship and State-Making in Thirteenth-Century Europe*. New York: Longman, 1998.

Face, Richard. "Secular History in Twelfth-Century Italy: Caffaro of Genoa." *Journal of Medieval History* 6 (1980): 169–84.

Garí, B. "Why Almería? An Islamic Port in the Compass of Genoa." *Journal of Medieval History* 18 (1992): 211–31.

Housely, Norman. *The Italian Crusades: The Papal-Angevin Alliance and the Crusades Against Christian Lay Powers, 1254–1343*. Oxford: Clarendon Press, 1982.

Law, John E. *The Lords of Renaissance Italy: The Signori, 1250–1500*. London: Historical Association, 1981.

———. *Venice and the Veneto in the Early Renaissance*. Burlington, Vt.: Ashgate/ Variorum, 2000.

Loud, G. A. "Continuity and Change in Norman Italy: The Campania During the 11th and 12th Centuries." *Journal of Medieval History* 22 (1996): 325–32. Repr. in *Conquerors and Churchmen in Norman Italy*. Brookfield, Vt.: Ashgate/Variorum, 1999. 313–43.

Oldfield, Paul. "An Internal Frontier? The Relationship Between Mainland Southern Italy and Sicily in the 'Norman' kingdom." *Haskins Society Journal* 20 (2009).

Ruggiero, Guido. *Violence in Early Renaissance Venice*. New Brunswick, N.J.: Rutgers University Press, 1980.

Thompson, Augustine. *Revival Preachers and Politics in Thirteenth-Century Italy: The Great Devotion of 1233*. Oxford: Clarendon Press, 1992.

Violence and Civil Disorder in Italian Cities, 1200–1500. Ed. Lauro Martines. Berkeley: University of California Press, 1972.

Waley, Daniel. "A Blood-Feud with a Happy Ending: Siena, 1285–1304." In *City and Countryside in Late Medieval and Renaissance Italy: Essays Presented to Philip Jones*, ed. Trevor Dean and Chris Wickham. London: Hambledon, 1990. 45–53.

Webb, Diana. "Cities of God: The Italian Communes at War." In *The Church and War*, ed. W. J. Sheils. Studies in Church History 20. Oxford: Blackwell for Ecclesiastical History Society, 1983. 111–27.

Section 5. Law and Order

Bellomo, Manlio. *The Common Legal Past of Europe, 1000–1800*. Trans. Lydia Cochrane. Washington, D.C.: Catholic University of America Press, 1995.

Briggs, Robin. *Witches and Neighbors: The Social and Cultural Context of European Witchcraft*. New York: Viking, 1996.

Crime, Society and the Law in Renaissance Italy. Ed. Trevor Dean and K. J. P. Lowe. Cambridge: Cambridge University Press, 1994.

Dean, Trevor, *Crime and Justice in Late Medieval Italy*. Cambridge: Cambridge University Press, 2007.

Jansen, Katherine L. "Florentine Peacemaking: The Oltrarno, 1287–1297." In *Pope, Church and City: Essays in Honour of Brenda M. Bolton*, ed. Frances Andrews, Christoph Egger, and Constance M. Rousseau. Leiden: Brill, 2004. 327–44.

Killerby, Catherine Kovesi. *Sumptuary Law in Italy 1200–1500*. Oxford: Clarendon Press, 2002.

Kirshner, Julius. *Privileges and Rights of Citizenship: Law and the Juridical Construction of Civil Society*. Berkeley, Calif.: Robbins Collection, 2002.

Kuehn, Thomas. *Law, Family, and Women: Toward a Legal Anthropology of Renaissance Italy*. Chicago: University of Chicago Press, 1991.

Lansing, Carol. "Concubines, Lovers, Prostitutes: Infamy and Female Identity in Medieval Bologna." In *Beyond Florence: The Contours of Medieval and Early Modern Italy*, ed. Paula Findlen, Michelle M. Fontaine, and Duane J. Osheim. Stanford, Calif.: Stanford University Press, 2003. 85–100.

McKee, Sally. *Uncommon Dominion: Venetian Crete and the Myth of Ethnic Purity.* Philadelphia: University of Pennsylvania Press, 2000.

Otis, Leah. *Prostitution in Medieval Society.* Chicago: University of Chicago Press, 1984.

Radding, Charles. *The Origins of Medieval Jurisprudence: Pavia and Bologna, 850–1150.* New Haven, Conn.: Yale University Press, 1988.

Stern, Laura. *The Criminal Law System of Medieval and Renaissance Florence.* Baltimore: Johns Hopkins University Press, 1994.

Trexler, Richard C. "Florentine Prostitution in the Fifteenth Century: Patrons and Clients." In Trexler, *Power and Dependence in Renaissance Florence*, vol. 2, *The Women of Renaissance Florence*. Binghamton, N.Y.: Medieval and Renaissance Texts and Studies, 1993. 31–65.

Wickham, Chris. *Courts and Conflict in Twelfth-Century Tuscany.* Oxford: Oxford University Press, 2003.

SECTION 6. THE BUILT ENVIRONMENT

Benton, T. "Three Cities Compared: Urbanism." In *Siena, Florence and Padua: Art, Society and Religion, 1280–1400*, ed.. Diana Norman. 2 vols. New Haven, Conn.: Yale University Press, 1995. Vol. 2, 7–28.

Bocchi, Francesca. "Regulation of the Urban Environment by the Italian Communes from the Twelfth to the Fourteenth Century." *Bulletin of the John Rylands Library University of Manchester* 72 (1990): 63–78.

Borsook, Eve. *Messages in Mosaic: The Royal Programmes of Norman Sicily, 1130–1187.* Oxford: Oxford University Press, 1990.

Bruzelius, Caroline. *The Stones of Naples: Church Building in the Angevin Kingdom, 1266–1343.* New Haven, Conn.: Yale University Press, 2004.

Caskey, Jill. *Art and Patronage in the Medieval Mediterranean: Merchant Culture in the Region of Amalfi.* Cambridge: Cambridge University Press, 2004.

———. "Steam and *Sanitas* in the Domestic Realm: Baths and Bathing in Southern Italy in the Middle Ages." *Journal of the Society of Architectural Historians* 58 (1999): 170–95.

Colafemmina, Cesare. "Hebrew Inscriptions of the Early Medieval Period in Southern Italy." In *The Jews of Italy: Memory and Identity*, ed. Bernard Dov Cooperman and Barbara Garvin. Potomac: University Press of Maryland, 2000. 65–81.

Friedman, David. *Florentine New Towns: Urban Design in the Late Middle Ages.* Cambridge, Mass.: MIT Press, 1988.

———. "Palaces and the Street in Late-Medieval and Renaissance Italy." In *Urban Landscapes, International Perspectives*, ed. W. R. Whitehand and P. J. Larkham. London: Routledge, 1992. 69–113.

Frugoni, Chiara. *A Distant City: Images of Medieval Experience in the Medieval World.* Trans. William McCuaig. Princeton, N.J.: Princeton University Press, 1991.

Marina, Areli. "Order and Ideal Geometry in Parma's Piazza del Duomo." *Journal of the Society of Architectural Historians* 65, 4 (December 2006): 520–49.

Miller, Maureen C. *The Bishop's Palace: Architecture and Authority in Medieval Italy*. Ithaca, N.Y.: Cornell University Press, 2000.

Tronzo, William. *The Cultures of His Kingdom: Roger II and the Cappella Palatina in Palermo*. Princeton, N.J.: Princeton University Press, 1990.

Nevola, Fabrizio. *Siena: Constructing the Renaissance City*. New Haven, Conn.: Yale University Press, 2007.

Wieruszowski, H. "Art and the Commune in the Time of Dante." *Speculum* 19 (1944): 14–33. Repr. in *Politics and Culture in Medieval Spain and Italy*. Rome: Edizioni di storia e letteratura, 1971. 475–502.

Section 7. Rome, the Papacy, and Papal Politics

Bolton, Brenda. "Carthusians at San Bartolomeo di Trisulti: Innocent III's Troublesome Gift." In *L'Ordine Certosino e il Papato: dalla fondazione alla schisma d'Occidente*, ed. Pietro di Leo. Atti del Convegno-Roma-Serra di San Bruno, May–October 2002. Rende, 2004. 235–60.

———. *Innocent III: Studies on Papal Authority and Pastoral Care*. Brookfield, Vt.: Variorum, 1995.

Brentano, Robert. *Rome Before Avignon: A Social History of Thirteenth-Century Rome*. New York: Basic Books, 1974. Repr. Berkeley: University of California Press, 1991.

Collins, Amanda. *Greater Than Emperor: Cola di Rienzo (ca. 1313–40) and the World of Fourteenth-Century Rome*. Ann Arbor: University of Michigan Press, 2002.

Gregorovius, Ferdinand. *History of the City of Rome in the Middle Ages*. Trans. Annie Hamilton. 8 vols. New York: Italica Press, 2000.

Kessler, Herbert and Joanna Zacharias, *Rome 1300: On the Path of the Pilgrim*. New Haven, Conn.: Yale University Press, 2000.

Krautheimer, Richard. *Rome: Profile of a City, 312–1308*. Princeton, N.J.: Princeton University Press, 1980.

Morris, Colin. *The Papal Monarchy: The Western Church from 1050 to 1250*. Oxford: Clarendon Press, 1989.

Musto, Ronald G. *Apocalypse in Rome: Cola di Rienzo and the Politics of the New Age*. Berkeley: University of California Press, 2003.

Pope, Church and City: Essays in Honor of Brenda Bolton. Ed. Frances Andrews, Christoph Egger, and Constance M. Rousseau. Leiden: Brill, 2004.

Stroll, Mary. *Symbols as Power: The Papacy Following the Investiture Contest*. Leiden: Brill, 1991.

Waley, Daniel. *The Papal State in the Thirteenth Century*. New York: St. Martin's Press, 1961.

Section 8. Disease and Medical Practice

Carmichael, Ann. *Plague and the Poor in Renaissance Florence*. Cambridge: Cambridge University Press, 1986.

Cipolla, Carlo. *Public Health and the Medical Profession in the Renaissance*. Cambridge: Cambridge University Press, 1976.

Cohn, Samuel K. *The Black Death Transformed: Disease and Culture in Early Renaissance Europe.* New York: Oxford University Press, 2002.

Collins, Minta. *Medieval Herbals: The Illustrative Traditions.* London and Toronto: British Library and University of Toronto Press, 2000.

Constantine the African and 'Ali ibn Al-'Abbas Al-Magusi: The "Pantegni" and Related Works. Ed. Charles Burnett and Danielle Jacquart. Studies in Ancient Medicine 10. Leiden: Brill, 1994.

Corner, George Washington. *Anatomical Texts of the Earlier Middle Ages.* Washington, D.C.: Carnegie Institution, 1927.

Green, Monica H. *Making Women's Medicine Masculine: The Rise of Male Authority in Pre-Modern Gynaecology.* Oxford: Oxford University Press, 2008.

———. *The "Trotula": An English Translation of the Medieval Compendium of Women's Medicine.* Philadelphia: University of Pennsylvania Press, 2002.

Herlihy, David. *The Black Death and the Transformation of the West.* Ed. Samuel K. Cohn. Cambridge, Mass.: Harvard University Press, 1997.

Park, Katherine. *Doctors and Medicine in Early Renaissance Florence.* Princeton, N.J.: Princeton University Press, 1985.

Practical Medicine from Salerno to the Black Death. Ed. Luis García-Ballester, Roger French, Jon Arrizabalaga, and Andrew Cunningham. Cambridge: Cambridge University Press, 1994.

Siraisi, Nancy G. *Medieval and Renaissance Medicine: An Introduction to Knowledge and Practice.* Chicago: University of Chicago Press, 1980.

Skinner, Patricia. *Health and Medicine in Early Medieval Southern Italy.* Leiden: Brill, 1997.

Section 9. Varieties of Religious Experience

Andrews, Frances. *The Early Humiliati.* Cambridge: Cambridge University Press, 1999.

Bornstein, Daniel E. *The Bianchi of 1399: Popular Devotion in Late Medieval Italy.* Ithaca, N.Y.: Cornell University Press, 1993.

Cossar, Roisin. *The Transformation of the Laity in Bergamo.* Leiden: Brill, 2006.

Cowdrey, H. E. J. "The Papacy, the Patarines and the Church of Milan." *Transactions of the Royal Historical Society* 5th ser. 18 (1968): 25–48. Repr. in Cowdrey, *Popes, Monks and Crusaders.* London: Hambledon, 1984.

Creative Women in Medieval and Early Modern Italy. Ed. E. Ann Matter and John Coakley. Philadelphia: University of Pennsylvania Press, 1994.

Henderson, John. *Piety and Charity in Late Medieval Florence.* Oxford: Oxford University Press, 1994.

Howe, John. *Church Reform and Social Change in Eleventh-Century Italy: Dominic of Sora and His Patrons.* Philadelphia: University of Pennsylvania Press, 1997.

Jansen, Katherine L. *The Making of the Magdalen: Preaching and Popular Devotion in the Later Middle Ages.* Princeton, N.J.: Princeton University Press, 2000.

Lansing, Carol. *Power and Purity: Cathar Heresy in Medieval Italy.* Oxford: Oxford University Press, 1998.

Little, Lester, K. *Liberty, Charity, Fraternity: Lay Religious Confraternities at Bergamo in the Age of the Commune.* Northampton, Mass.: Smith College, 1988.

Loud, G. A. *The Latin Church in Norman Italy.* Cambridge: Cambridge University Press, 2007.

Morse, Victoria. "The *Vita mediocris:* The Secular Priesthood in the Thought of Opicino de Canistris." *Quaderni di storia religiosa* 4 (1997): 257–82.

Powell, James M. *Albertanus da Brescia: The Pursuit of Happiness in the Early Thirteenth Century.* Philadelphia: University of Pennsylvania Press, 1992.

Schuchman, Anne M. "Politics and Prophecy in the Life of Umiliana dei Cerchi." *Florilegium* 17 (2000): 101–14.

Siena, Florence, and Padua: Art, Society, and Religion 1280–1400. Ed. Diana Norman. New Haven, Conn.: Yale University Press, 1995.

Thompson, Augustine. *Cities of God: The Religion of the Italian Communes, 1125–1325.* University Park: Pennsylvania State University Press, 2005.

Vauchez, André. *Sainthood in the Later Middle Ages.* Trans. Jean Birrell. Cambridge: Cambridge University Press, 1997.

Webb, Diana. *Patrons and Defenders: The Saints in the Italian City-States.* New York: Tauris Academic Studies, 1996.

Wolf, Kenneth B. *The Poverty of Riches: St. Francis of Assisi Reconsidered.* Oxford: Oxford University Press, 2003.

Women and Religion in Medieval and Renaissance Italy. Ed. Daniel Bornstein and Roberto Rusconi. Chicago: University of Chicago Press, 1996.

Section 10. Marriage, Family, and Children

Byrne, Joseph and Eleanor Congdon. "Mothering in the Casa Datini." *Journal of Medieval History* 25 (1999): 35–56.

Chabot, Isabelle. "Lineage Strategies and the Control of Widows in Renaissance Florence." In *Widowhood in Medieval and Early Modern Europe,* ed. Sandra Cavallo and Lyndan Warner. London: Longman, 1999. 127–44.

Chojnacki, Stanley. *Women and Men in Renaissance Venice: Twelve Essays on Patrician Society.* Baltimore: Johns Hopkins University Press, 2000.

Drell, Joanna. *Kinship and Conquest: Family Strategies in the Principality of Salerno During the Norman Period, 1077–1194.* Ithaca, N.Y.: Cornell University Press, 2002.

Herlihy, David and Christiane Klapisch Zuber. *Tuscans and Their Families: A Study of the Florentine Catasto of 1427.* New Haven, Conn.: Yale University Press, 1985.

Hughes, Diane Owen. "Domestic Ideals and Social Behavior: Evidence from Medieval Genoa." In *The Family in History,* ed. Charles E. Rosenberg. Philadelphia: University of Pennsylvania Press, 1975. 115–43.

———. "From Brideprice to Dowry in Mediterranean Europe." *Journal of Family History* 3 (1978): 262–96.

———. "Kinsmen and Neighbors in Medieval Genoa." In *The Medieval City,* ed. Harry A. Miskimin, David Herlihy, and A. L. Udovitch. New Haven, Conn.: Yale University Press, 1977.

————. "Urban Growth and Family Structure in Medieval Genoa." *Past and Present* 66 (1975): 3–28.

Kelly, Shona Wray. "Women, Family, and Inheritance in Bologna During the Black Death." In *Love, Marriage, and Family Ties in the Middle Ages*, ed. Miriam Muller and Isabel Davis. Turnhout: Brepols, 2003. 205–15.

Kertzer, David and Caroline Brettell. "Advances in Italian and Iberian Family History." *Journal of Family History* 12 (1987): 87–120.

Kertzer, David and Richard P. Saller. *The Family in Italy from Antiquity to the Present.* New Haven, Conn.: Yale University Press, 1991.

Klapisch Zuber, Christiane. *Women, Family and Ritual in Renaissance Italy.* Chicago: University of Chicago Press, 1985.

Molho, Anthony. *Marriage Alliance in Late Medieval Florence.* Cambridge, Mass.: Harvard University Press, 1994.

Skinner, Patricia. "Daughters of Sichelgaita: the Women of Salerno in the 12th Century." In *Salerno nel XII secolo: istituzioni, società, cultura*, ed. Paolo Delogu and Paolo Peduto. Salerno: Centro Studi Salernitani Raffaele Guariglia, 2004. 119–31.

————. *Family Power in Southern Italy: The Duchy of Gaeta and Its Neighbors, 850– 1139.* Cambridge: Cambridge University Press, 1995.

————. "Halt! Be Men! Sikelgaita of Salerno: Gender and the Norman Conquest of Southern Italy." *Gender and History* 12 (2000): 622–41.

————. *Women in Italian Medieval Society 500–1200.* New York: Pearson, 2001.

Section 11. Education and Erudition

Abulafia, David. *Frederick II: A Medieval Emperor.* Oxford: Oxford University Press, 1992.

Black, Robert. *Education and Society in Florentine Tuscany.* Leiden: Brill, 1997.

————. *Humanism and Education in Medieval and Renaissance Italy: Tradition and Innovation in the Latin Schools from the Twelfth to the Fifteenth Century.* Cambridge: Cambridge University Press, 2001.

Grendler, Paul. F. *Schooling in Renaissance Italy: Literacy and Learning, 1300–1600.* Baltimore: Johns Hopkins University Press, 1989.

————. *The Universities of the Italian Renaissance.* Baltimore: Johns Hopkins University Press, 1989.

Hyde, J. K. *Literacy and its Uses: Studies on Late Medieval Italy.* Ed. Daniel Waley. Manchester: Manchester University Press, 1993.

Intellectual Life at the Court of Frederick II Hohenstaufen. Ed. William Tronzo. Washington, D.C.: National Gallery of Art. 1994.

Kelly, Samantha. *The New Solomon: Robert of Naples (1309–1343) and Fourteenth-Century Kingship.* Leiden: Brill, 2003.

Kelly, Shona Wray. "*Speculum et Exemplar*: The Notaries of Bologna During the Black Death." *Quellen und Forschungen aus italienischen Archiven und Bibliotheken* 81 (2001): 1–28.

Mulchahey, M. Michèle. *"First the Bow Is Bent in Study": Dominican Education Before 1350.* Toronto: Pontifical Institute of Mediaeval Studies, 1998.

Petrucci, Armando. *Readers and Writers in Medieval Italy: Studies in the History of Written Culture.* New Haven, Conn.: Yale University Press, 1995.

Roest, Bert. *A History of Franciscan Education (c. 1210–1517).* Leiden: Brill: 2000.

Siraisi, Nancy F. *Arts and Sciences at Padua: The Studium of Padua Before 1350.* Toronto: Pontifical Institute of Mediaeval Studies, 1973.

Witt, Ronald G. "Boncompagno and the Defense of Rhetoric." *Journal of Medieval and Renaissance Studies* 16, 1 (1986): 1–31.

SECTION 12. SOCIAL MEMORY, HISTORY, COMMEMORATION

Banker, James R. *Death in the Community: Memorialization and Confraternities in an Italian Commune in the Late Middle Ages.* Athens: University of Georgia Press, 1988.

Birk, Joshua. "Borderlands and Borderlines: Narrating the Past in Twelfth-Century Sicily." In *Multicultural Europe and Cultural Exchange in the Middle Ages and Renaissance,* ed. James P. Helfers. Turnholt: Brepols, 2005. 9–32.

Bourdua, Louise. *The Franciscans and Art Patronage in Late Medieval Italy.* Cambridge: Cambridge University Press 2004.

Cassidy, Brendan. *Politics, Civic Ideals and Sculpture in Italy, 1240–1400.* London: Harvey Miller, 2007.

Chronicling History: Chronicles and Historians in Medieval and Renaissance Italy. Ed. Sharon Dale, Alison Williams Lewin and Duane J. Osheim. University Park: Pennsylvania State Uniiversity Press, 2007.

Cohn, Samuel K., *Death and Property in Siena, 1205–1800.* Baltimore: Johns Hopkins University Press, 1988.

———. *The Cult of Remembrance and the Black Death: Six Renaissance Cities in Central Italy.* Baltimore: Johns Hopkins University Press, 1992.

Coleman, Edward. "Sense of Community and Civic Identity in the Italian Communes." In *The Community, the Family, and the Saint: Patterns of Power in Early Medieval Europe: Selected Proceedings of the International Medieval Congress,* ed. Joyce Hill and M. Swan. Turnhout: Brepols, 1998. 45–60.

Drell, Joanna. "Cultural Syncretism and Ethnic Identity: The Norman 'Conquest' of Southern Italy and Sicily." *Journal of Medieval History* 25, 3 (1999): 187–202.

Epstein, Steven. *Wills and Wealth in Medieval Genoa, 1150–1250.* Cambridge, Mass.: Harvard University Press, 1984.

Fentress, James and Chris Wickham. *Social Memory.* Oxford: Blackwell, 1992.

Gardner, Julian. *Patrons, Painters and Saints: Studies in Medieval Italian Painting.* Brookfield, Vt.: Ashgate/Variorum, 1993.

Geary, Patrick. *Phantoms of Remembrance: Memory and Oblivion at the End of the First Millennium.* Princeton, N. J.: Princeton University Press, 1994.

Hyde, J. K. "Medieval Descriptions of Cities." *Bulletin of the John Rylands Library University of Manchester* 48 (1966): 308–40.

Lansing, Carol. *Passion and Order: Restraint of Grief in the Medieval Italian Communes.* Ithaca, N.Y.: Cornell University Press, 2008.

Loud, G. A. "The 'Gens Normannorum'—Myth or Reality?" *Proceedings of the Battle Conference on Anglo-Norman Studies* 4 (1981): 104–16. Repr. in Loud, *Conquer-*

ors and Churchmen in Norman Italy. Brookfield, Vt.: Ashgate/Variorum, 1999. 104–16.

Morse, Victoria. *Opicino de Canistris: In Praise of Pavia.* Trans. William North and Victoria Morse. New York: Italica Press, forthcoming.

Rubinstein, Nicolai. "Political Ideas in Sienese Art." *Journal of the Warburg and Courtauld Institutes* 21 (1958): 179–207.

Safran, Linda. "Language Choice in the Medieval Salento: A Sociolinguistic Approach to Greek and Latin Inscriptions." In *Zwischen Polis, Provinz und Peripherie: Beiträge zur byzantinischen Geschichte und Kultur,* ed. Lars M. Hoffman. Mainzer Veröffentlichungen zur Byzantinistik. Wiesbaden: Harrassowitz, 2005. 819–40.

Skinner, Patricia. "'And Her Name Was . . . ?' Gender and Naming in Medieval Southern Italy." *Medieval Prosopography* 20 (1999): 23–49.

———. "Gender, Memory and Family Identity: Reading a Southern Italian Jewish Family Chronicle." *Early Medieval Europe* 13 (2004): 277–96.

Starn, Randolph and Loren Partridge. *Arts of Power: Three Halls of State in Italy, 1300–1600.* Berkeley: University of California Press, 1992.

White, John. *Art and Architecture in Italy, 1250–1400.* 3rd ed. New Haven, Conn.: Yale University Press, 1993.

Wickham, Chris. "The Sense of the Past in Italian Communal Narratives." In *The Perception of the Past in Twelfth-Century Europe,* ed. Paul Magdalino. London: Hambledon, 1992. 173–89.

Wolf, Kenneth B. *Making History: The Normans and Their Historians in Eleventh-Century Italy.* Philadelphia: University of Pennsylvania Press, 1995.

Contributors

Gregory W. Ahlquist. Department of History, State University of New York, Geneseo.

Frances Andrews. Department of Mediaeval History, University of St. Andrews.

Lawrin Armstrong. Centre for Medieval Studies, University of Toronto.

Joshua C. Birk. Department of History, Smith College.

Brenda Bolton. Department of History, University of London.

Daniel E. Bornstein. Departments of History and Religious Studies, Washington University in St. Louis.

Louise Bourdua. Department of History of Art, University of Warwick.

Caroline Bruzelius. Department of Art, Art History and Visual Studies, Duke University.

William Caferro. Department of History, Vanderbilt University.

Jill Caskey. Department of Fine Art, University of Toronto.

Osvaldo Cavallar. Faculty of Policy Studies, Nanzan University.

Isabelle Chabot. Research Fellow, European University Institute, Florence.

J. H. Chajes. Department of Jewish History, University of Haifa.

Adele Cilento. Dipartimento di Studi storici e geografici, Università degli Studi di Firenze.

Amanda Collins. Former Junior Research Fellow in Intellectual History, Wolfson College, Oxford.

Eleanor A. Congdon. Department of History, Youngstown State University.

Roisin Cossar. Department of History, University of Manitoba.

Samuel K. Cohn. Department of History, University of Glasgow.

Edward Coleman. Department of History, University College Dublin.

George Dameron. Department of History, St. Michael's College.

Trevor Dean. School of Arts, Roehampton University, London.

Joanna Drell. Department of History, University of Richmond.

Robert Gibbs. Department of History of Art, University of Glasgow.

Sean Gilsdorf. Formerly Department of History, Smith College.

Tehmina Goskar. Centre for Antiquity and the Middle Ages, University of Southampton.

Monica H. Green. Department of History, Arizona State University.

Katherine L. Jansen. Department of History, Catholic University of America.

Samantha Kelly. Department of History, Rutgers University.

Catherine Kovesi Killerby. Department of History, University of Melbourne.

Julius Kirshner. Emeritus. Department of History, University of Chicago.

John E. Law. History Department, University of Wales at Swansea.

Catherine Lawless. Department of History, University of Limerick.

Lynn Marie Laufenberg. Department of History, Sweet Briar College.

G. A. Loud. School of History, University of Leeds.

Areli Marina. School of Architecture, University of Illinois, Urbana-Champaign.

Sally McKee. Department of History, University of California, Davis.

Christine Meek. School of Histories and Humanities, Trinity College Dublin.

Alex Metcalfe. History Department, University of Lancaster.

Maureen Miller. Department of History, University of California, Berkeley.

Anthony Molho. Emeritus. Brown University; European University Institute, Florence.

Victoria Morse. Department of History, Carleton College.

M. Michèle Mulchahey. Pontifical Institute of Mediaeval Studies, Toronto.

Fabrizio Nevola. Facoltà di Lettere e Filosofia, Università degli Studi di Siena.

William North. Department of History, Carleton College.

James M. Powell. Emeritus. Department of History, Syracuse University.

Emily O'Brien. Department of History, Simon Fraser University.

John Petruccione. Department of Greek and Latin, Catholic University of America.

Yolanda Plumley. Centre for Mediaeval Studies, University of Exeter.

Valerie Ramseyer. Department of History, Wellesley College.

David Routt. Department of History, University of Richmond.

Linda Safran. Department of Fine Art, University of Toronto.

Anne M. Schuchman. Department of Italian Studies, New York University.

Patricia Skinner. Formerly School of History, University of Southampton.

Alan Stahl. Curator of Numismatics, Princeton University.

Kenneth Stow. Emeritus. Department of Jewish History, University of Haifa.

Mary Stroll. Department of History, University of California, San Diego.

Augustine Thompson, O.P. Department of Religious Studies, University of Virginia.

Diana Webb. Emerita. Department of History, King's College, University of London.

Kenneth Baxter Wolf. Department of History, Pomona College.

Shona Kelly Wray. Department of History, University of Missouri, Kansas City.

Index

Page numbers in italics refer to visual images.

Acknowledgments

This book has been in the pipeline for a very long time, and owes much to many people. First, for their generosity, good will, and above all, *pazienza* we would like to offer our deepest thanks to our contributors, some of whose work unfortunately landed on the "cutting-room" floor. Special thanks are due to Bill North and Sean Gilsdorf who were particularly generous with their time and translations. Hugh West and Yucel Yanikdag of the UR History Department offered valuable advice.

Credit is also due to our support staff at the University of Richmond. Timothy Bronstetter, David Schilling, and June Weltner served as research assistants on the project, while the incomparable Debbie Govoruhk provided much needed secretarial and administrative skills. Financial support in the form of various grants-in-aid and subsidies came from Andrew Newcomb, UR Dean of Arts and Sciences and Department of History. The Office of Graduate Studies at Catholic University also provided a grant-in-aid, and the University of St Andrews provided leave at an early stage which allowed the project to get off the ground.

We are also grateful to our editor, Jerry Singerman at the University of Pennsylvania Press, who exhibited the patience of Job while awaiting the final version of this manuscript. We are indebted to the two anonymous readers of the manuscript whose suggestions—not always followed to the tee—made this a better volume. We also here acknowledge a debt to Olivia Remie Constable whose volume on *Medieval Iberia* was a model for our own.

Finally, we would like to thank Massimo, David, and Louise, who have been discussing and living this volume with us for longer than anyone should ever have done.